C++Builder™ 6
Developer's Guide

Satya Sai Kolachina

Wordware Publishing, Inc.

Library of Congress Cataloging-in-Publication Data

Sai Kolachina, Satya.
　　C++builder 6 developer's guide / by Satya Sai Kolachina.
　　　　p.　cm.
　　Includes bibliographical references and index.
　　ISBN 1-55622-960-7 (paperback)
　　1. Computer software—Development.　2. Delphi (Computer file).
　　3. Telecommunication
　　systems.　I. Title.
　　QA76.76.D47 M665　　2002
　　005.1--dc21　　　　　　　　　　　　　　　　　2002011
　　　　　　　　　　　　　　　　　　　　　　　　　　CIP

© 2003, Wordware Publishing, Inc.

All Rights Reserved

2320 Los Rios Boulevard
Plano, Texas 75074

No part of this book may be reproduced in any form or by
any means without permission in writing from
Wordware Publishing, Inc.

Printed in the United States of America

ISBN 1-55622-960-7

10 9 8 7 6 5 4 3 2 1
0211

C++Builder is a trademark of Borland Software Corporation in the United States and other countries. Other products mentioned are used for identification purposes only and may be trademarks of their respective companies.

All inquiries for volume purchases of this book should be addressed to Wordware Publishing, Inc., at the above address. Telephone inquiries may be made by calling:

(972) 423-0090

Dedication and Acknowledgments

It is my pleasure and responsibility to dedicate this book to a few people without who I am incomplete in several aspects.

First of all, I mention my father, Sri Venkata Lakshmana Murthy Kolachina, and mother, the late Srimathi Kamala Devi Kolachina, who gave me this invaluable life, taught me human values, and with whose blessings, efforts, and encouragement I am now what they envisioned I should be.

Next I mention Sri Vinai Bhushan VR Kanteti and his wife, Srimathi Swarajya Lakshmi Kanteti, who gave me a career and laid the foundation stone for my social status today.

There is a saying "Behind every successful man is a woman." It is also said that without a wife's cooperation, the husband is only an incomplete person. These words are very much true in my case, since my wife, Parvathi Devi Kolachina, has provided me encouragement and full cooperation at every step in my life, career, and even while writing this book. I express my gratitude to her whole-heartedly.

I am very proud of my children, Kamala Priyadarsini Kolachina and Satya Shilpa Kolachina, who always regarded their dad as a great person and always extended their love, affection, and cooperation, though I am a very normal person like millions of others in this world.

I next thank very much the reviewers, Damon Chandler and Thomas J. Theobald, who gave me their valuable suggestions to better present my thoughts. I also thank my close friends and relatives who provided me encouragement.

I thank Wordware Publishing and its staff for extending me their full cooperation throughout the process.

I am very thankful to Karen Giles at Borland Developer Relations, who provided me with the C++Builder 6 software and encouraged me to write this book.

I am a true believer that every human being is a representation of God. Therefore, I thank the creator of this universe who provided me so many well-wishers and a continuous flow of thoughts to keep my commitment to the publisher and to the reader community.

Contents

Contents

Contents

Part II
Advanced and Distributed Application Development

Contents

Contents

Introduction

My desire to write a book about C++Builder has some history. I have been very impressed with Borland since their first edition of C++ (and prior editions of C), because they have always made an effort to ensure quality. Unfortunately, there are very few books on the market about Borland C++ or C++Builder, compared to other products like Visual Basic or Visual C++. Since different authors have different viewpoints of a product, I always prefer to consult more than one book to gain in-depth knowledge, as every author provides a unique service with his or her expertise. Also, authors are limited by their own constraints; every book does not cover every aspect of the product. When I first used MIDAS a few years ago, there was not a book available to help me do my project. I spent a lot of time investigating answers for my questions in an iterative manner. I can say that my frustration over that prompted me to write this book on C++Builder.

As with every release, C++Builder 6 is very rich with features. Best of all, you can build distributed objects in different technologies in the real RAD (rapid application development) way. To my knowledge, this is the only C++ implementation that enables you to build C++ applications on the fly, just as easy as with Delphi or Visual Basic. For programmers who are apprehensive of C++, I would recommend learning C++ using this product. I paid exclusive attention to three main subject areas of C++Builder 6: Windows application development, database development, and distributed systems development. Throughout the duration of this project, I attempted to make the book useful for every type of reader—a novice in C++Builder, a programmer experienced with the product, and those who already have books on prior editions of C++Builder. The entire book contains 12 chapters. Some chapters are relatively larger than we normally see in many books. To keep the flow of my thoughts continuous (which is very helpful for the reader), I did not want to break the chapters into smaller pieces. I divided the 12 chapters into two parts. The first part presents topics on Windows application development as well as database development. The second part is dedicated to distributed systems development and a few miscellaneous topics. Thus, I present more than 200+ pages on several distributed architectures, including DataSnap, WebBroker, WebSnap, BizSnap, CORBA, and TCP/IP. I also created a number of example projects, which you may directly compile on your computer, either for learning or for use in your own projects. Most of the source code for the examples is presented in the book and provided on the companion CD. However, you may need to have the Enterprise edition of C++Builder 6 to work on most of the second part of the book, since it covers advanced topics.

For a couple of reasons, I did not present COM/ActiveX-related chapters in this book. The main reason is that almost all the available books on C++Builder present topics on COM-related technologies very well. In addition, Microsoft itself is drifting its focus away from COM-related technologies since they released the .NET framework, which would force many organizations to reduce the intensity of their COM-based application development. Slowly, many organizations will migrate their COM-based solutions to .NET or other distributed architectures.

Chapter Overview

As mentioned earlier, the 12 chapters in this book are divided into two parts. The first part contains chapters on topics related to Windows application development and database development. The second part contains chapters on topics related to the development of distributed objects and applications. Extensive sample applications are provided throughout the book, in all the chapters, for different programming scenarios. Let me now present an overview of each of the chapters to familiarize you with the contents of the book.

Chapter 1 serves as an introduction to programming in C++Builder 6 and an introduction to Windows programming with this tool. You will find topics on familiarizing yourself (and navigating) with the tool, new features added to the current release (C++Builder 6) compared to the previous release, creating projects, types of applications that can be created with the tool, compiling the projects, setting project options, installing third-party components onto the Component Palette, and creating simple Windows applications. The chapter is mainly focused on providing considerable introduction for professionals who are considering C++Builder 6 as their development platform.

In **Chapter 2**, I focus my attention on some advanced C++ programming concepts, such as templates, namespaces, casting, exception handling, pointers, references, virtual methods, C++Builder keyword extensions to the C++ language, and object construction sequence in a typical class hierarchy. I do not teach the C++ language itself, but I do discuss the importance of these advanced features in building efficient and enter-prise-class applications.

In **Chapter 3**, I present an in-depth discussion on the Visual Component Library (VCL), which provides a rich set of components and run-time routines to the developer. It is the VCL that makes C++Builder a distinct platform from its competition and also adds strength to the core C++ language. The chapter presents VCL's features, including the component architecture, object persistence, visual and non-visual components, interacting with the VCL Application object and the system resources, such as the screen, mouse, and clipboard, an in-depth discussion on the run-time type information, the VCL forms and frames, and more. The chapter is aimed at providing strong fundamentals in the VCL architecture and forms a foundation for the following chapters.

Chapter 4 is aimed at providing advanced VCL programming techniques. The enhanced features on Action Objects, action lists, and action manager enable you to design action-based applications that automate your task and minimize the programming need, since actions incorporate most of the coding within themselves. Windows drag and drop is another advanced feature discussed at length with full working projects. Then date and time management and file and directory management are discussed in great detail. Chapters 3 and 4 together are designed to raise your comfort level in building Windows applications using the VCL.

Chapter 5 introduces the concepts of database programming, VCL's architecture that supports database development, the different database architectures supported by VCL, data modules as containers of database components, the Borland Database Engine (BDE), and the ADO component set to connect to databases using Microsoft's ADO/OLE DB technology.

Chapter 6 provides advanced database development techniques. In this chapter, I discuss the new dbExpress framework from Borland, concepts of unidirectional datasets, and the IBExpress component set to connect to InterBase databases. I also present the data access components, client dataset, dataset provider, and basics required for building client-server applications. The discussion in this chapter forms a basis for future topics on distributed object development.

Chapter 7 marks the beginning of the second part, which is dedicated to a great extent to distributed object development. However, this chapter completely focuses on WebBroker application development, an overview of the HTTP protocol, building web applications using Borland's traditional WebBroker architecture, and different types of web applications including

Apache web modules. I also present an in-depth discussion on the producer and dispatcher components.

In **Chapter 8**, I focus completely on Borland's new WebSnap architecture for building web applications. The topics in this chapter include web page modules, web data modules, adapter components, content producers, an overview of server-side scripting, and VCL script objects.

Chapter 9 is aimed at developing DataSnap applications. The topics discussed in this chapter include what constitutes a DataSnap server module, IAppServer—the interface implemented by a typical remote server module, the threading model implemented by a server module, different ways a client can connect to the remote server, and implementing a web-based client to a DataSnap server.

Chapter 10 presents you with the distribution object development using the CORBA framework. The CORBA object model is discussed at length and includes the Basic Object Adapter (BOA), the Portable Object Adapter (POA), and other constituents of the framework. Though most of the discussion is generic in nature, Borland's VisiBroker is the base CORBA implementation to demonstrate the process with examples. The chapter also presents a detailed discussion on the development of a custom client-server model using simple TCP/IP sockets and finally presents a sample custom FTP client application.

Chapter 11 focuses on the BizSnap architecture introduced by Borland to implement SOAP-based web services. Initially, I present an overview of XML terminology and concepts of web services, and then I discuss the process of building web service (server) modules and web service clients using C++Builder. You will notice that, as with any other technology, C++Builder makes it very simple to build web services. I also discuss Borland's extension of the SOAP objects to DataSnap, thus creating SOAP-based DataSnap server modules. This is a very cool approach to web-enable your current DataSnap applications as web services.

Chapter 12, the last chapter in the book, provides a discussion on some miscellaneous and advanced topics. In this, chapter I present three main topics, including an overview of the Borland CLX (Component Library for Cross-platform development) introduced in C++Builder 6, which enables porting your Windows-based applications to Linux without pain. It includes BaseCLX, which is common mostly across VCL and CLX frameworks. I also present custom component development concepts and OLE objects and OLE containers.

Part I

Windows and Database Development

Chapter 1

Introduction to C++Builder 6

Introduction

As I mentioned in the introduction to this book, C++Builder 6 is a RAD tool to build your enterprise applications using the C++ language and the component libraries provided by Borland. We will go through the details of the component libraries in later chapters. At this time, we will discuss the different pieces of the product that work together to give you the desired result.

C++Builder 6 Overview

In this section, I will mostly go through the Integrated Development Environment (IDE) and other features useful in the application development process. If you are already a user of the product and familiar with these topics, you may skip this section and jump directly to the section titled "New Features."

The Main Window and Toolbars

Figure 1-1 shows the default menu bars and toolbars that appear in the main window when you start C++Builder. The individual toolbars are docked to the main window, and may be undocked if you desire. The toolbars provide quick access to certain frequently used menu items. The Component Palette is also docked to the main window in the default style. Figures 1-2 through 1-5 display the Standard, View, Debug, and Desktop toolbars, respectively. The Help toolbar is also docked to the main window; it contains only one button, which opens the online help manual.

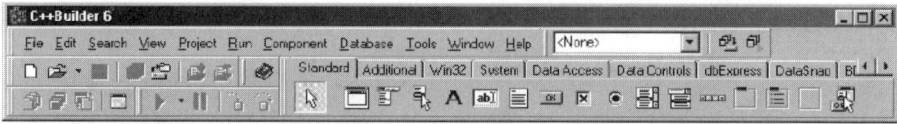

Figure 1-1: The main window in default style

The Standard toolbar contains shortcut buttons for operations such as creating new projects or project items, opening existing projects or files, adding files to the project, removing files from the project, and saving project files.

Figure 1-2: The Standard toolbar

The View toolbar contains shortcut buttons for operations such as viewing the forms or units in a project, adding new forms to the current project, and toggling the view between a form and its corresponding unit.

Figure 1-3: The View toolbar

The Debug toolbar contains shortcut buttons used while debugging your application.

Figure 1-4: The Debug toolbar

The Desktop toolbar may be used to save your current desktop settings (specific to C++Builder IDE) with a name. This is helpful for saving multiple desktop settings for future use.

Figure 1-5: The Desktop toolbar

Component Palette

The Component Palette is a container that holds all the components registered with the IDE. The components are arranged in different pages. C++Builder 6 comes in different editions, which dictate the set of components packaged with that edition. The Enterprise Edition is the highest level edition and contains all the components built with the system. Check with Borland about the components included in the specific edition you have. Components provide easy access to manage the objects from the IDE. Components may be visual and non-visual. In simple terms, visual components are those that participate in the visual presentation of your application and are visible during run time. Non-visual components do not participate in the visual presentation of your application; rather, they provide services in the background mode. But since they are components and available in the Component Palette, you can access them during application design.

Once you compile your application and start executing, the components' services are accessible only through your program, and they are not visible for user interaction or display. When you create your own components or buy components from third-party vendors, you may install them on the Component Palette, and they behave very naturally like the components supplied by Borland. Figure 1-6 displays the Component Palette with the default pages. A left and right arrow pair is provided at the top-right corner of the Component Palette to switch to pages that are not visible since the viewable size of the Component Palette is limited, particularly when you install a number of third-party components.

Figure 1-6: The Component Palette

Object Inspector

The Object Inspector serves two main purposes in the development process. For every component (visual or non-visual) that you are placing on your project form, you can set its properties during design time, and you can create empty event handlers in the corresponding program files where you can type in your implementation of the event handler. Figure 1-7 displays a simple view of the Object Inspector.

The Object Inspector has two tabbed pages and a combo box above these pages. The names of all the objects placed on the forms (including the forms) are listed in the combo box, and by selecting the appropriate object, its current property settings are displayed in the Object Inspector. The Properties page displays properties of the object, and the Events page displays available events for the object. When you choose a different object from the object list, the properties and the list of events change immediately to those corresponding to the selected object. The Object Inspector displays only the published properties of the components. Properties that should be allowed to be set during design time are published when building the components.

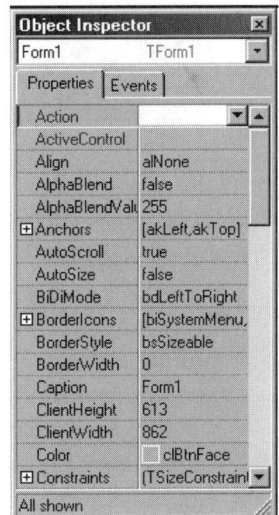

Figure 1-7: The Object Inspector

If a specific editor is required to set a particular property of an object, the appropriate editor is invoked automatically when you click the ellipsis button next to the property edit box. For some types of components, the component writers write special property editors. For example, the SQL property of a database query component requires that you enter multiple lines of query, since a query string constitutes a string list object. In such a case, when you click the ellipsis button in the corresponding edit box, or double-click in the edit box, the String List Editor associated with the SQL property is displayed, as shown in Figure 1-8.

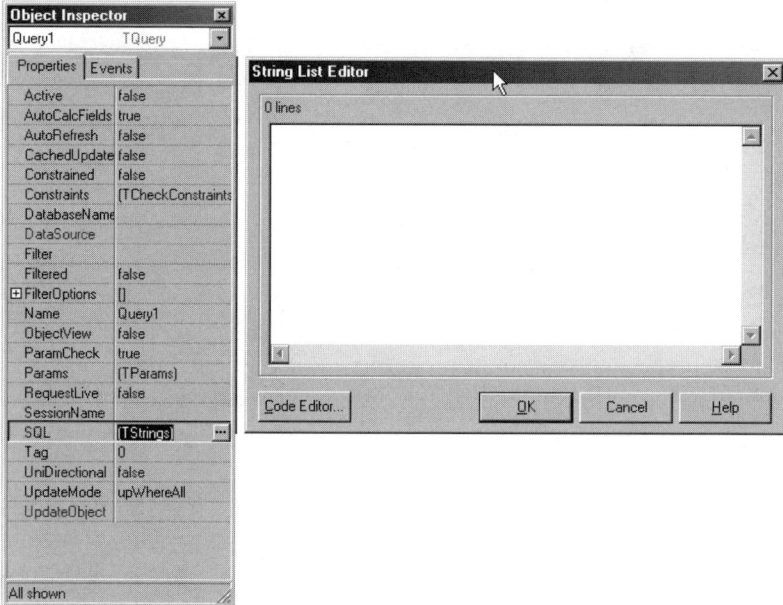

Figure 1-8: The Object Inspector with a property editor

When you switch to the Events page of the Object Inspector, you can create empty event handlers in the program file corresponding to the form that contains the object by double-clicking in the edit box next to the specific event for which you wish to create the event handler. Event handlers of objects are public methods in the associated form class file and provide a nice encapsulation of the objects within the form by exposing these event handlers (and other public methods you manually create) to the (current) application or an external application that can access this form if the form is embedded within a DLL. Most of the time, you don't have to invoke the event handlers yourself. They are automatically executed when the specific event is fired by the system or by the component itself. But, if your application design requires it, there are occasions that may demand manual invocation of an event handler.

Object TreeView

The Object TreeView provides another view of the objects placed on the forms. While the Object Inspector displays properties of a specific object, the Object TreeView displays the objects on the form in a hierarchical style. When you choose an object in the Object TreeView, its properties are displayed in the Object Inspector automatically. Some components behave like containers of other components. In the Object TreeView, you can reassign objects from one container to another, such as moving objects like buttons or list boxes from the form to a panel or group box, which is also placed on the form itself. Figure 1-9 displays the Object TreeView and Figure 1-10 displays the default IDE with the main menu, Object Inspector, Object TreeView, Component Palette, and the toolbars docked to the main window. The figure also displays the main form for the default project.

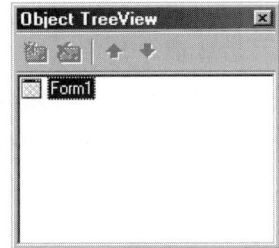

Figure 1-9: The Object TreeView

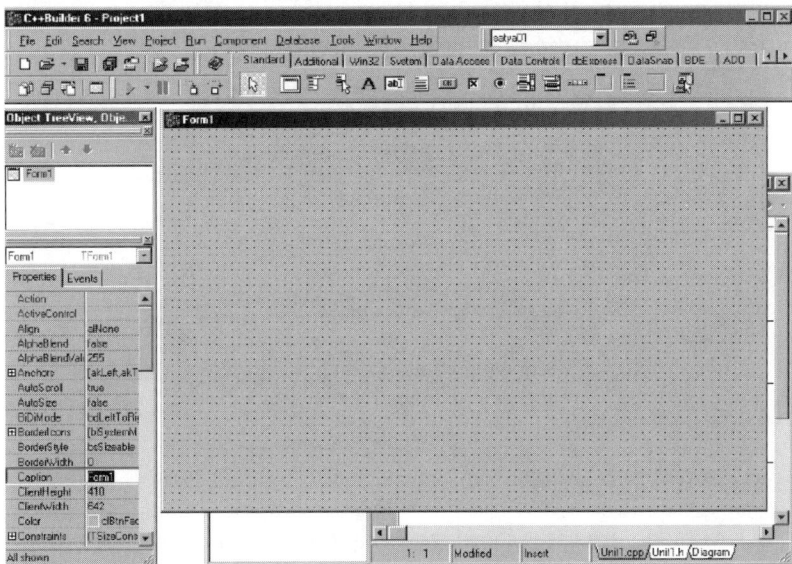

Figure 1-10: The IDE with a default project

To-Do List

The IDE also provides a way to maintain a to-do list of tasks, which is very useful in enterprise-level application development. You can invoke the To-Do List by selecting View | To-do List from the IDE main menu. The

To-Do List window is displayed. You can add, edit, and delete items on the list. The pop-up menu showing the tasks you can do with the to-do list is displayed when you click the right mouse button while the mouse pointer is placed on the to-do list view. The to-do list view and the pop-up menu are displayed in Figure 1-11. When you click the Add menu option from the pop-up menu, another dialog is displayed, which lets you add items to the list, as shown in Figure 1-12. You can assign names of individuals to tasks, prioritize the tasks, and also categorize them based on some criteria, such as project development phase, team name, and so on.

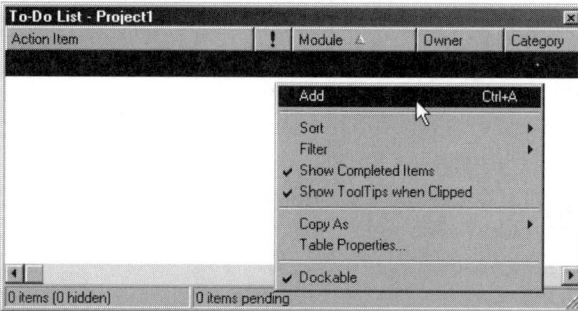

Figure 1-11: To-Do List with pop-up menu

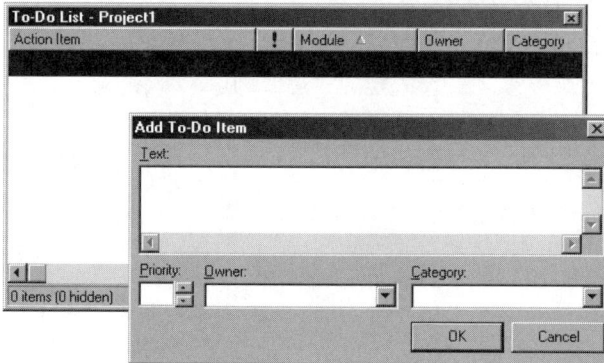

Figure 1-12: To-Do List with add item dialog

Alignment Palette

When components are placed, you may need to align them according to certain criteria, such as aligning a group of components along their left edge, right edge, vertical line passing through the center, horizontal line passing through the center, with reference to the form's dimensions, and so on. Without the alignment palette, you have to manually compute the pixels for exact component location and set the Left, Top, Right, and Bottom properties of the component in the Object Inspector. With the alignment palette, the task becomes simple. First select multiple components, then

invoke the alignment palette by choosing the
View | Alignment Palette menu option from the
main menu. The alignment palette is displayed, as
shown in Figure 1-13. Each of the buttons on the
alignment palette corresponds to a type of alignment, as explained before. While multiple
components are selected together (by holding
down the Shift key and selecting the required
components), click on the appropriate button that provides the type of
alignment you desire. All the components that you selected together are
then aligned automatically.

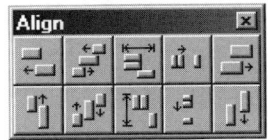

Figure 1-13: Alignment
palette

New Features

C++Builder 6 provides many new features and enhancements to the existing features of the product. In this section, we will go through some of
these new features by different categories. It is not possible to discuss all
the new features here.

Technology Additions

WebSnap and Enhancements to Internet Development

With C++Builder 6, you can continue to use the WebBroker architecture as
you did with C++Builder 5. In addition, the new WebSnap architecture is
provided, which brings advanced web development concepts into your
hands. You can develop complex web applications easier than before in a
very similar style to building VCL applications. This is a major feature
addition to the C++Builder programming community. The following features are provided by WebSnap:

- You can now create multiple web modules in a single web application
  by modularizing your development process and expanding your application's capabilities. However, you cannot add multiple web modules
  to WebBroker applications. To use the new feature, you should start
  developing your applications with the WebSnap framework. When you
  implement multiple web modules in your application, you can cross-
  reference components of one module in the other, and modules may be
  cached or created on demand.

- A number of wizards are added in support of the new framework. They
  include the WebSnap Application Wizard, which creates the main web
  server application, the WebSnap Data Module Wizard, which adds one
  or more data modules to your web application, and the WebSnap Page

Module Wizard, which adds one or more web page modules to your application. The New Items dialog contains a new page to host the WebSnap application wizards.

- In addition to the current web application types (such as ISAPI/NSAPI, CGI, and WinCGI), you can now develop web applications for deployment with the Apache web server. The new Web App Debugger executable module gives you the ability to debug web applications.

- A number of new components are provided in support of the new framework and are available in the WebSnap page of the Component Palette. The new components identify WebSnap framework-related elements, such as a web application page module, a web application data module, a simple page module, a data module, and a number of adapter components that provide scriptable interfaces, which act like a bridge between your VCL-style C++ program and the server-side scripts.

- You can now implement server-side scripts in your HTML pages, both in JavaScript and VBScript. In addition, your script can access C++Builder objects. A group of adapter components (including the adapter page producer) even automate your web page design process by creating required HTML code and server-side script to display the adapter fields and execute the adapter actions. In short, your business logic in the C++Builder program is exposed to the script through the adapter components. Other components include the new dispatcher components, such as the page dispatcher to automatically dispatch the incoming HTTP request messages to the appropriate page module and the adapter dispatcher component to automatically handle the HTML form submissions and requests for dynamic images by calling adapter action and field components. Also, the new XSL page producer component generates web page content by transforming data described with XML using an XSL (Extensible Stylesheet Language) template. There are other miscellaneous components provided for session management, user login process automation, and so on.

- Another new feature provided with this framework is that you are able to preview the HTML pages (embedded with script components) while designing the web module in the code editor. This is made possible by the WebSnap surface designers, which are part of the IDE and are invoked automatically when you attempt to preview the pages.

In simple terms, the WebSnap technology is a very valuable addition to the current C++Builder feature set. This new framework is discussed in depth in Chapter 8 with full working sample projects.

BizSnap

BizSnap is the name given by Borland to the web services technology. Now C++Builder programmers can build web services in the VCL application style and publish the WSDL (Web Services Definition Language) documents along with their web services. When you go through this new topic in Chapter 11, you will appreciate the simplicity of Borland's implementation of SOAP (Simple Object Access Protocol)-based application development.

Enhancements

Enhancement to DataSnap

Borland extended the web services technology to the DataSnap architecture to enable you to publish your DataSnap server services through SOAP protocol for access by the DataSnap clients over the Internet. You can easily add a web interface to your current client-server applications developed using the DataSnap architecture. The DataSnap architecture is discussed in Chapters 6 and 9, while its SOAP extension is discussed in Chapter 11.

New Database Support

C++Builder 6 includes support for dbExpress, the new data access technology introduced by Borland. The concept of unidirectional datasets is implemented in this technology, improving the data access speeds with the use of unidirectional cursors. Use of this technology requires new database drivers. C++Builder 6 comes with dbExpress drivers for InterBase, Oracle, Informix, DB2, and MySQL. More and more drivers for other popular architectures and database systems (such as Microsoft SQL Server, ODBC plug-in, and so on) are being added by third-party vendors and Borland itself. Chapter 6 discusses features of this technology in detail with sample applications.

STLPort Standard Template Library

The new STLPort standard template library has become popular due to its enhanced compliance with ANSI C++ and multi-platform support. C++Builder 6 includes this library as part of the product.

New Components and Wizards

The action component functionality is enhanced with a number of new features as well as components. The action main menu bar, action toolbar, action manager customization dialog, and a number of standard actions facilitate simplification of the user interface development process. This will be explained in Chapter 4 to a great extent. The value list editor, color combo box, and labeled edit box are some additional general-purpose components. The Object TreeView discussed earlier is a new addition in this release. The Object Inspector is enhanced with expanded inline components.

The Internet Direct (Indy) components are open source Internet components. Three new pages in the Component Palette provide Indy client components, Indy server components, and miscellaneous Indy components. The MIDAS page has been replaced by DataSnap due to the name change of the framework.

The new Component Library for Cross-platform development (CLX) is added to this version of C++Builder with the C++ version of the components. However, the library was first released with Delphi 6, then Kylix, and now C++Builder. This topic is discussed in Chapter 12.

The new XML (Extensible Markup Language) Data Binding Wizard generates interfaces and class definitions that correspond to the structure of an XML document or schema. The XML data bindings simplify the process of complex coding to access the XML documents using the DOM (Document Object Model) interfaces. This is accessible through the New Items dialog. The new XML document component also supports the simplified version of DOM interface implementation, which may be configured to use a customized third-party vendor-supplied DOM interface implementation. The XML concepts are discussed in Chapter 11. A new tool called XML mapper is supplied with C++Builder 6 and can be used to convert a data packet created by a client dataset component into an XML data packet, and vice versa. This is very useful to smoothly transition a traditional data model into an XML schema and vice versa, enabling you to elevate your DataSnap applications with XML-based interfaces. This topic is discussed in more detail in Chapter 9. CORBA development is enhanced with support to the new VisiBroker 4.5 architecture.

Working with Projects

Every application that we develop is in the form of a project. The project may be a simple Windows executable, a console application, or a DLL. Whatever the output is of your application, it is represented by a project.

What Constitutes a C++Builder 6 Project?

A C++Builder 6 project constitutes a set of files. Each file that becomes part of a project has a specific purpose and identification. The main project file has the .bpr file extension ("bpr" stands for Borland project). When the project is compiled and linked, the final (binary) executable file will have the same filename as the main project file with a different extension, such as .exe. If you create a Windows DLL application, an additional IDE-managed file with the .bpf extension is added to the project. When you create Borland packages, the .bpk file is created to store the project options, and the binary packages have the default file extension .bpl, similar to the way Windows DLLs are created with the default file extension .dll. Borland packages have a corresponding .bpi file (which is the import library for the package). The .bpi file corresponds to a .bpl file in a similar way to how an import library corresponds to a DLL file.

Every form added to the project will have three files: one .dfm file (which stores the form definition), one .h file (which is the header file for the form definition), and one .cpp file (which contains the form implementation code). These three files are collectively called a *unit* in a C++Builder application (similar to the Delphi unit). The main difference between a Delphi unit and a C++Builder unit is that the C++Builder unit contains an additional header file.

In addition to the standard files discussed above, a web project may have an HTML file to contain the HTML code (and any server-side script). When you compile a project, the IDE creates additional .obj files, which contain the intermediate object code. .lib files are created when you create statically bound DLLs, which are linked with the applications that use the DLL files.

Every time you save project files, a backup file is created with the ~ symbol as the first character of the file extension. For example, when you save a file by the name "unit1.cpp," the backup file is named "unit1.~cpp." There are other file types that may be created, depending on the type of project you are building. The beauty of the C++Builder environment is that it creates the minimum number of files, which are easily manageable.

Files contained within a project are managed with the help of the Project Manager window, which is displayed when you select the View | Project

Manager option from the IDE main menu. Multiple projects may be grouped together as a project group, and the project group definition file is saved with the .bpg file extension. You can give any name to a project group. You are not required to create a project group, but you must create a project if you need to build an application.

Project configuration options may be set using the Project Options dialog, which is displayed by selecting the Project | Options menu option from the IDE main menu. Figure 1-14 displays a typical Project Options dialog. When you select the Project | Edit Option Source option from the IDE main menu, the entire project configuration is displayed in the form of an XML document.

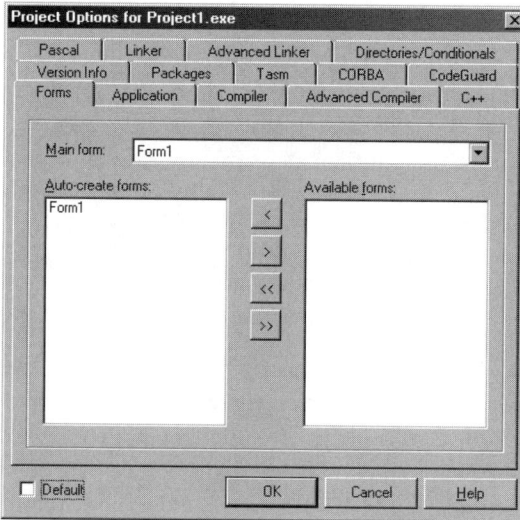

Figure 1-14: Project Options dialog

Setting Project Options

In this section we will go through some of the frequently used project options. The Project Options dialog displayed in Figure 1-14 has a number of pages, and each page has options for a specific need. The Forms page lets you specify which of the forms in the project should be autocreated. When you create a Windows application project, the application creates all the forms when the application is initialized by default. But you can control which forms should be created automatically from this page, since you can programmatically create forms on demand. This topic is discussed in Chapter 3.

The Application page lets you edit the application title, main help file, and application icon. The Compiler and Advanced Compiler pages let you change the default compiler settings/switches, as required by your application. The C++ page allows you to change the language-specific settings. The Directories/Conditionals page lets you add additional directories to search for the include files and library files. By default, the directories where C++Builder 6 is installed are listed in this page. If you change the default directory names, your project may not compile. The Linker and Advanced Linker pages let you edit the options used by the linker. The Packages page is used for two purposes: to install and uninstall packages (of components) in the Component Palette; this list is identified as design time packages. In addition, there is a check box towards the bottom captioned "Build with runtime packages" accompanied by an edit box and an Add button. When this check box is checked, your executable (or DLL/BPL) file size will be very compact because the linker does not include the code referenced from the packages (specified in the edit box by clicking the Add button) into your executable. Rather, your executable will only have a reference to the specific packages, which are loaded into memory dynamically at the time of execution. In this case, you will have to distribute the particular packages with your application for distribution. This is usually a preferable and recommended method. But, if you wish to distribute your application as a stand-alone executable without the run-time packages, then you have to uncheck the box so the code referenced from the packages will be included in your executable. In this case, your executable program size will usually be larger. This option may be acceptable for small-sized applications, but it is very inconvenient if you are building very large applications.

Borland Packages and Components

The components are usually built into larger containers called *packages*. Borland packages are special dynamic-link libraries (DLLs) created and used by Borland applications in C++Builder (and Delphi) environments. If you are building libraries to be used by external development environments, such as Microsoft Visual C++, then you are advised to create DLLs. If you are creating libraries for exclusive use by C++Builder (and Delphi) developers, then you are advised to create Borland packages, which have the default file extension .bpl. However, there are compatibility issues well-known in the developer community with regard to using DLLs developed in Microsoft Visual C++ in a C++Builder application and vice versa. There are also ways to overcome the majority of these problems, which are beyond the scope of this book.

Components form the major part of the C++Builder 6 development environment. *Components* are reusable objects (classes with specific features that enable them to be accessed through the Component Palette). With each edition of C++Builder 6, Borland provides a set of components. You may also buy components built and sold by third-party vendors, or you may build components yourself.

Borland provides two types of component frameworks: the Visual Component Library (VCL) and the Component Library for Cross-platform development (CLX). The VCL is designed exclusively for the Microsoft Windows operating system while the CLX is designed to work with both the Windows and Linux operating systems. Component architectures and their usage is discussed in detail in Chapters 3, 4, and 12. In addition, every chapter discusses some components relevant to the topic of the chapter. Therefore, components form a vital part of this development tool. You may also use the ActiveX components (built in any development environment); however, to use ActiveX components, you must first import them into C++Builder 6 and install them onto the Component Palette as local components.

Installing Third-Party Vendor Components

Installing third-party vendor components is a fairly easy process. Most of the vendor packages come with an installation program (or a self-extracting compressed executable file), which performs the installation task. If an installation package is not provided (as is usually the case with shareware components), you can install the packages yourself. Borland packages are identified with the file extension .bpl with the corresponding package import libraries having the file extension .bpi. The Install Packages dialog may be invoked two ways: either by selecting the Component | Install Packages menu option from the IDE main menu or by opening the Packages page in the Project Options dialog, as explained earlier. Either method opens the same dialog, in which you can use the Add and Remove buttons to add a new package to the Component Palette or remove an already installed package from the Component Palette. I advise you not to play with the default packages installed by C++Builder because if you accidentally remove an existing package, you may not be able to compile your applications. Once you install the packages, you don't have to repeat the procedure every time you start the C++Builder IDE; they are automatically loaded and made available for your project. Also, do not forget to add the directory/path information for the include files and libraries in the project options. If you do not do this, your projects may not compile or link, particularly when you use these components in your programs.

Types of Projects That C++Builder 6 Supports

C++Builder 6 is capable of building several application types, as listed here:

- Standard Windows executable files
- Console applications that execute at the Windows command prompt
- Windows dynamic-link libraries (DLLs) for use by any development platform that supports linking to DLLs
- Borland packages and components in VCL and CLX frameworks for exclusive use by Borland C++Builder and Delphi platforms
- ActiveX components for use by any development platform that supports ActiveX technology
- Applications using either VCL or CLX
- Multi-threaded applications
- Windows control panel applications
- Windows service applications
- ActiveX components and automation servers
- COM objects, COM+ event objects, COM+ subscription objects, and transactional objects
- CORBA servers and clients
- Three-tier client-server applications using Borland's proprietary DataSnap architecture
- Networking applications using many TCP/IP-based protocols, including socket-based applications (blocking and non-blocking), FTP clients and servers, SMTP clients and servers, NNTP clients and servers, Telnet clients and servers, HTTP clients and servers, and so on
- Web server applications of different types, including ISAPI/NSAPI, CGI, WinCGI, and Apache server modules using either WebBroker or WebSnap architecture
- Web service clients and server objects using the SOAP/HTTP architecture
- Applications providing OLE support and connecting to Microsoft Office Servers, such as Word, Excel, PowerPoint, and Outlook

Most of these project types are initiated from the New Items dialog, which is opened by selecting the File | New | Other menu option from the IDE main menu or by clicking the shortcut button in the Standard toolbar. Figure 1-15 displays the New Items dialog.

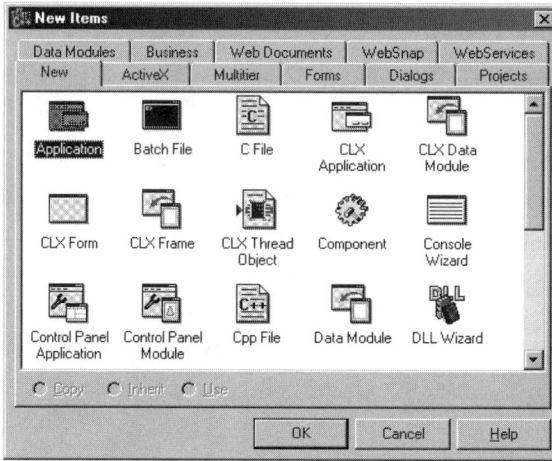

Figure 1-15: New Items dialog

Building User Interfaces

In this section, I only present an overview of the user interface design process because the details of building VCL-based applications are discussed in Chapter 3. Typically, a Windows application would have a form as the main component—at least one form. When we create a standard Windows application, a main form with the corresponding unit file and header file is automatically created for you, and the necessary code to create an instance of the form and initiate the application is added to the main application program. Please remember that a form does not constitute the main application program. A form is only an object within the main program, and the main program incorporates the WinMain function. You may add more forms to the project afterward, through either the New Items dialog or the IDE main menu.

The form acts as the main container of all the visual and non-visual components. Examples of visual components include edit boxes, check boxes, rich text edit boxes, list boxes, list views, simple buttons, radio buttons, and so on, while examples of non-visual components include database-related components, such as connections, tables, query objects, and so on.

Most of the visual components have some common properties with respect to positioning the component on the form (or on any other container placed on the form, such as panels and group boxes); these properties include Top, Left, Width, and Height, all integer values representing pixels. The Anchors property lets you fix the distance (in pixels) of the component from the four edges (left, right, top, and bottom). The Align property specifies how the component should be aligned with respect to its parent component. You may also use the alignment palette to align multiple components together, as discussed earlier. The Name property represents the name of the particular instance of the component and should be unique for the unit (or the form). You may, however, use the same component name in different units, and when you refer to them, you qualify the component name with the form name (as in Form2 → ADOConnection). Also, the Name property does not permit spaces in the property value (since this represents a class variable of the object within the form class). The Visible property makes the component visible during run time, if set to true. Remember, it is always visible during design time. The Tag property takes an integer value and may be used for any purpose you like. The Hint property is a text string and a run-time setting. When a value is set for this property, the hint text is displayed when the user moves the cursor over the component. However, to enable the hint text display, you must also set the ShowHint property to true.

Your First Windows Application

Almost all readers (including myself) expect to see the famous Hello World example when we first open a book about a new product. I don't want to deviate from this tradition. In this section, let me start demonstrating C++Builder with a much-awaited example. Let's go through the steps involved in building a simple Windows application.

From the New Items dialog, double-click the application icon. This will create a project with the main form and the unit files. Every time I create a project, the first thing I do is save the project files in an appropriate folder. When we save this project, we have to provide a name for the unit file and a name for the project file. The unit file is saved with the file extension .cpp, while the project file is saved with the .bpl file extension. From the IDE Standard toolbar, there is a button for the Save All operation. Click that button (or select the menu option File | Save All) to invoke the Save dialog. The Save All operation attempts to save all the files in the project that were modified since the last time they were saved. In the Save dialog, you first have to provide a name for the unit and then for the project. I named the unit file "HelloWorldUnit.cpp" and the project "HelloWorld.bpl." It is required that we give different names to both the files (even though they have different file extensions) because the IDE creates a .cpp file for the project with the same name as the project's .bpl file. To see the files created in the project, select the View | Project Manager option. This displays the Project Manager window, as shown in Figure 1-16.

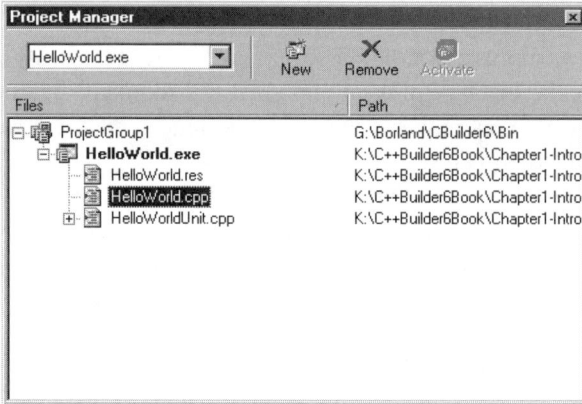

Figure 1-16: Project Manager window

To open a source file in the project, double-click the item in the list that shows the source filename. To add more source files or remove source files attached to a project, place the mouse cursor on the project name and right-click. You will see a pop-up menu of options for working with individual items in the project.

Let's reduce the size of the form since our example does not need a big form. In the Object Inspector, set the Height property to 300 and the Width property to 400. Also, set the Name property to "HelloWorldForm," and save the files. When you change the Name property of the form, notice that the .dfm filename is also changed to the form name.

From the Standard page of the Component Palette, drop a TLabel component and a TButton component onto the form. The TLabel component represents a label and TButton represents a button. When you drop a component from the Component Palette, the IDE sets a default name to the instance of the component by appending a serial number (starting from 1) to the component name and dropping the first character T. If you drop more instances of the same component, the serial number is increased by 1 for every instance. Thus, the TLabel's instance is named Label1, and TButton's instance is named Button1. You may change the name of the component by setting its Name property to a different (unique) value, as discussed earlier. It is normally advised to give meaningful names to the objects, since you will be referring to them in the program. Therefore, let's change the Name property of Label1 to HelloWorldLabel and Button1 to HelloWorldButton. Also, change the Caption property of the button to "Hello," and erase the Caption property of the label by deleting its value in the Object Inspector.

For the button component, double-click the OnClick event in the Events page of the Object Inspector. This will create an empty event handler in the program unit file and a corresponding entry in the public section of the form class in the unit header file. Let's now write a single line of code in the event handler to set the Caption property of the label. Two points are noteworthy at this time. The property of the object (such as Caption) is accessed through the arrow notation (→) since the label object is created on the heap and is accessed through the object's address. The label object is owned by the form and destroyed automatically when the form is destroyed. This is a feature of VCL forms and their objects. The VCL architecture is discussed in detail in Chapters 3 and 4. The second point is that the Caption property is an AnsiString object and is set as a string literal in this case. The traditional way of creating string objects using the standard strcpy() method is not used here. AnsiString is a powerful string class and is also discussed in detail in Chapter 3. While using C++Builder 6, you will notice that you will be using more sophisticated (prebuilt) VCL objects, and most of the time you will be working with the objects through their properties, methods, and events. The rest of the chapters in the book will provide enough detail in this respect.

Let's add another button component from the Component Palette and change its Name property to MessageClearButton and its Caption property to "Clear." In the OnClick event handler of this method, we will set the Caption of the label to a NULL string. The purpose of this event handler is to clear the label caption when clicked.

Build the project by selecting the Project | Make HelloWorld option from the IDE main menu. When you execute the project, you will see the two buttons; one button sets the "Hello World!" string, and the other button clears the string. The program is very simple, so I do not present the source code here, but the project is available on the companion CD.

Please note that usually when an application is executed, the objects belonging to the form have an initial state, which is set in the Object Inspector during design time. This means that properties set for the objects before the project was saved and compiled become initial settings. However, not every property of an object is accessible through the Object Inspector (if they are not published when the component is developed, as explained in Chapter 12). Such properties are called run-time properties and are accessible only through the program code, not during design time. When a component is dropped from the Component Palette, most of the properties are set with the corresponding default values during object construction as designed by the component writer (even the run-time components are set, but these are not visible in the Object Inspector). If we need to change the default setting of run-time properties, we can do so in the form constructor or in another form-level event appropriate to the circumstance.

Summary

Since this is the first chapter of the book, I made it more useful for newcomers to the C++Builder community in order to help them navigate through some of the toolbars and dialogs and familiarize them with the product's ability to build their applications. For those who don't need an introduction to the product, the new features of the current release are presented in summary.

This chapter began with an overview of the individual parts of the IDE. The next section outlined the new features that Borland introduced in this release, which was followed by an outline of how to build C++Builder 6 projects, the constituent elements of a project, the types of projects we can build using C++Builder 6, setting project options, and how to install third-party vendor components onto the Component Palette. Finally, the chapter concluded with a presentation of the Hello World application.

Chapter 2

C++ Advanced Concepts

Introduction

Before we jump on to discuss the core functionality offered by C++Builder 6, I would like to take the opportunity to present you with a high-level overview of some of the standard C++ language features and extensions made to the language in order to support the Visual Component Library framework. VCL is discussed in more detail in later chapters. I also want to make it clear that I do not intend to cover the core C++ language in this chapter; rather, I will highlight special features of the language that make the language better utilized by application developers. If you are new to the C++ language but familiar with another object-oriented language, you may not find it difficult to have a smooth ride with this book. But if you are new to object-oriented languages in general, I recommend that you refer to a book that exclusively teaches you the C++ language in addition to using this book.

I would also like to mention that the language is not that hard, though many programmers are scared to even consider learning it. I encourage such programmers with the simple words: "C++Builder makes learning C++ language a really simple and pleasant experience." Please do not think I am trying to market the product. I am not. It really is a cool tool. In my opinion, it is as simple to develop in C++Builder as it is in Visual Basic or Delphi.

At this time, I would like to mention Borland's Delphi, which is an Object Pascal-based RAD tool for Windows development. Borland maintains a tight, as well as loose, relationship between its two powerful development environments: Delphi and C++Builder. I call the relationship tight because the two component architectures are very similar in their features; components developed in one platform may be ported to the other easily. I also call the relationship loose because to use one platform, we do not have to use the other; in this sense, they are not dependent on each other. Familiarity with one of these platforms is advantageous when working with the other platform. To maintain the tight relationship between the platforms, Borland often provides features of one platform to the other. Also, component vendors take advantage of this relationship by developing their components on one platform (usually on Delphi) and porting them to the other. Because of such a relationship, I will often compare certain features between the two platforms throughout the book. My approach will only be advantageous to you as the reader, never disadvantageous.

Language Overview

In C++, most of the time you encounter classes and objects apart from standard C-like variables and language constructs. The *class* forms the basic structure of an object in a form similar to a design blueprint of an engineering component. An *object* of this class is an instance of the class. The process of creating an object from its class is called *object instantiation*. At any time in a program, a number of objects instantiated from the same class or different classes may co-exist. In fact, in a typical C++ program, many objects interact with one another and exchange data from other objects. In simple terms, a true object-oriented program involves three main tasks, as outlined here:

- Creation of objects from one or more classes, usually at different points of time during the entire life of the program. Objects may be instantiated on the stack or heap, as demanded by the application design. A program that has to execute by itself will have a main() function similar to a C program; a Windows GUI application has a WinMain() function instead.

- Exchange of data in a controlled fashion among the objects. The classes, which are better encapsulated, have better control of their private data elements than those that are loosely encapsulated. By loosely encapsulated, I mean that the class design exposes their internal data elements to external objects in a way that violates the object-oriented design principles.

- Destroying the objects when they are no longer required. Objects instantiated on the stack have limited scope and resources and are automatically destroyed by the application program after they go out of scope. However, objects instantiated on the heap have extended scope and resources but need to be destroyed explicitly by the application developer. The component libraries provided with C++Builder provide an ownership mechanism by which the owner of certain types of objects automatically destroys the objects that it owns when the owner itself is destroyed. This feature is explained in more detail in subsequent chapters.

Many of us know that the three main principles underlying the object-oriented language paradigm are encapsulation, polymorphism, and inheritance. *Encapsulation* is the principle of hiding information private to the class and providing methods that expose private data members in a controlled way to the external world. *Polymorphism* is the concept of one interface and multiple implementations. For example, we design a virtual base class, which dictates the minimum behavior to be implemented by its descendants without implementing that behavior by the base class itself. The descendant classes may all have different implementations having the same method signature as dictated by the virtual base class, and in addition may add their own features. *Inheritance* is the principle of defining new classes by acquiring features of existing classes. The process of acquiring features from existing classes is called *deriving from the base class*, where the base class is the existing class. This way, all the classes derived from a common base class will exhibit standard behavior, as described in the common base class, though the classes themselves have their own defined behavior. In the process, the derived class may override methods already implemented in the base class. Thus, when a method is executed on an object of the derived class, the method implemented by the derived class will be executed if one exists. Otherwise, the method implemented by the immediate ancestor class will be executed. This concept can be extended to any number of levels in the object hierarchy.

In a class hierarchy implementing polymorphic classes, the class occupying the highest position in the hierarchy is the *virtual base class*. The hierarchy may have any number of levels, and the class at the bottom of the hierarchy is the last derived class; it should not contain any pure virtual methods, since we have to create objects of this class. C++ implements the concept of polymorphism through *vtables*. The vtable for a derived class contains method pointers of all the parent classes in the hierarchy and pointers to its own methods. This may also be viewed as the base classes being embedded within the derived class as *subsets* of methods and the derived class as the *superset* of methods.

C++ Features That are Often Ignored

Like many other programming languages, C++ has undergone an evolutionary process, and many extensions have been made to the language. Some of these extensions are underutilized, either due to lack of understanding or their unavailability in some implementations. In this section, I discuss these additional features.

Templates

What are Templates?

Templates are generic parameterized types where the parameters are data types that are not yet specified at compile time. This means that we create class and function definitions with parameters whose data types are unknown when the program is compiled. The standard C++ program raises compile-time errors if we do not specify data types before compilation because C++ is a strongly typed language. But when we define our classes or functions as templates, the program can be compiled error-free because the compiler will not compile the code for any specific types; rather, the template code is only compiled for the types that are used. At this time, the compiler creates a separate version of the function for each type used in the program and compiles it. Templates can be defined for classes and functions. A class template is a pattern for class definitions; a function template is a pattern for function definitions. In either case, the pattern is usable for object types that do not exist when the template is created.

When to Use Templates

Templates are useful for avoiding situations that result in duplication of code. For example, function templates can be used to create a family of functions that apply the same logic (or algorithm) to different data types. Templates can also be used in functions to replace void pointers; when we use void pointers, the compiler cannot perform type checking or type-specific operations because the compiler cannot determine the type. With templates, we can create functions and classes that operate on typed data. Templates can also be used to implement custom collection classes. The Standard Template Library (STL), which is an extension to the initial C++ language specification, is implemented using templates. Therefore, knowledge of templates and their features are a minimum requirement to further understand the STL.

Listings 2-1 and 2-2 present examples of a class template and a function template, respectively. In defining templates, the generic parameter data type is defined as <class T>. However, we can use any data type, even though we specify the keyword class.

Listing 2-1: Class template

```
//--------------------------------------------------------------------------

#include <vcl.h>
#include <iostream>
#pragma hdrstop
using std::cout;
using std::endl;
//--------------------------------------------------------------------------
#pragma argsused
//--------------------------------------------------------------------------
template <class T> class StackTemplate
{
    T* StBuffer;
    int availPos;
    int maxSize;
public:
    StackTemplate(int n);        // constructor
    ~StackTemplate();            // destructor
    void push(T item );          // push an item to the stack top
    T pop( void );               // pop an item from the stack top
    int getSize();               // return the stack size
};
template <class T> StackTemplate<T>::StackTemplate(int n)
{
    availPos = n;
    maxSize = n;
    StBuffer = new T[n];
}
template <class T> StackTemplate<T>::~StackTemplate()
{
    delete[] StBuffer;
}
template <class T> void StackTemplate<T>::push(T item)
{
    if (availPos > 0) {
        StBuffer[maxSize - availPos] = item;
        --availPos;
    }
    return;
}
template <class T> T StackTemplate<T>::pop( void )
{
    if (availPos < maxSize) {
        T Obj = StBuffer[maxSize - (availPos+1)];
        ++availPos;
        return Obj;
    }
    else
        return NULL;
}
template <class T> int StackTemplate<T>::getSize()
```

```
{
    return (maxSize - availPos);
}
//----------------------------------------------------------------------------
int main()
{
    StackTemplate <AnsiString> stringStack(5);

    AnsiString fStr;
    fStr = "Borland C++Builder";
    stringStack.push(fStr);
    fStr = "Borland JBuilder";
    stringStack.push(fStr);
    fStr = "Borland Delphi";
    stringStack.push(fStr);
    fStr = "Borland Kylix";
    stringStack.push(fStr);

    int stackSize = stringStack.getSize();
    cout << "Number of items on the string stack = " << stackSize << endl;
    cout << "Items on the string stack are listed from top to bottom " << endl;
    for (int j=0; j < stackSize; ++j) {
        cout << stringStack.pop().c_str() << endl;
    }

    StackTemplate <TComponent*> compStack(5);
    TListBox* fListBox = new TListBox(Application);
    TButton* fButton = new TButton(Application);
    compStack.push(fListBox);
    compStack.push(fButton);

    TComponent* fComp;
    AnsiString fCompName;

    stackSize = compStack.getSize();
    cout << "Number of items on the component stack = " << stackSize << endl;
    cout << "Items on the component stack are listed (from top to bottom) " << endl;
    for (int j=0; j < stackSize; ++j) {
        fComp = compStack.pop();
        fCompName = fComp->ClassName();
        cout << fCompName.c_str() << endl;
    }
    return EXIT_SUCCESS;

}
//----------------------------------------------------------------------------
```

In the class template example displayed above, I defined a template class for a stack object and demonstrated it in the main() function by using it to create one stack for the AnsiString object type and another stack for objects of TComponent descendant classes. When executed, the program creates the stack object, pushes the items onto the stack, and finally pops all the items from the stack. Please note that the example is written just to demonstrate the use of templates.

Listing 2-2: Function template

```
//----------------------------------------------------------------

#include <vcl.h>
#include <iostream>
#pragma hdrstop
using std::cout;
using std::endl;


//----------------------------------------------------------------

#pragma argsused
//----------------------------------------------------------------
template <class T> void SwapTemplate(T& obj1, T& obj2) {
    T TempObject;
    TempObject = obj1;
    obj1 = obj2;
    obj2 = TempObject;
}
//----------------------------------------------------------------
int main()
{
    int x = 10;
    int y = 5;
    SwapTemplate<int> (x, y);
    cout << "Swap int type variables " << endl;
    cout << "x = " << x << "; y = " << y << endl;

    AnsiString str1("Borland C++Builder");
    AnsiString str2("Borland Delphi");
    SwapTemplate<AnsiString> (str1, str2);
    cout << "Swap AnsiString type variables " << endl;
    cout << "str1 = " << str1.c_str() << endl;
    cout << "str2 = " << str2.c_str() << endl;
    return EXIT_SUCCESS;
}
//----------------------------------------------------------------
```

In the function template example, I created a function template to swap the values of the two input objects. For the swap function to work for a particular data type, the data type should support the assignment operator. In both of these examples, I used the namespace std. The following section explains namespaces.

Namespaces

During application development in C++, it is likely that we will come across classes or functions with the same name, particularly when several developers are working on individual parts of the same application within the same organization. To allow for duplication of names, we use namespaces. A *namespace* is a declarative region that uniquely identifies any names defined within its scope by qualifying such names with the name of the namespace. This also mandates that we ensure uniqueness of names within a namespace. The namespace mechanism allows an application to be partitioned into a number of subsystems. Each subsystem can define and operate within its own scope. Developers of each of these subsystems are free to define identifiers that are convenient within that subsystem (or namespace) without worrying about duplication of the names by developers of other subsystems. Listing 2-3 displays a namespace definition.

Listing 2-3: Namespace declaration

```
//-----------------------------------------------------------------

#include <vcl.h>
#pragma hdrstop

//-----------------------------------------------------------------
#pragma argsused
//-----------------------------------------------------------------
namespace ns1 {
    class String {
        private:
            char* buffer;
            int length;
        public:
            String();
            int getLength();
    };
    //
    // member function implementation
    //
}
//-----------------------------------------------------------------
namespace ns2 {
    class String {
        private:
            char* StrBuffer;
            int StrLength;
        public:
            String();
            int getLength();
    };
    //
    // member function implementation
    //
}
//-----------------------------------------------------------------
int main()
{
    ns1::String st1;
    ns2::String st2;
    return 0;
}
//-----------------------------------------------------------------
```

From the example, note that we are able to define two different classes with the same name each in a different namespace; while using the class names within a program, we qualify the member class name with the namespace name. If we use more members of a namespace within the same program, it is more convenient to use the *using namespace* directive, as shown here:

```
using namespace ns1;
```

When we use the using namespace directive, we do not have to qualify any of the names defined within that namespace. Also, when we use the namespace with the using directive, we automatically get access to all of the namespaces included by the using directive within that namespace. Thus, the using directive is transitive in nature. However, the using directive may introduce unintended ambiguities, particularly when namespaces are nested and the same identifiers are used within both the namespaces.

When we are using multiple namespaces containing identifiers having the same names within an application, we can also use the *using* declaration (instead of the using namespace directive) within the local scope of a function to specify which identifier we are going to use. Since the using declaration is specific to individual identifiers, it does not introduce ambiguities. The using declaration syntax is shown here:

```
using ns1::function1;
using ns2::function2;
```

There is a single global namespace defined automatically within the context of a C++ application. This is the reason that all the global names must be unique within the scope of the application. A namespace definition may be nested within another namespace definition. Every namespace definition must appear within the context of another namespace or within a file context. When we define nested namespaces, the names within the inner namespace are accessed by double qualifiers, as in outer_ns::inner_ns::function(), where outer_ns is the name of the outer namespace and inner_ns is the name of the inner namespace. When we define nested namespaces, we may explicitly mention the inner namespace name in the using clause, which permits us to use only the inner namespace. In this case, names defined within the inner namespace do not need to be qualified, whereas the names defined within the outer namespace must be qualified.

We can also create unnamed namespaces, which are namespaces without a name. We may define as many unnamed namespaces within a translation unit (or program unit) as we wish, but they all share the same single namespace. Thus, we have to keep the identifier names unique across all the unnamed namespaces within the program unit. The unnamed namespace allows variables and functions to be visible within the entire program unit, yet not visible externally. Though entities in an unnamed namespace might have external linkage, they are effectively qualified by a name unique to their translation unit and therefore cannot be seen from any other translation unit. Unnamed namespaces are a good replacement for static declaration of variables and function identifiers.

Namespaces can be extended after they are initially defined. If we redefine a namespace after it is first defined, the namespace is automatically extended. However, the namespace extension is possible within a single translation unit. If we extend a namespace after we start using it with the using directive, the extensions made to the namespace are not visible at the point where the using directive is used.

Casting in C++

Casting is the process of accessing methods of a class with a pointer to another class within the same class hierarchy. In a class hierarchy, a pointer to the base class can be used to call the implementation of base class virtual methods residing in the derived class object. Since the derived class contains the definitions of all the base classes from which it is derived, it is safe to cast a pointer up in the hierarchy to any of the parent (or base) classes. This is called upcasting because the pointer is moved up in the class hierarchy. Because base classes are subsets within the vtable of the derived class, upcasting is usually typesafe. On the other hand, if we try to access the derived class methods using a pointer to one of its parent (or base) class objects, we are downcasting the pointer because we are moving the pointer down in the class hierarchy. Since downcasting involves accessing methods not defined in the base class vtable, the object we are trying to cast should be of the correct type for the casting to be safe. C++ provides different casting operators for different situations.

dynamic_cast

The *dynamic_cast* operator may be used to perform the upcasting and downcasting within a class hierarchy. This operator also performs the run-time check necessary to make the operation safe. Since there is a run-time type check involved, there is also additional time needed to perform the check. Therefore, in cases where a simple static_cast (as explained in the following section) is sufficient, it is not required to do a dynamic_cast. The syntax to use this operator is:

```
dynamic_cast< T >(expression);
```

Here "T" must be a pointer or a reference to a previously defined class type or a pointer to void. The expression type must be a pointer if T is a pointer or an l-value if T is a reference. Listing 2-4 displays several examples showing how to use the dynamic_cast operator. Please note that the code is not complete and may not compile as given here. You need to complete the code to compile and test it.

Listing 2-4: dynamic_cast sample code

```
//---------------------------------------------------------------------------
// This is a class hierarchy example with 3 classes
// base class
class baseClass {
// class implementation
};
// first derived class
class derivedFirst : public baseClass {
// class implementation
};
// last derived class
class derivedLast : public derivedFirst {
// class implementation
};
//---------------------------------------------------------------------------
// code samples demonstrating the use of
// dynamic_cast operator
void func() {
    derivedLast* dLast = new derivedLast;
    // The following conversion (upcasting) is permitted because
    // derivedFirst is the direct base class
    derivedFirst* dFirst = dynamic_cast< derivedFirst* >(dLast);

    // The following conversion (upcasting) is permitted because
    // baseClass is the indirect base class in the hierarchy
    baseClass* base = dynamic_cast< baseClass* >(dLast);

    // Create an object of the derived class and assign to base class ptr
    derivedFirst* dFirst2 = new derivedFirst;
    baseClass* base2 = dFirst2;

    // The following conversion (downcasting) is permitted
    // if the base class has virtual functions
    // VCL event handlers usually pass the base TObject pointer for the
    // Sender parameter. The appropriate (derived) object pointer may be
    // obtained by syntax similar to this.
    derivedFirst* dFirst3 = dynamic_cast< derivedFirst* >(base2);

    // The following conversion is not permitted
    // because base2 does not point to derivedLast object
    derivedLast* dLast2 = dynamic_cast< derivedLast*>(base2);

    // The following conversion is permitted, but we cannot execute the
    // methods of base2 using the vPtr. The vPtr should be converted back
    // to a derivedFirst or baseClass ptr, in order to make method calls.
    void* vPtr = dynamic_cast< void* >(base2);
}
//---------------------------------------------------------------------------
```

static_cast

The *static_cast* operator is usually used for non-polymorphic type conversions, such as enum to int, int to float, and so on. It may also be used, with caution, in place of the dynamic_cast operator. In contrast to the dynamic_cast, the static_cast operator does not perform a run-time check to ensure safe casting. The operator relies on the types provided in the expression and on the programmer to ensure safe conversion. Therefore, the static_cast operator may be used in situations where you are certain that the expression of casting is really an object of the appropriate type or when you are certain that the conversion is not going to fail. In addition, if you try to perform a dynamic_cast on an ambiguous conversion, it will fail either by returning NULL in case of a pointer cast or by throwing a bad_cast exception in case of a reference cast. Hence, you know that the operation did not succeed. On the other hand, if a static_cast operation fails, it will return, as if nothing went wrong. This is more dangerous because using the pointer obtained from such an unsafe conversion would result in access violation situations, and the program may abnormally terminate. The syntax for this operator is:

```
static_cast< T >(expression);
```

const_cast

The *const_cast* operator must be used to add or remove the const and volatile modifiers from identifiers. The syntax for this operator is:

```
const_cast< T >(argument);
```

In this expression, T and argument must be of the same type, except if T is qualified as const and volatile; then the argument should not be qualified, and vice versa. The cast is resolved at compile time. The result of this expression is of type T. A pointer to const object can be converted to the identical object without the const modifier. A successful conversion results in a pointer to the original object. Listing 2-5 displays sample code to demonstrate the use of this operator. The const_cast operator works on the volatile modifier similar to the const modifier.

Listing 2-5: const_cast sample code

```
// sample code to show how the const_cast operator can be used
void func() {
    // In the following example the const variable x is converted to
    // a non-const variable y. The variable y can be modified in the
    // program, just as any other int variable
    const int x = 10;
    int y = const_cast<int>(x);

    // In the following example the non-const variable a is converted to
    // a const variable b. Now the variable b cannot be modified since it is a const.
```

```
    int a = 10;
    const int b = const_cast<const int>(a);

}
```

reinterpret_cast

The *reinterpret_cast* operator is used for simple reinterpretation of bits, which means casting any pointer type to any other pointer type; therefore, it is inherently unsafe. The resulting pointer after casting should not be used to directly access the object; rather, it should be used to cast the pointer back to the original type. In this sense, the operator may be an intermediate step. This operator may be used to convert an integer type to any pointer type, and vice versa. When we convert a pointer to an integer type, the resulting value may be bit-shifted and manipulated to produce a unique index value. We may write a hash function to encapsulate this feature. This may not be a foolproof approach for generating a unique index in enterprise applications involving millions of transactions, but in small applications, it may produce a fairly unique value and is worth considering.

The syntax to use this operator is:

```
reinterpret_cast< T >(argument);
```

Please keep in mind that by doing this casting, we are just reinterpreting the original type as another type and therefore it should only be used in special situations, as discussed above.

Exception Handling

C++ has built-in support to handle exceptional conditions requiring special handling. These are usually run-time errors, such as unavailability of system resources or attempts to execute illegal program instructions and so on. Exception handling enables you to write programs that communicate unexpected events to a higher execution context, which is in a better position to recover from such abnormal error conditions. The try, throw, and catch statements implement exception handling in C++. Listing 2-6 displays typical code that uses try, throw, and catch statements. In the try... catch block, code within the try block is a guarded section of the program and is executed with exception handling capability enabled, which means that code in this block may throw exceptions that will be caught in the catch block for handling purposes. The catch block should be repeated once for every type of exception thrown within the try block. We may design our own exception classes as required within our application framework. The set of exception classes provided by Borland's VCL and CLX frameworks are huge and work in conjunction with the try, throw, and catch framework.

Please note that the code in this example is only to demonstrate exception-handling syntax; it does not compile as it is given here.

Listing 2-6: Try, throw, and catch

```
void TryCatchFunction() {
    try {
        // processing logic
        FunctionThatThrowsException();
        // processing logic
    }
    catch (ExceptionCondition &ec) {
        HandleExceptions(ec);
    }
}
void FunctionThatThrowsException() {
    // processing logic
    if (ErrorCondition) {
        throw ExceptionCondition(ErrorCode, ErrorMessage);
    }
}
void HandleExceptions(ExceptionCondition &ec) {
    // processing logic
}
```

When the code within the try block is executed, if no exception condition occurs, the code within all the catch blocks associated with the previous try block are ignored. If an exception is thrown during execution of the try block or during execution of any routine called by code in this block, an exception object is created by the throw operand. At this time, the compiler looks for a catch block in a higher execution context (the try...catch block in this case) that can handle an exception of the type that is thrown. If a catch block is found, the exception is handled by code within the catch block. If a catch block is not found, the search continues to the next higher level try...catch block (if the try catch blocks were nested). If a suitable catch block is not found in any of the higher execution contexts, the predefined run-time function terminate() is called to abnormally terminate the program. Please note that the only way that the code in a catch block is executed is by throwing the corresponding exception. An exception handler (typically the catch block) may re-throw the same exception, either partially handling the exception condition or without handling. When an exception is re-thrown, the compiler searches for the next higher execution context, which can catch this exception. The syntax to re-throw an exception is the throw keyword followed by a semicolon (throw;).

It is important to note that the order in which we write catch blocks is important because when the matching catch block is found for an exception, the subsequent catch blocks are ignored. Therefore, when an exception object of a derived exception class is thrown, we should place the catch block for a derived exception class before the catch block for the base exception class. The derived exception class represents a more specific exception object, and the base exception class represents the more generic exception object.

A Word about Pointers

When anyone talks about programming in C++, at least one important feature comes to mind: pointers. This is perhaps the only feature that scares many programmers, with regards to programming in C++. Let me have the opportunity to present you with my approach to using pointers.

The stack memory is used mainly for two purposes: to store function parameters (also called arguments) and function stack frames and to store local variables and objects. Function parameters and stack frames go together. When a function is called from another function, the function parameters are the variables and objects whose values are copied (or pushed) onto the stack before the program control jumps to the called function. Stack frames contain data required by the processor to return to the calling function and resume its execution from where it was suspended before the control jumped to the called function. Along with the function arguments, the stack frame information is also pushed onto the stack.

During the execution of the called function, the processor retrieves (or pops up) the argument values from the stack. When the control has to return to the calling function, the stack frame information of the calling function is also retrieved from the stack. It is with the help of stack frame information that the processor will be able to clean up the stack and bring it to the state where it was before executing the function call. The internals of stack usage and management are out of the scope of this book. For more details on stacks and their management, I recommend referring to books and articles that exclusively discuss subjects such as assembly language programming or compiler internals. Also please note that stack management is more of a processor feature that specific language compilers implement in their own style. Now you understand the importance of the stack. Today's computing requirements demand simultaneous execution of several processes, and each of the processes have several function calls nested to many levels. The stack is a scarce resource and required for the basic execution of the program. What happens if we use up the stack memory by allocating our objects on the stack? It may lead to abnormal termination of the program, including stack overflow errors.

It is more inefficient if we pass objects (and not the pointers) as function arguments because the whole object is copied to the stack instead of the pointer. Imagine a situation in which you are passing this object across several layers of function calls. You will be making multiple copies of the same object and pushing onto the stack again and again. The stack does not clean up this garbage until you return to the first calling function. There are two disadvantages to this approach. The first one is misuse of the stack space, and the second is the time it takes for the called function to retrieve the whole object from the stack (multiple times if the argument is passed across several functions), thus impacting program performance. Instead, if we create our objects on the heap (with the new operator), obviously we create a pointer to access the object. In this case, the object is created on the heap with the pointer on the stack. However, depending on where the object pointer is declared within the source program and its storage class specifier, the scope of the pointer may vary, such as local, global to the program, or static. Typically in a C++ program, the object pointers declared in the class declaration are visible to all the member functions. The member functions may pass a pointer to the object (to objects of other classes), thus providing restricted access to the object pointer.

The object may need storage as large as several hundred bytes, but the pointer only occupies 4 bytes on a 32-bit machine, which is created on the stack. The amount of stack space used up when we pass object pointers across (several) function calls is insignificant compared to when we pass the object by value. Also, when we pass object pointers as function arguments, the called function has direct access to the original object through the pointer and can modify it, if required. However, the only time you may consider passing an object by value as a function argument is when you do not want the called function to have the ability to modify the original object. In my opinion, careful design of the program (such as using the const keyword) can avoid such situations.

We know that objects created on the heap have to be explicitly deleted using the delete operator. An error on the part of the programmer may lead to access violation exceptions, such as trying to access or delete an object that has already been deleted. In this case, it is good programming practice to check if the pointer is pointing to the object before trying to access or delete it; however, the delete operator checks if the pointer is NULL before trying to delete, and if the pointer is NULL, the delete operation is not performed. On the other hand, if we do not delete objects created on the heap once we are done with them, we introduce inherent memory leaks in the program. A *memory leak* is a situation where the allocated memory is not released, nor is it accessible to other programs. Some of us may have a misconception that objects have to be destroyed only in the destructor function. There is no hard-and-fast rule in this regard. Our design should be able to help us in determining the scope and lifetime of the object, and accordingly we have to delete it when we are done using it.

The following are typical situations where we might commit programming errors that lead to access violation errors or memory leaks:

■ Creating an object on the heap and assigning it to a pointer having local scope within a function. In this case, the object is not accessible once the execution of the function is over. In such a situation, either we have to delete the object before the function returns or save the object's address in a global pointer or in a global container object, which may contain a list of object pointers of the same object type. If we save the object address, we can still access the object through the stored pointer.

■ If you created an array of objects on the heap using the new [] operator (as in obj = new className[2];), then you must delete the array using the delete [] operator, as in (delete [] obj;).

■ If you created class definitions containing pointers to other objects as members, you need to make sure that before the main object gets destroyed, the objects assigned to the member pointers are destroyed; otherwise, we cannot reclaim the memory used by the objects assigned to the member pointers, nor can we access them. This is a potential memory leak situation. One way to avoid this situation is to delete all the internal objects in the destructor of the main object.

■ It is also a common practice that most of us use multiple pointers pointing to the same object, which means that you have created only one instance of the object but assigned this object to more than one pointer in the program. In this case, the object should only be deleted once, and all the pointers pointing to the object should be set to NULL explicitly. Here I am referring to object pointers having the same level of scope, such as pointers defined in the same function or pointers defined as members of the class. If we pass an object pointer as a function argument from a calling function to a called function, it is not a multiple pointer scenario because the pointer passed as function argument has scope limited to the called function only. However, in such a scenario, we may tend to delete the object in the called function. A good programming practice is to delete the object in the calling function after the control is returned from the called function.

Dynamic memory management is not something to be scared of, but it should be used cautiously because it comes with power and performance and imposes responsibility on the part of the programmer. The performance improvement while using the dynamic memory management feature in large C++ applications is significant.

References

In the previous section, we discussed dynamic memory management using pointers. In this section, we will focus our attention on the object references. In C++, we can pass objects as function arguments either by value or by reference. If we pass the object by value, we have noted earlier that the whole object is copied onto the stack, which does not help in situations when the object is fairly large or when we need the function to modify the contents of the original object instead of modifying a copy of the object. In such situations, we pass the object by reference. An object's *reference* is an alias of the object, or it refers only to the address of the object. Therefore, when we pass an object's reference, only the object reference is copied to the stack, not the object itself. This helps a lot in optimal usage of the stack, and the called function can directly modify the contents of the object.

When the program is compiled, the compiler stores all the identifier information in a symbol table. In the symbol table, object references are stored as entries that point to real compiled objects. Thus, a reference does not have an identity for itself.

Passing function arguments by reference is functionally not different from passing object pointers. However, with references, the compiler handles the details of passing pointers and dereferencing them; with pointers, you do it yourself. Also, when we pass object references as function arguments, there is no need to perform a NULL check on the reference in the called function; in contrast, with object pointers it is always good practice to check if the pointer is not NULL before we access the object. Thus, references are a higher-level abstraction than pointers. Listing 2-7 displays sample code differentiating function calls, passing objects by value, by reference, and by pointer. This is a working example, and the output of this program is shown in Figure 2-1.

Listing 2-7: Object references

```
//----------------------------------------------------------------------
#include <vcl.h>
#include <iostream>
#pragma hdrstop
using std::cout;
using std::endl;
//----------------------------------------------------------------------
#pragma argsused
//----------------------------------------------------------------------
class TestObject {
    private:
        int member;
    public:
        // class implementation
        TestObject() { };
```

```
            int getMember() { return member;};
            void setMember(int value) { member = value; };
};

void ObjectByValue(TestObject obj) {
    int member_value = obj.getMember();
    obj.setMember(12);
}

void ObjectByReference(TestObject& obj) {
    // when object references are passed, it is not required
    // to perform a NULL check as we do in case of object pointers.
    int member_value = obj.getMember();
    obj.setMember(22);
}

void ObjectByPointer(TestObject* obj) {
    // when pointers are passed, it is required to make sure that the
    // pointer is not NULL, before we access the object through the pointer
    if (obj != NULL) {
        int member_value = obj->getMember();
        obj->setMember(32);
    }
}
int main()
{
    TestObject obj;
    obj.setMember(20);
    cout << "Initial value of member = " << obj.getMember() << endl;
    // pass object by value
    ObjectByValue(obj);
    cout << "Value after passing (by value) to function = " << obj.getMember() << endl;
    // pass object by reference
    ObjectByReference(obj);
    cout << "Value after passing (by reference) to function = " << obj.getMember()
        << endl;
    // pass object by pointer
    ObjectByPointer(&obj);
    cout << "Value after passing (by pointer) to function = " << obj.getMember() << endl;
    return EXIT_SUCCESS;
}
//-------------------------------------------------------------------------
```

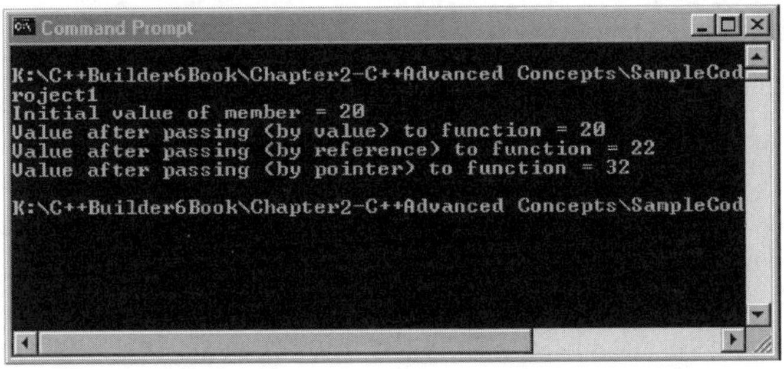

Figure 2-1: Output of a console application demonstrating the object references

Virtual Methods

Implementation of the virtual functions provides run-time polymorphic behavior in a class hierarchy. We have seen earlier that a pointer to the base class can be set to point to a class derived from that base class. However, such an assignment enables us only to access methods of the derived class, which are inherited from the base class. The base class pointer does not have any knowledge of the additional methods that the derived class may have declared.

Methods of the base class that are declared as virtual provide run-time polymorphic behavior when overridden by the derived classes. This means that if the derived class overrides a virtual method of the base class, and if we are accessing a derived class object through a base class pointer, a call to this method invokes the derived class implementation of the method, not the base class implementation. This is because of the run-time determination of which object the pointer is pointing to—the base class object or the derived class object. However, if the derived class did not override the virtual method, then the base class implementation is invoked automatically. Figure 2-2 displays how the vtable of the derived class contains the overridden version of the virtual method.

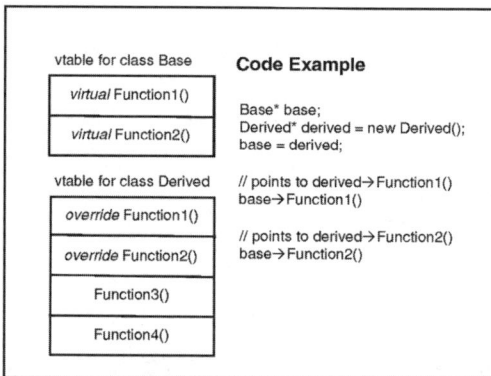

Figure 2-2: Vtable representation of base and derived classes

Let's validate our discussion with an example. In our example, I created a base class and three derived classes. The base class declares and implements a virtual method called DisplayMessage(). The purpose of this method is to tell us which version of the method is being executed. The first and second derived classes override this method with their own messages. The third derived class does not override this method. I created a main function, which creates a base class object initially and executes the method from the base class object. Following this, I created each of the three derived class objects sequentially, assigned them to the base class pointer, and then executed the method. (In the code you may notice that I am deleting the previous object before the next object is created, just to make sure that there is no memory leak in the program.)

The results support our discussion on the virtual methods. With the first two derived class objects assigned to the base class pointer, the method overridden in the respective class is executed. With the third derived class object, the method from the base class is executed because we have not overridden the method in this class. Listing 2-8 displays the sample code for our illustration, and Figure 2-3 displays console output when the program is compiled and executed. This is a working example, so you can try to compile and test this program.

Listing 2-8: Virtual functions

```
//-------------------------------------------------------------------------

#include <vcl.h>
#include <iostream>
#pragma hdrstop
using std::cout;
using std::endl;
//-------------------------------------------------------------------------
#pragma argsused
//-------------------------------------------------------------------------
class Base {
public:
    Base() { };
    virtual void DisplayMessage() {
        cout << "Displaying Message from an object of Base class" << endl;
    };
};
//-------------------------------------------------------------------------
class DerivedFirst : public Base {
public:
    DerivedFirst() { };
    void DisplayMessage() {
        cout << "Displaying Message from an object of DerivedFirst class" << endl;
    }
};
//-------------------------------------------------------------------------
class DerivedSecond : public Base {
public:
    DerivedSecond() { };
    void DisplayMessage() {
        cout << "Displaying Message from an object of DerivedSecond class" << endl;
    }
};
//-------------------------------------------------------------------------
class DerivedThird : public Base {
public:
    DerivedThird() { };
};
//-------------------------------------------------------------------------
int main()
{
```

```
// create a base class object
Base* bc = new Base();
bc->DisplayMessage();

// delete the base class object and assign it to DerivedFirst object
delete bc;
bc = new DerivedFirst();
bc->DisplayMessage();

// delete the base class object and assign it to DerivedSecond object
delete bc;
bc = new DerivedSecond();
bc->DisplayMessage();

// delete the base class object and assign it to DerivedThird object
delete bc;
bc = new DerivedThird();
bc->DisplayMessage();
delete bc;
return EXIT_SUCCESS;
}
//------------------------------------------------------------------------
```

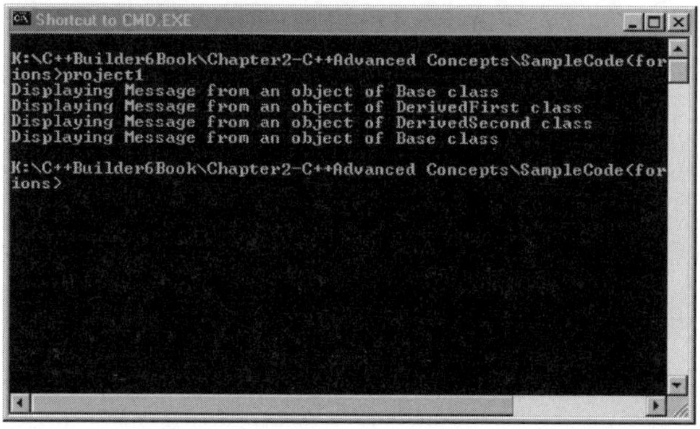

Figure 2-3: Console output of virtual methods example

If the base class does not implement the virtual method, then such a method is called a *pure virtual method* and is specified in the class definition with a declaration similar to the following:

```
virtual void PureVirtualFunction() = 0;
```

In this declaration, we are setting the method declaration to a value equal to zero, which conveys to the compiler that the base class does not implement this method. A class containing at least one pure virtual method is called an *abstract class*. Objects of abstract classes cannot be instantiated. The mere existence of abstract classes is to function as base classes, and every derived class from an abstract base class must implement all the pure virtual methods. This discussion is going to help us when we continue with the concepts of implementing Delphi interfaces in C++Builder.

C++ Language and C++Builder

Overview

In the previous sections, we discussed some core C++ language features that are sometimes ignored by many programmers. If you are not familiar with these features, I am sure you must have gained some knowledge on these topics. On the other hand, if you are already well conversant with these topics, the discussion may have helped to refresh your knowledge.

In this section, we will focus our attention on some of the C++ language features in the way that they are implemented in C++Builder 6. While C++Builder 6 certainly supports development of ANSI C and C++ compliant applications, two powerful component libraries—Visual Component Library (VCL for short) and Component Library for Cross-platform development (CLX for short)—are also provided with this product to enable rapid application development of Windows applications and cross-platform applications respectively. A detailed discussion of VCL and CLX is presented in later chapters. Please note that it is not mandatory to use VCL or CLX components to write a C++ application in C++Builder. To make this point clear, the different C++ application categories that are supported in C++Builder 6 and related features and issues are listed here. Each of these categories of applications may be an executable program or an object library, static or dynamic.

- A completely ANSI C or C++ compliant application without using VCL or CLX libraries. This type of application is portable across any platform and operating system that has a compiler in compliance with the appropriate ANSI standards. However, the compliance is usually at source-code level. Object-level compliance is possible only on the same platform. Please note that Win32-based applications do not fall in this category because Win32 library is Windows specific.

- A C++ compliant application without using VCL or CLX libraries but using Win32 core library, as provided by Microsoft Corporation. Applications developed in this category are portable across other C++ development environments on the Windows platforms, both at source level and object level. However, the compatibility is governed (and limited) by different Win32 library versions on different Windows operating systems (such as Windows 98, Windows NT, Windows 2000, and Windows XP).

- A C++ application making use of VCL core components. This type of application is not compatible with any other development platform on Windows, even at source level, because VCL is core Borland technology. But the object libraries developed in this category are usually compatible with other development environments within the Windows platforms with limitations already explained.

- A C++ application making use of CLX core components. This type of application is compatible across Windows and Linux operating systems at source level. (Borland is planning to release a version of C++Builder on Linux that builds applications using CLX components. At the time of publication, Borland had already released the Linux version of Delphi, called Kylix, using the CLX components). The object-level compatibility is, however, limited by the operating systems.

- I am not listing the COM, CORBA, and Web applications here because they all form part of the VCL/CLX architecture, with the exception that COM is not implemented in CLX due to platform portability requirements and since COM is a Microsoft Windows-based technology.

- It is easy to convert a VCL application into a CLX application to be portable to Linux due to similarities in these component libraries, provided the VCL application has minimum usage of direct Win32 function calls or direct operating system function calls.

- Due to the RAD (rapid application development) nature of the VCL and CLX libraries, application development using these libraries demands less time. Learning VCL and CLX architectures is not difficult and is usually fast. If you are already familiar with the VCL, learning CLX becomes an even simpler process.

- Both VCL and CLX are event-based architectures (similar to Java packages), and the components automatically trigger event handlers when the corresponding events occur. We can develop Windows GUI and console applications using either VCL or CLX libraries.

- C++Builder 6 is also equipped with two sets of Standard Template Libraries (STL). One set was originally developed by RogueWave but licensed through Borland in C++Builder. The second set is the open source version of STL, called STLPort. We can use the STL objects in any category of applications we discussed above without altering their ANSI compliance level, as STL is itself in compliance with ANSI standards.

Keyword Extensions

This section discusses ANSI-conforming keyword extensions implemented in C++Builder 6 to support the VCL and CLX architectures. Please note that these keyword extensions are specific to C++Builder and not to the standard C++ language. If you use one or more of these keywords in your application, your application may not be portable across other platforms.

__classid

The __*classid* operator is used by the compiler to generate a pointer to the vtable for the specified class name. This operator may also be used to obtain the metaclass from a class. The syntax to use this operator is shown in Listing 2-9. There are also other ways to obtain the metaclass of a class, as discussed in Chapter 3, "The VCL Explored."

Listing 2-9: Sample code

```
// code to declare and implement the TNewComponent1
// code to declare and implement the TNewComponent2
//
//
TMetaClass classes[2];                 // Create an array of classes
Classes[0] = __classid(TNewComponent1); // Assign first element to the first component
Classes[1] = __classid(TNewComponent2); // Assign second element to the second component

// The classes array may be used in registering the components with the component palette
```

__closure

Standard C++ permits us to assign a derived class instance to a base class pointer. If the base class member functions are defined as virtual, then we can access the member functions of the derived class through the base class pointer. But we cannot assign a derived class member function to a base class member function pointer. The __*closure* extension keyword may be used to facilitate this. In this context, the __closure keyword is used in the function pointer declaration. A function pointer declaration with the __closure keyword declares a generic function pointer with a specific signature (i.e., a set of input parameter types in specific sequence and a return value type). A member function that has the same signature (i.e., accepts the same set of input parameter types in the same sequence and the return value type) as the function declared with the __closure keyword prefix and belonging to any object (base or derived) can be assigned to the function pointer with the __closure prefix. Remember that the assignment is to an object instance's member function and not to the class member function. Then the closure function may be executed by its name and by providing the necessary input parameters. The return value may be assigned to a variable of the appropriate type. The sample code in Listing 2-10 helps you understand this concept. The output displayed on a console is shown in Figure 2-4.

Listing 2-10: __closure sample code

```
//-------------------------------------------------------------------------

#include <vcl.h>
#include <iostream>
#pragma hdrstop
using std::cout;
using std::endl;
//-------------------------------------------------------------------------

#pragma argsused
class Car {
public:
    Car();   // constructor
    void getBase();
    void setBase(int valueBase);
};
Car::Car(){
    cout << "executing base class constructor " << endl;
}
void Car::getBase() {
    cout << "executing base class get() " << endl;
}
void Car::setBase(int valueBase) {
    cout << "executing base class set() " << endl;
}
//-------------------------------------------------------------------------
class SportsCar : public Car {
public:
    SportsCar(); // constructor
    void getDerived();
    void setDerived(int value);
};
SportsCar::SportsCar() {
    cout << "executing derived class constructor " << endl;
}
void SportsCar::getDerived() {
    cout << "executing derived class get() " << endl;
}
void SportsCar::setDerived(int value) {
    cout << "executing derived class set() " << endl;
}
//-------------------------------------------------------------------------
int main(int argc, char* argv[])
{
    void (__closure *closureFunction1)(int);
    void (__closure *closureFunction2)(void);
    Car* myCar = new Car();
    SportsCar* spCar = new SportsCar();
    closureFunction1 = myCar->setBase;
    closureFunction2 = spCar->getDerived;
    closureFunction1(4);
    closureFunction2();
```

```
      return EXIT_SUCCESS;
}
//------------------------------------------------------------------------
```

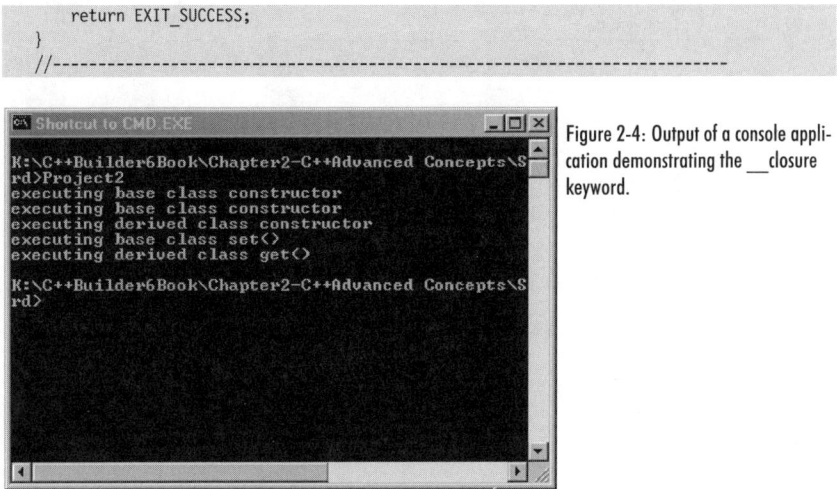

Figure 2-4: Output of a console application demonstrating the __closure keyword.

__property

Apart from being a powerful C++ implementation, C++Builder also contains a component framework. A few important characteristics of such a framework are to define the attributes of objects as properties and to enable the developer to publish these properties as required, so they can be manipulated in the IDE during design time. Properties are the way to access the private data members (or attributes) of objects using public member methods.

The __*property* keyword declares an attribute of a class through public member methods. The attributes declared by the __property keyword completely control access to the property, and therefore, there are no restrictions on how to implement the properties within a class. It means that the developers can expose an attribute of the class as a read-only property or read-write property as desired. Listing 2-11 displays sample code to declare a read-write property for a class attribute. The class attribute FCyl is exposed to the external world as the property Cyl. Also notice that I associate a read method and a write method with this property. The read method enables the users to get the value of the property, and the write method enables the user to set the value of the property. We will discuss more about properties in Chapter 12, "Miscellaneous and Advanced Topics" in the section "Custom Component Development."

Listing 2-11: Sample code

```
//---------------------------------------------------------------------
class Car {
private:
    int FCyl;
public:
    Car() {};
    void writeCyl(int cyl);
    int readCyl();

    __property int Cyl = {read=readCyl, write=writeCyl};
};
void Car::writeCyl(int cyl) {
    FCyl = cyl;
}
int Car::readCyl() {
    return FCyl;
}
//---------------------------------------------------------------------
```

__published

When properties are published, they are available in the Object Inspector of the IDE for the developer to set their values during design and development time and also during run time. Unpublished properties can only be accessed programmatically during run time. A standard C++ program can have only public, private, and protected sections to categorize its members. Programs written using the VCL or CLX component framework can also have the published section. The published section is identified by the __published keyword. Properties declared in this section will be made available through the Object Inspector during design time. Published members follow the same visibility rules as the public members.

The only difference between published and public members is that Object Pascal-style run-time type information (RTTI) is generated for data members and properties declared in the __published section. RTTI enables an application to dynamically query the data members, member functions, and properties of an otherwise unknown class type. No constructors or destructors are allowed in a __published section. Properties, Pascal intrinsic or VCL or CLX derived data members, member functions, and closures are allowed in a __published section. The type of a property defined in a __published section must be an ordinal type, a real type, a string type, a small set type, a class type, or a method pointer type.

__declspec

The __declspec keyword is used with special arguments to provide language support for the VCL. Macros for these __declspec arguments are defined in the sysmac.h header file. These arguments and their purpose are explained in Table 2-1.

Table 2-1: __declspec arguments with description

__declspec Argument	Description
__declspec(delphiclass)	Used for declarations for classes derived from TObject. These classes will be created with compatibility for (a) Object Pascal compatible RTTI, (b) VCL/CLX compatible constructor-destructor behavior, and (c) VCL/CLX compatible exception handling. This also means that the class was implemented as Delphi source file, and only a class declaration is provided in the header file. This declaration is identified by the macro RTL_DELPHICLASS in the sysmac.h header file.
__declspec(delphireturn)	This is used internally by VCL or CLX for declaration of classes that were created in C++Builder to support Object Pascal's built-in data types and language constructs because they do not have a native C++ type. These include Currency, AnsiString, Variant, TDateTime, and Set. This argument makes C++ classes for VCL or CLX compatible handling in function calls as parameters and return values. This modifier is needed when passing a structure by value to a function between Object Pascal and C++. This declaration is identified by the macro RTL_DELPHIRETURN in the sysmac.h header file.
__declspec(delphirtti)	This argument causes the compiler to include run-time type information in a class when it is compiled. When this argument is used, the compiler generates run-time type information for all the fields, methods, and properties that are declared in the published section. For interfaces, the compiler generates the run-time type information for all the methods. If a class is compiled with run-time type information, all its descendants also include the run-time type information. Since the class TPersistent is compiled with run-time type information, it means that there is no need to include this argument to compile any classes that have TPersistent as an ancestor. This declaration is identified by the macro DECLSPEC_DRTTI in the sysmac.h header file.
__declspec(dynamic)	This argument is used for declaration of dynamic functions. Dynamic functions are similar to virtual functions, except they are stored in the vtables for the objects that define them, not in the descendant object's vtables. If you call a dynamic function and that function is not defined in the object, the vtables of its ancestors are searched until the function is found. Dynamic functions are valid only for classes derived from TObject. This declaration is identified by the macro DYNAMIC in the sysmac.h header file.
__declspec(hidesbase)	This argument preserves the Object Pascal program semantics when porting Object Pascal virtual and override functions to C++Builder. In Object Pascal, virtual functions in the base class can appear in the derived class as a function with the same name but as a completely new function without any explicit relation to the earlier one. This declaration is identified by the macro HIDESBASE. The compiler generates this function with the HIDESBASE qualifier.
__declspec(package)	This argument indicates the code defining the class can be compiled in a package. This declaration is identified by the macro PACKAGE in the sysmac.h header file.
__declspec(pascal-implementation)	This argument indicates that the code defining the class was implemented in Object Pascal. This modifier appears in the Object Pascal portability header file for C++Builder.
__declspec(uuid)	This argument associates a class or interface with a globally unique identifier (GUID). Typically, this is used with classes that represent Object Pascal Interfaces. This declaration is identified by the macro INTERFACE_UUID in the sysmac.h header file.

Apart from the macros for the basic arguments described above, macros for combinations of basic arguments are also defined in the sysmac.h header file. They are listed in Table 2-2.

Table 2-2: Macros defining combinations of __declspec arguments

__declspec Argument	Macro
__declspec(pascalimplementation, package)	PASCALIMPLEMENTATION
__declspec(delphireturn, package)	DELPHIRETURN
__declspec(delphiclass, package)	DELHICLASS
__declspec(hidesbase, dynamic)	HIDESBASEDYNAMIC

__interface

Most of the time, we have to inherit the behavior of multiple base classes to a derived class when programming in a true object-oriented environment. This is due to the complex nature of the enterprise applications. Some object-oriented languages, such as Delphi and Java, support this require-ment through the interface construct, which is not supported by the standard C++ language specification. But C++ supports inheriting a class directly from multiple base classes. Apart from supporting multiple inheritance for the ANSI-compliant applications, C++Builder extends the concept of inter-faces to the VCL- and CLX-based applications through the _interface keyword. The __interface keyword is a macro definition that maps to the class keyword. When you program in Delphi, you can derive from one base class and implement any number of interfaces. The interfaces in Delphi take the role of additional base classes in a C++ program.

The Delphi interfaces contain all pure virtual methods with no imple-mentation and no data members. They are usually derived from the IInterface interface. By following certain conventions, we can make a class in C++Builder behave just like a Delphi interface construct. The conven-tions are described below.

- Declaring all the method signatures as pure virtual methods and not containing any data members

- Using the __interface keyword in place of the class keyword. By doing this, we are only trying to simulate an interface definition without vio-lating rules of the language.

- Starting the interface names with the letter I, as in IMyInterface. This helps us to a great extent by hinting that a particular (class) declaration refers to an interface and not a class. We can also find the same by going through the declaration, but we can save time by following the convention.

- Borland also recommends assigning a GUID (globally unique identi-fier) for an interface, since most of the code that works with interfaces expects to see an interface definition with a GUID.

■ The Delphi IInterface interface is also available in C++Builder. Deriving the interface from IInterface provides basic interface management methods.

■ It is also useful to define a class of DelphiInterface type that makes it convenient to work with the interfaces. When you use interfaces in Delphi, the Object Pascal compiler automatically handles interface-related tasks, such as incrementing the reference count every time an application acquires the interface pointer and decrementing it when the object reference goes out of scope. C++Builder provides the Delphi-Interface template class to do the same thing. The template class has a constructor, copy constructor, assignment operator, and destructor to implement the reference count manipulation as required. However, there are other operators provided by the template class to access the underlying interface pointer that do not perform the reference counting. In such cases, you have to explicitly call the AddRef and Release methods for this purpose.

■ By design, you cannot inherit VCL-style classes from multiple base classes. I do not want you to mistake the multiple inheritance feature of the ANSI C++ compliant program, which is implemented by C++Builder. If you have to derive a VCL-style class from VCL-style base classes, you can only derive from one VCL-style base class. However, you can implement multiple inheritance by deriving from one VCL-style base class and one or more interface style classes, which meet the criteria of an interface, as discussed earlier.

Object Construction Sequence in C++Builder

When a class is a member in a class hierarchy, it is important that we understand the object construction sequence. As I mentioned earlier, C++Builder has two flavors of C++ implementation: the standard ANSI-compliant style C++ and the VCL/CLX style. C++Builder acquired this dual nature because the VCL/CLX component libraries originated from Object Pascal as the base language of implementation.

In a standard (ANSI-compliant) C++ program, when we instantiate an object of a derived class, the typical order of object creation is from the virtual base class, then the base classes in the order as they exist in the class hierarchy, and finally the derived class object. The C++ syntax uses the constructor initialization list to call the base class constructors. The run-time type of the object is that of the class that is being constructed.

In a typical Object Pascal class hierarchy, only the constructor of the final derived object (which is being instantiated) is guaranteed to be called.

However, memory is allocated for each of the base classes. The immediate base class constructor is called only by explicitly using the inherited keyword in the constructor of the subsequent derived class. However, to make sure that all the base classes are constructed in the VCL/CLX architecture, the classes in these component libraries make it a convention to explicitly use the inherited keyword in a derived class to call the non-empty constructors of the immediate ancestor class, though it is not a requirement imposed by the Object Pascal language. The run-time type of the object is established as that of the class that is being instantiated and will not change as the constructors of the base classes are executed. There is a notable difference between C++ and Object Pascal language styles.

Now we will examine what happens to the object construction sequence in a typical VCL-based application in C++Builder. When we build our application in C++Builder, we are writing code in the C++ language, and hence our code is going to be compiled by the C++ compiler underlying the C++Builder product. However, the base classes that are ancestors to our C++ classes are libraries written, compiled, and packaged in Object Pascal style. What we have as our C++ interfaces are header files containing class definitions and method signatures translated to C++ style.

Now you can guess what happens when the C++ compiler takes charge of our derived C++ class (or classes). Since we are using the C++ compiler, the compiler tries to construct the base classes first (as per C++ syntax rules), followed by the derived classes. Since all the base classes are in Object Pascal, the object construction sequence is opposite to the C++ style. This means that the last (base) class in the VCL hierarchy is constructed first, and the sequence moves backward until it reaches TObject, which is the first VCL class in the hierarchy. After TObject is constructed, the attention is moved toward the set of C++ classes that we have built. Since these are written in C++, the sequence of object construction is forward, which means the first base C++ class is constructed first (after the TObject construction), and the sequence moves forward until it reaches the final derived class in the hierarchy, which is the leaf class. The run-time type of the object is established (in Object Pascal style) as that of the instantiated class and will not change through the object construction process. Listing 2-12 is sample code that illustrates the run-time type of the object with the help of virtual functions being called from the constructor. The example illustrates both standard C++ style and VCL-style classes.

Listing 2-12: unit1.cpp

```
//----------------------------------------------------------------------

#include <vcl.h>
#include <iostream>
#pragma hdrstop
using std::cout;
using std::endl;
//----------------------------------------------------------------------
#pragma argsused
// standard C++ style base class and derived class
class BaseCar {
public:
    BaseCar() { DisplayMessage(); };
    virtual void DisplayMessage() { cout << "C++ style - Base Car" << endl;};
};
class Toyota : public BaseCar {
public:
    Toyota() { };
    void DisplayMessage() { cout << "C++ style - Toyota Car" << endl;};
};
//----------------------------------------------------------------------
// VCL C++ style base class and derived class
class VCLBaseCar : public TObject {
public:
    VCLBaseCar() { DisplayMessage(); };
    virtual void DisplayMessage() { cout << "VCL style - Base Car" << endl;};
};
class VCLHonda : public VCLBaseCar {
public:
    VCLHonda() { };
    void DisplayMessage() { cout << "VCL style - Honda Car" << endl;};
};
//----------------------------------------------------------------------
int main()
{
    Toyota* toyota = new Toyota();
    VCLHonda* vclhonda = new VCLHonda();
    delete vclhonda;
    delete toyota;
    return EXIT_SUCCESS;
}
//----------------------------------------------------------------------
```

The output of this console program is displayed in Figure 2-5 on the following page.

From the output display, it is clear that in a standard C++ application, the run-time type is set to the class whose object is being constructed. When the base class constructor is called first, the base class version of the DisplayMessage() method is executed since the run-time type is the base class. Since the derived Toyota class has an empty constructor, there is no way to execute its version of the DisplayMessage() method. On the other hand, in the VCL application, the run-time type is set to the derived VCLHonda class. Even though the TObject is constructed first, we are not displaying any message in its constructor since it is part of the standard VCL package. For our example, the base VCLBaseCar class is constructed first, and its constructor is calling the derived class version of the Display-Message() method since run-time type is set to the derived class.

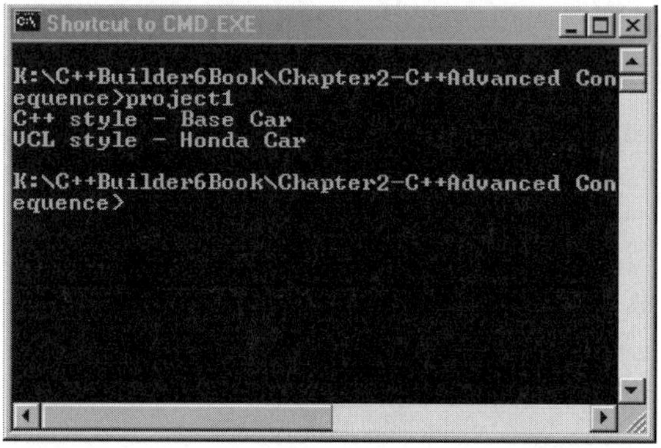

Figure 2-5: Output of a console application illustrating run-time type of the object

Summary

It is now time to summarize what we learned in this chapter. I started the chapter with an introduction on advanced C++ language features, followed by the language overview, which includes encapsulation, polymorphism, and inheritance.

The advanced features of the language, including templates, namespaces, casting, exception handling, pointers, references, and virtual methods, also were discussed, and example programs demonstrated the different programming scenarios.

Then we continued our discussion on Borland's extensions to the language, which enable us to maximize their component libraries. These features include an overview of types of C++ programs that we can build in C++Builder 6, keyword extensions, and interfaces that replicate Delphi-style functionality in C++Builder. Finally, we talked about object construction sequence in a typical C++ program and a VCL program.

As I mentioned at the beginning of the chapter, I focused attention on special topics instead of going into language semantics.

Chapter 3

The VCL Explored

Brief Introduction to VCL Architecture

The Visual Component Library (VCL) is the core set of objects that C++Builder 6 offers to its users on the Microsoft Windows-based operating system. This chapter describes features of the VCL framework and some frequently used components. The following chapter continues to present advanced features and components in an attempt to enable readers to draw the power of VCL into their Windows-based applications. Together, the two chapters cover most of the standard VCL functionality. However, specialized components for database access, web services, and Internet usage, etc. are reserved for later chapters that cover them in depth. To enable developers to port their code between Windows-based operating systems and Linux, however, C++Builder 6 offers a separate set of components, called CLX, Component Library for Cross-platform development, which is the subject of another chapter.

In its simplest form of definition, VCL is a library of classes that encapsulate the Microsoft Windows application programming interface (API) using the object-oriented approach. VCL is architected in a way so that both Delphi (Object Pascal) and C++Builder (C++) users can use them identically and effectively. In addition to the visual components (as the name suggests), VCL also provides powerful non-visual classes to make itself a real rapid application development (RAD) framework. Refer to the VCL architecture in Figure 3-1 in brief.

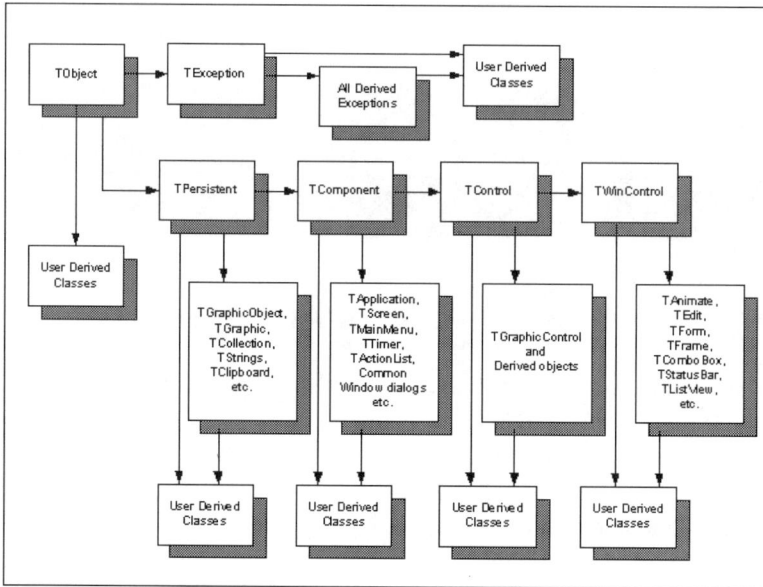

Figure 3-1: VCL architecture overview

VCL is more of a framework, rather than just a component library. The features provided and supported by this framework include the following:

■ VCL components are based on properties, methods, and events. Properties describe the state of the object at any point in time that can be set during design time and often at run time. Methods operate on these properties to enable the external world control and manipulate the properties. The events are triggered by either user actions or system actions. An example of an event is that generated by the windows messages or user keystrokes.

■ VCL components can be manipulated during design time or execution time of the application. Windows GUI applications are comprised of forms and components placed on the form. The state of the components and the form at any time can be saved to a form file (*.dfm) and restored in another programming session.

■ VCL components encapsulate the Windows API and messages in such a way that the standard windows message processing architecture is not visible to the developer; rather, a more sophisticated and object-based architecture is presented.

■ The VCL framework enables developers to implement custom components for specialized tasks and enhance the functionality of the framework itself. The custom components can also be stored in a repository for later reuse or sharing between developers.

■ VCL does not interfere with the standard Windows development architecture. Programmers who wish to use this traditional architecture can still do so. This also means that the core Windows API functions can be called directly, bypassing the VCL framework. Developers can also freely make direct Windows API calls from within a VCL-based application.

■ Having originated from Object Pascal, VCL also provides a flavor of Delphi-based objects, in addition to providing full C++ language support. Thus, VCL is a framework that supports two powerful language environments, C++ and Object Pascal. The power of VCL is almost identical between Delphi and C++Builder to a great extent, while some differences exist in order to preserve each language's identity and characteristics.

■ The set of VCL objects that are provided with C++Builder include the complete Win32 standard graphical user interface (GUI) controls, Windows standard dialogs, components that support database access in different ways (BDE, ODBC, ADO, and dbExpress), components to develop Internet-based applications, web server applications, web services using XML/SOAP architectures, Borland's DataSnap architecture for supporting multi-tier applications, and others. However, users should check with Borland for the specific set of components included in each edition of the product. The descriptions and examples in this book correspond to the richest edition of C++Builder, which is usually the Enterprise edition. Those who have other editions of the product will also find this book useful because features of those editions are included in the book by default. This also means that not every example from this book may work with every edition of the product.

■ VCL also permits the use of ActiveX components (developed in other development platforms like Visual Basic, Visual C++, etc.) in VCL-based applications. This is made possible by importing an ActiveX control into the C++Builder environment, which will transform the ActiveX control to a VCL control; from then on the control behaves like a natural VCL control.

■ VCL also permits development of ActiveX controls for use by other development environments like Visual Basic, Visual C++, etc.

VCL Objects

Before we continue discussing VCL architecture, we must keep in mind a few VCL-specific features with respect to the C++ programming language. In C++, a *class* defines the blueprint of how an object looks and behaves in the real programming world, and an *object* is an instance of the class. The state of an object is represented by its instance variables, and the object's methods operate on the instance variables to find or change the state of the object. When an object is created, its existence is governed by two characteristics: its scope and memory allocation. These two characteristics are interrelated. The *scope* of an object is its visibility (and persistence) with respect to other programming elements.

Every object created in the program occupies memory, as required by its structure and contents. There are two types of memory chunks available in the system: the stack and the heap. Objects created on the stack are automatically destroyed when they go out of scope, and objects created on the heap occupy the memory location(s) until explicitly destroyed by the program, even after they go out of scope. Therefore, it is the responsibility of the programmer to keep track of how the objects are being created and how they are destroyed. The C++ language leaves this responsibility in the hands of the programmer, along with the power of dynamic memory management. The following sample code demonstrates how the objects can be created on the stack and heap, respectively, in C++.

Listing 3-1

```
Class Car {
private:
    int Cylinders;  // instance variable
public:
    Car(void);      // constructor
    int getCylinders();        // gets Cylinders private variable
    void setCylinders(int cyl); // sets Cylinders private variable
};
```

Assuming that the member functions are implemented in the class implementation, the following code creates an object of this class on the stack and assigns a value to its instance variable.

```
Car newCar;
newCar.setCylinders(4);
```

The following code creates the object on the heap and assigns a value to the instance variable:

```
Car *newCar = new Car();
NewCar→setCylinders(4);
```

The new operator, as used in the previous code, is specific to object-oriented languages like C++. The *new* operator enables creation of objects on
the heap. Objects created using the new operator must be destroyed when
no longer needed by using the *delete* operator.

```
delete newCar;
```

All VCL objects must be created on the heap using the new operator (with
the exception of AnsiString, explained later in this section) and must be
destroyed using the delete operator. The size of the stack is always limited,
compared to the heap. In addition, when objects created on the stack are
passed as parameters to functions, new copies of the objects are created on
the stack, which may not always be the required way. When objects are created on the heap and the object pointers are passed as parameters to other
objects and functions, only these pointers are created on the stack, not the
objects. Therefore, it improves performance of the program when objects
are created once and accessed via object pointers. The performance gain
may not be visible in small applications, but complex, enterprise-level
applications will demonstrate a performance improvement. Also, in a complex object-oriented architecture like VCL, an object might not be a simple
class; most of the time, an object contains several objects within itself. This
object containment may span to many levels in very complex object structures. Therefore, using the heap for dynamic memory usage often results in
more effective use of memory. One of the strengths of the C++ language
itself is dynamic memory management. Some developers may not like the
fact that they have to take the responsibility of object destruction when the
object is no longer needed. In my opinion, the power of dynamic memory
management comes with the price of managing the memory
programmatically.

At first, it may appear to be a difficult task to take responsibility for freeing the objects when they are done being used. The VCL architecture has a
built-in feature that relieves the programmer from this burden to a great
extent. All VCL components (visual and non-visual) have a property called
Owner, which is another component that takes the responsibility of freeing
the components that it owns when the owner itself is destroyed. In a
VCL-based application, the form owns all components created on it during
design time. During run-time creation of components, the owner component pointer has to be passed as a parameter to the constructor. During run
time, there is an opportunity for the programmer to define another component, other than the form, as owner. Thus, run-time creation of components
using the new operator does not necessitate their explicit deletion by the
programmer, as their owner takes care of this task.

All other VCL objects that are not components by class (i.e., not a TComponent descendant) must be created using the new operator and destroyed using the delete operator explicitly by the programmer.

AnsiString

In addition to the Win32 String type or the std::string class, C++Builder provides the AnsiString class to create string objects. AnsiString is designed to function like the Delphi long string type. At a minimum, AnsiString requires four bytes to create the object pointer, even though the string is NULL. When the string contains data, it points to a dynamically allocated block of memory, a 32-bit length indicator and a 32-bit reference count. This memory is allocated on the heap, but its management is entirely automatic without requiring any user code. Because AnsiString variables are pointers, two or more of them can reference the same value without consuming additional memory. The compiler exploits this to conserve resources and execute assignments faster.

The new operator is not required to create AnsiString objects. The AnsiString object grows dynamically to any size as the string grows and is only limited by the available memory size. The object does not have any properties exposed; rather, it has methods (including the constructors) that provide functionality to manipulate the string objects very efficiently.

AnsiString can be instantiated in two ways, as shown here:

```
AnsiString str1;                          // the object is created on the stack
AnsiString *str2 = new AnsiString();      // the object is created on the heap
```

The constructor of the class is overloaded with different signatures. The example only shows the simple constructor without any arguments.

Table 3-1 displays some commonly used methods of this class.

Table 3-1: Methods of AnsiString

Method	Description
SubString(int index, int count)	Extracts a substring from the AnsiString objects from a specific (one-based) position to a specific number of bytes beyond the starting point
+ and + = operators	Concatenates AnsiString objects
= operator	Assigns one AnsiString object to another
TrimLeft()	Trims leading spaces and control characters
TrimRight()	Trims trailing spaces and control characters
Trim()	Trims both leading and trailing spaces and control characters
StringOfChar(char ch, int count)	Returns an AnsiString object of desired length containing same single character
LowerCase()	Returns the AnsiString object in all lowercase characters
UpperCase()	Returns the AnsiString object in all uppercase characters
ToInt()	Converts the AnsiString object to integer and returns as an integer value

Method	Description
ToDouble()	Converts the AnsiString object to floating-point value and returns as double value
Insert(const AnsiString& str, int index)	Inserts an AnsiString object into another AnsiString object at the desired (one-based) position
Length()	Returns the length of string in bytes as an integer value
IsEmpty()	Returns a Boolean value indicating whether the string is empty or not
c_str()	Returns a character pointer to a NULL-terminated character array

The value returned by the c_str() method is only a pointer to the internal data buffer of the AnsiString object. If the character array has to be used later, it is advised to create enough buffer to hold the returned value and do the string copy. An example is shown here:

```
const AnsiString str = "New String";        // create the AnsiString object
char *buffer = new char[str.Length()+1];    // create char buffer enough for the string
strcpy(buffer, str.c_str());                // string copy the value to the buffer

delete [] buffer;                           // delete the buffer after using it.
```

Notice that the buffer size allocated is one character more than the length of the string, in order to accommodate the NULL terminator for the C-style char array. The value copied to the buffer can be used in all functions that accept a character pointer.

There are other methods of the AnsiString object mentioned within the product manuals that the reader is encouraged to investigate and practice with.

What is TObject?

TObject is the abstract base class from which all VCL objects are derived. This class provides fundamental behavior of an object, like construction, destruction, run-time type information about the class itself, and message handling. Objects that descend directly from this class (as opposed to those that descend from the TPersistent class) cannot save their state; they can be created, used, and destroyed only at run time. Examples of classes that descend directly from TObject include TException and its descendants, TList, TQueue, TStack, TBits, TStream and its descendants, TPrinter, and TRegistry, among others.

The most common situation that programmers face during development is that they have to perform some task on an object, based on the class that instantiated it or the class that is one of its ancestors. Table 3-2 displays some commonly used methods.

Table 3-2: Commonly used TObject methods

Method	Description
ClassName()	Returns a ShortString that contains the name of the class of which the object is an instance
ClassNameIs(AnsiString fClassName)	Returns a Boolean value indicating whether or not the object is of the type identified by the fClassName argument
ClassParent()	Returns a pointer to the TMetaClass definition of the parent class from which the object's class is derived
InheritsFrom(TClass fAncestorClass)	Returns a Boolean value indicating whether the object's class is inherited from the class fAncestorClass or any one of its descendant classes
InstanceSize()	Returns the number of bytes required to instantiate an object of the current class
ClassType()	Returns a pointer to the TMetaClass definition of the object. However, it is usually not required to directly access the metaclass definition of an object because the methods provided by TMetaClass correspond to the static methods of the TObject class.

Listings 3-2 and 3-3 provide examples of using some of these methods:

Listing 3-2

```
TListBox* fListBox = new TListBox(this);
ShortString fClassName = fListBox->ClassName();
```

In this example, fClassName contains the value "TListBox" as ShortString.

> **Note:** ShortString is a Delphi data type and is usually used for strings of size 0 to 255 bytes. While the length of ShortString can be changed dynamically, its memory is allocated statically to 256 bytes when it is created. The first byte represents its length, and the remaining 255 bytes are available for characters. In contrast, AnsiString is considered a long string, and the memory is allocated dynamically as the string size increases. AnsiString objects can grow up to a maximum of 2GB in size.

TControl is the immediate ancestor class of TWinControl, the latter of which is the immediate ancestor class of TCustomListBox, from which TListBox is derived.

Listing 3-3

```
TListBox* fListBox = new TListBox(this);
bool fbool1 = fListBox->InheritsFrom(TWinControl);
bool fbool2 = fListBox->InheritsFrom(TList);
```

In this example, fbool1 contains the value true because the TListBox class descends (indirectly) from TWinControl. Similarly, fbool2 contains the value false because TList is not in the object hierarchy of TListBox.

TClass is defined as a pointer to TMetaClass. To obtain metaclass information for an object, use the ClassType() method of the object, which returns a pointer to TMetaClass. More on the run-time type information (RTTI) is discussed in a separate section later in this chapter.

Persistence of Objects—TPersistent Class

One of the key requirements to be met by objects in a component framework is the ability to save their state before the object is destroyed and to recreate the object, loading it from where it was saved earlier. The state information that is stored by the object is its own behavior, as identified by the properties assigned and modified during design time. Examples of properties include Caption, Name, Top, Left, Height, Width, etc. This ability is termed *persistence*. The TPersistent class is directly derived from TObject and adds persistence to the objects, in addition to the basic functionality provided by TObject. Examples of objects that are direct descendants of the TPersistent class include TGraphicsObject, TGraphic, TStrings, TClipboard, and TCollection.

Basic VCL Component—TComponent Class

In simple terms, a *component* is an object that has the ability to be hosted in the Component Palette in the IDE. The TComponent class derived from TPersistent incorporates the component behavior, which includes:

- The ability to be hosted in the Component Palette and manipulated in the form designer
- The ability to own (and contain) and manage other components, with enhanced streaming and filing capabilities
- The ability to be converted to an ActiveX object or other COM object

Both visual and non-visual components can coexist in the Component Palette. Visual components become part of a GUI application providing visual manipulation of data, whereas non-visual components appear on the screen only during design time and provide functionality that does not require visual representation of data during execution of the application. Though TComponent is the base ancestor class for all components, only non-visual components are derived directly from this class. The visual components must be derived from the TWinControl or TControl classes, which are further derived classes of TComponent, depending on whether the component has to behave as a windowed control or not. TWinControl is derived from TControl, which is derived from TComponent.

Non-Visual Components

Some of the commonly used non-visual components include TApplication, TScreen, TTimer, TActionList, and Windows common dialogs like TOpenDialog (to select a filename to open), TSaveDialog (to select a filename to save a file), TPrinterSetupDialog (to enable printer setup), and TPrintDialog (to select print options). Global instances of TApplication and TScreen objects are available in the application and are explained in detail later in the chapter. Each of the non-visual components provide a service that does not require visual presentation of data. For example, TTimer represents a Windows timer object, which enables the developer to time certain events as required in the application. TActionList maintains a list of actions used with components and controls; a separate section is devoted to the Action Objects and related components in Chapter 4.

It is important to note that non-visual components also may be available in the Component Palette to be dropped onto the form during design time; this does not mean that the component is visual. The component is available in the Component Palette for the convenience of the developer to drop it on the form during design time, but it will not show up on the form during run time. One of the common components that component designers create is a non-visual component that acts like a manager component to manage the behavior of a group of other visual components. TActionList is similar to that.

Visual Components—TControl and TWinControl Classes and Their Descendants

A *control* is a component that becomes visible during run time. The control receives input focus if it is a window-based control; it will not receive focus if it is not a window-based control but just a graphic image. What I mean is that only TWinControl descendants can receive input-related messages directly from Windows. Users can use the keyboard to interact with windowed controls. Also window-based controls have a window handle assigned by the operating system. The TControl class provides the basic functionality of a control and is derived directly from the TComponent class. TControl is the base class for all the visual components. All the visual components that do not receive input focus should be derived from the TControl class. Examples of such classes provided by VCL are TGraphicControl and its derivatives.

The primary purpose of most graphic controls is to display text or graphics. In this context, TGraphicControl provides a Canvas property to provide ready access to the control's drawing surface, and a virtual paint method is called in response to WM_PAINT messages received by the parent control. VCL controls that descend from TGraphicControl include TBevel, TImage, TPaintBox, TShape, TSpeedButton, TSplitter, and TCustomLabel, from which TDBText and TLabel are derived.

TWinControl is another direct descendant of the TControl class and provides base functionality for all controls that need to interact with the user. In addition to being able to receive input focus and interact with the user, the windowed controls can act as parent controls and hence contain other components. Thus, all the visual container objects are windowed controls. They also have a window handle, as identified by the Windows operating system. Several specialized (custom) controls are derived from TWinControl as base classes to provide additional base functionality as needed for the type of control sets. For example, TCustomEdit provides additional base functionality as needed for all edit controls, TCustom-ComboBox provides additional base functionality as needed for different types of combo boxes, and TCustomListBox provides additional base functionality as needed for different types of list boxes.

If a specialized (visual) custom control needs to be developed, it can be derived from TWinControl, and if a fully functional control needs to be developed, it can be derived from the corresponding custom control (such as TCustomEdit, TCustomComboBox, or TCustomListBox, etc.).

The Application—Global TApplication Instance

The C++Builder IDE enables the developer to create different types of applications. The basic types of applications that the developer usually works with are listed here:

- Windows GUI application
- Windows NT/2000 service application
- Web server application
- Windows Control Panel application
- WebSnap application
- SOAP server application
- CLX application
- Console application
- Windows dynamic-link libraries (DLLs)
- Borland packages (BPLs)

For the first seven types of applications, C++Builder automatically creates a global variable named *Application*. For the last three types of applications, no such variable is created. A console application is a program that executes at the command mode. Windows DLLs are libraries of functions and objects that are called by another application. Borland packages are Windows DLLs that are exclusively developed for users of Borland C++Builder and Borland Delphi.

The Application variable is intended to provide information to the developer specific to the application itself, and because of its global scope, it is available throughout the application. Based on the type of application created through the IDE, the appropriate unit header file containing the Application variable definition is included in the project. Table 3-3 displays the types of applications and the corresponding class name that the Application variable represents.

Table 3-3: Application variable for different application types

Application Type	Application Variable Description
Windows GUI application	The Application variable contains GUI application properties and is defined as an instance of TApplication class as defined in Forms.hpp (the header file located in the C++Builder include directory).
Windows NT/2000 service application	The Application variable contains properties of a service application and is defined as an object of TServiceApplication class.
Web application	The Application variable contains the properties of a web server application and is defined as an object of one of the derived classes of TWebApplication class, which are TISAPIApplication, TCGIApplication, and TApacheApplication. As the names suggest, each of these web application types contain properties specific to the respective type of web application.
Windows Control Panel application	The Application variable contains properties for a control panel application and is defined as an object of the TAppletApplication class.
WebSnap application and SOAP application	The Application variable contains the properties of one of the following: TISAPIApplication, TCGIApplication, TApacheApplication, or TApplication classes, depending on whether the web server type is ISAPI DLL, CGI executable, Apache server module, or web application debugger executable, respectively.
CLX application	The Application variable contains the properties of TApplication class as defined in the QForms.hpp header file.

If a Windows DLL instantiates a form object dynamically, the Application variable is available and accessible even in the DLL-based form application. This is because the Application variable is defined in the Forms.hpp file. But the Application→Run() method should not be called from a DLL-based form application because a DLL does not execute by itself; only its methods will be executed from another executable program. It should also be noted that applications should not host their main form from within a DLL; if this behavior is required, it is recommended that the developer use Borland packages rather than DLLs.

Properties, Methods, and Events of TApplication

This section discusses the TApplication class as defined in the Forms.hpp header file, which focuses mainly on Windows GUI applications. The behavior of other types of applications is discussed in chapters that focus specifically on those applications.

The properties and methods introduced in TApplication reflect the fundamentals established in the Windows operating system to create, run, sustain, and destroy an application. For this purpose, TApplication encapsulates the behavior providing the functionality listed here:

- Windows message processing
- Context-sensitive online help
- Menu accelerator and key processing
- Exception handling
- Managing the fundamental parts of an application, such as MainWindow, WindowClass, etc., as defined by the Windows operating system

When a Windows GUI application is created, the IDE automatically includes the Forms.hpp file. The application may contain more than one form object, but the first form object that is instantiated in the main project cpp file will be the form that is displayed first when executed, and the global Application variable is the one that is defined in the main form. Therefore, in a project containing multiple forms, the developer can easily change the main form by putting the desired form as the first form in the sequence while instantiating the forms using syntax similar to Listing 3-4.

Listing 3-4

```
#include <vcl.h>
#pragma hdrstop
USERES("Project1.res");
USEFORM("Unit1.cpp", Form1);
USEFORM("Unit2.cpp", Form2);
USEFORM("Unit3.cpp", Form3);
//-------------------------------------------------------------------------
WINAPI WinMain(HINSTANCE, HINSTANCE, LPSTR, int)
{
  try
  {
    Application->Initialize();
    Application->CreateForm(__classid(TForm3), &Form3);
    Application->CreateForm(__classid(TForm2), &Form2);
    Application->CreateForm(__classid(TForm1), &Form1);
    Application->Run();
  }
  catch (Exception &exception)
  {
```

```
    Application->ShowException(&exception);
  }
}
```

In this example, Form3 will be displayed as the main form of the application. This is a typical example of a VCL GUI application, and the example presents the project source code. The first statement is a call to the Application→Initialize() method. This method calls the InitProc procedure pointer, which is NULL by default. The purpose of having this method is to initialize any subsystems, such as OLE automation. In order to use the custom initialization, include the header file that defines the InitProc procedure pointer, create a custom initialization procedure that assigns a value to this procedure pointer, and add a call to this procedure to the project source prior to the call to Initialize. Only one instance of InitProc can be defined in an application. If more than one header file assigns a value to InitProc, only the last assignment will work. For projects that do not assign a value to InitProc, the call to Application→Initialize() can be safely deleted from the project source. The Application→CreateForm(__classid(TForm3), &Form3) statement invokes the Form3's constructor method because this is the time the form object is instantiated. When a new form is added, the IDE adds these statements to the project source by default. If you intend to instantiate only the main form and not the others at this time, the other lines can be deleted from the project source, and the other forms may be instantiated at run time before they are used, which is illustrated in a later section in this chapter.

When the Application→Run() method is executed, the program's main message loop begins, and it ends only when the application terminates. This method should not be called from another place in the project.

An application is active if the form or application has focus. An application becomes inactive when a window from a different application is about to become activated. This status is indicated by the property Application→ Active. Table 3-4 summarizes the important properties, methods, and events of the TApplication class.

Table 3-4: Properties, methods, and events of TApplication

Property	Description
MainForm	Returns a pointer to the main form of the application (read-only)
Handle	Returns a handle to the application's zero dimension form (read-only)
ExeName	Returns the executable filename of the application including the path information (read-only)
HelpFile	Returns the name of the help file that the application uses to display help. This can be set during design time using the Options dialog (Project | Options) or during run time.

Part 1

Property	Description
CurrentHelpFile	Read CurrentHelpFile to determine the name of the help file that is currently used by the application when it executes a help command (via the HelpCommand method) or brings up context-sensitive help (via the HelpContext or HelpJump method).
DialogHandle	Provides a mechanism for using non-VCL dialog boxes in a C++Builder application. Use DialogHandle when displaying a modeless dialog box that was created using the CreateDialog Windows API function. Assigning the handle of the modeless dialog box to DialogHandle allows the dialog to see messages from the application's message loop.

Method	Description
HandleMessage(), ProcessMessages()	HandleMessage() interrupts execution of the application while Windows processes a message in the Windows message queue before returning control to the application. If the message queue is empty, this method generates an OnIdle event and starts the process of updating the actions in the application. If the application goes idle, this method may take a long time to return. Therefore, do not call this method when waiting for something that is message-based while priority actions are also being processed. Instead, call ProcessMessages() when processing more than just messages to permit Windows to process the messages that are currently in the message queue. ProcessMessages() cycles the Windows message loop until it is empty and then returns control to the application. ProcessMessages() does not let the application go idle. Neglecting message processing affects only the application calling ProcessMessages(), not other applications. In lengthy operations, calling ProcessMessages() periodically allows the application to respond to paint and other messages.
Terminate()	This method calls the Windows API PostQuitMessage function to perform an orderly shutdown of the application. Terminate() is not immediate. Terminate() is called automatically on a WM_QUIT message and when the main form closes.
HelpContext(THelpContext *context)	Use HelpContext to bring up the help topic specified by the context parameter from the file specified in the CurrentHelpFile property. HelpContext generates an OnHelp event.
HelpCommand(int Command, int Data)	Provides quick access to any of the help commands in the WinHelp API. Use HelpCommand to send a command to WinHelp. Before sending the help command to the Windows help engine, HelpCommand generates an OnHelp event on the active form or on TApplication. Finally, the command is forwarded to WinHelp if there is no OnHelp event handler or if the OnHelp event handler indicates that WinHelp should be called.
HelpJump(AnsiString jumpId)	Call HelpJump to bring up a topic identified by its symbolic name. HelpJump displays the topic identified by the JumpID parameter from the file specified in the CurrentHelpFile property. HelpJump generates an OnHelp event either on the active form or on the Application object itself.
Minimize()	Minimizes the application to the task bar
Restore()	Restores the application to normal status
ShowException(Exception* e)	Displays a message box for the exceptions that are not caught by the rest of the application code

Event	Description
OnActivate	Provides you with the opportunity to perform tasks when the application first starts up
OnIdle	Provides you with the time window to perform any background tasks when the application is not busy
OnHelp	This event is generated when the application receives a request for help. The HelpContext, HelpCommand, and HelpJump methods generate this event.
OnMessage	Provides the opportunity to intercept queue-based windows messages

Event	Description
OnMinimize	Lets you perform tasks when the application's main window is minimized
OnRestore	Lets you perform tasks when the previously minimized application window is restored to normal state

Since Application is a global variable and not available through the IDE as a component, it is not possible to create the event handlers directly through the Object Inspector; for this reason, C++Builder provides a TApplication-Events component in the Additional page of the Component Palette. The location of this component on the Component Palette is shown in Figure 3-2.

TApplicationEvents

Figure 3-2: TApplicationEvents component in the Component Palette

When you add a TApplicationEvents object to a form, the Application object forwards all events to the TApplicationEvents object. Thus, each event of the TApplicationEvents object is the same as the event with the same name on the Application object. Each form in an application can have its own TApplicationEvents object. Each application event occurs for all the TApplicationEvents objects in the project. To change the order in which the different TApplicationEvents objects receive events, use the Activate() method. To prevent other TApplicationEvents objects from receiving a specific event, use the CancelDispatch() method. This means that in a typical application containing multiple forms, each with a different instance of the TApplicationEvents object, the form that is currently active can receive the Application object's events first in sequence when compared to the other forms when the Activate() method of TApplicationEvents object is called from the form's OnActivate event handler method. This, however, is not going to prevent other forms from receiving the Application object's events. It is only going to affect the sequence in which they receive the events. However, it is also possible to prevent any of the forms

' TApplicationEvents object from receiving the Application object's events by just calling the CancelDispatch() method of the corresponding TApplicationEvents object.

Other Global Variables—TScreen, TMouse, and TClipboard Instances

When a Windows GUI project is created, a global variable Screen of type TScreen is created. The *Screen* variable encapsulates the state of the screen on which the application is running. Therefore, the Screen variable is useful to capture and set the run-time screen state of the application. This variable is defined in the Forms.hpp header file. The properties provided by the Screen variable let the programmer access the screen-related system resources, such as Monitors, Cursors, Fonts, Resolution, etc., and application-level resources, such as Forms and DataModules instantiated by the application, etc. Most of these are lists of <u>read-only</u> objects, which can be iterated over an upper limit of a number of such objects identified by the Screen. Very few of these can be set programmatically, such as current mouse Cursor, IconFont, and HintFont.

For example, when a client application requests data from the server, the Cursor may be changed to a different shape (such as HourGlass, as used by most applications), indicating to the user that the request is being processed. Once the data is displayed, the Cursor may be changed back to default shape (the shape before it was changed), indicating that the request processing is complete. This is a very useful hint that most Windows-based applications provide to the user to let him or her know that the request is in process, the length of time that the request process is taking, or that the request failed due to a network-related problem (in which case the cursor takes an unusually long time to return back to the default shape). This is explained in Listing 3-5 with a code snippet.

Listing 3-5

```
Screen→Cursor = crHourGlass;    // indicates that the request is in process.
try {
//
// processing code goes here
//
}
__finally {
    Screen→Cursor = crDefault; // indicates that the processing is complete.
}
```

The first statement changes the cursor to HourGlass mode, and the second statement changes it back to default mode. The two statements are usually separated by code that makes the data request, receives and displays it in visual controls, or does some other processing, displays any messages, etc. In reality, the two statements of code are in different methods of the form or application.

It is possible to let the forms in the application be realigned with respect to the desktop properties, such as screen resolution. The TForm descendant objects have a property called Align (derived from the TControl ancestor class), which lets them align themselves (and hence their child components) according to their parent's position. Since the desktop screen is the parent for all the forms within an application, the forms naturally align themselves according to their Align property, whenever the parent resolution or alignment changes. The Screen variable has two methods to control this behavior: DisableAlign() to disable the forms from realigning themselves and EnableAlign() to set their ability to align themselves. These simple methods control the behavior of the entire GUI application. Because the forms are parents for their child components, their alignment controls the alignment of the child components. The OnActiveControlChange and OnActiveFormChange events provided by the Screen variable let the program recognize when the active control or active form changes.

Another application-level variable created automatically in a Windows GUI application is *Mouse*, which is an instance of TMouse class. The Mouse variable provides properties that expose the mouse characteristics, or how the application can respond to mouse messages. Programs can check whether a mouse is present, whether the mouse has a wheel, the number of lines that are scrolled with the wheel movement, and whether the drag operation should immediately start when the left button is pressed or after the mouse is moved a certain specified number of pixels after pressing the left button. There are no methods that the programmer should call from within an application.

Another useful global object is *Clipboard*, which is an instance of TClipboard class. However, this object is not instantiated automatically in an application. Rather, the programmer should call the Clipboard() function defined in the Clipbrd.hpp file, which must be included for applications that need to access the clipboard. When the Clipboard() method is called, an instance of the TClipboard object is returned. Every call to this function from within the application provides access to the same clipboard maintained by Windows. Thus, the global nature of the Windows clipboard is retained and maintained by the method.

The properties and methods of the TClipboard object enable the programmer to copy data into the global Windows clipboard and retrieve it later, either in the same application or in another application. Data in different formats can be copied into the clipboard. This is a standard feature that a majority of commercial applications provide to their users. The signatures of the method used to copy and retrieve text data are presented in Listing 3-6.

Listing 3-6

```
void __fastcall SetTextBuf(char * Buffer);
int __fastcall GetTextBuf(char * Buffer, int BufSize);
```

The SetTextBuf() method sets the character text into the clipboard, and GetTextBuf() retrieves the character text from the clipboard. The code to copy a bitmap to the clipboard and retrieve the bitmap from the clipboard to another bitmap object is described in Listings 3-7 and 3-8. To copy the bitmap to the clipboard, the Assign() method of the TClipboard is used, and to copy the bitmap from the clipboard to the bitmap object, the Assign() method of the TBitmap is used.

Listing 3-7: unit1.cpp

```
#include <vcl.h>
#pragma hdrstop

#include "Unit1.h"
//---------------------------------------------------------------------------
#pragma package(smart_init)
#pragma resource "*.dfm"
TForm1 *Form1;
//---------------------------------------------------------------------------
__fastcall TForm1::TForm1(TComponent* Owner)
    : TForm(Owner)
{
}
//---------------------------------------------------------------------------

void __fastcall TForm1::Button1Click(TObject *Sender)
{
    const AnsiString fGraphicFileName = "Graphic1.BMP";
    TFileStream* fGraphicFile = new TFileStream(fGraphicFileName, fmOpenRead);
    Graphics::TBitmap *Bitmap1 = new Graphics::TBitmap();
    try
    {
        Bitmap1->LoadFromStream(fGraphicFile);
        Canvas->Draw(10,10,Bitmap1);
        Clipboard()->Assign(Bitmap1);
    }
    catch ()
    {
        MessageBeep(0);
    }
    delete Bitmap1;
    delete fGraphicFile;

}
//---------------------------------------------------------------------------
void __fastcall TForm1::Button2Click(TObject *Sender)
{
```

```
    Graphics::TBitmap *Bitmap2 = new Graphics::TBitmap();
    try
    {
        Bitmap2->Assign(Clipboard());
        Canvas->Draw(200,200,Bitmap2);
    }
    catch ()
    {
        MessageBeep(0);
    }
    delete Bitmap2;

}
//---------------------------------------------------------------------------
```

Listing 3-8: unit1.h

```
#ifndef Unit1H
#define Unit1H
//---------------------------------------------------------------------------
#include <Classes.hpp>
#include <Controls.hpp>
#include <StdCtrls.hpp>
#include <Clipbrd.hpp>
#include <Forms.hpp>
//---------------------------------------------------------------------------
class TForm1 : public TForm
{
__published:          // IDE-managed Components
    TButton *Button1;
    TButton *Button2;
    void __fastcall Button1Click(TObject *Sender);
    void __fastcall Button2Click(TObject *Sender);
private:              // User declarations
public:               // User declarations
    __fastcall TForm1(TComponent* Owner);
};
//---------------------------------------------------------------------------
extern PACKAGE TForm1 *Form1;
//---------------------------------------------------------------------------
#endif
```

The project contains a form with two buttons: Button1 and Button2. When you click Button1, an image appears at a specific location identified by pixel position (10,10) relative to the top-left corner of the form's client area. At the same time, the image is copied to the clipboard. When you click Button2, the image is copied from the clipboard to another location identified by pixel position (200,200).

The clipboard provided by VCL has another interesting feature by which the programmer can copy a component from the form to the clipboard and later copy the component from the clipboard back to the form at some other location. This is one way to create identical copies of the component with the same set of properties. Listings 3-9 and 3-10 provide an example to illustrate this feature. The application contains a form with GroupBox, DBGrid, Button1, and Button2. When you click Button1, the DBGrid component is copied to another location in the form. When you click Button2, the component is copied into the GroupBox, and the GroupBox contains the new copy of the component. The copy can be done any number of times, but it is important to remember that every time a new copy of the component is made, it contains the same name as the source component; hence, you are required to change the name of the previously placed component to a different name because a form cannot have two components with the same name. If this is not taken care of, the program will throw an exception during run time.

Listing 3-9: unit1.cpp

```cpp
#include <vcl.h>
#pragma hdrstop

#include "Unit1.h"
//---------------------------------------------------------------------------
#pragma package(smart_init)
#pragma resource "*.dfm"
TForm1 *Form1;
//---------------------------------------------------------------------------
__fastcall TForm1::TForm1(TComponent* Owner)
    : TForm(Owner)
{
  // Register the TDBGrid class so that the clipboard can
  // read and write database-grid objects
  TMetaClass *MetaClass = __classid(TDBGrid);
  RegisterClass(MetaClass);
  count = 1;
  x=20;
  y=20;
}
//---------------------------------------------------------------------------

void __fastcall TForm1::Button1Click(TObject *Sender)
{
  count++;
  // copy the component to the clipboard
  Clipboard()->SetComponent(DBGrid1);
  // It is required to change the name of the
  // source component to a different name.
  const AnsiString fGridName = "DBGrid"+IntToStr(count);
  DBGrid1->Name = fGridName;
  // Now retrieve the component from the clipboard
  // and place it in a different location
  // Note that the component copied from clipboard
  // contains the name of the source component.
  Clipboard()->GetComponent(this, this);
  x += 10;
  y += 10;
  DBGrid1->Top = y;
  DBGrid1->Left = x;


}
//---------------------------------------------------------------------------
void __fastcall TForm1::Button2Click(TObject *Sender)
```

```
{
    count++;
    // copy the component to the clipboard
    Clipboard()->SetComponent(DBGrid1);
    // It is required to change the name of the
    // source component to a different name.
    const AnsiString fGridName = "DBGrid"+IntToStr(count);
    DBGrid1->Name = fGridName;
    // Now retrieve the component from the clipboard
    // and place it in a different location
    // Note that the component copied from clipboard
    // contains the name of the source component.
    Clipboard()->GetComponent(this, GroupBox1);
    x += 10;
    y += 10;
    DBGrid1->Top = y;
    DBGrid1->Left = x;

}
//---------------------------------------------------------------------------
```

Listing 3-10: unit1.h

```
#define Unit1H
//---------------------------------------------------------------------------
#include <Classes.hpp>
#include <Controls.hpp>
#include <StdCtrls.hpp>
#include <Forms.hpp>
#include <DBGrids.hpp>
#include <Clipbrd.hpp>
#include <Grids.hpp>
//---------------------------------------------------------------------------
class TForm1 : public TForm
{
__published:          // IDE-managed components
    TGroupBox *GroupBox1;
    TButton *Button1;
    TDBGrid *DBGrid1;
    TButton *Button2;
    void __fastcall Button1Click(TObject *Sender);
    void __fastcall Button2Click(TObject *Sender);
private:              // User declarations
public:               // User declarations
    __fastcall TForm1(TComponent* Owner);
    int count;
    int x,y;
};
//---------------------------------------------------------------------------
extern PACKAGE TForm1 *Form1;
//---------------------------------------------------------------------------
#endif
```

Getting the RTTI

Earlier in this chapter, the TObject class was introduced and we discussed how to make use of its methods to find out about the objects we are working with. That was an introduction to the run-time type information (RTTI), which is the information that the compiler stores about the objects in the application. VCL is a mature architecture in the sense that it provides a very structured and object-oriented approach to the majority of the programming needs of an enterprise.

One of the features of a mature architecture, in my opinion, should be the ability to let the programmer create and dynamically manage the behavior and lifetime of objects during run time. This is partly provided by the programming language specification and, more than that, the framework that implements it. Programmers should know the object characteristics to manage the behavior of objects during run time. VCL makes this easy due to its strong object hierarchy design. As most of us know, VCL was developed in Object Pascal and ported a seamless interface to the C++ programming world. The methods used to obtain the run-time type information are defined in the Typinfo.pas Pascal source file; C++ programmers can see the function definitions in the Typinfo.hpp file. This header file must be included in the application if additional information is required from the RTTI. This section discusses some more functions as defined in the RTTI that are useful for us.

Is a Specific Property Published for the Object?

If we need to know if a component has published a specific property, we can use the IsPublishedProp() function. This function is overloaded. It is defined as shown here:

```
bool __fastcall IsPublishedProp(System::TObject* Instance, const AnsiString PropName);
bool __fastcall IsPublishedProp(TMetaClass* AClass, const AnsiString PropName);
```

It takes two parameters; the first one is a pointer to the object, and the second one is the name of the property for which we are seeking information.

```
bool is_published = IsPublished(ListBox1, "Color");
```

This statement returns true because Color is a published property of the TListBox component. In this example, it is assumed that ListBox1 is an object of TListBox.

What is the Property Type?

TTypeKind is an enumeration that defines a list of property types that the RTTI supports to provide information. It is defined as shown here:

```
enum TTypeKind { tkUnknown, tkInteger, tkChar, tkEnumeration, tkFloat, tkString,
tkSet, tkClass, tkMethod, tkWChar, tkLString, tkWString, tkVariant, tkArray, tkRecord,
tkInterface, tkInt64, tkDynArray };
```

Is a Specific Property in an Object of a Specific Type?

Another useful function is PropIsType(). Its (overloaded) definition is given here:

```
bool __fastcall PropIsType(System::TObject* Instance, const AnsiString
    PropName, TTypeKind);
bool __fastcall PropIsType(TMetaClass* AClass, const AnsiString PropName,
    TTypeKind TypeKind);
```

This function takes three parameters; the first one is a pointer to the object, the second one is the name of the property that we are inquiring about, and the third is the property kind we are checking for the property. It returns a Boolean value, indicating whether or not the property is of a specified type in the object.

```
bool is_type = PropIsType (ListBox1, "Name", tkSet);
```

This statement returns false because the Name property of the TListBox component is of type tkString, not tkSet. In this example, it is assumed that ListBox1 is an object of the TListBox class.

What is the Type of a Specific Property in an Object?

PropType() is another useful function. Its (overloaded) definition is shown here:

```
TTypeKind __fastcall PropType(System::TObject* Instance, const AnsiString PropName);
TTypeKind __fastcall PropType(TMetaClass* AClass, const AnsiString PropName) ;
```

Is the Property Stored in the DFM File?

The method IsStoredProp() tells us if the property is stored in the form file (.DFM). Its signature is defined as shown here:

```
bool __fastcall IsStoredProp(System::TObject* Instance, const AnsiString PropName);
```

Getting and Setting Property Values for an Object

Now we examine the functions that will help us get and set the property values for different types of properties. The method GetPropValue() retrieves the property value as a Variant, and the method SetPropValue() sets the property value from a Variant. These methods are defined as shown here:

```
Variant __fastcall GetPropValue(System::TObject* Instance, const AnsiString PropName,
    bool PreferStrings);
void __fastcall SetPropValue(System::TObject* Instance, const AnsiString PropName, const
    Variant &Value);
```

The methods take an object pointer and the property name string as the first two parameters. The third parameter of the GetPropValue() method is a Boolean value that indicates if the result is preferred as a string. For example, if the property is a Boolean type, and if the result is preferred as a string value (i.e., if you pass true as the PreferStrings parameter), the GetPropValue() method will return a string containing "true" or "false," depending on the value of the property. On the other hand, if you pass false as the PreferStrings parameter, the GetPropValue() method will return the value of −1 for true and 0 for false. The SetPropValue() method takes, as its third parameter, the value of the property as a Variant. These methods can thus be used to get or set properties whose types are compatible with the Variant type.

Two similar methods that operate on Variant data types are GetVariantProp() and SetVariantProp(). The signatures of these methods are given here:

```
Variant __fastcall GetVariantProp(System::TObject* Instance, const AnsiString PropName);
void __fastcall SetVariantProp(System::TObject* Instance, const AnsiString PropName,
    const Variant &Value);
```

The GetVariantProp() method is different from GetPropValue() in that it does not return the value as a string, whereas the latter does, as discussed earlier. There is not much of a difference between the SetVariantProp() and SetPropValue() methods.

Get and set methods that operate on properties of specific types are given here for reference; their usage is self-explanatory from their signatures.

Get and Set Properties of Type Ordinal

```
int __fastcall GetOrdProp(System::TObject* Instance, const AnsiString PropName);
void __fastcall SetOrdProp(System::TObject* Instance, const AnsiString PropName, int
    Value);
```

Get and Set Properties of Type Enum

```
AnsiString __fastcall GetEnumProp(System::TObject* Instance, const AnsiString PropName);
void __fastcall SetEnumProp(System::TObject* Instance, const AnsiString PropName, const
    AnsiString Value);
```

Get and Set Properties of Type Set

```
AnsiString __fastcall GetSetProp(System::TObject* Instance, const AnsiString PropName,
    bool Brackets);
void __fastcall SetSetProp(System::TObject* Instance, const AnsiString PropName, const
    AnsiString Value);
```

The value returned by the GetSetProp() function is a comma delimited string of the values in the set. If the Brackets parameter is set to true, the whole string is enclosed between a set of square brackets. The SetSetProp()

function accepts the set values in a comma delimited string (without square brackets) and populates the set internally.

Get and Set Properties of Type Object

```
System::TObject* __fastcall GetObjectProp(System::TObject* Instance, const AnsiString
    PropName, TMetaClass* MinClass);
void __fastcall SetObjectProp(System::TObject* Instance, const AnsiString PropName,
    System::TObject* Value);
```

Get and Set Properties of Type String

```
AnsiString __fastcall GetStrProp(System::TObject* Instance, const AnsiString PropName);
void __fastcall SetStrProp(System::TObject* Instance, const AnsiString PropName, const
    AnsiString Value);
```

Get and Set Properties of Type Float

```
Extended __fastcall GetFloatProp(System::TObject* Instance, const AnsiString PropName);
void __fastcall SetFloatProp(System::TObject* Instance, const AnsiString PropName,
    Extended Value);
```

Get and Set Properties of Type Int64

```
__int64 __fastcall GetInt64Prop(System::TObject* Instance, const AnsiString PropName);
void __fastcall SetInt64Prop(System::TObject* Instance, const AnsiString PropName, const
    __int64 Value);
```

Get and Set Properties of Type Method

```
Sysutils::TMethod __fastcall GetMethodProp(System::TObject* Instance, PPropInfo
    PropInfo);
void __fastcall SetMethodProp(System::TObject* Instance, PPropInfo PropInfo, const
    Sysutils::TMethod &Value);
```

Refer to the section "Custom Component Development" in Chapter 12 for more information on component properties.

A Closer Look at Forms

Forms provide visual interface of the Windows GUI application. Form is the highest level of component in the visual component hierarchy. Forms can contain any other type of visual and non-visual VCL components. Forms can also contain ActiveX components developed in other platforms, as explained in the section "Using Office 2000 Automation Objects" in Chapter 12. When a form is created in the application using the IDE, C++Builder automatically creates the form in memory by including code in the WinMain() function. The WinMain() function is created in the project's main program file (e.g., Project1.cpp). Every time a new form is added to the application, the IDE adds code to the project's main program and makes the form part of the application, as explained earlier in the chapter. This is the default behavior. It also creates a global variable for every form with the same name as the form. This global variable is a pointer to an instance of the form object and is used to reference it when the application is running.

In applications containing multiple forms, every form is accessible in every other form through this global form variable. However, to make this possible, it is required to include the form's header file in the other form's program from where it is to be accessed.

If the application contains more than one form, it is also not always desirable to have the forms created and kept in memory, as it may cause performance problems for larger applications. Therefore, in such cases, we can create the first form automatically in the project's main program file, and the code that the IDE adds to create the other forms may be safely removed from the WinMain() function. The same thing can be achieved by choosing the Project | Options | Forms page and removing the specific form from the Auto-create forms list and putting it in the Available forms list. Later, when the other form needs to be displayed, it can be created and displayed at that time. The sample code given in Listing 3-11 explains how to dynamically create the form and display.

Listing 3-11

```
if (!Form2)
    Form2 = new TForm2(Application);
if (Form2→Visible == false) {
    Form2→Show();
}
Form2→SetFocus();
```

In this example, we used the global form variable Form2, which is automatically created and defined in the Form2's header file after the TForm2 class definition. This code ensures that the Form2 object is created only if the object does not exist. If the form is not displayed or obscured by other forms or windows, the form's Visible property would be false, in which case the form is displayed using the Show() method. The form may be visible but may not be receiving input focus, in which case the SetFocus() method brings the form to the front and makes it receive the user's keyboard focus.

If additional instances of the same form must be displayed at the same time, additional variables of the same form class may be declared and instantiated using code similar to the above example. The Show() method of the form displays the form in the modeless style, which means the input focus may be shifted to other forms of the same application while the form is displayed. However, there may be occasions when it would be desirable to show a form in the modal style, which means the input focus cannot be shifted to other forms of the same application while this form is displayed. To shift input focus to other forms, the modal form must be closed. To display a form in modal style, the ShowModal() method must be called instead of the Show() method. Also, if the form is used for limited functionality, a local variable of the form's instance will also serve the purpose and the default global variable does not have to be used. If a local variable is used to create the form and the form is displayed modally, the form's instance can be deleted after the form is closed, as shown in Listing 3-12.

Listing 3-12

```
TForm2* localForm2 = new TForm2(Application);
try {
    localForm2->ShowModal();
}
__finally {
    delete localForm2;
}
```

Creating Forms in a DLL

Real world enterprise-level applications usually contain a main form hosting the main menu and other forms serving each of the menu items in the main menu. This is typical of many applications. In such a case, there will be as many forms in the application as there are menu items or sub-items. There are applications hosting anywhere from 10 to 100—or even more—forms. In such a scenario, it is certainly not advisable to create and instantiate all the forms in the main application program at one time, for several reasons. The first and foremost reason is the amount of memory required to hold so many forms at one time. To hold about 100 forms at once, the client machines require a large amount of memory. The second reason is that usually in an enterprise application serving several functions, the same user or same set of users does not perform all the functions in the application. What I mean is only a small subset of functions (from the complete set of functions provided by the application) would be used by an individual or a group of individuals, which is usually controlled by the user and profile management functions of the application. Therefore, it is also not required to make all the form objects available in the application at one time. This prompts anyone with enough Windows development experience to create DLLs for every individual form. That is the option we are going to discuss in this section. Windows DLLs (dynamic-link libraries) are libraries of functions or objects that can be called or instantiated only when required and share the same address space as the main calling application. They are, therefore, not independent applications and cannot be executed on their own, as they do not run in their own address space.

In the typical scenario discussed here, one or more forms may be compiled into a single DLL (as desired by the application architect), and the form should be instantiated from the main form of the application. An example is presented here to help the reader understand how this can be

Part 1

achieved. The example presents the main pieces of code that are required to create and execute a form from a DLL. Creating DLL-based applications is demonstrated in Chapter 7, along with WebBroker applications.

Create a Windows DLL application using the DLL Wizard. The wizard creates a program with the DllEntryPoint() function alone. I added the function CreateForm(), which takes a pointer to a component object as an input parameter that we use in the function to serve as the owner for the form being created by the DLL. I also added an #include statement to include a header file FormDll.h (refer to Listing 3-13) and created the header file. The DLL Wizard does not create a header file for the program.

Listing 3-13: FormDll.cpp

```
#include <vcl.h>
#include <windows.h>
#pragma hdrstop
//---------------------------------------------------------------------------
//   Important note about DLL memory management when your DLL uses the
//   static version of the RunTime Library:
//
//   If your DLL exports any functions that pass String objects (or structs/
//   classes containing nested Strings) as parameter or function results,
//   you will need to add the library MEMMGR.LIB to both the DLL project and
//   any other projects that use the DLL. You will also need to use MEMMGR.LIB
//   if any other projects which use the DLL will be performing new or delete
//   operations on any non-TObject-derived classes which are exported from the
//   DLL. Adding MEMMGR.LIB to your project will change the DLL and its calling
//   EXE's to use the BORLNDMM.DLL as their memory manager. In these cases,
//   the file BORLNDMM.DLL should be deployed along with your DLL.
//
//   To avoid using BORLNDMM.DLL, pass string information using "char *" or
//   ShortString parameters.
//
//   If your DLL uses the dynamic version of the RTL, you do not need to
//   explicitly add MEMMGR.LIB as this will be done implicitly for you
//---------------------------------------------------------------------------
#include "FormDll.h"
#pragma argsused
int WINAPI DllEntryPoint(HINSTANCE hinst, unsigned long reason, void* lpReserved)
{
    return 1;
}
//---------------------------------------------------------------------------
void __stdcall CreateForm(TComponent* Owner)
{
    dllForm = new TDllDemoForm (Owner);
    dllForm->Show();
}
//---------------------------------------------------------------------------
```

The header file listing is given in Listing 3-14.

Listing 3-14: FormDll.h

```
#ifndef DllH
#define DllH

#include "DllForm.h"
TDllDemoForm* dllForm;
extern "C" __declspec(dllexport) __stdcall void CreateForm(TComponent *Owner);
//------------------------------------------------------------------------

#endif
```

The header file contains the function prototype of the CreateForm() function using the __declspec(dllexport) declarator. It also includes the header file for the form's class definition and creates a global variable of the DLL form. The __declspec(dllexport) declarator statement is required when statically linking the DLL to the main executable program.

When the DLL is compiled, the FormDll.dll and FormDll.lib files are created.

The DLL form may be invoked from the main form in two ways: by static linking and by dynamic linking. To link the DLL statically to the main executable program, the following tasks are involved:

1. Create the main executable program project. The project file in the example is DllStaticDemo.cpp, and the main form name is StaticMain.cpp.

2. Add the FormDll.lib file to the project.

3. In the StaticMain.cpp file, include the FormDll.h header file. This is where the manually created DLL header file is required. The StaticMain.cpp program main form contains a button to initiate the DLL calling function.

4. Compile the program and execute. When the button on the main form is clicked, the DLL form is displayed. Every click to the button instantiates a new copy of the DLL form.

In this example, we linked the DLL's library file to the main program; hence, it is called *static linking*. When a DLL is statically linked, the small footprint of the DLL (in the form of the library file) is included in the main program and remains in memory throughout the application's execution. The actual DLL form is loaded when the first call is made to the function. The application takes care of loading the DLL file into memory and the DLL remains in memory until the application terminates.

Listings 3-15 and 3-16 provide the cpp and header files, respectively, for the main executable program performing the static linking of the DLL.

Listing 3-15: StaticMain.cpp

```
//---------------------------------------------------------------------------

#include <vcl.h>
#pragma hdrstop

#include "StaticMain.h"
#include "FormDll.h"
//---------------------------------------------------------------------------
#pragma package(smart_init)
#pragma resource "*.dfm"
TForm1 *Form1;
//---------------------------------------------------------------------------
__fastcall TForm1::TForm1(TComponent* Owner)
    : TForm(Owner)
{
}
//---------------------------------------------------------------------------
void __fastcall TForm1::Button1Click(TObject *Sender)
{
    CreateForm(this);
}
//---------------------------------------------------------------------------
```

Listing 3-16: StaticMain.h

```
//---------------------------------------------------------------------------

#ifndef StaticMainH
#define StaticMainH
//---------------------------------------------------------------------------
#include <Classes.hpp>
#include <Controls.hpp>
#include <StdCtrls.hpp>
#include <Forms.hpp>
//---------------------------------------------------------------------------
class TForm1 : public TForm
{
__published:            // IDE-managed Components
    TButton *Button1;
    void __fastcall Button1Click(TObject *Sender);
private:                // User declarations
public:                 // User declarations
    __fastcall TForm1(TComponent* Owner);
};
//---------------------------------------------------------------------------
extern PACKAGE TForm1 *Form1;
//---------------------------------------------------------------------------
#endif
```

A DLL may also be loaded dynamically into memory by using the Windows LoadLibrary() function. Once in memory, a function of the DLL can be called by first obtaining a pointer to the DLL function (via the GetProcAddress() function) and then calling the function dynamically by using the function pointer. The system loads the DLL into memory only when the first call to LoadLibrary() is made for that DLL. Every subsequent call to

LoadLibrary() only increments a usage counter maintained internally by Windows. A loaded library may be unloaded with the FreeLibrary() call to the same DLL. Every call to FreeLibrary() decrements the usage counter of that library. When the usage counter reaches 0, Windows automatically unloads the DLL from memory. Therefore, the programmer can have control of the process of loading and unloading the DLL from the memory and hence manage the memory more effectively. Also, there is no need to link the import library file (.lib file) to the project. All we need is the DLL file and signature of the function to call.

To link the DLL dynamically to the main executable program, the following steps need to be performed:

1. Create the main executable program project. The project file in the example is DllDemo.cpp, and the main form name is MainForm.cpp.

    The MainForm.cpp program's main form contains a button to initiate the DLL calling function and a label to display a message if DLL loading fails.

2. Compile the program and execute it. When the button on the main form is clicked, the DLL form is displayed. Every click on the button instantiates a new copy of the DLL form.

Listings 3-17 and 3-18 provide the cpp and header files, respectively, for the main executable program performing the dynamic linking of the DLL.

Listing 3-17: MainForm.cpp

```
//---------------------------------------------------------------------------

#include <vcl.h>
#pragma hdrstop

#include "MainForm.h"
//---------------------------------------------------------------------------
#pragma package(smart_init)
#pragma resource "*.dfm"
TDLLDemoMainForm *DLLDemoMainForm;
//---------------------------------------------------------------------------
__fastcall TDLLDemoMainForm::TDLLDemoMainForm(TComponent* Owner)
    : TForm(Owner)
{
    Label1->Caption = "";   // set the message label to an empty string
}
//---------------------------------------------------------------------------
void __fastcall TDLLDemoMainForm::Button1Click(TObject *Sender)
{
    typedef void (*CALLEDFUNCTION) (TComponent* Owner);
    CALLEDFUNCTION DllFunctionPtr;
    AnsiString fDllName = "FormDll.dll";
    AnsiString fFunctionName = "CreateForm";
    AnsiString fMessage;
    char fDllNameStr[50];
```

```
        strcpy(fDllNameStr, fDllName.c_str());
        HINSTANCE DLLInst = NULL;
        DLLInst = LoadLibrary(fDllNameStr);
        if (DLLInst) {
            DllFunctionPtr = (CALLEDFUNCTION) GetProcAddress(DLLInst,fFunctionName.c_str());
            if (DllFunctionPtr) DllFunctionPtr(this);
            else {
                fMessage = "Could not obtain pointer for function ";
                fMessage += fFunctionName;
                fMessage += " in DLL ";
                fMessage += fDllName;
                Label1->Caption = fMessage;
            }
        }
        else {
            fMessage = "Could not load DLL ";
            fMessage += fDllName;
            Label1->Caption = fMessage;
        }
    }
//------------------------------------------------------------------------
```

Listing 3-18: MainForm.h

```
//------------------------------------------------------------------------

#ifndef MainFormH
#define MainFormH
//------------------------------------------------------------------------
#include <Classes.hpp>
#include <Controls.hpp>
#include <StdCtrls.hpp>
#include <Forms.hpp>


//------------------------------------------------------------------------
class TDLLDemoMainForm : public TForm
{
__published:            // IDE-managed Components
    TButton *Button1;
    TLabel *Label1;
    void __fastcall Button1Click(TObject *Sender);
private:                 // User declarations
public:                  // User declarations
    __fastcall TDLLDemoMainForm(TComponent* Owner);
};
//------------------------------------------------------------------------

extern PACKAGE TDLLDemoMainForm *DLLDemoMainForm;
//------------------------------------------------------------------------
#endif
```

Since the CreateForm() function calls the Show() method of the DLL form instead of the ShowModal() method, it may be noted that the DLL form would be displayed in modeless style; hence, the programmer has less direct control of when the form would be closed. In the case of dynamic linking of the DLL, the programmer should resort to other methods (that are beyond the scope of this book) to determine when to call the

FreeLibrary() function in order to unload the DLL programmatically. However, if the FreeLibrary() function is not called, the system unloads the DLL automatically when the main application terminates execution. Note that an application loading forms from DLLs must contain its own main form (or have it in a package file), and that form should not be loaded from a DLL itself.

There is one way we can ensure that the form unloads itself from the memory; it is to write an OnClose event handler for the form as shown here:

```
void __fastcall TForm1::FormClose(TObject *Sender, TCloseAction &Action)
{
    Action = caFree;
}
```

The statement that assigns the value caFree to the Action parameter instructs the form to unload itself from memory and free the memory allocated for it.

What are a Form's Characteristics?

Forms are inherited from the TForm class. Every time a form is added to the project, the IDE performs a series of tasks, as described here.

■ Creates a subclass of the TForm class and automatically names it TForm1, TForm2, etc., depending on the last created form index. The form's class declaration is stored in a header file.

■ Creates a global instance variable of the form in the header file

■ Creates a form definition file with the .dfm file extension (DFM stands for Delphi ForM file), which preserves the visual presentation of the form as an image. However, the file's contents may be viewed in graphical form or as text.

■ Creates the main program file for the form with the .cpp extension with an empty constructor. This is the file where the form's behavior is implemented as one or more event handlers.

Form is a container of components. In the hierarchy of an application's components, Form is the highest level of visual container in a Windows GUI application. By default, every component that is placed on the form by the designer is contained and owned by the form, and it takes the responsibility of destroying the component when the form itself gets destroyed. However, during run-time creation of components by the programmer, another component may be set as owner for the new component. The parent-child relationship of forms is different from ownership of components by the form. The differences are listed here:

- While ownership is a property introduced in the VCL at the TCompo-nent level and relates to the responsibility of the owner component to destroy the owned component, the parent-child relationship is defined at the TWinControl level where the parent always represents a win-dowed control of a child, which can be a windowed or non-windowed control, and the parent is responsible for saving the state of the control when the form is saved.

- A control that can behave as a parent of another control can also be that control's owner, but a component that is the owner of another compo-nent doesn't also have to be the component's parent (and vice versa).

- Most of the form's behavior is introduced in the TCustomForm class. The form's properties, methods, and events describe and control the following behavioral aspects of its contents:

  - The type of form, whether it is an SDI (Single Document Inter-face) form, MDI (Multiple Document Interface) parent form, or MDI child form, etc.

  - The display characteristics of the form, such as modal, modeless, resizable, Windows dialog type, iconized style, normal style, maxi-mized to occupy the entire desktop, etc.

  - Display position of the form on the desktop when executed

  - The lifetime management of the components

  - Provides direct access to the drawing area of the form to allow cus-tom drawing by the programmer

  - Lets the programmer access its components individually or collec-tively and change their properties through the Components array property. To access the properties defined in TComponent class or its ancestors, the individual elements of the Components array can directly be used. However, to properly identify and access the properties of components derived from TComponent, it is required to cast the elements of the Components array to the appropriate component type using the appropriate typecast opera-tor (e.g., dynamic_cast if you don't know whether a type conver-sion is defined or not, and static_cast if you know that the type conversion is defined).

  - Ability to reorganize its controls during run time. The controls can be rearranged at different positions or regrouped dynamically, cre-ating new visual containers at run time.

  - Lets the programmer interact with the form at several stages during its lifetime through the event handlers. The event handlers can be assigned dynamically at run time to the methods compiled into the code.

The individual properties, methods, and events are not discussed here, as they are readily available to the developer in the online manuals.

Frames in the VCL

Frame is a VCL control that was introduced by Borland in Delphi 5 and C++Builder 5. Like a form, it is a container of other components. It uses the same ownership mechanism as forms for automatic instantiation and destruction of the components on it and the same parent-child relationships for synchronization of component properties. In the VCL architecture, frames may be considered as intermediate components between forms and panels. Both forms and panels are containers; forms are self-sufficient units, whereas panels are not self-sufficient units. Frames are self-sufficient units without independent existence.

The characteristics that make frames distinct in the VCL architecture are listed here:

- The frame has no independent existence in an application during run time, but a form does. This means that a frame cannot be displayed on its own. It has to be contained within a form, another frame, or any hierarchy of frames, but ultimately it is displayed only through forms. In this respect, it behaves like a customized component.

- The frame can be considered a self-sufficient container. This means that the frame alone can be created in a single unit and contain other components. This gives the programmer the ability to create complex component groups within the project, even without creating and registering them to the Component Palette. Once a frame is created with required components, the frame can be included in any project and reused.

- Frames can also be added to the Component Palette or object repository for frequent reuse in multiple projects. This would increase productivity. Placing the mouse on the frame, click the right mouse button, and, from the menu of options displayed, choose Add to Palette to add the frame to the Component Palette. In this case, you are asked to enter a name for the frame component, choose a palette page where this component should be hosted, and change the icon if desired. If you choose Add to Repository to add the frame component to the repository, you are asked to provide information such as title, description, author of the frame component, and the repository page that should host the component.

- Because certain types of resources are shared between concurrent instances of frames, using frames to contain resources like images can help reduce the resource requirements to a great extent, particularly when the project contains repeated use of the same image like a company logo or background image that is displayed on every form.

Using Frames in a Project

As described earlier, the use of frames in a VCL project serves multiple purposes. Regardless of the purpose for which we use the frames, the steps involved are the same. For demonstration purposes, we will use a small example of creating a frame that contains a bitmap image as a background image in the application.

1. Create a VCL GUI application. This will automatically add a form to the project. Let's name the project FrameDemo.bpr and the form MainForm.cpp. The form class is named FrameDemoForm.

2. Add a frame unit to the project by choosing **File | New | Frame**. This will add a frame to the project. On the frame, drop a **TImage** component, assign a bitmap file to the Picture property, set the Stretch property to **true**, and set the Align property of the image object to **AlClient** so that the picture occupies the entire client area of the frame. Save the frame unit as **FrameUnit.cpp**. At this time, the frame appears as shown in Figure 3-3.

3. Now drop a frame object from the Component Palette Standard page. Whenever we try to drop a frame object from the Component Palette to the form, the system displays a list of all the frames (to choose from) defined in the project so far. At this time, the system displays Frame1. Choose **Frame1** and click **OK**.

4. The frame object created above would be dropped onto the form. To set this as a background image in the project, set the Align property of the frame to **AlClient**. At this time, the form appears as shown in Figure 3-4.

5. Now open the FrameUnit and add a **TLabel** object. Set its Caption property to any string, say "**Global Alliance Corporation**." Set the font size to **20** so that the label appears in a big size.

   Notice that when the contents of the frame are changed, the changes appear in the form instantaneously. This can be seen in Figure 3-5. This is a property exhibited exclusively by frames; when the defining frame class (which is inherited from TFrame) undergoes changes in its contents, the object instances are automatically updated by the IDE with the changes. In this example, we worked with only one instance of the TFrame-derived class, but the principle works with any number of instances created at the time.

This example also brings an interesting feature relevant to frames to our attention: Only one copy of the picture resource is compiled into the program in the FrameUnit.dfm file. The MainForm.dfm does not contain the binary resource. Imagine how compact the program would be in case of projects involving many forms, each having the same background image. The form (.dfm) files may be examined in text mode to notice this behavior.

Figure 3-3: Frame in the project

Figure 3-4: Inherited frame

Figure 3-5: Inherited frame adopts changes made in the base frame

The Value List Editor

VCL introduced another useful visual component in the Additional page of the Component Palette. It is the TValueListEditor, which is derived from the TCustomDrawGrid component. This is a nice visual editor for creating string list objects containing name-value pairs or saving them as property files. Most applications use property files to provide initial configuration information. If these files are made editable through the TValueListEditor component, then it adds even more flavor to your application. However, if your application's configuration needs to be saved in separate sections of name-value pairs, you may consider using INI files or even the system registry if your configuration data is more complex. The editor consists of two columns: One contains the names of the keys for each row and the other contains the values of the keys. By default, the editor adds a row on the top to display title captions. However, you may disable displaying the title row by excluding the doColumnTitles setting from the DisplayOptions set property. Let's examine the properties and methods of this component in more detail.

The ColCount and RowCount read-only properties describe the number of columns and rows (including the title row) in the object. The Cells[int col][int row] property gives us access to the specific cell identified by the column ID and row ID. The column identifier is 0 for the name column and

1 for the value column. The row identifier can be 0 for the title row or a value from 1 up to RowCount–1 to identify a specific row.

ItemProps[int row] specifies the item properties, such as whether the item is read-only, the maximum length of the string the user can enter into that item value, an edit mask, a fixed set of values such as a pick list from which the user can select a value, and whether the item lets the users drop down a pick list or launch a dialog to enter values. Listing 3-19 displays a code snippet to show how you can add a pick list as a row value to a TValueListEditor object.

Listing 3-19: Sample code to set a pick list for a ValueListEditor item

```
//-----------------------------------------------------------------------
void __fastcall TForm1::PickListItemBtnClick(TObject *Sender)
{
    ValueListEditor1->InsertRow("NEW PICKLIST", "", true);
    ValueListEditor1->ItemProps[6]->EditStyle = esPickList;
    ValueListEditor1->ItemProps[6]->PickList->Add("DB PARAM1");
    ValueListEditor1->ItemProps[6]->PickList->Add("DB PARAM2");
}
//-----------------------------------------------------------------------
```

The KeyOptions property is a set of values, which may include one or more of keyEdit, keyAdd, keyDelete, and keyUnique. The keyEdit option lets the user select and edit the key column where the name portion of the name-value pair may be changed. The keyAdd option lets the users add new name-value pairs. They can add new rows by pressing the Insert key or down arrow key. The keyDelete option lets the user delete a name-value pair. The keyUnique option makes sure that the key value remains unique across all the rows, and therefore the user is not permitted to create new keys with the same value of another existing key.

Keys[int row] specifies the key value for the row identified by the index value. The index may be a value from 0 up to RowCount–1.

The Strings property returns a TStrings object containing all the rows as name-value pairs in the form name=value.

The TitleCaptions property is a TStrings object and identifies the column headings. The default values are Key and Value, which can be changed during design time or run time.

The Values[const AnsiString key] property specifies the value of a particular row identified by the key value.

The InsertRow(const AnsiString key, const AnsiString value, bool Append) method adds a new row to the object. The first argument to the method is the key, the second argument is the value, and the third argument indicates whether to append the row at the end (if set to true) or insert the row before the current row.

The DeleteRow(int row) method deletes the row specified by the row index, which can be from 1 up to RowCount–1 (since 0 identifies the title row, it cannot be deleted). The method does not care about the keyDelete value in the KeyOptions property because that option is only used to control the user's ability to delete the row while using the editor during run time. The Refresh() method may be called to update the display to show any changes that have been made to the Strings property programmatically.

The FindRow(const AnsiString key, int &rowId) method attempts to locate a row with a specified key, and if the requested row is found, the method sets the index of the row in the rowId argument and returns the Boolean value true. If multiple rows are found with the specified key, the method sets the index of the first row to the rowId argument. If the specified key value is not found, the method returns false. The RestoreCurrentRow() method may be executed to undo any changes done to the current row.

Figure 3-6 displays a TValueListEditor during design time and Figure 3-7 displays the same during run time but with values. Setting the FixedCols property to 1 displays the first column in gray.

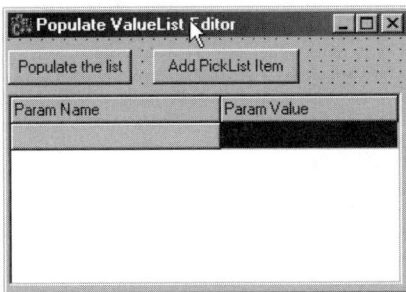

Figure 3-6: The TValueListEditor during design time

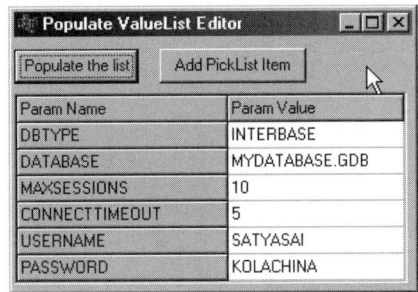

Figure 3-7: The TValueListEditor with values (during run time)

Summary

We started the chapter with an overview of the VCL architecture and discussed the features of the VCL framework, followed by an introduction to the VCL objects and how VCL's component ownership concept helps the programmer destroy objects.

Then AnsiString was given first in the discussion due to its profound use (and importance) in VCL-based applications, followed by a discussion on classes that formulate the core VCL foundation for visual and non-visual components.

A discussion of global application-level variables and components was addressed due to their importance in the VCL applications; these are Application, Screen, Mouse, and Clipboard instances, since these are used and required in any general VCL application, no matter the type of application we are writing (however, there are exceptions where some of these are not used in some types of applications).

We continued to discuss the RTTI in more detail and useful style, where we observed the method signatures that help the programmer use these methods to retrieve the run-time type information.

The discussion continued on forms and frames in more detail, with code examples to dynamically create forms' instances at run time. We provided screen shots for a frames project, where frame inheritance was explained. Finally, the Value List Editor component, which is a new addition in C++Builder 6, was discussed.

Some of these topics were discussed in detail and some were merely introduced. Some of the topics are covered in more detail in other chapters where the subject matter is relevant in the context of that chapter. The following chapter provides more information about advanced VCL features.

Chapter 4

Advanced VCL Features

Introduction

The previous chapter provided readers with introductory VCL features to enable them to feel comfortable with writing VCL applications. This chapter focuses on some of the advanced and additional VCL topics that are required in typical Windows applications, including the SYSUTILS and FILECTRL units. In the VCL architecture, these units provide very useful routines and objects that are needed to interact with the operating system.

Actions and ActionLists

Action Objects in VCL characterize the application's response to the most common user inputs, like clicking a mouse or a button or selecting an item from the main menu. Programmers usually come across situations where they have to provide some system response to multiple-user actions. The C++Builder IDE lets us assign the same event handler to multiple events. But there is a more structured and automated way of doing this task in the VCL, using Action Objects. Let's first identify the different objects that VCL provides for us to work with actions. Figure 4-1 describes the basic elements that form part of the action-triggering mechanism and the typical sequence of events that happens when Action Objects are used in the application.

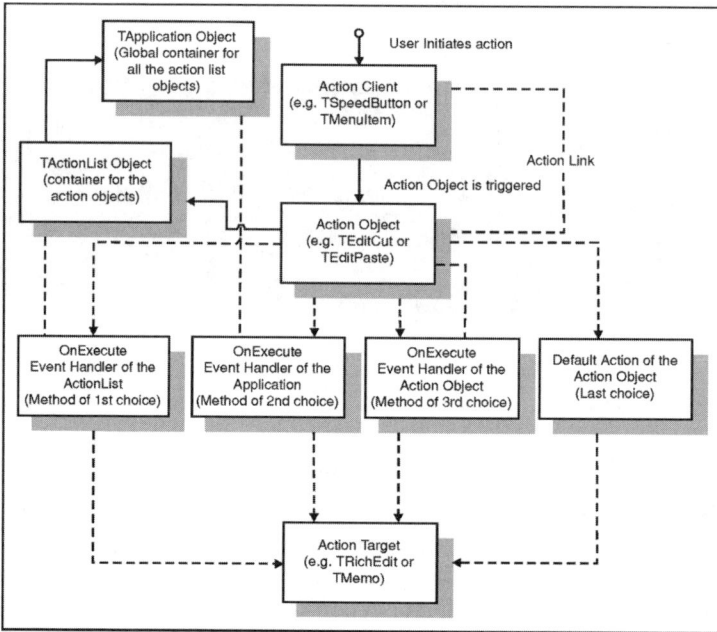

Figure 4-1: Basic elements of the action-triggering mechanism

Action Clients

The VCL controls that receive user input and initiate the linked Action Objects are called *action clients*. These controls have an Action property, which is a TAction Object or one of its descendants. When the Action property of the action client is assigned a valid Action Object, an action link is established internally. An *action link* is an instance of TActionLink or one of its descendants. It is this action link that connects the Action Object properties with the corresponding action client properties. The application programmer never uses the action link class directly. The Action Object internally uses action link. Component writers who wish to extend the action link behavior to other controls may create descendants of TActionLink. The VCL controls that behave like action clients include TSpeedBtn, TMenuItem, TButton, TBitBtn, TCheckBox, TRadioButton, and TForm.

Action Objects and TAction Class

The TAction class represents the basic action that can be assigned to an action client. In fact, one action can be assigned to more than one action client. Doing so would enable all the action clients to initiate the same TAction object in order to behave the same.

Types of Action Objects

There are two types of Action Objects that can be used in conjunction with action clients: standard actions and custom actions. *Standard actions* are predefined within the VCL framework and come with built-in functionality that can be used right away in your applications. These are instances of TAction descendant classes, such as TEditCut and TEditPaste. TEditCut and TEditPaste are descendants of TEditAction, which is further derived from TAction. The standard actions are grouped into categories of related tasks, such as the Edit category, which contains the standard actions relevant to edit controls, and the Format category, which contains the standard actions relevant to the formatting features of rich text, etc. Table 4-1 later in this chapter describes the standard actions and their categories, as available in the VCL in C++Builder 6. *Custom actions* are TAction instances that are assigned to the action clients but require the appropriate event handler to be implemented by the programmer. It is very easy to use either the standard actions or custom actions.

Action Targets

Action targets are those controls on which the Action Objects act upon. If the Action Object performs one of the edit functions, the action targets are descendants of TCustomEdit class, such as TEdit, TRichEdit, and TMemo, etc. In this case, a TEditCopy Action Object copies the selected text from the target edit control and stores it in the clipboard, and a TEditPaste Action Object pastes the clipboard contents at the current cursor location in the target edit control. This cycle of actions is described pictorially in Figure 4-2.

If we use standard Action Objects of the VCL, then for every category of actions, the set of action clients and the set of action targets are predetermined. For example, the standard actions in the Edit category are designed to work with the TSpeedBtn and TMenuItem, not with the TButton and TBitBtn action clients. The corresponding action targets are the edit controls that are descendants of the TCustomEdit class. Similarly, if we use the standard actions in the Window category, the corresponding action target must be the parent form of a Multiple Document Interface (MDI) application;

these standard actions disable themselves if the action target is not the parent form of an MDI application or if it does not contain MDI children.

If we use custom Action Objects, we need to write OnExecute event han-

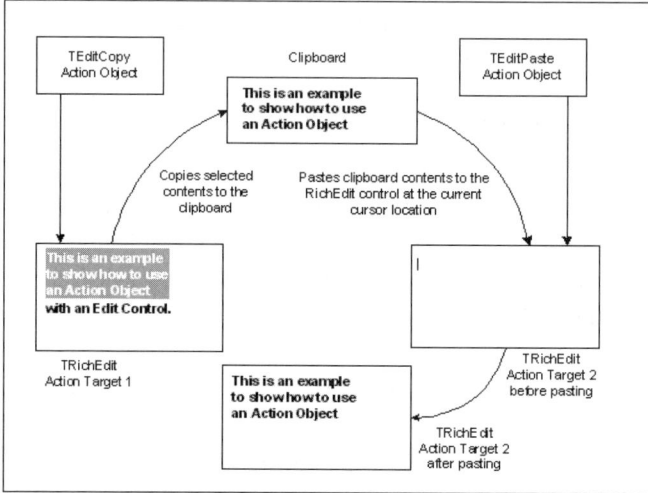

Figure 4-2: Example of standard edit Action Objects in action

dlers for the Action Object, the ActionList object that contains the Action Object, or the application that contains the Action Object.

ActionList Object

The ActionList object is an instance of the TActionList class. It is a container of Action Objects. ActionList is a non-visual VCL component that is dropped from the Standard page of the Component Palette. It is one of the two ways that C++Builder 6 supports the use of Action Objects. The other method is using the Action Manager and is discussed later in this chapter. It is easy to turn off or on all the actions in an ActionList object by setting the State property to asSuspended or asNormal, respectively.

Using the Standard Action Objects

Let's write a sample application that uses the standard Action Objects. Do the following tasks to complete the example:

1. Create a new application project in the C++Builder 6 IDE.

2. From the Standard page of the Component Palette, drop the **ActionList** component.

3. From the Win32 page of the Component Palette, drop an **ImageList** component onto the form. Double-click the **ImageList** component, add at least one image to the list, and click **OK** to close the ImageList. The image we are going to add in the list here is not necessarily going to be used to display the button images. We are just making sure that the image list is not empty. Select the **ActionList** component and set its Images property to the **ImageList** component just created. Doing so will enable the ActionList to automatically assign default button images to the standard Action Objects (only). The Images property must be set before choosing any standard actions in the ActionList component.

4. Double-click the **ActionList** component on the form. The ActionList editor is displayed, as shown in Figure 4-3.

5. Keeping the mouse pointer on the ActionList editor, click the right mouse button. A pop-up menu appears.

6. Choose **New Standard Action** from the menu. The Standard Action Classes list is displayed, as shown in Figure 4-4.

7. From the list, choose **TEditCopy** and **TEditPaste** from the Edit category and click the **OK** button.

    The selected Action Objects and their category are created and displayed in the ActionList editor, as shown in Figure 4-5.

8. From the Win32 page of the Component Palette, drop one **ToolBar** component and two **TRichEdit** components. The ToolBar component automatically aligns itself to the top of the form. Manually align both the TRichEdit components, and set their width and height both equal to **200** pixels in the Object Inspector. Double-click the **Lines** property of each of the TRichEdit components and clear the values from the editor so that the components have no initial data in the client window.

9. From the Additional page of the Component Palette, drop two **SpeedBtn** components onto the toolbar. In the Object Inspector, set their Width property to **75** pixels so that the components appear wider. Set the Action property of the first SpeedBtn component to **EditCopy1** and the second SpeedBtn component to **EditPaste1**. After assigning the Action property, each of the SpeedBtn components shows its respective caption text, which is obtained from the Action Objects.

10. At this time the form appears as shown in Figure 4-6. Save the project and compile.

11. Run the executable. It will look like a small text editor application without much functionality other than copying the selected content of the edit window and pasting it back in another edit window. Initially, the Copy button appears disabled. This button is enabled only after selecting text in an edit control. Since the edit controls are clear initially, type some text and test the copy and paste functionality, as in a traditional text editor. Two edit controls are placed on the form to show you that the Action Objects automatically know their action target once you select the text to be copied or identify the location to paste the contents.

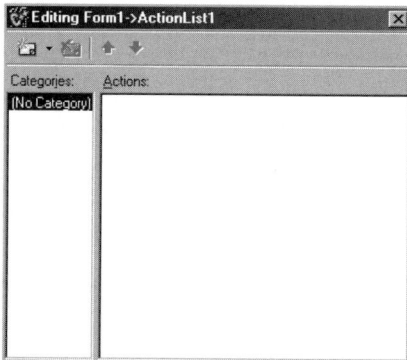

Figure 4-3: ActionList editor (with no actions)

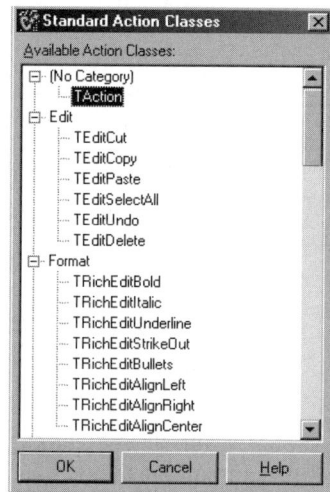

Figure 4-4: Standard Action Classes list

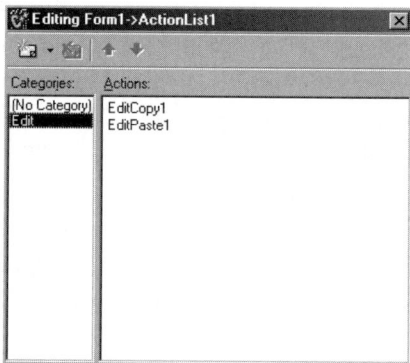

Figure 4-5: ActionList editor (actions assigned)

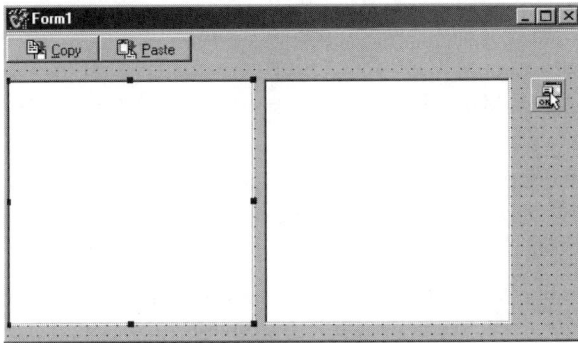

Figure 4-6: Form with actions, buttons, and TRichEdit controls

How Does the Application Find the Action Target for an Action Object?

The application follows a sequential order to find the action target. If no action target is found suitable for the action, then nothing happens. The sequence is given as follows:

- Active control is the first potential action target.

- If the active control is not the right action target, the application looks at the ActiveForm of the screen.

- Finally, the controls on the ActiveForm are searched if the form itself is not an action target.

Using the Custom Action Objects

Let's write a sample application to demonstrate the use of custom Action Objects. Perform the following tasks to create the sample application:

1. Create a new application project in the C++Builder 6 IDE.

2. From the Standard page of the Component Palette, drop the **ActionList** component.

3. Double-click the dropped component on the form. The ActionList editor is displayed. See Figure 4-3 in the previous example.

4. Keeping the mouse pointer on the ActionList editor, click the right mouse button. A pop-up menu appears.

5. Choose **New Action** from the menu. A new instance of a TAction object is created in the list and displayed. Every time we choose New Action, a new instance is created. Each of these instances represents a generic Action Object whose action needs to be defined in the code. For this sample application, let us write the action handler method for one Action Object.

6. From the Standard page of the Component Palette, drop two **Button** components onto the form. Set the Action property of both the Button objects to the same Action Object that we just created in the previous step.

7. Double-click the OnExecute() event handler of the Action Object in the Object Inspector, and write the small piece of code shown in Listing 4-1.

8. Compile the project and execute the application. When you click either of the buttons, you get the same result. Figure 4-7 displays the result screen.

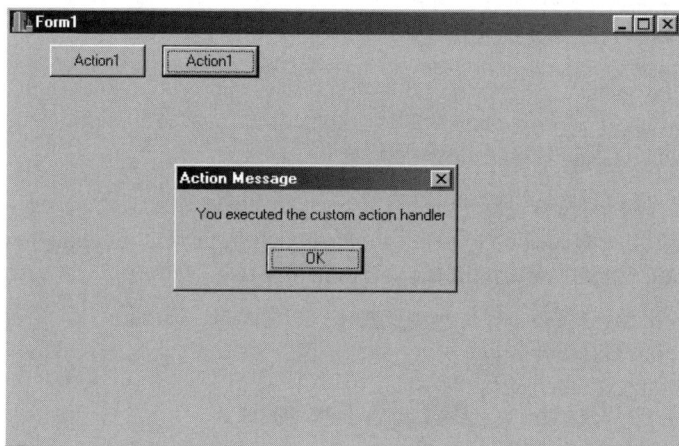

Figure 4-7: Custom action implementation

Listing 4-1

```
void __fastcall TForm1::Action1Execute(TObject *Sender)
{
    Application->MessageBox("You executed the custom action handler",
        "Action Message", MB_OK);
}
```

The point I am trying to make here is that you can provide the same action result through different channels. In this respect, any combination of action client objects can share the same action handler. By now, you may have also noticed that whenever the Action Object is assigned to the Action property of one or more action clients, the caption of the Action Object is copied to the caption of the action client. In fact, it is not just the Caption property that is copied; rather, all the corresponding properties are copied. Since the Caption property is visible, we have noticed it; the others are simply not visible. This copying of properties is handled by the Action Link object (which is an instance of TActionLink or its descendant), as discussed earlier in this section. However, the properties that are copied from the Action Objects may be overridden in the action clients either during design time or run time.

How Does VCL Identify the Appropriate Action Handler for an Action?

Now let's examine the criteria that VCL follows to identify the appropriate action handler method for an action. Whether we use custom actions or standard actions, we are free to write our own action handler method for the Action Object. When the user clicks an action client, VCL follows a dispatching sequence to find out the correct event handler to handle the action. An action handler method can be written at one or more of three different levels: ActionList level, Application level, or Action Object level.

The OnExecute() method at the ActionList and Action Object levels and the OnActionExecute() method at the Application level represent the event handlers for the Action Object. The dispatching sequence is: first the ActionList object, next the Application object, and finally the Action Object. The following rules are applied while executing the action handler at all these levels:

- If an action handler is defined at only one of these levels, VCL executes that action handler.

- If an action handler is defined at more than one level, it tries to execute them all in the dispatching sequence mentioned earlier, provided the action handler at a previous execution level lets it continue to the next level. By "lets it continue," I mean that if we set Handled = true at the previous execution level, the next level event handler is not executed since we are satisfied with the previous event handler. If we do not set Handled = true explicitly, or if we set Handled = false explicitly, the next level event handler is executed if we wrote that event handler. A simple example is that if we wrote all three event handlers and did not set Handled = true in any of them, it executes them all in the dispatching sequence.

- Another parameter to the OnExecute (or OnActionExecute) method is a pointer to the TBasicAction object. This parameter helps us in writing a single event handler (at the ActionList and Application levels) to handle more than one Action Object by explicitly writing blocks of code for each Action Object, as shown in Listing 4-2. This feature and the previous one together give us ample flexibility to control the Action Objects' functionality.

- The scope of applicability of action handler functionality includes all the Action Objects contained within the action handler level. However, one or more contained Action Objects may be explicitly included in (or excluded from) the scope, as mentioned previously.

- If we write a custom action handler at any one of the levels and an Action Object falls within the scope of this action handler, the action handler functionality overrides any default functionality carried by the Action Object (usually when the Action Object is one of the standard actions).

Listing 4-2

```
void __fastcall TForm1::ActionList1Execute(TBasicAction *Action, bool &Handled)
{
    if (Action == Action1)
        Application->MessageBox("You executed the custom action handler",
        "ActionList Message", MB_OK);
        Handled = true;
    }
}
```

Table 4-1: Standard VCL actions

Category	Standard Actions	Description and Default Action
Edit	TEditCut TEditCopy TEditPaste TEditSelectAll TEditUndo TEditDelete	The Action Objects in this category provide the standard edit actions, and they are used with edit control targets that are derived from TCustomEdit. TEditAction is the base class for the descendant Action Objects that override the ExecuteTarget method.
Format	TRichEditBold TRichEditItalic TRichEditUnderline TRichEditStrikeOut TRichEditBullets TRichEditAlignLeft TRichEditAlignRIght TRichEditAlignCenter	The Action Objects in this category provide the standard text formatting features to rich text edit objects. TRichEditAction is the base class for the descendant Action Objects that override the ExecuteTarget and UpdateTarget methods to implement the formatting feature.
Help	THelpContents THelpTopicSearch THelpOnHelp THelpContextAction	The Action Objects in this category provide the standard help functionality and can be used on any target. THelpAction is the base class for the descendants that each override the ExecuteTarget method to pass the command onto a Help system.
Window	TWindowClose TWindowCascade TWindowTileHorizontal TWindowTileVertical TWindowMinimizeAll TWindowArrange	The Action Objects in this category provide standard window actions. The target control for these Action Objects is the parent form of an MDI application. The actions are executed on the MDI child windows. TWindowAction is the base class for the descendants that each override the ExecuteTarget method to implement the respective action.

Category	Standard Actions	Description and Default Action
File	TFileOpen TFileSaveAs TFilePrintSetup TFileRun TFileExit	The Action Objects in this category are used to initiate the specific actions on the files, such as initiating the respective dialog or running an executable file if it is the File Run action or closing the application if it is the File Exit action.
Search	TSearchFind TSearchFindNext TSearchFindReplace TSearchFindFirst	The Action Objects in this category provide text search functions on the target edit control. TSearchAction is the base class for the descendants that each override the ExecuteTarget method to display a modeless dialog. This dialog enables the user to enter search criteria as provided by the action.
Tab	TPreviousTab TNextTab	The target controls for these objects are descendants of TCustomTab-Control, such as TPageControl and TTabControl. 　The Action Objects in this category provide the functionality to move the current page to the previous or next page. TTabAction is the base class for the descendants that each override the ExecuteTarget method to perform the necessary action.
List	TListControlCopySelection TListControlDeleteSelection TListControlSelectAll TListControlClearSelection TListControlMoveSelection TStaticListAction TVirtualListAction	The target control for the Action Objects in this category is a list control, such as ListBox, ListView, etc. The target control is identified by the ListControl property. Some of these Action Objects require a destination list control object, identified by the Destination property. When a destination list control is also used, the source list control is identified by the ListControl property. The functionality of these objects is explained here. (For simplicity's sake, the TListControl prefix is omitted here.) 　SelectAll selects all the items in the source list control. ClearSelection deselects all the selected items. CopySelection copies all the selected items from the source list control to the destination list control. Move-Selection moves all the selected items from the source list control to the destination list control. DeleteSelection deletes the selected items from the target list control. The TListControlAction is the base class for all the above descendant action classes in this category that override the ExecuteTarget method to provide the respective functionality. 　StaticListAction supplies a static list of the items created at design time to the list control. VirtualListAction supplies items dynamically to the list control, as coded in the OnGetItem event handler. The TCustom-ListAction is the base class for the TStaticListAction and TVirtualListAction objects.
Dialog	TOpenPicture TSavePicture TColorSelect TFontEdit TPrintDlg	The Action Objects in this category provide some Windows common dialogs in addition to those provided in the File category. The names of these objects are self-explanatory as to the actions that they support.
Internet	TBrowseURL TDownLoadURL TSendMail	TBrowseURL launches the default browser to open a page at the specified URL using the URL property. TDownLoadURL starts downloading the file at the specified URL and periodically generates the OnDownloadProgress event so that the users can be given feedback about the progress of the download process. The URL property indicates the file to be downloaded. TURLAction is the base class for these actions. 　Controls linked to the TSendMail Action Object cause the application to send a MAPI mail message containing the message specified in the Text property.

Category	Standard Actions	Description and Default Action
Dataset	TDataSetFirst TDataSetPrior TDataSetNext TDataSetLast TDataSetInsert TDataSetDelete TDataSetEdit TDataSetPost TDataSetCancel TDataSetRefresh	The Action Objects in this category provide record navigation features in descendants of TDataSet component. The dataset component must be associated to a TDataSource component, and the DataSource property of the Action Objects must be set to this TDataSource component. Each of these Action Objects provide action that corresponds to a dataset method with a similar name. The corresponding action client is disabled if a particular action is not relevant in a situation. For example, TDataSetFirst Action Object corresponds to the First() method of the dataset component. 　　If the dataset is already pointing to the first record, this action is not relevant at this time, and hence the action client that is connected to the TDataSetFirst Action Object is disabled. The same concept applies to all the Action Objects. TDataSetAction is the base class for the Action Objects in this category that override the ExecuteTarget method to provide the respective functionality.
Tools	TCustomizeActionBars	This Action Object is used in conjunction with the ActionManager to provide run-time customization of Action Objects.

Visual Components That Render Action Objects

In C++Builder 6, new VCL components are added to extend the Action Object functionality to visually design menus and toolbars at both design time and run time. Figure 4-8 shows the Component Palette page containing these components.

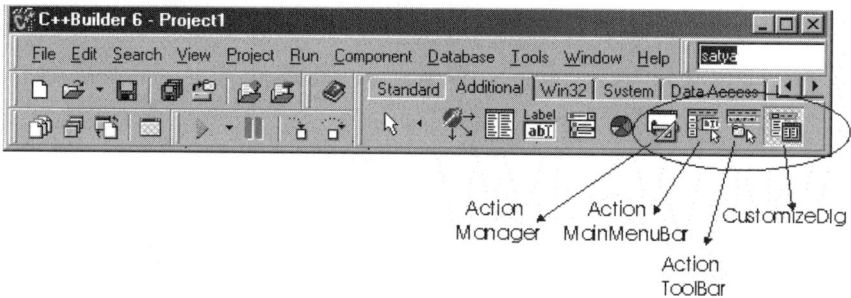

Figure 4-8: Action components in the Component Palette

These components are:

- ActionManager
- ActionMainMenuBar
- ActionToolBar
- CustomizeDlg

The ActionMainMenuBar is an instance of the TActionMainMenuBar class that contains the action client items and behaves very similar to the

TMainMenu object. The ActionToolBar is an instance of the TActionTool-Bar class and renders the action client items as tool buttons. Both these new container objects are linked to an ActionManager object, which is an instance of the TActionManager class. The ActionManager object houses all the action client items that are contained in the ActionMainMenuBar as well as the ActionToolBar. The action client items may be standard Action Objects or custom Action Objects. To add an ActionMainMenuBar component to the ActionManager, we have to drop the component onto the form that contains the ActionManager component. Later, when we assign ActionManager's Action Objects to the ActionMainMenuBar, VCL automatically creates a link from ActionMainMenuBar to the ActionManager. To add an ActionToolBar component to the ActionManager, we can do it the same way as we did the ActionMainMenuBar component, or we can add it through the ActionManager component itself, as explained in the following steps.

I am going to take you through the process of building a small Windows WordPad kind of application with a minimal amount of coding:

1. Create a new application project in the C++Builder 6 IDE. Save it anywhere on your hard disk with project and unit names of your choice.

2. From the Additional page of the Component Palette, drop an **Action-Manager** component and an **ActionMainMenuBar** component onto the form. The ActionMainMenuBar component automatically aligns itself to the top of the form. In the Object Inspector, set the following properties to make sure that the menu bar displays all four borders:

    ```
    EdgeBorders→ebLeft = true;
    EdgeBorders→ebTop = true;
    EdgeBorders→ebRight = true;
    EdgeBorders→ebBottom = true;
    ```

3. From the Win32 page of the Component Palette, drop an **ImageList** component onto the form. Double-click the **ImageList** component, add at least one image to the list, and click the **OK** button to close the ImageList. The image we are going to add in the list here is not necessarily going to be used to display the button images. We are just making sure that the image list is not empty.

4. Select the **ActionManager** component and set its Images property to the ImageList component created in the previous step. Doing so will enable the ActionManager to automatically assign default button images to the standard Action Objects. However, if we add any custom Action Objects to the ActionManager, no images are automatically set; we have to do it manually. In this example, we only use standard Action Objects.

5. Now double-click the **ActionManager** component. The Action-Manager property editor appears and looks like Figure 4-9. The property editor has three tab pages. Choose the **Toolbars** tab page. Click the **New** button twice. Two ActionToolBar components are created (named ActionToolBar1 and ActionToolBar2) on the form and listed in the property editor.

6. Now select the **Actions** tab in the property editor.

7. In the Object Inspector, for both the ActionToolBar components, set the following properties to make sure that the toolbars display all four borders:

```
EdgeBorders→ebLeft = true;
EdgeBorders→ebTop = true;
EdgeBorders→ebRight = true;
EdgeBorders→ebBottom = true;
```

8. Keeping the mouse pointer on the ActionList editor, click the right mouse button. A pop-up menu appears. Choose **New Standard Action** from the menu. The Standard Action Classes list is displayed, as shown in Figure 4-4. This is the same list that we saw in an earlier example.

9. From the list of standard actions, choose all the Action Objects under the File, Edit, and Format categories and the PrintDlg item from the Dialog category. More than one item can be selected from this list by pressing down the Shift or Ctrl key and selecting the appropriate item. The selected items are highlighted. After completing the selection, click the **OK** button, which closes this list and adds the selected items to the Actions tab page of the ActionManager property editor.

   You can browse through the Action Objects added to the list. You may notice that the property editor automatically assigned the appropriate images to the Action Objects. Since we assigned a non-empty ImageList object to the ActionManager, we indicated to the VCL that we wished to use default images for the action clients. You may also notice that the default shortcut keys are assigned to the Action Objects. At this time, the property editor looks like Figure 4-10.

10. Now the fun starts. Let's fill the menu bar and toolbars we created earlier. This can be done by a simple drag-and-drop operation. We can select action items individually or as a complete category, depending on how we wish to place the items on the menu bar and toolbars. I will follow a specific order to place the items; you may choose a different order if you wish. The drag-and-drop is achieved by selecting the desired item (action item or action category), holding the left mouse key, moving the mouse pointer to the menu bar or toolbar, and releasing the left mouse key.

I placed the File, Edit, and Format categories in the menu bar in that order. Then I placed the PrintDlg item from the Dialog category as a sub-item in the File menu below the Print Setup item.

I placed selected items from the File, Edit, and Dialog categories on the first toolbar. I finally placed selected items from the Format category on the second toolbar. Please refer to Figure 4-11 to check the order.

11. From the Win32 page, drop a **RichEdit** component onto the form and set its Align property to **alClient**. Using the Object Inspector, clear the Lines property of the RichEdit so that the edit window looks clean.

12. In the Object Inspector, set the following properties for the FileOpen1 Action Object to make sure that we work only with text files:

```
Dialog→DefaultExt = TXT;
Dialog→Filter = Text files (*.TXT)|*.TXT;
```

13. Repeat the step for the FileSaveAs1 Action Object.

Notice that I am not enclosing the string values with double quotes because I am setting these properties in the Object Inspector. However, you have to enclose any strings with double quotes to set string values during run time.

Now let's write a few event handlers to complete this project. Since we are using standard Action Objects, you may ask why we have to write event handlers. The Windows common dialogs are a little more than just copy and paste type of actions. Each of the dialogs that we have used in the application need some programming to react to the user's choices. We have to write event handlers to tell VCL what to do when the user makes choices or enters values in the dialog boxes. Also, if we need to incorporate extra functionality beyond what is provided by the standard Action Objects, we have to write code. But recall that if we write Action Object event handlers, we would be losing the default action functionality provided by the VCL.

To keep the coding simple, we will create event handlers for just three of the actions: FileOpen1, FileSaveAs1, and PrintDlg1. Each of these Action Objects has a Dialog property, which represents the corresponding Windows common dialog object provided by the VCL. Each of these Windows common dialogs has an Execute() method, which returns true if the user clicks the OK button and false if the user clicks the Cancel button. But we are not using these dialogs directly; rather, we are invoking them through the Action Objects. The Action Objects provide OnAccept() and OnCancel() event handlers corresponding to the true and false conditions. Therefore, we have to implement the

OnAccept() event handlers for the three dialogs to tell the VCL what to do in response to user inputs. I also created the custom member method PrintText(TCanvas* Canvas) for the main form class, which writes text lines from the TRichEdit component to the printer's canvas. This method is invoked by the OnAccept() event handler of the PrintDlg1. I will not discuss the code further here. Please refer to Listing 4-3 for the cpp file of the unit and Listing 4-4 for the corresponding header file.

14. Compile the project and execute. You may wonder how fast we are able to create a simple text editor with reasonable functionality. Please note that the print function we have incorporated here is not complete. More needs to be worked on to add features like controlling page size, page breaks, etc.

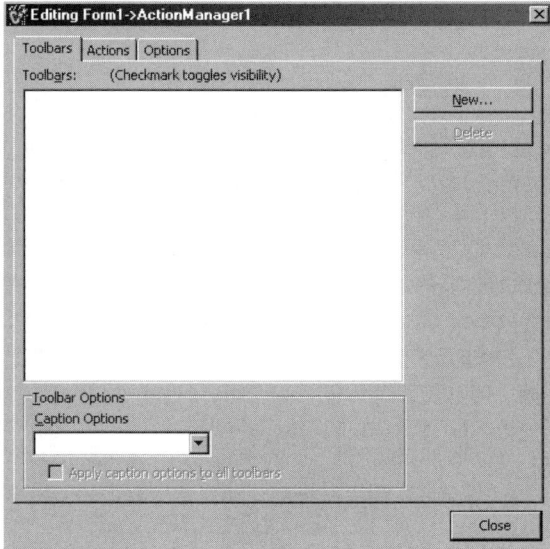

Figure 4-9: ActionManager property editor (with no actions)

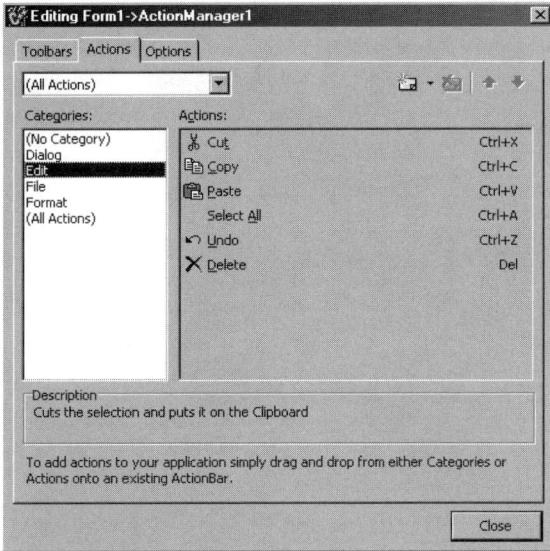

Figure 4-10: ActionManager property editor (with actions assigned)

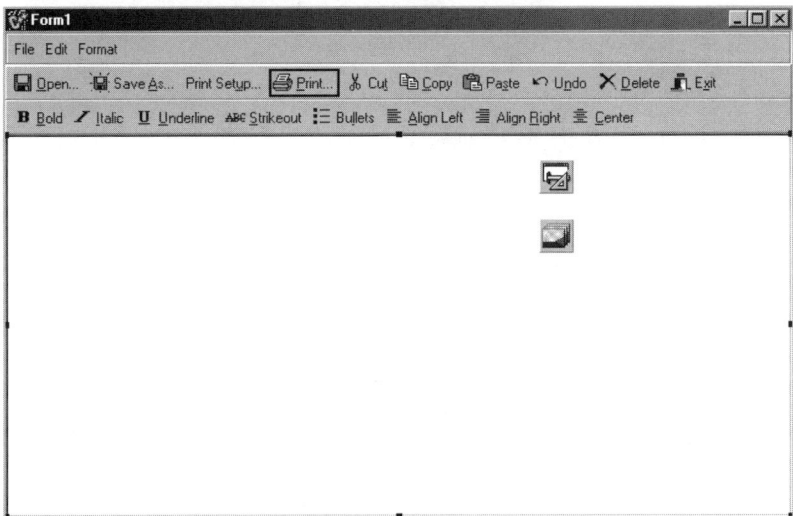

Figure 4-11: Simple text editor (with the components)

Listing 4-3: Unit1.cpp

```
//---------------------------------------------------------------------------

#include <vcl.h>
#pragma hdrstop

#include "Unit1.h"
//---------------------------------------------------------------------------
#pragma package(smart_init)
```

```
#pragma resource "*.dfm"
TForm1 *Form1;
//---------------------------------------------------------------------------
__fastcall TForm1::TForm1(TComponent* Owner)
        : TForm(Owner)
{
}
//---------------------------------------------------------------------------

void __fastcall TForm1::FileOpen1Accept(TObject *Sender)
{
        AnsiString fileName = FileOpen1->Dialog->FileName;
        RichEdit1->Lines->Clear();
        RichEdit1->Lines->LoadFromFile(fileName);
}
//---------------------------------------------------------------------------
void __fastcall TForm1::FileSaveAs1Accept(TObject *Sender)
{
        AnsiString fileName = FileSaveAs1->Dialog->FileName;
        RichEdit1->Lines->SaveToFile(fileName);
}
//---------------------------------------------------------------------------
void __fastcall TForm1::PrintDlg1Accept(TObject *Sender)
{
    TPrinter *APrinter = Printer();
    APrinter->Copies = PrintDlg1->Dialog->Copies;
    int i;
    for (i=0; i < APrinter->Copies; i++) {
        APrinter->BeginDoc();
        PrintText(APrinter->Canvas);
        APrinter->EndDoc();
    }
}
//---------------------------------------------------------------------------
void __fastcall TForm1::PrintText(TCanvas *Canvas)
{
    int i, x;
    AnsiString S("Text String");     // sample text to determine text height
    x = Canvas->TextHeight(S);
    for (i=0; i < RichEdit1->Lines->Count; i++) {
        S = RichEdit1->Lines->Strings[i];
        Canvas->TextOut(1, x * i, S);
    }
}
//---------------------------------------------------------------------------
```

Listing 4-4: Unit1.h

```
//---------------------------------------------------------------------------

#ifndef Unit1H
#define Unit1H
//---------------------------------------------------------------------------
#include <Classes.hpp>
#include <Controls.hpp>
#include <StdCtrls.hpp>
#include <Forms.hpp>
#include <ActnCtrls.hpp>
#include <ActnList.hpp>
#include <ActnMan.hpp>
```

```cpp
#include <ActnMenus.hpp>
#include <ToolWin.hpp>
#include <ImgList.hpp>
#include <ExtActns.hpp>
#include <StdActns.hpp>
#include <ComCtrls.hpp>
//---------------------------------------------------------------------------
class TForm1 : public TForm
{
__published:        // IDE-managed components
        TActionManager *ActionManager1;
        TActionMainMenuBar *ActionMainMenuBar1;
        TImageList *ImageList1;
        TActionToolBar *ActionToolBar1;
        TActionToolBar *ActionToolBar2;
        TEditCut *EditCut1;
        TEditCopy *EditCopy1;
        TEditPaste *EditPaste1;
        TEditSelectAll *EditSelectAll1;
        TEditUndo *EditUndo1;
        TEditDelete *EditDelete1;
        TRichEditBold *RichEditBold1;
        TRichEditItalic *RichEditItalic1;
        TRichEditUnderline *RichEditUnderline1;
        TRichEditStrikeOut *RichEditStrikeOut1;
        TRichEditBullets *RichEditBullets1;
        TRichEditAlignLeft *RichEditAlignLeft1;
        TRichEditAlignRight *RichEditAlignRight1;
        TRichEditAlignCenter *RichEditAlignCenter1;
        TFileOpen *FileOpen1;
        TFileSaveAs *FileSaveAs1;
        TFilePrintSetup *FilePrintSetup1;
        TFileRun *FileRun1;
        TFileExit *FileExit1;
        TPrintDlg *PrintDlg1;
        TRichEdit *RichEdit1;
        void __fastcall FileOpen1Accept(TObject *Sender);
        void __fastcall FileSaveAs1Accept(TObject *Sender);
        void __fastcall PrintDlg1Accept(TObject *Sender);
private:            // User declarations
public:             // User declarations
        __fastcall TForm1(TComponent* Owner);
        void __fastcall PrintText(TCanvas *Canvas);
};
//---------------------------------------------------------------------------
extern PACKAGE TForm1 *Form1;
//---------------------------------------------------------------------------
#endif
```

Since we have seen the ActionManager in action, we can now talk more about it. This component stores all the necessary information to effectively recreate the action-based user interface. The contents of the component can be saved to a stream object (such as a memory stream or file stream) and retrieved later to dynamically create the user interface. (Streams and streaming are discussed in Chapter 12 in more detail.) We can create multiple user interfaces and dynamically change them at run time, or we can pass the user interface layout from one process to another (even across the network) and enable a remote application dynamically to generate and display its user interface.

The last component in this set, CustomizeDlg is an instance of the TCustomizeDlg class. When connected to an ActionManager object through its ActionManager property, all the Action Objects created during design time will be available to the user for customization. However, the user cannot create new toolbars and new action items at run time but will be able to customize all components created during design time. This includes making the action clients and toolbars visible or invisible, removing the action clients from the toolbars, changing the order of appearance of the action clients on the toolbars, etc.

Windows Common Dialogs

In the previous section, we had the opportunity to work with some of the Windows common dialogs. I will now discuss them in detail. A *dialog* is a window that intercepts the application execution and asks the user for additional input. During the normal flow of application execution, sometimes the application cannot continue unless the user provides additional information, *usually* if the user wants to select specific system resources. For example, when the user wants to print the active document to the printer and selects the corresponding menu option, the application has to know which printer among the installed ones receives the document for printing. Often, dialogs are displayed modal because the application cannot continue without the user's input. C++Builder 6 comes with VCL objects for Windows common dialogs, as listed here:

- The TColorDialog component displays a Windows dialog box for selecting colors. When the Execute() method is called, the dialog is activated and appears on the screen. The user closes the dialog by clicking either OK or Cancel. The Execute() method returns true if the user made a choice or false if no choice was made.

- The TFindDialog component displays a modeless dialog window that prompts the user for a search string. When the Execute() method is called, the dialog is activated and displayed on the screen, and a Boolean value true is returned. When the user clicks the Find Next button, the FindText property is set to the search string that the user entered. The dialog remains open until the user clicks the Cancel button. Since the dialog is modeless, the user is able to get back to the application (usually a document) while the dialog is displayed; this enables the user to repeatedly execute the search function by clicking the Find Next button.

■ The TFontDialog component displays a Windows dialog box for selecting a font and style from the list of fonts loaded in the system. When the Execute() method is called, the dialog is activated and appears on the screen. The user closes the dialog by clicking either OK or Cancel. The Execute() method returns true if the user made a choice or false if no choice was made.

■ The TOpenDialog component displays a Windows dialog box to open a disk file. When the Execute() method is called, the dialog is activated and appears on the screen. The user closes the dialog by clicking either OK or Cancel. The Execute() method returns true if the user made a choice or false if no choice was made. The selected (or entered) filename is available in the FileName property. The Filter property controls which types of filenames must be displayed in the list. The DefaultExt property sets the default file extension if the user does not specify it.

■ The TPrintDialog component displays a Windows dialog box to send print jobs to the printer selected from a list. The dialog compiles the list of printers depending on the drivers installed on the machine. When the Execute() method is called, the dialog is activated and appears on the screen. The user closes the dialog by clicking either the Print or Cancel button. The Execute() method returns true if the user clicked the Print button and false if the user clicked the Cancel button.

■ The TPrinterSetupDialog component displays a Windows dialog box to select a printer from a list and set its configuration options. When the Execute() method is called, the dialog is activated and appears on the screen. The user closes the dialog by clicking either OK or Cancel. The Execute() method configures the printer and returns true if the user made a choice or false if no choice was made.

■ TReplaceDialog is a special version of TFindDialog that prompts the user for both a search string and a replace string. The ReplaceText property holds the new text that replaces the old text. Its value is set from the value entered by the user after the user clicks the Replace button or ReplaceAll button.

■ The TSaveDialog component displays a Windows dialog box to save a file to disk. When the Execute() method is called, the dialog is activated and appears on the screen. The user closes the dialog by clicking either OK or Cancel. The Execute() method returns true if the user made a choice or false if no choice was made. The selected or entered filename is available in the FileName property. The Filter property controls which types of filenames must be displayed in the list. The DefaultExt property sets the default file extension if the user does not specify it.

The TCommonDialog class encapsulates most of the functionality of the Windows common dialogs, and the descendant classes add new properties and methods or override methods in the base class to provide the necessary functionality.

If you wish to write your own version of Windows common dialogs, it is recommended that you descend from TCommonDialog in order to avoid the complexity of writing the component from scratch.

Windows Drag and Drop

Drag and drop is a very useful feature provided by the Windows operating systems. The mouse is used as an agent to coordinate the drag-and-drop operation between the two entities, the source and target objects. The *source object* is the one being dragged when the mouse button is held, and the *target object* is the one on which the source object is dropped when the mouse button is released. The drag-and-drop operation enables the application user to transfer or copy data elements from the source to the target without any data entry involved, thus improving user productivity and usability of the application. Drag and drop is considered to be one of the most useful GUI design principles. However, it should only be used where it is appropriate. The properties and methods supporting drag and drop are introduced in the TControl object and are available in all the descendant objects.

Properties and Methods of the Source Object

For the control to act as a drag source, the following property must be set:

```
DragKind = dkDrag;
```

To enable dragging, start automatically when the left mouse button is held; the DragMode property must be set to dmAutomatic. To manually control the drag operation, the property must be set to dmManual, which is the default value. If DragMode is set to dmManual, the dragging operation starts when the BeginDrag() method is called in the OnMouseDown() event. The signatures of these methods are given here.

BeginDrag() Method

```
void __fastcall BeginDrag(bool Immediate, int Threshold);
```

If the Immediate parameter is true, the dragging starts immediately after the user presses and holds the left mouse button. If the Immediate parameter is false, the dragging starts after the mouse is moved Threshold number of pixels after pressing and holding the left button.

OnMouseDown() Event

```
typedef void __fastcall (__closure *TMouseEvent)(System::TObject* Sender, TMouseButton
    Button, Classes::TShiftState Shift, int X, int Y);
__property TMouseEvent OnMouseDown = {read=FOnMouseDown, write=FOnMouseDown};
```

The Sender parameter is the drag source object. TMouseButton indicates whether the mouse button is the left, right, or middle button. TShiftState indicates the state of the Alt, Ctrl, and Shift keys and the mouse buttons. X and Y are the pixel coordinates of the mouse pointer in the client area of the sender. In this event handler, we can access the source object, the pressed mouse button, and the position coordinates of the mouse pointer, and hence the contents of the source object.

Event Handlers for the Drop Target

The control that is going to accept the dropped control is called the *drop target* or *drag target*. In the true sense of accepting a dropped control, it means that the drop target control is willing to take the data passed by the source control. For the drop target, there are no properties to be set and no methods to be called; we just have to implement two event handlers: the OnDragOver event handler and the OnDragDrop event handler.

When the mouse is moving over any control after capturing the drag source, the OnDragOver event handler is fired for that control. If we do not implement the OnDragOver event handler for any control, the drag operation goes to waste automatically without dropping the object anywhere. Therefore, we implement the OnDragOver event handler for the drop target control. This event handler has several parameters. The Source parameter is the control that is being dragged (if it is a simple drag) or a custom drag object (if we implement the custom drag object). The Sender parameter is the control for which we are implementing the event handler. Other parameters are the mouse positional coordinates X and Y and a Boolean parameter Accept, which is true by default. If we set the parameter Accept to true, the control acts as a drop target and accepts the dropped object. If we set Accept to false or if we do not implement this event handler, the control does not accept the drag source.

In the OnDragDrop event handler, we write the code to unpack (obtain) the values from the Source object and do whatever we intended to do in the drag-and-drop operation.

Custom Drag Objects

When the source control is dropped on a target, the source control is sent as a Source parameter in the target event handlers that receive the dragged object. We may face circumstances such as having to implement dragging from multiple controls and dropping on a single target, or we may have to implement drag and drop across controls hosted in separate DLLs or the main EXE file of the same application. Or, we may intend to implement custom drag images other than the default ones provided in C++Builder 6, etc. The point I am attempting to make here is that there may be complex drag-and-drop situations for which the default behavior of the source control object may not be sufficient. To accommodate such circumstances, VCL lets us implement custom drag objects through the TDragObject class and its descendants. If we intend to use this object, we have to implement the OnStartDrag event handler. Its signature is given here:

```
typedef void __fastcall (__closure *TStartDragEvent)(System::TObject* Sender,
    TDragObject* &DragObject);
__property TStartDragEvent OnStartDrag = {read=FOnStartDrag, write=FOnStartDrag};
```

Notice that the TDragObject object is one of the parameters to this event handler. If we implement this event handler, it is triggered when the user starts the drag operation. Create an instance of TDragObject object or one of its descendant classes (as we require) and set it to the DragObject parameter. Then, the Source parameter in the target event handlers will be this DragObject and not the control that is initiating the drag operation. If we use the TDragObject class itself, we may be doing minimal customization, but we can descend a class from this base class and add more customization, as we desire. Another feature of this class is that its Instance property returns the module handle of the executable (DLL or EXE) that contains this object.

The TDragControlObject and TDragControlObjectEx classes are notable descendants of the TDragObject class. They can be used to drop a control other than the control being dragged. We can instantiate an object of these classes by passing the control to be dropped as a parameter to the constructor. Both these classes provide the same functionality but differ in one characteristic. If we use the TDragControlObject (or its descendant), we will have to free its object after we are done with it. On the other hand, if we use TDragControlObjectEx (or its descendant), we do not have to free its object.

Let's work through an example to demonstrate customizing drag and drop. The following steps illustrate this:

1. Create a new VCL application. The IDE automatically creates the project and unit files. Save the project and unit files with names of your choice and in a directory of your choice. I named the project CustomDragAndDrop.bpr and the unit file CustDrag.cpp.

2. On the form, drop three drag source controls: one **TListBox** component, one **TEdit** component, and one **TBitBtn** component. The idea is to demonstrate dragging data items from different source controls.

3. For each of these objects, set the DragMode property to **dmManual**. This will give us the opportunity to demonstrate the implementation of manual drag.

4. Then drop a second **TListBox** component, which acts like a drop target.

5. Create a descendant of the TDragControlObjectEx class. I called this class TDerivedDragObject. Add a constructor method that accepts a TControl pointer as a parameter. Also add the member **fDragItem** of type AnsiString. Create a member variable of this class in the form header file. Hence, this definition must appear before the form class definition. I presume that I do not have to explicitly tell a C++ programmer how to organize the class definition and implementation code. For simplicity's sake, I included this code in the same form header file before the form class definition:

```
class TDerivedDragObject : public TDragControlObjectEx {
public:          // user defined memebers
     __fastcall TDerivedDragObject(TControl*fControl);
     AnsiString fDragItem;
};
```

6. In the form class definition, add a public member of type pointer to the class TDerivedDragObject:

```
TDerivedDragObject* fCustomDragObject;
```

7. Implement the simple constructor for the class we created. Again, for simplicity's sake, I included this code in the form cpp file itself:

```
__fastcall TDerivedDragObject::TDerivedDragObject(TControl* fControl)
     : TDragControlObjectEx(fControl)
{
}
```

Here I would like to mention that I implemented a very simple descendant class just to demonstrate how it can be implemented. You are free to extend this to include more complex data members to pass through this object.

8. For each of the three components placed on the form, implement the OnMouseDown and OnStartDrag event handlers. In the

OnMouseDown event handler, call the BeginDrag event handler of the component itself. In the OnStartDrag event handler, make sure that the data item you are passing is not NULL, and then set this data item to the fDragItem member of the drag object. Finally, set the custom drag object that we created to the DragObject parameter.

9. Now implement the OnDragOver event handler for the drop target list box. In this event handler, the important parameter is a Boolean value Accept. Set this value to true if the Source parameter is a drag object type; otherwise, set it to false. In this event handler, we decide whether the drop target is going to accept the dragged object or not.

    ```
    if (IsDragObject(Source))
        Accept = true;
    else
        Accept = false;
    ```

10. Finally, implement the OnDragDrop event handler for the drop target list box. Notice that the Source parameter is the custom drag object that we created earlier and not the control that is being dragged. From the Source object, extract the fDragItem data member and display the value in the target list box. This program clearly demonstrates that by implementing custom drag objects, we are able to package data items from different sources and send it to the drop target.

    The complete source code for the program is displayed in Listing 4-5 (CustDrag.cpp file) and Listing 4-6 (corresponding header CustDrag.h file).

Listing 4-5: CustDrag.cpp

```
//---------------------------------------------------------------------------

#include <vcl.h>
#pragma hdrstop

#include "CustDrag.h"
//---------------------------------------------------------------------------
#pragma package(smart_init)
#pragma resource "*.dfm"
TCustDragAndDrop *CustDragAndDrop;
//---------------------------------------------------------------------------
__fastcall TDerivedDragObject::TDerivedDragObject(TControl* fControl)
        : TDragControlObjectEx(fControl)
{
}
//---------------------------------------------------------------------------
__fastcall TCustDragAndDrop::TCustDragAndDrop(TComponent* Owner)
        : TForm(Owner)
{
}
//---------------------------------------------------------------------------

void __fastcall TCustDragAndDrop::ListBox1MouseDown(TObject *Sender,
```

```
                TMouseButton Button, TShiftState Shift, int X, int Y)
{
        TListBox* lb = (TListBox*)Sender;
        lb->BeginDrag(false,5);
}
//---------------------------------------------------------------------------

void __fastcall TCustDragAndDrop::ListBox1StartDrag(TObject *Sender,
    TDragObject *&DragObject)
{
        // Create an instance of TDerivedDragObject object and
        // pass it as the DragObject
        TListBox* flb1 = static_cast<TListBox*>(Sender);

        // Create the custom drag object instance for list box object
        fCustomDragObject = new TDerivedDragObject(flb1);

        // If the list box is empty or no item is selected do nothing
        if ((flb1->Items->Count <=0) || (flb1->ItemIndex <0)) {
                delete fCustomDragObject;
                return;
        }
        // Set the data to be passed to the drop target
        fCustomDragObject->fDragItem = flb1->Items->Strings[flb1->ItemIndex];
        // Set the drag object to the custom drag object
        DragObject = fCustomDragObject;
}
//---------------------------------------------------------------------------

void __fastcall TCustDragAndDrop::Edit1MouseDown(TObject *Sender,
    TMouseButton Button, TShiftState Shift, int X, int Y)
{
        TEdit* edit1 = (TEdit*)Sender;
        edit1->BeginDrag(true,5);
}
//---------------------------------------------------------------------------

void __fastcall TCustDragAndDrop::Edit1StartDrag(TObject *Sender,
    TDragObject *&DragObject)
{
        // Create an instance of TDerivedDragObject object and
        // pass it as the DragObject
        TEdit* edit1 = static_cast<TEdit*>(Sender);
        // Create the custom drag object instance for the edit box object
        fCustomDragObject = new TDerivedDragObject(edit1);

        // If the edit box is empty, do nothing
        if (edit1->Text == "") {
                delete fCustomDragObject;
                return;
        }
        // Set the data to be passed to the drop target
        fCustomDragObject->fDragItem = edit1->Text;
        // Set the drag object to the custom drag object
        DragObject = fCustomDragObject;
}
//---------------------------------------------------------------------------

void __fastcall TCustDragAndDrop::BitBtn1MouseDown(TObject *Sender,
```

```
          TMouseButton Button, TShiftState Shift, int X, int Y)
{
        TBitBtn* bbtn1 = (TBitBtn*)Sender;
        bbtn1->BeginDrag(true,5);
}
//-------------------------------------------------------------------------

void __fastcall TCustDragAndDrop::BitBtn1StartDrag(TObject *Sender,
     TDragObject *&DragObject)
{
        // Create an instance of TDerivedDragObject object and
        // pass it as the DragObject
        TBitBtn* bbtn1 = static_cast<TBitBtn*>(Sender);
        // Create the custom drag object instance for the bitbtn object
        fCustomDragObject = new TDerivedDragObject(bbtn1);

        // If the button caption is empty, do nothing
        if (bbtn1->Caption == "") {
                delete fCustomDragObject;
                return;
        }
        // Set the data to be passed to the drop target
        fCustomDragObject->fDragItem = bbtn1->Caption;
        // Set the drag object to the custom drag object
        DragObject = fCustomDragObject;
}
//-------------------------------------------------------------------------

void __fastcall TCustDragAndDrop::ListBox2DragOver(TObject *Sender,
     TObject *Source, int X, int Y, TDragState State, bool &Accept)
{
        // If the source is an instance of TDragObjet or its descendant
        // then accept the dragged item
        if (IsDragObject(Source))
                Accept = true;
        else
                Accept = false;
}
//-------------------------------------------------------------------------

void __fastcall TCustDragAndDrop::ListBox2DragDrop(TObject *Sender,
     TObject *Source, int X, int Y)
{
        TDerivedDragObject* fdo = static_cast<TDerivedDragObject*>(Source);
        AnsiString fDraggedItem = fdo->fDragItem;
        TListBox* flb2 = static_cast<TListBox*>(Sender);
        if (flb2->Items->Count > 0)
                flb2->Items->Clear();
        flb2->Items->Add(fDraggedItem);
}
//-------------------------------------------------------------------------
```

Listing 4-6: CustDrag.h

```cpp
//----------------------------------------------------------------------------

#ifndef CustDragH
#define CustDragH
//----------------------------------------------------------------------------
#include <Classes.hpp>
#include <Controls.hpp>
#include <StdCtrls.hpp>
#include <Forms.hpp>
#include <Buttons.hpp>
//----------------------------------------------------------------------------
class TDerivedDragObject : public TDragControlObjectEx {
public:          // user defined members
        __fastcall TDerivedDragObject(TControl*fControl);
        AnsiString fDragItem;
};
//----------------------------------------------------------------------------
class TCustDragAndDrop : public TForm
{
__published:          // IDE-managed components
        TListBox *ListBox1;
        TListBox *ListBox2;
        TEdit *Edit1;
        TBitBtn *BitBtn1;
        void __fastcall ListBox1MouseDown(TObject *Sender,
          TMouseButton Button, TShiftState Shift, int X, int Y);
        void __fastcall ListBox1StartDrag(TObject *Sender,
          TDragObject *&DragObject);
        void __fastcall Edit1MouseDown(TObject *Sender,
          TMouseButton Button, TShiftState Shift, int X, int Y);
        void __fastcall Edit1StartDrag(TObject *Sender,
          TDragObject *&DragObject);
        void __fastcall BitBtn1MouseDown(TObject *Sender,
          TMouseButton Button, TShiftState Shift, int X, int Y);
        void __fastcall BitBtn1StartDrag(TObject *Sender,
          TDragObject *&DragObject);
        void __fastcall ListBox2DragOver(TObject *Sender, TObject *Source,
          int X, int Y, TDragState State, bool &Accept);
        void __fastcall ListBox2DragDrop(TObject *Sender, TObject *Source,
          int X, int Y);

private:                // User declarations
        TDerivedDragObject* fCustomDragObject;
public:                 // User declarations
        __fastcall TCustDragAndDrop(TComponent* Owner);
};
//----------------------------------------------------------------------------
extern PACKAGE TCustDragAndDrop *CustDragAndDrop;
//----------------------------------------------------------------------------
#endif
```

Drag and Drop Across Modules in an Application

Another interesting aspect of custom drag and drop is the ability to implement dragging from one module and dropping onto another module of the same application, such as an application that has a main EXE program and a DLL. The concept can be extended easily to applications containing more than one DLL. I am presenting here a brief outline of the steps involved. The complete source code for both the projects is presented at the end of the discussion.

1. Create a class file (a simple unit file with corresponding header file) containing the definition and implementation of the TDerivedDrag-Object class. For simplicity's sake, I am reusing the same class definition as in the previous example. The only difference is that this time I am implementing it in separate unit and header files. The reason is that I have to include this class definition in two projects, one for the main EXE and the other for the DLL. Name the unit file **CustomDrag-Object.cpp**. The corresponding header file is automatically named CustomDragObject.h by the IDE. Listings 4-7 and 4-8 display these files, respectively.

2. Create a main application that generates an EXE program when built. Save the files in a directory of your choice with names of your choice. I named the project InterModuleDragExeProject.bpr and the main form source file InterModuleExeForm.cpp. Listings 4-9 and 4-10 display the cpp and header files, respectively. Add the **CustomDragObject.cpp** unit to this project and include the corresponding header file in the header file of the form. You need to also include the DLL source header file (as explained in the next step) in the form header file. Also, add a public member of type pointer to the class TDerivedDragObject in the form class definition:

    ```
    TDerivedDragObject* fCustomDragObject;
    ```

3. Drop a **TListBox** component on the form to act as the drag source object, and add a few items using the Object Inspector. Since we are implementing custom drag, this component is used to initiate the drag operation. Implement the OnStartDrag event handler for this component. Also, drop a **TButton** component on the form and implement its OnClick event handler with code to display the DLL form.

4. Create a DLL application and save the files with appropriate names in a directory of your choice. I named the project InterModuleDragDll-Project.bpr and the source unit containing the DLLEntryPoint function InterModuleDragDllSource.cpp. As we discussed in Chapter 3, I

manually created a header file for the latter program so that I can include it in the main form header file in the EXE application. This header file contains a declaration of a function that invokes the form embedded in the DLL. Listings 4-11 and 4-12 display the DLL source and header files, respectively.

5. Create a form to be added to the DLL project. I named this form InterModuleDragDllForm.cpp. Listings 4-13 and 4-14 display the cpp and header files, respectively. On this form, add a **TListBox** component to act as a drag target. Implement the OnDragOver and OnDragDrop event handlers for the list box.

6. Build the two projects and execute the main EXE program. When you click the button on the main form, the DLL form is displayed. Now you can test dragging the individual items from the main form list box to the DLL form list box.

Listing 4-7: CustomDragObject.cpp

```
//-----------------------------------------------------------------------
#pragma hdrstop
#include "CustomDragObject.h"
//-----------------------------------------------------------------------

#pragma package(smart_init)
  __fastcall TDerivedDragObject::TDerivedDragObject(TControl* fControl)
        : TDragControlObjectEx(fControl)
{
}
//-----------------------------------------------------------------------
```

Listing 4-8: CustomDragObject.h

```
//-----------------------------------------------------------------------
#ifndef CustomDragObjectH
#define CustomDragObjectH
#include <vcl.h>
#include <windows.h>
//-----------------------------------------------------------------------
class TDerivedDragObject : public TDragControlObjectEx {
public:          // user defined members
        __fastcall TDerivedDragObject(TControl*fControl);
        AnsiString fDragItem;
};
//-----------------------------------------------------------------------
#endif
```

Listing 4-9: InterModuleExeForm.cpp

```
//-----------------------------------------------------------------------
#include <vcl.h>
#pragma hdrstop

#include "InterModuleDragExeForm.h"
//-----------------------------------------------------------------------
```

```
#pragma package(smart_init)
#pragma resource "*.dfm"
TForm1 *Form1;
//---------------------------------------------------------------------------
__fastcall TForm1::TForm1(TComponent* Owner)
        : TForm(Owner)
{
}
//---------------------------------------------------------------------------
void __fastcall TForm1::Button1Click(TObject *Sender)
{
    CreateForm(this);
}
//---------------------------------------------------------------------------

void __fastcall TForm1::ListBox1StartDrag(TObject *Sender,
      TDragObject *&DragObject)
{
        // Create an instance of TDerivedDragObject object and
        // pass it as the DragObject
        TListBox* flb1 = static_cast<TListBox*>(Sender);
        // Create the custom drag object instance for list box object
        fCustomDragObject = new TDerivedDragObject(flb1);

        // If the list box is empty or no item is selected do nothing
        if ((flb1->Items->Count <=0) || (flb1->ItemIndex <0)) {
                delete fCustomDragObject;
                return;
        }
        // Set the data to be passed to the drop target
        fCustomDragObject->fDragItem = flb1->Items->Strings[flb1->ItemIndex];
        // Set the drag object to the custom drag object
        DragObject = fCustomDragObject;
}
//---------------------------------------------------------------------------
```

Listing 4-10: InterModuleExeForm.h

```
//---------------------------------------------------------------------------

#ifndef InterModuleDragExeFormH
#define InterModuleDragExeFormH
//---------------------------------------------------------------------------
#include <Classes.hpp>
#include <Controls.hpp>
#include <StdCtrls.hpp>
#include <Forms.hpp>
#include "CustomDragObject.h"
#include "InterModuleDragDllSource.h"
//---------------------------------------------------------------------------
class TForm1 : public TForm
{
__published:          // IDE-managed components
        TListBox *ListBox1;
        TButton *Button1;
        void __fastcall Button1Click(TObject *Sender);
        void __fastcall ListBox1StartDrag(TObject *Sender,
          TDragObject *&DragObject);
private:               // User declarations
        TDerivedDragObject* fCustomDragObject;
```

```
public:                  // User declarations
        __fastcall TForm1(TComponent* Owner);
};
//---------------------------------------------------------------------------
extern PACKAGE TForm1 *Form1;
//---------------------------------------------------------------------------
#endif
//---------------------------------------------------------------------------
```

Listing 4-11: InterModuleDragDllSource.cpp

```
//---------------------------------------------------------------------------
#include <vcl.h>
#include <windows.h>
#pragma hdrstop
//---------------------------------------------------------------------------
//    Important note about DLL memory management when your DLL uses the
//    static version of the RunTime Library:
//
//    If your DLL exports any functions that pass String objects (or structs/
//    classes containing nested Strings) as parameter or function results,
//    you will need to add the library MEMMGR.LIB to both the DLL project and
//    any other projects that use the DLL. You will also need to use MEMMGR.LIB
//    if any other projects which use the DLL will be performing new or delete
//    operations on any non-TObject-derived classes which are exported from the
//    DLL. Adding MEMMGR.LIB to your project will change the DLL and its calling
//    EXE's to use the BORLNDMM.DLL as their memory manager. In these cases,
//    the file BORLNDMM.DLL should be deployed along with your DLL.
//
//    To avoid using BORLNDMM.DLL, pass string information using "char *" or
//    ShortString parameters.
//
//    If your DLL uses the dynamic version of the RTL, you do not need to
//    explicitly add MEMMGR.LIB as this will be done implicitly for you
//---------------------------------------------------------------------------
#include "InterModuleDragDllSource.h"
#pragma argsused
int WINAPI DllEntryPoint(HINSTANCE hinst, unsigned long reason, void* lpReserved)
{
    return 1;
}
//---------------------------------------------------------------------------
void __stdcall CreateForm(TComponent* Owner)
{
    dllForm = new TDllForm (Owner);
    dllForm->Show();
}
//---------------------------------------------------------------------------
```

Listing 4-12: InterModuleDragDllSource.h

```
#ifndef DllH
#define DllH

#include "InterModuleDragDllForm.h"
TDllForm* dllForm;
extern "C" __declspec(dllexport) __stdcall void CreateForm(TComponent* Owner);
//---------------------------------------------------------------------------

#endif
```

Listing 4-13: InterModuleDragDllForm.cpp

```
//---------------------------------------------------------------------------

#include <vcl.h>
#pragma hdrstop

#include "InterModuleDragDllForm.h"
//---------------------------------------------------------------------------
#pragma package(smart_init)
#pragma resource "*.dfm"
TDllForm *DllForm;
//---------------------------------------------------------------------------
__fastcall TDllForm::TDllForm(TComponent* Owner)
      : TForm(Owner)
{
}
//---------------------------------------------------------------------------
void __fastcall TDllForm::ListBox1DragDrop(TObject *Sender,
    TObject *Source, int X, int Y)
{
      TDerivedDragObject* fdo = static_cast<TDerivedDragObject*>(Source);
      AnsiString fDraggedItem = fdo->fDragItem;
      TListBox* flb2 = static_cast<TListBox*>(Sender);
      if (flb2->Items->Count > 0)
            flb2->Items->Clear();
      flb2->Items->Add(fDraggedItem);
}
//---------------------------------------------------------------------------
void __fastcall TDllForm::ListBox1DragOver(TObject *Sender,
    TObject *Source, int X, int Y, TDragState State, bool &Accept)
{
      // If the source is an instance of TDragObject or its descendant
      // then accept the dragged item
      if (IsDragObject(Source))
            Accept = true;
      else
            Accept = false;
}
//---------------------------------------------------------------------------
void __fastcall TDllForm::FormClose(TObject *Sender, TCloseAction &Action)
{
      Action = caFree;
}
//---------------------------------------------------------------------------
```

Listing 4-14: InterModuleDragDllForm.h

```
//---------------------------------------------------------------------------

#ifndef InterModuleDragDllFormH
#define InterModuleDragDllFormH
//---------------------------------------------------------------------------
#include <Classes.hpp>
#include <Controls.hpp>
#include <StdCtrls.hpp>
#include <Forms.hpp>
#include "CustomDragObject.h"
//---------------------------------------------------------------------------
class TDllForm : public TForm
```

```
{
__published:          // IDE-managed components
        TListBox *ListBox1;
        void __fastcall ListBox1DragDrop(TObject *Sender, TObject *Source,
          int X, int Y);
        void __fastcall ListBox1DragOver(TObject *Sender, TObject *Source,
          int X, int Y, TDragState State, bool &Accept);
        void __fastcall FormClose(TObject *Sender, TCloseAction &Action);
private:              // User declarations
public:               // User declarations
        __fastcall TDllForm(TComponent* Owner);
};
//---------------------------------------------------------------------------
extern PACKAGE TDllForm *DllForm;
//---------------------------------------------------------------------------
#endif
```

Date/Time Management

Another useful feature that almost all the programmers are required to work with is date and time management and timestamp management. VCL has a powerful set of functions and the TDateTime class that handles these features. The date and time-related functions are defined in the SYSUTILS unit of VCL, and I will use them along with the TDateTime class in my discussion. Since the SYSUTILS unit is automatically included when we include vcl.h in our project, there is no need to explicitly include this unit.

TDateTime Class

The TDateTime class is provided in C++Builder to function like the TDateTime data type in the Object Pascal language that is used in Delphi. Similar to the AnsiString class discussed in an earlier chapter, there is no need to use the new operator to create objects of this class. Thus, you can instantiate this object in the following two ways:

```
TDateTime dateTime1;
TDateTime dateTime2 = new TDateTime();
```

The data member that stores the date-time value is a double data type. The reference timestamp that represents a TDateTime value of 0 is 12/30/1899 12:00 AM, which is also considered to be the midnight (0 hours) of 12/29/1899. When instantiated without any initial value, the date-time value is set to this reference value. The object can be instantiated with another date-time object, a double value, system date, system time, or system timestamp. The following examples illustrate the different ways to instantiate the TDateTime object:

```
TDateTime dateTime1 = Date();        // instantiates to the current date value.
TDateTime dateTime2 = Time();        // instantiates to the current time value.
TDateTime dateTime3 = Now();         // instantiates to current date and time value.
TDateTime dateTime4 = 2.25;          // instantiates to 01/01/1900 06:00 AM.
TDateTime dateTime5 = dateTime2;     // instantiates to another date-time object.
TDateTime dateTime6 = TDateTime(2001, 10, 23); // specific year, month and day.
```

The functions Date(), Time(), and Now() are VCL functions defined in the SYSUTILS unit that return the current system date, current system time, and current timestamp as TDateTime objects. These values can also be obtained from the methods CurrentDate(), CurrentTime(), and Current-DateTime(), respectively, on the TDateTime object.

TDateTime objects participate in arithmetic operations to give us flexibility in date-based or timestamp-based computations. The operands that participate with a TDateTime object are other date-time objects, double values, or integer values. When we add fractional values to a TDateTime object, the integer portion of the data member indicates the number of days past the reference date, and the decimal portion indicates the proportion of time past (out of 24 hours) since the last day at midnight.

```
TDateTime dateTime1;
DateTime1 += 0.25    // indicates 6:00 AM on 12/30/1899
```

If the result of arithmetic operations is a negative value (such as –2.25), the interpretation is slightly different. The negative sign applies only to the integer portion and hence to the number of days, indicating that the date is behind the reference date by the negative integer value (in this case, –2). The decimal fraction always represents the proportion of time past since the previous day at midnight. In this example, a value of –2.25 represents 12/28/1899 6:00 AM. Table 4-2 describes methods and some frequently used operators supported by the TDateTime object.

Table 4-2: Methods and operators of the TDateTime object

Method	Description
CurrentDate()	Returns the current system date as a TDateTime object
CurrentDateTime()	Returns the current system date and time as a TDateTime object
CurrentTime()	Returns the current system time as a TDateTime object
DateString()	Returns the date portion of the object as an AnsiString object
DateTimeString()	Returns the date and time value of the object as an AnsiString object
DayOfWeek()	Returns the day of the week for the date portion of the object as an integer. Sunday is treated as the first day of the week and Saturday as the seventh.
DecodeDate(unsigned short* year, unsigned short* month, unsigned short* day)	This is a very useful method to separate the day, month, and year of the object into individual items. Notice that the parameters to the method are pointers to unsigned short variables.
DecodeTime(unsigned short* hour, unsigned short* min, unsigned short* sec, unsigned short* msec)	This is very similar to the DecodeDate() method and is used to decode the time portion of the object into individual items.

Method	Description
FileDate()	Files stored on the disk have a timestamp associated with them. This method is used to convert the date-time value of the object to an integer value representing the file timestamp.
FileDateToDateTime()	Converts the file timestamp to a TDateTime object and stores in the current object
FormatString(AnsiString& format)	Returns the date and time value of the object as a formatted AnsiString object. The required format is provided as an input parameter to the method.
TimeString()	Returns the time portion of the object as an AnsiString object

Operator	Description
AnsiString()	Returns the date time value as an AnsiString Usage: ``` TDateTime dtime = Now(); AnsiString str = AnsiString(dtime); ```

double()	Returns the date time value as a double
	
	Usage:
	
	``
	TDateTime dtime = Now();
	double dbl = double(dtime);
	``

In addition to the TDateTime object, VCL has a wealth of functions defined in the SYSUTILS unit that provide date and time management functionality. Most of them are conversion utilities to convert date-time value to and from different formats. Table 4-3 is provided as a ready reference for these functions.

Table 4-3: Some useful SYSUTILS functions

SYSUTILS Function	Description
Date()	Returns current system date as TDateTime object
DateTimeToFileDate(System:: TDateTime DateTime)	Converts the TDateTime object that is passed as a parameter to this function to an integer value representing the DOS file timestamp. This integer can be used in the function FileSetDate(int Handle, int Age) to set the timestamp of a file. Handle represents the file, and Age represents the integer value of DOS date-timestamp. The FileSetDate() function is part of file management routines in the VCL. DOS file timestamp is discussed later in this section.
DateTimeToStr(System::TDate- Time DateTime)	Returns the TDateTime object that is passed as a parameter to this function as an AnsiString object
DateTimeToString(AnsiString &Result, const AnsiString Format, System::TDateTime DateTime)	Converts the TDateTime object that is passed as a parameter to this function to a formatted AnsiString object and stores it in the Result parameter. The Format parameter provides the required format. Formatting features are discussed later in this section.
DateTimeToSystemTime(System:: TDateTime DateTime, _SYSTEM- TIME &SystemTime)	Converts the TDateTime object that is passed as a parameter to this function to an instance of Win32 SYSTEMTIME structure type. The SYSTEMTIME structure and its uses are discussed later in this section.

SYSUTILS Function	Description
DateTimeToTimeStamp(System:: TDateTime DateTime)	Returns the TDateTime object that is passed as a parameter to this function as an instance of VCL TTimeStamp structure type. TTimeStamp stores individual date and time values as integers. The date value represents the number of days passed since the date 01/01/0001, and the time value represents the number of seconds elapsed since midnight. This structure is intended to give another form of representation for the current timestamp value.
DateToStr(System::TDateTime Date)	Returns the date portion of the TDateTime object that is passed as a parameter to this function as a formatted AnsiString object. The format is specified by ShortDateFormat global variable, which is obtained using the options Control Panel | Regional Settings | Date tab.
DayOfWeek(System::TDateTime Date)	Returns the day of the week for the TDateTime object that is passed as a parameter to this function as an integer value; 1 represents Sunday and 7 represents Saturday.
DecodeDate(System::TDateTime Date, Word &Year, Word &Month, Word &Day)	Converts the date portion of the TDateTime object that is passed as parameter to this function to individual day, month, and year components
DecodeTime(System::TDateTime Time, Word &Hour, Word &Min, Word &Sec, Word &MSec)	Converts the time portion of the TDateTime object that is passed as a parameter to this function to individual hour, minute, second, and millisecond components
EncodeDate(Word Year, Word Month, Word Day)	Returns a TDateTime object containing a date value that is constructed from the individual components of day, month, and year. The year must be between 1 and 9999. The month must be between 1 and 12. The day must be between 1 and 31, based on the month specified. If the specified values do not yield a valid date, an EConvertError exception is thrown.
EncodeTime(Word Hour, Word Min, Word Sec, Word MSec)	Returns a TDateTime object containing a time value that is constructed from the individual components of hour, minute, second, and millisecond. Valid hour values are 0 through 23. Valid min and sec values are 0 through 59. Valid MSec values are 0 through 999. The resulting object contains the decimal fraction value that conforms to the TDateTime object's time value rules. If the specified values are not within range, an EConvertError exception is thrown.
FormatDateTime(const AnsiString Format, System::TDateTime DateTime)	Returns a formatted AnsiString object representing the TDateTime object that is passed as a parameter. The format is specified by the Format parameter.
IncMonth(const TDateTime Date, int Months)	Returns a new TDateTime object that contains month values incremented by months. If the input day of month is greater than the last day of the resulting month, the day is set to the last day of the resulting month. If the incremented month value exceeds the current year (any following years), the year value is also set to the appropriate value.
IsLeapYear(Word Year)	Returns true if the specified year is a leap year
MSecsToTimeStamp(System::Comp MSecs)	Returns an instance of the TTimeStamp object that is constructed from the number of milliseconds (since 01/01/0001). The number of milliseconds is specified as a Comp data type. Comp is a C++ struct that implements the Object Pascal 64-bit integer data type. Comp can represent a value in the range $-2^{63}+1$ to $2^{63}-1$ (about $-9.2 * 10^{18}$ to $9.2 * 10^{18}$). Comp values can represent 19 significant digits.
Now()	Returns current timestamp as a TDateTime object
ReplaceDate(TDateTime &DateTime, const TDateTime NewDate)	Replaces the date portion of the first TDateTime object with the date portion of the second TDateTime object without changing the time
ReplaceTime(TDateTime &DateTime, const TDateTime NewTime)	Replaces the time portion of the first TDateTime object with the time portion of the second TDateTime object without changing the date

SYSUTILS Function	Description
StrToDate(const AnsiString S)	Returns a TDateTime object after converting the input string value that represents a date-time value containing the date. The string value S must consist of two or three numbers separated by the character defined by the DateSeparator global variable. The order for month, day, and year is determined by the ShortDateFormat global variable; possible combinations are m/d/y, d/m/y, and y/m/d. If the date contains only two numbers separated by the DateSeparator, it is interpreted as a date in the current year. If the specified string does not represent a valid date, an EConvertError exception is thrown. The global variables are obtained using the options Control Panel | Regional Settings | Date tab.
StrToDateTime(const AnsiString S)	Returns a TDateTime object after converting the input string value that represents a date-time value containing the date and time. The date portion of the string must follow formatting rules specified by the DateSeparator and ShortDateFormat global variables, and the time portion of the string must follow formatting rules obtained from the operating system Control Panel → Regional Settings → Date tab page. However, it is not necessary to indicate the time portion with AM or PM at the end, in which case the time must be specified in the 24-hour scale. If the specified string does not represent a valid date, an EConvertError exception is thrown.
StrToTime(const AnsiString S)	Returns a TDateTime object after converting the input string value that represents a date-time value containing the time. The rules for specifying the time string are the same as discussed for the previous function.
SystemTimeToDateTime(const _SYSTEMTIME &SystemTime)	Returns a TDateTime object after converting the input Win32 SYSTEMTIME struct data type
Time()	Returns the current time value as a TDateTime object
TimeStampToDateTime(const TTimeStamp &TimeStamp)	Returns a TDateTime object after converting the input TTimeStamp object
TimeStampToMSecs()	Returns the absolute number of milliseconds after converting both the date and time portions of the input TTimeStamp object. The returned value is an instance of the Comp structure, and the reference date for this value is 01/01/0001.
TimeToStr(System::TDateTime Time)	Returns an AnsiString object after converting the input TDateTime object containing a time value. The conversion uses the LongTimeFormat global value.

Constant	Description
DateDelta	The TDateTime object uses the reference date of 12/30/1899, and the TTimeStamp object uses the reference date of 01/01/0001; the DateDelta constant is provided to make date value corrections. It is defined in the SysUtils.pas file as the number of days between 01/01/0001 and 12/31/1899. Its value is 693594.
MSecsPerDay	This constant represents the number of milliseconds per day. Its value is 86400000.
SecsPerDay	This constant represents the number of seconds per day. Its value is 86400.

What is DOS File Timestamp?

DOS file timestamp is also known as DOS File DateTime value. It is the combination of two packed 16-bit values, one to store DOS File date and the other to store DOS File time. The individual bit values that comprise these structures are shown in Tables 4-4 and 4-5, as defined in the Microsoft documentation (MSDN Library).

Table 4-4: DOS File date

Bits	Contents
0-4	Day of the month (1-31)
5-8	Month (1 = January, 2 = February, etc.)
9-15	Year offset from 1980 (add 1980 to get actual year value)

Table 4-5: DOS File time

Bits	Contents
0-4	Second, divided by 2
5-10	Minute (0-59)
11-15	Hour (0-23 on a 24-hour clock)

Win32 Core Date-Time Management

Now let's discuss some of the Win32-based date and time management functions, which can be used in conjunction with the VCL functions to deliver easy-to-interface systems. SYSTEMTIME is a structure data type and is comprised of individual data members to represent day, month, year, etc. This structure is used by Win32 functions to store the timestamp values. The structure definition is shown here, followed by the functions that use this structure.

```
typedef struct _SYSTEMTIME {
    WORD wYear;
    WORD wMonth;
    WORD wDayOfWeek;
    WORD wDay;
    WORD wHour;
    WORD wMinute;
    WORD wSecond;
    WORD wMilliseconds;
} SYSTEMTIME;

VOID GetLocalTime(
    LPSYSTEMTIME lpSystemTime        // address of output system time structure
);

VOID GetSystemTime(
    LPSYSTEMTIME lpSystemTime        // address of output system time structure
);

BOOL SetLocalTime(
    CONST SYSTEMTIME *               // sets system time, using local time
);

BOOL SetSystemTime(
    CONST SYSTEMTIME *lpSystemTime // sets system time, using UTC time
);
```

The GetLocalTime() function retrieves the current local date and time from the clock in the computer where the operating system is loaded. The input parameter is a pointer to the structure SYSTEMTIME and contains the value returned by the function call. Most of the time, applications need to display (and use) the local time. However, there may be time-sensitive global (or internationalized) applications that require using the universal time. The GetSystemTime() function retrieves the current system date and time in terms of coordinated universal time (UTC). Microsoft documentation (MSDN) defines the UTC as follows: "*System time is the current date and time of day. The system keeps time so that your applications have ready access to accurate time. The system bases system time on coordinated universal time (UTC). UTC-based time is loosely defined as the current date and time of day in Greenwich, England.*" The SetSystemTime() function sets the system date and time, using the universal time value as input. The SetLocalTime() function sets the system date and time, using the local time as input.

Both the GetLocalTime and GetSystemTime functions do not return any value. Both the SetSystemTime and SetLocalTime functions return a non-zero value if the function succeeds and a zero value if the function fails. If the function fails, check the last error code using the Win32 GetLastError() function. Executing Win32 functions from a VCL application is discussed in Chapter 3.

Since VCL provides functions to convert date and time values between VCL formats and Win32 format, it becomes easy on the part of programmers to provide systems (and components) that can interact with the applications developed using Win32 SDK directly or with applications developed by other vendors. This type of data (object or structure) conversion is visible in other units of VCL as well, not just SYSUTILS.

Formatting Date-Time Strings

We have seen that date-time values can be retrieved as AnsiString objects. It is very useful to embed date-time values in message strings or as time-stamps to display to the user, etc. While converting the date-time value to a string, the format of the string can be specified using the FormatString() method. There are a number of format specifiers that VCL supports. A few examples are shown here. C++Builder 6 online documentation provides the complete list.

■ The specifier "c" indicates that the date-time value be displayed in the format given by the ShortDateFormat global variable.

```
TDateTime dt = Now();
AnsiString dts = dt.FormatString("c");
```

In this example, the string dts contains a value similar to "12-23-2001 4:35:33 PM." However, the actual format depends on how Regional Settings are set up in the Control Panel on your computer.

- The specifier "d" indicates that the day value be displayed without a leading zero if it is a single-digit value (such as "1-31"), as opposed to the specifier "dd," which indicates that the single-digit day value be displayed with a leading zero (such as "01-31").

- The specifier "am/pm" indicates that a 12-hour clock be used and the word "am" be appended to the string at the end for time values before noon and "pm" be appended to the string at the end for time values after noon.

- The specifier "ampm" indicates that a 12-hour clock be used and the string be appended with the global variable TimeAMString for time values before noon and the global variable TimePMString for time values after noon.

- Embedded constant string literals can be used to provide meaningful formats, as shown in the example here:

```
TDateTime dt = Now();
AnsiString dts = dt.FormatString("'on' dd-mm-yyyy 'at' hh:nn:ss", dt);
AnsiString msg = "The process started "+dts;
```

In this example, the string msg contains a value similar to "The process started on 23-01-2001 at 15:20:25."

Constants Defined in SYSUTILS

Here is a list of date- and time-related constants defined in the SYSUTILS unit, which may be used in conjunction with the functions discussed in this section.

- ShortMonthNames is a 12-element AnsiString array of short form of month names. The mmm format specifier in the format string uses the value obtained from this array. The default values are fetched from the LOCALE_SABBREVMONTHNAME system locale entries.

- LongMonthNames is a 12-element AnsiString array of long form of month names. The default values are fetched from the LOCALE_ SMONTHNAME system locale entries.

- ShortDayNames is a seven-element AnsiString array of short form of day names. The ddd format specifier in the format string uses the value obtained from this array. The default values are fetched from the LOCALE_SABBREVDAYNAME system locale entries.

- LongDayNames is a seven-element AnsiString array of long form of day names. The default values are fetched from the LOCALE_SDAY-NAME system locale entries.

- TimeAMString is the suffix string used for time values between 00:00 and 11:59 in a 12-hour clock format. The initial value is fetched from the LOCALE_S1159 system locale entry.

- TimePMString is the suffix string used for time values between 12:00 and 23:59 in a 12-hour clock format. The initial value is fetched from the LOCALE_S2359 system locale entry.

- ShortDateFormat is the format string used to convert a date value to a short string suitable for editing. The initial value is fetched from the LOCALE_SSHORTDATE system locale entry.

- LongDateFormat is the format string used to convert a date value to an AnsiString suitable for display, not for editing. The initial value is fetched from the LOCALE_SLONGDATE system locale entry.

Directory and File Management

Another set of features provided by the SYSUTILS unit is the functions and objects that enable access to the files and directories stored on the disk. We organize these functions by their functionality before starting our discussion. Apart from the SYSUTILS unit, the FILECTRL unit also provides some of these functions. I will highlight these differences wherever they exist. Unlike the SYSUTILS unit, including "vcl.h," the file does not automatically include the FILECTRL unit. We have to explicitly include the "filectrl.hpp" file.

Working with Directories

The CreateDir() function enables us to create a directory with the given name on the current drive. The signature of the function is given here:

```
bool __fastcall CreateDir(const AnsiString DirName);
```

The function returns true if it succeeds in creating the directory; otherwise, it returns false. The input parameter may specify just a simple name of the directory or the directory name preceded by the full or relative path name. If we specify just the directory name, the directory will be created in the current directory. If we include the full or relative path name, then each and every subdirectory in the path must exist prior to execution of this function. If not, an exception is thrown. To avoid this situation, use the Force-Directories() function if the subdirectories need to be created, or check for the existence of subdirectories using the DirectoryExists() function before trying to create the directory (or subdirectory). Following are descriptions of these functions.

- The ForceDirectories() function forces the system to create any subdirectories specified in the directory path if they do not already exist, thus avoiding an exception condition. The signature of the function is given here. The path specified may be the full path or a relative path.

  ```
  bool __fastcall ForceDirectories(const AnsiString DirName);
  ```

- The DirectoryExists() function returns true if the specified directory exists on the drive; otherwise, it returns false. This function is provided in the FILECTRL unit.

  ```
  bool __fastcall DirectoryExists(const AnsiString DirName);
  ```

- The GetCurrentDir() function returns the (fully qualified) current directory name.

  ```
  AnsiString __fastcall GetCurrentDir();
  ```

- The ChDir() function changes the current directory to the directory specified in the input parameter. The signature of the function is given here:

  ```
  void __fastcall ChDir(const AnsiString DirName);
  ```

- The SetCurrentDir() function sets the current working directory to the name specified as a parameter. If the current directory is set successfully, the function returns true; otherwise, it returns false. The signature of the function is described here:

  ```
  bool __fastcall SetCurrentDir(const AnsiString DirName);
  ```

- The RemoveDir() function deletes the directory specified in the input parameter. The directory must be empty before this function is called. The signature of the function is given here:

  ```
  bool __fastcall RemoveDir(const AnsiString DirName);
  ```

- The SelectDirectory() function displays a directory selection dialog box to the user. There are two variations of this function. Signatures of both the variations are shown here:

  ```
  bool __fastcall SelectDirectory(AnsiString &Directory, TSelectDirOpts Options, int
  HelpCtx);
  ```

This variation of the function has three parameters: a directory name string, a set of directory selection options, and a help context ID. The directory name string parameter contains the initial directory that the user sets. When the user clicks the OK button, the dialog sets this string parameter with the newly selected directory name, including the full path. A sample code snippet is shown in Listing 4-15. When executed in a program, the dialog appears as shown in Figure 4-12.

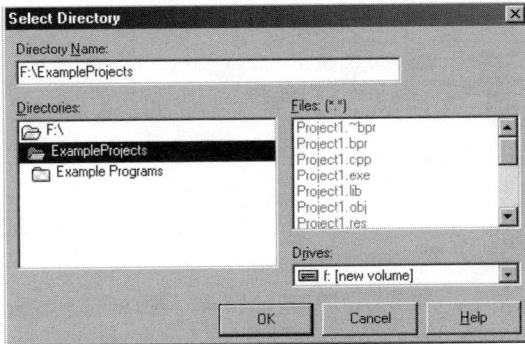

Figure 4-12: SelectDirectory dialog (flexible form)

Listing 4-15

```
//-------------------------------------------------------------------------
const SELDIRHELP = 10;
AnsiString Dir = "F:\\ExampleProjects";
if (SelectDirectory(Dir, TSelectDirOpts() << sdAllowCreate << sdPerformCreate
    << sdPrompt,SELDIRHELP)) {
    Label1->Caption = Dir;
}
//-------------------------------------------------------------------------
```

The second form of the function is described here:

```
bool __fastcall SelectDirectory(const AnsiString Caption, const WideString Root,
    AnsiString &Directory);
```

In this form of the function, we provide a caption to the dialog box, a root directory from where to display the subdirectory tree, and an AnsiString variable that stores the user-selected (fully qualified) directory name. The sample code is shown in Listing 4-16 and the corresponding dialog box is displayed as in Figure 4-13.

Figure 4-13: SelectDirectory dialog (simple form)

Listing 4-16

```
//--------------------------------------------------------------------------
const WideString Root = " F:\\ExampleProjects";
AnsiString Dir;
const AnsiString capt = "Select Directory dialog";
if (SelectDirectory(Caption, Root, Dir)) {
    Label1->Caption = Dir;
}
//--------------------------------------------------------------------------
```

In the first form of the function, the current directory is set to the directory selected by the user. This is not the case with the second form. Also, the second form is limited in functionality and does not show the drive selection combo box or the files in the selected directory. We have to choose the appropriate form of the function as needed. This function is provided in the FILECTRL unit.

In all these functions, the directory (or subdirectory) names in the path name must be separated by "\\" instead of "\", in order to provide for the escape sequence.

Working with Files

Now we will discuss the functions that support file management. As far as file management is concerned, a number of routines are provided and we categorize them based on the sub-functions.

Functions That Work with File Existence and Search

The FileCreate() function creates a file with the given name. If it succeeds in creating the file, the file handle is returned; otherwise, –1 is returned. If the filename includes a full (or relative) path, the file is created in the directory (or subdirectory) specified. Otherwise, the file is created in the current directory. The signature of the function is given here:

```
int __fastcall FileCreate(const AnsiString FileName);
```

The FileExists() function returns true if the specified file exists on the disk; otherwise, it returns false. If the filename includes the full (or relative) path, then the file search is performed in the appropriate directory (or subdirectory). Otherwise, the search is performed in the current directory. The signature of the function is provided here:

```
bool __fastcall FileExists(const AnsiString FileName);
```

The FileSearch() function searches the specified directory list for the specified filename. If the file is found in the list specified, the fully qualified path name is returned. Otherwise, it returns an empty string. The input directory list is a single AnsiString object with individual directory names separated by semicolons. The signature of the function is provided here:

```
AnsiString __fastcall FileSearch(const AnsiString Name, const AnsiString DirList);
```

WIN32_FIND_DATA Structure

The WIN32_FIND_DATA structure describes a file found by one of the Win32 functions FindFirstFile, FindFirstFileEx, or FindNextFile. The structure is defined as shown here:

```
typedef struct _WIN32_FIND_DATA {
    DWORD    dwFileAttributes;
    FILETIME ftCreationTime;
    FILETIME ftLastAccessTime;
    FILETIME ftLastWriteTime;
    DWORD    nFileSizeHigh;
    DWORD    nFileSizeLow;
    DWORD    dwReserved0;
    DWORD    dwReserved1;
    TCHAR    cFileName[MAX_PATH];
    TCHAR    cAlternateFileName[14];
} WIN32_FIND_DATA, *PWIN32_FIND_DATA;
```

The dwFileAttributes member contains the file attributes. The next three structure members determine the file creation time, the last access time, and the last write time, respectively, as the names suggest. These times are reported in coordinated universal time (UTC), which was discussed earlier. Windows stores file size in two members: nFileSizeHigh and nFileSizeLow. The full filename is stored as a NULL-terminated string in the cFileName member, and the DOS8.3 format filename is stored as a NULL-terminated string in the cAlternateFileName member.

VCL defines a structure of type TSearchRec that includes the WIN32_FIND_DATA structure as one of its members. It also contains the filename as an AnsiString object and file size as a single integer (32-bit) variable indicating the number of bytes. If the size of a file is expected to exceed the 32-bit integer value, then compute the file size using the formula (nFileSizeHigh * (MAXDWORD+1)) + nFileSizeLow), as defined in the MSDN documentation.

VCL provides three functions to search for files that match a set of specific attributes. They are FindFirst(), FindNext(), and FindClose(). The signatures of these functions are given here:

```
int __fastcall FindFirst(const AnsiString Path, int Attr, TSearchRec &F);
int __fastcall FindNext(TSearchRec &F);
void __fastcall FindClose(TSearchRec &F);
```

FindFirst() searches the given path for files matching the required attributes. If a file is found, its info is returned in the TSearchRec structure. The TSearchRec structure contains the returned file information. FindNext() returns the next entry matching the path and attributes specified. Hence, it must be used in conjunction with the FirstFirst() method. Both methods return 0 if successful and a Windows error code if they failed. FindClose() terminates the FindFirst/FindNext sequence and releases the memory allocated.

File Attributes

A set of file attributes characterizes a given file. For example, one attribute may indicate if the file is hidden, and another attribute may indicate if the file is read-only, etc. In Win32 SDK, there are 13 file attributes (and a reserved attribute) provided to characterize files and directories. However, VCL supports a subset of most frequently used attributes through its functions. This subset of attributes is represented as an int data type in VCL, each of them identified by a bit value. To combine more than one attribute, we must use the bitwise or operator (|). The list of Win32 attributes is displayed in Table 4-6, indicating which of them are supported by VCL functions.

Table 4-6: Win32 File attributes

Win32 File Attribute	Description	VCL Attribute
FILE_ATTRIBUTE_ARCHIVE	The file or directory is an archive file or directory. Applications use this attribute to mark files for backup or removal.	faArchive
FILE_ATTRIBUTE_COMPRESSED	The file or directory is compressed. For a file, this means that all of the data in the file is compressed. For a directory, this means that compression is the default for newly created files and subdirectories.	
FILE_ATTRIBUTE_DEVICE	Reserved; do not use.	
FILE_ATTRIBUTE_DIRECTORY	The handle identifies a directory.	faDirectory
FILE_ATTRIBUTE_ENCRYPTED	The file or directory is encrypted. For a file, this means that all data streams in the file are encrypted. For a directory, this means that encryption is the default for newly created files and subdirectories.	
FILE_ATTRIBUTE_HIDDEN	The file or directory is hidden. It is not included in an ordinary directory listing.	faHidden
FILE_ATTRIBUTE_NORMAL	The file or directory has no other attributes set. This attribute is valid only if used alone.	
FILE_ATTRIBUTE_NOT_CONTENT_INDEXED	The file will not be indexed by the content indexing service.	

Win32 File Attribute	Description	VCL Attribute
FILE_ATTRIBUTE_OFFLINE	The data of the file is not immediately available. This attribute indicates that the file data has been physically moved to offline storage. This attribute is used by Remote Storage, the hierarchical storage management software in Windows 2000. Applications should not arbitrarily change this attribute.	
FILE_ATTRIBUTE_READONLY	The file or directory is read-only. Applications can read the file but cannot write to it or delete it. In the case of a directory, applications cannot delete it.	faReadOnly
FILE_ATTRIBUTE_REPARSE_POINT	The file has an associated reparse point.	
FILE_ATTRIBUTE_SPARSE_FILE	The file is a sparse file.	
FILE_ATTRIBUTE_SYSTEM	The file or directory is part of or used exclusively by the operating system.	faSysFile
FILE_ATTRIBUTE_TEMPORARY	The file is being used for temporary storage. File systems attempt to keep all of the data in memory for quicker access rather than flushing the data back to mass storage. A temporary file should be deleted by the application as soon as it is no longer needed.	

In addition to the attributes identified in the table, VCL has two others. The attribute faVolumeID indicates the file is a volume ID and the attribute faAnyFile indicates any file on the disk. These attributes are used in the FileGetAttr() function to find out the attributes of the file or directory. VCL's FileSetAttr() function internally calls the Win32 SetFileAttributes() function. The SetFileAttributes() function sets only eight of the above 13 file attributes; the remaining five attributes must be set using other Win32 SDK functions, as described in the following discussion. The corresponding Win32 GetFileAttributes() function, however, retrieves all the attributes that are set on the device (file or directory).

Setting the Advanced Attributes

As mentioned earlier, these advanced attributes must be set using the Win32 function calls, since the VCL does not directly support them.

FILE_ATTRIBUTE_COMPRESSED Attribute

Use the DeviceIoControl() function with the FSCTL_SET_COMPRESSION operation as the dwIoControlCode parameter. This function sends a control code directly to a specified device driver, causing the corresponding device to perform the corresponding operation.

```
BOOL DeviceIoControl(
    HANDLE hDevice,             // handle to device
    DWORD dwIoControlCode,      // operation
    LPVOID lpInBuffer,          // input data buffer
    DWORD nInBufferSize,        // size of input data buffer
    LPVOID lpOutBuffer,         // output data buffer
    DWORD nOutBufferSize,       // size of output data buffer
    LPDWORD lpBytesReturned,    // byte count actually returned
```

```
   LPOVERLAPPED lpOverlapped     // overlapped information
);
```

- hDevice is the handle to the directory or file whose attribute must be set as compressed.

- lpInBuffer is the pointer to the input data buffer. In this case, it should be NULL.

- nInBufferSize is the size of the input buffer. In this case, it is 0.

- lpOutBuffer is the pointer to the output data buffer. In this case, it should be NULL.

- nOutBufferSize is the size of the output buffer. In this case, it is 0.

- lpBytesReturned is a variable that receives the size, in bytes, of the data stored into the buffer pointed to by lpOutBuffer.

- lpOverlapped is the pointer to the OVERLAPPED structure if the hDevice was opened with the FILE_FLAG_OVERLAPPED flag. In this case, it must be NULL.

FILE_ATTRIBUTE_ REPARSE_POINT Attribute

Use the DeviceIoControl() function with the FSCTL_SET_REPARSE_ POINT operation. On a Windows 2000 NTFS volume, a file or directory can contain a *reparse point*, which is a collection of user-defined data. The format of this data is understood by the application, which stores the data, and a file system filter, which you install to interpret the data and process the file. When an application sets a reparse point, it stores this data, plus a reparse tag that uniquely identifies the data that it is storing. When the file system opens a file with a reparse point, it attempts to find the file system filter associated with the data format identified by the reparse tag. If such a file system filter is found, the filter processes the file directed by the reparse data. If no such file system filter is found, the file open operation fails. If we wish to make use of the reparse points on a file or directory, this flag must be set on the file. If we set the reparse point on a directory, that directory must be empty. More detail on the reparse points can be obtained from the Microsoft documentation (MSDN). The reader is encouraged to understand the concepts of reparse points before trying to implement them.

FILE_ATTRIBUTE_ SPARSE_FILE Attribute

Use the DeviceIoControl() function with the FSCTL_SET_SPARSE operation. A file (typically very large) in which a lot of data is all zeros is said to contain a sparse data set. An example is a matrix in which some or much of the data is zeros. Applications that use sparse data sets include image processors and high-speed databases. Windows 2000 NTFS introduces another solution called a sparse file. When the sparse file facilities are used, the system does not allocate hard drive space to a file, except in regions where it contains something other than zeros. The default data value of a sparse file is zero.

FILE_ATTRIBUTE_DIRECTORY Attribute

By setting this attribute, files cannot be converted to directories. By just using the functions to create a directory, as we discussed earlier in this section, the attribute is set.

FILE_ATTRIBUTE_ ENCRYPTED Attribute

To create an encrypted file, the file should be created with the FILE_ ATTRIBUTE_ENCRYPTED attribute in the Win32 function call CreateFile(). When we create a file using VCL's FileCreate() function, this attribute is not supported, and hence, after creating the file we can convert it to an encrypted file using the EncryptFile() Win32 function.

Filename Manipulation Functions

In this section we focus our attention on how to manipulate the parts of a filename. I present this set of functions in Table 4-7.

Table 4-7: Filename manipulation functions

Function	Description
ChangeFileExt(const AnsiString FileName, const AnsiString Extension)	Changes the file extension of the input FileName string to the new value, as specified in the Extension parameter. The function does not change the existing filename. The new filename is returned as an AnsiString value.
DosPathToUnixPath(const AnsiString Path)	Converts a DOS-compatible path specification from the input parameter to a UNIX-compatible path specification. All the backslash characters ("\") are converted to forward slash characters ("/"). The return value is the path specification. It is recommended to not include the drive letter in the input DOS path because the function does not discard the drive letter, and in UNIX, the drive letter has no meaning.
ExcludeTrailingBackslash(const AnsiString S)	Returns the modified path string without the trailing backslash. Borland discourages the use of this function in new applications, which should use the ExcludeTrailing-PathDelimiter() function instead.
ExcludeTrailingPathDelimiter (const AnsiString S)	Returns the modified path string without the trailing path delimiter, which is the "\" character. This function gives the same result as the previous one. Borland recommends that all new applications should use this function instead of ExcludeTrailingBackslash. This function is introduced in C++Builder 6.
ExpandFileName(const Ansi-String FileName)	Returns the fully qualified path name of the input filename, which contains the relative path name
ExpandUNCFileName(const AnsiString FileName)	Returns the fully qualified path name using the Universal Naming Convention for the network filenames. The network server name and share name replace the drive name. For local disk files, this function produces the same result as the previous one.
ExtractFileDir(const AnsiString FileName)	Returns the drive and fully qualified path names as a string for the input filename

Function	Description
ExtractFileDrive(const AnsiString FileName)	Returns the drive name portion of the input filename string. For local disk files, the drive letter is retrieved, and for network files, the result is in the form "\\<server name>\<share name>."
ExtractFileExt(constAnsiString FileName)	Returns the file extension portion of the input filename. The resulting string includes the period that separates the filename from the extension. If the file has no extension, the result string is empty.
ExtractFileName(const AnsiString FileName)	Extracts the name and extension parts of the filename and returns it as a string. The resulting string does not contain the drive and directory path information.
ExtractFilePath(const AnsiString FileName)	Extracts the drive and directory parts of the filename and returns it as a string. The returned string includes the backslash or colon that separates the path from the filename and extension.
ExtractRelativePath(const AnsiString BaseName, const AnsiString DestName)	Converts a fully qualified path name identified by the DestName parameter to a relative path name with respect to the path name identified by the BaseName parameter. The BaseName may or may not contain the filename but must include the final path delimiter. The converted value is returned as an AnsiString object.
ExtractShortPathName(const AnsiString FileName)	Converts the path containing the long filename (and directory names) to the path containing the short filename (and directory names) in DOS 8.3 format. The converted value is returned as an AnsiString object.
IncludeTrailingBackslash(const AnsiString S)	This function ensures that the path name ends with the trailing backslash character ("\"). Borland discourages the use of this function in new applications. Rather, use the IncludeTrailingPathDelimiter() function.
IncludeTrailingPathDelimiter (const AnsiString S)	This function ensures that the path name ends with the trailing path delimiter, which is the backslash character ("\"). Borland recommends using this function instead of the previous one. This function is introduced in C++Builder 6.
IsPathDelimiter(const AnsiString S, int Index)	Checks whether the character at Index position is a path delimiter character ("\"). The index is 0-based. (i.e., we should specify the index between 0 and string length −1). Since we use two backslash characters ("\\") in the string for the delimiter in order to provide for the escape sequence, the function reports the second backslash as the delimiter character and not the first one. It is important to note this feature in order to use the function in the proper way.
MatchesMask(const AnsiString StringToMatch, const AnsiString Mask)	This is a very useful function that checks if a given string StringToMatch matches the pattern specified by the Mask parameter. The pattern specifies how each individual character in the string must match the corresponding matching element in the mask. The mask elements may be individual character literals, sets of character literals, sets of character ranges, or wildcard characters * and ?. Each of the sets must enclose itself with square brackets [], e.g., [a-e]. Individual elements of a set must not be separated by a space or comma. A single mask may contain any combination of these types. Here is an example of the mask: "b[a-f]*[hu]??[o-r]". This mask indicates that the string must start with the character "b," followed by any character between "a" and "f" followed by any number (and combination) of characters (because of the wildcard character *) followed by the character "h" or "u," followed by any two characters (because of the wildcard characters ??), followed by any single character between "o" and "r."
MinimizeName(const AnsiString Filename, Graphics::TCanvas* Canvas, int MaxLen)	This is another very useful function that shortens a (long) filename so that it can be drawn on a surface to fit the size specified in the number of (length-wise) pixels. Replacing directories in the path portion of the filename with dots until the resulting name fits the specified number of pixels in length shortens the length of the filename.
ProcessPath(const AnsiString FileName, char &Drive, Ansi-String &DirPart, AnsiString &FilePart)	This function parses the input filename and separates the three portions of the string: the drive portion as a character and the directory and file portions as AnsiString objects.

Function	Description
UnixPathToDosPath(const AnsiString Path)	Converts a UNIX-compatible path specification from the input parameter to a DOS-compatible path specification. All the forward slash characters ("/") are converted to backslash characters ("\"). The return value is the DOS-path specification.

File Content Management

In this sub-section, we discuss the functions that operate on the file contents. These include opening a file, file open modes, positioning the file pointer within a file, reading from and writing to the file, and finally closing the file.

The FileOpen() function opens the specified file in the specified mode. The access mode can be read-only or write-only, or read-write, deny-read, deny-write, deny-none (means give full access to all), or share-exclusive (means deny read and write). Internally, VCL calls the Win32 CreateFile() method to convert the VCL access mode to the Win32 access mode value. If successful, the method returns the file handle; otherwise, it returns a value of –1. The signature of this function is given here:

```
int __fastcall FileOpen(const AnsiString FileName, int Mode);
```

The FileSeek() function positions the current file pointer at the requested position in the file that is already open. Upon successful completion, it returns the new file pointer position; otherwise, it returns –1. The signature of the function is given here:

```
int __fastcall FileSeek(int Handle, int Offset, int Origin);
```

The file pointer usually indicates the position in the file from where the next read or write operation can be performed. When the file is opened initially, the pointer is at the beginning of the file. If the file is not empty when opened, it is very important to position the pointer appropriately so that the next read operation is successful or so the new contents are written without damaging existing contents of the file. The Handle parameter represents the file handle, the Offset parameter is the number of bytes the file pointer should be moved, and the Origin parameter indicates from where the Offset bytes are to be counted. If Origin is 0, the Offset must be counted from the beginning of the file; if Origin is 1, the Offset must be counted from the current file pointer position; if Origin is 2, the Offset must be counted from the end of the file toward the beginning (i.e., backward counting).

The FileRead() function reads the specified number of bytes from the specified file and places them in a buffer. The signature of the function is given here:

```
int __fastcall FileRead(int Handle, void *Buffer, int Count);
```

The Handle parameter represents the file handle. The buffer of count size must have been created before trying to read the file. Otherwise, an access violation error occurs. The function returns the number of bytes actually read (which may be less than the requested number of bytes) if the read was successful; otherwise, it returns –1.

The FileWrite() function writes the specified number of bytes from the buffer to the specified file at the current file pointer position, and the file pointer is advanced by the number of bytes written to the file. The signature of the function is given here:

```
int __fastcall FileWrite(int Handle, const void *Buffer, int Count);
```

The function returns the number of bytes actually written to the file if the write was successful; otherwise, it returns –1.

The FileClose() function closes the file specified by the handle. The signature of the function is given here:

```
void __fastcall FileClose(int Handle);
```

Summary

We started the chapter with an introduction to the Action Objects, followed by the ActionList object and how it simplifies system responses to user input actions. We also discussed the standard Action Objects provided by VCL and saw how to implement the custom Action Objects. Then a new feature introduced in C++Builder 6, ActionManager, was discussed and we walked through an example that showed us how to implement most of the standard features required for a Win32-based applications.

We then discussed the VCL way of implementing the Windows common dialogs.

Afterward, we spent a considerable time discussing the VCL support to implement Windows drag and drop and saw how to develop custom drag-and-drop features in our applications. We demonstrated the custom drag and drop with a couple of very useful example applications.

Following this, we discussed how two major aspects of SYSUTILS and FILECTRL units make our programming easier with respect to working with date and time functions and directory and file management routines. Though we focused our attention on VCL features, we also discussed how some of the direct Win32 functions could be intermixed in our applications to develop applications that can be easily interfaced with those developed on other platforms.

Chapter 5

Simple Database Development

Introduction to Database Development

Traditionally, database development has been referred to as the development of applications that rely on database management systems to cater to the data management requirements. Since the advent of mid-range computers, distributed computing started attracting the industry as a reasonable and efficient alternative to centralized mainframe-based computing architecture. The two architectures have their own merits and drawbacks, but this book is not intended to discuss them in detail. However, we will discuss the process of implementing distributed and desktop-level computing as one of the key topics in the book. In this chapter, we will begin our discussion and continue the discussion in further chapters.

One of the key aspects of distributed computing architecture is the ability to slice the database into logical units of data on the basis of an application's requirements and store them in relatively smaller databases distributed across the enterprise's network. This feature brings the concept of localizing a database to the application, which means bringing the data close to the application where it belongs. These distributed applications may become part of the complex enterprise architecture or may be completely dedicated to a local department's needs. In an enterprise environment, many times applications are interdependent on each other in terms of data as well as functional tasks. This necessitated the development of distributed objects using the well-established object-oriented paradigm. If we stretch this concept of localization further, we will arrive at desktop applications, which are usually designed for very small shops or individuals. While we concentrate on enterprise computing, however, we should not neglect the small shop requirements.

The varied needs of distributed applications had given the database vendors a way to develop database management systems that vary in their features. Desktop databases give us the ability to develop completely localized applications useful for a single user or very limited number of users. These databases usually do not provide features that are required for large databases, such as security, multiple connections, load balancing, backup and recovery, and replication. Examples of such database management systems are Paradox, dBase, FoxBASE, and Access. These databases are usually suitable for two-tier applications. Also, the desktop databases do not usually agree on a common programming API or language and are completely vendor specific.

On the other hand, SQL-based databases, also known as server-based databases, provide features that are demanded by large-size distributed applications. These features include (but are not limited to) multiple connection and session management, user-level security, backup and recovery, replication, and load balancing. These databases are suitable for the development of three-tier and multi-tier enterprise-level distributed applications (intranet), web-based applications (Internet), and applications that interact with business partners (business-to-business, or B2B). SQL-based databases usually follow the standard SQL specification at the minimum and provide the vendor-specific features on top of this.

Two-tier, Three-tier, and Multi-tier Applications

Each tier of an application represents an application component layer. The top tier is the layer that communicates with an external entity (end user in most cases); the bottom tier is the database itself. In a two-tier application, only these two layers are present, and hence the top tier is heavily loaded with presentation logic as well as business logic. This type of application is usually developed for desktop access to small or limited-user databases. Since these are usually single-user based systems, there is no need to administer the flow of information in such applications.

In a three-tier application, a middle tier is designed to function as an application server layer, which controls and administers the flow of information and access to the database, and introduces enterprise basic features, such as security and load balancing. In addition, the business logic and database access are shifted from the top tier to the middle tier, thereby reducing the size and complexity of the top tier. This makes the deployment of the top tier on client machines easy and drastically improves the performance of the application because the top tier, which communicates with the end user, is very light. A typical enterprise application hosted on its intranet is an example of a three-tier application. Such applications usually do not have a security threat from the external world, as they run within the secure zone of the enterprise. However, user-level security is provided and handled (mostly by the database server and sometimes partly by the application server) in order to give different levels of access to the data to individual employees performing different roles.

Multi-tier applications are an extension of the three-tier concept and truly represent a distributed object-based computing environment. Instead of a single middle tier, there will be multiple layers in between. The layer that is closest to the database acts as the application server in terms of controlling the database connectivity and session management. The intermediate layers between the top tier and the application server act as independent automation servers or object brokers. Their job is to coordinate with the application server (or another layer representing an object broker) to request a specific piece of information. If all the tiers are hosted within the enterprise secure zone, they are governed by the same rules of security as the three-tier applications. However, many times this type of system interacts with object brokers across the Internet or a network external to the enterprise. In such cases, additional security measures have to be implemented within the object brokers and the application server in order to

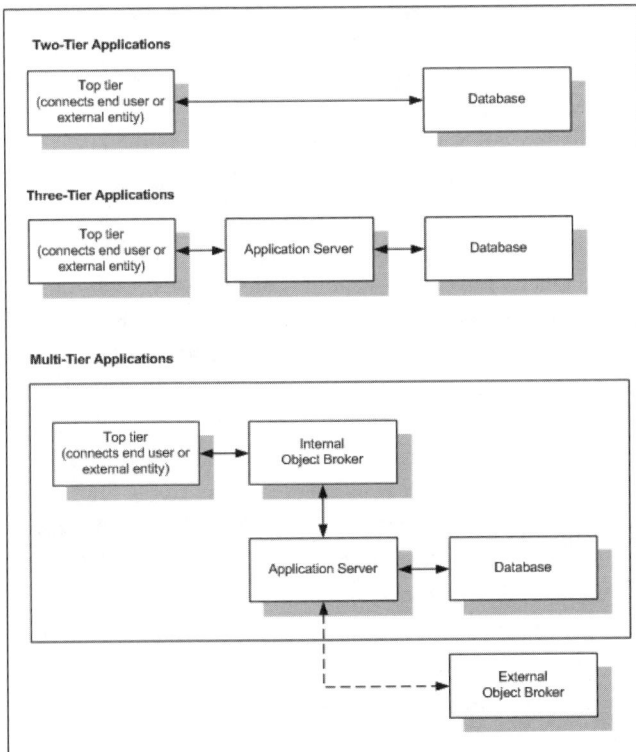

Figure 5-1: Two-tier, three-tier, and multi-tier applications

restrict the access and provide tight security to the enterprise data. Also in this type of scenario, the object brokers as well as the application server handle two types of service: internal service requests and external service requests. Figure 5-1 displays the different types of applications we discussed here.

In this chapter we concentrate our discussion on the general database access architecture as provided by the VCL, followed by two-tier application development.

VCL Architecture for Database Development

In this section, I focus on the similarities that VCL architecture maintains across the different frameworks. A word of appreciation goes to Borland in this regard, due to their efforts to provide a uniform set of components that work very similarly with respect to the developer's point of view and still protect the integrity and specificity of the respective framework. This makes it very easy for the developer to change the back-end database with minimal code changes. However, at this point, I would caution developers and architects to pay special attention to the database-/framework-specific features while making such changes. An example of such a change may be migrating a system that is written for a desktop database to a server-based database. As long as we use VCL components, such changes will be easier. Again, migrating a two-tier system to a three-tier system is not an easy step due to an additional layer that we introduce as a result of the change.

VCL provides a wealth of components for database development. Apart from a framework like VCL, we also need to have database drivers to connect to specific databases. The database drivers are usually libraries provided by the respective database vendors (or third-party vendors) to enable external applications to connect to the database and interact with it for the purposes of executing queries or performing administration or maintenance functions in the background mode. When I say background mode, I mean without knowledge of the foreground (or front-end) processes. There are even general frameworks designed by different organizations (or vendors) to enable software houses to develop database drivers for commercial databases. Examples of such frameworks are BDE, ODBC, and Microsoft ADO. Starting with Delphi 6, Borland has introduced a new database access framework named dbExpress.

With respect to database development using VCL architecture, we primarily use three sets of components. These are:

- Database connection components

- Data access components
- Data-aware controls

The database connection components are used to connect to the database and its objects and execute queries or commands on the database. The data-aware controls are usually visual components such as a grid or edit control, combo box, etc. that display data to the user. The data access components play the intermediary role between the other two sets as conduits of data. The second and third sets of components are generic in nature, and the first set of components varies based on the framework we use to connect to the database. In the Component Palette, the components located in the BDE page are used to connect to the database using the BDE and ODBC frameworks; the components located in the ADO page are used for the ADO and ODBC frameworks; the components located in the InterBase page are exclusively provided to connect to the Borland InterBase database; and the components located in the dbExpress page are used to connect using the dbExpress framework. Note that some databases have multiple choices for the architecture by which applications can attach to them. For example, InterBase has dbExpress, BDE, and ODBC drivers.

In this chapter, we will concentrate on BDE, ODBC, and ADO technologies, and in the following chapter we will discuss dbExpress and InterBase Express components.

Database Connection Components

Database Connection Frameworks Supported in VCL

The database connection components typically consist of a component to establish a persistent connection to the database, a component to execute a query on the database, a component to execute a stored procedure, and a component to extract contents from a table or view. There are variations across components that support different frameworks; there may be some additional components for each of the frameworks. These differences are due to the specific nature of the framework that the component set supports. Tables 5-1 through 5-4 display the similarities and differences among these component sets.

Table 5-1: BDE/ODBC components

Database Function	Component for BDE/ODBC
Establish persistent connection with database	TDataBase
Execute a SQL query on the database	TQuery
Retrieve data from a table or view	TTable
Execute a stored procedure on the database	TStoredProc
Framework-specific components	TSession, TBatchMove, TUpdateSQL, TNestedTable, TBDEClientDataSet

Table 5-2: ADO/ODBC components

Database Function	Component for ADO/ODBC
Establish persistent connection with database	TADOConnection
Execute a SQL query on the database	TADOQuery
Retrieve data from a table or view	TADOTable
Execute a stored procedure on the database	TADOStoredProc
Framework-specific components	TADODataSet, TADOCommand

Table 5-3: dbExpress components

Database Function	Component for dbExpress
Establish persistent connection with database	TSQLConnection
Execute a SQL query on the database	TSQLDataSet
Retrieve data from a table or view	TSQLDataSet
Execute a stored procedure on the database	TSQLDataSet
Framework-specific components	TSQLClientDataSet, TSQLMonitor

In addition to TSQLDataSet, there are dbExpress components such as TSQLTable, TSQLQuery, and TSQLStoredProc that are similar to the BDE components TTable, TQuery, and TStoredProc, respectively, and are provided to aid in migrating existing applications from BDE-specific components to dbExpress components.

Table 5-4: InterBase Express components

Database Function	Component for InterBase Express
Establish persistent connection with database	TIBDataBase
Execute a SQL query on the database	TIBQuery
Retrieve data from a table or view	TIBTable
Execute a stored procedure on the database	TIBStoredProc
Framework-specific components	TIBUpdateSQL, TIBDataSet, TIBSQL, TIBDatabaseInfo, TIBSQLMonitor, TIBEvent, TIBExtract, TIBClientDataSet, TIBTransaction

Figure 5-2 displays the different ways to establish a database connection using the different frameworks supported in the VCL.

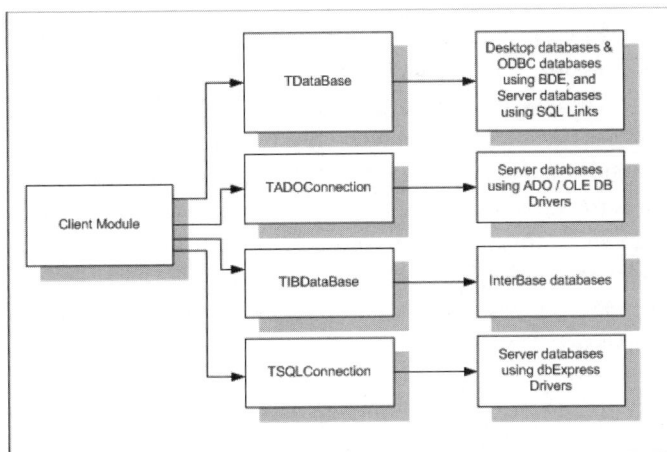

Figure 5-2: Different ways to connect to databases in the VCL framework

The BDE framework uses Borland Database Engine, which is a set of DLLs designed by Borland that is traditionally used to connect to the databases since the early days of Delphi. Compared to other frameworks, the BDE is bulkier in size. BDE is usually shipped with standard drivers for desktop databases like dBase, Paradox, FoxPro, Access, and simple text files. With the enterprise release of C++Builder and Delphi, a set of SQL drivers is also shipped to enable connecting to server-based SQL databases like InterBase, Oracle, Informix, and DB2. It also includes a built-in ODBC socket to enable developers to connect to the ODBC drivers using the BDE framework.

The ADO framework (sometimes referred to as "dbGo for ADO") stands for Microsoft's ActiveX Data Objects technology and is designed to work with COM to provide data access services to Windows-based systems. This framework uses OLE DB drivers to connect to the database. If you have an OLE DB driver to a database, you can use the ADO framework, whether it is a desktop database or server-based database. You can also use an ODBC driver in place of an OLE DB driver with the ADO framework. However, the OLE DB technology is known to be more performance oriented than the ODBC technology. The set of components provided by Borland to use the ADO framework is very powerful, and you will be amazed to note that ADO was never this easy to use in a C++ application. In simple terms, you will use the ADO framework the Borland way. These components are available to work with Delphi 5 and C++Builder 5 onward.

The dbExpress framework is the most recent technology designed by Borland and is available to work with Delphi 6, C++Builder 6, and Kylix. Some of the important features of this framework include being lightweight, high performance, and cross-platform portable. When I say "cross-platform portable," I mean the programs written using this technology with CLX components are portable across Windows and Linux operating systems at source code level. However, the VCL components are specific to Windows only. Borland is currently providing drivers for InterBase, Informix, Oracle, DB2, and MySQL in this framework. The specific set of drivers shipped with each edition of the product varies, and you have to check with Borland.

The IBExpress framework is exclusively designed to work with the Borland InterBase database. The components do not use BDE/ODBC/ADO frameworks. Rather, they are designed to work with the InterBase client libraries directly and provide you with high-performance database connection and transaction support. If your organization has InterBase installations, it is recommended you use the IBExpress framework to achieve performance gain.

How Do You Connect to a Database?

Each of the frameworks is distinct in its connection characteristics and underlying technology that it supports. But the VCL architecture provides components with similar properties and access methods so that the developer will not have much difficulty in switching from one framework to another. TDataBase, TADOConnection, TIBDataBase, and TSQLConnection represent the first component that we use with each of the frameworks in order to establish a database connection. These components are all derived from a single base class, TCustomConnection, which is designed to establish a connection with a remote data source; it may be a desktop database, server database, the application server in a three-tier (or multi-tier) application, or an interface such as the one used by the ADO framework.

The purpose of this object is to provide:

- Methods to connect to (and disconnect from) a remote data source
- Login support to the data sources that require login
- Properties to keep track of datasets that are using the connection

The descendant connection components implement the database-/framework-specific connection features. The details of establishing a database connection are explained in the sections about the respective frameworks.

What is TDataSet?

TDataSet is the base class for any database object that we use in any of these frameworks. In VCL, a dataset is designed to contain a record structure and a set of records that conform to the record structure. This suggests that a dataset represents a record set in this sense. An object of this class cannot be directly instantiated, as it contains pure virtual methods. However, objects of its descendant classes can be created, provided those classes have overridden the pure virtual methods. Thus, in the process of overriding the pure virtual methods of the TDataSet class, the descendant classes are expected to provide the source (e.g., a specific table from a database) from where the record structure is created and also from where and how the data is retrieved. That means that the generic TDataSet class should be converted to a specific data object before we try to use it. This also suggests to us that we can create customized descendants of this class to handle data objects that we may create on the fly in an application.

Typically, the properties and methods of this object enable us to work through the record structure and navigate the record set. The events implemented for these objects are triggered when a significant task is performed on the dataset (e.g., there is an event that is fired when the dataset is opened or an event that is fired before inserting a new record into the dataset). Though a number of events are provided, giving us flexibility to handle the dataset's behavior throughout its lifetime, we only implement (or write) the required ones in our application. When implemented, these event handlers enable us to perform specific tasks like data validation before insert or update and forced cleanup or refresh of the dataset per the application's need, etc. Another significant feature of this component is that it stores a record buffer locally, which in a descendant class could be used to enable us to disconnect from the database after getting the data and work in an offline mode, if desired. However, such advanced features are only available if provided by the descendant classes.

Figure 5-3 on the following page displays how the TDataSet functions as a base class for the different frameworks to manage the database objects.

All of the frameworks typically derive three fundamental types of components from TDataSet. These are tables, queries, and stored procedures, which are common in most of the databases. We may find databases on the market that do not support queries or stored procedures. We are not considering such databases in our discussion here.

Tables represent a static snapshot of data obtained at a specific point of time. The properties and methods enable us to connect to a specific database (or connection) component, set the table that we are interested in

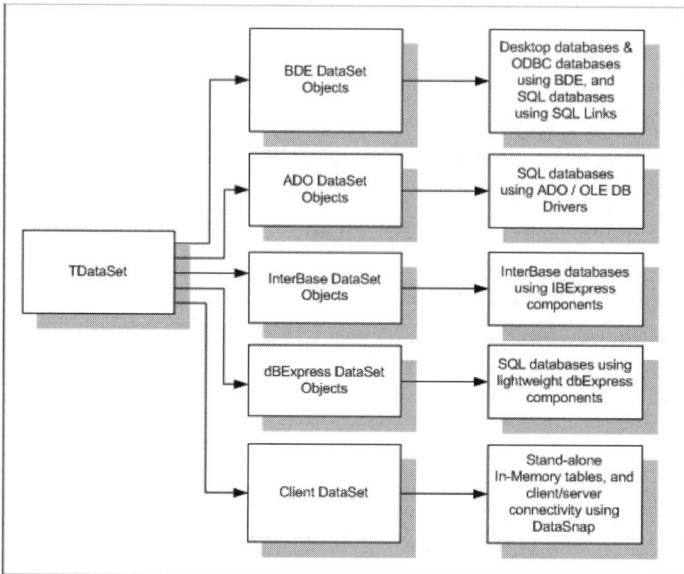

Figure 5-3:
TDataSet as base class to manage data objects in different frameworks

reading (and/or updating online), and refresh the data as frequently as we need in the application. Opening a table may be performed in online or offline mode. In online mode, the updates that we perform on the table are immediately applied to the database (for simplicity's sake, I am not discussing the transaction support at this point). In offline mode, the updates do not happen immediately, but are applied at a later point of time.

Queries are mainly of two types. The first type of query retrieves a set of records from the database (which is usually called a SELECT query), and once the data is retrieved, it works like an offline mode table, and we can navigate through the record set as we do in a table. However, it is also possible to process a query that retrieves records for update, as supported by the respective database. The second type of query is usually a data manipulation language (DML) statement and is used to update or delete one or more records that satisfy specific criteria. Such queries do not retrieve a record set; rather, they just retrieve a result code and associated message (as thrown by the database) indicating whether the query execution has been successful or not. Therefore, the query components implement properties and methods to connect to a specific database (or connection) component, contain an SQL statement, input parameters to the statement, and execute the statement on the database. The ability to contain and navigate the record set (as derived from the base TDataSet component) is preserved in addition to the added functionality.

Stored procedures usually represent individual code blocks to perform more complicated tasks than a simple query or update. These may include multiple queries, control statements, etc. implemented in a procedural language (specific to the database). We may be able to pass one or more input parameters or expect multiple return values in output parameters. We may also expect a return record set. To enable us to perform all these tasks, these components implement properties and methods to connect to a specific database (or connection) component, contain input parameters to the stored procedure, contain placeholders to accept output parameters, and execute the stored procedure on the database. The ability to contain and navigate the record set (as derived from the base TDataSet component) is preserved in addition to the added functionality.

Dataset States

Dataset objects have a State property, which indicates the current state of the dataset when inquired. It is very important to know these states to avoid related exception situations. In this section, we will discuss some of the frequent occurrences of the state. The states not discussed here are usually specific to certain circumstances or temporary states used by the component internally.

When the state is dsInactive, it means that the dataset is closed, and hence we cannot perform any task related to the data or the record structure. The only permitted tasks are those that bring the dataset to one of the active states, such as opening the dataset.

When the state is dsBrowse, it means that the dataset is open and available for browsing only. This is the default state when the dataset is first open. In this state, the records in the dataset cannot be changed (it must be in dsEdit mode for changes to be made, which is discussed below). Also, the dataset attains this state after a successful execution of the Post() or Cancel() method.

When the state is dsInsert, it means that the active record has just been inserted into the dataset and is available to populate field values. A dataset attains this state when a new record is added through the Append() or Insert() method. However, the active record is only a record buffer and is still not part of the current record set. To make the active record part of the current record set, you have to execute the Post() method after populating the field values.

When the state is dsEdit, it means that the active record can be modified. A dataset attains this state when the Edit() method is called to edit the active record. The changes will be made to the record set only after executing the Post() method.

When the state is dsOpening, the dataset is in the process of opening but has not finished yet. This state occurs when the dataset is opened for asynchronous fetching.

The active record in a dataset is always the record to which the record pointer is currently pointing. The record pointer is accessible only when the dataset is open and contains a record set of one or more records. The dsInsert and dsEdit states of the dataset are only applicable to the active record. When the dataset is in one of these two states, it is not possible to successfully execute methods that try to move the record pointer. We have to Post() or Cancel() the changes before we try to navigate the dataset.

Synchronous and Asynchronous Modes

When the dataset is connected to a data source in synchronous mode, setting properties or executing methods on the dataset will make these changes impact the database objects directly. If the dataset is disconnected from the database after retrieving the data, or if the dataset is populated from the database through a middle tier, the dataset is considered to be in asynchronous mode, with respect to the database. In this case, since the dataset is not directly connected to the database, any changes applied to the dataset will not directly update the database; rather, a middle tier will apply the changes later asynchronously.

Figure 5-4 displays how dataset changes are applied to the database in a typical scenario where a dataset is connected to the database synchronously.

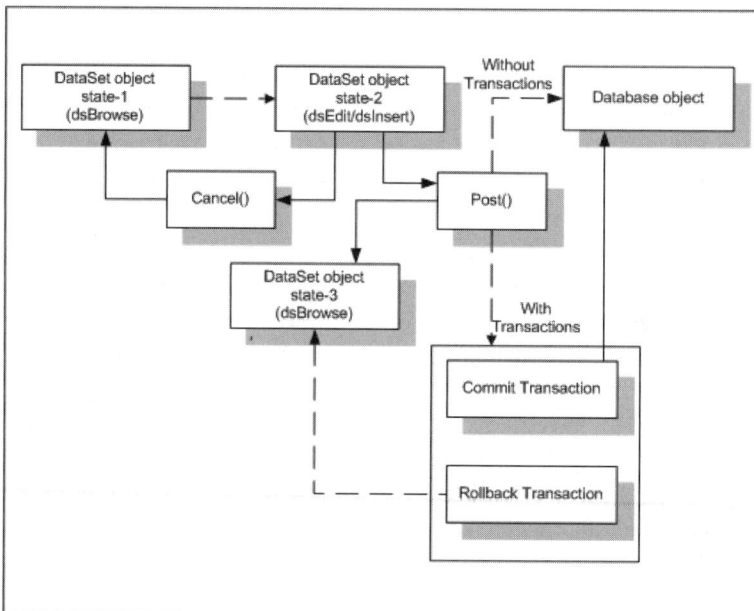

Figure 5-4:
Applying dataset
changes to the
database

Figure 5-4 shows the situation with transaction support and without transaction support. When the transaction support is disabled, the execution of the Post() method on the dataset will apply changes directly to the database in addition to applying the changes on the dataset itself. In this scenario, the only way to avoid such a direct update is by executing the Cancel() method of the dataset. When the transaction support is enabled, the execution of the Post() method on the dataset applies the changes to the dataset only, and the corresponding database update takes place when the transaction is committed the next time (which is usually executed through the database connection component in the VCL). If the transaction is rolled back, we come back to the point where the changes were applied to the dataset.

Properties, Methods and Events

Now let's examine some of the generic features supported by the TDataSet component, as outlined in Table 5-5, before we move on to the specifics of the frameworks/databases. Please note that some of these features depend on the descendant classes for the implementation and hence may not be available in all the descendant objects.

Table 5-5: Properties, methods, and events of TDataSet

Property	Description
Active	Use this property to find out if the dataset is open or not. Setting this property to true opens the dataset. If the dataset is a table, this action retrieves the records from the database table. The series of actions that take place include generating a BeforeOpen event, setting the dataset state to dsBrowse, establishing a way to fetch the data, typically by opening a cursor, and generating an AfterOpen event. Calling the Open() method has the same effect. Setting this property to false closes the dataset. The series of actions that take place include generating a BeforeClose event, setting the dataset state to dsInactive, closing the cursor, and generating an AfterClose event. Calling the Close() method has the same effect.
AggFields	This property represents a TFields object, which contains an array of aggregate fields, which are usually defined to represent summarized values over groups of records. Aggregate fields are calculated fields. Use this property to access the values of aggregate fields in the current record.
Bof	This is a Boolean property. It indicates whether the dataset is currently pointing to the first record. If the dataset has records, this property returns true when the dataset is first opened.
Eof	This is a Boolean property. It indicates whether the dataset is currently pointing to the last record.
FieldCount	This property indicates the number of fields associated with the dataset, as represented by the Fields property. It does not include calculated fields. In applications that use dynamically generated dataset components, it is recommended to read this property just before its use because the field count varies in the number of fields in the dataset.
FieldDefList	This property represents the flattened list of field definitions contained in the dataset. Any nested (child) field definitions are shown as siblings to the parent field definition. In addition, this property should be used only to read the field definitions, not values in a record.

Property	Description
FieldDefs	This property represents the hierarchical list of field definitions. In this representation, the nested field definitions are shown with their appropriate parent-child relationship. An example of nested field definitions is the abstract field types defined by the user and supported by the underlying database. When an application creates a dataset object by calling either CreateTable() or CreateDataSet(), as supported by the descendant class, this property is used to create the dataset structure. If this property is not defined, the Fields property is used. Therefore, this property should only be changed in those applications that create a dataset programmatically. In all other cases, this property should be used for read-only purposes. In addition, this property should be used only to read the field definitions and not values in a record.
FieldList	This property can be used in a similar manner as the Fields property, but the field's array is arranged sequentially.
Fields	This property should be used to read field values in the active record or set the field values when the record is in edit mode. It contains a TFields component, which is an array of TField components. The fields in the array can be arranged hierarchically or as a flattened list, depending on whether the ObjectView property of the dataset is set to true or false. This property does not contain the aggregate fields.
FieldValues	This property represents the value of a field and can be used to access all the fields, including the aggregate and non-aggregate fields. Use this property to read and write the individual field values of the active record, where the name of the field is known. The value of the field is read and accepted as a Variant type and is therefore used to access fields of any data type. This property is very useful where the field type is not known or a generic routine has to be written for handling different data types.
Filter	This property should be used to set a dataset filter. It describes the filter condition, and hence only those records that match the condition are available in the dataset. It is an AnsiString object. The syntax for setting the filter text is very similar to the WHERE clause of a SELECT statement in a standard SQL query. Value comparison operators, such as $<, >, =, >=, <=, <>$, can be used in addition to the normal mathematical operators of $+, -, *,$ and $/$. Complex filter conditions can be built using AND, OR, and NOT to join simple filter conditions. An example of filter text is: `EMPLOYEE_ID < 100 AND EMPLOYEE_ID > 50`. The filter text can also be built and set dynamically, based on the user input. Filters are not supported in unidirectional datasets.
FilterOptions	This property can be used to set how the filter text should be used to compare the string values of fields. This is a set of values and can include foCaseInsensitive to indicate that string comparisons be performed case insensitive and foNoPartialCompare to indicate that wildcard characters in the filter text must be treated as part of the string text and not as wildcard characters. The absence of each of these filter options indicates that the opposite meaning of these options should be taken as the default setting.
IsUniDirectional	This indicates whether the dataset object is unidirectional or not. Some of the descendants of TDataSet are unidirectional datasets. Components of the dbExpress framework, such as TCustomSQLDataSet and its descendants, are examples in this category.
RecNo	This indicates the active record number in the dataset. The descendant classes must implement this property to correctly return the value.
RecordCount	This property indicates the total number of records in the dataset. The descendant classes must implement this property to correctly return the value.
RecordSize	This indicates the record size in bytes. The descendant classes must implement this property to correctly return the value.
State	This indicates the current state of the dataset. This property is very useful in determining what can be done with the dataset or current record. It can be effectively used to avoid exception conditions.

Method	Description
Append()	Adds a new, empty record at the end of the current record set. The dataset state is set to dsInsert, and the record is now editable.
AppendRecord(TVarRec* values, int size)	Adds a new record at the end of the current record set, populates it with the values from the input parameters, and executes the Post() method. The first parameter is an array of TVarRec objects, and the second parameter is the index of the last element in the input array. The index is always one less than the number of array elements.
Cancel()	Cancels all the changes done to the active record after the dataset state has become dsInsert or dsEdit, and sets the state to dsBrowse
ClearFields()	Clears the contents of all the fields in the active record if it is in the dsInsert or dsEdit state
Close()	Closes the dataset and sets the Active property to false
Delete()	Deletes the active record and positions the record pointer on the next record. If the deleted record was the last record, the pointer is positioned on the previous record. Calls the BeforeDelete event handler before deleting the record and the AfterDelete event handler after deleting the record.
DisableControls()	Every time data changes in the active record, the data-aware controls change the displayed data. If such changes are done through a large number of controls, there will be screen flicker. By calling this method, the screen flicker can be avoided and performance can be improved because the associated controls do not show the updates until the corresponding Enable-Controls() method is called. DisableControls() can be nested any number of times but must equal the number of calls to the EnableControls() method. Until then, the data-aware controls do not show the updates. Disabling a master dataset in a master-child relationship causes the child dataset(s) also to be disabled.
Edit()	Puts the active record in edit mode and sets the dataset state to dsEdit. The active record is then editable.
EnableControls()	Every call to this method must correspond to an earlier call to the DisableControls() method. After all the necessary calls to this method are executed, the data-aware controls display any changes made to the dataset(s).
FieldByName(AnsiString fieldName)	This method returns the TField component of the specified field. It can be used to retrieve any field (one that belongs to the Fields property or the AggFields property and also a subfield of an object field). This can be used to retrieve the field value or set the field value.
FindField(AnsiString fieldName)	Call this method to determine if the specified field exists in the dataset. If the specified field exists in the dataset, the method returns the corresponding TField component; otherwise, it returns NULL.
First()	Moves the record pointer to the first record and sets Bof to true
Insert()	Inserts a new, empty record at the current record position. The dataset state is set to dsInsert and the record is now editable.
InsertRecord(TVarRec* values, int size)	Inserts a new, empty record at the current record position, populates it with the values from the input parameters, and executes the Post() method. The first parameter is an array of TVarRec objects, and the second parameter is the index of the last element in the input array. The index is always one less than the number of array elements.
IsEmpty()	This is a Boolean property that indicates whether the dataset is empty or not.

Method	Description
IsLinkedTo(TDataSource * fdataSource)	A dataset is usually linked to a data source to enable the data to be displayed in data-aware controls. The data source acts as a conduit between the dataset and controls. This method can be used to check if the dataset is linked to the specified data source given as the parameter.
Last()	Moves the record pointer to the last record and sets Eof to true
Locate(AnsiString keyFields, Variant &keyValues, TLocateOptions options)	This method should be called to locate a specific record containing the matching key values for the specified key fields. The options may indicate whether the search is case insensitive or whether to allow partial key values to be matched. This method is inherited directly in bidirectional datasets and is commonly overridden in unidirectional descendants to provide indexing criteria.
Next()	Moves the record pointer to the next record from its current position. If Eof is already true, then calling this method has no impact.
Open()	Gives the same result as setting the Active property to true
Post()	Applies all the changes to the dataset and sets the state to dsBrowse
Prior()	Moves the record pointer to the previous record from its current position. If Bof is already true, then calling this method has no impact.
Refresh()	Refreshes the dataset records from the underlying dataset

Event	Description
AfterCancel	This event is triggered after canceling changes made to the current record in the dataset.
AfterClose	This event is triggered after successfully closing the dataset and setting the dataset state to dsInactive.
AfterDelete	This event is triggered after deleting the active record.
AfterEdit	This event is triggered after the active record is put in edit mode.
AfterInsert	This event is triggered after inserting a new record in the dataset.
AfterOpen	This event is triggered after the dataset is opened, and its state is set to dsBrowse.
AfterPost	This event is triggered after posting changes to the current record in the dataset.
BeforeCancel	This event is triggered before canceling changes to the current record in the dataset through the Cancel() method.
BeforeClose	When the Close() method is called or the Active property is set to false, this event is triggered before the dataset is closed.
BeforeDelete	This event is triggered before deleting the active record by executing the Delete() method.
BeforeEdit	This event is triggered before the active record is put in edit mode by executing the Edit() method.
BeforeInsert	This event is triggered before inserting a new record in the dataset and setting the dataset state to dsInsert. Both the Insert() and Append() methods generate this event.
BeforeOpen	This event is triggered before opening the dataset.
BeforePost	This event is triggered before posting changes to the current record in the dataset through calling the Post() method. This is the ideal time to perform validity checks on data before posting the changes.

We have seen an exhaustive list of features that are available to most of the TDataSet descendant classes. We now better understand that a dataset is an abstract definition of a set of records, obtained from a database or otherwise, and we can use these common features and any specific features introduced by the descendant classes to manipulate the fields and their contents.

Data-aware Controls and DataSource

TDataSet and its descendants are non-visual components. If we do not need to visually display data to the user, we can work with the dataset descendant classes directly in the background mode, which we do anyway in many cases. It is also equally important in many situations to display data to the user for browsing or for update, or both, or for populating new data from user input. In all such cases, we need the data-aware controls, which provide visual display on the screen. The most commonly used controls are TDBGrid, TDBNavigator, TDBListBox, TDBEdit, TDBComboBox, TDBCheckBox, TDBRadioGroup, and TDBText. This is not a complete list; more controls can be seen in the Data Controls page in the Component Palette. In all these components, one important property is DataSource, which acts like a conduit between the dataset object and the data-aware control.

Figure 5-5 displays how data flows between a dataset object and data-aware control through the data source.

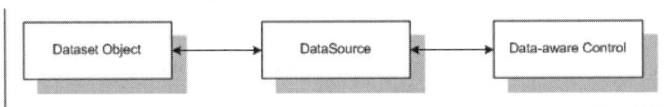

Figure 5-5: Data flow through data source

The TDataSource component has the DataSet property, which must be set to the source dataset object. The DataSource property of the data-aware control must be set to the data source component that we created earlier. That is how the connectivity should be established. A dataset component can be assigned to more than one data source component at the same time. But a data source component accepts only one dataset component assignment at the same time, and a data-aware control accepts only one data source component assignment at the same time. These assignments can be changed dynamically during run time based on the application needs. However, it is recommended that the dataset be closed before changing such assignments to avoid exception conditions.

Data Module—The Non-visual Container

A typical VCL-based Windows application contains a form component, which is derived from the TForm component, as we noticed in earlier chapters. Similarly, when you add a data module to a project, the wizard creates a descendant class from the TDataModule component. The data module is a container that can hold the non-visual components of the application, such as database components including datasets, connection components, and providers, networking components like sockets, and other simple components like timers and so on. The data module itself is a non-visual component. It is not a requirement to place non-visual components on the data modules; rather, it is a convenience. Use of data modules makes grouping related non-visual components together and keeps the main user interface forms clean during design time. If your application uses just one or two non-visual components, you may not notice the difference. But if you use a number of non-visual components, particularly datasets, data sources, and so on, you would certainly feel very comfortable in placing them separately on a data module so that your main form is clean.

A simple data module may be used in a Windows GUI application, whereas there are other components derived from the TDataModule that are intended for specific types of projects, such as the TWebDataModule, which is used in WebSnap applications, the TCRemoteDataModule, which is used in DataSnap applications, and the TSoapDataModule, which is used in BizSnap applications while building web services. We will learn about these different types of data modules as we discuss the associated topics in later chapters.

Borland Database Engine (BDE) Framework

BDE Components

BDE components are not new in this release of C++Builder. Rather, is the standard framework provided traditionally since very early releases of Delphi and C++Builder. BDE provides mainly three types of connectivity, as explained here:

- Connectivity to desktop databases such as Paradox, Access, and dBase
- Connectivity to server-type databases such as Oracle, InterBase, and DB2 using SQL Links drivers
- Connectivity to any database having an ODBC driver using the ODBC library

In this section, we examine how to establish connectivity using the BDE framework. To establish a BDE connection in any of the three ways, we need to first set up a BDE alias. A BDE alias is a configuration setting that we set up using BDE Administrator. It acts like a database driver for all practical purposes. BDE Administrator is installed along with C++Builder and is accessible from the Start menu or the Control Panel.

Setting Up a BDE Alias for InterBase SQL Links Driver

Start the BDE Administrator. It works like a wizard, although it is a complete application by itself. In the application window, the left pane contains two tabs: Databases and Configuration. The Configuration tab displays native drivers and ODBC drivers as installed along with System settings. In this tab, we can change configuration settings for these drivers. The native drivers include the desktop drivers and SQL Links drivers. The Databases tab lets us create aliases to the drivers defined in the Configuration tab. A set of predefined database aliases is displayed in this tab within a hierarchical tree named Databases. A configuration setting that defines how to use a database driver for a specific database is called a *database alias*. Thus, using the same InterBase driver, we can create one alias for each database, at a minimum. In this section, I am going to demonstrate this procedure step by step:

1. With the mouse, right-click on **Databases** in the Databases tab. A menu of options appears.

2. In the drop-down menu, choose the **New** option. A dialog appears with a list of database configurations as predefined in the Configuration tab.
   The list contains the native drivers supplied by Borland (for both the desktop databases and SQL databases) and ODBC datasets defined using the ODBC Administrator Wizard.

3. From this list, choose the one for **InterBase database**. If you have installed InterBase Client and C++Builder 6 Enterprise edition, you will see this option. If you do not see this option in the list, make sure that you installed these products properly or choose another database driver. Click **OK** in this dialog.

4. A new item is created in the left pane under the database alias list. Give a name to the new alias that we just created. I named it IBNative. Right-click this item with the mouse and choose **Apply** from the menu to save the changes. Click **OK** on the confirmation screen.
   The right pane always displays the specific database alias and its parameters that are selected on the left pane. Some of these include the

database name and user ID. The database name here means the specific database (or an instance) that we wish to connect with this alias.

Each database management system has its own way of identifying its database. An InterBase database is identified by the data file with the .gdb extension. An InterBase server or a client application can connect to this database. An Access database is identified by the data file with the .mdb extension. An SQL Server database is identified by its name as created and displayed in the Enterprise Manager Console. An Oracle database is identified by its global database name or SID or the service name as defined in the Net8 Configuration. Among different releases of Oracle, there may be slight variations, and you are advised to check with Oracle documentation. An important thing to remember here is in order to properly create the BDE alias for a database, you should have installed the appropriate client software for that database. If you are not sure of the database name, please check with your database administrator.

5. For the new alias we created, make sure that the database name is properly updated in the right pane.

The new database alias is now ready for use in our application. The entire procedure is demonstrated in Figures 5-6 through 5-9.

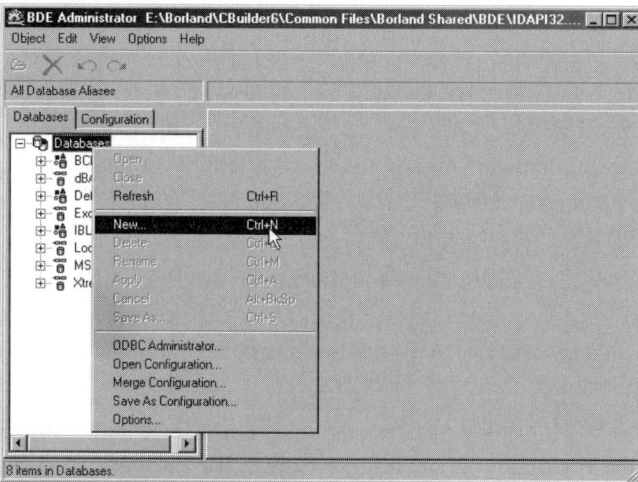

Figure 5-6: Creating a new database alias in the BDE Administrator

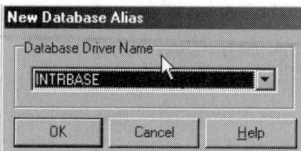

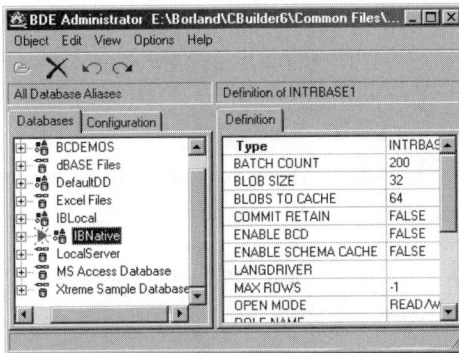

Figure 5-8: Giving an appropriate name to the BDE alias

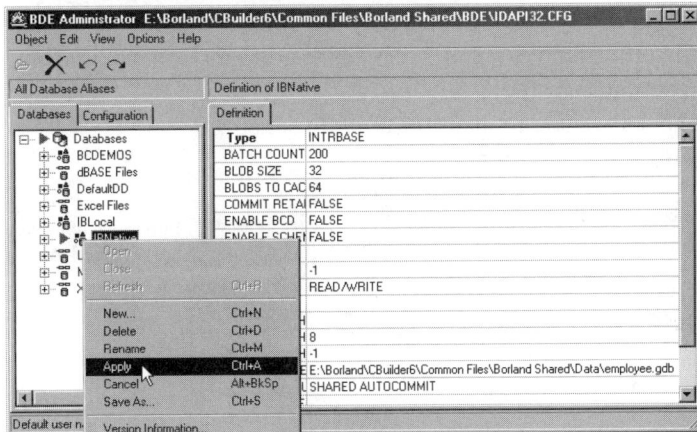

Figure 5-9: Updating the appropriate database name for the BDE alias

Setting Up a BDE Alias for MS Access ODBC Driver

Setting up a BDE alias for a database containing an ODBC driver is similar to setting up one for a BDE native driver. The only additional step required is to set up an ODBC DSN using the ODBC Data Source Administrator Wizard. This wizard is located in the Windows Control Panel and Administrative Tools in Windows 2000. On other Windows operating systems such as Windows NT, Windows 98, and Windows XP, it is located through the Control Panel.

1. Start the ODBC Administration Wizard. When executed, the screen looks like Figure 5-10. In this screen, choose the **System DSN** tab. This tab lists all the system data sources currently defined. A system data source is to ODBC as a BDE alias is to BDE. When we define a system data source, we link a database to the corresponding pre-installed ODBC driver. Now we are trying to define a system data source to a Microsoft Access database.

2. Click the **Add** button. The Create New Data Source screen will be displayed, as shown in Figure 5-11. In this screen, all the pre-installed ODBC drivers are listed. Choose the one that says **Microsoft Access Driver (*.mdb)** and click the **Finish** button.

3. The ODBC Microsoft Access Setup screen is displayed, as shown in Figure 5-12. In this screen, enter a name for the data source and an optional description, and click the **Select** button to choose the database file (*.mdb file) from the desired location. This file is your Access database.

4. After you select your database, click **OK** to complete the setup. Now your ODBC system DSN is ready. Remember that if your database name or location changes, you need to edit this DSN and re-select the correct database file.

   The procedure remains the same to set up a system DSN for any ODBC driver connection.

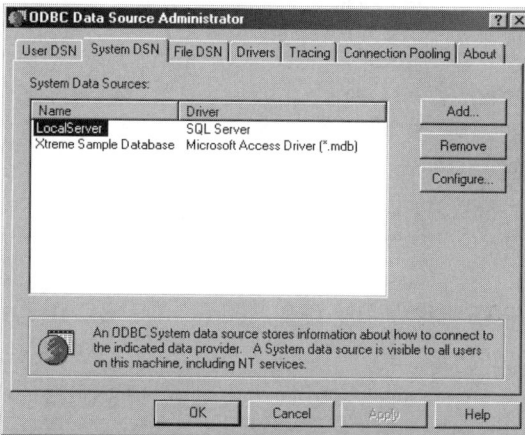

Figure 5-10: ODBC Data Source Administrator dialog

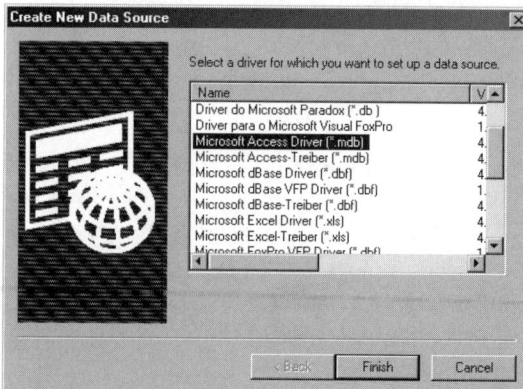

Figure 5-11: Create New Data Source dialog

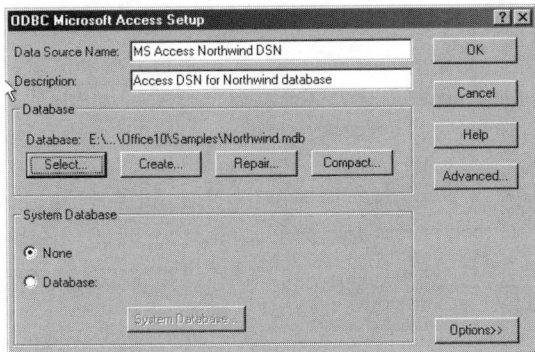

Figure 5-12: ODBC Microsoft Access Setup dialog

Once the ODBC system DSN is set up, the BDE Administrator picks it automatically and displays in the database alias list. You do not have to do anything else.

Sample Application Using BDE Framework

Let's now demonstrate how to use the BDE framework in creating a simple two-tier database application. In this example, we use the BDE alias that we created earlier for the InterBase database, IBNative. Perform the following steps to create the application:

1. Create a new project, and save the files in a location of your choice.

2. Set the height and width of the main form to the size of your choice. I set the height to 470 pixels and width to 385 pixels.

3. From the BDE page of the Component Palette, drop a **TDatabase** and **TTable** onto the form; from the Data Access page, drop a **TDataSource**; from the Data Controls page, drop a **TDBGrid** and **TDBNavigator**; from the Standard page, drop a **TListBox** and two **TLabel** components, and from the Additional page, drop two **TBitBtn** components. You can also use the TButton component in place of TBitBtn. I am using a TBitBtn because I am setting images to the buttons.

4. Set the properties of the TDatabase component: AliasName = **IBNative**; Params: **USER NAME = SYSDBA**; PASSWORD = **masterkey**; LoginPrompt = **false**; DatabaseName = **SampleIBData-Base**. Here I am setting default values to the user name and password as initially set by InterBase during installation. Also, when we set the user name and password either during design time or run time, we can disable the login prompt so that we can avoid the login screen from appearing before connecting the database. For the TDatabase to establish the connection, we have to set either the AliasName or the

DriverName property. In the Object Inspector, the drop-down list displayed for the DriverName property is the same list displayed in the BDE Administrator as configured databases. The items in this list represent general drivers and do not necessarily represent a specific database or database instance. On the contrary, the drop-down list displayed for the AliasName property is the same list of database aliases that we configured in the BDE Administrator. By creating a BDE alias and using it for the AliasName property, we are attempting to connect to the specific database we are interested in.

At this point, we are still not trying to establish a database connection. We will do it in the program.

5. Set the properties of the TTable component: DatabaseName = **SampleIBDataBase**. The list of database names displayed in the Object Inspector for this property contains the database alias names. The TDatabase component that we set up in the previous step is also displayed in the list. For the TTable component to connect to the database, it is not necessary to have a TDatabase component. By assigning a BDE alias for the DatabaseName property itself, we can establish the connection. But having a TDatabase component gives us flexibility so that the database component represents the back-end database and allows us to have control of centralized login. At this point, we do not attempt to set the database table name because we did not establish a database connection in the earlier step.

6. Set the properties of the TDataSource component: DataSet = **Table1**. Here we are setting the table component that we created earlier.

7. Set the properties of BitBtn1: Caption = **Connect**; Name = **ConnectBtn**. Set the Glyph property to a desired bitmap.

8. Set the properties of BitBtn2: Caption = **Disconnect**; Name = **DisconnectBtn**. Set the Glyph property to a desired bitmap.

9. Set the properties of Label1: Caption = **Tables in the Database**. Position this label above the ListBox component.

10. Set the properties of Label2: Caption = **<NULL>**; Visible = **false**. Position this label above the DBGrid component. We will use this label to display the table name programmatically. Therefore, we will make it invisible when the application is started.

11. Set the properties of the TDBGrid component: DataSource = **DataSource1**; Visible = **false**. We will use this grid to display data from the selected table. Therefore, we will make it invisible when the application is started.

12. Set the properties of the TDBNavigator component: DataSource = **DataSource1**; Visible = **false**. We will use this component to navigate the selected table. Therefore, we will make it invisible when the application is started.

13. Set the Caption property of the main form to "**Sample Database Application Using BDE Framework**."

    The main form should now look like Figure 5-13.

14. Write an event handler for the ConnectBtnClick event. In this event handler, we try to connect to the database. If an exception is raised, then we display a message box. If we succeed in connecting to the database, then we display a list of tables in ListBox1 and make the Label2, DBGrid1, and DBNavigator1 components visible, along with disabling ConnectBtn and enabling DisconnectBtn. While displaying the table names in the list box, we purposefully excluded system tables so that we do not do any damage to them in our example.

15. Write an event handler for the DisconnectBtnClick event. In this event handler, clear the list box, disconnect from the database, make the Label2, DBGrid1, and DBNavigator1 components invisible, disable DisconnectBtn, and enable ConnectBtn. If an exception is raised, then we display a message box.

16. Write an event handler for the ListBox1DblClick event. The list box contains names of user tables in the database. Therefore, in this event handler, we extract the name of the selected table, assign it to Table1, and open the table. When we open the table, the contents are automatically displayed in the grid box through the DataSource property, which acts like a conduit between the database table and the data control. Since we assigned the same data source to DBGrid1 and DBNavigator1 at the same time, we will be able to navigate the table data while viewing the same in the grid.

    The cpp and header files for this program are displayed in Listings 5-1 and 5-2, respectively.

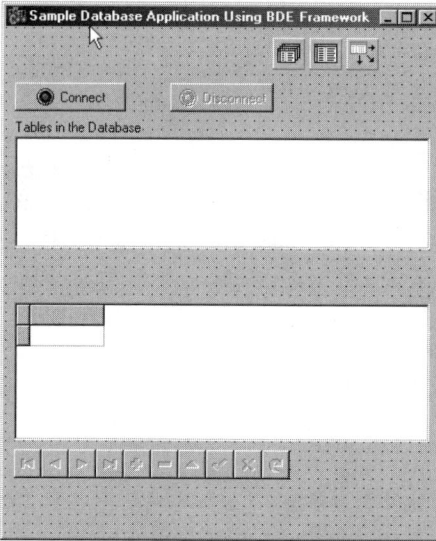

Figure 5-13: The main form of the simple database application using the BDE framework

Listing 5-1: Unit1.cpp

```cpp
//---------------------------------------------------------------------------

#include <vcl.h>
#pragma hdrstop

#include "Unit1.h"
//---------------------------------------------------------------------------
#pragma package(smart_init)
#pragma resource "*.dfm"
TForm1 *Form1;
//---------------------------------------------------------------------------
__fastcall TForm1::TForm1(TComponent* Owner)
                : TForm(Owner)
{
}
//---------------------------------------------------------------------------

void __fastcall TForm1::ConnectBtnClick(TObject *Sender)
{
    // Try connecting to the database. Any exceptions raised
    // will be displayed to the user in the message box.
    try {
        Database1->Connected = true;
        ListBox1->Items->Clear();
        // Display table names in the list box.
        // Do not display system tables.
        Database1->GetTableNames(ListBox1->Items, false);
    }
    catch (Exception& e) {
        MessageDlg(e.Message, mtError,
        TMsgDlgButtons() << mbOK, 0);
        return;
```

```
        }
        ConnectBtn->Enabled = false;
        DisconnectBtn->Enabled = true;
        Label2->Caption = "";
        // Make these controls visible
        Label2->Visible = true;
        DBGrid1->Visible = true;
        DBNavigator1->Visible = true;
}
//---------------------------------------------------------------------------

void __fastcall TForm1::DisconnectBtnClick(TObject *Sender)
{
    // Try disconnecting from the database. Any exceptions raised
    // will be displayed to the user in the message box.
    try {
        if (Database1->Connected) {
            ListBox1->Items->Clear();
            Database1->Connected = false;
        }
    }
    catch (Exception& e) {
            MessageDlg(e.Message, mtError,
            TMsgDlgButtons() << mbOK, 0);
            return;
    }
    ConnectBtn->Enabled = true;
    DisconnectBtn->Enabled = false;

    // Make these controls invisible
    Label2->Visible = false;
    DBGrid1->Visible = false;
    DBNavigator1->Visible = false;
}
//---------------------------------------------------------------------------
void __fastcall TForm1::ListBox1DblClick(TObject *Sender)
{
    // Read the selected table name from the list items
    // Set it to the table name of Table1 and open the table.
    TListBox* fListBox = (TListBox*)Sender;
    int selectedItem = fListBox->ItemIndex;
    if (selectedItem < 0)
        return;
    AnsiString fTableName = fListBox->Items->Strings[selectedItem];
    try {
        if (fTableName != "") {
            Table1->Active = false;
            Table1->TableName = fTableName;
            Table1->Active = true;
            Label2->Caption = "Data from Table " + fTableName;
        }
    }
    catch (Exception& e) {
            MessageDlg(e.Message, mtError,
            TMsgDlgButtons() << mbOK, 0);
            return;
    }
```

```
    }
//------------------------------------------------------------------------
```

Listing 5-2: Unit1.h

```
//------------------------------------------------------------------------

#ifndef Unit1H
#define Unit1H
//------------------------------------------------------------------------
#include <Classes.hpp>
#include <Controls.hpp>
#include <StdCtrls.hpp>
#include <Forms.hpp>
#include <Buttons.hpp>
#include <DB.hpp>
#include <DBTables.hpp>
#include <DBGrids.hpp>
#include <Grids.hpp>
#include <DBCtrls.hpp>
#include <ExtCtrls.hpp>
//------------------------------------------------------------------------
class TForm1 : public TForm
{
__published:              // IDE-managed components
        TDatabase *Database1;
        TTable *Table1;
        TDataSource *DataSource1;
        TBitBtn *ConnectBtn;
        TBitBtn *DisconnectBtn;
    TListBox *ListBox1;
    TLabel *Label1;
    TDBGrid *DBGrid1;
    TLabel *Label2;
    TDBNavigator *DBNavigator1;
        void __fastcall ConnectBtnClick(TObject *Sender);
    void __fastcall DisconnectBtnClick(TObject *Sender);
    void __fastcall ListBox1DblClick(TObject *Sender);
private:                  // User declarations
public:                   // User declarations
        __fastcall TForm1(TComponent* Owner);
};
//------------------------------------------------------------------------
extern PACKAGE TForm1 *Form1;
//------------------------------------------------------------------------
#endif
```

In this example, we have seen how a two-tier database application is developed. Typically in a two-tier application, we write all the business logic, including database logic, in the client. The database tier does not offer anything more than what a database system offers. The BDE run-time files have to be distributed on every client machine. This makes the client application bulky.

Creating BDE Components Programmatically

Like other VCL components, BDE components can also be created and used programmatically during run time, such as establishing a database connection, opening existing tables, and creating new tables. Take a look at an example where we create the database component using the BDE alias definition IBNative and create a table called Phone_Book_Entries programmatically.

The cpp and header files for this program are displayed in Listings 5-3 and 5-4, respectively.

Listing 5-3: Unit1.cpp

```cpp
//------------------------------------------------------------------------
// Example code to create a table dynamically
// to store phone book entries.
// This code should be compiled in a form-based application
//------------------------------------------------------------------------

#include <vcl.h>
#pragma hdrstop

#include "Unit1.h"
//------------------------------------------------------------------------
#pragma package(smart_init)
#pragma resource "*.dfm"
TForm1 *Form1;
//------------------------------------------------------------------------
__fastcall TForm1::TForm1(TComponent* Owner)
    : TForm(Owner)
{
}
//------------------------------------------------------------------------

void __fastcall TForm1::Button1Click(TObject *Sender)
{
    try {
        TDatabase* newDb = new TDatabase(this);
        newDb->AliasName = "IBNative";
        newDb->Params->Add("USER NAME=SYSDBA");
        newDb->Params->Add("PASSWORD=masterkey");
        newDb->DatabaseName = "SampleDB";
        newDb->LoginPrompt = false;
        newDb->Connected = true;
    }
    catch (Exception& e) {
        MessageDlg(e.Message, mtError,
        TMsgDlgButtons() << mbOK, 0);
        return;
    }
    try {
        TTable* newTable = new TTable(this);
        newTable->Active = false;
        newTable->DatabaseName = "SampleDB";
        newTable->TableName = "Phone_Book_Entries";
        if (!newTable->Exists) {
```

```
                newTable->FieldDefs->Clear();
                TFieldDef *newField = newTable->FieldDefs->AddFieldDef();
                newField->Name = "First_Name";
                newField->DataType = ftString;
                newField->Size = 25;
                newField->Required = true;

                newField = newTable->FieldDefs->AddFieldDef();
                newField->Name = "Last_Name";
                newField->DataType = ftString;
                newField->Size = 25;
                newField->Required = true;

                newField = newTable->FieldDefs->AddFieldDef();
                newField->Name = "Home_Phone";
                newField->DataType = ftString;
                newField->Size = 25;
                newField->Required = true;

                newField = newTable->FieldDefs->AddFieldDef();
                newField->Name = "Work_Phone";
                newField->DataType = ftString;
                newField->Size = 25;
                newField->Required = true;

                newTable->CreateTable();
        }
    }
    catch (Exception& e) {
        MessageDlg(e.Message, mtError,
        TMsgDlgButtons() << mbOK, 0);
        return;
    }
}
//---------------------------------------------------------------------------
```

Listing 5-4: Unit1.h

```
//---------------------------------------------------------------------------

#ifndef Unit1H
#define Unit1H
//---------------------------------------------------------------------------
#include <Classes.hpp>
#include <Controls.hpp>
#include <StdCtrls.hpp>
#include <Forms.hpp>
#include <DB.hpp>
#include <DBTables.hpp>
//---------------------------------------------------------------------------
class TForm1 : public TForm
{
__published:            // IDE-managed components
    TButton *Button1;
    void    fastcall Button1Click(TObject *Sender);
private:                 // User declarations
public:                  // User declarations
    __fastcall TForm1(TComponent* Owner);
};
//---------------------------------------------------------------------------
```

```
  extern PACKAGE TForm1 *Form1;
//-----------------------------------------------------------------------------
  #endif
```

ActiveX Data Objects (ADO) Framework—dbGo

Microsoft ADO Components

Now we will focus our attention on the ADO framework. The basis for the ADO framework is the Microsoft ActiveX Data Objects concepts, and it works in conjunction with COM technology. ADO is a high-level, easy-to-use interface to OLE DB, which is a low-level, high-performance interface to a variety of data stores. Also, ADO provides a layer of abstraction between the client or middle-tier application and the low-level OLE DB interfaces and uses a small set of automation objects. ADO and OLE DB both can work with relational (tabular) and hierarchical (stream) data.

The components of this framework, as implemented by Microsoft, are Connection, Command, Recordset, Record, Stream, Parameter, Field, Property and Error objects, and Fields, Properties, Parameters, and Errors collections.

Simplified Borland ADO Components

Borland implemented a robust interface to this framework that fits very well within the VCL component architecture. In this exercise, Borland has really done very commendable work. We can use our VCL-based skills in implementing ADO-based database applications without much knowledge of ADO architecture or COM architecture. Here we discuss Borland ADO components.

How Do We Make a Database Connection?

TADOConnection is the component that should be used to establish a database connection with any kind of data store that has an OLE DB driver installed on the system. Functionally, this component can be considered on par with the TDatabase component of the BDE framework, though there are differences. Multiple dataset objects in an application can share a single connection component.

The ConnectionString property represents a set of connection parameters (separated by a semicolon), as expected by the ADO framework. A typical connection string to connect to an SQL Server 2000 database is shown in Listing 5-5. The ConnectionString is an AnsiString object containing the string value, as mentioned.

Listing 5-5: Connection string for SQL Server 2000 database

```
Provider=SQLOLEDB.1;Password=password;Persist Security Info=True;User ID=userid;
Initial Catalog=dbname;Data Source=WIN2KSERVER;Use Procedure for Prepare=1;
Auto Translate=True;Packet Size=4096;Workstation ID=WORKSTN_ID;
Use Encryption for Data=False;Tag with column collation when possible=False
```

In this string, the parameter Provider represents the OLE DB provider name (or OLE DB driver), Initial Catalog represents the database name, Data Source represents the server machine name where the SQL Server is installed, and Workstation ID represents the client machine name that is going to open the connection with the server.

Listing 5-6 displays a typical connection string for an Oracle8i database.

Listing 5-6: Connection string for Oracle8i database

```
Provider=OraOLEDB.Oracle.1;Password=password;Persist Security Info=True;
User ID=userid;Data Source=orcl_sid
```

In the connection string for an Oracle database, the Data Source parameter represents an Oracle SID or global database name or a service name as defined on the client machine using the Oracle Net8 configuration assistant. A connection string can be built using the Data Link Properties dialog from the IDE, or it can be built manually in a text editor. If we are building the connection string manually we need to know all the necessary parameters that we have to set in order to establish the connection. I always recommend building the connection string using the IDE and then saving it to a data link file because the wizard takes care of most of the required parameters. After building the string using the wizard, we can manually edit it if we need to make changes later. The wizard can be initiated by clicking the ellipsis button next to the ConnectionString property in the Object Inspector.

The ConnectionTimeout property represents the time (in seconds) that can expire before a connection attempt can be considered unsuccessful. The default timeout period is 15 seconds. If a connection could not be established before the timeout period, an exception is thrown.

Mode is another useful property. It indicates the mode in which the connection should be opened; for example, mode cmReadWrite should be used to allow both read and write operations through the connection, mode cmShareExclusive should be used to prevent others from opening a connection while this connection is active, and so on. However, the mode is also governed by the user ID and password we are using in the connection string and the level of access provided by the underlying database for that user ID. If the selected mode does not match the permissions given to that user by the database, an exception will be raised.

Most of the server-type databases support transactions, and the ADO framework also extends that support. A *transaction* is a set of tasks (such as INSERT, UPDATE, DELETE, and SELECT) grouped together to represent a logical unit of work so that all the tasks must be executed successfully to complete a given task. If all the tasks are executed successfully, the transaction will be *committed* to the database, which means all the updates are posted to the database. If any one of the tasks in the transaction fails, then the transaction will be *rolled back*, so none of the tasks are posted to the database. This kind of behavior is required to ensure data integrity within the application.

In large enterprise-level applications, several transactions will be in process at the same time, initiated by different clients. The *transaction isolation level* determines how a transaction interacts with other simultaneous transactions when they work with the same tables and how much it can see the work performed by other transactions. A transaction isolation level of ilReadUncommitted means the transaction can see the uncommitted work performed by other transactions; a transaction isolation level of ilReadCommitted (and ilCursorStability) means the transaction can see the changes performed by other transactions only after they are committed; a transaction isolation level of ilSerializable means that the transactions are conducted in isolation from other transactions; and a transaction isolation level of ilRepeatableRead means that changes made in other transactions are visible only after they are committed and the dataset is refreshed by requerying. The IsolationLevel property of the TADOConnection component helps us in this regard. However, the transaction isolation levels supported by the underlying database take precedence in determining the isolation level actually used while processing a transaction. Also, the methods BeginTrans(), CommitTrans(), and RollbackTrans() provide support to implement transactions. The BeginTrans() method initiates a new transaction. All the database activity performed through this connection component will be committed to the database when CommitTrans() is executed successfully. Execution of RollbackTrans() cancels database updates and rolls back the database to the sync point where it was before the previous BeginTrans() was executed.

The ConnectionObject property gives us direct access to the underlying Connection object of the Microsoft ADO framework. We have to remember that by using Borland's ADO framework, we are making our life easier, but at the same time, we can directly access the underlying Microsoft ADO objects through the interfaces provided by C++Builder if we have enough knowledge of these low-level objects, if we need functionality that is not exposed by Borland's ADO objects, and if we are confident that we are not going to "mess up" the object's contents. In my opinion, most of the time we do not have to access the low-level ADO objects.

Other properties include ConnectOptions to indicate whether the connection should be established synchronously or asynchronously, Keep-Connection to indicate whether the connection should be kept alive with the database or not when no datasets are open, and CursorLocation to indicate whether we wish to open a client-side cursor or server-side cursor.

The connection is initiated by setting the Connected property to true or executing the Open() method of the connection component. A variation of the Open() method also accepts the user login ID and password as two parameters, which will override the values specified in the connection string. When we explicitly pass the user ID and password through the connection component, it is recommended that the LoginPrompt property be set to false to avoid the default login dialog provided by C++Builder. You can also implement your own login dialog to be used in your application to suit your business needs.

Though we set all the necessary properties of the connection component before we attempt to establish the connection, we still get an opportunity to programmatically control any of the properties before making the connection by implementing the OnWillConnect event handler. Similarly, the OnConnectionComplete event handler is executed after successfully establishing the connection.

Obtaining Metadata from the Database

The connection component provides methods to extract simple metadata from the database. The GetTableNames(TStrings* list, bool sysTables = false) method retrieves the names of all the tables in the database as a list, which is passed as the first parameter to the method. The second parameter is a Boolean variable and indicates whether or not the list should include system tables. Similar to this method is the GetProcedureNames(TStrings* list) method, which retrieves all the stored procedure names, as defined in the database. The third method in this category is GetFieldNames(Ansi-String tableName, TStrings* list), which retrieves the field names for the specific database table. There is another method, OpenSchema(TSchema-Info schema, const OleVariant &restrictions, const OleVariant &schemaId, TADODataSet* dataset), which can be used by a variety of schema info types, such as catalogs, table constraints, check constraints, referential constraints, and many more.

Here I will discuss more on the OpenSchema() method with example syntax so that you can make use of this method more effectively. This method is a VCL wrapper to the underlying ADO connection object's OpenSchema() method, and therefore the usage requirements of this method are very much guided by the underlying implementation.

The first parameter of this method is the type of schema information you are interested in retrieving. Examples of this include siTables, siColumns, siIndexes, and siTableConstraints, among others. If you use siTables, the method retrieves metadata about tables in the database; if you use siColumns, the method retrieves metadata about columns in the tables and their properties; if you use siIndexes, you will get index definitions on the tables; and if you use siTableConstraints, you will get the constraints (such as unique and check constraints) defined on the tables. The record set returned is placed in the TADODataSet component provided as the fourth parameter to the method. This record set is a structure containing columns defined in the MSDN documentation and varies depending on the schema information we are requesting. For example, if we use the siColumns value for the first parameter, the resulting record set will contain 28 columns. I will discuss some of these column names here, and I advise you to refer to MSDN documentation for the rest. The COLUMNS record set contains columns such as TABLE_CATALOG, TABLE_SCHEMA, TABLE_NAME, COLUMN_NAME, ORDINAL_POSITION, IS_NULLABLE, DATA_TYPE, CHARACTER_MAXIMUM_LENGTH, NUMERIC_PRECISION, and NUMERIC_SCALE, among others. TABLE_CATALOG represents the catalog name if the underlying database supports catalogs. In the case of Microsoft SQL Server, the catalog name is the database name itself. TABLE_SCHEMA is usually the owner of the table schema. Other names mentioned above are self-explanatory.

For each of the schema types that we may request, there are some restrictions that we may impose in our method call so that the returned data can be filtered. For example, for the siColumns schema info, the restriction columns are TABLE_CATALOG, TABLE_SCHEMA, TABLE_NAME, and COLUMN_NAME. We can consider the restriction columns similar to the WHERE clause of a SELECT statement. If we want to use the restriction columns, we can use one or more of them in any combination. Since ADO is a COM-based architecture, VCL accepts these restrictions as an OleVariant data type. For example, we can create an array of these restrictions as a single OleVariant object and send it. Listing 5-7 gives an example of passing the restrictions to the Open Schema() method. The third parameter to the method is the GUID (globally unique ID) of a provider-schema query not defined by the OLE DB specification and should only be used if the first parameter is siProviderSpecific. In all other cases, this parameter is not used, and hence we can use EmptyParam in its place. EmptyParam is a global variable defined in the SYSTEM unit; it indicates that the optional parameter is not used in the current method call. We can also use Empty-Param in place of the second parameter, indicating that we do not want to put any restrictions on the returned metadata record set; in this case, all the records in the specific schema query are retrieved.

Listing 5-7

```
    int bounds[2] = {0,3};
    OleVariant ov1 = VarArrayCreate(bounds,1,varVariant);
    ov1.PutElement("employees",2);
    ADOConnection1->OpenSchema(siColumns, ov1, EmptyParam, ADODataSet1);
```

It is important to note that we must honor the ordinal position of the restrictions when we set them in our array variables. In the current example, TABLE_NAME is the third restriction that I am setting, and hence I am using the index value 2 in the PutElement method call on the OleVariant (since the array is 0 index based). Similarly, if I want to use the restriction on the TABLE_SCHEMA column, I will use the index value 1 since its ordinal position is 2.

Note: Please note that the specific schema info queries available through an ADO connection object are dependent on the underlying OLE DB provider. If we try to use a schema info query that is not supported by the underlying OLE DB provider, an exception is raised. It is my observation that some of the OLE DB providers do not support all the schema info queries. Therefore, I advise the use of database-specific system views in order to get more granular detail on the metadata, rather than relying on the OpenSchema() method of the ADO Connection object. You may also use the ADOX objects provided by MDAC (Microsoft Data Access Components) as an extension to the ADO. ADOX objects are COM components and can be imported from their type libraries. ADOX components are not in the scope of the current discussion. However, an example is provided later in this chapter to demonstrate the use of the database's system views to extract more granular metadata.

> **Note:** You may notice a similarity in the schema info queries
> and the INFORMATION_SCHEMA views provided in Microsoft
> SQL Server architecture. This similarity may be attributed to the
> fact that both the OLE DB specification and the SQL Server
> database have been provided by the same vendor, Microsoft.

What Dataset Objects are Available in the ADO Framework?

TCustomADODataSet is derived from TDataSet and serves as an ancestor class for all the dataset objects in the ADO framework. Since it is a virtualized base class, it cannot be instantiated as an object. It publishes most of the properties, methods, and events from the TDataSet class and adds new properties, methods, and events relevant to the framework. In this section, we discuss the new features added to this class.

The Connection property should be used to set the TADOConnection component that provides an established connection to the database, or the ConnectionString property can be set similar to the way that we did for the connection component. The property MaxRecords should be set to indicate the maximum number of records to be returned in the result set. A value of 0 should be used for unlimited number of records.

The MarshalOptions property should be used to tell which records must be sent back to the server when the local record set is modified and we are using the client-side cursor. A value of moMarshalAll indicates that all the records in the local record set must be sent back to the server, and a value of moMarshalModifiedOnly indicates that only the modified records must be sent to the server.

The IndexName property indicates the currently active index on the record set. By setting the index name to a specific index, the records in the record set can be retrieved in the order specified by the index. It is recommended that the dataset be closed before setting or changing this property, as some databases may throw an exception if you try to change the index while the dataset is open and connected to the database in online mode. Setting this value to an empty string retains the natural order of records in the dataset or makes the primary index of the table active, as determined by the underlying database.

The RecordSet property is Borland's implementation of an interface to the ADO RecordSet object and is published by this class. Similarly, the Properties property is Borland's implementation of an interface to the ADO Properties object. The majority of circumstances do not mandate the need to use these properties. But users familiar with the ADO technology may try to use them if they are convinced that they need them. Another useful property is RecordStatus, which gives us the status of the current row in the record set. The status rsOK indicates that the record update was successful; the status rsNew indicates that the row is a new insert into the recordset; the status rsModified indicates that the record is modified, and so on.

The Sort property contains a string representation of sort order on the record set. We can specify sorting on multiple fields; each of them can be controlled individually, as ascending or descending sort. For example, we can specify a sort string "First_Name ASC, Age DESC" while retrieving employee data from the Employee table. The retrieved rows are sorted first by First_Name in ascending order and then by Age in descending order. While sorting is for ordering the retrieved records, index-based retrieval applies to the retrieving sequence from the database.

TCustomADODataSet introduces properties relevant to command execution and setting parameters for commands to be executed, but it does not publish these properties. Rather, the descendant classes publish these properties. The different dataset objects derived from TCustomADODataSet are TADOTable, TADOQuery, TADODataSet, and TADOStoredProc.

TADOTable implements a base table, and when connected to a database, retrieves data from an underlying table or view. Most of the server-based databases consider views on par with tables, at least for reading purposes. In such cases, this component can be used to retrieve records from a view. However, the update criteria are governed by the rules of the underlying database. There are some databases that consider views as different object types. In those cases, you may not be able to access the views using this component, but other dataset components can be used. When connected online with the database, changes made to the records in the TADOTable component can be applied directly to the base table in the database and may also be incorporated within a transaction through event handlers.

The TableName property indicates the name of the base table in the database. Before trying to open the dataset, this property must be set to a valid table name. During design time, the list of pre-existing tables is displayed in the Object Inspector for this property after successfully establishing the connection. The ReadOnly property of this component may be set to true to make the dataset non-modifiable, even though the underlying base table is modifiable. If the table is the child of a master-child relationship, the MasterSource property indicates the TDataSource component whose DataSet property is the master table.

The TADOQuery component lets us execute an SQL statement on the database objects, including metadata objects. The statements we can use include SELECT, UPDATE, DELETE, ALTER TABLE, and CREATE TABLE. The property SQL is a TStrings object and contains an SQL statement spanning across several lines. There is no limit to the size of an SQL statement. There may be restrictions imposed by the underlying database on nested SQL statements or JOINS. Therefore, if the SQL statement fails at the database level, an exception will be raised. If the SQL statement contains input or output parameters (or both), then these parameters can be passed by setting values to the Parameters collection property. After setting the SQL statement and parameter values, we execute the query by executing the method ExecSQL(). If the SQL statement is of SELECT type, the retrieved records can be navigated using the TDataSet navigation methods, and the fields can be accessed and manipulated by the corresponding properties and methods of TDataSet that we have seen earlier in this chapter. If the SQL statement does not retrieve any rows, the successful execution of the method indicates that the action specified in the SQL statement is complete. In addition, the RowsAffected property indicates how many rows were updated or deleted by the SQL statement. If there was an error in the update or delete action, a corresponding exception will be raised, and RowsAffected is set to –1.

This is a very appropriate component that we frequently use for back-end programming in a server module and to implement transaction-based processing. An example shown in the next section will help you understand the typical use of this component.

The TADOStoredProc component should be used to execute a stored procedure on the database. Stored procedures are more versatile and complex than queries because they are programs written in a procedural language (as supported by the database); they handle multiple and complex queries with the help of control structures that are precompiled and stored in the database as objects. Use of stored procedures is very popular in large systems, as they bring about performance improvement due to their precompiled nature.

The ProcedureName property is a string containing the name of the stored procedure to be executed on the database. A stored procedure may have input or output parameters or both. After setting the procedure name, we set the input parameters using the Parameters property and call the ExecProc() method to execute the procedure. If the procedure returns any output parameter values, they are available in the Parameters property in the corresponding placeholders that we created earlier. If the execution of the stored procedure returns a record set, it is available in the RecordSet property, and we can navigate it using the TDataSet navigation methods and access the fields and their values using the corresponding properties and methods discussed earlier.

The TADODataSet component is the more generic type used to retrieve data from one or more tables or views. If we are accessing a table, the CommandText property represents the table name, and CommandType represents what type of command we are executing using the component. The typical values of CommandType are cmdText to indicate an SQL statement, cmdTable to indicate a table name, cmdStoredProc to indicate a stored procedure name, and so on. Based on the command type we are setting, we have to populate the value for the CommandText property with an SQL statement, table name, or stored procedure name accordingly. This component is not suitable for executing data manipulation language (DML) statements, such as INSERT, UPDATE, and DELETE. The RDS-Connection property identifies the Microsoft Remote Data Service (RDS) Data Space object, as implemented by the TRDSConnection class.

The TADOCommand Component

The TADOCommand component is a more generic type and is derived directly from TComponent. Therefore, it does not have any dataset-related behavior like the other dataset objects we have discussed so far. But it can be used to execute a command that returns a record set. In that case, the record set must be assigned to another TADODataSet component's RecordSet property in order to access the returned records. To avoid such complications, it is recommended not to use this component to execute commands on databases that return a record set. Ideally, this component must be used to execute data definition language (DDL) statements or SQL statements and stored procedures that do not return a record set.

The CommandObject property identifies the Microsoft ADO's Command object through Borland's implementation of the interface. Another useful property is ExecuteOptions, which specify the characteristics of an execution operation, such as eoAsyncExecute to execute the command asynchronously, eoExecuteNoRecords to discard any records returned by the command execution, and so on. Other properties are similar to the TCustomADODataSet class.

Sample Application Using ADO Components

Now I will demonstrate how to establish an ADO connection using the IDE and how to use this connection string in a console application. Steps to establish the connection are discussed here. If you have SQL Server 2000 installed on your system, the example can be run directly without much modification. Otherwise, you will have to change the connection parameters, database name, and table and column names specific to your database.

1. Create a new Windows GUI application. There is no need to save this project, since we are not going to continue with the GUI application in this example.

2. From the ADO page in the Component Palette, drop an **ADOConnection** component on the form. Double-click the component or click the ellipsis next to the ConnectionString property of the component in the Object Inspector. This will bring up the wizard that helps us build the connection string. The screen looks like Figure 5-14. In this screen, select the **Use Connection String** radio button and click the **Build** button.

3. The Data Link Properties dialog is displayed, as shown in Figure 5-15. It is the first page in the dialog and is used to select the provider for our database connection. In this screen, select the **Microsoft OLE DB Provider for SQL Server** item in the list and click the **Next** button.

4. The next page in the dialog is displayed as shown in Figure 5-16. In this page, enter the server name (localhost if your database is on the same machine where you are running C++Builder 6) and database login information. After entering these details, the databases currently hosted by the server are listed in item 3 for the Select the database on the server radio button. Choose the database of your choice. I chose the Northwind database, which is installed automatically during SQL Server 2000 installation.

5. Click the **Test Connection** button. If the parameters are entered properly and the database server is running, the connection test succeeds and you will see a message box similar to Figure 5-17.

6. Click **OK** to close the message box, and click the **OK** button in the Data Link Properties dialog box to close the dialog and assign the connection string automatically to the ConnectionString property in the Object Inspector.

7. Now copy the ConnectionString text into a text file and save it. I named this file connection.txt, since it contains the connection string.

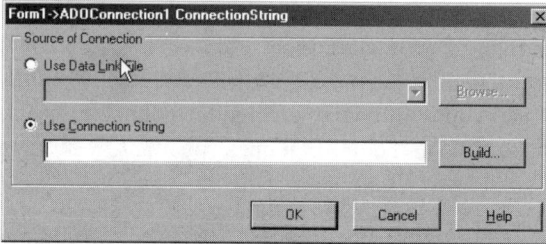

Figure 5-14: Wizard to build ADO Connection string

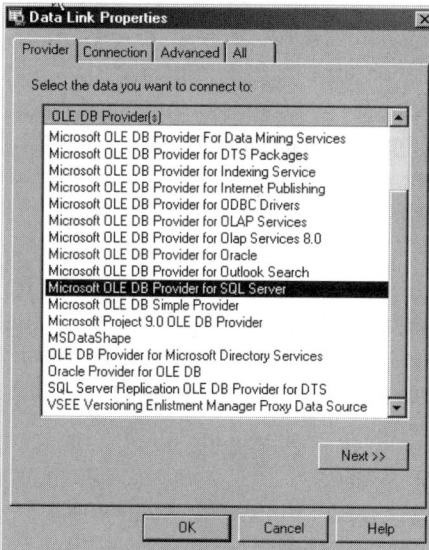

Figure 5-15: Data Link Properties dialog Provider page

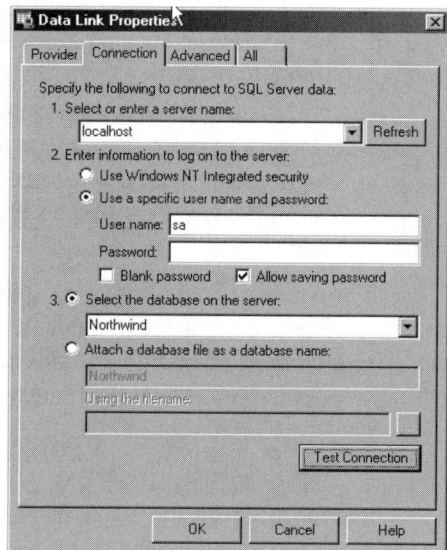

Figure 5-16: Data Link Properties dialog Connection page

Figure 5-17: Test connection success message box

ADO components are used in a Windows form-based application very similar to a BDE-based application. However, in this demonstration, I intend to show you how ADO components can be used in a server module without having to use forms. The Forms.hpp file is included to enable the use of the application global variable.

> **Note:**   Please note that BDE components also can be used in a console-based application in a way similar to ADO components demonstrated in this example.

Listing 5-8 is a console application that I developed to demonstrate this concept. The same functionality can be incorporated in a DLL or Borland package application. In this application, I demonstrated several concepts that we discussed in this section.

First, I demonstrated the use of ADO components in a console-based application. When we create ADO components programmatically and not through the IDE, we have to call the Windows COM library initialization function CoInitializeEx(void* pvReserved, DWORD dwCoInit) before creating any of the ADO components. This is because ADO components are built upon the COM architecture, and the COM library must be initialized at the beginning of the program and uninitialized at the end of the program. The function to uninitialize the COM library is CoUninitialize(). There are two parameters to initialize the COM library; the first parameter is reserved by Microsoft for later use and should be NULL in our call, and the second parameter indicates the threading model that our program should use, such as COINIT_MULTITHREADED for the multi-threaded model and COINIT_APARTMENTTHREADED for the apartment-threaded model. There are no parameters to be passed while unitializing the COM library.

Second, I demonstrated how to use a connection string stored in a text file, create a connection component programmatically, and establish the connection. Third, I demonstrated the use of TADOQuery and setting parameters to the query, and finally we have seen how simple it is to extract metadata from the database's system views. Metadata can be extracted from any database in a similar way; the only difference is the names of the system views and their columns.

Listing 5-8: Unit1.cpp

```
//---------------------------------------------------------------------------
// This example is designed to explain the use of ADO components in a server
// module, completely in background mode.
//---------------------------------------------------------------------------

#include <vcl.h>
#include <iostream>
#include <ADODB.hpp>
#include <DB.hpp>
#include <Forms.hpp>
#include <memory>
#pragma hdrstop

using std::cout;
//---------------------------------------------------------------------------
```

```cpp
#pragma argsused
int main(int argc, char* argv[])
{
    if (argc < 2) {
        cout << "Usage : <program name> <option> \n";
        cout << "Option - 1 for sample column values \n";
        cout << "         - 2 for table meta data \n";
        return EXIT_SUCCESS;
    }

    const AnsiString option = argv[1];

    // Initialize the COM library, and the Application
    CoInitializeEx(NULL, COINIT_APARTMENTTHREADED);
    Application->Initialize();
    Application->Run();

    // Create the ADO connection object
    TADOConnection* adoConn = new TADOConnection(Application);

    // Open the connection parameter file and read - begin
    const AnsiString connParamFile = "connection.txt";
    std::auto_ptr<TFileStream> connParamFileStream(
        new TFileStream(connParamFile, fmOpenRead)
        );
    const std::size_t size = connParamFileStream->Size;
    char* buffer = new char[size+10];
    try
    {
        connParamFileStream->Read((void*)buffer, size);
        strcat(buffer, "\0");
        adoConn->ConnectionString = buffer;
        delete [] buffer; buffer = NULL;

        // Read the connection string from the file - complete

        // connect to the database
        adoConn->LoginPrompt = false;
        adoConn->Connected = true;

        if (option == "1") {
            // Create a table component and open a table
            TADOTable* adoTable = new TADOTable(Application);
            adoTable->Connection = adoConn;
            adoTable->TableName = "Customers";
            adoTable->Active = true;
            cout << "Sample data retrieval is in process ...\n";

            // retrieve data from the table
            for (int i=0; i < adoTable->RecordCount; i++) {
                cout << "Customer ID : ";
                cout << adoTable->FieldByName("CustomerID")->AsString.c_str();
                cout << "   ";
                cout << "Contact Name: ";
                cout << adoTable->FieldByName("ContactName")->AsString.c_str();
                cout << "\n";
                adoTable->Next();
            }
            delete adoTable;
```

```
                MessageDlg("Data Extraction is complete ...", mtInformation,
                    TMsgDlgButtons() << mbOK, 0);
        }
        else if (option == "2") {
            // Create a query component and open a table
            TADOQuery* adoQuery = new TADOQuery(Application);
            adoQuery->Connection = adoConn;
            AnsiString queryStr = "SELECT DATA_TYPE, CHARACTER_MAXIMUM_LENGTH, ";
            queryStr += "NUMERIC_PRECISION, NUMERIC_SCALE, IS_NULLABLE ";
            queryStr += "FROM INFORMATION_SCHEMA.COLUMNS ";
            queryStr += "WHERE TABLE_NAME = :table AND COLUMN_NAME = :column";
            cout << "Sample Meta data retrieval is in process ...\n";

            adoQuery->Close();
            adoQuery->SQL->Clear();
            adoQuery->SQL->Add(queryStr);
            adoQuery->Parameters->ParamByName("table")->Value = "Customers";
            adoQuery->Parameters->ParamByName("column")->Value = "ContactName";
            adoQuery->Open();
            const AnsiString dataType = adoQuery->FieldByName("DATA_TYPE")->AsString;
            const int maxLength = adoQuery->FieldByName("CHARACTER_MAXIMUM_LENGTH")
                            ->AsInteger;
            const int precision = adoQuery->FieldByName("NUMERIC_PRECISION")->AsInteger;
            const int scale = adoQuery->FieldByName("NUMERIC_SCALE")->AsInteger;
            const AnsiString isNullable = adoQuery->FieldByName("IS_NULLABLE")->AsString;

            cout << "Table Name     : Customers\n";
            cout << "Column Name    : ContactName\n";
            cout << "Data Type      : " << dataType.c_str() << "\n";
            cout << "Max Length     : " << maxLength << "\n";
            cout << "Precision      : " << precision << "\n";
            cout << "Scale          : " << scale  << "\n";
            cout << "Is Nullable ?  : " << isNullable.c_str() << "\n";

            delete adoQuery;
            MessageDlg("Sample Meta Data Extraction is complete ...", mtInformation,
                TMsgDlgButtons() << mbOK, 0);
        }
    }
    catch (Exception& e)
    {
        Application->ShowException(&e);
        CoUninitialize();
        delete [] buffer;
        return EXIT_FAILURE;
    }

    // Uninitialize the COM library and free the resources
    CoUninitialize();
    return EXIT_SUCCESS;
}
//--------------------------------------------------------------------------
```

Summary

We started the chapter with a discussion on general concepts of database development and two-tier, three-tier, and multi-tier applications, followed by VCL's architecture for database development. In the VCL's database development architecture, we discussed the similarities between the different database development frameworks, BDE, ADO, dbExpress, and IBExpress components. We have also learned the general features provided by the base classes TCustomConnection and TDataSet, as used by their descendant classes in different frameworks.

We spent considerable time in understanding the dataset states, synchronous and asynchronous modes, and dataset properties, methods, and events. Then our discussion continued on data controls and data sources.

Next, we focused our attention on the BDE framework, in which we demonstrated how to set up BDE aliases for a native SQL Links driver and an ODBC data source. Then I demonstrated an example application using the BDE framework.

We continued our discussion with the ADO framework and learned how Borland's ADO components simplified the Microsoft ADO framework, followed by the ADO component suite, a demonstration of establishing database connection, and a console application using ADO components.

Chapter 6

Advanced Database Development

Introduction

In the previous chapter, we discussed the traditional BDE framework along with Borland's implementation of Microsoft ADO objects. VCL database architecture provides a similarity in the components designed in each of these architectures. This similarity makes it easy for developers to migrate systems developed using one framework to the other, in addition to the ability to develop complex interfaces. In the current enterprise development environment, there is a continuous need for application migration due to new and enhanced database architectures coming up on the market. For various internal reasons, several organizations have, and are continuing to have, a mix of database systems running in their corporate environments. Often, a particular database is more suitable for working with a particular framework, though most of the databases work with more than one particular framework. As developers, it is our job to continuously support the organizations with a mix of frameworks.

We will devote this chapter to two more database frameworks developed by Borland for different purposes. While IBExpress framework is exclusively developed for Borland's InterBase database, the dbExpress framework is the most recent addition to the VCL's database architecture. The IBExpress components interact with InterBase libraries directly, instead of connecting through an intermediate layer, such as ODBC or ADO, and therefore provide a very efficient interface with the database. The dbExpress components are unique in the sense that they are designed to provide a unidirectional interface with the database servers and are very suitable to work with intermediate provider components.

Data Access Components

The components in the Data Access page on the Component Palette play a vital role in advanced database development. In this section, we discuss these components in detail. Understanding the data access components in depth helps us build client and server modules in a multi-tier application.

What is TClientDataSet?

The TClientDataSet component implements a database-independent dataset. The source of data for this component is multi-fold; it can obtain data from a provider component of a server module or from data files, or it can work as an in-memory table. When it works in conjunction with a provider component, the client dataset functions like a data consumer located in the client module. The provider, however, plays the role of server module. When it works with data files or as an in-memory table, it functions like a stand-alone dataset. This feature of the client dataset enables us to create briefcase model applications, where we can retrieve the data from a provider when the application is online with the server, save the data to one or more data files, and detach the client module from the server module. Now the client module can be restarted in offline mode (with the assumption that we developed the application to work in offline mode) when the user is not connected to the server. In the offline mode, the user can work with a local copy of the dataset(s), save them to local disk, and when connected to the server again, the dataset(s) can be synchronized with the server to resolve updates made by the client applications. However, it is the responsibility of the developer to make the application work in the offline mode and design the server module to be capable of handling simultaneous offline mode access to the same dataset. This means that if more than one user makes offline copies of the same dataset at the same time or during overlapping time intervals, the designer should adopt appropriate strategy while resolving updates to the same data records by different users.

It is also possible to develop stand-alone applications that just use data files alone or in-memory tables. In-memory tables are very useful data structures to store tabular data with navigation capabilities similar to database tables. Another use of a TClientDataSet component is to provide for caching (or buffering) of records from a unidirectional dataset in order to simulate the traditional BDE-style two-tier application model. This feature is very useful when we work with dbExpress components, since they provide unidirectional database cursors to maximize the performance of large queries.

TClientDataSet as an In-memory Table

The TClientDataSet component can be used as a stand-alone in-memory table in any application. In this sense, it functions similar to a container with a record navigation feature. It is possible to create a TClientDataSet component at design time and run time. Whether we create the client dataset visually on the form or during run time in the program, the steps involved are the same. In the visual approach, we use the visual tools provided by VCL, and while creating the program, we set necessary properties and execute the relevant methods. There are primarily two steps involved: define all the fields in the dataset and create the dataset.

Creating a ClientDataSet on a Form

1. Create a new VCL application. Save the project in a folder of your choice. Name the form unit and the project as you desire.

2. From the Data Access page in the Component Palette, drop a **ClientDataSet** object onto the form. Like any other dataset component, this is a non-visual component. It is visible only during design time and run time, so we can interact with it through the program code. Right-click on the component. From the pop-up menu that appears, choose the item **Fields Editor**. The Fields Editor is displayed, as shown in Figure 6-1.

3. Right-click on the **Fields Editor**. A pop-up menu appears. The items displayed initially in this menu are Add Fields, New Field, and Add All Fields. Other editing-related menu items are disabled. After we add one or more fields in the editor, the other relevant items will be enabled. The only menu item that is used when creating an in-memory table from scratch is the New Field item. The other two items are useful when creating a client dataset from another dataset that already exists on the form.

4. Choose the **New Field** item in the Fields Editor pop-up menu. The New Field entry dialog, shown in Figure 6-2, is displayed. In the New Field entry dialog, we can add as many fields as we like to our dataset. In this dialog, we can enter field properties like Field Name, Data Type, and Size. The Type combo box provides a vast list of data types that most of the databases support. There is a radio button that lets you choose the field type. If the field type is Data, it means the field is stand-alone and not dependent on other fields. Another useful field type is Lookup, which means that the value for this field is obtained from another dataset.

If we mark a field as Lookup type, it means that the value for this field is retrieved from a field belonging to another dataset, and hence we have to fill in the lookup definition information for that field. The lookup definition contains four fields: the lookup dataset name that is going to be the source for the new field, the key field or fields in the new dataset that map to the corresponding field or fields in the lookup dataset, the corresponding field or fields in the lookup dataset, and finally the field in the lookup dataset whose value is to be copied into the new field. Every time a new field is added to the client dataset, it appears in the Fields Editor.

5. After we enter all the required fields, the Fields Editor looks similar to Figure 6-3. Right-click on the client dataset component; from the pop-up menu, choose the **Create DataSet** item to create the dataset. The dataset is created and ready for use.

Once the dataset is created, it is now available to add data records, navigate through the records, locate a specific record, and so on.

Figure 6-1: Client Dataset Fields Editor (before adding new fields)

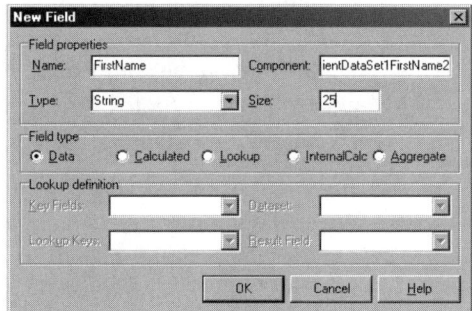

Figure 6-2: New Field properties dialog

Figure 6-3: Client Dataset Fields Editor (after adding new fields)

Programmatically Creating a ClientDataSet

We can create a client dataset programmatically as simple as any other VCL object. The following steps illustrate an example program that I developed for demonstration.

1. Create a new VCL application and save the project and unit files in a folder of your choice with names of your choice. Drop six **TButton** components from the Standard page in the Component Palette. Drop a **TDataSource** component from the Data Access page, one **TDbGrid** and one **TDbNavigator** from the Data Controls page, and one **TOpenDialog** and one **TSaveDialog** from the Dialogs page in the Component Palette.

2. To make the application more friendly, let's set meaningful captions to the buttons. Set the Button1 caption to "**Create Table**," Button2 to "**Delete Table**," Button3 to "**Save to file**," Button4 to "**Load from file**," Button5 to "**Close Table**," and Button6 to "**ReOpen Table**."

3. Set the DataSource property of the DbNavigator1 and DbControl1 components to the DataSource1 component that we dropped onto the form. At this time, we do not set the DataSet property of the DataSource1 component because we do not have that component yet. We will create that component in the program and then set it.

   We will use Button1 to create the dataset, Button2 to delete the dataset, Button3 to save the dataset to a file, and Button4 to create (or load) the dataset from a file, as the captions suggest.

4. Now implement all the event handlers as mentioned above. In addition to the event handlers, I also wrote a private member function, AddFieldToDataSet(), which helps in building the field definitions of the dataset. The complete program source is presented in Listing 6-1 (cpp file) and Listing 6-2 (header file).

Listing 6-1: Unit1.cpp

```
//-------------------------------------------------------------------

#include <vcl.h>
#pragma hdrstop

#include "Unit1.h"
//-------------------------------------------------------------------
#pragma package(smart_init)
#pragma resource "*.dfm"
TForm1 *Form1;
//-------------------------------------------------------------------
__fastcall TForm1::TForm1(TComponent* Owner)
        : TForm(Owner), pDataSet(NULL)
{
```

```
}
//---------------------------------------------------------------------------

void __fastcall TForm1::Button1Click(TObject *Sender)
{
    if (pDataSet)
        delete pDataSet;
    pDataSet = new TClientDataSet(this);
    AddFieldToDataSet(pDataSet, "First_Name", ftString, 30, true);
    AddFieldToDataSet(pDataSet, "Last_Name", ftString, 30, true);
    AddFieldToDataSet(pDataSet, "Home_Phone", ftString, 15, true);
    AddFieldToDataSet(pDataSet, "Work_Phone", ftString, 15, false);
    AddFieldToDataSet(pDataSet, "Age", ftInteger, 0, false);
    AddFieldToDataSet(pDataSet, "Birth_Date", ftDateTime, 0, false);
    pDataSet->CreateDataSet();
    pDataSet->Open();
    DataSource1->DataSet = pDataSet;
}
//---------------------------------------------------------------------------
void __stdcall TForm1::AddFieldToDataSet (TClientDataSet *fDataSet, AnsiString
    fFieldName,
    TFieldType fFieldType, int fSize, bool fReqd)
{
    TField* fField = NULL;

    switch (fFieldType) {
        case ftString:
            fField = new TStringField(fDataSet);
            break;
        case ftSmallint:
            fField = new TSmallintField(fDataSet);
            break;
        case ftInteger:
            fField = new TIntegerField(fDataSet);
            break;
        case ftDate:
            fField = new TDateField(fDataSet);
            break;
        case ftDateTime:
            fField = new TDateTimeField(fDataSet);
            break;
        case ftFloat:
            fField = new TFloatField(fDataSet);
            break;
        case ftBlob:
            fField = new TBlobField(fDataSet);
            break;
        case ftBoolean:
            fField = new TBooleanField(fDataSet);
            break;
    }

    if (fField != NULL) {
        fField->Name = fFieldName;
        fField->FieldName = fFieldName;
        fField->DataSet = fDataSet;
        fField->Required = fReqd;
        fField->Size = fSize;
    }
```

```cpp
}
//-----------------------------------------------------------------------------
void __fastcall TForm1::Button2Click(TObject *Sender)
{
    if (pDataSet == NULL)
        return;
    // Close the dataset
    if (pDataSet->Active)
        pDataSet->Close();
    delete pDataSet;
    pDataSet = NULL;
}
//-----------------------------------------------------------------------------
void __fastcall TForm1::Button3Click(TObject *Sender)
{
    // Determine the current directory, from where the program is executed
    AnsiString fCurrDir = ExtractFileDir(Application->ExeName);
    if (pDataSet == NULL || !pDataSet->Active)
        return;
    // set the initial directory of the save dialog to current directory
    SaveDialog1->InitialDir = fCurrDir;
    if (SaveDialog1->Execute()) {
        pDataSet->SaveToFile(SaveDialog1->FileName);
    }


}
//-----------------------------------------------------------------------------
void __fastcall TForm1::Button4Click(TObject *Sender)
{
    // If the dataset is not created, create one.
    if (pDataSet == NULL) {
        pDataSet = new TClientDataSet(this);
    }
    // If the dataset is already open, close it.
    if (pDataSet->Active)
        pDataSet->Close();

    // Determine the current directory, from where the program is executed
    AnsiString fCurrDir = ExtractFileDir(Application->ExeName);

    // set the initial directory of the open dialog to current directory
    OpenDialog1->InitialDir = fCurrDir;

    // Load the dataset from file
    if (OpenDialog1->Execute()) {
        AnsiString fFileName = OpenDialog1->FileName;
        pDataSet->LoadFromFile(fFileName);
        DataSource1->DataSet = pDataSet;
    }
    else {
        if (pDataSet)
            delete pDataSet;
    }
}
//-----------------------------------------------------------------------------
void __fastcall TForm1::Button5Click(TObject *Sender)
{
    if (pDataSet != NULL)
        pDataSet->Close();
```

```
}
//----------------------------------------------------------------------------

void __fastcall TForm1::Button6Click(TObject *Sender)
{
    if (pDataSet != NULL)
        pDataSet->Open();
}
//----------------------------------------------------------------------------
```

Listing 6-2: Unit1.h

```
//----------------------------------------------------------------------------

#ifndef Unit1H
#define Unit1H
//----------------------------------------------------------------------------
#include <Classes.hpp>
#include <Controls.hpp>
#include <StdCtrls.hpp>
#include <Forms.hpp>
#include <DB.hpp>
#include <DBClient.hpp>
#include <DBCtrls.hpp>
#include <DBGrids.hpp>
#include <ExtCtrls.hpp>
#include <Grids.hpp>
#include <Dialogs.hpp>
//----------------------------------------------------------------------------
class TForm1 : public TForm
{
__published:    // IDE-managed components
    TButton      *Button1;
    TButton      *Button2;
    TDBGrid      *DBGrid1;
    TDBNavigator *DBNavigator1;
    TDataSource  *DataSource1;
    TButton      *Button3;
    TOpenDialog  *OpenDialog1;
    TSaveDialog  *SaveDialog1;
    TButton      *Button4;
    void __fastcall Button1Click(TObject *Sender);
    void __fastcall Button2Click(TObject *Sender);
    void __fastcall Button3Click(TObject *Sender);
    void __fastcall Button4Click(TObject *Sender);
    void __fastcall Button5Click(TObject *Sender);
    void __fastcall Button6Click(TObject *Sender);
private:        // User declarations
    TClientDataSet* gDataSet;
    void __stdcall AddFieldToDataSet (TClientDataSet *fDataSet,
        AnsiString fFieldName, TFieldType fFieldType, int fSize, bool fReqd);
public:         // User declarations
        __fastcall TForm1(TComponent* Owner);
};
//----------------------------------------------------------------------------
extern PACKAGE TForm1 *Form1;
//----------------------------------------------------------------------------
#endif
```

When we drop a TClientDataSet component onto a form, we can also create the record structure and copy data from another dataset. Right-click on the client dataset component and choose the Assign Local Data menu item. A dialog box containing a list of all the pre-existing datasets is displayed. Select a dataset from this list from where you wish to copy the record structure and/or data into the client dataset. Then when you invoke the Fields Editor, you can use the Add Fields and Add All Fields options. In addition to these options, the Fields Editor provides field-editing options, such as Select All, Cut, Copy, Paste, and Delete.

When we create lookup fields in a client dataset as discussed earlier, we do not usually populate values for the lookup field values when we append new records or edit existing records. We only make changes to the key field or fields that make up the lookup key with corresponding fields in the lookup dataset. Then the lookup field value is automatically pulled from the lookup dataset by the client dataset.

Before we move on to the more advanced features of the client dataset, let's deviate for a while to discuss the basics of the provider component so that we can visualize how the client dataset and provider duo works.

TDataSetProvider in Advanced Database Development

The TDataSetProvider component plays an important role in developing multi-tier applications and applications with unidirectional datasets. In a client-server model, the dataset provider is the server-side equivalent to the client dataset on the client side. It provides data from the dataset to the client and resolves updates to the dataset or database server. In other words, it serves as a data broker between a remote database server and a client dataset. Also, it is the dataset counterpart of an XML Transform Provider component that is used to transform data from XML documents. We will discuss the XML Transform Provider component in more detail in a later chapter. In this chapter, we will concentrate our attention on the dataset provider. The dataset provider interacts with the datasets through the IProviderSupport interface, which is implemented by the dataset that provides data to the provider. In other words, any dataset that implements this interface will be able to provide data to a client dataset through the provider component. The TDataSet class implements the IProviderSupport interface with simple, protected stub methods that do nothing. It is the responsibility of the dataset classes that descend from TDataSet to expose these methods and provide proper implementation. Thus, most of the dataset classes, such as the BDE datasets, ADO datasets, dbExpress datasets, and IBX datasets, provide their own implementation of the IProviderSupport interface methods, as appropriate to the specific data access architecture. The dataset provider may exist in the client application (usually in the case of a two-tier application) or may be contained in an application server module, as in a three-tier application.

The TDataSetProvider-TClientDataSet Duo

Now we will be able to visualize the relationship between the provider and the client dataset components. The client dataset communicates with the provider through the IAppServer (or its descendant) interface. If the provider is contained in the same client module that also contains the client dataset, an IAppServer object is automatically created internally to handle the communication between the client dataset and the provider components. But, if the provider is contained in an application server module, as in a multi-tier application, the server module also implements a descendant of the IAppServer interface to handle requests from the client dataset. Figure 6-4 displays a typical multi-tier application server module. The application server module is a descendant of the TCRemoteDataModule component, which does not implement the IAppServer interface by itself; rather, it creates a descendant of IAppServer to handle the client requests. The provider is contained in the remote data module along with the dataset that provides data to the provider. This dataset can be any TDataSet descendant that is connected to a database and has implemented the IProviderSupport interface.

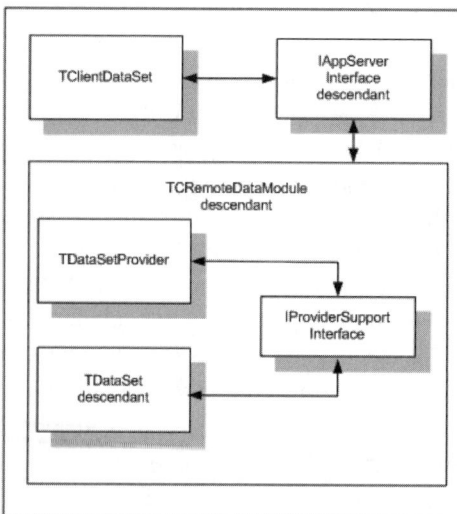

Figure 6-4: TClientDataSet and TDataSetProvider in a multi-tier application

Now let me present a high-level overview of the typical sequence of actions that take place when we use a dataset provider and a client dataset together in a client-server application. More details are provided while we discuss individual properties, methods, and events of these components.

- The provider receives data from the dataset when the dataset is opened (with appropriate settings, such as table name if it is a table or executing a query or stored procedure that returns a record set).

- If a client dataset is connected to the remote data module's provider component, the client dataset can be built using the Fields Editor options Add All Fields and Add Fields.

- When the provider receives a request from a client dataset for data packets, it packages the data received from the underlying dataset and sends it to the client. The provider can add custom information to the data packet before sending it to the client dataset in its OnGetDataSet-Properties event handler. Also, the provider can edit the data packet, if desired, in its OnGetData event handler before sending it to the client dataset.

- The client dataset receives data from the underlying dataset through the provider in the form of data packets when we execute the Open() method, set the Active property to true on the client dataset, or request additional data packets either explicitly by calling the GetNextPacket() method or implicitly by navigating through the client dataset.

- Then it reconstructs the data in the data packet to a local, in-memory table for the user's use. Therefore, the data that we see through a client dataset is a local copy of the data and is cached by the client dataset. This is a very useful feature that enables us to work with the unidirectional datasets, such as those provided by the dbExpress framework similar to a BDE- or ADO-based dataset. The unidirectional nature of the dbExpress dataset is hidden and taken care of by the provider, since the provider knows how and when to make updates to the dataset.

- The client dataset maintains a change log of any changes made by the user on the cached copy of the data. When the changes are done, we can initiate the updates through the provider. The client dataset can also send custom information to the provider in its OnBeforeApplyUpdates event handler, which the provider can retrieve in its corresponding event handler.

- The provider performs updates, and the update errors are reported back to the client dataset. How the provider applies the updates, to what extent the provider's functions can be influenced by the client dataset, and how the errors are reported back can be configured programmatically using the provider options. The provider can also send custom information to the client dataset along with the data packet in its OnAfterApplyUpdates event handler, which the client dataset can retrieve in its corresponding event handler.

■ Please note that once the connectivity is established between the client dataset and the provider, methods on the provider are invoked or event handlers are triggered on the provider when the corresponding methods are called or properties are set on the client dataset. This way, execution of the provider object functions is performed (partially influenced) through the client dataset. Since a client module does not directly communicate with the server module or provider object, the client dataset serves as a gateway.

Our discussion in this section will help us better understand the DataSnap (formerly known as MIDAS) applications, discussed in Chapter 9.

Properties, Methods, and Events of TClientDataSet

In this section, I present the most commonly used properties, methods, and events of the client dataset component in more detail. The items discussed in Table 6-1 have more relevance when the client dataset is used in conjunction with a provider component than as an in-memory table.

Table 6-1: Properties, methods, and events of TClientDataSet

Property	Description
Aggregates	Aggregates represent summary values on groups of records in the client dataset. The Aggregates property represents a collection of TAggregate objects that are available for the client dataset. When a client dataset is connected to a provider, for every aggregate field defined in the client dataset, the Fields Editor automatically adds an aggregate object.
AppServer	Returns the IAppServer interface that the client dataset interacts with in order to communicate with the provider. Applications do not usually have to access this interface directly. The properties and methods of the client dataset are automatically translated into method calls as implemented by this interface. For in-memory datasets, this property is not used.
ChangeCount	Client dataset maintains a local cache of the records provided by the provider. The ChangeCount property represents how many modifications are pending to be synchronized with the database since the last time they were synchronized (or cancelled). Every field value that is different from the corresponding value of that field since the last synchronization (or cancellation) counts as a change to the local copy of the data.
ChangeCount (cont.)	Whenever the client dataset is synchronized with the database by calling the ApplyUpdates() method, cancels all modifications with a call to the CancelUpdates() method, or makes changes permanent by merging the delta packet with the data packet with a call to the MergeChange-Log() method (but still not synchronized with the database), the ChangeCount property is reset to zero.

Property	Description
CommandText	This is an SQL Query string, a table name, or stored procedure name that is sent to the provider to be run on the target dataset that the provider represents, if the provider permits the client dataset to send dynamic queries. One of the provider options, poAllowCommandText, indicates this property. If this property is not included, that means the provider does not accept client-specific queries, and hence the CommandText property has no impact on the execution of the query on the target dataset. If the provider accepts dynamic client query strings, the command text is executed when the Execute() method is called or the dataset is opened, whichever is the appropriate case.
ConnectionBroker	Represents an object of TConnectionBroker component, which is used to centralize connections to remote providers to more than one client dataset at the same time. It is not necessary to use this component to establish a connection with a remote provider, but in larger client modules having multiple client datasets interacting with the different providers hosted on the same server or connecting with the same connection component, using a connection broker will make it easy to centralize the connection.
Data	Represents the data of the client dataset in a transportable format. It is an OleVariant-type value and stores the entire set of records returned by the provider. The source of the data may be a provider, a disk file, or data entered by the user into an in-memory table.
DataSize	This indicates the size in bytes required to hold the data. This integer value is useful in determining the buffer size to be allocated before copying this data to a fixed size buffer. However, if we are using a dynamically increasing buffer, it is not required to use this value.
Delta	The Delta property represents a change log on the client dataset. This is also an OleVariant type value and contains all changes made by the user to the Data property through online updates using data controls or by any other means. In fact, the Delta property represents a change log on the Data property. This value is sent to the provider when the updates are requested on the target dataset. When the updates are successful, the Delta is cleared. If any update errors occur, Delta contains all the changes that failed in the update process. When the updates are cancelled by the client dataset, the Delta property is cleared. In file-based applications or in-memory tables, the MergeChangeLog() method makes the changes permanent in the client dataset and clears the Delta property. The Delta property is not maintained by the client dataset if the LogChanges property is set to false, in which case all the user updates are directly made to the Data property since a change log is not maintained.
FetchOnDemand	This is a Boolean property and indicates whether the client dataset should automatically fetch the next set of records when required (for example, when the user navigates to the end of the current data packet and scrolls further down). This is true by default. If the application needs to have control before fetching the next packet of records, then this property should be set to false, and the next packet must be fetched programmatically by calling the GetNextPacket() method. If this property is false, and the provider does not include the BLOB fields by default, the BLOB fields must be fetched by explicitly calling the FetchBlobs() method. Similarly, if the provider does not include nested detail sets by default when this property is false, then the nested detail sets must be fetched by explicitly calling the FetchDetails() method. The provider includes BLOB fields or nested detail sets when the provider options poFetchBlobsOnDemand and poFetchDetailsOnDemand, respectively, are not included.
FileName	Identifies the name of a file that stores the data of the client dataset. If the dataset always reads from and writes to a specific file, then use this property to set the filename. If a valid filename is set, then every time the client dataset is closed, the data is written to the same file, and every time the client dataset is opened, the data is read from the same file. If it is not always the same file to be used, then use the SaveToFile() and LoadFromFile() methods to save data to and read data from a file. Whether we use a single file method or different file method, the file-based IO makes an application function as a briefcase model application.

Property	Description
IndexDefs	This is an array of index definitions on the target dataset. The index definitions on the client dataset can be set by calling the IndexDefs→Update() method or synchronizing the index definitions from the target dataset directly using the provider connection.
LogChanges	This is a Boolean property indicating whether the client dataset must maintain a separate change log to contain the changes made by the user. By default, it is true for client datasets that work with remote providers. If this property is false, the user's changes are immediately applied to the Data property, and the resulting data packet is unable to be sent to apply changes to the database. Setting this property to false is only useful in two-tiered file-based or in-memory tables to conserve resources.
MasterFields	If the MasterSource property is set for a client dataset, the MasterFields property represents one or more fields in the master table to link with corresponding fields in the client dataset in order to establish the master-detail relationship.
MasterSource	The MasterSource property identifies a TDataSource whose DataSet property represents the master table in a master-detail relationship.
PacketRecords	If this value is −1, then all the records from the target dataset are returned by the provider in a single fetch. If this value is 0, then only the metadata of the target dataset is returned. If this value is more than zero, the provider returns only as many records as the value specifies in a single fetch.
Params	Represents a collection of TParam objects. Each of the Param objects represents an input (or output) parameter as required by the corresponding query or stored procedure. Params can be set manually or automatically. To set Params automatically, execute the FetchParams() method, which sets the parameters as required by the target dataset object. Params can also be set manually during design time or run time. When setting Params manually, it is required to set the Param objects exactly as expected by the target dataset object. Any mismatch in the data type of the Param object results in a run-time exception being raised. If the target dataset object is a table (instead of a query or stored procedure), then we can use Param objects to represent individual fields and limit records of selection by setting specific values to these Param objects.
ProviderName	Identifies the name of the provider object with which the client dataset communicates for fetching data and applying updates. The name is exactly the same as it is defined in the remote data module.
RemoteServer	Identifies the TCustomRemoteServer descendant that serves as the connection component for the client dataset to connect to an application server. This is the connection object that can be centralized by using a ConnectionBroker object, as discussed earlier. Examples of the connection objects are TSocketConnection, TDCOMConnection, or TWebConnection. These components are discussed in detail in Chapter 10, which focuses on developing distributed applications.
SavePoint	This is an integer value and represents the current state of edits made to the client dataset when logging changes. The save point can be effectively used to roll back changes made to the client dataset since the last save point by setting its value to the previously saved value.
XMLData	This property is the same as the Data property, except the data packet is in XML format instead of binary format as used internally by the client dataset component.

Method	Description
ApplyUpdates(int MaxErrors)	Call this method when the user is done with any changes to the client dataset's records to apply the updates to the underlying target dataset. The Delta property is the source of all the client dataset changes. Before the provider is called for update, the BeforeApplyUpdates event is triggered on the client dataset. This event may be used to send client-specific data to the provider. Then the provider is called to apply updates to the dataset. At this time the BeforeApplyUpdates event on the provider is triggered and the provider receives the client-specific data sent by the client dataset in its BeforeApplyUpdates event handler. Thus, the client dataset can communicate to the provider, and the provider can take any necessary action before the updates are actually applied to the target dataset. Then the provider performs the updates, packages any errors reported by the database server, and sends it back to the client dataset. Before sending the packet to the client dataset, the AfterApplyUpdates event handler is triggered on the provider so that it can send any custom information to the client dataset or respond to the custom information sent by the client dataset in the BeforeApplyUpdates event handler. Then the AfterApplyUpdates event handler is triggered on the client dataset so that it can take necessary action based on the custom information sent by the provider. Thus, at this time, the provider gets a chance to communicate back to the client dataset after the updates are performed. Both the client dataset and the provider communicate with each other using the OleVariant data type, which is suitable to package any type of data. The input parameter indicates the maximum number of errors tolerated before the update process should be aborted. It should be set to −1 to indicate no limit on errors. The value returned by this method is an integer representing the actual number of errors encountered.
CancelUpdates()	The CancelUpdates() method cancels all the pending updates to the dataset, clears the Delta property, and resets the ChangeCount property to 0.
Close()	Close the client dataset. When the client dataset is created as an in-memory table, the structure and data of the table is preserved even after executing a Close() call on the dataset. When it is reopened with the Open() method, the structure and data are preserved to what they were before executing Close().
CreateBlobStream (TField* Field, TBlob-StreamMode Mode)	The CreateBlobStream() method creates a stream object for reading or writing a BLOB field in the dataset, identified by the Field parameter. The Mode parameter indicates whether the stream should be used to read or write or both. The acceptable modes are bmRead, bmWrite, and bmReadWrite. The return value is a stream object, which should be deleted explicitly after you are done with it.
CreateDataSet()	The CreateDataSet() method should be called when we are creating a client dataset object explicitly as an in-memory dataset. Before calling this method, the field definitions must be added. It also means that the FieldDefs and/or Fields property must be non-empty. If the IndexDefs property contains values, these values are used to create indexes. It is not required to explicitly create a client dataset object when used in a client module in conjunction with a provider object (either remote or local provider).
DataRequest(Ole-Variant Data)	Call the DataRequest() method to trigger an OnDataRequest() event on the provider object. The Data parameter is an OleVariant and is passed to the provider through the event handler.
EmptyDataSet()	The EmptyDataSet() method removes all the records from the dataset. The structure of the dataset is still preserved.
Execute()	The Execute() method triggers execution of an SQL command on the provider. If the provider's Options property includes poAllowCommandText, and the CommandText property contains a valid SQL command (along with the Params property to supply any parameters to the command identified by the CommandText property), the SQL command is executed by the provider. Otherwise, by default the SQL command or stored procedure associated with the underlying dataset object is executed. This method is intended to run SQL commands that do not return a result set. When the method is executed, a BeforeExecute event is triggered on the client dataset first, where it can build custom data objects to be passed to the provider before execution of the command begins.

Method	Description
Execute() (cont.)	Then the provider is passed the execution request, which triggers a BeforeExecute event on the provider. In this event handler, the provider has the opportunity to retrieve the data sent by the client dataset and take any necessary action before processing the request, and the provider executes the command (either the command associated with the target dataset or the command set by the client dataset). Then the AfterExecute event is triggered on the provider where it can package custom data to be sent back to the client dataset. Finally, the AfterExecute event on the client dataset is triggered where it receives the custom data packaged by the provider. When the provider executes the command, any output parameters are set in the Params property of the client dataset. Therefore, the custom data passed between the client dataset and the provider does not include the input or output parameters of the command.
FetchParams()	The FetchParams() method retrieves current parameter values from the underlying dataset, which means the Params property of the client dataset is refreshed by the provider. This is very useful, particularly when we wish to set the parameters and their data types. When the client dataset executes this method, the BeforeGetParams event is triggered on the client dataset, where it can package custom information for the provider, and then the provider is requested to fetch the parameters. The BeforeGetParams event is then triggered on the provider, where it gets the opportunity to retrieve the custom information sent by the client dataset before actually fetching the parameters. After fetching the parameters, the AfterGetParams event is triggered on the provider to enable it to send custom information to the client dataset. The parameters are then sent to the client dataset, and the AfterGetParams event is triggered on the client dataset, enabling it to retrieve the custom information sent by the provider. To obtain output parameter values, call the Execute() method.
GetNextPacket()	The GetNextPacket() method retrieves the next set of records from the provider. The maximum number of records to be retrieved is controlled by the PacketRecords property. The method returns an integer value indicating the number of records retrieved.
LoadFromFile (const AnsiString FileName)	Loads the dataset from a file. The file should have been saved before by the SaveToFile() method on this or another client dataset. This is because the data should have been saved in the client dataset's internal format. Files saved by other components will not work with this method.
LoadFromStream (TStream* Stream)	Loads the dataset from a stream. The file should have been saved before by the SaveToStream() method on this or another client dataset. This is because the data should have been saved in the client dataset's internal format. Streams saved by other components will not work with this method.
MergeChange-Log()	When the client dataset's data is populated, it formulates a baseline for the changes made later on. All the changes made to the data are contained in the Delta property (when the LogChanges property is true). Call MergeChangeLog() to merge all the changes with the data so that a new data baseline is established for the next set of changes. When this method is executed, the Delta property is cleared. When the client dataset is used as an in-memory table or file-based table, and when LogChanges is true, this method should be called explicitly in order to make sure that the updates are applied to the client dataset.
RevertRecord()	The RevertRecord() method undoes all the edits done in the current record. To undo only the last change made to the current record, call UndoLastChange() instead. If the changes are already applied to the underlying dataset or merged to the client dataset, then execution of this method has no impact.
SaveToFile(AnsiString FileName, TData-PacketFormat Format = dfBinary)	Call the SaveToFile() method to save the client dataset to a disk file. The file can be saved in binary or XML format. This feature is useful for developing briefcase model applications.

Method	Description
SaveToStream(TStream * Stream, TDataPacket-Format Format = dfBinary)	Call the SaveToStream() method to save the client dataset to a stream. The stream can be saved in binary or XML format. It is very useful to save the client dataset to a stream to facilitate transmission of this data over a network to other applications.
UndoLastChange(bool FollowChange)	The UndoLastChange() method undoes the last change to the current record. The change may be a single edit, insertion of a new record, or deletion of the current record. The input Boolean parameter indicates whether to reposition the cursor on the restored record. If it is true, the cursor is positioned on the restored record; otherwise, it is positioned on the current record.

Event	Description
AfterApplyUpdates	After the ApplyUpdates() method is executed on the provider in response to a client dataset's request, the provider can send custom information packaged in its own AfterApplyUpdates event handler. Then the AfterApplyUpdates event is triggered on the client dataset, which gets the opportunity to retrieve the custom data sent by the provider. The custom data is transferred between the provider and the client dataset as an OleVariant object in the second argument to the event handler. The first argument is the object for which the event is triggered (i.e., the client dataset or the provider).
AfterExecute	After the provider executes the SQL command in response to a client dataset's call, the provider can send custom information packaged in its own AfterExecute event handler. Then the AfterExecute event is triggered on the client dataset, which gets the opportunity to retrieve the custom data sent by the provider. The custom data is transferred between the provider and the client dataset as an OleVariant object in the second argument to the event handler. The first argument is the object for which the event is triggered (i.e., the client dataset or the provider).
AfterGetParams	After the provider fetches the parameters in response to a client dataset's call, the provider can send custom information packaged in its own AfterGetParams event handler. Then the AfterGetParams event is triggered on the client dataset, which gets the opportunity to retrieve the custom data sent by the provider. The custom data is transferred between the provider and the client dataset as an OleVariant object in the second argument to the event handler. The first argument is the object for which the event is triggered (i.e., the client dataset or the provider).
AfterGetRecords	After the provider fetches data for a client dataset, the provider can send custom information packaged in its own AfterGetRecords event handler. Then the AfterGetRecords event is triggered on the client dataset, which gets the opportunity to retrieve the custom data sent by the provider. The custom data is transferred between the provider and the client dataset as an OleVariant object in the second argument to the event handler. The first argument is the object for which the event is triggered (i.e., the client dataset or the provider). The AfterGetRecords events on the client dataset and the provider are triggered every time the provider fetches a set of records, whether the fetch was automatic or initiated by the client dataset.
BeforeApplyUpdates	When the client dataset calls the ApplyUpdates() method, the BeforeApplyUpdates event is triggered on the client dataset so that it can package custom information for the provider, which the provider can use before applying the updates on the underlying dataset. The custom data is transferred as an OleVariant object in the second argument to the event handler. The first argument is the client dataset itself.
BeforeExecute	When the client dataset calls the Execute() method to execute a command on the target dataset, the BeforeExecute event is triggered on the client dataset so that it can package custom information for the provider, which the provider can use before executing the command on the underlying dataset. The custom data is transferred as an OleVariant object in the second argument to the event handler. The first argument is the client dataset itself.

Event	Description
BeforeGetParams	When the client dataset calls the FetchParams() method to fetch the parameters from the target dataset, the BeforeGetParams event is triggered on the client dataset so that it can package custom information for the provider, which the provider can use before fetching the parameters for the client dataset. The custom data is transferred as an OleVariant object in the second argument to the event handler. The first argument is the client dataset itself.
BeforeGetRecords	Every time a set of records is fetched by the client dataset from the target dataset, the BeforeGetRecords event is triggered on the client dataset so that it can package custom information for the provider, which the provider can use before fetching the next set of records from the underlying dataset. The custom data is transferred as an OleVariant object in the second argument to the event handler. The first argument is the client dataset itself.
OnReconcileError	When the provider executes the ApplyUpdates() method, any errors reported by the underlying database are sent to the client dataset as an OleVariant object, and the Reconcile() method on the client dataset is automatically called with these errors as the input parameter. The Reconcile() method triggers the OnReconcileError event once for every error record. In this event handler, we can take one of a set of possible actions on the failed record. The possible actions include raCancel to cancel all changes to this record, raRefresh to cancel all changes to this record and refresh the record from the server, and raCorrect to replace the record with the (corrected) record in the event handler, among others.

Properties and Events of TDataSetProvider

Since most of the provider's functionality is similar to the client dataset's functionality, in this section we will present only those features not yet discussed. Table 6-2 describes the features of the dataset provider in additional detail.

Table 6-2: Properties and events of TDataSetProvider

Property	Description
DataSet	The underlying dataset (a descendant of TDataSet), which provides data to the provider. In order for the dataset to communicate with the provider, the dataset should have overridden the IProviderSupport interface methods as provided in the TDataSet. If not, the provider would not be able to apply updates to the dataset.
Exported	This is a Boolean property. When set to true, it indicates that the provider is made available to the clients of the remote data module that owns it, and the clients can specify the provider as a target for calls made through the IAppServer interface. When this property is set to false, IAppServer calls that specify the provider cause an exception.
Options	The Options property is a way of configuring the provider component with respect to how it communicates with the client dataset or to what extent it exposes itself to the client dataset. These options include poIncFieldProps to include the field properties (such as DisplayLabel, DisplayFormat, Visible, EditMast) with the returned data packet; poCascadeDeletes to enable the provider to delete all the detail records when the corresponding record in the master table is deleted, if the provider represents the master table in a master-detail relationship and the underlying database supports cascaded deletes as part of referential integrity constraints; poCascadeUpdates to enable the provider to update detail records automatically when the key values of a record in the master table are updated if the provider represents the master table in a master-detail relationship and the underlying database supports cascaded updates as part of referential integrity constraints; poDisableEdits prevent clients from modifying the records of the underlying dataset; poDisableInserts prevent clients from inserting new records into the underlying dataset; and poAllowCommandText to allow the client dataset to send a dynamic SQL command to be executed on the underlying dataset.

Property	Description
ResolveToDataSet	When the client dataset requests to apply updates, the provider is required to apply updates either directly to the underlying dataset or through the database server. For this purpose, it employs a resolver component, which is an object of TDataSetResolver if the ResolveToDataSet is true or an object of TSQLResolver if the ResolveToDataSet is false. If we need to make use of the underlying dataset's events (such as AfterDelete, AfterPost, and so on), we need to apply the updates directly to the dataset to trigger these event handlers at appropriate times.
UpdateMode	This property determines how the provider should locate records in the underlying dataset in order to apply the updates. The modes include upWhereAll to indicate that all columns are used to locate the record, upWhereChanged to indicate that only key field values and original values of fields that have changed are used to locate the record, and upWhereKeyOnly to indicate that only key fields are used to find the record.

Event	Description
AfterUpdateRecord	This event handler is triggered after a record is updated against the target dataset. The event handler has four arguments; the first argument is the provider itself, the second argument is the underlying dataset, the third argument is the delta packet of the client dataset, and the fourth argument is the kind of update that is performed, such as Insert, Update, or Delete. You may implement this event handler to do any special processing after the successful update of a record.
BeforeUpdateRecord	This event handler is triggered once for every record before making the update. At this time, the provider gets an opportunity to make any changes to the record or parameter values. For example, if the update query has a parameter for the current timestamp, and if it is required that the timestamp be set by the server module rather than the client dataset, then this event handler should be implemented setting the specific parameter value with the current timestamp as obtained in the provider module. The event handler has five arguments; the first argument is the provider itself, the second argument is the underlying dataset, the third argument is the client dataset Delta property, the fourth argument is the update type, and the fifth argument is a Boolean value indicating whether a change is applied to the record. Set this value to true if you applied the update explicitly in the event handler.
OnGetData	This event handler is triggered once every time the provider retrieves a data packet from the underlying dataset. At this time, the provider has the opportunity to edit any (or all) of the dataset records before sending the data packet to the client dataset. The event handler has two arguments; the first argument is the provider itself, and the second argument is the data packet from the underlying dataset in the form of a client dataset object. Even though the client does not seek to filter the retrieved data packet, the provider may be programmed (as designed) to suppress any of the records that it does not want to send to the client dataset.
OnGetDataSetProperties	This event handler should be implemented if we desire to include application-specific information in the data packets. This information is stored in the client dataset as optional parameter(s) and can be retrieved later by the provider from the client dataset delta packet using the GetOptionalParam() method of the client dataset. The event handler has three arguments. The first argument is the provider itself, the second argument is the underlying dataset, and the third argument is an OleVariant containing an array of Variant array called Properties. Each Variant array element is itself an array containing three elements; the first element is the name of the custom parameter as a string, the second element is the value of the parameter as a Variant, and the third parameter is a Boolean value indicating whether the custom parameter will be included in the delta packet sent by the client dataset when requesting updates. If we wish to access the custom parameter later in the delta packet, we should mark its third array element as true.

Event	Description
OnGetTableName	When the provider is about to apply updates to the database, it sets a resolver component. If the underlying dataset is based on a single table, such as TTable or TADOTable, the resolver will be able to identify the table name against which the updates should be made. But if the underlying dataset is a multi-table query or stored procedure, the resolver cannot determine the name of the table targeted for updates. In such a situation, this event handler should be implemented to tell the resolver the name of the table. This event handler has three arguments; the first argument is the provider itself, the second argument is the underlying dataset component, and the third argument is an AnsiString. Setting the third argument to the table name passes this information to the resolver.
OnUpdateData	This event handler is triggered once every time the provider is about to begin applying updates from the delta packet from the client dataset. At this time, the provider has the opportunity to edit any (or all) of the dataset records before applying updates to the underlying dataset. The event handler has two arguments; the first argument is the provider itself, and the second argument is the delta packet from the client dataset in the form of a client dataset object.
OnUpdateError	This event handler is triggered for every record that failed to update. The event handler has five arguments; the first argument is the provider itself, the second argument is the client dataset, the third argument is the error object, the fourth argument is the update type, and the fifth argument is the resolver response. We set the response value to inform the resolver what action it should take. The possible responses include rrSkip to indicate skipping the current record update, rrAbort to indicate aborting the entire update operation, rrIgnore to indicate that the current record should neither be updated nor sent back to the client dataset for resolving, and rrApply to indicate that the current record must be updated with new values (or settings) made in this event handler. Therefore, the provider will get the opportunity to fix the failed record within the purview of provider design, before reporting the error to the client dataset.

So far we have discussed the client dataset and provider component features, but we will make an attempt to go through examples in support of our discussion in Chapters 9 and 10, where we cover DataSnap applications and custom client-server applications.

If we are going to discuss code examples in later chapters, then why did we start the discussion in this chapter? Because we first need to understand these components before we can discuss unidirectional datasets, as presented by the Borland dbExpress framework.

Methods Supported by IProviderSupport Interface

Table 6-3 provides a description of the methods supported by the IProviderSupport interface and mostly applicable while developing traditional client-server applications. There are more methods than those discussed in the table. Please note that these methods are internally called by the provider component in your application, and you do not need to call them explicitly. However, the forthcoming discussion is going to help you if you are writing custom components that would be descended from a provider or a dataset component. Since the methods of this interface are implemented by the corresponding dataset, the dataset component exposes its features and characteristics through these methods. For example, the ADO dataset objects provided in C++Builder 6 expose the features and behavior of Microsoft ADO-based objects. If you desire to expose any additional features (or suppress any of the already exposed features), you may design your own descendant dataset components from TDataSet and implement the IProviderSupport interface in a way that suits your requirements.

Table 6-3: Methods supported by the IProviderSupport interface

Method	Description
PSEndTransaction(bool Commit)	The provider executes this method to end a transaction that was started earlier by a call to the PSStartTransaction() method. The method takes a Boolean parameter, which indicates to commit the updates when set to true or roll back when false.
PSExecute()	The PSExecute() method is implemented by the corresponding dataset component to execute the associated SQL or stored procedure, as appropriate. It can also execute the command text supplied by the client (through the provider) if the client is permitted to supply custom command text.
PSExecuteStatement (AnsiString sql, TParams* params, void * result)	This method is called by the provider to execute the SQL statement that it generates for a client request if the value of its ResolveToDataSet property is false. The method takes three arguments; the first argument is an AnsiString containing the SQL statement, the second argument is a pointer to a TParams object (TParams contains the parameters required to bind to the SQL statement before execution), and the third parameter is a void pointer. If the execution of the SQL statement results in a result set, this method creates a new dataset object containing the retrieved records and makes this pointer point to the new dataset. The provider that is calling this method is responsible for freeing the object after using it.
PSGetIndexDefs (TIndexOptions * indOpt)	This method is called by the provider to get definitions of all the indexes defined in the database for the object identified by the dataset. This method takes a single parameter, which is a set that specifies the different types of indexes the provider is interested in getting. This information is necessary for the provider to know the affected rows when the field values are changed by the client.
PSGetKeyFields()	The provider calls this method to obtain a list of fields from the dataset that uniquely identify a record. The default implementation retrieves all the field components whose ProviderFlags property includes the pfInKey value. The ProviderFlags property of a field component is designed to let the provider know how the field component may be used. In the current discussion, this property is used to retrieve the list of key fields on a dataset. The value returned is an AnsiString containing the field names separated by semicolons.
PSGetParams()	The provider calls this method to obtain a pointer to the dataset parameters, as identified by the TParams object. If the dataset does not have any parameters set, the NULL value is returned. When the dataset implements this interface, it should only return a pointer to the existing TParams object and should not create a new object. The provider itself has a GetParams() method, which returns the pointer (to the TParams object) as obtained from the dataset.
PSGetTableName()	This method returns the table name that this dataset represents and as it appears in the generated SQL statements. The value returned is an AnsiString. The provider uses this value in generating SQL statements that correspond to the client dataset requests. If the dataset does not return a table name, the OnGetTableName event handler of the provider must be implemented by the developer where the table name is explicitly set by the developer. Then the provider will use that table in its generated SQL statements.
PSInTransaction()	This method returns a Boolean value indicating if there is already a transaction in process. This is useful to know, particularly if the provider wants to start a transaction on the dataset.

Method	Description
PSIsSQLBased()	This method returns a Boolean value indicating whether the dataset (and the underlying database) provides native SQL support. This is a very important method for a provider because it has to generate SQL statements to fulfill the client's requests. In a typical situation, such as BDE-enabled desktop databases, the dataset may provide SQL support even if the underlying database does not. This is possible because the SQL support is provided in the dataset descendant class in this example through the BDE engine. However, the way the SQL statement is formed and processed is different in both cases when the SQL support is provided at the database level or the dataset level. The provider uses this information to construct the SQL statements appropriately.
PSReset()	The provider calls this method to reposition the dataset to the first record before fetching the records.
PSSetCommandText (AnsiString commText)	The provider may allow its client dataset to send a custom SQL statement as command text if its Options property includes the poAllowCommandText setting. When the client calls the GetRecords() or Execute() method with a custom SQL statement, the provider in turn calls the PSSetCommandText() method on the dataset, passing the client's SQL statement as a parameter, and then calls the PSExecute() method to execute the SQL statement. The value of the SQL statement replaces the dataset's SQL property (if it exists) or replaces the name of the table or stored procedure that the dataset represents.
PSSetParams(TParams *params)	The provider calls this method to set the dataset parameters. The method takes a single argument, which is a TParams object.
PSSQLSupported()	This method is used to determine if the dataset is able to execute SQL statements. If so, the PSExecuteStatement() method may be called safely. If not, an exception is raised if the provider tries to execute an SQL statement. If this method returns false, the provider's ResolveToDataSet property must be set to true so that the updates are not sent to the database server.
PSStartTransaction()	The provider executes this method to start a new transaction before applying the updates requested by the client dataset. Before executing this method, the provider makes sure that there is no currently active transaction by executing the PSInTransaction() method. The transaction support provided by this interface does not assume that nested transactions are supported in the underlying database.
PSUpdateRecord (TUpdateKind* updKind, TDataSet* delta)	When the client initiates an update, the provider calls this method to give the dataset a chance to provide (and execute) a custom update event handler before it generates the SQL statement for an update. If the method returns true, the provider assumes that the dataset has undertaken the responsibility of making the update and hence does not generate the update SQL. If the method returns false, the provider understands that the dataset did not perform the custom update and hence generates its own update SQL statement and calls the PSExecuteStatement() method. If the specific dataset descendant object is designed to provide a chance to an event handler (implemented by the user) to make custom updates, then it calls that event handler. If the user did not implement the custom update event handler, or if the dataset itself is not designed to provide such a feature to the user, then this method returns false. If the user implemented a custom update event handler, the dataset executes that event handler and returns true to the calling provider. For example, the BDE- and IBX-based datasets provide the OnUpdateRecord event handler and pass the updates sent by the provider to this event handler, which permits the developer to implement custom update logic.

The TDataSource Component

Before we take a look at the dbExpress architecture, let's have a birds-eye view of the TDataSource component since it is a very useful component and we use it predominantly in our code examples as well as real-life applications.

The data source component functions like a conduit between the datasets and data-aware controls. It also links two datasets in a master-detail relationship. Every dataset must be associated with a data source component in order to make its data displayed through data-aware controls, and every data-aware control must be associated with a data source in order to receive data for displaying and manipulation by the user. While only one dataset can be associated with a data source component at any point in time, more than one data-aware control can share the same data source component. This feature demonstrates the one source and multi-view capability of this component.

The DataSet property of the data source component should be used to set or identify the associated dataset. For all the data-aware controls that share the same data source component, the source of input data can be changed any time in the program by resetting the DataSet property of the data source to the appropriate dataset object. The State property represents the dataset state of the associated dataset. The Enabled property is a Boolean value and indicates whether the associated data-aware control can display the data. If this property is set to false, all the data-aware controls associated with this data source will be blank. The IsLinked(TDataSet* DataSet) method may be used to check if the data source is linked to a particular dataset.

There are three event handlers—OnDataChange, OnUpdateData, and OnStateChange—that will be triggered on a data source component when the associated dataset undergoes a change in its current record, when the current record in the associated dataset is about to be posted, and when the associated dataset state changes, respectively. Normally, it is preferable to implement the event handlers on a dataset to acknowledge the record changes or state changes. But it is convenient to implement the event handlers on the data source component when our code does not represent or depend on a particular dataset.

XML-based Data Access Components

The Data Access page in the Component Palette has XML-based data access components, in addition to traditional dataset-based components. These components are discussed in detail in Chapter 9, which covers applications development using the Borland WebSnap architecture.

Borland dbExpress Architecture

Overview

Starting with Kylix, Delphi 6, and C++Builder 6, Borland introduced a new database access architecture, dbExpress, which is a high-speed, small-footprint database access technology. The drivers are written to work exclusively with the unidirectional dbExpress dataset components. The features of dbExpress datasets are as follows:

- They are unidirectional and do not provide the ability to buffer records. We can navigate the result set in the forward direction only. That means that the only navigational methods permitted on these datasets are Next() and Last().

- An attempt to navigate backward or call First() or Prior() will raise an exception. Also, an attempt to position the cursor at a particular record is not permitted. Therefore, bookmarks are not supported by these datasets.

- Filters and lookup fields are not supported because they require record buffering.

- Since the unidirectional datasets use unidirectional cursors, the record access is faster and less resource intensive.

- dbExpress datasets cannot be connected to data-aware controls directly. Rather, they can be connected to a client dataset-provider duo in order to provide caching and display in data-aware controls. An alternate way to use dbExpress drivers is the use of TSQLClientDataSet, which is not a unidirectional dataset; it employs a client dataset to internally access the dbExpress drivers.

dbExpress Components

Having seen the features of the architecture, let's now discuss the components available in this architecture. The components of the dbExpress framework are very similar to the BDE or ADO framework. There is a connection component, TSQLConnection, which should be used to obtain a connection to the database. The connection component represents the database that we are planning to connect to, and therefore specifies the connection-related parameters, such as driver, user ID, password, and so on. To enable the traditional BDE-based systems to be migrated smoothly to the new dbExpress-based architecture, Borland provides components such as TSQLTable to migrate TTable-based code, TSQLQuery to migrate TQuery-based code, and TSQLStoredProc to migrate TStoredProc-based code. As the names suggest, these components are useful for accessing the complete table, executing a specific SQL command, and executing a stored procedure, respectively. I am talking about migrating a BDE-based application to the dbExpress framework. By making use of the similarities in the components, we may even try to migrate an ADO-based application to a dbExpress framework. The ADO framework is somewhat different from the rest of the frameworks because it is completely dependent on the Microsoft ADO architecture. Therefore, we may have to put more efforts in migrating an ADO-based application to dbExpress. You might wonder what the reason is for such a migration. In fact, due to the robustness of the ADO framework and Borland's implementation of ADO components, it is really not required to do such a migration except for specific reasons, such as if you wish to eliminate COM dependence of your application (since ADO runs on COM framework) or if you wish to make your application portable to a Linux operating system.

There is a general-purpose dataset, TSQLDataSet, that can be used to perform any SQL command or retrieve any table data. This is the most versatile component of the suite and is recommended in all the new applications. As mentioned earlier, there is another component, TSQLClientData-Set, that may be treated as a compound component containing the features of the generic TSQLDataSet, a client dataset (supporting record buffering), and an internal provider. This component is not a unidirectional dataset; rather, it is derived from TCustomClientDataSet and contains all the features of a client dataset. In addition, it uses an internal provider to work with the dbExpress TSQLConnection component.

Configuring a dbExpress Connection

dbExpress comes with a set of drivers, one for each of the supported databases. At the time of publication, Borland shipped drivers for InterBase, Oracle, DB2 Universal Database, Informix, PostgreSQL/RedHat Database, and MySQL with the Enterprise Edition of the product. The specific drivers shipped with a different edition may differ. Please check with Borland for more details. Since this is an emerging architecture, we can expect to have more drivers in the future for other database systems, either from Borland or third-party vendors. When C++Builder 6 is installed, the shipped dbExpress drivers are installed into the \bin directory of the product. Two configuration files, dbxdrivers.ini and dbxconnections.ini, are installed in the \Common Files\Borland Shared\DBExpress directory. The dbxdrivers.ini file contains definitions of all the installed drivers for the dbExpress framework. The dbxconnections.ini file contains all the connection definitions as configured on the system.

Here we need to understand the difference between a driver and a connection. A *driver* is a dbExpress library file (built to dbExpress specifications), which connects to the vendor-supplied database client software with vendor- (driver-) specific parameters. Therefore, for every database server, there is one driver definition entry in the dbxdrivers.ini file. A *connection* is specific to a database or a schema hosted by the database. For example, an Oracle client installed on the system allows us to configure service definitions to different databases hosted on different hosts or even different environments. Each service definition uniquely identifies the database to which it connects. In other words, Oracle identifies different database connections as services. A system having Oracle client software installed on it will be able to make connections to multiple databases (through the respective service definitions) using a single dbExpress Oracle driver. In such a scenario, there is only one entry in the dbxdrivers.ini file, whereas each database (service) connection is to be configured in the dbxconnections.ini file with an entry of its own. Therefore, we rarely change the driver configuration file, but we update the connection configuration file every time we add or update a connection. However, we have to change the driver configuration file if a driver's specific parameters change. Also, please note that the difference between the driver definition and connection definition is very minute. An analogy for a driver and its connection is the class and an instance of that class in the object-oriented paradigm.

Let's walk through the steps involved in configuring a database connection:

1. Create a new project in the IDE. Since this demonstration is only for establishing a connection, it is not required to save the project and unit files.

2. From the dbExpress tab in the Component Palette, drop an **SQLConnection** component. Double-click this component to display the connection parameter editor dialog. The displayed screen looks like Figure 6-5.

    In the connection parameter editor, a combo box lets you choose a driver name (as defined in the dbxdrivers.ini file). In the list box below the combo box, a list of predefined connections for the selected driver is displayed. You can also view all the connections in this list. In the right pane, a list of connection parameters is displayed; they are self-explanatory.

The most common connection parameters that we have to set are Database, User_Name, and Password. For Oracle, Database is the Oracle Service name and for InterBase, it is the database filename, and so on.

3. Click the **OK** button to close the dialog.

4. Test the connection by setting the Connected property to **true**. If the connection parameters are set properly and the component is able to load the dbExpress driver properly, the connection is established immediately. Otherwise, the appropriate error message is displayed; change the connection parameters to make the connection work.

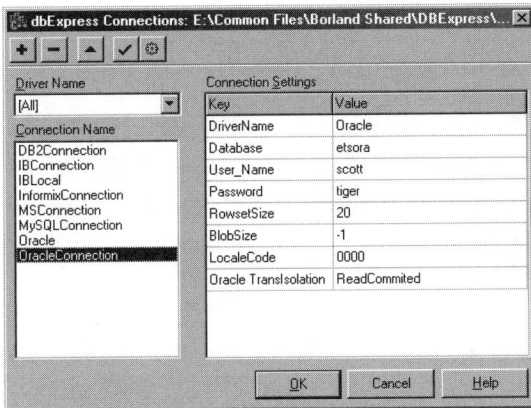

Figure 6-5: dbExpress Connection parameter editor

Using Unidirectional Datasets with Data-aware Controls

As we discussed earlier, unidirectional datasets do not provide a record buffer. Therefore, we can only do a forward navigation of the record set. Because of this, we cannot directly connect the TCustomSQLDataSet descendants to a data source that is linked to data-aware controls. If we try to do this, an exception is raised either during design time or run time.

We have two ways to display data using the dbExpress drivers through data-aware controls. We will discuss both of them here.

Through TSQLClientDataSet

TSQLClientDataSet falls in the hierarchy of TCustomClientDataSet and hence is not a unidirectional dataset. This component encapsulates the combined functionality of three individual components: a TClientDataSet, a TDataSetProvider, and a TSQLDataSet. Figure 6-6 describes how a

TSQLClientDataSet component can be used to display data using data-aware controls.

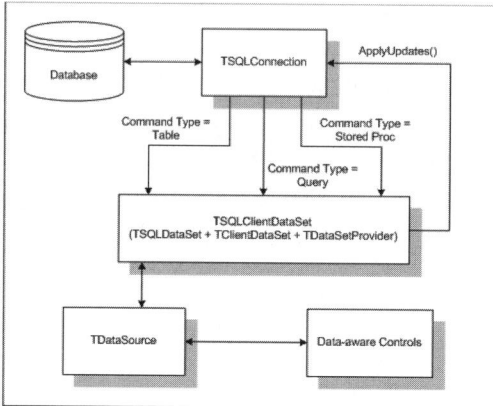

Figure 6-6: Using TSQLClientDataSet to display data using a TSQLConnection

The TSQLClientDataSet has the record-buffering feature similar to TClientDataSet, the ability to interact with a dbExpress driver similar to TSQLDataSet, and the ability to apply updates and resolve update errors similar to TDataSetProvider.

The DBConnection property should be set to a valid TSQLConnection component in order to establish connection with the target database. The CommandType property should be used to specify which type of command we wish to execute with this dataset. When set to ctTable, we can access the whole table; when set to ctQuery, we can execute a query on the target database; and when set to ctStoredProc, we can execute a stored procedure. We should use the CommandText property to identify the table or stored procedure that we are going to work with on the target database and to set the SQL statement when we are executing a query. During design time, if the connection is already established and the CommandType is set to ctTable, the CommandText property displays a drop-down list of all the existing tables within the database. Since the TSQLClientDataSet has the record-buffering capability, we can use bookmarks, set filters, and navigate the dataset backward with the Prior() and First() methods. The Params property can be used to pass input parameters or as placeholders for output parameters in conjunction with a query or stored procedure.

Note: Please note that the Params property as exposed by the TCustomClientDataSet descendants and TCustomSQL-DataSet descendants is an object of TParams, which is a collection of TParam objects. This is different from the Parameters property as exposed by the TCustomADODataSet descendants, which is an object of TParameters representing a collection of TParameter objects.

The changes applied to the dataset by the Post() method are only internal to the record buffer but will not be applied to the target database until we perform the ApplyUpdates() method on the dataset. Since the provider component is internal to this dataset component, we only implement one set of events corresponding to BeforeApplyUpdates, AfterApplyUpdates, or other such events we have seen with the client dataset and provider duo. This means we do not have any control over the provider-specific events. If your application is complex and you need such control over the provider-specific events, then you are advised to use the client dataset and dataset provider separately, which will be discussed in the following sub-section.

Now let's walk through an example to demonstrate what we discussed here:

1. Create a new VCL project. Save the project and unit files with names of your choice in a directory of your choice. I saved them with the default names provided by C++Builder IDE.

2. From the dbExpress page in the Component Palette, drop an **SQLConnection** component and an **SQLClientDataSet** component. From the DataAccess page, drop a **DataSource** component. From the DataControls page, drop a **DBGrid** component and a **DBNavigator** component. Finally, from the Standard page, drop four **Button** components, a **Memo** component, and a **Label** component.

3. For the sake of clarity, let's change the captions on the buttons, since these are the components that interact with the user. Set the caption of Button1 to "**Table**," the caption of Button2 to "**Query**," the caption of Button3 to "**ApplyUpdates**," and the caption of Button4 to "**CancelUpdates**."

4. For the SQLClientDataSet component, set the DBConnection property to **SQLConnection1**. For the DataSource component, set the DataSet property to **SQLClientDataSet1**. For both the DBGrid and DBNavigator components, set the DataSource property to **DataSource1**.

5. I enhanced the font size and set the style as bold for the Caption property of the Label component. For the Memo component, set BevelInner and BevelOuter to **bvLowered**, BevelKind to **Flat**, and ScrollBars to **ssVertical**.

6. Set a suitable caption for the form.

7. Now implement the event handlers. The complete source code for the sample application is presented in Listing 6-3 (cpp file) and Listing 6-4 (header file).

Listing 6-3: Unit1.cpp

```cpp
//---------------------------------------------------------------------------

#include <vcl.h>
#pragma hdrstop

#include "Unit1.h"
//---------------------------------------------------------------------------
#pragma package(smart_init)
#pragma resource "*.dfm"
TForm1 *Form1;
//---------------------------------------------------------------------------
__fastcall TForm1::TForm1(TComponent* Owner)
        : TForm(Owner)
{
}
//---------------------------------------------------------------------------

void __fastcall TForm1::FormActivate(TObject *Sender)
{
    SQLConnection1->LoginPrompt = false;
    SQLConnection1->Connected = true;
}
//---------------------------------------------------------------------------
void __fastcall TForm1::Button1Click(TObject *Sender)
{
    SQLClientDataSet1->Close();
    SQLClientDataSet1->CommandType = ctTable;
    SQLClientDataSet1->CommandText = "customer";
    Label1->Caption = "Table Name";
    Memo1->Lines->Clear();
    Memo1->Lines->Add("customer");
    SQLClientDataSet1->Open();
}
//---------------------------------------------------------------------------
void __fastcall TForm1::Button2Click(TObject *Sender)
{
    SQLClientDataSet1->Close();
    SQLClientDataSet1->CommandType = ctQuery;
    Label1->Caption = "Query SQL";
    Memo1->Lines->Clear();
    Memo1->Lines->Add("select * from employee ");
    Memo1->Lines->Add("where job_country = 'USA' ");
    SQLClientDataSet1->CommandText = Memo1->Text;
    SQLClientDataSet1->Open();
}
//---------------------------------------------------------------------------
void __fastcall TForm1::Button3Click(TObject *Sender)
{
    SQLClientDataSet1->ApplyUpdates(-1);
}
//---------------------------------------------------------------------------
void __fastcall TForm1::Button4Click(TObject *Sender)
```

```
  {
    SQLClientDataSet1->CancelUpdates();
  }
//---------------------------------------------------------------------------
```

Listing 6-4: Unit1.h

```
//---------------------------------------------------------------------------

#ifndef Unit1H
#define Unit1H
//---------------------------------------------------------------------------
#include <Classes.hpp>
#include <Controls.hpp>
#include <StdCtrls.hpp>
#include <Forms.hpp>
#include <DB.hpp>
#include <DBClient.hpp>
#include <DBLocal.hpp>
#include <DBLocalS.hpp>
#include <DBXpress.hpp>
#include <Provider.hpp>
#include <SqlExpr.hpp>
#include <DBGrids.hpp>
#include <Grids.hpp>
#include <DBCtrls.hpp>
#include <ExtCtrls.hpp>
//---------------------------------------------------------------------------
class TForm1 : public TForm
{
__published:            // IDE-managed components
    TSQLClientDataSet *SQLClientDataSet1;
    TSQLConnection *SQLConnection1;
    TDataSource *DataSource1;
    TDBGrid *DBGrid1;
    TDBNavigator *DBNavigator1;
    TButton *Button1;
    TButton *Button2;
    TButton *Button3;
    TButton *Button4;
    TMemo *Memo1;
    TLabel *Label1;
    void __fastcall FormActivate(TObject *Sender);
    void __fastcall Button1Click(TObject *Sender);
    void __fastcall Button2Click(TObject *Sender);
    void __fastcall Button3Click(TObject *Sender);
    void __fastcall Button4Click(TObject *Sender);
private:                 // User declarations
public:                  // User declarations
    __fastcall TForm1(TComponent* Owner);
};
//---------------------------------------------------------------------------
extern PACKAGE TForm1 *Form1;
//---------------------------------------------------------------------------
#endif
```

Through TClientDataSet and TDataSetProvider

In the previous section, we saw how we can make use of the compound component TSQLClientDataSet to work with dbExpress connections. There we have not really used a unidirectional dataset.

In this section, we will discuss how we can use the client dataset and provider components separately but in conjunction with each other to enable us to use the dbExpress unidirectional datasets. Figure 6-7 describes this scenario pictorially.

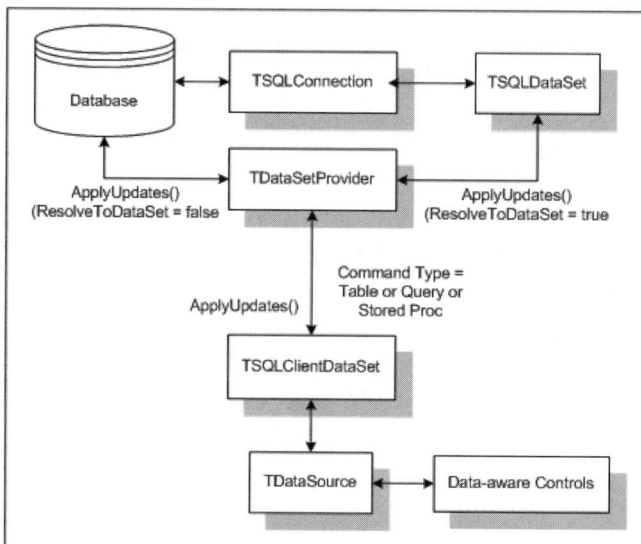

Figure 6-7: Using unidirectional datasets with client dataset and dataset provider

TSQLDataSet is the most versatile unidirectional dataset. When connected to a TSQLConnection component through the SQLConnection property, it establishes the database connection through a dbExpress driver. The CommandType and CommandText properties work together in a way similar to what was explained in the previous section for the TSQLClient-DataSet. In Figure 6-7 and in the following sample program, I used TSQLDataSet for demonstration purposes. I did this purposely instead of using TSQLTable, TSQLQuery, and TSQLStoredProc individually. The primary reason is that Borland recommends using the TSQLDataSet in all future development work, and the individual components TSQLTable, TSQLQuery, and TSQLStoredProc are provided for easy migration of current BDE-based systems to dbExpress framework. Also, it is usually easy to use individual components rather than a more generic component in different ways. Therefore, I wanted to show you how a general-purpose (but versatile) component can be used in a context like this. By the time you complete reading this section, I am sure that you will be able to figure out how to use the individual components in place of the general-purpose component.

The TDataSetProvider is an external entity in this case and provides the dataset connectivity to the TSQLDataSet component. The TClientDataSet component now communicates with the TDataSetProvider with respect to retrieving data and applying updates. We can also note from Figure 6-7 that we can apply updates to the dataset directly if we set the ResolveToDataSet property of the provider to true; otherwise, by default the updates are applied through the database, which enhances performance. The rest of the details in the figure are self-explanatory.

Now I will demonstrate the concept programmatically. The sample program is a two-tier application with SQLDataSet, DataSetProvider, and ClientDataSet on the same form.

1. Create a new VCL project. Save the project and unit files with names of your choice in a directory of your choice. I saved them with the default names provided by C++Builder IDE.

2. From the dbExpress page in the Component Palette, drop an **SQLConnection** component and an **SQLDataSet** component. From the Data Access page, drop a **DataSource** component, a **DataSet-Provider** component, and two **ClientDataSet** components. From the Data Controls page, drop a **DBGrid** component and a **DBNavigator** component. Finally, from the Standard page, drop five **Button** components, a **Memo** component, and a **Label** component.

3. For the sake of clarity, let's change the captions on the buttons, since these are the components that interact with the user. Set the caption of Button1 to "**Table**," the caption of Button2 to "**Query**," the caption of Button3 to "**StoredProc**," the caption of Button4 to "**ApplyUpdates**," and the caption of Button5 to "**CancelUpdates**."

   ClientDataSet1 is used to retrieve the record buffer as sent by the provider and is used in conjunction with table retrieval or a select query that returns a result set. ClientDataset2 is used to display the output parameter values as retrieved by the stored procedure. Therefore, the structure of the ClientDataSet2 component is built during design time itself, and you may refer to the source code for the same.

4. For the SQLDataSet component, set the SQLConnection property to **SQLConnection1**.

5. For both the DBGrid and DBNavigator components, set the Data-Source property to **DataSource1**. At this time, we are not setting the

DataSet property of DataSource1. We will do that in the program because we are using two ClientDataSets for different purposes. The DataSource component connects one of the two ClientDataSets to the data controls.

6. I enhanced the font size and set the style to bold for the Caption property of the Label component. For the Memo component, set BevelInner and BevelOuter to **bvLowered**, BevelKind to **Flat**, and ScrollBars to **ssVertical**.

7. Set a suitable caption for the form.

8. Now implement the event handlers. The event handlers are similar to the previous program to some extent. But notice that the Command-Type and CommandText properties are set on the SQLDataSet instead of the ClientDataSet. Also, after opening the SQLDataSet, we have to open the ClientDataSet in order to accept the data packet from the provider.

To keep the program simple, I am not setting the CommandText property of the ClientDataSet. However, by doing so we can influence the data access logic of the SQLDataSet. We will see this in an example in Chapter 10, "Developing Distributed Applications."

The complete source code for the sample application is presented in Listing 6-5 (cpp file) and Listing 6-6 (header file).

Listing 6-5: Unit1.cpp

```cpp
//-------------------------------------------------------------------------

#include <vcl.h>
#pragma hdrstop

#include "Unit1.h"
//-------------------------------------------------------------------------
#pragma package(smart_init)
#pragma resource "*.dfm"
TForm1 *Form1;
//-------------------------------------------------------------------------
__fastcall TForm1::TForm1(TComponent* Owner)
    : TForm(Owner)
{
}
//-------------------------------------------------------------------------

void __fastcall TForm1::FormActivate(TObject *Sender)
{
    SQLConnection1->LoginPrompt = false;
    SQLConnection1->Connected = true;
}
//-------------------------------------------------------------------------

void __fastcall TForm1::Button1Click(TObject *Sender)
```

```
{
    ClientDataSet2->Close();
    SQLDataSet1->Close();
    SQLDataSet1->CommandType = ctTable;
    SQLDataSet1->CommandText = "customer";
    Label1->Caption = "Table Name";
    Memo1->Lines->Clear();
    Memo1->Lines->Add("customer");
    SQLDataSet1->Open();
    ClientDataSet1->Close();
    if (ClientDataSet1->Params->Count > 0)
        ClientDataSet1->Params->Clear();
    ClientDataSet1->Open();
    DataSource1->DataSet = ClientDataSet1;
}
//---------------------------------------------------------------------------
void __fastcall TForm1::Button2Click(TObject *Sender)
{

    ClientDataSet2->Close();
    SQLDataSet1->Close();
    SQLDataSet1->CommandType = ctQuery;
    Label1->Caption = "Query SQL";
    Memo1->Lines->Clear();
    Memo1->Lines->Add("select * from employee ");
    Memo1->Lines->Add("where job_country = 'USA' ");
    SQLDataSet1->CommandText = Memo1->Text;
    SQLDataSet1->Open();
    ClientDataSet1->Close();
    if (ClientDataSet1->Params->Count > 0)
        ClientDataSet1->Params->Clear();
    ClientDataSet1->Open();
    DataSource1->DataSet = ClientDataSet1;
}
//---------------------------------------------------------------------------
void __fastcall TForm1::Button3Click(TObject *Sender)
{
    SQLDataSet1->Close();
    SQLDataSet1->CommandType = ctStoredProc;
    Label1->Caption = "Stored Proc Name";
    Memo1->Lines->Clear();
    Memo1->Lines->Add("MAIL_LABEL");
    SQLDataSet1->CommandText = "MAIL_LABEL";
    SQLDataSet1->Prepared = true;
    SQLDataSet1->Params->Items[0]->AsInteger = 1001;
    SQLDataSet1->ExecSQL(false);
    ClientDataSet1->Close();
    ClientDataSet1->FetchParams();

    ClientDataSet2->ReadOnly = false;
    ClientDataSet2->Close();
    ClientDataSet2->Open();
    ClientDataSet2->EmptyDataSet();

    ClientDataSet2->Append();
    const AnsiString Line1(ClientDataSet1->Params->ParamByName("LINE1")->AsString);
    ClientDataSet2->FieldByName("LabelLineValue")->AsString = Line1;
    ClientDataSet2->Post();

    ClientDataSet2->Append();
```

```
        const AnsiString Line2(ClientDataSet1->Params->ParamByName("LINE2")->AsString);
        ClientDataSet2->FieldByName("LabelLineValue")->AsString = Line2;
        ClientDataSet2->Post();

        ClientDataSet2->Append();
        const AnsiString Line3(ClientDataSet1->Params->ParamByName("LINE3")->AsString);
        ClientDataSet2->FieldByName("LabelLineValue")->AsString = Line3;
        ClientDataSet2->Post();

        ClientDataSet2->Append();
        const AnsiString Line4(ClientDataSet1->Params->ParamByName("LINE4")->AsString);
        ClientDataSet2->FieldByName("LabelLineValue")->AsString = Line4;
        ClientDataSet2->Post();

        ClientDataSet2->Append();
        const AnsiString Line5(ClientDataSet1->Params->ParamByName("LINE5")->AsString);
        ClientDataSet2->FieldByName("LabelLineValue")->AsString = Line5;
        ClientDataSet2->Post();

        ClientDataSet2->Append();
        const AnsiString Line6(ClientDataSet1->Params->ParamByName("LINE6")->AsString);
        ClientDataSet2->FieldByName("LabelLineValue")->AsString = Line6;
        ClientDataSet2->Post();
        DataSource1->DataSet = ClientDataSet2;
        ClientDataSet2->ReadOnly = true;
        ClientDataSet2->First();
}
//---------------------------------------------------------------------------
void __fastcall TForm1::Button4Click(TObject *Sender)
{
    if (ClientDataSet1->Active)
        ClientDataSet1->ApplyUpdates(-1);
}
//---------------------------------------------------------------------------
void __fastcall TForm1::Button5Click(TObject *Sender)
{
    if (ClientDataSet1->Active)
        ClientDataSet1->CancelUpdates();
}
//---------------------------------------------------------------------------
```

Listing 6-6: Unit1.h

```
//---------------------------------------------------------------------------

#ifndef Unit1H
#define Unit1H
//---------------------------------------------------------------------------
#include <Classes.hpp>
#include <Controls.hpp>
#include <StdCtrls.hpp>
#include <Forms.hpp>
#include <DB.hpp>
#include <DBXpress.hpp>
#include <FMTBcd.hpp>
#include <SqlExpr.hpp>
#include <DBGrids.hpp>
#include <Grids.hpp>
#include <DBClient.hpp>
#include <Provider.hpp>
```

```
#include <DBCtrls.hpp>
#include <ExtCtrls.hpp>
//---------------------------------------------------------------------------
class TForm1 : public TForm
{
__published:            // IDE-managed components
    TSQLConnection *SQLConnection1;
    TSQLDataSet *SQLDataSet1;
    TDataSource *DataSource1;
    TDBGrid *DBGrid1;
    TButton *Button1;
    TButton *Button2;
    TButton *Button3;
    TButton *Button4;
    TButton *Button5;
    TClientDataSet *ClientDataSet1;
    TDataSetProvider *DataSetProvider1;
    TDBNavigator *DBNavigator1;
    TMemo *Memo1;
    TLabel *Label1;
    TClientDataSet *ClientDataSet2;
    TStringField *ClientDataSet2LabelLineValue;
    void __fastcall FormActivate(TObject *Sender);
    void __fastcall Button1Click(TObject *Sender);
    void __fastcall Button2Click(TObject *Sender);
    void __fastcall Button4Click(TObject *Sender);
    void __fastcall Button5Click(TObject *Sender);
    void __fastcall Button3Click(TObject *Sender);
private:                // User declarations
public:                 // User declarations
    __fastcall TForm1(TComponent* Owner);
};
//---------------------------------------------------------------------------
extern PACKAGE TForm1 *Form1;
//---------------------------------------------------------------------------
#endif
```

Using Unidirectional Datasets without Data Controls

Every application is not just a GUI application. The unidirectional datasets can be used in background processing. There are numerous applications that need data retrieval in background mode. For example, you may have to generate address labels from a mail database, generate a flat file containing credit card transactions across the network to a financial institution, generate reports for management's review, and so on.

In such cases, you have to process the result set in just one direction, the forward direction. When the unidirectional dataset is opened, the record cursor points to the first record. We process each record in a loop in the forward direction until we reach the end of the result set. We are not constrained from interacting with other objects by the unidirectional navigation restriction. If we need update records from the current result set or records in another table, we can create objects and call methods on these objects that work in isolated transactions. The only restriction is that we should not try to edit records in the current result set. We can refresh the current result set at any point in time, if our programming logic demands so.

By designing a unidirectional cursor-based architecture, Borland is providing us with a faster way of accessing data by avoiding unwanted record-buffering when not required. When record buffering is required, we are augmenting the unidirectional dataset with client dataset and provider duo.

Borland InterBase Express for InterBase

Overview

Now we will focus our attention on another high-performance data access architecture, InterBase Express (or IBX). As the name suggests, the framework is designed to work exclusively with Borland InterBase databases. If you know that you are going to use InterBase databases exclusively in your application, you can make use of this architecture. If you are migrating your application from another database to InterBase, it is worthwhile to consider using this framework. There are many factors that make InterBase a good choice for many organizations. It is a very lightweight, high-performance database and provides a very cost-effective solution, even for larger applications. For details on actual licensing costs, please check with Borland Corporation. Moreover, Borland has made it available through the open source channels for people who are very serious about open source products.

Until now, we have been discussing database frameworks that mandate the use of at least one driver (if not more) to access a database. The core of any database driver is a set of API (application programming interface) functions provided by the database vendor. Whether we use ADO, BDE, or dbExpress, we are using the components of these frameworks to interact with the database driver API to provide us with access to the database, which means we are using the framework driver API in conjunction with the database driver API. But the components in the IBX framework directly interact with the database call level API, thus avoiding at least one layer of access. We do not use any framework-specific drivers when we use IBX components. IBX components are available from Delphi 5 and C++Builder 5 onward. Since the IBX components are VCL based, they can be used only with Delphi and C++Builder. The CLX versions of these components are also available for Delphi 6, C++Builder 6, and Kylix platforms.

IBX Components

There are similarities in the IBX component set and the database component sets that we have discussed so far. However, by using IBX components, we are able to access more InterBase-specific features since they are designed exclusively for Borland InterBase databases.

TIBDatabase, TIBDatabaseInfo, and TIBTransaction

The TIBDatabase component represents a single connection to a database. But more than one dataset can be connected to the database simultaneously using this component. This component is derived from TCustomConnection and behaves similarly to other connection components. However, this component does not need a connection string or driver setup information; rather, you directly assign an InterBase database to its DatabaseName property. To establish a database connection, the minimum requirement is the user_name and password values in the Params property. These values can be set during design time or run time. If the LoginPrompt property is set to false, then the user_name and password are expected to be preset. If it is true, we have the opportunity to implement the OnLogin event handler, in which case the login dialog is not prompted during run time. If we set LoginPrompt to true and we do not implement the OnLogin event handler, then the default login dialog will be prompted. The OnLogin event handler may be implemented to dynamically set the user name and password values from encrypted strings.

> **Note:** In fact, the OnLogin event handler is derived from TCustomConnection and overridden. Therefore, it may be implemented in a similar way in applications using TADOConnection and TSQLConnection components.

The Handle property gives us the database handle that can be used to make direct calls to the InterBase API. This is a distinct advantage to using the IBX components over other frameworks.

The TIBDatabaseInfo component may be used to obtain the database information, such as database characteristics, environmental characteristics, performance statistics, and database operation counts about the database attached to the corresponding TIBDatabase component. Since most of the properties and methods of this component provide us with only read-only data, we should use this component mainly for informational purposes. We will quickly run through some of the properties and methods that may be of use to us. The Allocation property gives the number of pages allocated as a long integer. The BaseLevel property gives the database version number as a long integer. The DBSiteName property gives the database site name as a string, which is typically the name of the server that is hosting the database. The Handle property gives the database handle, which may be used in some direct InterBase API calls. The NoReserve property is a long integer value; a value of 0 indicates that space is reserved on each database page for holding backup versions of modified records (which is the default value), and a value of 1 indicates that no space is reserved. The PageSize property is a long integer indicating the number of bytes per page. The Version property is the database version as a string. The CurrentMemory property is a long integer indicating the amount of server memory currently in use. MaxMemory property is a long integer indicating the maximum amount of memory used at one time since the first process attached to the database. The NumBuffers property is a long integer indicating the number of memory buffers currently allocated. The UserNames property is a TStringList object containing the names of all users currently attached to the database.

The performance statistics are values that have accumulated since the database was first attached to any process, and they include four properties: Reads, Writes, Fetches, and Marks. The Reads property is a long integer indicating the number of page reads that have taken place since the current database was first attached to any process. The Writes property is a long integer indicating the number of page writes that have taken place since the current database was first attached to any process. The Fetches property is a long integer indicating the number of reads from the memory buffer cache. The Marks property is a long integer indicating the number of writes to the memory buffer cache. The database operation counts are values on operations that have taken place within the context of currently calling processes, and are calculated on a per-table basis. These values include DeleteCount, InsertCount, and UpdateCount, which indicate the number of deletes, inserts, and updates, respectively; ReqdSeqCount, which indicates the number of sequential database reads done on each table; and ReadIdxCount, which indicates the number of sequential database reads done via an index.

Every dataset in the IBX family executes commands within a transaction identified by the TIBTransaction component. When we create a TIBTransaction object in an application, its DefaultDatabase property should be set to a valid TIBDatabase component. All the IBX datasets have a Database property to assign a TIBDatabase component and a Transaction property to assign a TIBTransaction component, with the exception of TIBClientDataSet, which has the corresponding property names of DBConnection and DBTransaction, respectively. Before we attempt to use a dataset in the IBX family, we must set these properties at a minimum.

All the updates, inserts, and deletes on a dataset are performed within the context of the transaction object. The StartTransaction() method on the transaction object marks the beginning of a transaction. A transaction ends either by rolling back all the changes by calling the Rollback() method or committing the changes by calling the Commit() method. If we desire to roll back or commit the changes without ending the transaction, we may use RollbackRetaining() or CommitRetaining(), respectively, in place of Rollback() or Commit(). An attempt to start a transaction while a transaction is already in progress raises an exception. An attempt to commit or roll back the changes while either keeping the transaction context or ending the transaction context, while a transaction is not yet started, also raises an exception. The InTransaction property returns true or false, according to whether a transaction is in progress or not. Therefore, this property value should be checked before calling any of the above methods. Also remember that the CommitRetaining() and RollbackRetaining() methods do not end the transaction. They should only be used if the data must be saved to the database or changes be cancelled intermittently, as per the application. If we do not explicitly start the transaction associated with a dataset, then every individual insert, update, and delete is executed within the context of an implicit transaction associated with the TIBTransaction component. More than one dataset can share the same transaction component, in which case the context of the transaction is applied to all the datasets using the specific transaction object.

A database connection (identified by a TIBDatabase component) may open multiple transactions (identified by separate TIBTransaction objects) at the same time. The simultaneous transactions are independent of each other and may conflict with each other's work if updates in these transactions are applied against common tables. The isolation level of a transaction determines to what extent it is impacted by updates made by other transactions. It is one among many parameters that determine the behavior of a transaction. The transaction parameters are identified by the Params property of the TIBTransaction component, which is a TStrings object. Adding one or more of these parameter names to the Params property enables the corresponding parameters. This may be done during design time or run time. If we do not set Params explicitly for a transaction before it is started, a set of default parameters is set by the TIBTransaction component itself when it is started. The default parameter set includes isc_tpb_write, isc_tpb_concurrency, and isc_tpb_wait.

Table 6-4 lists the parameters of a transaction that may be used while setting the Params property. The parameters fall into four main categories:

access method specifiers, access mode specifiers, transaction isolation level specifiers, and lock resolution specifiers.

Access method specifiers describe how the current transaction shares access to a table along with other simultaneously executing transactions, such as shared, protected, or exclusive access on a table. *Access mode specifiers* describe the actions that can be performed by the functions associated by the transaction, such as read-only or read-write. *Isolation level specifiers* describe the view of the database seen by a transaction as it relates to actions performed by other simultaneously occurring transactions. *Lock resolution specifiers* describe how a transaction should react if a lock conflict occurs.

Table 6-4: Parameters of a transaction in InterBase

Parameter	Description
isc_tpb_shared	This model allows concurrent, shared access of a specified table among all transactions. This model may be used in conjunction with isc_tpb_lock_read and isc_tpb_lock_write to establish the lock option. This is an access method specifier.
isc_tpb_protected	This model permits concurrent, restricted access of a specified table. This model may be used in conjunction with isc_tpb_lock_read and isc_tpb_lock_write to establish the lock option. This is an access method specifier.
isc_tpb_exclusive	This model permits exclusive access of a specified table. This model may be used in conjunction with isc_tpb_lock_read and isc_tpb_lock_write to establish the lock option. This is an access method specifier.
isc_tpb_wait	This model specifies that the transaction has to wait for the conflicting resource to be released before retrying an operation. This is a lock resolution specifier.
isc_tpb_nowait	This model specifies that the transaction should not wait for the conflicting resource to be released. Rather, it indicates that an update conflict error be thrown. This is a lock resolution specifier.
isc_tpb_read	This model enables the transaction to start in the read-only access mode and only permits selecting data from tables. This is an access mode specifier.
isc_tpb_write	This model enables the transaction to start in the read-write access mode and permits selecting, inserting, updating, and deleting table data. This is an access mode specifier.
isc_tpb_lock_read	This model enables the transaction to start in the read-only access mode of a specified table. This parameter may be used in conjunction with the isc_tpb_shared, isc_tpb_protected, and isc_tpb_exclusive parameters to establish the lock option. This is an access mode specifier.
isc_tpb_lock_write	This model enables the transaction to start in the read-write access mode of a specified table. This parameter may be used in conjunction with the isc_tpb_shared, isc_tpb_protected, and isc_tpb_exclusive parameters to establish the lock option. This is an access mode specifier.
isc_tpb_consistency	This is a table-locking transaction model and is hence serializable. This is an isolation-level specifier.
isc_tpb_concurrency	This is a high throughput, high-concurrency transaction model with repeatable-read concurrency. This model takes full advantage of the InterBase multi-generational transactional model. It is one of the default parameters. This is an isolation-level specifier.
isc_tpb_read_committed	This is a high throughput, high-concurrency transaction model that can read changes committed by other concurrent transactions. However, transactions in this mode do not provide repeatable read. This is an isolation-level specifier.

Parameter	Description
isc_tpb_rec_version	This model enables an isc_tpb_read_committed transaction to read the most recently committed version of a record, even if other uncommitted versions are pending. This is an isolation-level specifier.
isc_tpb_no_rec_version	This model enables an isc_tpb_read_committed transaction to read only the latest committed version of a record. If an uncommitted version of a record is pending and isc_tpb_wait is also specified, the transaction waits for the pending record to be committed or rolled back before proceeding. Otherwise, a lock conflict error is reported at once. This is an isolation-level specifier.

Listing 6-7 displays example code to set the transaction parameters and start the transaction explicitly. To compile this code, you must include the ibheader.hpp header file if you are writing a server module without dropping IBX components from the IDE. If you are dropping IBX components from the IDE, this file is automatically included in the form header file.

Listing 6-7

```
IBTransaction1->Params->Add("isc_tpb_write");
IBTransaction1->Params->Add("isc_tpb_read_committed");
IBTransaction1->Params->Add("isc_tpb_rec_version");
IBTransaction1->StartTransaction();
```

A Word about Transaction Isolation Levels

Let me take the opportunity to explain the transaction isolation levels to enable you to make better use of them while setting the transaction parameters.

The transaction isolation level of isc_tpb_concurrency means it allows concurrent transactions to share data. In this mode, a transaction sees a stable view of the database as of the instance it starts and can share read/write access to tables with simultaneous transactions. This is the default isolation level if we do not set one.

The transaction isolation level of isc_tpb_read_committed does not provide a consistent view of the database. Unlike a concurrency transaction, a read-committed transaction sees changes made and committed by transactions that were active after this transaction started. Either isc_tpb_rec_version or isc_tpb_no_rec_version should be used with this transaction to obtain refined control over the committed changes a transaction is permitted to access. When we use isc_tpb_rec_version, the transaction can see the latest committed version of a row, even if a more recent uncommitted version is pending. When we use isc_tpb_no_rec_version, the transaction waits for any pending but uncommitted changes (to the row) to be committed or rolled back before any operation is performed. This is the default refinement to an isc_tpb_read_committed transaction if we do not set one. This default setting may result in a deadlock situation.

The deadlock situation may, however, be avoided by also using the isc_tpb_nowait parameter.

The transaction isolation level of isc_tpb_consistency is a restrictive isolation level. It prevents the transaction from accessing tables if they are being written to by other transactions. It also prevents other transactions from writing to a table once this transaction starts writing to it. This isolation level is designed to guarantee the highest requirements for transaction consistency, which means if a transaction writes to a table before other simultaneous read and write transactions, then only it can change a table's data. Since this isolation level restricts shared access to tables, it should be used with care.

Before we set the transaction parameters, we have to consider each transaction's isolation level and access mode carefully for all the transactions in the application that may access the same tables simultaneously in order to avoid possible lock conflicts.

Datasets in the IBX Family

With enough understanding of the database connection and transaction components, now it is time to continue our discussion on the datasets and their features provided in the IBX family of components.

IBX offers standard dataset components such as TIBTable for accessing a database table, TIBQuery for executing a query on the database, and TIBStoredProc for executing a stored procedure. In addition, IBX offers TIBDataSet as a generic dataset to process select, insert, update, and delete SQL statements, and TIBSQL to process SQL statements with minimal overhead. The functioning of TIBTable, TIBQuery, and TIBStoredProc are very similar to their counterparts in the BDE architecture, with the exception of the IBX-specific features. Here we discuss some features that are more relevant in the IBX context.

When more than one TIBTable component is linked to the same database table in the underlying database and each of them has its own data source component linking to a data control, such as a TDBGrid, then each of the table components has its own cursor position within its view of the table data. This is usually advantageous because each of the data controls may be pointing to a different record as navigated by the user(s). However, if we need to synchronize all the table components to point to the same record, we can achieve this by executing the GoToCurrent(TIBTable *OtherTable) method on a table component to synchronize its cursor position with another table component, as specified in the method argument and linked to the same database table. For this feature to work, it is required that the

Database and TableName properties be the same for both the table components. This method is only available for the TIBTable component. During design time, we can set the table name by selecting one from the drop-down list in the Object Inspector after setting the Database and Transaction properties. By default, the drop-down list displays only user tables in the current database schema. We can make it display system tables and/or user views by setting the corresponding values to true in the TableTypes property. The EmptyTable() method of the TIBTable deletes all the records in the underlying database table, and the DeleteTable() method deletes the underlying table.

The Prepare() and Unprepare() methods of the TIBQuery component are used to prepare a query for allocating resources to execute the query and to "unprepare" the query so that the resources previously allocated are released. The StmtHandle property of the TIBQuery component gives us the query statement handle to be used in an InterBase API call. By design, the TIBQuery component provides a read-only dataset. If you have to perform updates on a read-only dataset, then set its UpdateObject property to a valid TIBUpdateSQL component, which is discussed later in this chapter. The Params property of the TIBQuery component is a TParams object, and it should be used to set arguments used in the SQL statement.

The TIBStoredProc component should not be used with stored procedures that return a result set. It should only be used with stored procedures that do not return a result set. Therefore, do not use the Active property or Open() method on a TIBStoredProc component. Rather, you should use the ExecProc() method only. The Params property of the TIBStoredProc component is a TParams object, and it should be used to set arguments in the SQL statement. The StmtHandle property of the TIBStoredProc component gives us the statement handle of the stored procedure to be used in an InterBase API call.

We will now discuss the properties and methods common to all the TIBCustomDataSet descendants. Executing the IsSequenced() method determines whether the records in the underlying database table are sequenced or not. The return value of this method is a Boolean value. If this method returns true, we can locate a record by setting the RecNo property to that record number. All the updates to a dataset can be cached by setting the CachedUpdates property to true. Thus, when CachedUpdates is enabled, all the updates are stored in an internal cache within the client application, and they are all sent to the database table at once when the ApplyUpdates() method is executed on the dataset. The CancelUpdates() method cancels all the pending updates within the cache. To cancel the update on a single record, execute the RevertRecord() method instead of CancelUpdates(). Even after the ApplyUpdates() method is executed, the updates are not committed to the database; rather, they are controlled within the transaction linked to the dataset. When Commit() or CommitRetaining() is called on the transaction objects, the updates are finally committed. Since the client cache contains more than one record, we have the method CachedUpdateStatus() that executes on the current record and gives us the status of the pending action on this record. The possible status values include cusDeleted to indicate that the current record will be deleted when the updates are applied and committed, cusInserted to indicate that the record will be inserted, cusModified to indicate that the record will be modified, cusUninserted to indicate that the record was inserted and deleted, and cusUnmodified to indicate that the record will not be modified. The FetchAll() method may be used to fetch all the records and store locally within the client application when cached updates are used. This reduces network traffic. However, if the client resources are scarce, it is not a good idea to execute this method.

The TIBDataSet is a generic dataset component that may be used to execute select, insert, update, delete, and refresh statements. The statement to be executed is identified by the SelectSQL, InsertSQL, UpdateSQL, DeleteSQL, and RefreshSQL properties, respectively. Each of these properties is a TStrings object whose value can be set in the Object Inspector during design time or programmatically during run time. Please note that calling the Refresh() method of the dataset without setting RefreshSQL will raise an exception. In fact, this is true with every dataset operation described above. Also, the LiveModes property determines which of these SQL statements are permitted by the specific client application. The LiveModes property is a set that may include one or more of the following: lmInsert to allow the user to insert records, lmModify to allow the user to modify records, lmDelete to allow the user to delete records, and lmRefresh to allow the user to refresh records from the dataset. The ForcedRefresh property is a Boolean value; when set to true, it indicates that the dataset should force a refresh after posting every single record. If this property is false, the dataset refreshes only when the Refresh() method is executed explicitly.

The TIBSQL component is an alternate to TIBQuery and TIBDataSet, and is designed to work with minimal resource usage. It does not belong to the TDataSet hierarchy, and therefore the dataset features available in the other datasets in the IBX family are not available in this component. It has been built exclusively for the IBX family. It can execute any type of SQL statement. The statement to be executed must be assigned to the SQL property, and the SQLType property should be set to the appropriate SQL statement type. The valid SQLType values include SQLSelect, SQLUpdate, SQLInsert, SQLDelete, and SQLDDL, among others. For example, when we set the SQL statement to create a table within the database, then we must set the SQLType to SQLDDL. The result set returned by a SELECT statement is not a standard result set manipulated by a TDataSet. It is an object of the TIBXSQLDA class. In addition, the result set is unidirectional. For these reasons, we cannot navigate the data returned by executing an SQL statement through the TIBSQL component or through a data control such as TDBGrid. Using the TIBSQL component for background processing, where unidirectional cursors are enough, is ideal; it can also be used to work with raw input files and raw output files, as a medium of data transfer between datasets. For example, the input parameters of a query processed through the TIBDataSet component may be populated (in raw form) using a raw output file generated by a TIBSQL component, or vice versa.

Executing Stored Procedures That Return a Result Set

Normally, it is good practice to use a query-based component, such as TIBQuery, TIBDataSet, or TIBSQL, to execute SQL commands that return result sets and to use stored procedures to execute SQL commands that do not return a result set. Also, stored procedures may be defined with much more complex logic involving a group of SQL commands to perform a specific task. But sometimes we face circumstances where we have to execute a stored procedure that returns a result set. In such situations, we can still execute a query component, such as TIBQuery, where the query string includes a SELECT statement, and we use the stored procedure name in place of the table name. An example of such a query would be:

```
select * from CUST_PROJ_LIST(CUST_ID);
```

In this example, CUST_PROJ_LIST represents a stored procedure name, which accepts a single parameter, CUST_ID (say an integer value), and returns a result set. The example stored procedure syntax is given in Listing 6-8.

Listing 6-8

```
CREATE PROCEDURE CUST_PROJ_LIST(CUST_ID INTEGER)
RETURNS (PROJ_NAME CHAR(100))
AS
BEGIN
    FOR SELECT PROJ_NAME
    FROM CUST_PROJECT
    WHERE CUST_ID = :CUST_ID
```

```
        INT :PROJ_NAME
      DO
          SUSPEND;
   END
```

Please note that the procedure CUST_PROJ_LIST should have already been defined in the database. The procedure may also include any number of columns in its result set and may retrieve from any number of tables; in fact, it can be a complex SELECT statement with inner and outer joins, as required by our application. Since we are linking the stored procedure to our TIBQuery (instead of TIBStoredProc), we can navigate the result set using the normal bidirectional cursor.

Updating a Read-only Dataset

The TIBQuery component returns a result that is by default (and by design) read-only. When we display this result set to the user through a data source and a data control, such as a TDBGrid component, the user may have a need to update the dataset. The IBX component family has the component TIBUpdateSQL, which enables us to modify data in a read-only dataset.

Let's discuss the programming steps involved in making such an update happen through a read-only dataset by writing a small sample application.

1. Create a new Windows application using the IDE and save the project and unit files in a directory of your choice with names of your choice.

2. From the InterBase page in the Component Palette, drop a **TIBData-base** component, **TIBQuery** component, **TIBTransaction** component, and **TIBUpdateSQL** component onto the form. From the Data Access page, drop a **TDataSource** component. From the Data Controls page, drop one each of **TDBGrid** and **TDBNavigator** components. Finally, drop five **Button** components from the Standard page. We leave the default names of the components, as assigned by the IDE, as a standard practice.

3. For the sake of clarity, let's give some captions to the button components, since they interact with the user. In the Object Inspector, set the caption property of Button1 to "**Query-NoUpdate**," the caption of Button2 to "**Query-EnableUpdate**," the caption of Button3 to "**Close the Query**," the caption of Button4 to "**Apply Updates**," and the caption of Button5 to "**Cancel Updates**."

    To distinguish this sample from the others, I set the caption of the Form1 to "IBX Demo—Update ReadOnly dataset."

4. Now assign a database to the DatabaseName property of the IBDatabase1. This must be a file with the .gdb extension, as defined by

InterBase normally. In this example, I am using the EMPLOYEE.gdb sample database provided by Borland, which is installed in the <InterbaseHome>\examples\Database directory by default. Set the Params property using the property editor with values of user_name= sysdba and password=masterkey (which are default values for an InterBase database). If these are different in your installation, use your values. Set the LoginPrompt property to **false** to prevent the login dialog from prompting us. You may test the database for connectivity at this stage by setting the Connected property to true. But I would prefer to connect the database in the program.

5. Set the Database property of the IBTransaction1 component to **IBDatabase1**.

6. For the IBQuery1 component, set the SQL property to a SELECT query string. In the example, I set it to "SELECT * FROM CUSTOMER," using the SQL property editor. Also, set the Database and Transaction properties to the respective component names.

7. If you want to test whether the query is working or not, you can do it at this stage by setting the Active property to true. After testing, you can set the Active property back to false. The UpdateObject property should be set to the IBUpdateSQL1 component name in order to enable updating of this read-only dataset. I would prefer to do that in the program, as I am planning to demonstrate the read-only feature of the dataset along with its ability to update when we desire.

8. For the IBUpdateSQL1 component, set the ModifySQL property to a valid SQL statement. Remember, the column names that you are setting in this SQL will only be allowed to be modified by the user when we make the dataset modifiable. Listing 6-9 displays the SQL that I set to modify the dataset.

9. For the DataSource1 component, set the DataSet property to the IBQuery1 component to establish the link between the dataset and the data controls.

10. For the DBNavigator1 component, set the DataSource property to the DataSource1 component. Also disable the Insert, Delete, and Refresh buttons in the navigator bar by setting the corresponding options to **false** in the VisibleButtons property, since we are only implementing the ModifySQL statement in the IBUpdateSQL1 component. If we implement the corresponding SQL statements in this component, then the corresponding buttons may be made visible. I am trying to keep the example as simple as possible.

11. For the DBGrid1 component, set the DataSource property to the DataSource1 component.

Now it is time to work on the event handlers. I will be brief here with what I implemented in order to make it easy for you to follow through. In the OnActivate event handler of Form1, I established the database connection. In the OnClick event handler of Button1, I opened the IBQuery1 dataset without connecting to an UpdateObject. Therefore, when we click Button1, the dataset is opened in the read-only mode and will not let you make any changes. In the OnClick event handler of Button2, I opened the IBQuery1 dataset after setting the UpdateObject. Therefore, when we click Button2, the dataset is opened in the update mode, but it will enable only three columns for editing, as described in Listing 6-9. The OnClick event handler for Button3 is implemented with logic to close the dataset.

Finally, I implemented the event handlers for Button4 and Button5 to apply updates and cancel updates, respectively.

Please note that I tried to demonstrate how to start, commit, and roll back the transaction, though it is not really required in this small application. You can implement the program by removing all the lines related to transaction processing. The program still works. You can try this variation of the program, if you wish to do so. In this case, the IBTransaction1 object uses an implicit transaction processing, as we discussed earlier in this chapter.

The source listings for the program are provided in Listing 6-10 for the cpp file and Listing 6-11 for the header file.

Listing 6-9: ModifySQL syntax

```
update customer set
customer = :customer,
contact_first = :contact_first,
contact_last = :contact_last
where cust_no = :Old_cust_no
```

Listing 6-10: Unit1.cpp

```
//---------------------------------------------------------------------------

#include <vcl.h>
#pragma hdrstop

#include "Unit1.h"
//---------------------------------------------------------------------------
#pragma package(smart_init)
#pragma resource "*.dfm"
TForm1 *Form1;
//---------------------------------------------------------------------------
__fastcall TForm1::TForm1(TComponent* Owner)
    : TForm(Owner)
{
```

```
}
//-------------------------------------------------------------------------

void __fastcall TForm1::FormActivate(TObject *Sender)
{
    IBDatabase1->Connected = true;
}
//-------------------------------------------------------------------------
void __fastcall TForm1::Button1Click(TObject *Sender)
{
    IBQuery1->Active = false;
    IBQuery1->CachedUpdates = false;
    IBQuery1->UpdateObject = NULL;
    IBQuery1->Active = true;
}
//-------------------------------------------------------------------------
void __fastcall TForm1::Button2Click(TObject *Sender)
{
    if (!IBTransaction1->InTransaction)
        IBTransaction1->StartTransaction();
    IBQuery1->Active = false;
    IBQuery1->CachedUpdates = true;
    IBQuery1->UpdateObject = IBUpdateSQL1;
    IBQuery1->Active = true;
}
//-------------------------------------------------------------------------
void __fastcall TForm1::Button4Click(TObject *Sender)
{
    if (!IBTransaction1->InTransaction)
        IBTransaction1->StartTransaction();
    IBQuery1->ApplyUpdates();
    IBTransaction1->Commit();
}
//-------------------------------------------------------------------------
void __fastcall TForm1::Button5Click(TObject *Sender)
{
    IBQuery1->CancelUpdates();
    if (IBTransaction1->InTransaction)
        IBTransaction1->Rollback();
}
//-------------------------------------------------------------------------
void __fastcall TForm1::Button3Click(TObject *Sender)
{
    if (IBTransaction1->InTransaction)
        IBTransaction1->Rollback();
    IBQuery1->Close();
}
//-------------------------------------------------------------------------
```

Listing 6-11: Unit1.h

```
//-------------------------------------------------------------------------

#ifndef Unit1H
#define Unit1H
//-------------------------------------------------------------------------
#include <Classes.hpp>
#include <Controls.hpp>
#include <StdCtrls.hpp>
#include <Forms.hpp>
```

```
#include <DB.hpp>
#include <IBCustomDataSet.hpp>
#include <IBDatabase.hpp>
#include <IBQuery.hpp>
#include <DBCtrls.hpp>
#include <DBGrids.hpp>
#include <ExtCtrls.hpp>
#include <Grids.hpp>
#include <IBUpdateSQL.hpp>
//---------------------------------------------------------------------------
class TForm1 : public TForm
{
__published:            // IDE-managed components
    TIBTransaction *IBTransaction1;
    TIBQuery *IBQuery1;
    TDataSource *DataSource1;
    TDBNavigator *DBNavigator1;
    TDBGrid *DBGrid1;
    TIBDatabase *IBDatabase1;
    TIBUpdateSQL *IBUpdateSQL1;
    TButton *Button1;
    TButton *Button2;
    TButton *Button3;
    TButton *Button4;
    TButton *Button5;
    void __fastcall FormActivate(TObject *Sender);
    void __fastcall Button1Click(TObject *Sender);
    void __fastcall Button2Click(TObject *Sender);
    void __fastcall Button4Click(TObject *Sender);
    void __fastcall Button5Click(TObject *Sender);
    void __fastcall Button3Click(TObject *Sender);
private:                 // User declarations
public:                  // User declarations
    __fastcall TForm1(TComponent* Owner);
};
//---------------------------------------------------------------------------
extern PACKAGE TForm1 *Form1;
//---------------------------------------------------------------------------
#endif
```

TIBClientDataSet at a Glance

Recall that we discussed the TSQLClientDataSet, which belonged to the family of TCustomClientDataSet and was a very useful component in building simple two-tier applications with the provider-resolver architecture. In this section, I would like to mention a similar component in the IBX family. It is the TIBClientDataSet component. It is a compound component encapsulating the behavior of a TClientDataSet and TDataSetProvider with the ability to connect to an InterBase database using TIBDatabase and TIBTransaction components. Therefore, it is very ideal for briefcase model applications.

The three cached dataset types—TIBClientDataSet, TSQLClient-DataSet, and TBDEClientDataSet—provide similar behavior with respect to data retrieval, managing the data and making updates in a true client-server style, and also in developing briefcase model applications. They differ mainly in the architecture used to connect to the database and hence the drivers (or the API) used on the server side. Therefore, these components are very useful in helping organizations migrate their systems based on one architecture to the other.

Summary

Now I will take the opportunity to summarize what we discussed in this chapter. I wanted to present advanced concepts of database development, particularly those that are useful in developing client-server applications, using unidirectional datasets, developing briefcase model applications, addressing Borland's emerging technologies in database development, and so on.

We started our discussion with an introduction to advanced concepts, followed by data access components designed by Borland to facilitate client-server programming in which we put considerable effort into understanding the client dataset, the relationship between the client dataset and provider components, and their properties. We also discussed the very powerful feature of the client dataset as an in-memory dataset that can be used alone or in conjunction with a provider in building briefcase model applications. This extensive discussion on data access components will help us understand how to develop DataSnap applications in Chapter 9.

Then we moved on to the dbExpress architecture introduced by Borland with Delphi 6 and C++Builder 6 which is a high-performance data access technology suitable in a true client-server environment, without losing the features provided by already existing data access technologies. This will help current users of Borland products, particularly users of Delphi and C++Builder, to consider migrating their current systems to a new and efficient architecture. In this section, we also discussed unidirectional datasets and their use in client applications in conjunction with cached client datasets.

Finally, we focused our attention on the IBX family of components, which are exclusively designed to provide high-performance data access technology on similar grounds, like the other data access technologies supported by Borland.

We supported our discussion with four sample applications in an attempt to demonstrate as many concepts as possible in a short chapter that covers vast technology features.

Part II

Advanced and Distributed Application Development

Chapter 7

Building WebBroker Applications

Introduction

Aside from developing Windows-based GUI applications, today's industry is in need of web-based applications or web-enabled applications. Web-based applications usually have only one interface to the users (i.e., through the Internet alone). Web-enabled applications usually represent the web interface to a traditional client-server system. In either case, it is our job as software professionals to provide a web-based interface to an application. During the past several years, web development has undergone many changes, with almost all the software companies participating to some extent.

The challenges faced by the web development community are many. In a traditional client-server application, we build the client module as well as the server module ourselves. When we do this, we have a lot of control over the protocol between the client and the server modules. If required, we can even build one internally because we know that the client module design is completely in our control. But in a web application, the client is a browser usually developed by external organizations (however, to a standard specification agreed by the industry); there are even multiple versions of the browser used extensively by users worldwide, and most important of all, our application is accessed by users whose expectations are unknown by the web development professionals. Securing the information passage over the Internet is the next big challenge for web developers, because once the data leaves one end of the connection between the client (the browser) and the server (web server), they have absolutely no control over the network path followed by the data stream before it reaches the other end. The software industry is continuously developing security measures and techniques, and as professionals, it is our utmost responsibility to safeguard the information of our customers and users. In a traditional client-server application,

255

a user session is stateful, and hence maintaining secure connections is much easier than in a web application where the session is stateless by default.

A typical web application includes a set of server components deployed in a web server environment. If the application produces dynamic pages based on data retrieved from a database, the database is also considered part of the application. Typically, when we refer to the web application components, we mean the HTML pages (perhaps intermixed with client-side scripts written in a scripting language, such as JavaScript or VBScript), web server modules, and any configuration files. The web server modules, having appropriate access to a database, provide the dynamic content in the web pages.

Uniform Resource Identifiers (URIs)

Overview

A *Uniform Resource Identifier* (URI) is simply a formatted string that identifies a resource or an object on the Internet via a name, location, or any other characteristic specific to the resource. Many times, web server applications produce content from more than one source, and the final result does not reside in a particular location but is created as necessary. URIs may describe resources that are not location specific. We also use the term Uniform Resource Locator (URL) to locate resources. There is not much of a difference between the terms URI and URL.

Parts of a URL

The *Uniform Resource Locator* (URL) is typically a string that we type in the browser to open a resource located somewhere on the Internet. However, URLs may also be used to locate resources on the local computer or on one of the computers within the local network. The URL may be considered the address of a particular resource with the most specific request for the information required. Figure 7-1 shows the parts of a typical URL. The first part of the URL is the protocol used. For an HTTP request, this string is http; for an FTP request, it is ftp. The server name follows the protocol identifier; they are separated by the separator string. Please note that the host name may be appended optionally by a colon and the port number that the server is listening to. Though an HTTP server listens to port 80 by default, we are usually free to configure the server to listen to a different port.

The web server module is the executable program, a script, or a shared library loaded by the web server. It is this module that communicates with the web server in retrieving the client request information and sending back responses to the client. This part of the string may include one or more sub-directories on the host computer where the program or script is located. However, the first subdirectory in the program path starts from the default home directory configured for the web server. This default home directory is usually called the default document root directory. Following the module name is the pathinfo string, which is intended to identify different requests made to the same module. Ideally, this is something similar to the situation where different functions within a program execute to process different requests or messages. The string following the pathinfo is the query string. There is a ? separator between the pathinfo and the query string. Since the query string is the last part of a URL, it can occupy the rest of the URL string and is limited by the maximum URL size imposed by the web server. The client can send parameter name-value pairs in the query string in support of the specific request (i.e., pathinfo). These terms will become more clear in later sections when we discuss web modules in detail.

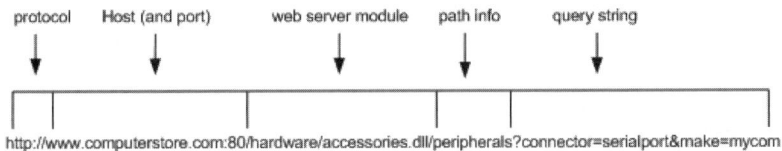

Figure 7-1: Parts of a URL

The HTTP Protocol

A *protocol* is a set of rules established for communication between two agencies. In terms of Internet technology, the Hypertext Transfer Protocol (HTTP) defines the rules for the clients (the browsers) and the servers (the web servers) to communicate with each other. This is a very simple definition of the protocol. In reality, the protocol specifies rules for proxies and other agents to take part in the communication between the server and the client. HTTP protocol is an application-level protocol implemented over the lower-level TCP/IP protocol. The TCP/IP protocol is in fact two parts: the Transmission Control Protocol (TCP) and the Internet Protocol (IP). While the Internet Protocol handles the task of moving data packets from one system to another, the Transmission Control Protocol ensures that the information is transferred reliably. In this section, we focus our discussion on the HTTP protocol to the extent that it will empower you to build robust web server applications; if you need more information about the protocol, please refer to the World Wide Web Consortium (W3C) specification.

> **Note:**   The W3C HTTP specification may be accessed at the following web site: http://www.w3.org/Protocols/HTTP/.

The HTTP protocol enables almost any kind of information to be transferred over the Internet, including (but not limited to) text messages, graphic images, streamed data, and so on. Messages sent by the client to the server are HTTP requests, and the messages returned by the server to the client are HTTP responses. Before initiating a request, the client establishes a TCP connection with the server. After completing each round of the message exchange (a request and response pair), the client may continue to use the same TCP connection as of HTTP version 1.1, but the protocol itself is stateless by default, which means that the server responds to a request based solely on the information provided within that request without reference to other requests from the client. In other words, the server does not maintain or carry the client's state from one request to another. The stateless nature of the HTTP protocol is its main distinction from the traditional client-server systems in which the servers maintain the client's state.

The HTTP Methods

There are four basic types of operations the clients perform while communicating with the server. The operations are also called *methods*. They are listed in Table 7-1 with appropriate descriptions.

Table 7-1: Basic client operations in HTTP

Operation	Description
GET	When the client intends to retrieve an object from a server on the Internet, it formulates an HTTP GET request. The request contains the URL of the object to be retrieved. As part of the URL, a program or script name is provided with any other parameters the program may need in order to process the request. The parameters sent to the server are formulated into a query string and appended to the URL. Therefore, it is important to note that the parameter names and values are visible in the URL. Also, the number of parameters that we can send in a GET request may be limited by the size of the URL string, as limited by the web server. The server may respond with a status code of success or failure, along with any relevant data, such as a message specially formatted by the server.
POST	The HTTP POST operation enables the clients to use HTML forms, which let the user fill in values in the form fields. When the user is done entering values, a button click may invoke a POST operation, posting the field values to the server. With a POST request, we may send as many field names and values as desired. They are not appended to the URL string; rather, they are filled within the request content. Thus, it may be beneficial to use a POST request in place of a GET request, although we do not use HTML forms in a specific request due to the additional flexibility.

Operation	Description
POST (cont.)	However, it is noteworthy that the field values embedded within the HTTP request are not free from hackers, though they are not visible to the end user who is browsing the Internet. If an HTTP request is accessible to hackers before it reaches the server, usually the complete contents are accessible. The only way to secure the information sent to a server is by using a reliable encryption scheme, such as Secured Socket Layer (SSL). The server may respond with a status code of success or failure, along with any relevant data, such as a message specially formatted by the server.
PUT	The HTTP PUT operation allows us to upload a resource from the local user system to the server. Along with a PUT request, we also send a URL, which tells the server where to put the resource. The resource we use in a PUT request is a file most of the time. The server may respond with a status code of success or failure along with any relevant data, such as a message specially formatted by the server.
DELETE	The HTTP DELETE operation permits a client to request that the server delete a resource on the Internet identified by the associated URL. The server may respond with a status code of success or failure along with any relevant data, such as a message specially formatted by the server.

The HTTP Request

A typical HTTP request contains three parts. The first part is a request-line, which includes the method type (such as GET or POST), the URL, and the HTTP version supported by the client browser. The second part is optional and may include one or more request headers. The third part is also optional and includes the request body. There is a blank line between the request header and the request body. Each of the request headers may apply to the specific request or request body. A list of the most frequently used request message headers is provided in Table 7-2. Please note that the list provided in the table reflects the request message headers typically supported by C++Builder 6 components. Some of the request headers are also valid response headers. I discuss the common request/response headers in this section, and discuss the response headers exclusive to HTTP response objects in the next section.

Part 2

Table 7-2: HTTP request message headers

Request Message Header	Description
Accept	The values assigned to this header indicate which types of content the client can accept in the response sent by the server. Multiple content types may be specified, each separated from the previous value by a comma. Each type may have associated parameters separated from the type value by a semicolon. A very useful parameter is the q factor, which indicates the quality factor of the content media type permissible by the client. The q value is a factor between 0 and 1, the highest indicating 100%. Here are some examples of Accept values: `Accept: text/plain; q=0.7, text/html` This header value indicates that the client can accept plain text format with a quality markdown of 30 percent and HTML text format without any quality markdown. An Accept header value of */* indicates that the client can accept all types of content.
Authorization	The Authorization header contains credentials provided by the client to authenticate the users. There are two types of authentication: Basic and Digest. With Basic authentication, the client provides the username and password in Base64 encoding format using printable characters.

Request Message Header	Description
Authorization (cont.)	As the name suggests, this type of encoding is really basic and should not be used when building secure web sites. With Digest authentication, the encrypted user credentials are sent over the Internet, using the Secure Socket Layer (SSL) protocol or Transport Layer Security (TLS) protocol.
Cache-Control	The Cache-Control header functions like a master header that provides one or more directives as supported by the HTTP specification to control all the caching mechanisms along the request and response chain for the request. Each of the directives is separated by a comma. Example directives for this header look like this: ■ max-age=2000 indicates that the request is invalid after 2000 seconds. ■ max-stale=1200 indicates that the client can accept a response up to 1200 seconds after it expires. If no value is specified, the client request does not expire. ■ min-fresh=200 indicates that the client does not accept a response that expires earlier than 200 seconds. ■ no-cache indicates that the request may not be cached. ■ no-store indicates that the request contains sensitive information and may not be stored on any permanent medium.

Connection	The default connection behavior in HTTP 1.1 is to maintain persistent connections, which means that the same connection is continuously used by the client for every subsequent request after the first request, unless the server wants to close. The server may choose to close the connection after a specific request by setting this header value to close. Also, in order to support HTTP versions older than 1.1, we may use a value of Keep-Alive for this header and optionally set a value for the Keep-Alive header, as in the following example:
	`Keep-Alive: timeout=5, max=200`
	`Connection: Keep-Alive`
	The Keep-Alive header is not available in the HTTP 1.1 specification, as it is no longer required.

Content-Encoding	This header indicates which encoding mechanisms are applied to the request message body. The permissible values are described here: ■ compress indicates that the UNIX compress program is used to produce the encoded message. ■ deflate indicates that the zlib encoding format defined in RFC 1950 is used in combination with the deflate compression mechanism described in RFC 1951. ■ gzip indicates that the encoding format produced is the same as that produced by the gzip (GNU zip) file compression format, which is described in RFC 1952. This format is Lempel-Ziv coding with a 32-bit CRC.
Content-Length	The Content-Length header gives the size of the message body in bytes and provides a way for the recipient to determine the length of the message being received. This is particularly helpful to determine the end of the message when the content type is not HTML. However, there are other rules that enable us to determine the end of the message: ■ If the server closes the connection, the end of the message is identified by the last byte received by the client. ■ A response message, which must not include a message body, is always terminated by the first empty line after the header fields. Other rules may be checked in the HTTP 1.1 specification.
Content-Type	The Content-Type header indicates the type of data that is sent in the message body. The values for this header follow the same rules as mentioned for the Accept header. However, we may use additional parameters with this header, such as Charset.
Cookie	Cookies are used to provide a state management feature to the web application, where the server sets cookies on the client machine (if the client permits) when the first request from that client is processed. The client then sends these cookies in its subsequent requests to the server so that the server knows the client before processing the request. The Cookie header may contain multiple fields separated by semicolons. The Cookie fields include the Cookie attributes, name-value pairs to uniquely distinguish the cookie from other cookies.

Request Message Header	Description
Cookie (cont.)	Typically, the multiple cookies set by a server in a request-response exchange may all have the same attributes but different name-value pairs. The values for the name, as well as all the attributes, must be strings in double quotes. The attributes that may be used in a cookie are described here: ■ The Version attribute indicates to which version of the state management specification the cookie conforms. For HTTP 1.1 specification, the value is 1. If a cookie is set, this attribute is required. ■ The Secure attribute does not have a value. If present, it indicates that the client should send the cookie only in secure sessions for subsequent requests. This is an optional attribute. ■ The Path attribute specifies the subset of URLs to which this cookie applies. This is an optional attribute. ■ The Max-Age attribute defines the lifetime of the cookie in seconds. The value for this attribute is a decimal non-negative integer. A value of 0 means that the cookie should be discarded immediately. This is an optional attribute. ■ The domain attribute specifies the domain for which the cookie is valid. This is an optional attribute. ■ The Comment attribute stores a documented comment about the cookie. Since cookies are usually used to store private information about a user or user machine, the comment helps the client to determine whether to use the cookie or not. This is an optional attribute.
Date	The Date header specifies the timestamp at which the sender of the message (client or server) originally generated the message. A sample date header is given here: `Date: Wed, 14 Feb 2001 05:36:24 GMT`
Expires	The Expires header specifies the timestamp after which the message becomes stale, which means not valid. This does not mean that the original message ceases to exist after this timestamp; it simply means that the sender of the message provides no assurance for the validity of the information provided in the message after the specified date and time, and therefore, the recipient must refresh the message content from the sender.
From	If provided, this header should contain an e-mail address of the sender. It is used by the server modules for the purpose of logging or to identify the source of the requests in order to filter unwanted requests. Since most users do not want to reveal their identity, this header is usually not used.
Host	This header contains the host name and port number of the requested resource. This feature enables the server to distinguish the incoming requests for the different web sites hosted on the same server (using the virtual hosts principle). This header must always be present when the client declares its support for HTTP 1.1 specification.
If-Modified-Since	This header specifies that a request may be processed if the resource associated with the request is modified after the date and time, as specified by the value in the header.
Referer	The Referer request header field allows the client to specify the address of the resource (URL) from which the requested URI was obtained. This is useful to generate lists of back links to resources for the purpose of tracking, logging, optimized caching, and so on. The value may be absolute URL or relative URL. If the value is a relative URL, it must be interpreted with respect to the request URL.
User-Agent	The User-Agent header identifies the specific HTTP implementation that the client is using. This header field is useful for the server to trace protocol violations and automated recognition of user agents for the purpose of tailoring the responses to avoid a specific user agent's limitations.

Part 2

A typical HTTP request is provided in Listing 7-1.

Listing 7-1: HTTP request example

```
GET /index.html Http1.1
Host: www.httpexampleserver.com
Accept: image/gif, image/jpeg
```

```
Content-Encoding: gzip, deflate
User-Agent: Mozilla/4.0 (compatible; MSIE 5.5; Windows NT 4.0)
Date: Wed, 14 Feb 2001 05:36:24 GMT
```

The HTTP Response

A typical HTTP response contains three parts. The first part is a status-line, which includes the status code and a reason phrase. The second part is optional and may include one or more response headers. The third part is also optional and includes the response body. There is a blank line between the response headers and the response body. Each of the response headers may apply to the specific response or the response body. Table 7-3 provides a list of response message headers with a description. The list provided in the table reflects the list of response message headers typically supported by C++Builder 6 components; however, I am omitting the message headers that have already been discussed in the request header table, since they are functionally identical.

Table 7-3: HTTP response message headers

Response Message Header	Description
Last-Modified	This header field indicates the date and time that the server believes the original resource specified in the URI was last modified. The exact meaning of this field depends on the implementation of the server of origin and the nature of the original resource. For files, it may be just the file system last-modified time. For entities with dynamically included parts, it may be the most recent of the set of last-modified times for its component parts. For database objects, it may be the last-update timestamp of the record.
Location	The Location response header field is used to redirect the recipient to a location other than the requested URL for completion of the request. The Content-Location header field differs from Location in that Content-Location specifies the original location of the entity enclosed in the request.
Server	The Server header specifies the HTTP server implementation that is processing the client's requests. This is the server-side equivalent of User-Agent on the client side. The field can contain multiple product tokens and comments identifying the server and any sub-products listed in the order of significance and separated by spaces. Product identifiers take the form of ProductName/Version-Number.
WWW-Authenticate	This header must be included with a 401 Unauthorized response message, asking the client to resend the request with proper authentication credentials. The field value consists of at least one challenge that indicates the authentication scheme(s) and parameters applicable to the request URL. The challenge indicates whether it is a Basic or Digest authentication, and the parameters are similar to the ones supplied by the client in the Authorization header.

The HTTP Response Status Codes

Every HTTP response includes a status-line as the first line. The status-line contains status code and a reason phrase. The status code is a three-digit code, and the first digit represents a specific type of status, as outlined here:

- 1xx—Informational messages. The request was received and is being processed.

- 2xx—Success. The request was successfully received, understood, and accepted.

- 3xx—Redirection. Further action must be taken in order to complete the request.

- 4xx—Client Error. The request contains bad syntax or cannot be fulfilled.

- 5xx—Server Error. The server failed to fulfill an apparently valid request.

Web Development in C++Builder 6

Overview

Borland C++Builder 6 comes with two sets of components called WebBroker components and WebSnap components. The WebBroker components were also available in the previous release of C++Builder, but the WebSnap components are the new set introduced in C++Builder 6. WebBroker forms the foundation for WebSnap technology. Due to the added features in the WebSnap framework, Borland recommends that you use the WebSnap framework rather than just the WebBroker framework in all your new web applications. It is also easy to migrate your existing WebBroker applications to the WebSnap framework because WebBroker components are also part of the WebSnap framework. In this chapter, we will discuss the WebBroker framework in detail, including sample applications. We will pay exclusive attention to the WebSnap framework in the next chapter using the foundation laid out in this chapter.

The WebBroker framework enables us to develop a web application in any of the following technologies:

- A Common Gateway Interface (CGI) application, which is a stand-alone executable file, such as an EXE file on Windows operating systems. Almost all the web servers on a variety of operating systems permit us to deploy CGI applications in the cgi-bin directory, as specified by the particular web server. The web server passes the client request objects to the CGI application through the STDIN (standard input), and response objects are returned from the CGI application to the web server through the STDOUT (standard output). Since almost all the development platforms enable us to develop applications that can read from STDIN and write to STDOUT, this is the most versatile way to develop web applications in Windows or UNIX, or any operating system. An object of the VCL class TCGIApplication handles the responsibility of evaluating the client requests and creating the TCGIRequest and TCGIResponse objects. Every individual client request is serviced by a separate instance of the application in a separate thread. The Borland Kylix development platform on the Linux operating system also enables us to build this type of application.

■ A WinCGI application (CGI application designed specific to the Windows platform alone), which is also a stand-alone executable file. The main difference between this type of web application and a standard CGI application is that the client request objects are written to configuration (INI) files, and the TCGIApplication object reads these INI files and creates the TWinCGIRequest and TWinCGIResponse objects. Every individual client request is serviced by a separate instance of the application in a separate thread, similar to the CGI application. We cannot develop this type of application on any other operating system.

■ An ISAPI/NSAPI (Microsoft Internet Server API or Netscape API) application, which is a DLL. The dynamic library created by this type of application is loaded by the corresponding web server (Microsoft IIS Server or Netscape server). Both of these APIs are wrapped within a single API in C++Builder. An object of the class TISAPIApplication receives the client request from the web server and creates TISAPIRequest and TISAPIResponse objects.

■ An Apache web server module, which is a DLL on Windows-based operating systems. The Apache web server loads this type of module when a client request is received to access the services of the module. An object of the class TApacheApplication handles the responsibility of creating a TApacheRequest object when a request is received from the Apache web server and creating the TApacheResponse object to bundle the response to be sent to the client. The Apache web server is an open source web server and is used by many organizations, such as Borland and IBM, as a base for their HTTP server design. Also, the Apache web server runs on a variety of operating systems, such as Windows and several clones of UNIX including the open source Linux. On UNIX-based operating systems, the Apache web server modules are shared libraries similar to DLLs on Windows. Currently, the Borland Kylix platform also enables us to build Apache web server modules for the Linux operating system. The Borland Kylix 3 platform on the Linux operating system also supports Apache web server module development.

Whatever type of web application we choose to develop among the ones listed above, the fundamental concepts of the web module remain the same. Notice that I am using the terms "application" and "module" synonymously in this sense. In the context of a WebBroker application, this is true, but in the context of a WebSnap application, an application may contain multiple web modules. In some cases, the module may be a stand-alone executable, and in some cases, it may be a shared library file loaded dynamically by the web server. The shared library files are usually preferable because they do not have the overhead of being loaded every time a client request is received and being executed in a separate thread by itself. This process is in contrast to stand-alone executables (programs or scripts in general) where the executables are loaded fresh for every client request and unloaded after serving the request. The advantage with the stand-alone executables is that they don't crash the web server if they fail due to access violations or any other reason; the thread that fails is the only one that crashes. On the contrary, if a shared module crashes, it would potentially crash the web server itself (because it runs in the address space of the web server) and would force a restart of the server.

A Typical Web Application

When the web server receives a client request, the identified module is started by the server (as a separate process in a separate thread if it is a stand-alone executable, or loaded dynamically into the address space of the server if it is a shared library file), and the request information is passed to the module. The request information includes mainly the pathinfo and the query string. The module then builds the corresponding request object and response object specific to the type of web application that we are building. Corresponding to every individual client request (i.e., pathinfo string), there will be an action item that we build in the web module. Our web module in C++Builder comprises one or more such action item event handlers that we wish to support in our application. The code in the action item event handlers analyzes the request parameters, (sometimes) analyzes the request header, performs any database retrievals or updates, and formulates the response content (usually in HTML format). As part of the web module, there is a web dispatcher whose main task is to invoke the action item event handler corresponding to a request pathinfo string and pass the response object to the web server when the action item event handler finishes its execution.

Now let's examine the VCL components that perform the individual tasks of a web module. The components required for web application development are located in the Internet and InternetExpress pages of the Component Palette. Only non-visual components are used in a web application. A web module is identified by the TWebModule component that is derived from TCustomWebDispatcher, which in turn is derived from TDataModule. The TWebModule component performs two main functions: contains any non-visual components and dispatches the HTTP request messages to the action items. In Chapter 9, "Developing DataSnap Applications," we will discuss the data module in detail and note that it is used to centralize all the non-visual components in an application so that the main application form is not cluttered with such components. It is also noteworthy to mention here that a TDataModule containing TWeb-Dispatcher may replace a TWebModule component in a web application. One web module can contain only one web dispatcher component. Since TWebModule contains a web dispatcher component inherently, if you try to place a web dispatcher component manually in the IDE, an error message is displayed and you will not be permitted to add the component. Similarly, since TDataModule does not contain a web dispatcher inherently, you can place, at the most, one web dispatcher component in it. If your program tries to add an additional web dispatcher during run-time, the web server application generates a run-time exception.

When we need to create a new web application, we do so by invoking the Web Server Application Wizard. First, we open the New Items dialog by clicking the speed button representing a new item or by selecting the File | New | Other menu item in the IDE. The New Items dialog is displayed, as shown in Figure 7-2.

Figure 7-2: New Items selection dialog

This is the dialog we invoke several times when we create new project types or add new items to a project. The dialog contains several pages, each of which contains icons representing new project-type wizards or new items in a project. The Web Server Application Wizard icon is located in the page titled New toward the bottom of the page. When we double-click this icon or click the OK button while this icon is selected, the Web Server Application Wizard is invoked; it looks like Figure 7-3.

Figure 7-3: Web Server Application Wizard

Since this wizard creates a new type of project, any currently opened project in the IDE must be closed before starting this wizard. Otherwise, the IDE automatically closes the current project (if already saved) before creating the new project; if the current project is not saved, a reminder dialog is displayed where you should confirm saving the current project or discarding all the unsaved changes. When the new web application project is created, a TWebModule object is automatically created and added to the project without regard to the type of web application that we have chosen in the wizard. Normally in new web applications, I do not see a reason why you should replace the TWebModule object with a TDataModule and TWebDispatcher combo. However, when you are trying to reuse the TDataModule objects that were already created and used in your existing traditional client-server applications, you may have to replace the TWebModule object with the corresponding TDataModule object in your new web application. This replacement is very simple. Just remove the TWebModule object from the project manager and add the TDataModule object. After adding, drop a new TWebDispatcher component from the Internet page of the Component Palette. We can also replace the automatically generated web module with a web module stored as a template in the repository or with a web module that is used in another web application. This feature makes it very simple to convert a web application from one type to another (e.g., from ISAPI to CGI or from CGI to Apache, and so on) without changing the action item event handlers. Here we notice that the VCL architecture and component framework offers in a lot of advantages and productivity, even for the web application development scenario.

The base classes that represent an HTTP request and an HTTP response are the TWebRequest and TWebResponse classes, respectively. When the web application (represented by TISAPIApplication, TCGIApplication, or TApacheApplication) receives the HTTP request from the web server, it creates the request object of the corresponding descendant class of TWebRequest (such as TISAPIRequest, TCGIRequest, TWinCGIRequest, or TApacheRequest, depending on the application type). It also creates the corresponding response object that is a descendant of the TWebResponse class (such as TISAPIResponse, TCGIResponse, TWinCGIResponse, or TApacheResponse, depending on the application type). Then the web application passes the request and response objects to the web dispatcher—in fact, to an object of the class that is a descendant of TCustomWebDispatcher. Since the TWebModule and TWebDispatcher are both descendants of TCustomWebDispatcher, I will call both of these objects simply a web dispatcher; either of them (whichever is present in the application) receives the request and response objects from the server. The only functional difference between the two is that a TWebDispatcher is used to enable an existing data module with the functionality of a TWebModule, thereby web-enabling existing applications.

The Actions property of the web dispatcher represents an object of the TWebActionItems class, which is a collection of TWebActionItem objects. During design time, we can invoke the collection editor to edit the individual action items by double-clicking in the client area of the TWebModule component or double-clicking the TWebDispatcher component placed in a data module. We can also add action item objects during run time if we design a completely automated web site. Every time the web dispatcher receives the set of request and response objects, it identifies the appropriate action item or an auto-dispatching component that is designed to handle the request message, and passes the request and response objects to the identified event handler so that it can perform any requested actions and formulate a response message. C++Builder also provides specialized content producer components that aid the action items in dynamically generating the content of response messages, which may include custom HTML code or other MIME content. We will look at the content producer components a little later after we completely understand the mechanics of processing the request and response objects. It is necessary to understand some important features of these components before we can work on example programs. Table 7-4 lists the properties, methods, and events of a web dispatcher component.

Table 7-4: Properties, methods, and events of TCustomWebDispatcher

Property	Description
Action[int index]	This property retrieves an individual action item (TWebActionItem) from the action item list, as identified by the index.
Actions	This property represents a collection of web action items (TWebActionItems). Since it represents a collection object, we can use the methods relevant to collections, such as add, delete, clear, and query for a particular action item, to work with individual action items during run time.
Request	Provides access to the HTTP request currently being handled as an object of one of the descendant classes of TWebRequest and is used to read request information while generating the response content. This property usually represents an object of a descendant class of TWebRequest, depending on the type of web application.
Response	Provides access to the HTTP response object built by the web application and is specifically used to set the response content to be sent to the client. Many times, it is also needed to set the response object properties before the response is sent. This property usually represents an object of a descendant class of TWebResponse, depending on the type of web application.

Method	Description
ActionByName (AnsiString Name)	This property retrieves the specific action item object as identified by the name. By accessing an action item either by name or any other way, it is possible to enable or disable the action item or set its properties to control the way the dispatcher can identify action items for the client requests.

Event	Description
AfterDispatch	This event is fired after the action item or items complete the task of generating the response content and before the response has been sent to the client. This is the last chance to change the response before it is sent or stop sending the response by setting the Boolean parameter Handled to false. However, this event is not fired if all of the action items matching the pathinfo (and including the default action item) set the Handled parameter to false; such a situation (or when we stop sending the response in this event handler) would result in a page not found or resource not found error condition. If the response has not yet been sent by the action item(s), we can explicitly send the response in this event handler, either by setting the Handled parameter to true or by executing the SendResponse() method of the response object.
BeforeDispatch	This event is fired before the dispatcher tries to match any of the action items to the request pathinfo. If we set the response content in this event handler itself, we can send the response either by setting the Handled parameter to true or by executing the SendResponse() method of the response object, in which case the dispatcher will not attempt to pass the request to any of the action items since the request has already been handled. This event handler also provides an opportunity for us to set the properties of the action items (either individually or collectively) to control the way the request will be handled. It is also possible to bypass all the action items and send program control to the AfterDispatch event handler; for this to happen, we have to set the Handled property to true without explicitly sending the response in the BeforeDispatch event handler.

Let's now take a look at the action item objects and their properties, methods, and events, as listed in Table 7-5.

Table 7-5: Properties, methods, and events of a TWebActionItem object

Property	Description
Default	This is a Boolean property. When set to true, it indicates whether the action item should handle any request that is not handled explicitly by any other action item. Also, when we explicitly set the Handled parameter to false in the action item event handler(s) related to a specific request, it is likely that the OnAction event handler of the default action item completes the task by setting the Handled parameter to true or explicitly executing the SendResponse() method of the response object.
Enabled	This is a Boolean value that indicates whether the action item can respond to HTTP requests that match the PathInfo and MethodType properties. This is an effective way to enable/disable action items during run time in a completely automated web application. The web dispatcher ignores action items when this property is set to false.
MethodType	Indicates the type of HTTP request that is handled by the action item. The permitted request types are mtGet, mtPost, mtHead, mtPut, and mtAny. For example, the value mtGet indicates that the action item should handle the HTTP request with the METHOD header value of GET, and the request parameters are retrieved from the URL query string; the value mtPost indicates that the encoded form data is passed in the body of the HTTP request, not as a query string in the URL.
PathInfo	This is an AnsiString value and represents the pathinfo portion of the URL string. The pathinfo and the method type together determine a one-to-one match between an HTTP request and an action item. It is also possible to assign more than one action item to service a single request.
Producer	The Producer property and the ProducerContent property are mutually exclusive. Only one of these should be used at any time for an action item object. If we use content producer to generate the response object content, and the producer is an object of a descendant class to the TCustomContent-Producer, then the Producer property can be set to the appropriate producer component, which generates the response content automatically. If Producer is set to a valid producer component, then after the action item receives a request message from the web dispatcher, the action item object first sets the response content to the content value returned by the producer component. It then receives the OnAction event handler, where it can set other properties of the response object. A content producer object can only be associated with one action item at a time. However, we can use the same content producer to produce content for different action items, and in such a case, we should always make sure that the content producer is assigned to only one action item at any point in time.
ProducerContent	This property and the Producer property are mutually exclusive. If we use the content producer to generate the response object content and the producer is an object of a class that implements the IProduceContent interface, the ProducerContent property can be set to the appropriate producer component, which generates the response content automatically. Setting this property to a valid producer component has the same effect as the Producer property, explained above.

Method	Description
AssignTo (TPersistent * Dest)	This method copies the properties of the current action item object to the destination object, which is passed as a parameter to the method if the destination object is an action item.

Event	Description
OnAction	The OnAction event is fired when the web dispatcher identifies the action item suitable to service an HTTP request by matching the PathInfo and MethodType properties or when the action item is set as the default action item. When the action item is set as the default action item, then for any HTTP request that does not have a matching action item, the OnAction event handler is fired for this (default) action item. When a valid producer component is assigned to the action item, the OnAction event is fired only after the response object's content is populated by the content returned by the producer's Content() method.

At this time, we study the features of the request and response objects, identified by the base classes TWebRequest and TWebResponse, respectively, since these classes determine the standard minimum characteristics of the request and response objects. Whenever appropriate, we discuss the specific features of the descendant classes, such as TISAPIRequest, ICGIResponse, and so on.

Table 7-6 lists the features of TWebRequest and Table 7-7 lists the features of the TWebResponse classes. In these tables, I present the features of the request and response objects as needed by a web application developer, not as need by a component writer.

Table 7-6: Properties and methods of a TWebRequest object

Property	Description
Accept	This is a read-only (AnsiString) property that provides the HTTP Accept header field value.
Authorization	This is a read-only (AnsiString) property that provides the HTTP Authorization header field value.
CacheControl	This is a read-only (AnsiString) property that provides the HTTP Cache-Control header field value.
Connection	This is a read-only (AnsiString) property that provides the HTTP Connection header field value.
Content	This is the unparsed message body of the request object (in the form of an AnsiString). The data in the Content property should be interpreted by the type of HTTP method used. If the MethodType is mtPost, it means that a set of fields and values are posted by the client browser and are available in the Content property. The individual field-value pairs may be accessed using the ContentFields property. If the MethodType is mtPut, the value in the Content property will replace the resource identified by the URL property.
ContentFields	ContentFields is a TStrings object and contains a list of name-value pairs, which are usually a set of fields and corresponding values posted by the client browser.
ContentLength	This is a read-only (int) property that provides the HTTP Content-Length header field value.
ContentType	This is a read-only (AnsiString) property that provides the HTTP Content-Type header field value.
Cookie	This is a read-only (AnsiString) property that provides the HTTP Cookie header field value. The individual cookie fields may be obtained from the CookieFields property.
CookieFields	This is a TStrings property that contains a list of strings, each of which is a field-value pair. When the request object is built, the individual cookie fields are extracted from the Cookie message header.
Date	This is a read-only (TDateTime) property that provides the HTTP Date header field value.
Expires	This is a read-only property that provides the HTTP Expires header field value.
Files	This is the set of files uploaded by the client in the HTTP request. This is an object of a descendant class to the TAbstractWebRequestFiles class. The implemented descendant class is TWebRequestFiles, which is available in WebSnap applications. Each of the elements in this collection object is an object of a descendant class to TAbstractWebRequestFile. Again, an implemented descendant to this class is TWebRequestFile which is available only in WebSnap applications.
From	This is a read-only (AnsiString) property that provides the HTTP From header field value.
Host	This is a read-only (AnsiString) property that provides the HTTP Host header field value.
IfModifiedSince	This is a read-only (TDateTime) property that provides the HTTP If-Modified-Since header field value.

Part 2

Property	Description
Method	This is the specific HTTP method (or operation) that the client is performing in the request. The typical (AnsiString) values are OPTIONS, GET, HEAD, PUT, DELETE, and POST. If the Method value of a request does not match the list specified in the Allow property of the response object, the request cannot be serviced by the web application.
MethodType	This is an encoded (enumerated, TMethodType) value representing the HTTP method, as identified in the Method property. The permitted method types are mtGet, mtPost, mtHead, mtPut, and mtAny. If the method type is mtAny in a request object, then the Method property value gives the exact method type.
PathInfo	This is an AnsiString value that represents the pathinfo portion of the URL string. The pathinfo and the method type together determine a one-to-one match between an HTTP request and an action item.
Query	This is an AnsiString object that contains the query string that is appended to the URL after the pathinfo string and following the ? separator. The individual fields of the query string may be accessed from the QueryFields property.
QueryFields	This is a TStrings object containing the field-value pairs provided with the HTTP GET request.
Referer	This is a read-only (AnsiString) property that provides the HTTP Referer header field value.
RemoteAddr	This is the IP address of the remote client associated with the HTTP request as an AnsiString object.
RemoteHost	This reports the fully qualified reverse domain lookup of the client associated with the HTTP request message (in the form of an AnsiString). This property may be used to compose URI values for back-links to the source of the request when the Referer property is not specified.
ScriptName	This is an AnsiString object that returns the web application, including the path, from the URL string. This string must be interpreted relative to the default document root directory of the web server; it is not an absolute path to the application.
ServerPort	This (int) property represents the server port in which the web server is listening to the HTTP requests. If the user explicitly entered the port number appended to the host name in the URL, the port number is also visible in the Host property.
URL	This is an AnsiString object that contains the URL that the client browser has provided in the HTTP request. This is the unparsed string as sent by the client. The individual parts of the URL are accessible using different properties of the object.
UserAgent	This is a read-only (AnsiString) property that provides the HTTP User-Agent header field value.

Method	Description
ExtractContentFields (TStrings *fields)	This method should be called to fill the fields parameter with the individual field-value pairs from the Content property. The method assumes that the fields are separated by ampersands (&), as it is the format used when the MethodType is mtPost. If the Content property is not assigned, the method does nothing.
ExtractCookieFields (TStrings *fields)	This method should be called to fill the fields parameter with the individual field-value pairs from the Cookie property. The method assumes that the fields are separated by semicolons, as it is the format used by the client sending the cookie fields. If the Cookie property is not assigned, the method does nothing.
ExtractFields (const TSysCharSet &sep, const TSysCharSet &whspace, char * content, TStrings *strings)	Call this method to parse and extract the multi-valued string into its constituent fields. This is a general-purpose method and may be used to separate fields from any string. The first parameter is a set containing one or more separators that should be used in the field extraction process. The second parameter is a set containing one or more characters that should be considered white spaces and are ignored while parsing the string. The third parameter is the string buffer that should be parsed. The fourth parameter is a TStrings object that will hold the individual fields obtained after parsing.

Method	Description
ExtractQueryFields (TStrings *fields)	This method should be called to fill the fields parameter with the individual field-value pairs from the query string in the Query property. The method assumes that the fields are separated by ampersands (&), as it is the format used by the client sending the query string. If the Query property is not assigned, the method does nothing.
GetFieldByName (AnsiString Name)	This method retrieves the value of a specific HTTP header identified by the Name parameter.

Table 7-7: Properties and methods of a TWebResponse object

Property	Description
Allow	Lists the HTTP request methods that the web application can service (in the form of an AnsiString). Within the string, the individual method names are separated by a comma.
Content	Contains the information sent to the web client. The response content can be a string of HTML commands, the name of an HTML file, graphic content such as a bit stream, or any other MIME content type. If the ContentStream property is set, it supersedes the value of the Content property, and only the ContentStream is sent to the client. This is an AnsiString object. To append to the content already set, you should create a local copy of the content, append to it, and then set it to the Content property of the response object. In the case of requests that do not require any content to be sent to the client (such as responses to the operations PUT, DELETE, or OPTIONS), the content is not set, and the response data is contained within the response header itself.
ContentStream	If the response message body should contain data retrieved from a bit stream, use the ContentStream property instead of the Content property. This property represents a descendant of the TStream object. An example is a JPG image retrieved from a database BLOB data field and formulated into a stream for the purpose of sending to a web client or multimedia content including images and sound.
ContentType	This is a read-only (AnsiString) property that provides the HTTP Content-Type header field value.
Cookies	This is a TCookieCollection object containing one or more cookies, which are objects of the TCookie class. This cookie collection will be sent to the client in the response.
CustomHeaders	CustomHeaders is a collection object and may be used to add one or more name-value pairs, which are custom for the application. This is a TStrings object and may contain any number of name-value pairs. Usually, this property is useful for providing header fields that do not fit into the standard message headers.
Date	This is a read-only (TDateTime) property that provides the HTTP Date header field value.
Expires	This is a read-only (TDateTime) property that provides the HTTP Expires header field value.
HTTPRequest	Provides access to the HTTP Request object in the form TWebRequest instance
LastModified	This is a read-only (TDateTime) property that provides the HTTP Last-Modified header field value.
Location	This is a read-only (AnsiString) property that provides the HTTP Location header field value.
Realm	This is a set of protected access URIs (in the form of AnsiString), including the URL of the current request. These URIs are only available after providing a password or authentication.
StatusCode	This (int) property indicates the status code for the status-line of the response object.
Title	This is an AnsiString value that identifies the response with a title. The property is optional.
WWWAuthenticate	This is a read-only (AnsiString) property that provides the HTTP WWW-Authenticate header field value.

Part 2

Method	Description
GetCustomHeader (AnsiString Name)	This method retrieves the value of the custom header identified by the Name parameter. The value returned is an AnsiString object.
SendRedirect (AnsiString URI)	Call this method to redirect the web request to another URI.
SendResponse()	Call this method to explicitly send the response object. If the web action item(s) and the web dispatcher event handlers set the Handled parameter to true, the web dispatcher automatically sends the response, and there is no need to explicitly send the response. Calling this method provides an explicit control in your hands as a programmer to send the response when you desire.
SendStream (TStream* Stream)	This method should be called to explicitly send a stream (such as a graphic image) in the response object. Before calling this method, call the SendResponse() method to set the properties of the response object. Alternately, you can set the ContentStream property to the stream to be sent and then call the SendResponse() method.
Sent()	This method returns a Boolean value indicating whether the response has been sent or not.
SetCookieField (TStrings *values, AnsiString domain, AnsiString path, TDateTime* expires, bool secured)	This method should be called to add a Cookie header to the cookie collection to be sent to the client. Each Cookie header contains a set of name-value pairs. The domain is the set of domains that the client may send to the cookie in its request, and the path is the set of URL paths on which the cookie is valid on the domains. The fourth parameter is the time after which the cookie expires, and the last parameter indicates whether the client should use a secure connection to send the Cookie header.
SetCustomHeader (AnsiString Name, AnsiString Value)	This method should be called to add or change a custom header to the set of custom headers identified by the CustomHeaders property. If the custom header already exists in the custom header list, it is replaced by the new custom header; if one does not exist with the same name, the new one is added to the list. The name of the custom header is identified by the Name parameter, and the corresponding value is identified by the Value parameter.

Web Dispatcher in Action

Let's now focus our attention on how the web dispatcher identifies the web action items to provide the response content. As I mentioned earlier, the Actions property of the web dispatcher is a collection object (an instance of the TWebActionItems class) and contains the list of TWebActionItem objects. When a request is received, the dispatcher tries to locate a web action item with PathInfo and MethodType properties that match the request object. If a matching action item is found, the dispatcher executes the event handler associated with that action item. If a matching action item is not found, it tries to locate the default action item. If a default action item exists, the dispatcher executes the event handler associated with the default item. If both the matching action item and the default action item are present, the matching action item is executed first. If the Handled parameter in the matching action item event handler is set to false, the default action item is also executed.

It is also possible to split the task of generating the response content among multiple action items. This is done by setting the PathInfo and MethodType properties of all such action items to the (same) corresponding values of the request object. In such a case, the dispatcher executes all the matching action items sequentially (based on the index position of the action item in the action item collection), as long as the Handled parameter in the previous matching action item event handler is set to false. The default action item event handler is executed only after executing all the matching action item event handlers and the Handled property in all those event handlers are set to false.

It is important to note that the response content generation task is carried forward to the next action item only if the previous action item event handler sets its Handled parameter to false. Therefore, we can stop this chain of execution of event handlers at any point desired by setting the Handled parameter to false in a specific event handler; if we do not explicitly set this parameter in a particular event handler, the default value of true is assumed. In either case, it is considered that the request has been successfully handled, and therefore the AfterDispatch event handler of the web dispatcher is fired. If we explicitly set this parameter to false in all the matching event handlers, the default action item event handler is also executed. If the Handled parameter is set to false in the event handlers for all the matching action items, including the default action item, the dispatcher assumes that the request has not been successfully handled, and therefore the AfterDispatch event handler of the dispatcher is not fired. The AfterDispatch event handler of the dispatcher is the last chance for us to change the response content before it is sent to the client. Please note that an explicit call to the SendReponse() method of the response object is equivalent to setting the Handled parameter to true in the action item event handler.

To append the response content in an event handler without losing the pre-existing content, we have to extract the pre-existing content string into a local AnsiString object, append to it any new content string, and reset the response content string to this new string value.

Sample Web Applications

Overview

By now, we have enough knowledge about building a web application using C++Builder components to try building a few live examples illustrating the principles discussed so far. I will demonstrate how to build a CGI application and an Apache application, how to convert a CGI application to an ISAPI DLL, and finally how to use the producer components that produce HTML content using the data from a database. We will demonstrate a different set of applications in the following chapter, "Building WebSnap Applications."

CGI Application

Follow the steps outlined here to create the sample CGI application:

1. Create a new web application of type CGI stand-alone executable. The IDE automatically creates a project cpp file, a web module, and the corresponding unit1.cpp and unit1.h files. In this application, the unit1.dfm is the web module. As we discussed earlier, we can use the web module just like a data module and place any non-visual components on it. In this example, I will demonstrate how the action item event handlers are coded to produce the response content.

2. From the IDE, choose the **Project | Options** menu item to change a couple of important options. In the Project Options dialog in the Linker page, uncheck the **Use dynamic RTL** selection. This is to make sure that the RTL code is linked into the program executable. In the Packages page, uncheck the **Build with runtime packages** selection. This is to make sure that the appropriate object code is directly linked in your program from the corresponding libraries so that we can avoid the complexity of distributing these libraries.

3. Save the project and unit files with names of your choice in a directory of your choice. For the sake of simplicity, I saved the files with default names.

4. This example needs SQL Server 7/2000 running on the network connected to your desktop. Drop a **TADOConnection** component and two **TADOQuery** components. Set the connection component's properties to connect to the sample Northwind database running on the SQL Server.

5. In the WebModuleCreate event handler of the web module, implement the code to establish the database connection; in the WebModuleDestroy event handler, implement the code to close the database connection.

6. Double-click anywhere on the web module. The Actions collection editor is displayed. Add three web action items by clicking the **Add New** icon in the collection editor three times. For the WebActionItem1, set the Default property to **true**. For WebActionItem2 and WebAction-Item3, set the PathInfo property to **/categories** and **/products**, respectively.

7. For the ADOQuery1 and ADOQuery2 components, set the SQL property to the appropriate select statements, as displayed in Listing 7-2.

8. Now implement the three action item event handlers, as displayed in Listing 7-3. The header file for the program is given in Listing 7-4.

9. Listing 7-5 is displayed to show the project cpp file for this project. In the next section, we will discuss how to convert one web application type to another without much modification to the code. This listing is useful in that discussion.

Listing 7-2: SQL statements

```
// For the ADOQuery1 component
select CategoryName, Description from Categories;

// For the ADOQuery2 component
select Categories.CategoryID, Categories.CategoryName,
Products.ProductID, Products.ProductName
from Categories, Products
where Products.CategoryID = Categories.CategoryID
order by CategoryName, ProductName;
```

Listing 7-3: Unit1.cpp

```
//---------------------------------------------------------------------------
#include "Unit1.h"
//---------------------------------------------------------------------------
#pragma package(smart_init)
#pragma resource "*.dfm"
TWebModule1 *WebModule1;
//---------------------------------------------------------------------------
__fastcall TWebModule1::TWebModule1(TComponent* Owner)
                     : TWebModule(Owner)
{
}
//---------------------------------------------------------------------------

void __fastcall TWebModule1::WebModuleCreate(TObject *Sender)
{
    ADOConnection1->Connected = true;
}
//---------------------------------------------------------------------------

void __fastcall TWebModule1::WebModuleDestroy(TObject *Sender)
{
    ADOConnection1->Connected = false;
}
//---------------------------------------------------------------------------

void __fastcall TWebModule1::WebModule1WebActionItem1Action(
    TObject *Sender, TWebRequest *Request, TWebResponse *Response,
    bool &Handled)
{
    // default action - display selection buttons
    AnsiString fRespStr = "<HTML>";
    fRespStr += "<TITLE>CGI Web Application (Executable)</TITLE>";
    fRespStr += "<BODY BGCOLOR=\"#CCCCBB\">";
    fRespStr += "<H1>Northwind Bakery</H1>";
    fRespStr += "<BR>";
```

```
        fRespStr += "<H2>Choose one of the Options</H2>";
        fRespStr += "<BR>";
        fRespStr += "<UL>";
        fRespStr += "<LI><A HREF=\"/cgi-bin/Project1.exe/categories\">Product
                    Categories</A>";
        fRespStr += "<LI><A HREF=\"/cgi-bin/Project1.exe/products\">Products in
                    Categories</A>";
        fRespStr += "</UL>";
        fRespStr += "</BODY>";
        fRespStr += "</HTML>";
    Response->Content = fRespStr;
}
//---------------------------------------------------------------------------

void __fastcall TWebModule1::WebModule1WebActionItem2Action(
    TObject *Sender, TWebRequest *Request, TWebResponse *Response,
    bool &Handled)
{
    // action to display categories
    AnsiString fRespStr = "<HTML>";
    fRespStr += "<TITLE>CGI Web Application (Executable)</TITLE>";
    fRespStr += "<BODY BGCOLOR=\"#CCCCBB\">";
    fRespStr += "<H1>Northwind Bakery</H1>";
    fRespStr += "<BR><H2>Product Categories</H2>";
    fRespStr += "<BR>";

    if (ADOConnection1->Connected) {
        ADOQuery1->Open();
        if (ADOQuery1->RecordCount <= 0) {
            fRespStr += "</BODY>";
            fRespStr += "</HTML>";
            Response->Content = fRespStr;
            return;
        }
        fRespStr += "<TABLE BORDER=2>";
        fRespStr += "<TR>";
            fRespStr += "<TH>Item ID</TH>";
            fRespStr += "<TH>Category Name</TH>";
            fRespStr += "<TH>Category Description</TH>";
        fRespStr += "</TR>";

        for (int i=1; i <= ADOQuery1->RecordCount; i++) {
            fRespStr += "<TR>";
                fRespStr += "<TD>" + IntToStr(i) + "</TD>";
                fRespStr += "<TD>" + ADOQuery1->FieldByName("CategoryName")->AsString
                        + "</TD>";
                fRespStr += "<TD>" + ADOQuery1->FieldByName("Description")->AsString
                        + "</TD>";
            fRespStr += "</TR>";
            ADOQuery1->Next();
        }
        fRespStr += "</TABLE>";
    }
    fRespStr += "</BODY>";
    fRespStr += "</HTML>";
    Response->Content = fRespStr;
}
//---------------------------------------------------------------------------
void __fastcall TWebModule1::WebModule1WebActionItem3Action(
```

```
            TObject *Sender, TWebRequest *Request, TWebResponse *Response,
            bool &Handled)
{
    // action to display products
    AnsiString fRespStr = "<HTML>";
    fRespStr += "<TITLE>CGI Web Application (Executable)</TITLE>";
    fRespStr += "<BODY BGCOLOR=\"#CCCCBB\">";
    fRespStr += "<H1>Northwind Bakery</H1>";
    fRespStr += "<BR><H2>Categorized Products</H2>";
    fRespStr += "<BR>";

    if (ADOConnection1->Connected) {
        ADOQuery2->Open();
        if (ADOQuery2->RecordCount <= 0) {
            fRespStr += "</BODY>";
            fRespStr += "</HTML>";
            Response->Content = fRespStr;
            return;
        }
        fRespStr += "<TABLE BORDER=2>";
        fRespStr += "<TR>";
            fRespStr += "<TH>Product ID</TH>";
            fRespStr += "<TH>Category Name</TH>";
            fRespStr += "<TH>Product Name</TH>";
        fRespStr += "</TR>";

        for (int i=1; i <= ADOQuery2->RecordCount; i++) {
            fRespStr += "<TR>";
                fRespStr += "<TD>" + ADOQuery2->FieldByName("ProductID")->AsString
                    + "</TD>";
                fRespStr += "<TD>" + ADOQuery2->FieldByName("CategoryName")->AsString
                    + "</TD>";
                fRespStr += "<TD>" + ADOQuery2->FieldByName("ProductName")->AsString
                    + "</TD>";
            fRespStr += "</TR>";
            ADOQuery2->Next();
        }
        fRespStr += "</TABLE>";
    }
    fRespStr += "</BODY>";
    fRespStr += "</HTML>";
    Response->Content = fRespStr;
}
//---------------------------------------------------------------------------
```

Listing 7-4: Unit1.h

```
//---------------------------------------------------------------------------
#ifndef Unit1H
#define Unit1H
//---------------------------------------------------------------------------
#include <SysUtils.hpp>
#include <Classes.hpp>
#include <HTTPApp.hpp>
#include <ADODB.hpp>
#include <DB.hpp>
//---------------------------------------------------------------------------
class TWebModule1 : public TWebModule
{
```

```
__published:          // IDE-managed Components
   TADOConnection *ADOConnection1;
   TADOQuery *ADOQuery1;
   TADOQuery *ADOQuery2;
   void __fastcall WebModuleCreate(TObject *Sender);
   void __fastcall WebModuleDestroy(TObject *Sender);
   void __fastcall WebModule1WebActionItem1Action(TObject *Sender,
         TWebRequest *Request, TWebResponse *Response, bool &Handled);
   void __fastcall WebModule1WebActionItem2Action(TObject *Sender,
         TWebRequest *Request, TWebResponse *Response, bool &Handled);
   void __fastcall WebModule1WebActionItem3Action(TObject *Sender,
         TWebRequest *Request, TWebResponse *Response, bool &Handled);
private:                // User declarations
public:                 // User declarations
                        __fastcall TWebModule1(TComponent* Owner);
};
//--------------------------------------------------------------------------
extern PACKAGE TWebModule1 *WebModule1;
//--------------------------------------------------------------------------
#endif
```

Listing 7-5: Project1.cpp—CGI application

```
//--------------------------------------------------------------------------
#include <condefs.h>
#include <stdio.h>
#include <stdlib.h>
#include <string.h>
#include <SysUtils.hpp>
#include <WebBroker.hpp>
#include <CGIApp.hpp>
#pragma hdrstop
USEFORM("Unit1.cpp", WebModule1); /* TWebModule: File Type */
//--------------------------------------------------------------------------
#define Application Webbroker::Application
#pragma link "cgiapp.obj"
#pragma link "webbroker.obj"
#pragma link "ReqMulti.obj"
#pragma link "WebSnap.lib"
#pragma link "WebDSnap.lib"
//--------------------------------------------------------------------------
int main(int argc, char* argv[])
{
  try
  {
    Application->Initialize();
    Application->CreateForm(__classid(TWebModule1), &WebModule1);
    Application->Run();
  }
  catch (Exception &exception)
  {
    Sysutils::ShowException(&exception, System::ExceptAddr());
  }
  return 0;
}
//--------------------------------------------------------------------------
```

Since this is a CGI application, any web server should be able to deploy this application. I tested this application with two web servers: the Microsoft Internet Information Server and the Apache 1.3 Web Server. On my desktop, I configured an IIS site to listen to port 8040 and the Apache server to listen to port 7779. I deployed this program (Project1.exe) to the /cgi-bin directory from the document root directory in both cases. Notice that we implemented three action items. The first one is the default action item and displays two options to further display categories and products, respectively. The second and third action items are implemented to display the categories and products, respectively. In the Internet Explorer window, I typed the URL http://localhost:7779/cgi-bin/Project1.exe. The result is displayed in Figure 7-4. This is the output when the application is deployed to the Apache web server. Similar results are obtained when I type the URL http://localhost:8040/cgi-bin/Project1.exe in the IE window.

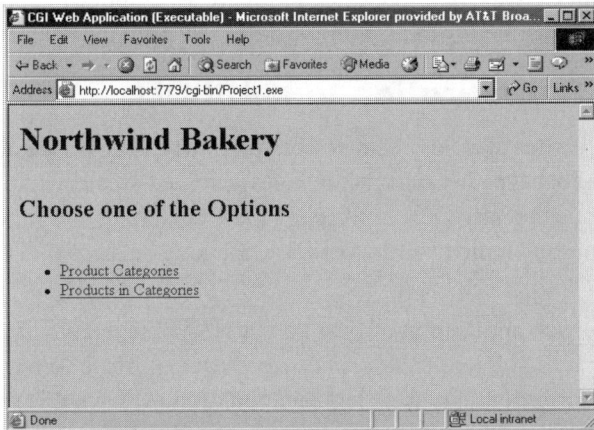

Figure 7-4: Internet Explorer window displaying the CGI application

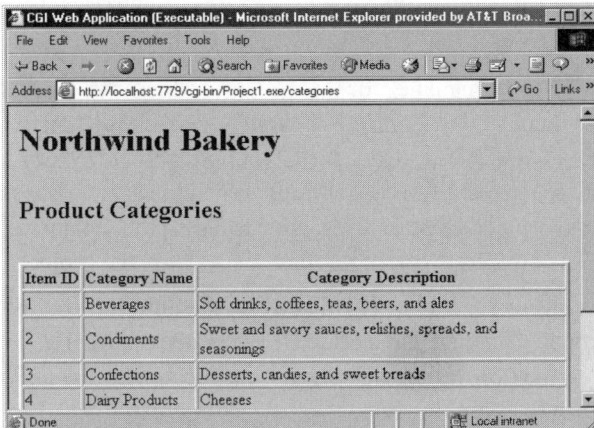

Figure 7-5: Internet Explorer window displaying categories

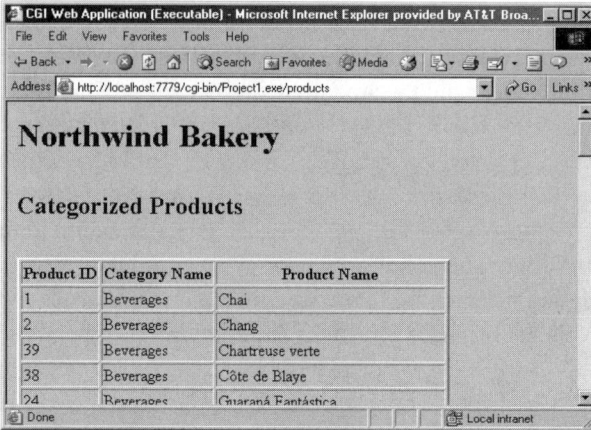

Figure 7-6: Internet Explorer window displaying products

When each of the links are clicked in the initial IE window, the corresponding pages are displayed, as in Figure 7-5 and Figure 7-6. Notice that these HTML pages are dynamically built with the data read from the database.

Convert the CGI Application to ISAPI DLL

As we discussed earlier, it is very easy to convert one type of WebBroker application to another type because the changes involved are very minimal. Let me demonstrate this to you by converting the CGI application we created in the previous example to an ISAPI DLL. Follow the steps outlined here to make this conversion happen:

1. Create a new web application of type ISAPI/NSAPI Dynamic Link Library. The IDE automatically creates a project cpp file, a web module, and the corresponding unit1.cpp and unit1.h files. Save this project in a directory of your choice. I saved the project in a different directory. The project name this time is Project2.cpp, and the web module is Unit1.

2. Now open the project manager for this project and remove Unit1 from the project, as displayed in Figure 7-7. Now copy the **Unit1.dfm**, **Unit1.cpp**, and **Unit1.h** files from the CGI application directory to this directory (where Project2 files are stored). When the system asks for confirmation to replace existing files, choose **Yes**. This replaces the default unit files created by the IDE when we created the project.

3. Now open the project manager again and add the unit that you just copied to the project. Thus, we have effectively connected our existing web module to the new project. There are just a couple more tasks we have to perform to complete this.

In the Unit1.cpp file, we have the WebActionItem1 that acts as a default action item and displays the initial page. This action item also defines links to the other two pages. You have to change the program name from Project1.exe to Project2.dll because our executable is the dynamic library in this case. Also, the title of the application should be changed wherever there is a reference. With these changes we are done changing the project type from a CGI application to an ISAPI application.

4. Now copy the program **Project2.dll** to the directory where you deployed the IIS server. This program does not run with the Apache server. We will see a separate example for the Apache server in the next section.

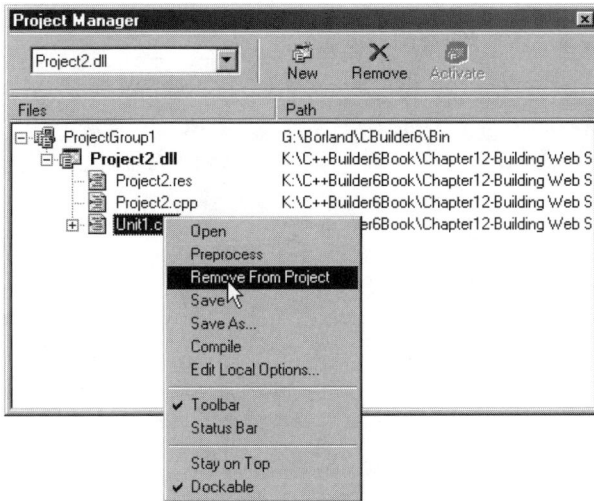

Figure 7-7: Removing the unit file from the application project definition

Part 2

I present the Project2.cpp file in Listing 7-6 to show you the differences between this listing and Listing 7-5, which is the CGI project file; the first difference is in the included header files and linked object files. The CGIApp.hpp header file in the CGI type web application declares the Application global variable of type TCGIApplication object, and in the ISAPI type web application the Application global variable represents the TISAPIApplication object. The ISAPI application declares the application as multi-threaded, whereas the CGI application runs separate instances for every request. The CGI application declares the main function because it is a console application, and the ISAPI application declares the DllEntryPoint function because it is a Windows DLL type application. Additionally, the

ISAPI application file declares three other functions: GetExtension-
Version() is called by the web server to obtain the application name and
version number for the HTTP functions in the run-time library, the
HTTPExtensionProc() function is called by the web server when it receives
an HTTP request to create the TISAPIRequest and TISAPIResponse objects
for further processing of the request and filling the response content, and
the TerminateExtension() function is called by the web server when it is
finally required to terminate the web application.

The important point to remember here is that the conversion of a web
application is automatically handled by the IDE by creating an appropriate
project file, and the logic in the web module is not changed significantly;
we may even write the web module in such a way as to also avoid the minimal changes.

Listing 7-6: Project2.cpp—ISAPI/NSAPI application

```
//--------------------------------------------------------------------------
#include <ActiveX.hpp>
#include <ComObj.hpp>
#include <WebBroker.hpp>
#include <ISAPIApp.hpp>
#include <ISAPIThreadPool.hpp>
#include <Isapi2.hpp>
#pragma hdrstop

USEFORM("Unit1.cpp", WebModule1); /* TWebModule: File Type */
//--------------------------------------------------------------------------
#define Application Webbroker::Application

#pragma link "isapiapp.obj"
#pragma link "isapithreadpool.obj"
#pragma link "webbroker.obj"
#pragma link "ReqMulti.obj"
#pragma link "WebSnap.lib"
#pragma link "WebDSnap.lib"
//--------------------------------------------------------------------------
int WINAPI DllEntryPoint(HINSTANCE hinst, unsigned long reason, void*)
{
  try
  {
    if (reason == DLL_PROCESS_ATTACH) {
      CoInitFlags = COINIT_MULTITHREADED;
      Application->Initialize();
      Application->CreateForm(__classid(TWebModule1), &WebModule1);
      Application->Run();
    }
  }
  catch (Exception &exception)
  {
  }
  return 1;
}
//--------------------------------------------------------------------------
extern "C"
```

```
{
  BOOL __declspec(dllexport) WINAPI GetExtensionVersion(Isapi2::THSE_VERSION_INFO &Ver)
  {
    return Isapithreadpool::GetExtensionVersion(Ver);
  }
  //-------------------------------------------------------------------------
  unsigned __declspec(dllexport) WINAPI
            HttpExtensionProc(Isapi2::TEXTENSION_CONTROL_BLOCK &ECB)
  {
    return Isapithreadpool::HttpExtensionProc(ECB);
  }
  //-------------------------------------------------------------------------
  BOOL __declspec(dllexport) WINAPI TerminateExtension(int dwFlags)
  {
    return Isapithreadpool::TerminateExtension(dwFlags);
  }
}
//-------------------------------------------------------------------------
#undef Application
//-------------------------------------------------------------------------
```

Apache Application

Apache HTTP server has become very popular on the Linux operating system and other UNIX clones. Many vendors have now started providing Apache-based HTTP servers, even on Windows operating systems. In an earlier section, I demonstrated how a CGI web application executable could be developed and deployed by the Apache web server. In addition, the Apache web server can also deploy shared modules (dynamic libraries on Windows and shared libraries on Linux and UNIX operating systems).

In this section we will see how to create a web application that runs on an Apache HTTP server as a shared module. This application type is also available in the CLX component architecture and currently in Kylix. On Windows it is available in C++Builder 6 and Delphi 6. It is also available in Kylix 3, the Linux version of C++.

The steps involved in the development of an Apache web application are outlined here. Again, the contents of the project cpp file are the main difference, and there are a few other steps when deploying the module to the web server. In this example, I will demonstrate an application using a BDE connection to a database.

In the IDE, create a web server application of type Apache Shared Module (DLL). Save the project files in a directory of your choice and with a name of your choice. I saved them with default names.

Notice that a web module is created similarly to the previous examples and assigned to the project. I replaced the web module with a pre-existing data module. To convert the data module to render web action items, I dropped a TWebDispatcher component from the Internet page of the Component Palette. The data module already contained a TTable component

Part 2

connected to the DBDEMOS database, as it was used in an existing application. We will use this component and try to populate the web pages with data from different tables in this database. Using the action editor of the web dispatcher component, I created four web action items. The first action item is the default one and provides a path to access the other action items. Since the code is very similar, I am not providing it here, but you can access the code on the companion CD. Remember that I am just demonstrating a simple Apache shared module. We will see the producer components in the next section, which automate most of the HTML work.

Let's take a look at the project file shown in Listing 7-7. The Apache shared module application includes the header file ApacheApp.hpp, which defines the global Application variable of type TApacheApplication. Also, the application provides two important declaratives that should be used in the httpd.conf file, which is the default configuration file to configure the features and functionality of an Apache HTTP server.

Every shared (dynamic) module must be loaded by the Apache web server when it is started. This is indicated to the server by means of the LoadModule directive in the configuration file. The LoadModule directive must specify an internal module name and associate it with the DLL filename. We have to add this directive to the httpd.conf file effectively after the ClearModuleList directive because the ClearModuleList directive clears all the previously loaded default modules. The module name specified in the LoadModule directive is automatically determined by a global declarative when the application is created in the C++Builder IDE. The module name is _<project name>_module. For example, if the project name is Project1, the module name then becomes _Project1_module. Similarly, another global declarative, <project name>-handler, is also created by the IDE in the project; when the project name is Project1, the handler declarative becomes Project1-handler. This variable must be used in the configuration file to specify a virtual directory name associated with the handler using the Location directive. Figure 7-8 shows the relationship between these project declaratives and the configuration file directives. The syntax of the LoadModule and Location directives in the configuration file is shown in Listing 7-8.

The global directives defined by the C++Builder application may be changed, if you desire, by one line of code for each of them. This must be coded in the DLL entry point function and in the __declspec directive, as shown in Listing 7-9. Compare this listing with Listing 7-7 to make things clear. It is important to remember that whatever module name you define, you must precede it with an underscore in the LoadModule directive in the configuration file. These global declaratives provide the link between the web application, the web server, and the URL we type in the browser to execute the program, as displayed in Figure 7-8. In the LoadModule directive, we may provide either the absolute path or the relative path to the program location. Similarly, the virtual directory name defined in the Location directive serves as the virtual program name that we type in the URL after the server name. For example, I defined the virtual directory name /apachedemo in the configuration file for this application, making the URL http://localhost:7779/apachedemo. In this URL, you may notice that we are not exposing the program name. The subsequent path assigned to an action item is appended to this URL, such as http://localhost:7779/apachedemo/ customers. Accessing each of these URLs produced HTTP pages, which are displayed in Figure 7-9 and Figure 7-10, respectively.

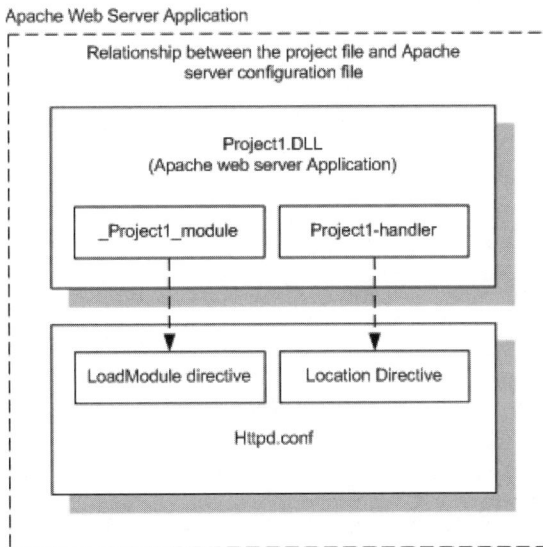

Figure 7-8: Relationship between the Apache server application and configuration file

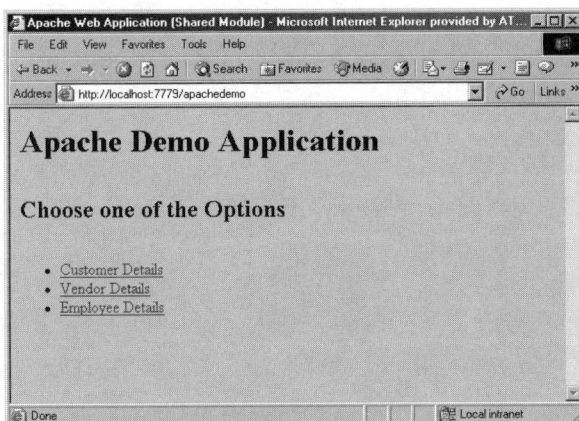

Figure 7-9: Apache web application main page

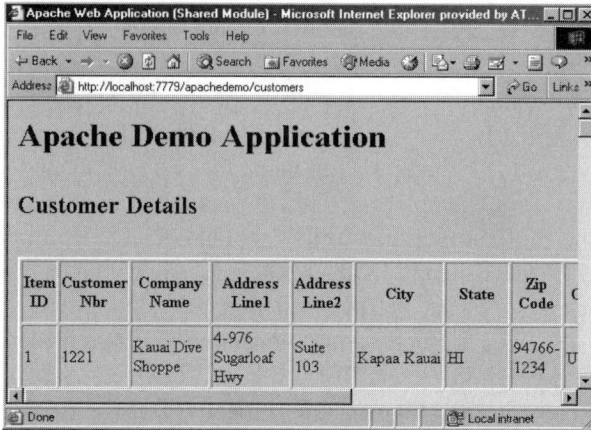

Figure 7-10: Apache web application subsequent page (first action item)

Listing 7-7: Project1.cpp—Apache shared module

```cpp
//---------------------------------------------------------------------------
#include <WebBroker.hpp>
#include <ApacheApp.hpp>
#pragma hdrstop

USEFORM("Unit1.cpp", DataModule1); /* TDataModule: File Type */
//---------------------------------------------------------------------------
#define Application Webbroker::Application

#pragma link "ApacheApp.obj"
#pragma link "webbroker.obj"
#pragma link "ReqMulti.obj"
#pragma link "WebSnap.lib"
#pragma link "WebDSnap.lib"


//---------------------------------------------------------------------------
extern "C"
{
  Httpd::module __declspec(dllexport) Project1_module;
}


//---------------------------------------------------------------------------
int WINAPI DllEntryPoint(HINSTANCE hinst, unsigned long reason, void*)
{
  try
  {
    if (reason == DLL_PROCESS_ATTACH) {
        Apacheapp::set_module(&Project1_module);
        Application->Initialize();
        Application->CreateForm(__classid(TDataModule1), &DataModule1);
        Application->Run();
    }
  }
  catch (Exception &exception)
  {
  }
  return 1;
}
```

```
//--------------------------------------------------------------------------
#undef Application
//--------------------------------------------------------------------------
```

Listing 7-8: LoadModule and Location directives in the httpd.conf file

```
# The LoadModule directive provides a link between the web application
# and the Apache web server. The linking element is the module name
# _Project1_module as mentioned in the directive. In the example
# the dll name is mentioned using relative path.
#
LoadModule _Project1_module htdocs/bcb6dg/Project1.dll
#
# LoadModule directive is complete here.
#
# Other directives of the file continue here.
#
# The Location directive provides a virtual directory name (or program
# name) to include in the URL. The directive should not be placed
# immediately after the LoadModule directive. The Location directive
# must be placed along with other Location directives in the file.
#
<Location /apachedemo>
          SetHandler Project1-handler
</Location>
#
# Location directive is complete here.
```

Listing 7-9: Sample code to change the module name and handler name

```
//--------------------------------------------------------------------------
#include <WebBroker.hpp>
#include <ApacheApp.hpp>
#pragma hdrstop

USEFORM("Unit1.cpp", DataModule1); /* TDataModule: File Type */
//--------------------------------------------------------------------------
#define Application Webbroker::Application

#pragma link "ApacheApp.obj"
#pragma link "webbroker.obj"
#pragma link "ReqMulti.obj"
#pragma link "WebSnap.lib"
#pragma link "WebDSnap.lib"


//--------------------------------------------------------------------------
extern "C"
{
  Httpd::module __declspec(dllexport) satya_module;
}
//--------------------------------------------------------------------------
int WINAPI DllEntryPoint(HINSTANCE hinst, unsigned long reason, void*)
{
  try
  {
    if (reason == DLL_PROCESS_ATTACH) {
        strcpy(ContentType, "satya-handler");
        strcpy(ModuleName, "satya_module");

        Apacheapp::set_module(&satya_module);
```

Part 2

```
        Application->Initialize();
        Application->CreateForm(__classid(TDataModule1), &DataModule1);
        Application->Run();
    }
  }
  catch (Exception &exception)
  {
  }
  return 1;
}
//---------------------------------------------------------------------------
```

Producer Components

Overview

So far we have seen the web dispatcher and its action items provide support in building the response object to specific HTTP requests. However, there are more powerful components that aid in automating the page generation process and separate the data from its visual presentation layer. These components also belong to the WebBroker family and are specifically useful in building dynamic page content by using data from the databases. After understanding the functionality of these components, we can appreciate that we will be relieved of most of the burden when building complex pages while retrieving data from the database.

PageProducer Components

The page producer components are designed to generate HTML strings of commands based on an input HTML template document. The input template document contains one or more placeholders called tags enclosed in a pair of angle brackets (< and >), such as <#tagname param1=value1, param2=value2 ...>. The angle brackets make the tag transparent to HTML browsers that do not recognize the <#tagname> construct. They are meant to be used by the VCL producer components only. As shown here, these tags may contain input parameter-value pairs. There can be as many of such parameter-value pairs as are required. Please note the syntactic rules when using the tags. There should not be any space between the opening bracket (<) and the pound sign (#) and between the pound sign and the tag name. Similarly, there should not be any space between the parameter name and the equal sign (=) and between the equal sign and the parameter value. There can be one or more spaces between any two consecutive parameter-value pairs. Again, after the last parameter-value pair, the closing bracket must follow without any space. When a producer component parses the HTML template in its OnHTMLTag event handler, it replaces the tag with the appropriate HTML string, as coded by the programmer.

The TCustomContentProducer class is the base class for all the producer components. We will examine the three virtual methods that are introduced in this class and implemented by all the subclasses. The Content() method returns the HTML string representing the content produced by the producer component. This is the content that will be sent through the response object. The ContentFromStream(TStream *stream) method returns the HTML string representing the content produced by the producer component based on the information provided in the input stream object. Similarly, the ContentFromString(const AnsiString str) method returns the HTML string representing the content produced by the input string.

The descendant classes of TCustomContentProducer override these methods to provide the HTML string that is appropriate to the component's functionality. There are two main categories of producer components derived from this base class: the page producers generate a standard HTML page and may include the content from a stream, and the table producers generate an HTML table containing records of data retrieved from a database table or as a result of a database query. The table producers may be used in conjunction with any of the TDataSet descendant objects. We will continue our discussion here with the page producer components and discuss the table producers in the following sub-section.

Remember one important point: It is not required to use an HTML template in order to use the producer components, but by using the templates containing tags, we can automate the HTML page generation process in large, complex systems. Also, we can use the OnHTMLTag event handler only if we provide the template. Providing the HTML template is very simple, either as a TStrings object (containing multiple lines of HTML text) through the HTMLDoc property or as an HTML file through the HTMLFile property. Depending on the HTTP request, we have the ability to change the template dynamically, thus providing different templates for different requests, as demonstrated in the example in this section.

Among the WebBroker component set, there are two page producers that are widely used: the TPageProducer and the TDataSetPageProducer components; the former is used to generate any custom HTML page content, and the latter is used to directly link the dataset record fields to the tag names in the template. Since we can drop any non-visual components onto the web module, even the TPageProducer component can be used to retrieve data from the database and replace the tag fields in the HTML template. However, if we use tag names that are the same as the field names of the dataset connected to the TDataSetPageProducer component, we do not have to manually replace the tag fields. The sample program provided later in this section also demonstrates how I was able to extract data from a database using both types of the page producer components described above.

TableProducer Components

The table producer components are designed to generate HTML tables using the data retrieved from the database. There are three types of such components: The TDataSetTableProducer component produces an HTML table with data obtained from a TDataSet descendant component, the TQueryTableProducer component produces an HTML table with data obtained from a TQuery component in the BDE Component Palette page, and the TSQLQueryTableProducer component produces an HTML table with data obtained from a TSQLQuery component in the dbExpress family. Since a database query can be processed using any of the three categories of components, as mentioned above, all three table producer components together support the different types of queries that we perform in a VCL-based application.

We will now look at an example that demonstrates the use of a page producer, a dataset page producer, and a table producer component. I have designed this example to cover many of the features in a single application. Of the table producer components, I demonstrate the TDataSetTable-Producer; the other two table producer components are similar in functionality.

1. Create a web application of type CGI stand-alone executable, and save the project files in a directory of your choice with names of your choice. Though we are building this application as a CGI executable, ideally this example would be built in any of the web application types supported by C++Builder 6. As usual, I saved the application with default names provided by the IDE. This saves me a lot of time.

2. In this application, we use an ADO-based database connection to a SQL Server database, the pubs database that is installed by the default SQL Server installation. Drop an **ADOConnection** object and three **ADOQuery** objects from the ADO page in the Component Palette and a **PageProducer** object, a **DataSetPageProducer**, and a **DataSetTableProducer** object from the Internet page in the Component Palette.

3. To the application project file, add three HTML documents from the Web Documents page in the New Items dialog. I named these HTML document files publishers.html, authors.html, and employee.html,

respectively. These HTML documents serve as HTML templates for our page producer objects. Please note that it is not required to attach these files to the project; C++Builder does not compile these files anyway. They may be created separately and deployed in the cgi-bin directory of your web server along with the program executable. I only attached them to the project since I initially created them in the project directory and used C++Builder's New Items dialog to create them.

4. Set the ConnectionString property of the ADOConnection1 object and test that the connection is working properly. Also make sure that the LoginPrompt property is set to false to avoid the login dialog displaying during run time. In the example, I set the user ID and password in the connection string during design time, but in real-world applications you may set the connection string during run time.

5. Set the Connection property of the three ADOQuery objects to the ADOConnection1 object. I will use the ADOQuery1 object to illustrate the PageProducer1 object and also how we can use the single query component to handle different action items. Therefore, I am not setting its SQL property during design time. I will use the ADOQuery2 object to illustrate the use of the DataSetTableProducer1 object, and finally I will use the ADOQuery3 object to illustrate the use of the DataSetPageProducer1 object.

6. Set the SQL property of the ADOQuery2 and ADOQuery3 components to the code provided in Listings 7-10 and 7-11.

7. Create six web action items in the action item property editor of the web module. The first action item is the default one and provides the initial page with options to the user. The second and third action items are implemented to set the publishers and authors pages, respectively. In the event handlers of these action items, I am also setting the HTMLFile property of the PageProducer1 object dynamically since the content for these objects is produced by the PageProducer1 object. The fourth action item is implemented to demonstrate how the DataSet-TableProducer1 object generates the HTML table for the result dataset obtained from executing the SQL statement in the ADOQuery2 object. The fifth action item is implemented to display a single employee record from the result dataset of the ADOQuery3 object. Finally, the sixth action item is implemented to display a single record as navigated by the user.

The HTML template in the publishers.html and authors.html files is very similar to a single tag—<#publishers> and <#authors>, respectively. I

Part 2

implemented the PageProducer1 object's OnHTMLTag event handler that
provides the HTML string, which replaces these placeholder tags. The
HTML string typically contains an HTML table displaying records
obtained from the database. The HTML template files are shown in Listings
7-12 and 7-13, respectively.

Listing 7-14 displays the Header property HTML string for the DataSet-
TableProducer1 object. Since the table producer component produces the
actual HTML table, the component provides two properties: Header and
Footer. The Header property may contain an HTML string that should be
displayed before the HTML table, and the Footer property may contain an
HTML string that should be displayed after the HTML table. Listing 7-15
displays the employee.html file content, which is the HTML template for
the employee record display page. In this HTML template, we notice that a
single record is displayed at a time.

In the sixth action item event handler, I implemented the logic to display
one record at a time. When the user clicks the record navigation buttons,
like Next and Prior, which indicate moving the record pointer from the current record, the program should know the current record position before
moving the record. Since the HTTP protocol is stateless, the program automatically closes the dataset after the current request is serviced; therefore, I
used a cookie by the name BookMark, which is used to store the last name
of the current employee record. This cookie is stored on the user's machine
(provided the users enable cookies in their browsers) and retrieved every
time this particular action item is invoked.

Listings 7-16 and 7-17 provide the complete listing of the cpp and
header files for the web module program.

Listing 7-10: SQL statement for the ADOQuery2 component

```
select authors.au_id, authors.au_lname, authors.au_fname,
titles.title_id, titles.title, titles.price
from authors, titles, titleauthor
where
titleauthor.au_id = authors.au_id and
titleauthor.title_id = titles.title_id and
price is not null
```

Listing 7-11: SQL statement for the ADOQuery3 component

```
select authors.au_id, authors.au_lname, authors.au_fname,
titles.title_id, titles.title, titles.price
from authors, titles, titleauthor
where
titleauthor.au_id = authors.au_id and
titleauthor.title_id = titles.title_id and
price is not null
```

Listing 7-12: publishers.html

```html
<!DOCTYPE HTML PUBLIC "-//W3C//DTD HTML 4.01 Transitional//EN">
<HTML>
  <HEAD>
    <TITLE>Registered Publishers
    </TITLE>
  </HEAD>
    <BODY BGCOLOR="#CCCCBB">
    <H2>This page uses TPageProducer component</H2>
    <BR>
    <H3>List of Publishers</H3>
    <BR>
    <#publishers>
    <BR>
  </BODY>
</HTML>
```

Listing 7-13: authors.html

```html
<!DOCTYPE HTML PUBLIC "-//W3C//DTD HTML 4.01 Transitional//EN">
<HTML>
  <HEAD>
    <TITLE>Registered Authors
    </TITLE>
  </HEAD>
    <BODY BGCOLOR="#CCCCBB">
    <H2>This page uses TPageProducer component</H2>
    <BR>
    <H3>List of Authors</H3>
    <BR>
    <#authors>
    <BR>
  </BODY>
</HTML>
```

Listing 7-14: Header property for the TDataSetTableProducer

```html
<HEAD>
    <TITLE>Authors and Titles</TITLE>;
    </TITLE>
  </HEAD>
    <BODY BGCOLOR="#CCCCBB">
    <H2>This page uses TDataSetTableProducer component</H2>
    <BR>
    <H3>Authors and Titles</H3>
    <BR>
```

Listing 7-15: employee.html

```html
<!DOCTYPE HTML PUBLIC "-//W3C//DTD HTML 4.01 Transitional//EN">
<HTML>
  <HEAD>
    <TITLE>Employees
    </TITLE>
  </HEAD>
    <BODY BGCOLOR="#CCCCBB">
    <H2>This page uses TDataSetPageProducer component</H2>
    <BR>
    <H3>Employee Details</H3>
```

Part 2

```
     <H4>
     <BR>First Name     : <#fname>
     <BR>Middle Initial : <#minit>
     <BR>Last Name      : <#lname>
     <BR>Job Description : <#job_desc>
     <BR>Hire Date      : <#hire_date>
     </H4>
     <FORM METHOD="POST" ACTION="/cgi-bin/Project1.exe/recsel">
     <INPUT TYPE="SUBMIT" NAME="First" VALUE="First">
     <INPUT TYPE="SUBMIT" NAME="Prior" VALUE="Prior">
     <INPUT TYPE="SUBMIT" NAME="Next" VALUE="Next">
     <INPUT TYPE="SUBMIT" NAME="Last" VALUE="Last">
     </FORM>
   </BODY>
</HTML>
```

Listing 7-16: Unit1.cpp

```cpp
//---------------------------------------------------------------------------
#include "Unit1.h"
//---------------------------------------------------------------------------
#pragma package(smart_init)
#pragma resource "*.dfm"
TWebModule1 *WebModule1;
//---------------------------------------------------------------------------
__fastcall TWebModule1::TWebModule1(TComponent* Owner)
                    : TWebModule(Owner)
{
}
//---------------------------------------------------------------------------

void __fastcall TWebModule1::WebModuleCreate(TObject *Sender)
{
    ADOConnection1->Connected = true;
}
//---------------------------------------------------------------------------

void __fastcall TWebModule1::WebModuleDestroy(TObject *Sender)
{
    ADOConnection1->Connected = false;
}
//---------------------------------------------------------------------------

void __fastcall TWebModule1::WebModule1WebActionItem1Action(
    TObject *Sender, TWebRequest *Request, TWebResponse *Response,
    bool &Handled)
{
    // default action - display selection buttons
    AnsiString fRespStr("<HTML>");
    fRespStr += "<TITLE>CGI Web Application - Using Producer Components</TITLE>";
    fRespStr += "<BODY BGCOLOR=\"#CCCCBB\">";
    fRespStr += "<H1>Publications Database - SQL Server</H1>";
    fRespStr += "<BR>";
    fRespStr += "<H2>Choose one of the Options</H2>";
    fRespStr += "<BR>";
    fRespStr += "<UL>";
    fRespStr += "LI><A HREF=\"/cgi-bin/Project1.exe/publishers\">Registered Publishers
            (Uses PageProducer)</A>";
    fRespStr += "<LI><A HREF=\"/cgi-bin/Project1.exe/authors\">Registered Authors (Uses
            PageProducer)</A>";
```

```
        fRespStr += "<LI><A HREF=\"/cgi-bin/Project1.exe/authortitles\">Authors and Titles
            (Uses DataSetTableProducer)</A>";
        fRespStr += "<A HREF=\"/cgi-bin/Project1.exe/employees\">Employee Details (Uses
            DataSetPageProducer)</A>";
        fRespStr += "</UL>";
        fRespStr += "</BODY>";
        fRespStr += "</HTML>";
        Response->Content = fRespStr;
}
//--------------------------------------------------------------------------

void __fastcall TWebModule1::WebModule1WebActionItem2Action(
    TObject *Sender, TWebRequest *Request, TWebResponse *Response,
    bool &Handled)
{
    PageProducer1->HTMLFile = "publishers.html";
    Response->Content = PageProducer1->Content();
}
//--------------------------------------------------------------------------
void __fastcall TWebModule1::WebModule1WebActionItem3Action(
    TObject *Sender, TWebRequest *Request, TWebResponse *Response,
    bool &Handled)
{
    PageProducer1->HTMLFile = "authors.html";
    Response->Content = PageProducer1->Content();
}
//--------------------------------------------------------------------------
void __fastcall TWebModule1::WebModule1WebActionItem4Action(
    TObject *Sender, TWebRequest *Request, TWebResponse *Response,
    bool &Handled)
{
    if (ADOConnection1->Connected) {
        ADOQuery2->Open();
        Response->Content = DataSetTableProducer1->Content();
    }
}
//--------------------------------------------------------------------------
void __fastcall TWebModule1::PageProducer1HTMLTag(TObject *Sender,
    TTag Tag, const AnsiString TagString, TStrings *TagParams,
    AnsiString &ReplaceText)
{
    AnsiString fTagText;
    if (CompareText(TagString, AnsiString("publishers")) == 0)
    {
        if (ADOConnection1->Connected) {
            ADOQuery1->Close();
            ADOQuery1->SQL->Add("select * from publishers");
            ADOQuery1->Open();
            if (ADOQuery1->RecordCount <= 0) {
                ReplaceText = fTagText;
                return;
            }
            fTagText = "<BR>";
            fTagText += "<TABLE BORDER=2>";
            fTagText += "<TR>";
            fTagText += "<TH>Item ID</TH>";
            fTagText += "<TH>Publisher Name</TH>";
            fTagText += "<TH>City</TH>";
            fTagText += "<TH>State</TH>";
```

Part 2

```
            fTagText += "<TH>Country</TH>";
            fTagText += "</TR>";

            for (int i=1; i <= ADOQuery1->RecordCount; i++) {
                fTagText += "<TR>";
                fTagText += "<TD>" + IntToStr(i) + "</TD>";
                fTagText += "<TD>" + ADOQuery1->FieldByName("pub_name")->AsString
                        + "</TD>";
                fTagText += "<TD>" + ADOQuery1->FieldByName("city")->AsString + "</TD>";
                fTagText += "<TD>" + ADOQuery1->FieldByName("state")->AsString + "</TD>";
                fTagText += "<TD>" + ADOQuery1->FieldByName("country")->AsString
                        + "</TD>";
                fTagText += "</TR>";
                ADOQuery1->Next();
            }
            fTagText += "</TABLE>";
            ReplaceText = fTagText;
        }
    }
    if (CompareText(TagString, AnsiString("authors")) == 0)
    {
        if (ADOConnection1->Connected) {
            ADOQuery1->Close();
            ADOQuery1->SQL->Add("select * from authors");
            ADOQuery1->Open();
            if (ADOQuery1->RecordCount <= 0) {
                ReplaceText = fTagText;
                return;
            }
            fTagText = "<BR>";
            fTagText += "<TABLE BORDER=2>";
            fTagText += "<TR>";
            fTagText += "<TH>Item ID</TH>";
            fTagText += "<TH>Author LastName</TH>";
            fTagText += "<TH>Author FirstName</TH>";
            fTagText += "<TH>Phone</TH>";
            fTagText += "<TH>Address</TH>";
            fTagText += "<TH>City</TH>";
            fTagText += "<TH>State</TH>";
            fTagText += "<TH>Zip Code</TH>";
            fTagText += "</TR>";

            for (int i=1; i <= ADOQuery1->RecordCount; i++) {
                fTagText += "<TR>";
                fTagText += "<TD>" + IntToStr(i) + "</TD>";
                fTagText += "<TD>" + ADOQuery1->FieldByName("au_lname")->AsString
                        + "</TD>";
                fTagText += "<TD>" + ADOQuery1->FieldByName("au_fname")->AsString
                        + "</TD>";
                fTagText += "<TD>" + ADOQuery1->FieldByName("phone")->AsString + "</TD>";
                fTagText += "<TD>" + ADOQuery1->FieldByName("address")->AsString
                        + "</TD>";
                fTagText += "<TD>" + ADOQuery1->FieldByName("city")->AsString + "</TD>";
                fTagText += "<TD>" + ADOQuery1->FieldByName("state")->AsString + "</TD>";
                fTagText += "<TD>" + ADOQuery1->FieldByName("zip")->AsString + "</TD>";
                fTagText += "</TR>";
                ADOQuery1->Next();
            }
            fTagText += "</TABLE>";
```

```
                ReplaceText = fTagText;
            }
        }
    }
}
//------------------------------------------------------------------------

void __fastcall TWebModule1::WebModule1WebActionItem5Action(
        TObject *Sender, TWebRequest *Request, TWebResponse *Response,
        bool &Handled)
{
    DataSetPageProducer1->HTMLFile = "employee.html";
    if (ADOConnection1->Connected) {
        ADOQuery3->Open();
        Response->Content = DataSetPageProducer1->Content();
    }
}
//------------------------------------------------------------------------

void __fastcall TWebModule1::WebModule1WebActionItem6Action(
        TObject *Sender, TWebRequest *Request, TWebResponse *Response,
        bool &Handled)
{
    if (Request->MethodType != mtPost)
        return;

    AnsiString oldCookie = Request->CookieFields->Values["BookMark"];

    if (!ADOQuery3->Active)
        ADOQuery3->Open();
    AnsiString paramValue =
        Request->ContentFields->Values[Request->ContentFields->Names[0]];

    if (paramValue == "First")
        ADOQuery3->First();
    else if (paramValue == "Next") {
        if (!oldCookie.IsEmpty()) {
            TLocateOptions fLO;
            ADOQuery3->Locate("LNAME", oldCookie, fLO);
            ADOQuery3->Next();
            if (ADOQuery3->Eof)
                ADOQuery3->First();
        }
        else
            ADOQuery3->First();
    }
    else if (paramValue == "Prior") {
        if (!oldCookie.IsEmpty()) {
            TLocateOptions fLO;
            ADOQuery3->Locate("LNAME", oldCookie, fLO);
            ADOQuery3->Prior();
            if (ADOQuery3->Bof)
                ADOQuery3->Last();
        }
        else
            ADOQuery3->Last();
    }
    else if (paramValue == "Last")
        ADOQuery3->Last();
    else
```

Part 2

```
            return;

    TCookie *newCookie = Response->Cookies->Add();
    newCookie->Name = "BookMark";
    newCookie->Value = ADOQuery3->FieldByName("LNAME")->AsString;
    newCookie->Secure = false;
    newCookie->Expires = Now() + 1;

    DataSetPageProducer1->HTMLFile = "employee.html";
    Response->Content = DataSetPageProducer1->Content();


}
//---------------------------------------------------------------------------
```

Listing 7-17: Unit1.h

```
//---------------------------------------------------------------------------
#ifndef Unit1H
#define Unit1H
//---------------------------------------------------------------------------
#include <SysUtils.hpp>
#include <Classes.hpp>
#include <HTTPApp.hpp>
#include <ADODB.hpp>
#include <DB.hpp>
#include <HTTPProd.hpp>
#include <DBBdeWeb.hpp>
#include <DBWeb.hpp>
#include <DSProd.hpp>
//---------------------------------------------------------------------------
class TWebModule1 : public TWebModule
{
__published:          // IDE-managed components
    TPageProducer *PageProducer1;
    TADOConnection *ADOConnection1;
    TADOQuery *ADOQuery1;
    TADOQuery *ADOQuery2;
    TDataSetTableProducer *DataSetTableProducer1;
    TDataSetPageProducer *DataSetPageProducer1;
    TADOQuery *ADOQuery3;
    void __fastcall WebModuleCreate(TObject *Sender);
    void __fastcall WebModuleDestroy(TObject *Sender);
    void __fastcall WebModule1WebActionItem1Action(TObject *Sender,
        TWebRequest *Request, TWebResponse *Response, bool &Handled);
    void __fastcall WebModule1WebActionItem2Action(TObject *Sender,
        TWebRequest *Request, TWebResponse *Response, bool &Handled);
    void __fastcall WebModule1WebActionItem3Action(TObject *Sender,
        TWebRequest *Request, TWebResponse *Response, bool &Handled);
    void __fastcall PageProducer1HTMLTag(TObject *Sender, TTag Tag,
        const AnsiString TagString, TStrings *TagParams,
        AnsiString &ReplaceText);
    void __fastcall WebModule1WebActionItem4Action(TObject *Sender,
        TWebRequest *Request, TWebResponse *Response, bool &Handled);
    void __fastcall WebModule1WebActionItem5Action(TObject *Sender,
        TWebRequest *Request, TWebResponse *Response, bool &Handled);
    void __fastcall WebModule1WebActionItem6Action(TObject *Sender,
        TWebRequest *Request, TWebResponse *Response, bool &Handled);
private:              // User declarations
```

```
public:                    // User declarations
                           __fastcall TWebModule1(TComponent* Owner);
};
//-------------------------------------------------------------------------
extern PACKAGE TWebModule1 *WebModule1;
//-------------------------------------------------------------------------
#endif
```

A nice feature is provided by C++Builder in the **TDataSetTableProducer** component. The Columns property is a **THTMLTableColumns** object and can be accessed at design time by clicking the ellipsis in the Object Inspector. The HTML columns property editor enables editing the individual column properties of the HTML table generated by the IDE automatically when the dataset is made active in the IDE. The same property editor also functions as a simple browser that displays the HTML page containing the HTML table, including the Header and Footer property HTML strings. The HTML columns property editor is displayed in Figure 7-11. Also please note that the MaxRows property contains a default value of 20 and should be set to –1 to display all the rows. A final point to remember is that we have to deploy the HTML files to the web server along with the program.

Figures 7-12 through 7-16 are the screenshots when this program is executed using a web server.

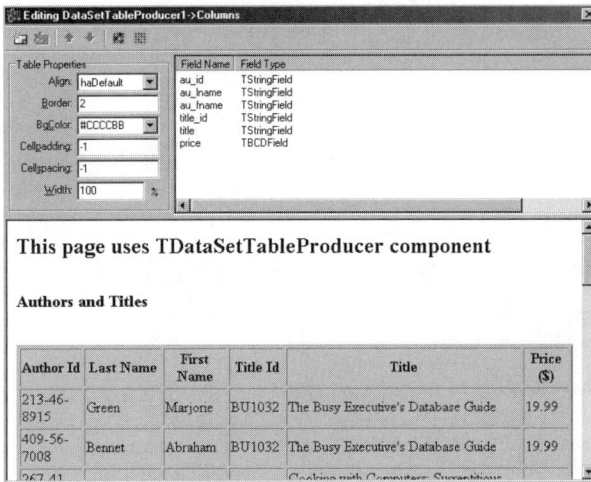

Figure 7-11: HTML columns property editor

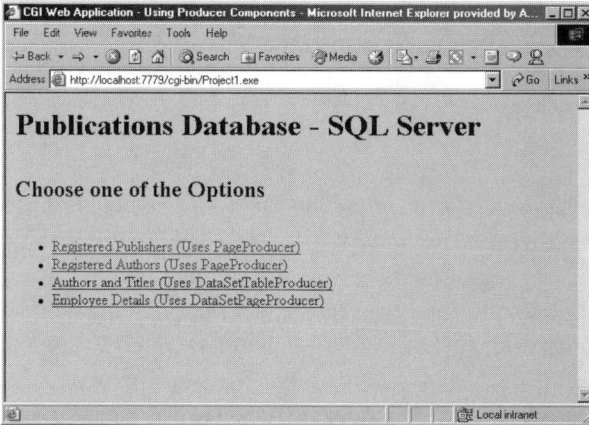

Figure 7-12: Application main page

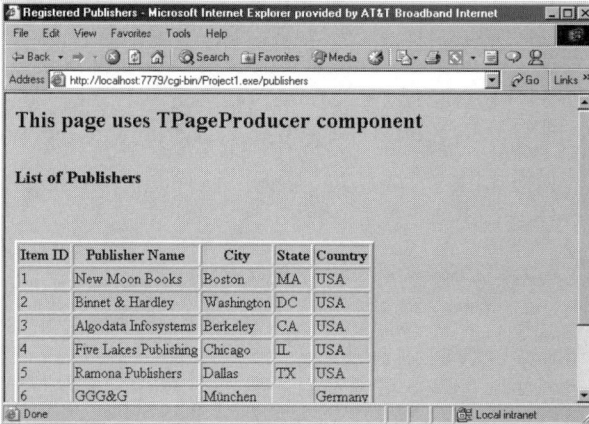

Figure 7-13: Publishers page

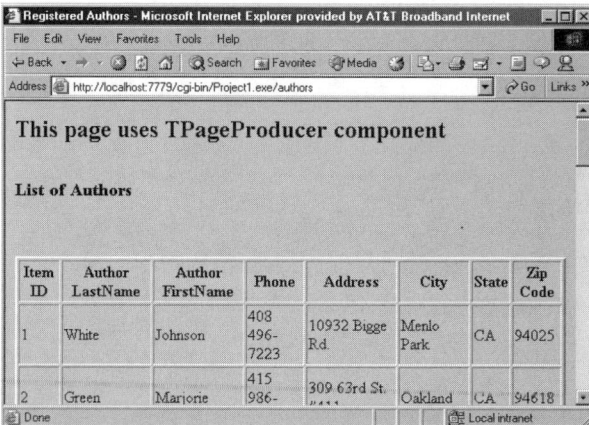

Figure 7-14: Authors page

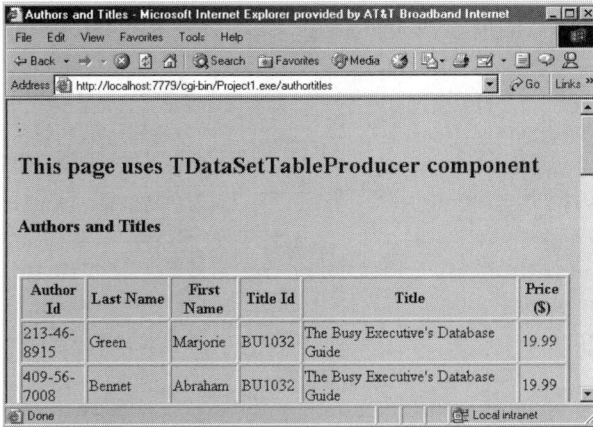

Figure 7-15: Author titles page

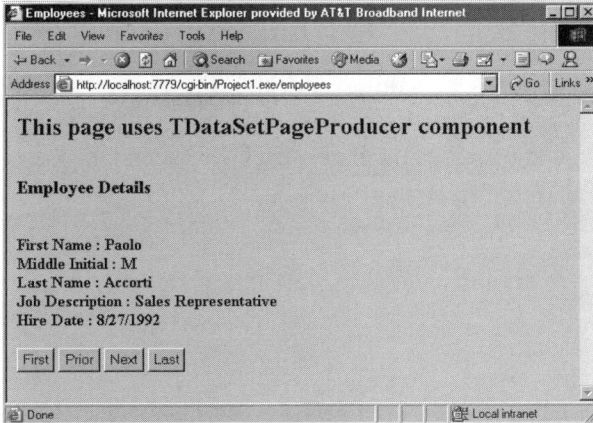

Figure 7-16: Single employee record page

Part 2

Summary

Let's now recapitulate what we have discussed in this chapter. We started the chapter with an overview of web programming and the challenges faced by the web developers. Then we examined the parts of a URL. We continued our discussion with an overview of the HTTP protocol, the HTTP methods, request and response headers, and the response codes to provide a high level of understanding.

Following the general discussion of the HTTP protocol, we began to understand how C++Builder 6's WebBroker architecture works. The different web application types, the web dispatcher component, the web action item objects, and their properties, methods, and events were all discussed in this section. We also discussed how the web dispatcher performs its key role in dispatching the request objects to the action items and how the response objects are passed back to the web server.

Then we looked at a sample application, in which I provided enough example code to understand the web development principles in the C++Builder 6 development environment. The sample applications include a standard CGI executable and an ISAPI/NSAPI DLL converted from a CGI application, followed by development of an Apache server DLL.

The last section of the chapter focused on the producer components, such as HTML page producers and HTML table producers. I presented a master program that demonstrates the use of the different types of producer components as well as implementing cookies.

Throughout the chapter, I provided numerous screenshots along with the example programs to enable a novice programmer to learn web development in a step-by-step manner. This may seem to be too much detail for a skilled programmer in this field, but I believe that as an author, I have to address the needs of readers with different skill levels.

While in this chapter I concentrated exclusively on the WebBroker architecture; in the following chapter, I will give exclusive attention to the new and more powerful WebSnap architecture from Borland.

Chapter 8

Building WebSnap Applications

Introduction

In the previous chapter we discussed how to build web applications using Borland's WebBroker architecture. The WebBroker technology is also available in C++Builder 5. Starting with Delphi 6 and C++Builder 6, Borland introduced a more robust web development architecture within the VCL framework. This new architecture is called WebSnap. The WebSnap framework has been designed upon the existing concepts of WebBroker architecture with additional features. In the previous chapter we learned that the primary task of dispatching the HTTP request and HTTP response between the application server and the action items was handled by the web dispatcher component, and the individual tasks (identified by the pathinfo strings) are handled by the individual web action items tied together by the web dispatcher. Also, one web application cannot handle more than one web module.

The concepts described in the WebBroker architecture are extended in the new WebSnap architecture, where we can handle more than one module within a web application. The individual tasks (identified by the pathinfo strings) are now handled by individual page modules and the contained page producer objects. The task of dispatching the HTTP requests and responses by invoking the corresponding page modules is handled by the page dispatcher. The HTML templates that work with the page producer components can now include server-side scripts written in scripting languages, such as JScript or VBScript. Moreover, the HTML templates are now included as part of the project files and created automatically whenever we create web page modules. We then have the new adapter components that provide an interface between the server-side application and the scripts embedded in the HTML files by enabling the scripts to access the data fields defined within the adapter components. We will discuss all these new concepts in the following sections of this chapter.

Since the WebSnap architecture introduces a number of new definitions, concepts, and components, I would like to spend a considerable amount of time in the initial sections to explain these concepts to help you get ready to start using the wizards and building sample applications.

WebSnap Components at a Glance

Overview

The WebSnap page in the Component Palette hosts the components that we are going to discuss in this chapter. Figure 8-1 shows a view of the Component Palette with these components.

Figure 8-1: WebSnap components

Let's now focus more attention on the components that make up the WebSnap architecture. The four fundamental component categories that form a basis to this architecture are web page modules, web data modules, adapter components, and content producers. In the process of understanding this framework, please do not try to compare the terminology one-to-one with the WebBroker framework; when promoting the WebBroker architecture to WebSnap, some terms were redefined with a broader sense than they were defined in the WebBroker framework. For example, the term "web module" in WebBroker means an object derived from the TWebModule class or a TDataModule object containing a TWebDispatcher component within itself, whereas in terms of a WebSnap application, a web module is either a web page module that is responsible for generating content for the web page or the web data module that contains one or more non-visual components to be shared by other web modules in the application. In the upcoming sections, we will discuss these topics in detail.

Web Page Modules

A *web application module* is typically a TWebAppPageModule object or a
TWebAppDataModule object. The TWebAppPageModule component
should be used if our application is to generate at least one web page; in
other words, our application is of page module type. Most of the web-based
applications fall in this category and hence must use this component. However, we may have to develop background server applications that just provide database-related (or similar) services to other server applications that
generate web pages. In all such cases, we can use the other type of web
application module, TWebAppDataModule. In other words, our application will be of data module type. It is important to note that TWebApp-
PageModule and TWebAppDataModule should not be confused with the
global Application variable. The global Application variable has the same
meaning that we defined in the WebBroker applications; for example, it is
an instance of TCGIApplication class, TISAPIApplication, or
TApacheApplication type (and so on), depending on the type of web application we are developing. When we invoke the WebSnap Application Wizard, in addition to choosing the type of web application (such as CGI or
Apache or ISAPI/NSAPI type), we also choose whether our application is
of page module type or data module type, based on the distinction we just
mentioned above.

In this chapter, we mainly concentrate on web applications that generate
web pages; therefore, we choose our application to be of page module type.
A page module type web application contains one or more page modules
(very similar to one or more action items of a WebBroker application). The
WebSnap Application Wizard automatically creates the first page module
when we choose the application to be of page module type. You may add
any number of additional page modules to the application later on. Excluding the first page module, each additional page module is an instance of
TWebPageModule, and the first page module is an instance of
TWebAppPageModule. The first page module contains an object of the
TWebAppComponents class, which is used to identify certain WebSnap
components as active and assigned to certain specific tasks at the application level; it initially contains the individual WebSnap components selected
in the wizard at the time of creating the application.

For example, a page dispatcher component identifies the default page to
be displayed when the URL does not specify a pathinfo string; if the
DefaultPage property of the page dispatcher is not set, the first page is identified as the default page. In addition to identifying the default page, the
page dispatcher also invokes the page corresponding to the pathinfo string

in the URL by matching the pathinfo string to the name of the page module. We need only one such page dispatcher component per application, but we are not restricted from dropping one page dispatcher in every page module. In such a case, the application has to be told which page dispatcher must be used at the application level. By default, the page dispatcher contained in the first page module (assuming that the default page dispatcher selected in the application wizard was not unchecked) is identified as the active page dispatcher. If we do not accept the default setting, we can change it by setting the PageDispatcher property of the WebAppComponents object to the corresponding page dispatcher. Similarly, we can also set the Application-Adapter and AdapterDispatcher properties to the appropriate objects. In fact, all of the components that were checked in the WebSnap Application Wizard may be set/reset as properties of the WebAppComponents object. Please note that it is only necessary to set these properties if we do not accept the default ones set by the wizard in order for the application to produce default behavior as desired. However, in the context of the application, we do not have to be concerned about those components that provide functionality at the page level.

Both the TWebAppPageModule and TWebPageModule components are designed to function as page modules. A WebSnap application that generates at least one web page can have one and only one instance of the TWebAppPageModule component (at the application level) and as many instances as desired of the TWebPageModule components (to serve as additional individual pages). When we add each page module to the application, the wizard automatically adds a producer component to the page module, which is responsible for generating the page content. The type of producer component that is automatically added to the page module is dependent upon the type that we choose in the wizard while creating the page, such as TPageProducer, TAdapterPageProducer, TDataSetPage-Producer, and so on. Each of the different types of producer components is designed to provide a specific type of page content. For example, the TAdapterPageProducer component automatically generates the server-side script as demanded by the adapter components, whereas the TPagePro-ducer component should be used to manually write custom server-side scripts and process any transparent custom tags in the HTML file. However, the adapter page producer component permits us to build a prototype web page using adapter components in a way that is similar to building a standard VCL form using the VCL components. We will discuss these topics in more detail in the later sections of the chapter.

When a page module is added to the project, an HTML file is also automatically created and assigned to the unit file corresponding to the page module. This is in contrast to WebBroker applications where we noticed that we have the option of creating the HTML file external to the application and using it internally within the program. The HTML file created by the wizard in a WebSnap application is automatically associated with the corresponding page producer component. Also, these HTML files may contain transparent tags, as demonstrated in the HTML template in the WebBroker application, and in addition, they may contain server-side scripts written in JScript(default)/VBScript; the transparent tags act as placeholders for the dynamic HTML content produced by the producer component, and the scripts provide more powerful control in accessing the data elements in the page module through the adapter components. It is important to note that when we use the page producers in a WebSnap application, we do not use the HTMLDoc or HTMLFile properties of these components because we have an HTML file that is automatically created and associated with the page producer by the wizard.

Web Data Modules

Web data modules are similar to the standard data modules and are containers of non-visual components, typically the database and dataset-related components. However, they are different from the standard data modules in the structure of the program unit and the interfaces that they support. All the other modules in the application can share the components placed on a web data module. The web data module also registers a factory to specify how the module should be managed by the WebSnap application, such as a flag that indicates whether to cache the module for later reuse or destroy the module after a request has been serviced. The unit file of the web data module defines a function with the same name as that of the web data module itself and returns a pointer to the appropriate instance of a class that is being referenced. This is a requirement to identify the particular instance of the module because more than one instance of the module may coexist in a multi-threaded web application.

Adapter Components

What are Adapters?

The next set of components of interest is the *adapters*, which provide an interface between the page producers and the scripts in the HTML files. For example, you can use an adapter to define data fields to be displayed on the HTML page. Adapters also support actions that execute commands, such as clicking a hyperlink or submitting an HTML form, which can initiate adapter actions. Then a script embedded within the HTML page can make

Part 2

calls to the adapter component in order to retrieve the data from the data fields or execute adapter actions associated with the commands. The component that automatically handles HTML form submissions and requests for dynamic images is an adapter dispatcher object, which is an instance of the TAdapterDispatcher class. A WebSnap application cannot execute adapter actions or obtain images from adapter fields unless it includes an adapter dispatcher. When you create a WebSnap application using the wizard provided through the IDE, an adapter dispatcher is automatically included (unless you uncheck the corresponding check box).

A typical WebSnap application includes an adapter dispatcher, one or more adapter components, and one or more page producer components, depending on the number of pages you are including in your application. Figure 8-2 describes the relationship between the adapters and the page producers.

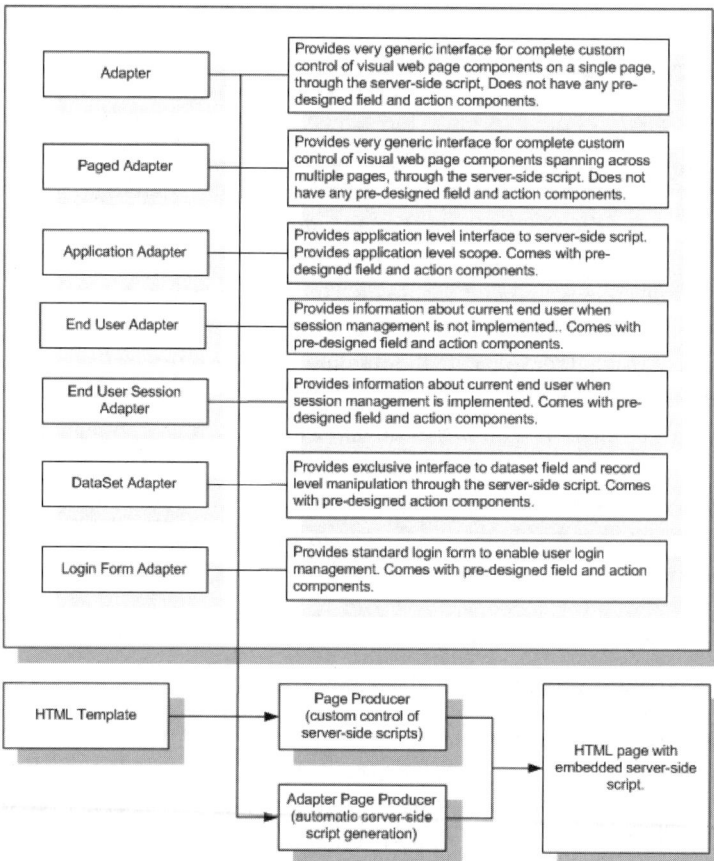

Figure 8-2: Adapters and page producers

If you use a generic page producer, you are going to write a custom server-side script as depicted in Figure 8-3. If you use the adapter page producer, the server-side script is automatically written by the page producer component itself, as shown in Figure 8-4.

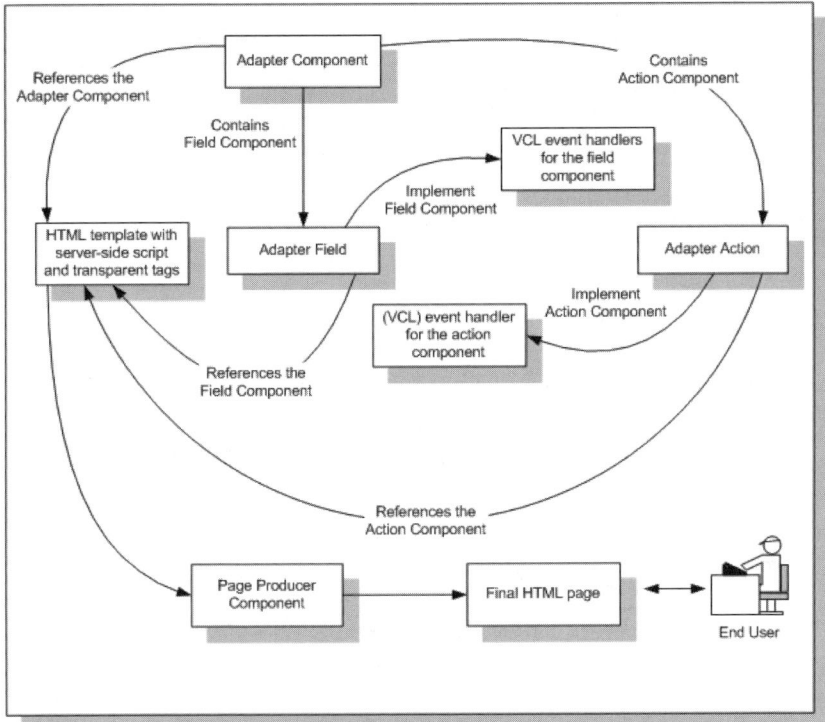

Figure 8-3: Scenario while using an adapter in a custom server-side script

Adapters are the new way of writing object-oriented code through the server-side scripts that the WebSnap architecture introduces. Without adapters, the same task should be performed through the object-oriented C++ code written within the C++Builder event handlers, as we did in the case of WebBroker applications. By using adapters, the web development process has been made a balanced mix of C++ expertise and scripting expertise; therefore, your development team can now include script-based developers working independently of the C++ developers without losing the features of integration of your web development project. The C++ developers can easily provide the adapter-side code while the script developers can access the adapters from their scripts and HTML code.

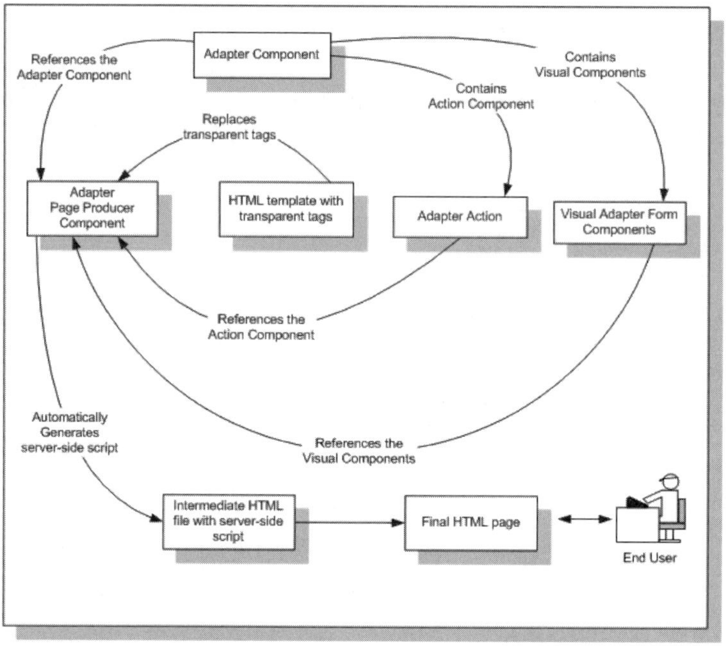

Figure 8-4: Scenario while using an adapter page producer to generate server-side script

Types of Adapters

There are primarily two types of adapter components: Generic adapters let you build customized applications and specific adapters provide prebuilt functionality that you can use directly in the application. Table 8-1 describes the different adapter types available in the WebSnap architecture. Any of these adapter types can be dropped into your WebSnap application from the WebSnap page in the Component Palette.

Table 8-1: WebSnap adapter types

Adapter Type	Description
TAdapter	This is a very general-purpose adapter. For each field component added to this component, you must implement a custom event handler to access the field values. Similarly, for each action component added to this adapter, you must implement a custom event handler to execute the command. When an HTML form with embedded server-side script containing adapter commands is submitted, the TAdapterDispatcher automatically calls the corresponding adapter actions to execute the commands. There is no built-in functionality available to fields and actions contained by this adapter. All the fields contained by a TAdapter object must be laid out on a single web page. If you wish to span the fields across multiple pages, you should use the TPagedAdapter component instead.

Adapter Type	Description
TApplicationAdapter	The TApplicationAdapter is a container for field and action components that are available through the Application script variable, which is different from the Application global variable within the C++ program. The global Application variable in a server-side script represents the application adapter object, whereas in the C++ program, it represents the type of web application. We can define custom fields and actions to this adapter to provide them with global scope so that they are accessible in every page (or script) within the application.
TDataSetAdapter	This adapter component is a scriptable interface to a TDataSet component and is designed to provide fields corresponding to dataset fields (or columns in the corresponding table or query), a data grid (in the form of an HTML table) to represent multiple records, actions to represent record navigation and processing commands, and so on. The dataset adapter comes with prebuilt functionality associated with the fields and actions. However, you can freely add any custom fields and actions, in which case you have to provide event handlers to access the fields and execute the actions.
TEndUserAdapter	The TEndUserAdapter component provides default information about the current end user, such as the user ID, user name, and whether the user logged in. We can add additional adapter fields and actions if our application needs them, in which case we have to write event handlers to access the fields and execute the actions. The LoginPage property of this component should be set to direct the end user to the page that contains the TLoginForm-Adapter (or any custom login adapter) object. This component is used in applications that do not support session management, such as CGI stand-alone executables. If we need to support sessions, we should use the TEndUserSessionAdapter component instead.
TEndUserSessionAdapter	The TEndUserSessionAdapter component is used to provide the end user information, just like the TEndUserAdapter component, in applications where we need to provide session management. To provide session management, we also have to include the TSessionsService component in our WebSnap application.
TLoginFormAdapter	The TLoginFormAdapter component provides default login fields to be included on a web form. The default fields include UserName, Password, and NextPage. The NextPage field provides a list of available pages to enable the user to select the next page after a successful login. The default login action is also provided by the adapter to execute the protected LogIn(const Variant &UserId) method of the end user adapter. However, you can override the default login function by implementing the OnExecute event handler of the Login Action component, in which case the previously mentioned LogIn() method will not be called.
TPagedAdapter	The TPagedAdapter object should be used in place of a TAdapter when you have a large amount of data (or a number of adapter fields) to span across multiple web pages.

Figure 8-5 depicts the default relationship between two adapters.

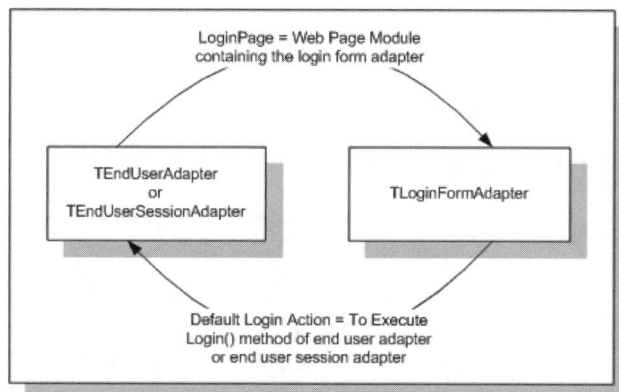

Figure 8-5:
EndUserAdapter and
LoginFormAdapter

An adapter can have one or more fields and actions. With the exception of the TAdapter and TPagedAdapter components, all the other adapter types come with predesigned fields and actions. The adapter fields may contain data item values to be displayed to or edited by the user or just hidden values that may be passed across pages, and the adapter actions represent commands, which may contain logic to execute specific tasks. The default actions provided with many adapter components provide the default functionality, which can be overridden by implementing the OnExecute event handler of the corresponding adapter action component.

The adapters, adapter fields, and adapter actions are accessible in the page module event handlers, just like any other VCL components; they are also accessible in the server-side scripts with the associated object names, as defined by the WebSnap architecture. Table 8-2 presented later in this chapter describes these objects and their definitions.

Content Producers

Content producers are the components that produce content for a web page. There are different types of content producers, such as page producers that are used in pages requiring more manual control of the content generation process and adapter page producers that may be used to visually design the web page and produce most of the content automatically. In the previous chapter, we discussed other producer components, such as dataset page producers, dataset table producers, and query table producers, which automate the process of presenting data from the database on a web page. Since page producers are meant to produce content for a web page, they should be contained in a page module. Ideally, one page producer is required for a single page module, as identified by the PageProducer property. This is the default page producer for the page module, but we can include more than one page producer and conditionally switch the default page producer as required in the application. However, we may have other producer components as determined by the page design logic. The content producer components may be contained within a web data module and shared by other modules, if we design the application to minimize the number of components.

The IPageDispatcher Interface

IPageDispatcher plays an important role in WebSnap applications and is intended to allow the WebSnap applications to interface with the page dispatcher. The TPageDispatcher component implements this interface. The interface allows a WebSnap application to dispatch request messages. The pathinfo portion of a URL identifies the page name, which establishes the connection between the page dispatcher and the actual web page module with that name. Let's examine the methods supported by this interface that are frequently used in our applications.

The DispatchPageName() method fills the response message with a page requested in the method, which means that the requested page will be displayed in the client browser. The method takes three parameters. The first parameter is an AnsiString object representing the name of the page, the second parameter is a pointer to the TWebResponse object representing the HTTP response in the current context, and the third parameter is an object of the TDispatchPageFlags set that contains attributes of the page to be retrieved. Only one attribute, dpPublished, is currently supported. If we set this attribute, the requested page is retrieved only if it is published. By default, this attribute is not set. The method returns a Boolean value indicating whether the requested page is successfully retrieved and filled in the response. We use this method in an example later in the chapter to display a page that is not published.

The PageNameOfRequest() method may be used to retrieve the name of the web page module to which the specific request object is addressed. The method takes one parameter, which is a pointer to the TWebRequest object, and returns the page name as an AnsiString object.

The RedirectToPageName() method fills out the response message so that it redirects the user to another page in the application. The method takes four parameters. The first parameter is the name of the web page module, and the second parameter is a reference to a TStrings object that contains application-defined name-value pairs as parameters. These name-value pairs supply the query fields of the redirected request message. The third parameter is a reference to the TWebResponse object, which represents the response message in the current context. The fourth parameter is an object of TDispatchPageFlags, which we discussed earlier. The method returns a Boolean value indicating whether the page redirection is successful or not.

Server-side Scripting

One of the very important features introduced in the WebSnap architecture is server-side scripting. The HTML files associated with the page modules may also contain server-side scripts written in the JScript or VBScript languages in addition to the static HTML text and transparent tags. These scripts are called server-side scripts because they are executed by your web server application before the final translated HTTP response is sent to the client. The advantages of using the server-side scripts are manyfold. The

scripting languages are object-oriented and provide the conditional, looping, and other language constructs similar to those supported by other
object-oriented languages, such as C++. The page producer executes the
script in response to a request for the producer content. Scripts enable you
to access database data through the adapter components. Also, since scripts
are embedded within an external HTML template file, you can update the
scripts without recompiling and redistributing the application if the script
was custom built by your developers; the limitation here is that you are
advised not to update the scripts generated by the adapter page producer
object or its descendants because the adapter page producer may update the
script during run time, as required by the application.

The script engine, which is responsible for generating the HTML code,
parses and evaluates any code embedded between the script delimiters <%
and %>. The code embedded between the script delimiters is called a *script
block*. The script engine does not touch any code outside the script block
delimiters. Also, the page producer translates any transparent tags after all
the script blocks are evaluated and translated into HTML commands. A
script block (which is a programming construct that forms a logical block
of code) may be intercepted by HTML commands and transparent tags.
Consider the following couple of code blocks (Listings 8-1 and 8-2). When
you create page modules using the WebSnap Application Wizard, the wizard automatically adds these code blocks into the HTML template file. If
your application requires, you may comment these lines in the script.

Listing 8-1: Sample login check code block with embedded HTML code

```
<h1><%= Application.Title %></h1>

<% if (EndUser.Logout != null) { %>
<%   if (EndUser.DisplayName != '') { %>
  <h1>Welcome <%=EndUser.DisplayName %></h1>
<%   } %>
<%   if (EndUser.Logout.Enabled) { %>
  <a href="<%=EndUser.Logout.AsHREF%>">Logout</a>
<%   } %>
<%   if (EndUser.LoginForm.Enabled) { %>
  <a href=<%=EndUser.LoginForm.AsHREF%>Login</a>
<%   } %>
<% } %>
```

Listing 8-2: Sample script block to display page links

```
<table cellspacing="0" cellpadding="0">
<td>
<% e = new Enumerator(Pages)
   s = ''
   c = 0
   for (; !e.atEnd(); e.moveNext())
   {
      if (e.item().Published)
```

```
    {
      if (c>0) s += ' | '
      if (Page.Name != e.item().Name)
        s += '<a href="' + e.item().HREF + '">' + e.item().Title + '</a>'
      else
        s += e.item().Title
      c++
    }
  }
  if (c>1) Response.Write(s)
%>
</td>
</table>
```

A careful examination of the code blocks reveals the following features:

- The first code block attempts to perform a basic login check for pages that require logging and contains HTML code interspersed within a logical script code unit. This is perfectly accepted by the script engine.

- The second block of code enumerates all the published page modules and generates a hyperlink so that all the published pages are displayed in HTML tabular form. Published pages automatically respond to HTTP requests when the page name matches the pathinfo string of the URL since they are managed by the page dispatcher. Pages that should not automatically respond to the HTTP requests and should only respond when requested by other WebSnap application objects should not be published.

- Global application objects, such as Application, Page, Pages, and their properties, may be accessed in the script, just like any other program variables. These objects are available in every module of the application. The global objects available to a WebSnap application are described in Table 8-2.

It is very important to recognize the link between script objects used in a script embedded in an HTML template and the WebSnap components implemented using the standard VCL framework. This link is a set of interfaces implemented as the adapter family of components. C++Builder 6 comes with predesigned adapter components used for some very common web development needs. As with any other VCL component, you can easily create custom adapter components (derived from those provided by the WebSnap framework) that make your web development easy and leave you with a set of reusable adapter components. The adapter components and their properties (and methods) are accessible in script blocks through the Object.Property (and Object.Method()) notation. We will focus our attention on this notation and the link between the script objects and adapter components more in subsequent sections when we discuss the adapter components in detail.

Part 2

Table 8-2: Predefined global objects in a WebSnap application

Global Object	Description
Application	The Application object provides information about the application. The most common property of this object is Title, which may be used to retrieve the application title and display it in every page. The ModulePath property provides access to the current path of the web application on the server host, which enables the web application to build path names for files or images. The ModuleFileName property provides the name of the web application. The TApplicationAdapter component, which is automatically included in your WebSnap application by default, provides properties for this object. You can add additional custom properties to this object by way of adding additional fields and actions.
EndUser	The EndUser object provides information about the end user that is currently logged in. The important properties of this object are DisplayName, which displays the name of the end user, LoggedIn (which is a Boolean value indicating whether the user is logged into the page or not), LoginFormAction (which directs the user to a form after successful login), and LogoutAction (which is used to log out a user). It is your responsibility to maintain the login user IDs and passwords and perform password validation when you actually implement such login forms. The TEndUserAdapter component encapsulates and provides properties for this object. This adapter is not automatically added to your application. You may need to add it manually. You may also have a different end user adapter for each page. The EndUserAdapter property of the WebAppComponents object determines the default end user adapter used for the application.
Modules	The Modules object is a collection object and provides access to all the modules (both the data modules and page modules) that have been instantiated to service the current HTTP request. A particular module is referenced by its name as a property of the Modules object. For example, if we have modules such as authors and publishers in our WebSnap application, the authors module is accessed as Modules.authors, and the publishers module is accessed as Modules.publishers, and so on. All the modules of an application may be enumerated using an Enumerator construct with this object.
Page	The Page object refers to the current page module. Every page module may have a title and can be accessed by the Title property. The HREF property may be used to get the URL of the page and is useful for building a hyperlink to the current page itself. The Boolean property Published indicates whether the page is published. The DefaultAction property identifies the associated adapter Action Object that provides default action for this page. In addition, there are other Boolean properties, such as Login-Required and CanView, that are associated with authentication of the page.
Pages	The Pages object is a collection object and provides access to all the page modules registered in the application. Individual page objects may be accessed by name as a property of the Pages object. All the pages of an application may be enumerated using an Enumerator construct with this object. This object is very similar to the Modules object except that Pages is a collection of page modules and Modules is a collection of page and data modules.
Producer	The Producer object provides access to the page producer of the current page. Use the Producer object to append the content with text containing transparent tags using the Write() method. The Content property may be used to read or set the content being sent to the client.
Request	The Request object provides access to the HTTP request. The properties directly accessible are Host, which exposes the TWebRequest's Host header value, Pathinfo, which retrieves the pathinfo portion of the URL, and ScriptName, which retrieves the web application name (from the URL).
Response	The Response object provides access to the HTTP Response object of the current request. Use the Response object to append to the content using the Write() method. If the content contains transparent tags, use the Producer object instead. The Content property may be used to read or set the content being sent to the client.
Session	The Session object is used to keep track of information about the end user for a short duration of time and provides access to the current session ID and any values stored in the session as name-value pairs.

Overview of the Scripting Language

As mentioned earlier, the WebSnap architecture supports JScript and VBScript. JScript is a slightly modified version of ECMAScript (or JavaScript), which is implemented by Microsoft Corp. It is fully compatible with ECMAScript, as long as we do not use Microsoft's additional features. For the sake of developers, I will take the opportunity to highlight some important features of JScript, which is the default scripting language in WebSnap applications. However, this section is not intended to discuss the JScript language in detail. For a complete discussion of the language, I would strongly recommend referring to JScript documentation or a similar source dedicated to the language. Also, I am not presenting scripting examples at this time, since I am going to discuss sample WebSnap applications in the latter sections of the chapter.

■ JScript is an object-based scripting language. Since it is a scripting language, we cannot write stand-alone applications in this language; an interpreter (or script engine) is always required to execute the scripts. For example, the script blocks written in WebSnap applications are interpreted and executed by Microsoft's ActiveScripting Engine.

■ JScript is an untyped (or loosely typed) language, which means you do not explicitly declare data types. The script engine automatically performs most of the data type conversions. The data types supported by JScript include String, Boolean, Number, Object, Array, and NULL.

■ JScript supports a variety of programming constructs, including control statements such as if...else, if...else if, and switch; looping statements such as while, do...while, for, and for...in; loop execution control statements such as break and continue; error handling statements such as try, catch, finally, and throw; and miscellaneous statements such as a function statement to declare functions, a with statement to establish a default object for a statement, and a this statement to refer to the current object

■ Variables are used to associate programming elements to values and are usually declared explicitly with the var statement (or declaration). If the var keyword is omitted while declaring a variable, the variable is implicitly declared for you, and it is assumed to have global scope. In comparison, a variable declared within a function (including function parameters) is considered to be local to the function. Also, variables declared anywhere in the script, except within a function, are considered to have global scope.

Part 2

■ JScript functions are similar to functions in any other programming language and contain a piece of executable code written to perform a specific task. The functions are declared once and invoked any number of times, as required.

■ Arrays in JScript are simple (ordered) collections of data elements, which are individually accessed by an index. The index of an array element indicates its relative position in the array. The array index is zero based; for example, an index of 0 means the element occupies first position, and an index of 1 means the element occupies second position, and so on.

■ JScript supports objects, which are defined as (unordered) collections of properties and methods. An object is constructed to represent a complex data item, whose data elements are called properties and functions are called methods. The property and method of an object are accessed using the notation Object.Property or Object.Method(). Thus, the properties of an object are accessed by their names, while the data elements of an array are accessed by their index. Please note that objects are one of the fundamental data types in JScript. JScript does not have a class construct, but the concepts of instantiating objects still exists, even with the object data type, which means we can instantiate objects of object data types. JScript provides a number of built-in objects for specific needs.

■ JScript objects are constructed using the new keyword. We can delete an object or its properties using the delete keyword. If we delete the property of an object, that property is not accessible for that instance of the object.

■ The Date object can be used to access the current system date and time and manipulate date and time values in the application and date- and time-related math operations. The getMonth() method retrieves the (zero-based) index of the month associated with the date object. Similarly, the getDay() method retrieves the index of the day of week (0 being Sunday and 6 being Saturday), the getDate() method retrieves the day of the month, and the getFullYear() method retrieves the full four-digit year. The Date object provides a very rich set of methods for which you may refer to the JScript documentation.

■ The Math object provides a rich set of mathematical constants and methods, which permit us to compute the absolute value, exponent, and logarithm of a number, round a number, and use trigonometric computations and random numbers.

■ The String object methods provide a variety of features, such as searching (and replacing) a substring, converting the string to all lowercase or all uppercase, determining the position of a character or substring within a string, and so on.

■ We create an enumeration object by the new Enumerator(collection) notation. Once an enumeration object is created, we can use the for loop to loop through all the items of the enumeration.

VCL Script Objects

In the previous section, we noticed that the scripting language is equipped with several script objects to perform a number of generic tasks. In addition, your WebSnap programs written in C++Builder 6 (or Delphi 6) can access a number of VCL objects as script objects. Since these objects are VCL and WebSnap based, you should remember that the server-side scripts developed using these objects would not function in other environments. Only WebSnap applications developed in conjunction with these scripts can work with these script files.

Another important feature regarding these script objects is that although you access the same VCL objects in the C++Builder application and the script file, not all the properties and methods exposed in the C++ program are available to the scripts. WebSnap exposes only selective properties and methods of these objects to the scripts.

Therefore, I would like to take the opportunity to present you with the different objects and their properties and methods to some extent. For a complete understanding of these features, I recommend that you refer to the C++Builder 6 documentation and the VCL source files. In my discussion, for every script object I would associate the corresponding VCL component in order to enable you to establish a link between the VCL objects and script objects. There are instances where a script object property or method may not have the corresponding VCL object property or method, which means that the property is only accessible from the script and not from the C++ program. In such cases, I would mention None. Following the discussion on the objects, we will continue with the sample code blocks as well as complete example projects.

The Application object refers to the TApplicationAdapter component. We include only one component of this type in a WebSnap application. Table 8-3 describes the properties and methods available in the scripts. As we discussed earlier, these properties and methods are accessible in the C++ programs belonging to your WebSnap application.

Part 2

Table 8-3: Application object

Script Object Property or Method	Corresponding VCL Object Property or Method	Description
Title	ApplicationTitle	Provides the title of the application as an AnsiString
ModuleFileName	None	Returns the fully qualified module name in the URL. Usually, this represents the WebSnap application name with path representing the directory location on the web server. Only the module name is identical to that in the URL; the path is the absolute path and not the virtual path.
ModuleFile	None	Returns the substring containing only the path portion of the previous string, excluding the module filename
QualifyFileName	QualifyFileName	Converts a relative filename or a directory reference to include the fully qualified path name. In VCL, the Application Adapter component does not support this method. Rather, a global function with this name is provided to do the same task.

The Adapter object refers to one of the descendants of the TCustomAdapter component. Every adapter component added to the web module is accessible by its name in its corresponding script. An adapter component belonging to another web module is referenced by the notation <Module Name>.<Adapter Name>, where <Module Name> represents the name of the web module and <Adapter Name> represents the name of the VCL adapter component. For example, if your application has two pages, the Home page containing the HomeAdapter and the Second page containing the SecondAdapter, then the HomeAdapter is accessed in the Second page script as Home.HomeAdapter.

Table 8-4 describes the properties and methods of the Adapter object.

Table 8-4: Adapter object

Script Object Property or Method	Corresponding VCL Object Property or Method	Description
Actions	Actions	This is an enumerator object and is useful for enumerating through a loop for each of its items, which are individual adapter Action Objects created in the C++ program. Within the loop, properties of each of the Action Objects are accessible. If we need to access only one specific Action Object, we can access it by name as a member of the adapter.
Fields	Data	This is an enumerator object and is useful for enumerating through a loop for each of its items, which are individual adapter field objects created in the C++ program. Within the loop, properties of each of the field objects are accessible. If we need to access only one specific field object, we can access it by name as a member of the adapter.
Errors	Errors	This is an enumerator object and is useful for enumerating through a loop to process each of the errors captured by the adapter.

Script Object Property or Method	Corresponding VCL Object Property or Method	Description
Records	None	If the adapter represents an object of the TDataSetAdapter component, the Records property is provided as an enumerator object and can be used to enumerate each of the records within a loop. In the C++ program, the equivalent way is to navigate the corresponding dataset object within the loop.
ClassName	ClassName()	Identifies the class name of the adapter component. The ClassName() method of the TObject class gives the same value in the C++ program.
Mode	Mode	Some adapters support Mode. For example, if the adapter is an object of the TDataSetAdapter component, the mode represents string values such as Edit, Browse, Insert, and Query. We can get or set these values in the script. The corresponding values of the VCL dataset are amEdit, amBrowse, amInsert, and amQuery.
CanView	ViewAccess	This property checks whether the user has a right to view this adapter field. It is a Boolean property in the script object and evaluated by the script based on the value set in the VCL object. In the VCL object, this is an AnsiString indicating the access rights.
CanModify	ModifyAccess	This property checks whether the user has rights to modify this adapter field. It is a Boolean property in the script object and evaluated by the script based on the value set in the VCL object. In the VCL object, this is an AnsiString indicating the access rights.

Part 2

The AdapterField object refers to one of the descendants of the TAdapter-UpdateField component. Adapters may contain one or more fields assigned to them as child components. An adapter field is used to display data to the user in display mode or edit mode or store hidden data fields to be passed between the script and the C++ program or between web modules. All the HTML input types, such as simple text, wide text areas, images, select lists, radio buttons, and so on, are represented as adapter fields in a WebSnap application. In simple terms, *adapter fields* form the bridge for data transport between the HTML file (containing server-side scripts) and the C++ program, which serves as the web server application. The adapter architecture separates the presentation layer (HTML and the script) from the application business logic (implemented in the C++ Builder or Delphi program).

An adapter field can be accessed in a script by its name qualified by the adapter name as set in the C++ program. Table 8-5 describes the properties and methods of the AdapterField object. Please note that not all the properties are relevant for every adapter type field. Some field types may provide some additional properties, whereas some other field types provide a different set of properties. I am putting my best effort into providing you with a clear understanding of a superset of these properties.

Table 8-5: AdapterField object

Script Object Property or Method	Corresponding VCL Object Property or Method	Description
CanModify	ModifyAccess	This property checks whether the user has a right to modify this adapter field. It is a Boolean property in the script object and evaluated by the script based on the value set in the VCL object. In the VCL object, this is an AnsiString indicating the access rights.
CanView	ViewAccess	This property checks whether the user has a right to view this adapter field. It is a Boolean property in the script object and is evaluated by the script, based on the value set in the VCL object. In the VCL object, this is a string indicating the access rights.
DisplayLabel	DisplayLabel	Provides a text label for display for this adapter field
DisplayStyle	None	The DisplayStyle property should be used to determine the read-only style of an editable field, such as simple text, an image, or list item, as indicated by the property values Text, Image, and List, respectively.
DisplayText	None	The DisplayText property is a string value to be used while displaying a read-only value for the field. This value may be used to dynamically create any display field. This property is typically supported by a TDataSetAdapterField component, based on the data from the dataset.
DisplayWidth	DisplayWidth	Indicates the display width for an input type field. A value of −1 indicates unlimited width.
EditText	None	The EditText property is a string value to be used while displaying an editable value for the field. However, the field must also be an editable field. This property is typically supported by a TDataSet-AdapterField component based on the data from the dataset.
InputName	None	The InputName property should be used to set the name attribute of an input field in the HTML code.
InputStyle	None	This property indicates the type of the input field, such as text box, text area, radio button, or check box. The built-in adapter objects in the C++ program set this value for use in the script. For example, the TDataSetAdapterField object sets the suggested input style of its fields, based on the data from the dataset. Also, if we add a custom adapter field of specific type, the input style is automatically set to that type. For example, if we add a custom field of type TAdapter-MemoField, the input style is set to text area.
MaxLength	None	Indicates the maximum length of the field allowed for data entry. This is governed by the incoming data source requirements.
Required	Required	This is a Boolean property and indicates whether the user must enter a value in the field.
Value	Value	Returns the value of the field entered or edited by the end user
Values	Values	Returns a list of field values and is only available in the script if the corresponding VCL adapter field component supports multiple values, such as in the case of multi-valued fields to provide a list of values in a select list (or a combo box style).
ValuesList	ValuesList	Represents a ValuesList object. In VCL, this is typically a TStrings-ValuesList component. This is a very useful object for passing a list of values or name-value pairs across pages, and works as a good communication media between the C++ program and the script. I will discuss the usage of this component in an example.

Script Object Property or Method	Corresponding VCL Object Property or Method	Description
ViewMode	None	Suggests how to display the adapter field value. The possible values are Input and Display. It is typically supported by a TDataSetAdapter-Field component based on the data from the dataset.
Visible	None	This property indicates whether the field should be visible to the user. It is typically supported by a TDataSetAdapterField component based on the data from the dataset.

The AdapterAction object refers to one of the descendants of the TCustom-AdapterAction object. An adapter action represents one or more commands that can be executed by the user or automatically by the script. The Action Object is implemented in the C++ program, and a means to execute the action (or the command associated with the action) is provided through the script. In simple terms, adapter actions form the bridge to transform user interaction events received through the web page into object actions (or reactions) in the C++ program, which serves as the web server application. For example, we can provide a hyperlink or a button to the user with a reference to the C++ Action Object; when the user clicks the button or hyperlink, the command associated with the Action Object in the C++ program is executed. If the action has a built-in command, as in the case of the default Action Objects belonging to a TDataSetAdapter component or TPagedAdapter component, we don't have to provide any implementation logic. However, we can override the default behavior of the command by implementing the OnExecute event handler of the Action Object, in which case the event handler takes precedence. We can also implement a custom Action Object by creating child objects of a TAdapterAction component in the C++ program, in which case we have to implement the OnExecute event handler of the Action Object. I will discuss an example to demonstrate how to implement event handlers for a custom Action Object.

The Action Object can be accessed in a script by its name qualified by the adapter name, as set in the C++ program. Table 8-6 describes the properties and methods of the AdapterAction object.

Table 8-6: AdapterAction object

Script Object Property or Method	Corresponding VCL Object Property or Method	Description
Array	None	This property represents an array of commands for an adapter action that supports multiple commands. It is an enumeration object and used to enumerate within a loop. Each item of the array represents a single command. Using this property, we can build a set of hyperlinks or buttons in the page.

Part 2

Script Object Property or Method	Corresponding VCL Object Property or Method	Description
AsFieldValue	None	This property returns the name of the Action Object in a string form. The main use of this value is to be set in the hidden field __act. When the form is submitted, the action name and associated parameters are sent through the HTTP Request object that is extracted by the adapter dispatcher in the WebSnap application, which locates the associated Action Object and executes its command.
AsHREF	None	This property returns the name of the Action Object as a string to be used in building a hyperlink by putting this value in an anchor tag. Therefore, the action is only activated when the user clicks the hyperlink.
CanExecute	ExecuteAccess	This property identifies the rights defined to execute the Action Object. It is a Boolean property in the script object and evaluated by the script based on the value set in the VCL object. In the VCL object, this is an AnsiString indicating the execute rights.
DisplayLabel	DisplayLabel	Provides a text label to be displayed for this action
DisplayStyle	None	The display style identifies the suggested style that this Action Object should use, either as an anchor or as a button. The adapter objects, having built-in adapter actions in the C++ program, set this value for use in the script.
Enabled	None	This Boolean property indicates whether the action is enabled or not so that the user interface element, such as a button, can be enabled in the script.
LinkToPage(sPage, fPage)	None	This method specifies that after successful execution of the action, the sPage should be processed. If there were errors during the execution of the action, the fPage should be processed.

The Page Object

The Page object represents a web page module. A page can be referenced by its (web page module) name as created in the application or as an item in the Pages enumeration object. There are also the similar objects Modules and Module. Modules is an enumeration object; each of its items represents a registered Module object, which can be either a page module or data module.

The two Boolean properties CanView and LoginRequired indicate whether the user has rights to view the page and if the page requires a login before displaying the contents, respectively. Published is another Boolean property, which indicates whether the page is published. Not all the pages in a web application may be published, which means that they are not all available for the user directly by name. We may have some pages that would be displayed depending on how the user navigates or where the user is looking in the page. It may be such that we never have to display some pages if the user does not show interest in some part of our application.

The DefaultAction property identifies the default Action Object associated with the page, and the HREF property provides us with a URL that can be used to generate a hyperlink to the page, which is useful for providing dynamic links to unpublished pages.

The Module Object

The Module object represents a page module as well as a data module. One very useful property is the Objects enumerator, which can be used to enumerate all the scriptable objects of the module. For example, if you have to know all the scriptable objects of a web page module, use the Objects property of the Module object, rather than working with the Page object.

Other Objects

The Request object represents an HTTP request and provides access to properties such as Host, PathInfo, and ScriptName. The Response object provides access to the HTTP response, and the Producer object provides access to the content producer that is producing the current page. Both of these objects provide (set/get) access to the response content through the Content property and the Write() method to append to the content. If we use transparent tags, we should work through the Producer object; otherwise, it should be through the Response object. If you go through the sample code in Listing 8-2, which is automatically generated by the IDE when you create (or add) a new web page in a WebSnap application, you notice that a list of hyperlinks is generated for all the published pages in the application and appended to the response content by executing the Response.Write(s) method, where the parameter to the method contains the generated hyperlinks.

The EndUser object provides information about the current end user and represents the fields and actions of the end user adapter object if one is used in the application. The Session object represents a user session. Session objects enable web applications to behave like stateful applications. The user sessions are created and managed by the C++Builder WebSnap application when you use the TSessionsService component. You may implement the OnStartSession and OnEndSession event handlers of this component if you need to do any initialization and cleanup tasks related to a user session, respectively. However, it is not required that you implement these event handlers to implement simple session management functionality. The Session script object provides access to the session created in the application. Through this object, we can access the current values stored in the user session.

Part 2

Building WebSnap Applications

WebSnap Application Wizards

Though I have not discussed the WebSnap architecture in depth, I am confident that the concepts discussed so far will be helpful in understanding how to develop WebSnap applications, which is the subject of the rest of the chapter.

Refresh your memory with Figure 8-1, presented at the beginning of the chapter, which shows you the set of components provided in the C++Builder 6 and Delphi 6 products.

> ■ **Note:**   The WebSnap components may only be available in specific editions of C++Builder 6 and Delphi 6. I would advise you to check with Borland Corp. for more details.

At this time, we will discuss the WebSnap Application Wizard, which is a useful tool in building our WebSnap applications. Figure 8-6 shows the WebSnap page in the New Items dialog, which is displayed when we attempt to create a new project from the IDE.

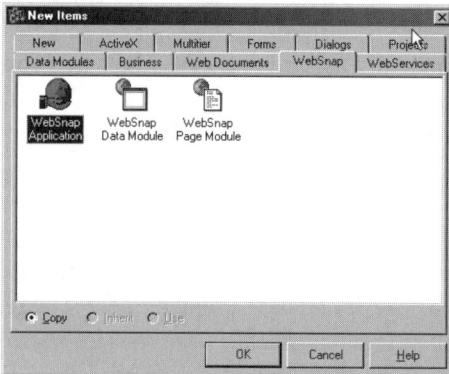

Figure 8-6: WebSnap page in the New Items dialog

There are three icons to choose from on this page: WebSnap Application, WebSnap Data Module, and WebSnap Page Module. The names clearly indicate what is going to be created when you choose each of these options. WebSnap Application should be selected every time you create a new WebSnap application, which also adds the first page if your application is of page module type. WebSnap Page Module should be selected every time you want to add an additional page to a web page module-type application. WebSnap Data Module should be selected every time you wish to add a data module container to your application.

When you select WebSnap Application and click OK, the New WebSnap Application dialog is displayed, which looks similar to Figure 8-7.

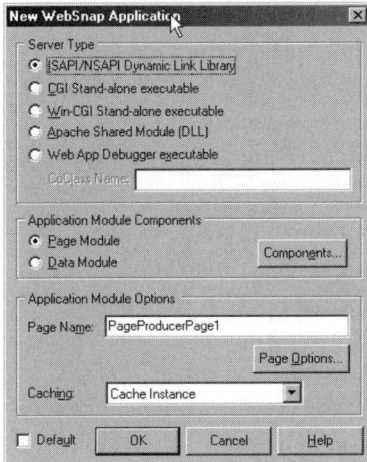

Figure 8-7: New WebSnap Application dialog

In this dialog, you will set/choose the following information.

- The Server Type group box enables you to select the type of web application you are building, such as ISAPI/NSAPI Dynamic Link Library or CGI Stand-alone Executable, and so on. These options are similar to what you have encountered while building the WebBroker applications. The project file and its default contents created by the wizard depend on the selection you make at this point. Please note that you still have the freedom to convert one web application type to another, as you have done in the WebBroker applications. However, there may be limitations imposed by WebSnap architecture while doing such a conversion. For example, WebSnap supports sessions and session objects, which is not a concept supported in the CGI stand-alone executable, since each HTTP request runs in a separate thread in the case of CGI stand-alone executables. Therefore, a DLL-type application built using sessions cannot be converted to a CGI stand-alone executable type.

- The Application Module Components group box enables you to select whether the application is of page module type or data module type. You also find a button labeled Components. When you click this button, the Web App Components dialog will be displayed, as shown in Figure 8-8, where you can select one or more components that can be placed on the web module. The wizard selects the default components required for the web application module, such as the Application

Adapter, the Page Dispatcher, and the Adapter Dispatcher. If you do not select a component in this dialog, you can add them later by dropping the corresponding component from the Component Palette. Please note that the default components selected by the wizard are required for the application to run properly. Therefore, I do not recommend deselecting the default components. You may, however, select additional components if you so desire. You can click OK to close this dialog after completing your selection to return to the New WebSnap Application dialog.

■ The Application Module Options group box enables you to select page-level options for the first page. In this group box, you can set the Page Name, which will become the name of the page and also the pathinfo portion of the URL; the Caching option may be selected to Cache Instance to enable module caching or Destroy Instance to disable module caching. If you desire to keep the module in memory between user sessions, enable caching; if you desire to destroy the module from memory after ending the active session, disable caching. The default option is to enable caching. There is also a button labeled Page Options. When you click this button, the Application Module Page Options dialog is displayed, which looks similar to Figure 8-9. In the Application Module Components group box, if you select a Data Module type, the Page Name box and the Page Options button are both disabled, as they are not appropriate for a data module.

The Application Module Page Options dialog enables you to select page-level options for the new page. This dialog has three group boxes, each for a different type of entry or selection. The Producer group box lets you choose the type of producer component, such as TPageProducer, TAdapterPageProducer, TDataSetPageProducer, TInetXPageProducer, and TXSLPageProducer. We already know the functionality behind the first three types. The TInetXPageProducer component should be used to produce an HTML document containing live database information from an application server, such as a DataSnap-based server. The TXSLPageProducer should be used to generate web page content by transforming data from an XML document using an XSL style template. You can also select the Script Engine to be JScript or VBScript. The adapter page producer currently generates only JScript-based script. Two other important options you can select in this dialog are the Published and Login Required check boxes. The Published property marks the page as published, which means the page is available to the user by its name and the user can directly request the page by typing the page name as the pathinfo in the URL. The Login Required option requires you to implement a login page by using either the TLoginFormAdapter or a similar component.

If you are adding an additional page to an existing WebSnap application, the New WebSnap Page Module dialog displayed will be slightly different, as shown in Figure 8-10. The only difference is that it adds the options to choose caching style and module creation style, indicating whether you want the module to be created in the startup or only on demand when the first reference to the module is made.

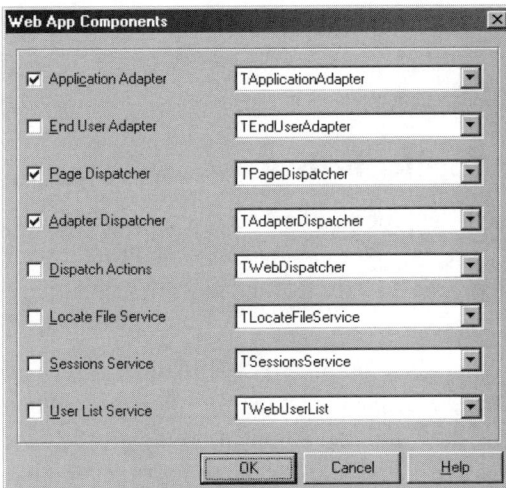

Figure 8-8: Web App Components dialog

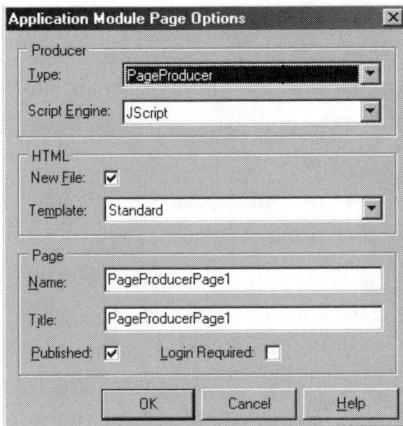

Figure 8-9: Application Module Page Options dialog

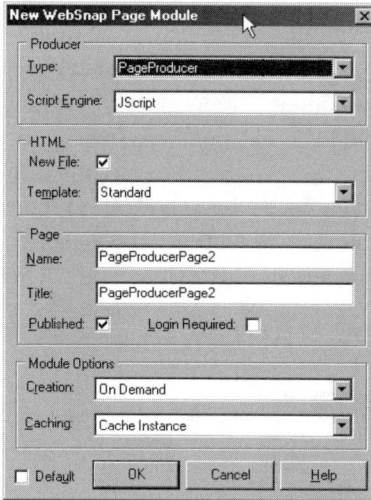

Figure 8-10: New WebSnap Page Module dialog

A Simple WebSnap Application

I will now walk you through the process of creating a simple WebSnap application containing two pages. In the first page, you will enter your first name and last name and then click a button to display the second page with a welcome message.

1. Create a new WebSnap application of ISAPI/NSAPI DLL type and page module type. Change the page name to **SimpleHome**. When you create the project using the WebSnap Application Wizard, as discussed in the previous section, the wizard creates the project file, unit header, cpp, form, and HTML files for the first page. Save all the project files in a directory of your choice. I named the project SimpleWeb-SnapAppl, and the unit SimpleHomePage. Set the ApplicationTitle property of the application adapter object to a string of your choice. This property will be used in the script to display the title in the web browser title bar.

2. Add a second web page module to the application. Set the page name as **WelcomePage**, and save the unit file as **WelcomePageModule**.

3. To the first page module, add one each of the **TAdapter** and **TSessionsService** components. We can continue with the default names of these objects: Adapter1 and SessionsService1. In the Object TreeView, the adapter object automatically displays the items Actions and Fields. These are group objects, and you can add one or more items to these group objects. Right-click on the **Adapter1→Actions** object, and select the **New Component** option. Select **AdapterAction** from

the list. For a simple adapter component, this is the only action type you can add. Later on when you use other special adapter types, you will see more options in this list. Right-click on the **Adapter1→Fields** object, and select the **New Component** option. You will see a bunch of adapter field types; these are all basic field types that are available for any adapter in general. From the list, select the **AdapterField** item. Repeat this last step again to add a second adapter field.

4. In the Object Inspector, change the names of the adapter action and the two adapter fields to **SubmitAction**, **FirstName**, and **LastName**, respectively. You may change the DisplayLabel property of these objects as you wish, and we will use this property to display a label on the web page when we are referencing them in the script. By now, you might be guessing that we use the two field objects to capture user input and the Action Object to call the second page. You are very much correct. Let's see how we do that.

5. Since we are using the basic adapter component without any built-in functionality, we have to provide functionality for the OnExecute event handler of the Action Object. Create the event handler from the Object Inspector as you would do for any other VCL object. Refer to Listing 8-3 to see the code for this event handler. Every request in a web application is stateless, which means that the web server does not know anything about prior requests from the same user and will process the current request exclusively based on the information available within the current request. Therefore, it is normal practice to use session objects to save data between requests from the same user. The TSessionsService object that we dropped onto the first page performs this task automatically.

In the OnExecute event handler of the Action Object, I am capturing the user-entered field values by accessing the ActionValue property of the action field, which is the implementation of the IActionFieldValue interface. The value (or values) associated with the field are obtained from the variant Values property of the interface. The SafeRedirect() global method invokes the page that is identified in the URL parameter to this method; in this example, we are invoking the welcome page. The WebContext() global method returns the context object associated with the current web context.

I also implemented the OnSessionStart event handler for the sessions service object, where I am initializing the session variables every time the session is started.

Similar to the SubmitAction button on the first page, I implemented an OKAction button with a simple adapter object on the welcome page so that when the user clicks the OK button, the first page is invoked.

Listings 8-3 through 8-6 provide the page module implementation for both the pages and corresponding scripts. To conserve space, I am not providing the header files here; you may refer to them in the project files on the companion CD.

6. Compile the application; deploy it to the Microsoft IIS server.

Listing 8-3: SimpleHomePage.cpp—first page

```cpp
//---------------------------------------------------------------------------
#include <vcl.h>
#pragma hdrstop

#include "SimpleHomePage.h"
#include <WebInit.h>
#include <WebReq.hpp>
#include <WebCntxt.hpp>
#include <WebFact.hpp>
#include "WelcomePageModule.h"

USEADDITIONALFILES("*.html");
const char* cFname = "F_NAME";
const char* cLname = "L_NAME";


//---------------------------------------------------------------------------
#pragma package(smart_init)
#pragma resource "*.dfm"

TSimpleHome *SimpleHome()
{
    return (TSimpleHome*)WebContext()->FindModuleClass(__classid (TSimpleHome));
}


static TWebPageAccess PageAccess;
static TWebAppPageInit WebInit(__classid(TSimpleHome), caCache, PageAccess
                     < wpPublished /* < wpLoginRequired */, ".html", "", "", "", "");
void __fastcall TSimpleHome::SubmitNameExecute(TObject *Sender,
      TStrings *Params)
{
    if (FirstName->ActionValue)
        Session->Values[cFname] = FirstName->ActionValue->Values[0];
    if (LastName->ActionValue)
        Session->Values[cLname] = LastName->ActionValue->Values[0];

    SafeRedirect(WebContext()->Response,
        WebContext()->Request->InternalScriptName + '/' + WelcomePage()->Name);
}
//---------------------------------------------------------------------------
void __fastcall TSimpleHome::SessionsService1StartSession(TObject *ASender,
      TAbstractWebSession *ASession)
{
//    WelcomePage()->FieldValues->Strings->Clear();
```

```
        Session->Values[cFname]= "";
        Session->Values[cLname]= "";
}
//-------------------------------------------------------------------------
```

Listing 8-4: SimpleHomePage.html—HTML for the first page

```
<html>
<head>
<title>
<%= Application.Title %>
</title>
</head>
<body bgcolor="#CCCCBB">
<h1><%= Application.Title %></h1>

<h2><%= Page.Title %></h2>

<form name="SimpleHomeAdapterForm" method="post">
<input type="hidden" name=__act>

<h3><%=Adapter1.FirstName.DisplayLabel%></h3>
<input type="text" name="<%=Adapter1.FirstName.InputName%>"
    size="45" maxlength=100>
<BR>
<h3><%=Adapter1.LastName.DisplayLabel%></h3>
<input type="text" name="<%=Adapter1.LastName.InputName%>"
    size="45" maxlength=100>
<BR>

<% if (Adapter1.SubmitName.Visible) { %>
  <input type="submit"
    value=<%=Adapter1.SubmitName.DisplayLabel%>
    name=<%=Adapter1.SubmitName.DisplayName%>
    class=submitButton
    onclick="SimpleHomeAdapterForm.__act.value=
    '<%=Adapter1.SubmitName.AsFieldValue%>'">
<% } %>

</body>
</html>
```

Listing 8-5: WelcomePageModule.cpp—second page

```
//-------------------------------------------------------------------------
#include <vcl.h>
#pragma hdrstop

#include "WelcomePageModule.h"
#include <WebInit.h>
#include <WebReq.hpp>
#include <WebCntxt.hpp>
#include <WebFact.hpp>
#include "SimpleHomePage.h"

USEADDITIONALFILES("*.html");
//-------------------------------------------------------------------------
#pragma package(smart_init)
#pragma resource "*.dfm"
```

Part 2

```
TWelcomePage *WelcomePage()
{
  return (TWelcomePage*)WebContext()->FindModuleClass(__classid (TWelcomePage));
}


static TWebPageAccess PageAccess;
static TWebPageInit WebInit(__classid(TWelcomePage), crOnDemand, caCache,
                  PageAccess < wpPublished /* < wpLoginRequired */, ".html", "", "",
                  "", "");
void __fastcall TWelcomePage::OkActionExecute(TObject *Sender,
    TStrings *Params)
{
    if (FieldValues->Strings->Count > 0)
        FieldValues->Strings->Clear();
    SafeRedirect(WebContext()->Response,
    WebContext()->Request->InternalScriptName + '/' + ·
    SimpleHome()->Name);
}
//-------------------------------------------------------------------------
```

Listing 8-6: WelcomePageModule.html—HTML for the second page

```
<html>
<head>
<title>
<%= Application.Title %>
</title>
</head>
<body bgcolor="#CCCCBB">
<h1><%= Application.Title %></h1>

<h2><%= Page.Title %></h2>

<form name="WelcomeAdapterForm" method="post">
<input type="hidden" name=__act>

<!--
 Build the Welcome string by concatenating
 the first name and last name
-->
<h3>
Welcome
<%=" "%>
<%=Session.Values("F_NAME")%>
<%=" "%>
<%=Session.Values("L_NAME")%>
</h3>
<br>

<% if (Adapter1.OkAction.Visible) { %>
  <input type="submit"
    value=<%=Adapter1.OkAction.DisplayLabel%>
    name=<%=Adapter1.OkAction.DisplayName%>
    class=submitButton
    onclick="WelcomeAdapterForm.__act.value='<%=Adapter1.OkAction.AsFieldValue%>'">
<% } %>

</body>
</html>
```

When you examine the source code for this application, you will notice an important feature. In the traditional VCL-based Windows application, an object of the form is created, and every time you access the form, a reference to the same form is returned, unless you take the responsibility of explicitly creating and destroying the form. In a WebSnap application, multiple instances of a web module may coexist in multiple threads, and we try to obtain an instance of the module within the current web context. A web context stores information about the components that are available in a WebSnap application and about the current request that is being processed. Applications do not create instances of the web context. Rather, they access the current web context object by calling the global WebContext() function. The web context object provides access to objects such as current request, current response, current end user, current session, and so on. When the FindModuleClass() method of the web context is executed, the application checks if an instance of the specified module is already created; if one is already created in the current context, it returns a reference to that object; if not, it creates a new instance and returns its reference. Therefore, in a WebSnap application the wizard automatically creates a function with the same name every time we add a web module, which returns an instance of the module in the current web context.

Figures 8-11 and 8-12 display how the application looks when you access the application in a web browser.

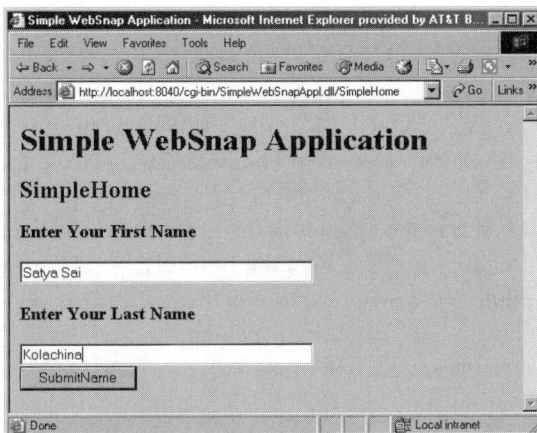

Figure 8-11: Simple WebSnap Application—SimpleHome page

Part 2

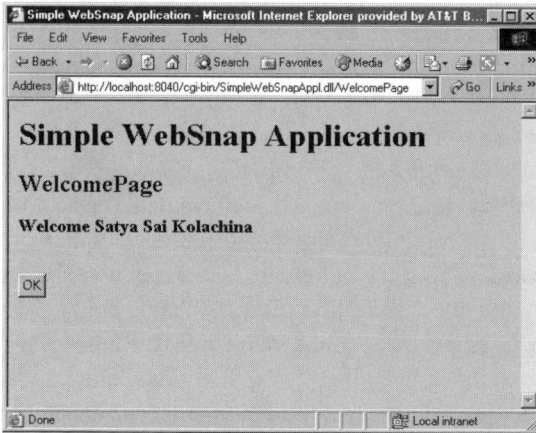

Figure 8-12: Simple WebSnap Application—Welcome page

An Improved Way to Save the State Information

In the previous example, we saved the user-entered field values in session variables and retrieved them in the welcome page script. We can achieve the same result using an improved approach. The WebSnap architecture has a component of type TStringsValuesList, which can store a list of string values. This is a very general-purpose component; it can be used to store a list of name-value pairs and can also be used to pass a set of values from one page to another page. When you set the ValuesList property of an adapter field component to an object of TStringsValuesList, an adapter page producer can automatically generate HTML/JScript code to access the list values associated with the strings list object.

In the improved approach, I created a TStringsValuesList object with a set of name-value pairs of all the values that I am interested in saving in the session. Then I created a variant object of the entire content of the strings values list object and saved it in the session in the first web module. Then, in the welcome page module, I implemented the BeforeDispatchPage event handler for the web module. This event handler is fired before the page producer is called to generate the web page. In this event handler, I am retrieving the session variable saved in the first page as a string value and rebuilding the strings values list object, then finally setting the Handled parameter to false in order to make sure that the page producer generates the page normally. For the purpose of rebuilding the strings values list object, I dropped a TStringsValuesList object onto the second web module from the Component Palette. Using this approach, we can bundle any number of values in a single session variable instead of creating several individual session variables, thereby providing compact and maintainable code, especially when you have several adapter fields to be passed between pages. I am not presenting the code here in order to conserve space, but the code can be accessed from the companion CD.

We can also directly access the strings values list object (or any component in general) of the second page from the first page and set its values or properties. But in this case, since we are not using a session variable to save the state information, the changes we make to the string list are permanent for the application as a whole and not limited to a specific user's session. If your application needs such a global change of variables, you can use this approach.

A WebSnap Application Connecting to a DataSource

We will now build a WebSnap application that can connect to a database, which acts as the persistent data store. Again, I am using the Northwind demo database that is shipped with Microsoft SQL Server and connecting to it through the ADO components. Please note that this is a simple example, and I am demonstrating several aspects that we discussed in this chapter. Follow the guidelines described here to create the application:

1. Create a WebSnap application of the ISAPI/NSAPI DLL type and the web page module type. Save the application files in a directory of your choice. I named the project WebSnapDbAppl.bpr and the first page HomePage.cpp. The page is identified in the application as "home."

2. Add a web data module, and name it **datacontainer**. This module contains all the database components and can be referenced from all the page modules. If you are building an enterprise class application, it is a good idea to categorize your database components into multiple web data modules. Save this module as **DbModule.cpp**.

3. In the header file of the web data module, add a **TClientDataSet** component as a public variable belonging to this module. In this demo, I am using a client dataset to store the user IDs and passwords, since the Northwind database does not have such a table. The fact is that I do not want to change the default database installed with the SQL Server. But, if you want, you may create a user table in the Northwind database (or any database you connect to) and use it in the application to store user IDs and passwords. In real-world applications, it is necessary to store the user IDs and passwords in a more secure way than just storing them as plain text in a database table.

4. Add the second page as **LoginPage.cpp** and name the page **login**. I used the TAdapterPageProducer to generate the login page. You have to select this option in the wizard while adding the page. Drop a **TLoginFormAdapter** from the Component Palette. The TLoginForm-Adapter component comes with the prebuilt fields UserName, Password, and NextPage. In the Object TreeView, open the branch for the login form adapter component you just added by clicking the plus sign to the left of the component name. You will see the two items Actions and Fields. Each of these is a group item. The Actions group item holds one or more adapter Action Objects and the Fields group item holds one or more adapter field objects.

5. Right-click on the **Fields** item, and you will see a pop-up menu similar to Figure 8-13. Click the **New Component** selection in the pop-up menu and a list of items is displayed, as shown in Figure 8-14, which are simply the types of adapter field objects that you can add to the Fields group item in addition to the default fields supported by this adapter. Click the **Add Fields** selection in the pop-up menu and you will see the prebuilt field objects in the list. If you have not yet added any of the prebuilt fields, you will see all of them in the list; but if you added one or more of them to the group item, you will see the remaining prebuilt field objects in the list. Click the **Add All Fields** selection from the pop-up menu to add all the prebuilt fields to the group item. In our demo, we only add the UserName and Password fields from the prebuilt list. Also in our example, we are not using the prebuilt login adapter action. Rather, just add a simple AdapterAction object by clicking the New Component selection in the pop-up menu for the adapter action selection. I am doing this because I am going to implement my own login action event handler.

Figure 8-13: Adding adapter fields to the Fields group item

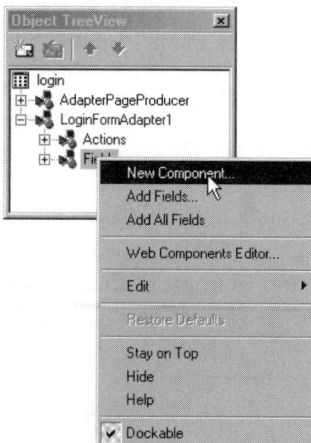

Figure 8-14: Adapter field types

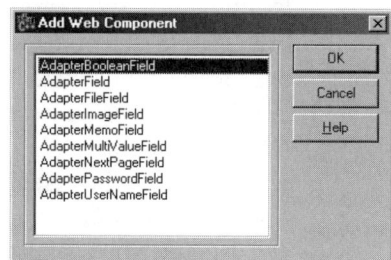

6. Now add an Adapter Action Object to the Actions group item. Follow the procedure similar to the earlier description, and add the **Login** Action Object.

   The adapter page producer component contains the display elements, such as one or more individual fields or a data grid to display data from a dataset, which produces the HTML objects to display the data retrieved from the adapter fields and also contains the command elements, such as adapter action buttons, which produce the HTML buttons to provide user clicks and bind them with the adapter actions. The individual fields will be translated to HTML input fields, radio buttons, select fields, and so on. A data grid will be translated into an HTML table.

   When we bind an adapter action button to an Adapter Action Object, the Action Object's OnExecute event handler is executed when the user clicks the corresponding button. If we do not implement this event handler, the prebuilt action of the Action Object is executed if the adapter provides prebuilt functionality. If we use the TAdapter object instead of a prebuilt adapter object, we have to implement the OnExecute event handler.

7. Now add some display elements to the adapter page producer. To add the display elements, add an Adapter form first. Then add a Field group to hold one or more fields for data entry. Finally, add a Command group item, which can hold one or more command items, such as adapter buttons. To the command group, add an adapter Action button, and to the field group, add two adapter display fields, one to accept the user ID and the other to accept the password. The display field can be used both for display and edit.

8. Now we have to bind the login form adapter and the adapter page producer. The binding is done at the field group and command group level. This is because you can have multiple field groups (and Command groups), and each can bind to a different adapter. This provides you with the flexibility to accept data from multiple sources or stream the data to multiple destinations. In our example, set the Adapter property of the field group to the login form adapter. The command group binding is against the specific field group instead of the adapter directly. Therefore, set the Display Component property of the command group item to the field group component.

9. Now implement the OnExecute event handler for the Login Action Object that we added to the Login form adapter. Please refer to the source code presented in Listing 8-7 for a complete understanding of

Part 2

the login page module. Since the page script is automatically generated by the adapter, I am not presenting it here, but it can be referenced in the project source files provided on the companion CD.

10. Set the DefaultPage property of the PageDispatcher component to the Login page. This will force the page dispatcher to display the Login page as the first page of the application. Drop a **TSessionsService** component onto the home page module so that session management is automatically enabled.

11. After login, the application will display a page with two buttons. Clicking the first button should display records from the customer table, and clicking the second should display records from the supplier table. Therefore, drop a **TADOConnection** component and two **TADOTable** components onto the data container module. Set the connection string of the connection component to connect to the SQL Server database, and rename the table components **CustomerTable** and **SupplierTable**, respectively. Set the Connection and TableName properties of the table components appropriately, and test the settings by activating the connection and opening the tables. I have an SQL Server 2000 installation, and the application is tested with it. If you do not have an SQL Server installation or if you do not have the Northwind demo database on your SQL Server installation, you can convert this application to work with any other database of your choice, but you have to make changes in a number of places to represent the database and tables appropriately.

12. Continue to add other page modules. Add a new web page module containing a simple PageProducer component to the application and name the page **LoginSuccess**. Save the module as **LoginSuccess-Module.cpp**. As the name suggests, this page should be displayed only after a user successfully logs in. Therefore, the Published check box must be unchecked when you add this page to the application. After we make sure that the login ID of the user is valid and the user entered the correct password, we display the page programmatically. If you do not uncheck the Published check box, the page is displayed when the user types in the page name as the pathinfo string in the URL. On the other hand, if the user tries to access a page that is not published, an exception is raised with a message similar to "Web Page not found: <page name>."

On the LoginSuccess page, I dropped a TAdapter component and added two adapter actions to this adapter, one to display customers and the other to display suppliers. I implemented the OnExecute event handlers for both of these adapter actions, in which I am invoking the method DispatchPageName() of the IPageDispatcher interface. Since we did not publish the web page, we are obtaining the instance of the page in the current context and dispatching it to the user through the response message in the current context. This is the same way that the LoginSuccess page is displayed in the OnExecute event handler of the login adapter action. Listing 8-8 presents the program source code for this module.

Since we are not using the adapter page producer in this module, the page script is not automatically generated; rather, we have to write custom script. Refer to Listing 8-9, which presents the page script for this module.

13. Next, add the two pages **customers** and **suppliers**. Each of them has an adapter page producer and a dataset adapter. The dataset adapter connects to the dataset representing the corresponding database table, and the adapter page producer contains a grid to display records from the table. In addition, I implemented two buttons and the corresponding actions: the Done button to display the previous page and the Logoff button to display the login page. I am not presenting the code listings for these modules here, but you can access them from the companion CD.

I also added an ErrorPage module, which is displayed when an exception is raised anywhere in the application and caught by the OnException event handler of the TWebAppComponents object located on the home page. The code listings for these modules also can be accessed from the companion CD.

Listing 8-7: LoginPage.cpp—login page

```
//---------------------------------------------------------------------------
#include <vcl.h>
#pragma hdrstop

#include "LoginPage.h"
#include <WebInit.h>
#include <WebReq.hpp>
#include <WebCntxt.hpp>
#include <WebFact.hpp>
#include "DbModule.h"
#include "LoginSuccessModule.h"

USEADDITIONALFILES("*.html");
//---------------------------------------------------------------------------
#pragma package(smart_init)
#pragma resource "*.dfm"

Tlogin *login()
{
  return (Tlogin*)WebContext()->FindModuleClass(__classid (Tlogin));
```

```
    }

    static TWebPageAccess PageAccess;
    static TWebPageInit WebInit(__classid(Tlogin), crOnDemand, caCache, PageAccess
        < wpPublished /* < wpLoginRequired */, ".html", "", "", "", "");
    void __fastcall Tlogin::LoginExecute(TObject *Sender, TStrings *Params)
    {
        // Empty the previous (possibly empty) user id session variable
        Session->Values[cUserId] = "";

        // Define and initialize local string variables to capture the
        // user-entered login information
        AnsiString userId("");
        AnsiString passwd("");

        // If the user entered values in the login page, capture the values
        // into local strings
        if (AdaptUserId->ActionValue)
            userId = AdaptUserId->ActionValue->Values[0];
        if (AdaptPassword->ActionValue)
            passwd = AdaptPassword->ActionValue->Values[0];

        // Obtain a pointer to the user id dataset.
        TClientDataSet* fUserIdTable = datacontainer()->UserIdTable;
        // If the user id exists and the valid password is entered, set the
        // user id session variable. Otherwise, throw appropriate exceptions.
        TLocateOptions fLo;
        if (fUserIdTable->Locate(cUserId, userId, fLo)) {
            if (fUserIdTable->FieldByName(cPassword)->AsString != passwd)
                throw Exception("Invalid password for the User " + userId);
            Session->Values[cUserId] = userId;

            TDispatchPageFlags AFlags;
            DispatchPageName(LoginSuccess()->Name, Response, AFlags);
        }
        else {
            AnsiString ErrorMsg("User ");
            ErrorMsg += userId;
            ErrorMsg += " not defined in the system !";
            throw Exception(ErrorMsg);
        }
    }
    //---------------------------------------------------------------------------
```

Listing 8-8: LoginSuccessPage.cpp—LoginSuccess page

```
    //---------------------------------------------------------------------------
    #include <vcl.h>
    #pragma hdrstop

    #include "LoginSuccessModule.h"
    #include <WebInit.h>
    #include <WebReq.hpp>
    #include <WebCntxt.hpp>
    #include <WebFact.hpp>
    #include "CustomersPage.h"
    #include "SuppliersPage.h"

    USEADDITIONALFILES("*.html");
    //---------------------------------------------------------------------------
```

```
#pragma package(smart_init)
#pragma resource "*.dfm"

TLoginSuccess *LoginSuccess()
{
  return (TLoginSuccess*)WebContext()->FindModuleClass(__classid (TLoginSuccess));
}

static TWebPageAccess PageAccess;
static TWebPageInit WebInit(__classid(TLoginSuccess), crOnDemand, caCache, PageAccess /*
    < wpPublished < wpLoginRequired */, ".html", "", "", "", "");
void __fastcall TLoginSuccess::DispCustActionExecute(TObject *Sender,
    TStrings *Params)
{
    // This action executes when the user tries to view
    // customer details page, clicking customer display button.
    TDispatchPageFlags AFlags;
    DispatchPageName(customers()->Name, Response, AFlags);
}
//---------------------------------------------------------------------------

void __fastcall TLoginSuccess::DispSupplActionExecute(TObject *Sender,
    TStrings *Params)
{
    // This action executes when the user tries to view
    // vendor details page, clicking vendor display button.
    TDispatchPageFlags AFlags;
    DispatchPageName(suppliers()->Name, Response, AFlags);
}
//---------------------------------------------------------------------------
```

Listing 8-9: LoginSuccessPage.html

```
<html>
<head>
<title>
<%= Application.Title %>
</title>
</head>
<body bgcolor="#CCCCBB">

<h2><%= Application.Title %></h2>
<h2>Northwind Database - Microsoft SQL Server</h2>
<br>
<h2>Choose one of the Options</h2>
<br>
<form name="LoginSuccessForm" method="post">
<input type="hidden" name=__act>

<% if (UserOptionsAdapter.DispCustAction.Visible) { %>
  <input type="submit"
    value=<%=UserOptionsAdapter.DispCustAction.DisplayLabel%>
    name=<%=UserOptionsAdapter.DispCustAction.DisplayName%>
    class=submitButton
    onclick="LoginSuccessForm.__act.value='<%=UserOptionsAdapter.DispCustAction.
                AsFieldValue%>'">
<% } %>
<br>
<br>
```

```
<% if (UserOptionsAdapter.DispVendAction.Visible) { %>
  <input type="submit"
    value=<%=UserOptionsAdapter.DispVendAction.DisplayLabel%>
    name=<%=UserOptionsAdapter.DispVendAction.DisplayName%>
    class=submitButton
    onclick="LoginSuccessForm.__act.value='<%=UserOptionsAdapter.DispVendAction.
           AsFieldValue%>'">
<% } %>


</body>
</html>
```

Summary

In this chapter I intended to spend sufficient time and resources to get the readers familiarized with the new WebSnap architecture, particularly since it is just emerging in the Borland developer community. It is not only new, but it is also fairly large compared to some other features added by Borland in this release of C++Builder. I admit that my attempt to present it as a single chapter is only an experiment. As readers, you are the best judges as to whether I am successful in my endeavor.

We started our discussion by identifying the differences between the WebBroker architecture and the new WebSnap architecture and continued discussing the components that make up this framework. In the process we learned several new concepts, including a broader definition of the web module, the new adapter components, content producers, the IPage-Dispatcher interface, and server-side scripting. The discussion continued with a very high-level overview of the scripting language and how the script interfaces with the C++ program through the adapters; we also examined the various script objects introduced in this framework.

We finally worked through a couple of example programs, where we paid additional attention to manually implementing adapter event handlers and conditionally dispatching the pages from within the C++ program. As I already mentioned, the examples do not attempt to demonstrate all the features, but I hope they will provide a good beginning to develop your enterprise web applications.

Chapter 9

Developing DataSnap Applications

Introduction

Today's industry is in absolute need of robust distributed application development. C++Builder 6 is a platform that provides and supports robust and varied distributed application development architecture and enables enterprises to build distributed server objects as well as client applications. In this chapter, we will discuss the DataSnap architecture, and in the following chapter we will continue our discussion on distributed application development using CORBA objects and simple TCP/IP applications.

DataSnap Applications

DataSnap architecture is not new to the Borland developer community. If you are familiar with Multi-tier Distribution Application Services (MIDAS), DataSnap is its enhanced version. For those of you not familiar with MIDAS, DataSnap is the proprietary middleware from Borland used to enable faster development of typical three-tier client-server applications. Borland implemented the DataSnap architecture using Microsoft's Component Object Model (COM) and Active Template Library (ATL) -based automation server framework. Using DataSnap architecture, you can develop multi-tier client-server systems very easily. In Chapter 6 we discussed most of the individual components that comprise the DataSnap architecture. In this chapter, we will discuss the IAppServer interface in more detail. We will also examine the relationship between this interface and the client dataset and provider components. Finally, we will go through a typical DataSnap application example.

Connecting to the Remote Application Server

In a typical DataSnap application, the application that implements a remote data module serves as the remote application server. The remote data module exposes its features through the IAppServer interface. The client application connects to the remote application server through a connection component. The DataSnap architecture supports different types of connections, such as a DCOM connection (using Microsoft Distributed COM architecture), a simple socket connection (using simple TCP/IP sockets), a web connection (using the HTTP protocol), and a SOAP connection to connect to a web service (using the SOAP protocol). In this chapter we will learn about the first three types of connections; we will defer discussion on the SOAP connection to Chapter 11, which is exclusively dedicated to web services.

The TDispatchConnection forms the base class of the three connection types: DCOM connection, socket connection, and web connection components. However, none of the three connection components directly descend from this base class. The TCOMConnection, which forms the base for the DCOM connection, and the TStreamedConnection, which forms the base for the other two, are direct descendants of the TDispatchConnection component. The TDispatchConnection component implements all the generic infrastructure required for logging on to an application server, obtaining an IAppServer interface, calling the application server's interface, and managing a remote connection. On the client side, it also introduces the ability to work with one or more client datasets. The immediate descendants of TDispatchConnection formulate the basis for the type of data transport mechanism. For example, the TCOMConnection descendant adds the ability to work with COM objects in addition to the generic capabilities inherited from the TDispatchConnection. Similarly, the TStreamedConnection descendant forms the basis for components that can handle their own marshalling. However, it still cannot connect to the application server by itself; such an ability is introduced by its descendant components. Going further, the simple definition of *marshalling* is the process of creating, managing, and transporting data packets between the client and server modules. Custom marshalling means implementing logic on both the client-side and server-side modules so that they understand precisely what their counterpart on the other side is communicating and respond in a similar way.

The TSocketConnection component, derived from the TStreamedConnection, implements the simplest type of connection using the TCP/IP protocol as the client-side component; it overrides the CreateTransport()

method of its parent class and obtains the ITransport interface. The matching server-side module is the ScktSrvr.exe program, which is shipped with the Enterprise Edition of C++Builder 6. Therefore, if you try to connect your client application to the server using the TSocketConnection component, make sure that the ScktSrvr.exe program is running along with your server module on the host where the server is deployed. In a similar way, the TWebConnection component is also derived from TStreamedConnection and establishes a connection using the HTTP protocol; it also overrides the CreateTransport() method of its parent class and obtains the ITransport interface. When you try to connect your client application using the TWebConnection component, make sure that the HTTPSrvr.DLL is placed in the directory identified by the URL mentioned in the client connection component's URL property. The modules ScktSrvr.exe and HTTPSrvr.dll perform the server-side marshalling as required by the respective protocols. They work in conjunction with your application server and provide server-side marshalling. Thus, we now understand that if we wish to provide our own custom connection mechanism, we need to derive a connection component from TStreamedConnection (or a higher level component if desired), override the CreateTransport() method to obtain the ITransport interface, and finally provide a server-side module that provides server-side marshalling.

For the most part, we do not need to do this exercise since the DataSnap architecture already provides built-in support to a variety of protocols. The scenario with TDCOMConnection is very similar. In this case, the client and the server communicate using the Microsoft DCOM architecture. The TConnectionBroker component centralizes the connections to multiple client datasets that all use the same connection. If you wish to use the connection broker component, set the RemoteServer property of the client dataset to the connection broker, instead of the actual connection object, and set the Connection property of the connection broker to the actual connection object. Also, you will implement the event handlers for the connection broker object instead of the actual connection object. By doing so, you are free to change the actual connection object (that establishes the connection with the server) without rewriting the event handlers. Without a connection broker, the event handlers should be implemented for the specific connection object, which we are going to use to establish the connection. In case you have to change the connection object, you would have to reimplement the event handlers. But when you use the connection broker object, you are centralizing the connections, and hence you only write the event handlers once, even if you change the connection object.

What is Contained in the DataSnap Server Module?

The remote data module plays an important role in DataSnap applications.

A normal VCL-based GUI application can be converted to a DataSnap server object by adding a remote data module to the application. When a remote data module is added to the application, using the Remote Data Module Wizard, the wizard automatically creates two classes; the first class is a descendant of TCRemoteDataModule, and the second class is its implementation interface. A traditional C++ program does not support interfaces, but a VCL-based C++ program does because the concept of interfaces is inherited from the Delphi interfaces, as we discussed in an earlier chapter. The implementation interface class is derived from the VCL interface class IAppServerImpl (and other COM ATL classes), thus providing IAppServer support and COM support. The IAppServer support is provided by the IAppServerImpl class, and the automation object features (such as object creation, reference count, object management through the Interface ID, and automatic destruction of the object when no more references exist) are inherited from the COM ATL classes. Though the wizard creates both the remote data module class and its interface class within the same header file, the program unit file is used to implement the contents of the remote data module alone since the interface implementation is automatically provided for you. However, if you understand the fundamentals of the implementation class, you will be comfortable working with the application in general.

Let's take a look at the wizard. Initiate the New Items dialog from the IDE and switch to the Multitier page, which displays several icons representing different multi-tier object wizards, including CORBA and Remote Data Module. Figure 9-1 on the following page displays the appearance of this dialog. When we discuss the CORBA objects later in this chapter, we will pay additional attention to the CORBA-related icons. For now, the only icon of interest is the Remote Data Module. Select the Remote Data Module icon and click OK. Now the Remote Data Module Wizard appears, as shown in Figure 9-2 on the following page.

This is a very simple wizard and asks for very little input. The two main fields you have to pay attention to are CoClass Name and Threading Model. Since the DataSnap architecture uses a COM automation framework to build the server objects, CoClass Name is the name of the automation server object as published with COM and must be provided. As shown in the figure, I am providing the name Satya for the automation object. The second field of interest is the threading model that we are supporting in our application server. We will discuss the threading model in a separate section later in this chapter. For now, let's accept the default Apartment threading model. The third field is used to enter a brief description of the object and is not a required field. The last option is a check box indicating whether to generate event support code; this is also discussed later. When you click the OK button, the wizard automatically generates a unit file and header file for the remote data module, in addition to some other files (such as the type library file for the project). The unit file is named SatyaImpl.cpp and the header file is named SatyaImpl.h. Since we have not added any functionality to our remote data module, let's examine the header file, as presented in Listing 9-1, for the time being.

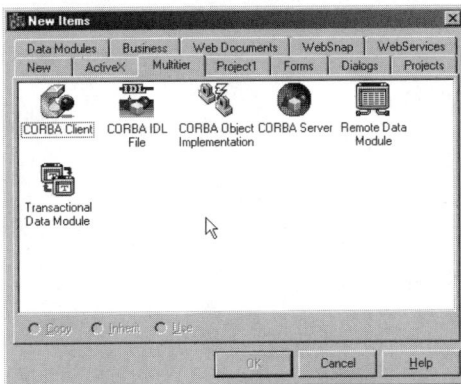

Figure 9-1: The Multitier page in the New Items dialog

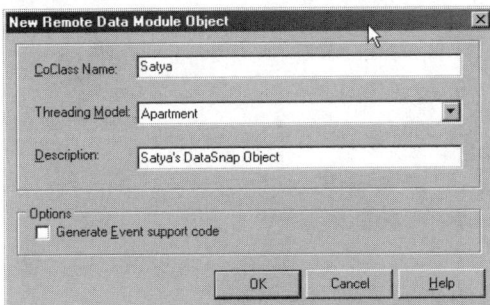

Figure 9-2: Remote Data Module Wizard

Listing 9-1: SatyaImpl.h—remote data module header file

```
// SATYAIMPL.H : Declaration of the Satya

#ifndef SatyaImplH
#define SatyaImplH

#define ATL_FREE_THREADED
#include <Classes.hpp>
#include <Controls.hpp>
```

```
#include <StdCtrls.hpp>
#include <Forms.hpp>
#include <MidConst.hpp>

#include "Project1_TLB.H"
#include <atl/atlvcl.h>



// Forward ref. of IAppServer implementor


/////////////////////////////////////////////////////////////////////
/////////////////////////////////////////////////////////////////////
class TSatya : public TCRemoteDataModule
{
__published:   // IDE-managed components
private:        // User declarations
public:         // User declarations
  __fastcall TSatya(TComponent* Owner);

__published:
};


/////////////////////////////////////////////////////////////////////
/////////////////////////////////////////////////////////////////////
extern PACKAGE TSatya *Satya;


/////////////////////////////////////////////////////////////////////
// TSatyaImpl     Implements ISatya, default interface of Satya
// ThreadingModel : Apartment
// Dual Interface : TRUE
// Event Support  : FALSE
// Default ProgID : Project1.Satya
// Description    : Satya's DataSnap Object
/////////////////////////////////////////////////////////////////////
class ATL_NO_VTABLE TSatyaImpl: REMOTEDATAMODULE_IMPL(TSatyaImpl, Satya, TSatya, ISatya)
{
public:

BEGIN_COM_MAP(TSatyaImpl)
  RDMOBJECT_COM_INTERFACE_ENTRIES(ISatya)
END_COM_MAP()

  // Data used when registering object
  //
  DECLARE_THREADING_MODEL(otApartment);
  DECLARE_PROGID(_T("Project1.Satya"));
  DECLARE_DESCRIPTION(_T("Satya's DataSnap Object"));

  // Function invoked to (un)register object
  //
  static HRESULT WINAPI UpdateRegistry(BOOL bRegister)
  {
    TRemoteDataModuleRegistrar regObj(GetObjectCLSID(), GetProgID(), GetDescription());
    // Disable these flags in order to disable use by socket or web connections.
    // Also set other flags to configure the behavior of your application server.
```

```
    // For more information, see atlmod.h and atlvcl.cpp.
    regObj.Singleton = false;
    regObj.EnableWeb = true;
    regObj.EnableSocket = true;
    return regObj.UpdateRegistry(bRegister);
  }


// ISatya
protected:
};

#endif  // SatyaImplH
```

Notice that the remote data module derived from TCRemoteDataModule is named TSatya, where Satya is the name we entered as the CoClass Name. TSatyaImpl is the interface class name, which is derived from the IAppServerImpl interface. The IAppServerImpl interface is implemented as a template class within the atlvcl.h header file, and we will examine the method calls implemented by this interface in the following section. The interface implementation declares the threading model and program ID and description from the values we entered in the wizard. The program ID is used in the client connection component's ServerName property and is available to the client through the registry. The program ID represents the specific individual remote data module within the application and is identified as <project name>.<rdm name>, where "rdm" stands for remote data module. It is registered in the server's registry when it is first time executed. Once the program is registered in the registry, it can be invoked automatically when the first client accesses it. If you create multiple remote data modules within a single project, each of the remote data modules has its own program ID and is hence individually visible to the client connection component.

The program is accessible through the server-side marshalling module (such as ScktSrvr.exe or HTTPSrvr.dll). For example, if you are trying to access the remote data module through TSocketConnection, the ScktSrvr.exe program must be running and listening for client requests (through the default port 211, which can be changed). The Update-Registry() method automatically registers or unregisters the object as needed. Let's take a close look at the properties of the registration object that we are setting in order to register (or unregister) the object. The EnableWeb and EnableSocket properties are Boolean, and when set to true will make this automation object available through the respective client connection component we discussed earlier. The RegisterPooled property is also Boolean and can be set to true to indicate that we enable the server that is pooling (or caching) the automation server object instances. In this case,

Part 2

a client request may be serviced by the immediate available instance of the object, and hence we should consider this as similar to stateless protocol. The Max property indicates the maximum number of object instances the server can cache in case the caching is enabled. The Timeout property indicates the maximum number of minutes the object may remain in cache (before being destroyed) when caching is enabled. The server checks every six minutes for the timeout value, and hence the object may exist (without a client interaction) for a maximum of six minutes longer than the Timeout value. The Singleton property is also Boolean; when set to true, it indicates that the object can be shared by multiple clients at the same time, in which case the Max and Timeout properties are ignored. The wizard adds only the default properties, but you can modify the code to change the default properties or add other supported property settings.

The remote data module is a container for the non-visual components. As its name suggests, it is a data module used in a remote server application. Most of the time, we place database and provider components on the module. The program unit file is the place where we implement the event handlers for all the components placed on the remote data module, such as provider event handlers and dataset event handlers.

The IAppServer Interface

The IAppServer interface (or its descendant) is implemented by the remote data module or its descendant, which is created by the Remote Data Module Wizard, as we discussed in the previous section.

The methods on this interface may be executed by the client application, which obtains a pointer to this interface through the connection object. Most of the time, it is not necessary to execute the interface methods directly, since they are automatically handled by the objects, when the appropriate sequence of events occur in the application. But in case you implement any custom methods for this interface, you should call them directly using the interface pointer, as shown in the example code in Listing 9-2.

Listing 9-2: Calling a custom method on the IAppServer interface from the client module

```
// The connection object is ConnectionObject
// The remote data module is AppServer
// The implementation interface remote data module is IAppServer
// The dispatch interface for the app server interface is IAppServerDisp
// The custom method you would be calling is CustomMethod(param1, param2)

IDispatch* dispInt = (IDispatch*)(ConnectionObject->AppServer)
IAppServerDisp appSrvr( (IAppServer*)dispInt);
appSrvr.CustomMethod(param1, param2);
```

Since the IAppServer interface reflects the client dataset's calls in terms of invoking corresponding methods or event handlers on the provider objects, the interface methods should know which provider the client dataset is trying to access. Therefore, a call to every method of this interface includes the provider name as the first argument in addition to other arguments, with an exception of the AS_GetProviderNames() method, which retrieves all the available provider names to the caller. Any data transferred between the client dataset and the provider through this interface is of OleVariant type, which is a special descendant of the Variant class and designed to be used specifically to pass data across the COM interface. When passing a TParams object across the COM interface, convert the TParams object to an OleVariant object using the PackageParams() method and perform the reverse conversion using the UnpackParams() method. These conversions are automatically performed by the client dataset methods, and you do not have to do anything explicitly. However, if you are writing your own custom descendant of a dataset that would have functionality similar to the client dataset, then you may have to use these methods explicitly in your implementation if such a need occurs. The PackageParams() method takes two arguments. The first argument is a pointer to the TParams object to be converted. The second argument is an object of the TParamTypes set, which may include one or more related values, such as ptInput, ptOutput, ptInputOutput, ptResult, and ptUnknown. The method returns an OleVariant object. The UnpackParams() method takes two arguments. The first argument is the OleVariant object to be converted, and the second argument is a pointer to the TParams object to hold the result after conversion.

The AppServer property of the connection component is a Variant object, and you should obtain the dispatch interface from this Variant. From the listing, notice that first we are obtaining a pointer to IDispatch interface by casting the Variant value; then we are constructing the dispatch interface object for your application server. The wizard automatically generates template code with standard filenames and attaches them to the project. If your remote data module is AppServer, then the implementation unit is TAppServer, its interface is IAppServer, and its dispatch interface is IAppServerDisp. It is recommended that you do not change any of these names, since the naming convention is tightly integrated with the DataSnap/COM architecture. If you change the names, your application may not be usable or may not behave as predicted.

Table 9-1 provides a description of the methods supported by the IAppServer interface. If you extend the default interface, you may add new methods as your application demands.

Part 2

Table 9-1: Methods supported by the IAppServer interface

Method	Description
AS_ApplyUpdates (const WideString prName, const OleVariant delta, int maxErr, int &errCount, OleVariant &ownerData, OleVariant &result)	Applies updates received from the client to the underlying dataset through the associated provider object. The method takes six arguments. The first argument identifies the provider that is associated with the dataset. The second argument contains all the changes made to the dataset. The third argument indicates the maximum number of errors that may be permitted before terminating the update process. The fourth argument is the address of an integer variable where the method stores the actual number of errors that occurred when the update was performed. The fifth argument contains any custom information supplied by the client application captured through the BeforeApplyUpdates event handler of the client dataset. The sixth argument is used by the method to return the set of records that could not be updated. When this method is invoked, the BeforeApplyUpdates event handler on the provider object is invoked, and the ownerData argument (client custom data) is passed to the event handler where you can implement logic that makes use of client custom data before the actual update process is initiated.
AS_DataRequest (const WideString prName, const OleVariant data, OleVariant &result)	The client dataset is capable of requesting data directly from the provider through a call to its own method DataRequest(). This method takes a single argument of type OleVariant, which can be any type of object. When the client dataset makes such a request, it is in turn invoking the AS_DataRequest() method of the IAppServer interface. This method further invokes the OnDataRequest event handler on the corresponding provider, passing the client's data argument to the event handler. If you implemented the provider's OnDataRequest event handler, the result returned by the event handler is passed back to the calling client through this interface method. In a way, this interface method acts like a conduit for smooth passage of a client's request to the provider and the provider's response back to the client. The method takes three arguments. The first argument is the provider name, the second argument is the client's custom data, and the third argument is used by the method to return the result returned by the provider's event handler.
AS_Execute (const WideString prName, const WideString cmdText, OleVariant &params, OleVariant &ownerData)	The client dataset is capable of executing an SQL command or stored procedure (or a client-supplied SQL command if the provider permits) directly on the provider object through a call to its own method Execute(). When the client dataset executes this method, it is in turn invoking the AS_Execute () method of the IAppServer interface, which further invokes the Execute() method on the corresponding provider object. The AS_Execute() method takes four arguments. The first argument is the provider name, the second argument is the client's custom SQL command, the third argument is the client's Params property containing any parameters required by the provider to execute the command, and the fourth argument is the client's custom data that may be useful for the provider to perform special execution logic. Please note that the Execute() method sequence that we just discussed is only useful for executing SQL commands or stored procedures that do not return a result set of records from the database.
AS_GetParams (const WideString prName, OleVariant &ownerData, const OleVariant result)	The client dataset's FetchParams() method results in a call to the AS_GetParams() method of the interface, which fetches the current parameter values from the corresponding provider object. Before the interface method is called, the BeforeGetParams event handler on the client dataset is invoked, which is where you would get the opportunity to pack any custom information to be sent to the provider. This interface method takes three arguments. The first argument is the name of the provider, the second argument is the OleVariant object containing the custom data provided by the client, and the third parameter is an OleVariant that holds the parameters returned by the provider. Please note that you should not try to fetch parameters using this method from a provider that is part of a stateless application server because in a stateless application server, the parameters might be changed by other clients. In such a situation, use the Execute() method on the client dataset instead.
AS_GetProviderNa mes (OleVariant &prNames)	This method returns a list of provider objects available from the specific application server connected to the connection object. The provider names obtained in this list may be used in other methods of this interface to make provider-specific requests. The method takes one argument, which holds the returned provider name list in an OleVariant array.

Method	Description
AS_GetRecords (const WideString prName, int count, int &recsOut, int options, const WideString cmdText, OleVariant &params, OleVariant: &ownerData, OleVariant &result)	This method is called to retrieve a specified number of records. It returns the requested records, starting with the current record of the provider's dataset. When working with a stateless remote data module, you may need to reposition the cursor or re-execute a query or stored procedure in the provider's BeforeGetRecords event handler. This method takes eight arguments. The first argument is the provider name. The second argument indicates the number of records or type of data. If it is −1, it indicates that all records must be retrieved. If it is 0, it indicates no records should be retrieved and only metadata should be retrieved. A positive value indicates the maximum number of records to be retrieved. The third argument is a pointer to an integer value that holds the number of records returned. The fourth argument indicates what must be included in the returned packet in addition to data. It may be a combination of values, such as MetaDataOption (to include metadata), ResetOption (to start from the first record disregarding the last record position in the previous data packet), XMLOption (to send the data packet as an XML string instead of OleVariant), and XMLUTF8Option (to send the data packet as an XML string and encode extended characters using UTF-8). The fifth argument is the command text of the SQL command or stored procedure name. The sixth argument contains the parameters, the seventh argument contains the client custom data, and the eighth argument is a pointer to the OleVariant to hold the data packet returned by the provider.
AS_RowRequest (const WideString prName, OleVariant Row, int requestType, OleVariant: &ownerData, OleVariant &result)	Client datasets call this method automatically to implement their FetchBlobs(), FetchDetails(), or RefreshRecord() methods to get information from a specified record of the dataset. The method takes five arguments. The first argument is the provider name. The second argument describes the current record in the client dataset. The third argument is the request type, which is the byte representation of the set object TFetchOptions. These options may include foRecord (to fetch field values from the current record), foBlobs (to fetch Blob field values from the current record), and foDetails (to fetch nested dataset fields for the current record). The third argument is set by casting the TFetchOptions object to a byte and then to an integer. The fourth argument contains any custom data sent by the client dataset in its BeforeRowRequest event handler. The fifth argument is an OleVariant object that holds the result from the provider.

Part 2

The Threading Model of Server Objects

Since the DataSnap applications are built on Microsoft COM-based architecture, the threading model applied to DataSnap applications is directly related to the COM threading model. An application process comprises of virtual memory, code, data, and other system resources. Within a process, the code that executes in a sequential manner is called a *thread*, which means the instructions belonging to the thread are executed sequentially, and as long as the process has only one thread running, there is no resource sharing involved. However, when the process runs multiple threads simultaneously, each of them sharing the resources available to the process, the application is termed a multi-threaded application and calls for special handling of the resources (as supported by the Windows operating system). All the server objects belonging to an application process may be grouped into units called *apartments*. An object lives in (or belongs to) only one apartment, but an apartment may contain more than one object. Also, an apartment may have multiple threads running simultaneously. The methods of an object may be called directly by any thread that belongs to the apartment to which the object also belongs. If a thread in an apartment needs to call the methods of an object that does not belong to the same apartment (or belongs to another apartment), the call must go through the proxy and stub-based marshalling mechanism.

We have already discussed that when we create a DataSnap server application, each time you add a remote data module, you will be providing the wizard with a name, a threading model, and a description. The threading model that we select at this point is registered with COM so that COM can handle the client requests accordingly. Therefore, we should also implement the code according to the threading model we select. Inconsistencies between the code and the threading model may result in unpredictable results. The following is a description of the different threading model options supported by the DataSnap Application Wizard.

- In the *single-threaded model*, the server object provides no threading support to the client calls, and all the client requests are serialized by COM. When this model is implemented, the process behaves like any standard single-threaded application, and hence you do not have to take any additional care to preserve the integrity of the global variables, as you would normally do in a multi-threaded application. In other words, your application is thread-safe.

- In the *apartment model* (also considered a single-threaded apartment model), an apartment consists of exactly one thread, which also means that each thread lives in its own apartment; the server objects can receive method calls from only one thread that belongs to the apartment. This is ensured by COM. In addition, COM also synchronizes all the method calls coming from the single-thread (that belongs to the apartment) with the Windows message queue. It is also logical to group objects that need to work in sync with each other in a single apartment. While implementing objects in this threading model, the global data must be protected using critical sections or another way that serializes the requests to global variables. However, object instance data can be safely accessed by the objects. Every client request is serviced by a different instance of the server object. The object's instances may be pooled, depending on the setting we made for the RegisterPooled property of the remote data module registrar object in the UpdateRegistry() method in the implementation interface.

- In the *free-threading model* (also considered a multi-threaded apartment model), an apartment may consist of more than one thread. In this case, an object may receive direct calls from more than one thread belonging to the same apartment. Calls to an object's method are not serialized by default and therefore offer multi-threaded object concurrency, which means the highest level of performance benefits. Also, the interface pointers across multiple threads are passed directly instead of through marshalling, adding to performance benefits. But objects must protect all the instance and global data using critical sections or some other form of serialization as supported by the Win32 operating system, such as mutexes, semaphores, and so on. Also, since the object does not control the lifetime of threads anyway, objects do not store the thread state information. In this threading model, apartments do not receive calls while making calls on the same thread.

- In the *both-threading model*, which is similar to the free-threading model, the outgoing calls, such as callbacks, are guaranteed to execute in the same thread. This model offers maximum performance and flexibility and also does not require the application to provide thread support for parameters supplied to outgoing calls.

- The *neutral-threading model* is supported under COM+ and falls between the apartment-threading model and the free-threading model. Like the free-threading model, this model allows multiple threads to access the object at the same time, without the extra marshalling requirement, to transfer to the thread on which the object was created. COM+ guarantees that it will receive no conflicting calls. While implementing objects in this threading model, you do not need to guard the object instance data against thread conflicts if it can be accessed by different methods in the object's interface.

DataSnap Application Logic Flow

Having understood the basics of the DataSnap architecture, it is now time to look at the specifics of how the client and server modules establish the connection and communicate with each other. Despite the existence of multiple connection object types due to the differences in the protocol and marshalling architectures, the features discussed here are going to be the same in all the DataSnap applications. However, I will bring any architecture-specific features to your attention when it is appropriate.

Before the client tries to establish a connection with the server, the server must be running. If we design our client to use the socket connection component, then the ScktSrvr.exe program must also be running. If our server application is not running when the first client makes a call, the server application is automatically started. The ScktSrvr.exe program should be started either manually or set up as a Windows service to start automatically, but the client cannot start this program through its call. Similarly, if your client application tries to connect using the web connection component, the wininet.dll must have been installed on the client system (if the client system is running Internet Explorer 3 or above this file already exists on the system), the server must be running IIS4 or above or Netscape Enterprise 3.6 or higher, and the HTTPSrvr.dll must be installed with the web server in the directory that is pointed to by the URL the client web connection uses.

A server object is identified by a remote data module, which may host one or more providers; each of the providers typically connects to a dataset. The provider is usually a TDataSetProvider or a TXMLTransformProvider component. For example, we may have one provider to connect to a single table and another provider to connect to a query object, which executes a complex SQL select statement joining multiple tables. Either the table or query object is represented by the general dataset object, which is usually a TDataSet descendant. This dataset object should have implemented the IProviderSupport interface in order to make its services available to the client through the provider object. Most of the dataset objects shipped with C++Builder 6 expose the methods of this interface.

The client obtains an interface pointer to the server object, which is the remote data module. Typically, the client uses an object of the TClient-DataSet component, which communicates with the providers through the IAppServer interface. Most of the time, we do not have to explicitly call the IAppServer methods on the server object, but in typical situations such as when we extend the IAppServer interface with custom methods, we have to explicitly call these methods using the interface pointer obtained through the connection component.

Figure 9-3 displays the typical sequence of events that occur in a DataSnap client-server application. In the figure, notice the bold line that separates the client module from the server module. The figure does not show the connection between the dataset and the database table and the sequence of events that happen during the provider and dataset interaction. Also, note that for every method call on the client dataset where there is a corresponding action associated with the server interface, similar types of events occur. You are free to plug in your business rules in the appropriate event handlers both on the client side and server side. Just like any other VCL event handler, if you implement a specific event handler, the system will invoke your event handler, and if you do not implement one, it either ignores it or takes the default action.

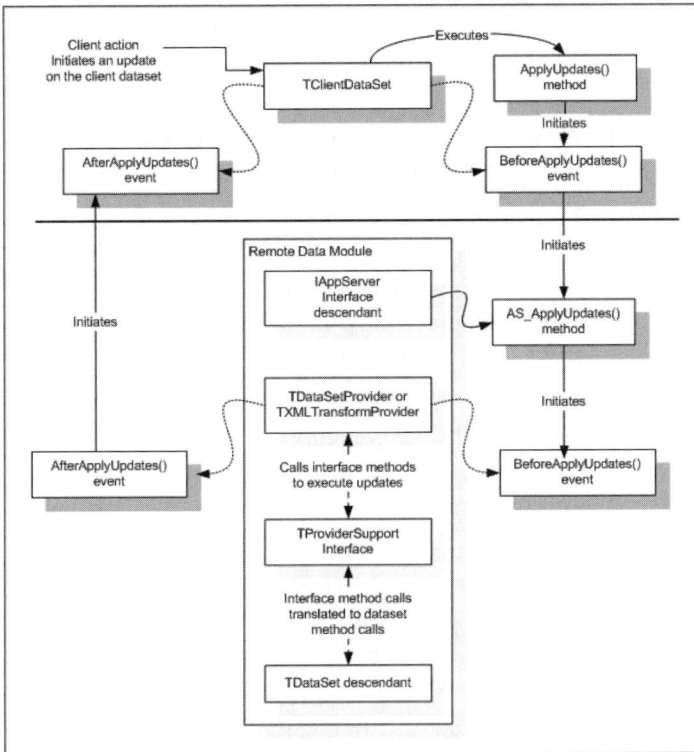

Figure 9-3: Typical sequence of events in a client-server application

Sample DataSnap Application

Let's now go through the process of creating a simple client and a simple server application. The server application will implement a remote data module containing a couple of providers connected to a table and query object. In this example, I am using an InterBase database employee.gdb, which is automatically installed in the InterBase \examples\database directory. Since I will be making updates to this database, I copied the database and index files to the directory where the server application is saved. Follow the steps outlined here to create the DataSnap server application.

1. Create a standard Windows GUI application. Save the project files with names of your choice in a directory of your choice. I saved the file in directory ..\DataSnapServer\. I named the project DataSnapServer.bpr.

2. Add a remote data module to the application with a name of your choice. I named it serverRDS. The wizard creates all the necessary files.

3. From the InterBase page in the Component Palette, drop a **TIBDatabase** component, a **TIBTransaction** component, a **TIBTable** component, and a **TIBQuery** component onto the remote data module. From the Data Access page, drop two **TDataSetProvider** components.

4. For the TIBDataBase component, set the DefaultTransaction property to the TIBTransaction object, the user_name to **SYSDBA**, and password to **masterkey** in the Params property. We are not setting the database name property at this time. We will do it at run time.

5. For the TIBTable and TIBQuery components, set the Database property to the TIBDatabase component and the Transaction property to the TIBTransaction component.

6. Change the name of DataSetProvider1 to **TableProvider** and the name of DataSetProvider2 to **QueryProvider**. For the TableProvider component, set the Dataset property to the TIBTable component, and for the QueryProvider component, set the Dataset property to the TIBQuery component.

7. In this example, we are just creating two providers, one for the table and one for the query. The table dataset component retrieves data by setting the table name, and the query dataset component performs any query that we can send from the client. For both the provider components in the Object Inspector, set the poAllowCommandText option to **true** in the Options property because we would like to send the command text (either the table name or the SQL command) from the client.

8. In the constructor of the remote data module serverRDS, implement the logic to connect to the database if the connection is not already established, as displayed in Listing 9-3. For the simple implementation of the server, you don't have to do anything else. As we continue with our discussion on additional topics, we will examine how the server module code is implemented.

9. Compile the server module and run it. Also remember to start the ScktSrvr.exe module, which may be located in the bin directory of C++Builder 6.

> ■ **Note:** When you try to compile and execute the examples, you might notice that the executables built on your machine with the source files as shipped on the companion CD may not run properly, since you may have connection problems between the server and client. This is because the globally unique identifiers (GUIDs) generated for the project may contain machine-specific information, and since they were originally built on my computer, it may cause the problem. Therefore, as a word of caution, I would advise you to recreate the project files and type libraries fresh on your system, and then copy the source files (cpp and header files) over your existing files if you saved your files with the same names as I did. Or just copy and paste the content of the files if the filenames differ, whichever is suitable for you.

Listing 9-3: serverRDSImpl.cpp—constructor method

```
__fastcall TServerRDS::TServerRDS(TComponent* Owner) : TCRemoteDataModule(Owner)
{
    if (!IBDatabase1->Connected) {
        const AnsiString currDir(ExtractFileDir(Application->ExeName));
        SetCurrentDir(currDir);
        AnsiString dbName(currDir);
        dbName += "\\data\\employee.gdb";
        IBDatabase1->DatabaseName = dbName;
        IBDatabase1->Connected = true;
    }
}
```

Part 2

Follow the steps outlined here to create the DataSnap client application:

1. Create a new windows GUI application and save the project files with names of your choice in a directory of your choice. I saved the file in directory ..\DataSnapClient-SocketConnection\. I named the project DataSnapClient.bpr.

   The main form of the client application looks similar to Figure 9-4. From the Component Palette, I dropped several components onto the form. They include a TPanel to hold all the components, one TMemo to enter the SQL command, one TMemo to display messages, one TEdit to enter the table name, one TDBGrid to display retrieved records, one TClientDataSet to connect to a provider on the server, one TDataSource to connect the data grid with the client dataset, one TSocketConnection to establish connection with the server module, one TDBNavigator to navigate the records, one TOpenDialog to open a saved client dataset local file, one TSaveDialog to save a client dataset to a local file, and finally ten TButton components. The buttons are used to initiate user actions, including connect, disconnect, get table, run query, update table, cancel updates, clear SQL, clear messages, save to file, and load from file.

2. In this example, I am demonstrating the socket connection component to establish the connection. For this component, set the Host property to the host computer name (I set it to localhost, since I am running the server module on the same machine as the client module); then when you click on the drop-down list for the ServerName property, you see the server name automatically in the notation <server application name>.<remote data module name> if the server and the ScktSrvr.exe programs are already running.

3. Implement the event handlers as shown in the Listing 9-4. I implemented the Form Create event handler to establish connection with the server module and set the Filter property for both the File Open and File Save dialogs. The OnClick event handlers for the Connect and Disconnect buttons are implemented to connect to and disconnect from the server module. Both the Get Table and Run Query button event handlers are similar. They check if the table name or SQL query are filled in properly before trying to connect to the provider. Then they close the client dataset first, set the CommandText and ProviderName properties on the client dataset, and open the dataset. Any exceptions are captured in the catch block of the try ... catch construct, and the message is displayed in the message box (TMemo component).

You may notice that even after disconnecting from the server module, if you initiate a request through the client dataset, such as get table or run query, the client dataset automatically invokes the connection and provides you with the result. This is the default behavior of the client dataset. I did not want to complicate the code. You can manually write code to avoid this behavior if the connection is closed, as desired by your application.

I also implemented the event handlers to apply the updates to the database, cancel the updates, save the client dataset to a local disk file, and load the client dataset back from the disk. The saving and reloading feature provides briefcase model functionality.

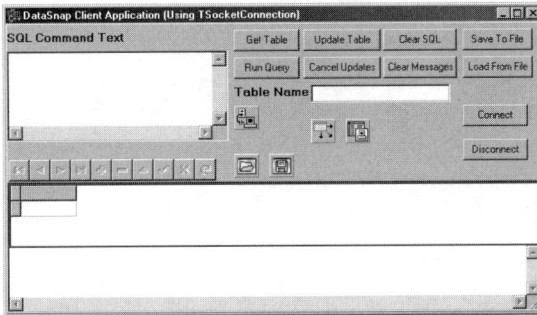

Figure 9-4: The DataSnap client main form

Listing 9-4: DataSnapClientMain.cpp

```cpp
//---------------------------------------------------------------------------

#include <vcl.h>
#pragma hdrstop

#include "DataSnapClientMain.h"
#include "ReconcileErrorDialog.h"
//---------------------------------------------------------------------------
#pragma package(smart_init)
#pragma resource "*.dfm"
TDSClientForm *DSClientForm;
//---------------------------------------------------------------------------
__fastcall TDSClientForm::TDSClientForm(TComponent* Owner)
    : TForm(Owner)
{
    try {
        if (!SocketConnection1->Connected) {
            SocketConnection1->Host = "localhost";
            SocketConnection1->Connected = true;
        }
        MsgList->Lines->Clear();
        MsgList->Lines->Add("Connected established with the server module");

        ConnectBtn->Enabled = false;
        const AnsiString currDir(ExtractFileDir(Application->ExeName));
        SetCurrentDir(currDir);
        OpenDialog1->InitialDir = currDir;
        SaveDialog1->InitialDir = currDir;
        OpenDialog1->Filter = "Data files (*.dat)|*.DAT";
        SaveDialog1->Filter = "Data files (*.dat)|*.DAT";
    }
    catch (Exception &ex) {
        MsgList->Lines->Add(ex.Message);
    }
}
//---------------------------------------------------------------------------
void __fastcall TDSClientForm::FormResize(TObject *Sender)
{
    if (Height < 410)
        Height = 410;
    if (Width < 620)
        Width = 620;
```

```
    }
    //----------------------------------------------------------------------------
    void __fastcall TDSClientForm::ClearSQLBtnClick(TObject *Sender)
    {
        SQLText->Lines->Clear();
    }
    //----------------------------------------------------------------------------
    void __fastcall TDSClientForm::ClearMsgBtnClick(TObject *Sender)
    {
        MsgList->Lines->Clear();
    }
    //----------------------------------------------------------------------------
    void __fastcall TDSClientForm::GetTableBtnClick(TObject *Sender)
    {
        try {
            const AnsiString tableName(TableNameEdit->Text);
            ClientDS->Close();
            if (tableName == "") {
                MsgList->Lines->Add("Table name empty. Please enter table name");
                return;
            }
            SocketConnection1->Connected = false;
            ClientDS->ProviderName = "TableProvider";
            ClientDS->CommandText = tableName;
            ClientDS->Active = true;
        }
        catch (Exception &ex) {
            MsgList->Lines->Add(ex.Message);
        }
    }
    //----------------------------------------------------------------------------
    void __fastcall TDSClientForm::RunQueryBtnClick(TObject *Sender)
    {
        try {
            const AnsiString sqlCommandText(SQLText->Text);
            ClientDS->Close();
            if (sqlCommandText == "") {
                MsgList->Lines->Add("Please enter SQL Command ");
                return;
            }
            SocketConnection1->Connected = false;
            ClientDS->ProviderName = "QueryProvider";
            ClientDS->CommandText = sqlCommandText;
            ClientDS->Active = true;
        }
        catch (Exception &ex) {
            MsgList->Lines->Add(ex.Message);
        }
    }
    //----------------------------------------------------------------------------
    void __fastcall TDSClientForm::UpdateTableBtnClick(TObject *Sender)
    {
        if (ClientDS->Active) {
            if ((ClientDS->ProviderName == "TableProvider") &&
                (ClientDS->CommandText != "")) {
                // If the client dataset is currently connected to the table provider
                // with a table name and is open, then you can initiate updates
                    const int errors = ClientDS->ApplyUpdates(0);
                    if (errors > 0)
```

```
                            MsgList->Lines->Add("One or more records failed to update");
                    else
                            MsgList->Lines->Add("All changes applied to the database");
        }
        else {
            MsgList->Lines->Add("Dataset not open. Update not possible");
        }
    }
}
//---------------------------------------------------------------------------

void __fastcall TDSClientForm::CancelUpdatesBtnClick(TObject *Sender)
{
    // if no records changed, there is no need to call CancelUpdates
    if (ClientDS->ChangeCount > 0)
        ClientDS->CancelUpdates();
}
//---------------------------------------------------------------------------
void __fastcall TDSClientForm::SaveBtnClick(TObject *Sender)
{
    try {
        if (SaveDialog1->Execute()) {
            ClientDS->SaveToFile(SaveDialog1->FileName);
            MsgList->Lines->Add("Client dataset saved to local file " +
                                SaveDialog1->FileName);
        }
        else
            MsgList->Lines->Add("Saving client dataset to local file cancelled");
    }
    catch (Exception &ex) {
        MsgList->Lines->Add("Exception occurred while saving client dataset to local
                            file");
        MsgList->Lines->Add(ex.Message);
    }

}
//---------------------------------------------------------------------------

void __fastcall TDSClientForm::LoadBtnClick(TObject *Sender)
{
    try {
        if (OpenDialog1->Execute()) {
            ClientDS->LoadFromFile(OpenDialog1->FileName);
            MsgList->Lines->Add("Client dataset loaded from local file " +
                                OpenDialog1->FileName);
        }
        else
            MsgList->Lines->Add("Loading client dataset from local file cancelled");
    }
    catch (Exception &ex) {
        MsgList->Lines->Add("Exception occurred while loading client dataset from local
                            file");
        MsgList->Lines->Add(ex.Message);
    }
}
//---------------------------------------------------------------------------

void __fastcall TDSClientForm::ConnectBtnClick(TObject *Sender)
{
```

Part 2

```
        try {
            if (!SocketConnection1->Connected) {
                SocketConnection1->Host = "localhost";
                SocketConnection1->Connected = true;
            }
            MsgList->Lines->Clear();
            MsgList->Lines->Add("Connected established with the server module");

            ConnectBtn->Enabled = false;
            DiscBtn->Enabled = true;
            AnsiString currDir = ExtractFileDir(Application->ExeName);
            SetCurrentDir(currDir);
            OpenDialog1->InitialDir = currDir;
            SaveDialog1->InitialDir = currDir;
            OpenDialog1->Filter = "Data files (*.dat)|*.DAT";
            SaveDialog1->Filter = "Data files (*.dat)|*.DAT";
        }
        catch (Exception &ex) {
            MsgList->Lines->Add(ex.Message);
        }
}
//-------------------------------------------------------------------------

void __fastcall TDSClientForm::DiscBtnClick(TObject *Sender)
{
        try {
            if (SocketConnection1->Connected) {
                SocketConnection1->Connected = false;
            }
            ConnectBtn->Enabled = true;
            DiscBtn->Enabled = false;
            MsgList->Lines->Clear();
            MsgList->Lines->Add("Disconnected from the server module");
        }
        catch (Exception &ex) {
            MsgList->Lines->Add(ex.Message);
        }
}
//-------------------------------------------------------------------------
```

We have seen a simple example that used the default server functionality provided by the DataSnap architecture, for the most part. In the following sections, we will discuss how to implement the event handlers on the client side and server side, providing you with the control to incorporate custom data and logic.

Connecting to the Server through DCOM

In the previous example we built the client application to connect to the server through the socket connection component. Without changing the server-side code, we now see how simple it will be to connect to the server using the DCOM connection component. What you have to change on the client side is very minimal. In place of the TSocketConnection component, use the TDCOMConnection component. Set the ServerName property just as you did for the socket connection component. In the program, replace all the references to the socket connection component to the DCOM connection component. Recompile the program and execute. You will not notice any difference from the end-user perspective. Moreover, you do not have to run the ScktSrvr.exe program on the server side, since both the client and server communicate through the Microsoft DCOM architecture, which performs the necessary marshalling. Thus, you can develop the multi-tier application using one type of connection component and can later change it to use a different connection component without much effort.

Applying Updates and Reconciling Errors

In our simple example I implemented a button-click event handler, where I invoked the ApplyUpdates() method on the client dataset, which in turn executes the AS_ApplyUpdates() method on the IAppServer interface. In the ApplyUpdates() method call, we are passing an integer argument indicating the maximum number of errors that are permitted before cancelling the update process. Set this value to –1 to indicate that the maximum permissible number of errors is unlimited. A value of zero indicates that the update process is aborted when the first error is encountered. When the ApplyUpdates() method is called on the client dataset, the client dataset passes the set of changed records (known as the delta data packet) to the provider through the application server interface. This delta data packet would have the same record structure as the client dataset (or the dataset that the provider supports).

We can implement the event handlers on the provider to control the update process required by the business rules. For example, when the user deletes a record from the Employee table, we can impose a record-level check on the provider before deleting the record to validate whether the delete operation is authorized by the user. If the delete operation on the particular record is not valid, we can cancel the update on that single record alone simply by throwing an exception with a custom-built error message. On the server side, I demonstrated this feature by implementing the BeforeUpdateRecord event handler for the provider. This event handler is executed once before the server attempts to update every record in the DeltaDS argument. The DeltaDS argument contains the set of records, which are modified by the user and tracked by the client dataset. When the DeltaDS is passed to this event handler, the record pointer points to the specific record that is being validated. In my example (see Listing 9-5), I am checking if the department number represents either the Engineering department (department number 600) or the Marketing department (department number 180); in either case, I do not permit the update process.

Part 2

In the sense of DataSnap applications, both a record-level update or delete operation are collectively considered an update process.

It is also possible that the update may automatically fail if the delete or update you are performing violates the database integrity principles. In that case, the OnUpdateError event handler should be implemented to process any custom logic. In the end, you may set the Response argument (which is one of the arguments to this event handler and is of TResolverResponse type) to a value that indicates which action the resolver component should take. Permitted values include rrSkip to skip the current record and leave the record changes in the cache without updating, rrAbort to abort the entire update process, and rrAply to update the current value as changed in the event handler instead of updating the value sent by the client dataset. This event is also executed if we throw any exceptions in the BeforeUpdate-Record event handler.

Listing 9-5 displays the two event handlers that I discussed in the previous paragraphs. However, please note that in the current example, it is not required to implement the OnUpdateError event handler; I just did so for a demonstration, since it has no impact on the business logic.

Listing 9-5: BeforeUpdateRecord and OnUpdateError event handlers

```
void __fastcall TServerRDS::TableProviderBeforeUpdateRecord(
    TObject *Sender, TDataSet *SourceDS, TCustomClientDataSet *DeltaDS,
    TUpdateKind UpdateKind, bool &Applied)
{
    if (UpdateKind == ukDelete) {
        // identify current record's department name
        // if it is Engineering or Marketing, then do not delete record
        const AnsiString fDept(DeltaDS->FieldByName("DEPT_NO")->AsString);
        if ((fDept == "600") || (fDept == "180")) {
            AnsiString fErrMsg("You are not authorized to delete records ");
            fErrMsg += "from Engineering and Marketing Departments";
            throw Exception(fErrMsg);
        }
    }
}
//----------------------------------------------------------------------------
void __fastcall TServerRDS::TableProviderUpdateError(TObject *Sender,
    TCustomClientDataSet *DataSet, EUpdateError *E,
    TUpdateKind UpdateKind, TResolverResponse &Response)
{
    Response = rrSkip;
}
//----------------------------------------------------------------------------
```

Since I am throwing an exception in this example, it should be caught somewhere. In multi-tiered applications, the client may catch the exception thrown by the server (or provider). Therefore, on the client side, you will implement the OnReconcileError event handler, which cycles through all the records that failed in the update process. For each kind of update (such as delete, insert, or modify the record), we can implement different logic. Since we have access to the client dataset, we can also attempt to correct the record and try the update again, or we can cancel the update for the current record. The Action argument passed in the event handler's arguments should be set to one of the following values: raSkip to skip the current record without doing anything but leaving it in the change log, raAbort to abort the entire error reconcile process, raCancel to cancel all changes to the current record, raRefresh to cancel all changes to the current record and refresh fresh values from the database, and so on. Also, please note that if you set raSkip, the record remains in the change log and may again be attempted for an update the next time you call the ApplyUpdates() method, and if you set raRefresh, you may get the most recent values of the record fields from the server, which may have been changed by some other user since you last obtained the record from the database.

Listing 9-6 shows the action that I am taking in my client application. Remember that I implemented the client application through two approaches, using the socket connection and using the DCOM connection. This example is implemented in the DCOM connection-based client application. In this event handler, I am taking action on the error record without giving the opportunity to the user. However, you may also give an opportunity to the user to see the error record in a separate window and take necessary action, such as correcting the record or cancelling the update. C++Builder 6 comes with a prebuilt Reconcile Error dialog in the object repository for this purpose. You may use this dialog as it is given, or you may inherit from it or change it as necessary. Figure 9-5 displays the Dialogs page and where to find it in the New Items dialog. This example is implemented in the client application using the socket connection, so you can see both ways of implementing this event handler.

Listing 9-6: OnReconcileError event handler on the client dataset

```
//--------------------------------------------------------------------------
void __fastcall TDSClientForm::ClientDSReconcileError(
    TCustomClientDataSet *DataSet, EReconcileError *E,
    TUpdateKind UpdateKind, TReconcileAction &Action)
{
    // if the update is of delete kind, just display the error message
    // and cancel the update for the current record
    if (UpdateKind == ukDelete) {
        MsgList->Lines->Add(E->Message);
        Action = raCancel;
    }}
//--------------------------------------------------------------------------
```

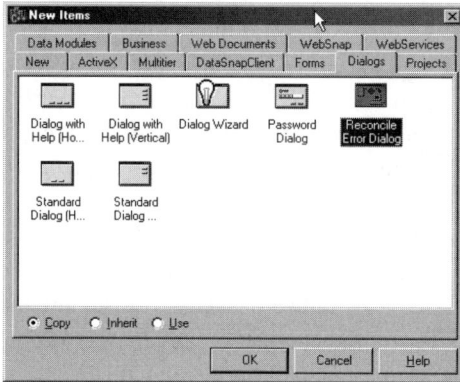

Figure 9-5: The Dialogs page in the New Items dialog

Web Client to a DataSnap Server

In the previous section we saw how to build a traditional client-server application, where a simple Windows-based client application can work with a provider resident in the server application in exchanging data from a database. However, the DataSnap architecture is not limited to the simple client-server model. In fact, you can build a web-based client application that can work with the same DataSnap server and simplify the web development process in the Windows operating environment. The web client can be a WebBroker or WebSnap application.

For the purpose of creating web-based clients using the DataSnap architecture, C++Builder 6 provides two components on the InternetExpress page of the Component Palette. They are TXMLBroker, which fetches XML data packets from the provider located in the server module, and TInetX-PageProducer, which generates a web page by using the XML data packets from the XML broker component, JavaScript libraries supplied with C++Builder 6, and the HTML template file with transparent tags. To build web-based clients for a DataSnap server, it is not required to be proficient in XML rules, since the XML parsing is internally done by the components and you do not have to write any XML documents. However, you can refer to Chapter 11, "Building BizSnap Applications," which provides some insight into XML documents.

TXMLBroker Component

The TXMLBroker component is the web client counterpart of the TClient-DataSet, which means that the XML broker can be used in the web modules in a similar way that we use the client dataset in a traditional Windows GUI application. When placed on a web module, the XML broker automatically registers itself with the web module as an auto-dispatching object, which means that the web module (or the web dispatcher) forwards all incoming HTTP messages directed to the XML broker automatically. For example, when the user clicks the button that initiates the Apply-Updates action on the displayed web page, the generated HTTP request, along with the associated delta packet, is automatically forwarded to the XML broker, which in turn applies the changes logged in the delta packet to the database through the IAppServer interface of the server module and the associated provider component.

The MaxRecords property of the XML broker component identifies the maximum number of records to be retrieved in one packet. If this value is set to –1, all the records in the underlying dataset are retrieved. Setting this value to 0 retrieves only the metadata without any records. Since the client application runs in a web browser, which downloads the data packets over the Internet, it is recommended that the maximum number of records be limited to a reasonable value, particularly if the dataset is too large. However, since the client is HTTP-based, the provider is stateless. Hence, every time we attempt to get the next set of records, we should provide a way for the provider to understand where to start the next data packet. This is done by setting a value in the OwnerData argument of the GetXMLRecords() or RequestRecords() method, since these are the methods that we execute to obtain the next data packet. The RemoteServer property should be set to one of the connection components that we discussed in the beginning of the chapter. The ProviderName property identifies one of the providers on the remote data module. When the Connected property is set to true, the XML broker is ready to fetch data packets from the provider when the producer component requests or when the HTTP request is received. Similar to the client dataset, the AppServer property gives you access to the IAppServer interface of the remote server. The Params property is an object of TXMLParams and contains the parameters that are to be sent to the server when executing the query or stored procedure associated with a provider.

The GetXMLRecords() method is called to retrieve an XML data packet from the server. The method returns the data packets as an AnsiString object in a form that is ready for insertion into an HTML document. The ApplyXMLUpdates() methods should be called to send an XML delta packet containing updated or newly inserted records and records marked for deletion to the server. The Params property is set automatically when the FetchParams() method is executed. For a description of the arguments passed to these methods or information about additional methods, please refer to the documentation that comes with the product or the product source files.

Part 2

TInetXPageProducer Component

The TInetXPageProducer is responsible for generating the HTML content from the XML data packets received through the XML broker. In a way, this component may be used similar to the adapter page producer, which we used in building a web page in the WebSnap architecture. For example, you can visually design the page using a web page editor associated with this component, but we are limited to only a certain type of component as compared to the adapter page producer. The generated HTML pages and the contained web items make use of a set of JavaScript libraries built and shipped with C++Builder 6. These files may be located in the source\webmidas sub-directory of the C++Builder home directory. Typically, these files are xmldb.js, xmldisp.js, xmldom.js, xmlerrdisp.js, and xmlshow.js. These files should be deployed along with the web client application, and the URL of their location should be set in the IncludePathURL property of the InetX page producer. Please note that failure to do this task will result in failure to run the web client application. It can take an input HTML template in the HTMLDoc parameter or in an external file identified by the HTMLFile parameter. But the page producer has a default HTML template that contains a set of transparent tags that the InetX page producer uses to assemble an HTML document, including content produced by other components. The default transparent tags include <#INCLUDE>, <#STYLES>, <#WARNINGS>, <#FORMS>, and <#SCRIPT>. Each of these transparent tags is translated by the page producer to replace the relevant code. For example, the <#INCLUDE> tag is replaced by code similar to that in Listing 9-7. This makes it clear how the page producer uses the JavaScript library files mentioned above.

Listing 9-7: The code that replaces the <#INCLUDE> tag

```
<SCRIPT language=Javascript type="text/javascript" SRC="IncludePathURL/xmldom.js">
    </SCRIPT>
<SCRIPT language=Javascript type="text/javascript" SRC="IncludePathURL/xmldb.js">
    </SCRIPT>
<SCRIPT language=Javascript type="text/javascript" SRC="IncludePathURL/xmldisp.js">
    </SCRIPT>
```

The <#STYLES> tag generates the statements that make use of the styles defined in the Styles property or in the file identified by the StylesFile property. The <#WARNINGS> tag generates any warning messages during design time, which we commonly notice during development; this tag has no impact during run time. The <#FORMS> tag generates HTML code produced by the components in the web page editor. The HTML from each component is generated in the same order as you add the components into the web page editor. The HTML generated by these components uses a set of JavaScript declarations that are generated by the producer in place of the <#SCRIPT> transparent tag. Collectively, all these tags may be replaced by a single <#BODYELEMENTS> tag if you are replacing the default HTML template with a custom HTML template designed by you. As a word of caution, please remember that when you are using your own HTML template, you have to place the collective tag or individual tags as discussed above; otherwise, your web client may not function as you would expect.

Let's now go through example applications where we first build a DataSnap server application suitable for use by web clients and then a WebBroker client and a WebSnap client that connect to this server. I could have reused the server that we built earlier in the chapter, but we cannot use some features like the provider option, such as poAllowCommandText, which we used in the traditional DataSnap server, in a server to be accessed by web-based clients.

1. Create a new Windows GUI application and add a remote data module. Save the files in a directory of your choice with names of your choice. I named the project DataSnapInetXServer.bpr.

    The components that I used in the server are very similar to what I used in the previous DataSnap server module, except I am using two TIBTable components in this example instead of one TIBTable and one TIBQuery. In the constructor, I am setting the TableName property for both the TIBTable components and opening them if they are not already open. This is the only difference; in the previous example, we permitted the user to provide the table name property, whereas in this example, we are statically setting these values. The server module constructor code is displayed in Listing 9-8.

Listing 9-8: The DataSnapInetXServer module constructor

```
__fastcall TserverRDSInetX::TserverRDSInetX(TComponent* Owner) :
        TCRemoteDataModule(Owner)
{
    if (!IBDatabase1->Connected) {
        const AnsiString currDir(ExtractFileDir(Application->ExeName));
        SetCurrentDir(currDir);
        AnsiString dbName(currDir);
        dbName += "\\data\\employee.gdb";
        IBDatabase1->DatabaseName = dbName;
        IBDatabase1->Connected = true;
        IBTable1->TableName = "employee";
        IBTable2->TableName = "customer";
        IBTable1->Open();
        IBTable2->Open();
    }
}
```

Now we will build a WebBroker client that accesses this server module, as outlined in the steps here.

1. Create a WebBroker application of ISAPI/NSAPI DLL type. Add three web action items to the web module. Save the application files in a directory of your choice with names of your choice. I named the application project DataSnapInetXWebBrokerClient.bpr.

2. Drop a **TSocketConnection** component, two **TXMLBroker** components, and two **TInetXPageProducer** components. One set of page producer and XML broker components would generate the employee list page, and the other set would generate the customer page.

3. For the first web action item, set the pathinfo as **/home** and implement the OnAction event handler with custom HTML code to display two options: list the employees and list the customers. For the remaining two web action items, set the PageProducer property to each of the page producers that we dropped earlier.

4. Each of the page producers is used to design the page using the corresponding web page editor component, and we set the corresponding XML broker to the display component's XMLBroker property. Figure 9-6 displays the web module components and the server module components in different windows. Listing 9-9 displays the web module code.

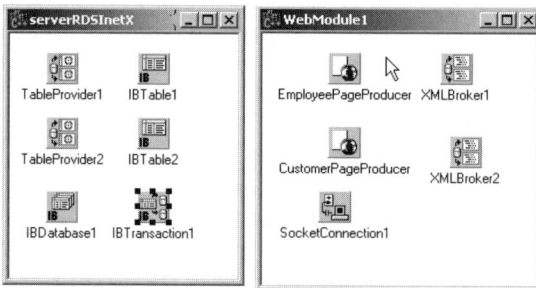

Figure 9-6: WebModule and RemoteDataModule of the DataSnapInetX application

Listing 9-9: DataSnapInetXWebBrokerClient.cpp

```cpp
//---------------------------------------------------------------------------
#include "InetXClientWebModule.h"
//---------------------------------------------------------------------------
#pragma package(smart_init)
#pragma resource "*.dfm"
TWebModule1 *WebModule1;
//---------------------------------------------------------------------------
__fastcall TWebModule1::TWebModule1(TComponent* Owner)
                    : TWebModule(Owner)
{
    SocketConnection1->Connected = true;
```

```
    XMLBroker1->Connected = true;
    XMLBroker2->Connected = true;
}
//-------------------------------------------------------------------------
void __fastcall TWebModule1::WebModule1WebActionItem1Action(
    TObject *Sender, TWebRequest *Request, TWebResponse *Response,
    bool &Handled)
{
    // default action - display selection buttons
    AnsiString fRespStr("<HTML>");
    fRespStr += "<TITLE>InetX Web Client Application (ISAPI/NSAPI DLL) </TITLE>";
    fRespStr += "<BODY BGCOLOR=\"#CCCCBB\">";
    fRespStr += "<H2>InetX Web Client Application</H2>";
    fRespStr += "<H2>InterBase Employee Database</H2>";
    fRespStr += "<BR>";
    fRespStr += "<H2>Choose one of the Options</H2>";
    fRespStr += "<BR>";
    fRespStr += "";
    fRespStr += "<A HREF=\"/cgi-bin/InetXClient.dll/employee\">Employee List</A>";
    fRespStr += "<A HREF=\"/cgi-bin/InetXClient.dll/customer\">Customer List</A>";
    fRespStr += "</UL>";
    fRespStr += "</BODY>";
    fRespStr += "</HTML>";
    Response->Content = fRespStr;
}
//-------------------------------------------------------------------------
```

The application is very simple but provides you with the basic knowledge to build WebBroker-based client applications for a DataSnap server. Figures 9-7 through 9-9 display the screens as they look when the application is deployed to the IIS server and executed through a web browser.

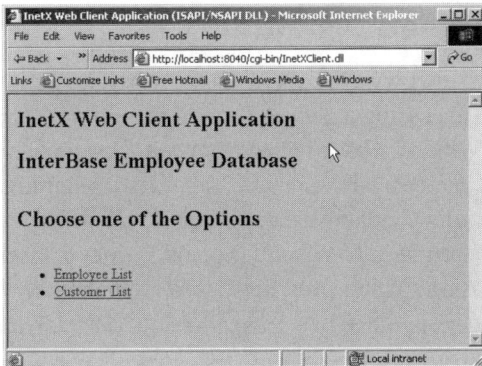

Figure 9-7: WebBroker client main page

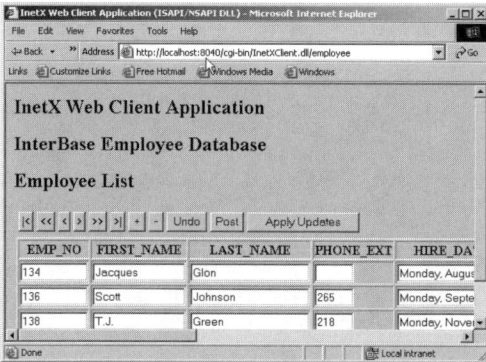

Figure 9-8: WebBroker client Employee List page

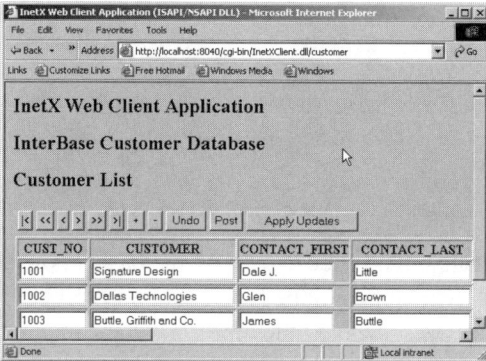

Figure 9-9: WebBroker client Customer List page

A Word on the XML-based Provider

In the previous sections we saw how the dataset-based provider component played an important role in accessing a dataset located in a remote data module from a traditional Windows-based client or a web-based client application. A dataset provider typically connects to a database table or query component and performs the database operations, such as select, update, delete, and insert. Starting in C++Builder 6 and Delphi 6, Borland provides a wonderful extension to their provider-based architecture, where we can use an XML document in place of a dataset and the TXMLTransformProvider in place of the TDataSetProvider, thus making our dataset-based server application an XML document-based server application. The client application may use either the TClientDataSet or the TXMLBroker component to access data from the XML-based provider. Figure 9-10 displays how a client dataset or an XML broker on the client application can access data from a dataset provider or XML transform provider.

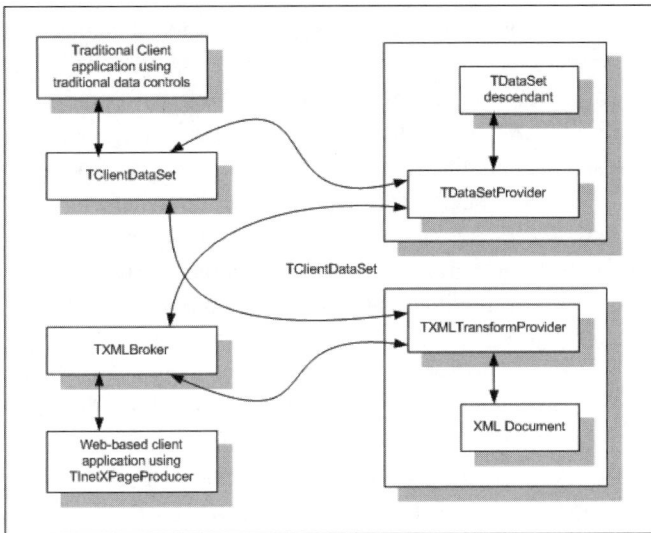

Figure 9-10: Combinations of data access between client and server modules

Part 2

The TXMLTransformProvider component performs the translation between the XML document and the client (which is the client dataset or XML broker). The XMLDataFile property identifies the XML document that serves as the base data source for the provider. The TransformRead property identifies an object of the TXMLTransform component that is used by the provider to transform the source XML document contents into a data packet. The TransformWrite property identifies an object of the TXMLTransform component that is used by the provider to transform the data packet into an XML document. The TransformationFile property of the TXMLTransform component should be set to the file, which is used by the provider while performing the data transformation. If the transformation files are not set properly, the transformation will not work and your server application will fail.

Let's discuss how we would get the transformation files that we need in the process. C++Builder 6 is shipped with a tool called XmlMapper.exe, which may be located in the C++Builder 6\bin directory, along with other executables. This is a simple Windows-based application that we may use to create the XML transformation files. When executed, the tool displays three vertical window panes. The first pane is designed to display the XML document structure, the third pane is designed to display the data packet structure, and the middle pane is designed to display the mapping information generated by the transformation process. We can use the utility to perform a transformation from one side to the other side. The buttons and menu options provide us with features such as opening the source file (XML document file or data packet file), setting the transformation options (defined in the bottom portion of the middle pane), initiating the transformation process, and saving the output files. The output files may be the files that result from the transformation process or the transformation mapping file. The source file may be an XML document, which is created using any commercial utility or converted from the data packet using the XmlMapper utility, or it might even be created manually using any text editor; if the source file is a data packet file, it would be created by saving the client dataset using the SaveToFile() method. If we open a data packet file in this utility, the third pane is filled with the structure of the data packet; then we can choose the fields that we want to be included in the transformation by double-clicking on the specific fields. At this time, the chosen fields would appear in the left pane, which displays the XML document structure. Then we can create the transformation mapping information by choosing the Create | Transformation menu option. Finally, we can transform the input file into the output format by clicking the Create and Test Transformation button in the bottom of the middle pane, which displays the transformed data in a separate window. We can save both the transformed file and the transformation mapping file by using the File | Save menu option and choosing the appropriate save file type. We can follow a similar procedure to create a data packet file from an XML document.

Now I will demonstrate how to build an application with a client dataset accessing data from an XML document. For the purpose of demonstration, I created a data packet file from the client dataset (through one of the DataSnapClient applications) for the Employee table in the employee.gdb database. This file is named employee.cds. Using the XmlMapper.exe utility, I created an XML document file and named it employee.xml. I also saved the transformation files XMLToDpkt.xtr, which contains transformation mapping to transform the XML document to a data packet, and DpktToXML.xtr, which contains transformation mapping to transform the data packet to an XML document. I saved all these files in the XML-Transform directory, where we are going to create our application. Now, let's go through the steps of creating the example application. I would like to simplify the example by creating a Windows GUI application and using the client dataset and XML transform provider in the same form:

1. Create a Windows GUI application and save the project and unit files with names of your choice. I saved all the files in the XMLTransform directory.

2. From the Data Access page in the Component Palette, drop a **TXML-TransformProvider**, a **TClientDataSet**, and a **TDataSource** onto the main form.

3. From the Data Controls page, drop a **TDBGrid** component. Establish connections between the data grid, data source, and client dataset components. For the client dataset, set the ProviderName property to the XML transform provider component's name.

4. Drop four **TButton** components, and set their names and captions as shown in the following listing. These buttons are used to provide user initiation to open the client dataset, close the dataset, apply updates, and cancel updates.

5. Implement the form constructor and other event handlers, as shown in Listing 9-10.

Listing 9-10: XMLTransformMain.cpp

```cpp
//---------------------------------------------------------------------------

#include <vcl.h>
#pragma hdrstop

#include "XMLTransformMain.h"
#include "ReconcileErrorDialog.h"
//---------------------------------------------------------------------------
#pragma package(smart_init)
#pragma resource "*.dfm"
TForm1 *Form1;
//---------------------------------------------------------------------------
__fastcall TForm1::TForm1(TComponent* Owner)
    : TForm(Owner)
{
    const AnsiString currDir(ExtractFileDir(Application->ExeName));
    SetCurrentDir(currDir);
    AnsiString xmlFile(currDir);
    AnsiString xmlTransInFile(currDir);
    AnsiString xmlTransOutFile(currDir);
    xmlFile += "\\employee.xml";
    xmlTransInFile += "\\XMLToDpkt.xtr";
    xmlTransOutFile += "\\DpktToXml.xtr";
    XMLTransformProvider1->XMLDataFile = xmlFile;
    XMLTransformProvider1->TransformRead->TransformationFile =
        xmlTransInFile;
    XMLTransformProvider1->TransformWrite->TransformationFile =
        xmlTransOutFile;
}
//---------------------------------------------------------------------------
void __fastcall TForm1::OpenBtnClick(TObject *Sender)
{
    ClientDataSet1->Open();
}
//---------------------------------------------------------------------------
```

Part 2

```
void __fastcall TForm1::CloseBtnClick(TObject *Sender)
{
    ClientDataSet1->Close();
}
//-------------------------------------------------------------------------

void __fastcall TForm1::UpdateBtnClick(TObject *Sender)
{
    ClientDataSet1->ApplyUpdates(0);
}
//-------------------------------------------------------------------------

void __fastcall TForm1::ClientDataSet1ReconcileError(
        TCustomClientDataSet *DataSet, EReconcileError *E,
        TUpdateKind UpdateKind, TReconcileAction &Action)
{
    Action = HandleReconcileError(this, DataSet, UpdateKind, E);
}
//-------------------------------------------------------------------------

void __fastcall TForm1::CancelBtnClick(TObject *Sender)
{
    ClientDataSet1->CancelUpdates();
}
//-------------------------------------------------------------------------
```

The example is implemented in a very simple form to show you how to set the connections and make use of the XML transform provider.

Summary

Let me summarize what we discussed in this chapter. We started the chapter with a brief introduction to DataSnap applications, the different connection objects, and the connection broker, which centralizes the connections. We then continued our discussion on the remote data module and examined the typical contents of the implementation interface of the remote data module. Our discussion continued with IAppServer interface details and the different threading models supported by COM while building DataSnap applications.

We then focused our attention on the logic flow of control in a typical DataSnap application, including the sequence of events between the client and the server modules. Following this, we created the DataSnap server module and two client modules, one using the socket connection and the other using the DCOM connection; then we discussed the process of applying user updates to the dataset and reconciling the errors in case of exceptions thrown by the server.

We discussed the TInetXPageProducer component and created two web client applications, one using the WebBroker architecture, the other using the WebSnap architecture, and both connecting to the same server module.

The discussion continued on the XML transform provider component, and we built an example to see how the XML transform provider could replace the dataset provider in connecting to an XML document within the robust DataSnap architecture.

Part 2

## Chapter 10

Developing Distributed Applications (CORBA and TCP/IP)

Introduction

Developing distributed applications is not a simple task, particularly when the industry is posing challenges to the developer community and evolving every day with new technologies, platforms, and architectures. Therefore, it is necessary for the software vendors and the developer community to provide the industry with tools and technologies that protect the investment of the industry over a period of time, make the job of the programmers easy, and at the same time not compromise the quality of the product delivered to the industry. In the previous chapter we discussed Borland's proprietary architecture DataSnap that is built to run on the Windows-based Microsoft COM framework. In this chapter we will continue our discussion on distributed application development using the Common Object Request Broker Architecture (CORBA), and we will also focus our attention on the custom development of a middleware client-server model using simple TCP/IP sockets.

The CORBA framework emerged as a uniform, universal middleware architecture which enables systems across multiple platforms and multiple development environments to communicate with each other without difficulty. Borland has done tremendous work in providing CORBA services to the industry through its VisiBroker implementation, which has become a leading CORBA implementation. As most of you know, CORBA is an open specification and may be implemented to run on any platform. C++Builder supports CORBA development, among other Borland tools. In

385

this chapter we will first discuss the principles behind this technology and then focus our attention on Borland's VisiBroker-based applications. Since VisiBroker is compliant with OMG's CORBA specification, I will presume that our discussion in this chapter will also help you to a great extent in understanding other CORBA implementations. I will also presume that you have an installation of VisiBroker for your use to test the examples. If you do not have a VisiBroker installation, you can obtain an evaluation copy from Borland Corporation (which may be licensed for a short duration) for the purpose of testing the examples from this chapter.

CORBA Overview

In simple terms, CORBA is a specification designed and maintained by the Object Management Group (OMG) and developed over the standard Internet Inter-ORB Protocol (IIOP), which makes the objects developed on one specific hardware and software platform accessible by objects developed in other hardware and software platforms. This means that objects and their clients can be built in different programming languages, such as C, C++, Object Pascal, Java, COBOL, Python, Smalltalk, and so on, in different operating systems, such as Windows, UNIX, Linux, and so on, running on different hardware platforms. The traditional way of thinking that the CORBA server <u>must</u> be running on a server machine and is accessible by its clients running on the workstations is no longer true. The persistence of objects widened this concept so much that in today's scenario, the object that provides a specific service is the server object, which may be located anywhere on the network and is accessible by clients from anywhere within the network; a legacy mainframe application written in COBOL language may become the client of a CORBA object running on a workstation. Having said that, I will elaborate on a couple of points here. The term "network" is very loosely defined and is considered to be the local network of an enterprise in this context, since the local network is usually within the demilitarized zone (DMZ) and is expected to be more secure within the boundaries of a firewall; if we need to extend object accessibility beyond the firewall, it is still possible, but we need to ensure that our objects do not act as back doors for hackers into the internal network. In fact, the concept of web services is growing tremendously, which exposes objects to the external world. We dedicate our attention to web services in Chapter 11.

Again, CORBA is a framework, and this framework should be provided by a vendor since OMG provides only a specification of the framework. Borland's VisiBroker provides the complete implementation of the framework to develop CORBA server objects and clients; in addition, it provides some extensions. Therefore, throughout my discussion, I will be using the words CORBA and VisiBroker interchangeably.

I will now discuss the process of building CORBA objects and what happens when a client attempts to connect to a server object in terms of the VisiBroker framework; in the process, we will identify the individual components that make up the framework.

The CORBA Object Model

How are object interoperability and portability achieved in this heterogeneous world? Let's focus our attention on the concepts behind the CORBA object model. Most of us are familiar with the word "interface" in the object-oriented programming world (though the C++ language itself does not explicitly support interfaces). A very general definition of the term suggests that an interface is a contract that the object developer is signing with everyone who is going to use the object, which means the interface exposes its functionality in terms of method signatures without any implementation. In most programming languages, interfaces do not contain member variables. The CORBA interfaces are slightly different in the sense that they can contain member variables as part of the contract along with the methods that represent the object's services.

Since CORBA is language independent, the object's interface is defined in an Interface Definition Language (IDL) for which the OMG has defined a specification. This interface definition should then be compiled by a compiler that is language specific. This language-specific compiler compiles the single interface definition source file into two source program files, one for the object and the other for its client. For example, the idl2cpp compiler generates two sets of C++ source files (which can be used with C++Builder or any other C++ compiler). One set of files comprises the C++ class file for the stub (which is used by the client module) and the corresponding header file, and the other set of files comprises the C++ class file for the skeleton (which is used by the server object) and the corresponding header file. It is this stub and skeleton that perform the marshalling of data packets between the client and the server using the CORBA framework. The IDL compilers are usually developed and supported by vendors that provide an implementation of CORBA. In our example, it is Borland Corporation that implements CORBA through its VisiBroker product.

The *skeleton* forms the base class for the class that implements the server object; in other words, declare the object implementation class as a descendant of the skeleton class. The methods of the skeleton class are capable of

Part 2

interacting with the Object Request Broker (ORB) through the Basic Object Adapter (BOA) or the Portable Object Adapter (POA). The ORB and BOA (or POA) are a set of libraries belonging to the VisiBroker framework. We do not have to be concerned about how they have been implemented, as Borland implemented them to the OMG's specification. Once we build the server object and start the server, the object is registered with the VisiBroker smart agent known as *osagent*.

The stub provides the definitions of variables related to the object (and the associated classes) so that the client can access the object through these variables. The client never instantiates the server object. Rather, it obtains a reference to the object through the ORB. On the other hand, when the client attempts to obtain a reference of the object through the interface on behalf of the client, the ORB tries to locate an implementation of that interface through the smart agent. If the object is already registered with the smart agent and the ORB successfully establishes a connection to the object with the client, the ORB creates a proxy object and provides its reference to the client. There may be multiple smart agents running on the network, and multiple instances of the object may have been registered with more than one smart agent. The ORB accepts the response from the smart agent that responds first to the request. Once the client receives the object reference, it will be able to make requests to the server object or execute the server methods. We will examine the contents of the stub and skeleton in the sections that follow.

The Interface Definition Language

The Interface Definition Language (IDL) is a descriptive language in which we describe the interfaces that the object is going to implement. Earlier in the chapter, I mentioned that the interfaces are language independent, which means that the interface descriptions and the IDL specifications do not specify which programming language should be used to implement them. We are free to implement the interfaces in a programming language of our choice, provided there is an IDL compiler to create the stub and skeleton files from the interface description, and the programming language is capable of making use of these files to communicate with the CORBA framework libraries. Since this book is written for C++Builder programmers, I will always be describing the IDL to C++ mapping process. However, the IDL itself is designed after the C++ language; hence, you would find a lot of similarity between the two languages, though there are substantial differences too. Interfaces are stored in IDL files, which have the .idl extension. A single IDL file may contain multiple interface descriptions. Listing 10-1 displays a sample IDL file containing multiple interface descriptions. Listing 10-2 displays a sample IDL file containing multiple interfaces housed within a module description.

Listing 10-1: Sample IDL file with simple interfaces

```
interface employee {
    attribute string name;
    attribute string curr_project;
    attribute long emp_hours;
};
interface project {
    attribute string name;
    long total_hours();
    long emp_hours(in string emp_name);
};
```

Listing 10-2: Sample IDL file with module description

```
module Department {
    interface employee {
        attribute string name;
        attribute string curr_project;
        attribute long emp_hours;
    };
    interface project {
        attribute string name;
        long total_hours();
        long emp_hours(in string emp_name);
    };
};
```

Part 2

To make understanding IDL syntax easy, I would like to compare it with the C++ language. The *interface* keyword maps to the *class* keyword in C++. Since the module description contains the interfaces within itself, I will map the *module* keyword to a namespace or higher-level class in a hierarchy of nested classes; VisiBroker does the latter. Since CORBA interfaces can have member variables, the interface may define attributes in terms of member variables, which are identified by the *attribute* keyword. When you map to a C++ class, the attributes are like class variables and may represent the properties. A declaration that does not contain the keyword attribute is considered to be a method declaration. The IDL permits the string data type (as most of the current object-oriented languages do), which maps to a char* in C++. When you use string data types, you will have to make special method calls to allocate and deallocate memory to the strings, which we will discuss later in the chapter. The short, long, float, double, unsigned short, unsigned long, and char data types map to the corresponding data types with the same name in C++. For other data type mappings, you may check the VisiBroker manuals.

IDL to CPP Translation

The idl2cpp compiler translates the IDL file to the C++ class and header files to be used in building the server object and client applications. While building the client module, we just use the stub class file (and the corresponding header file) only, whereas while building the server object, we use both the stub and skeleton classes (and the corresponding header files). This is because the classes and variables defined in the stub file are used in the skeleton file. You should never modify the contents of the stub and skeleton files; they are generated and maintained by the idl2cpp compiler. Should you need to change the interface definition, the change should only be applied to the idl file, and the stub and skeleton should be regenerated. If you name the interface file intfile.idl, the skeleton file is named intfile_s.cpp (the corresponding header file is intfile_s.hh), and the stub file is named intfile_c.cpp (the corresponding header file is intfile_c.hh). In this section, we will examine the contents of these files, since they play the key role in transforming our application to a CORBA client-server application. We are doing this exercise only to acquire some knowledge of these files. Also, since we have to make use of these classes in our client and server modules, apart from that, we are not going to manually update these files for any reason.

The Stub File Classes

The <interface-name> Class

The stub file contains a class with the same name as the interface name. This class represents the object for which the interface is defined. For example, if you defined an interface employee, the stub contains the employee class. This class is derived from the CORBA::Object class (or CORBA_Object) and implements a number of generic methods in addition to the methods that represent your interface methods and attributes.

When the client application invokes the _bind() method, the ORB attempts to locate the object through the osagent and returns a pointer to the object; at this time, the reference count of the object is set to 1, indicating that currently one client is using the object reference. If the server module that is hosting the object is not started, if we registered the object implementation with the Object Activation Daemon (OAD), and if the OAD is running at the time the _bind() request is being handled by the ORB, the server application is automatically started, the object under reference is activated, a proxy object is created by the client-side ORB, and a reference to this proxy object is returned to the client. All these actions take place without the knowledge of the client. We can also use the naming service and interface to automatically activate the objects when a client invokes the _bind() method. We will discuss the OAD and the naming service later in the chapter. This is one of the generic methods implemented in all the stubs. Any method calls to the object should be performed only after the _bind() method and only through the reference to the client-side proxy object, which would be packaged and sent to the server by the client-side ORB; the server-side ORB unpacks the method call and recreates it within the address space of the server so that the server executes the method as if it executes a local method call.

The _nil() method may be called to obtain a nil object reference. A nil object reference is a NULL value that is cast to the object pointer. The _duplicate() method increments the reference count of the object and returns a pointer to the same object; incrementing the reference count means indicating that the object reference is going to be used by another client, and therefore the object should not be destroyed until that reference is also released. The reference obtained by calling the _duplicate() method may be passed to another client application. The method takes a single parameter, which is the object pointer. The _ref_count() method returns the current reference count of the object. The release() method decrements the reference count of the object and releases the object reference. Once the object reference count becomes 0, VisiBroker automatically deletes the object and its reference. The this() method returns a pointer to the current object. The _clone() method creates an exact copy of the entire object's state and establishes a new separate connection to the object. This method takes a single parameter, which is a pointer to the object.

Since this class is derived from the CORBA_Object class in addition to the methods implemented in the stub class, you may also call the CORBA_Object methods, such as _interface_name() to obtain the interface name of the object, boa() to obtain a pointer to the Basic Object Adapter (BOA), desc() to obtain the object type information as a pointer to the CORBA::TypeInfo object, the _object_name() method to return the object name, and the _repository_id() method to return the repository ID corresponding to the object. The _is_local() method returns a CORBA::Boolean value of true (1) if the object implementation is in the same process where the method is invoked and false (0) if not. Similarly, the _is_remote() method returns true if the object implementation is on a remote server and false if not.

A pointer to the object is created by the name <interface-name>_ptr, and a reference type is defined by the name <interface-name>Ref, which is a typedef equivalent to the pointer type. For the employee interface, these definitions are employee_ptr and employeeRef, respectively.

Part 2

Object Reference Widening and Narrowing

A CORBA object hierarchy is nothing but a C++ class hierarchy. The interface object is inherited from the CORBA::Object. We discussed the concept of upcasting and downcasting an object pointer in a class hierarchy in Chapter 2. Widening a CORBA object reference is the same as upcasting, and narrowing is the opposite process, which is downcasting. Widening is permitted on all CORBA objects by default because casting an object up in the hierarchy is legal in object-oriented programming. Narrowing is permitted only if the object is really of the type to which it is narrowing. The _narrow(object_ptr _ptr) method narrows the argument object and returns the downcast pointer. If the downcast was not permitted, the result of this method call would be a nil reference. If the _narrow() method is successful in downcasting the object reference, it constructs a new object and returns its reference. After we are done using the reference, we should release the object reference.

The <interface-name>_var Class

Another class that the IDL compiler generates in the stub file is named <interface-name>_var. If your interface name is employee, this class is named employee_var. This class is derived from the CORBA::_var class. It automatically manages the memory associated with the dynamically allocated object reference, and this may be used in place of the <interface-name>_ptr variable. A _var type can be constructed using a _ptr type variable, by assigning a _ptr type variable, or through another _var type object. In short, this class functions like a smart pointer.

The Skeleton Classes

The classes generated by the IDL compiler for the server object are saved in the skeleton file. The skeleton classes use definitions made in the stub file, and the skeleton header file includes the stub header file. Therefore, while compiling the server object, you should include both the stub and skeleton files in the project, whereas while compiling the client module, you need to include just the stub file in the project.

The POA_<interface-name> Class

This is an abstract base class generated by the IDL compiler from which the object skeleton class is derived. The methods representing the operations on the object are defined as well as the methods to set and get values for the attributes. This class is derived from a servant class, PortableServer_ServantBase, which provides the necessary methods to receive and interpret client requests on server object operations.

The _sk_<interface-name> Class

This is the object skeleton class derived from the POA_<interface-name> class and a base servant class PortableServer_RefCountServantBase. This class serves as the immediate ancestor for the object implementation that we provide in the server application. Also, it implements the object reference counting methods.

The CORBA Server Application

Similar to the way a COM server hosts COM objects, a CORBA server application is required to host a CORBA object. It may be a console application or a Win32 application. In this section, we will see how to build a CORBA server application. Figure 10-1 displays the Multitier page in the New Items dialog. Note that we will be using the first four icons in this chapter while building the CORBA servers and clients. A CORBA server project is created by selecting the CORBA Server icon and clicking the OK button.

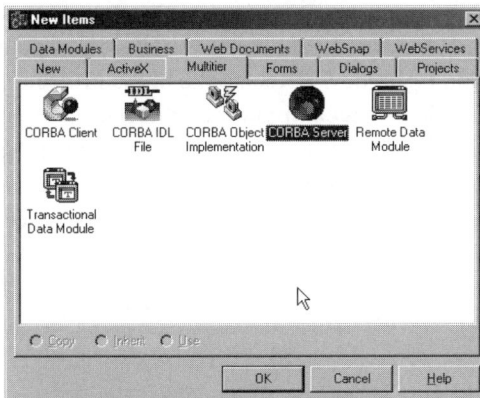

Figure 10-1: The Multitier page in the New Items dialog

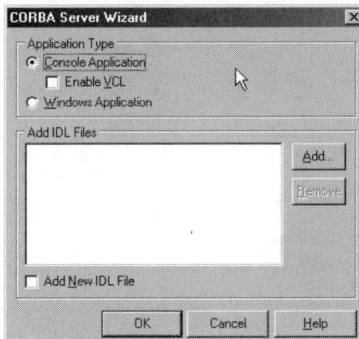

Then the CORBA Server Wizard appears, as displayed in Figure 10-2. This is a simple wizard, where you specify whether you would like to build a console application or a Windows application to host your CORBA objects. Accordingly, the wizard creates the project files and includes the necessary header files. At this point, I would like to mention that C++Builder 6 makes it very easy to build CORBA implementations by creating all the necessary framework in your project and program files, as outlined by the VisiBroker architecture. You have to implement the operations on your object as you specify in the interface. Similarly, building the CORBA clients is very easy; you incorporate object calls into your client application. Listing 10-3 displays a simple application source file generated by the CORBA Server Wizard when you choose the Console Application option. From the source listing, you may notice that the default ORB adapter used by the wizard is the Basic Object Adapter (BOA), which was used prior to the CORBA 2.3 specification. VisiBroker 4.5 is CORBA 2.3 compliant and can let you build applications that use the Portable Object Adapter (POA), which replaced the BOA. However, BOA support is provided in VisiBroker 4.5 for backward compatibility. In order to allow smooth transition for users of earlier versions of VisiBroker, the wizard generates the BOA-compliant server by default. Also, if you open the CORBA page in the Project Options dialog, you will see additional compilation option -boa in the Addition IDL options category, as shown in Figure 10-3. To use POA in place of BOA, we have to remove this compilation option and manually edit the code generated by the project wizard, which is discussed in a later section.

Listing 10-3: Sample CORBA server application

```
//--------------------------------------------------------------------------

#include <corbapch.h>
#pragma hdrstop

//--------------------------------------------------------------------------

#include <corba.h>
#include <condefs.h>
#pragma argsused
main(int argc, char* argv[])
{
        try
        {
                // Initialize the ORB and BOA
                CORBA::ORB_var orb = CORBA::ORB_init(argc, argv);
                CORBA::BOA_var boa = orb->BOA_init(argc, argv);
                // Wait for incoming requests
                boa->impl_is_ready();
        }
        catch(const CORBA::Exception& e)
        {
```

```
                Cerr << e << endl;
                return(1);
        }
        return 0;
}
//-----------------------------------------------------------------------
```

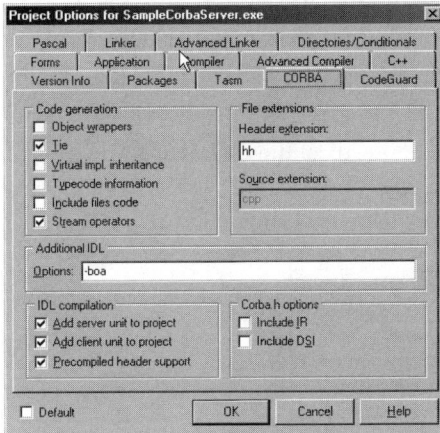

Figure 10-3: Project Options dialog CORBA page

From Listing 10-3, we see that the server initializes the ORB first and then initializes the BOA. For every CORBA server, the ORB and object adapter (BOA or POA) must be initialized before we run the server. The method call boa→impl_is_ready() enables the BOA to listen for client calls. Therefore, we must initialize our objects before this statement.

We will now continue our discussion on creating a CORBA server and client applications. Listing 10-4 describes the simple IDL file that we are going to use in our application. In this file, I defined an interface having three attributes and one operation. Two of the attributes represent the minimum and maximum values within which the server object generates a random number. These values are long integers. The third attribute represents the user name as entered by the user of the client module and is a string variable.

Listing 10-4: RandInterface.idl

```
interface randNumber {
        // name of the visitor (user of client module)
        attribute string visitorName;
        // random number range lower limit
        attribute long randMin;
        // random number range upper limit
        attribute long randMax;
        // get the random number within
        // the lower and upper limits
        long getRandNbr();
};
```

Now let's create the server application following the steps outlined earlier. I saved the server application files as SimpleCorbaServer.bpr for the project and SimpleCorbaServer.cpp for the program.

1. Assign the IDL file to the project.

2. In the project manager view, right-click on the **IDL** file and choose **Compile**. The stub and skeleton files are generated. The project creates BOA-based code by default. Let's leave it like that for this example.

3. Let's now add the server object implementation. In the New Items dialog, go to the Multitier page, and select the **CORBA Object Implementation** icon. Click the **OK** button. The CORBA Object Implementation Wizard is displayed, as shown in Figure 10-4.

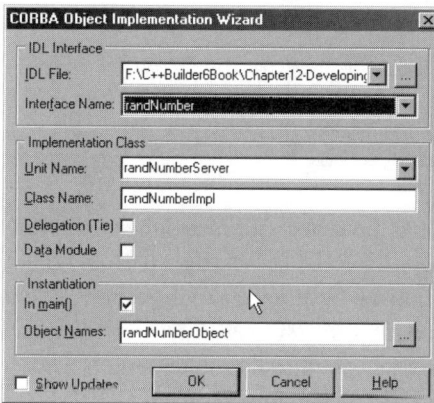

Figure 10-4: The CORBA Object Implementation Wizard

In the wizard, you will see three sections: the IDL Interface section, where you will choose the IDL file and the interface name from within the IDL file for which you are going to implement the object; the Implementation Class section, where you will enter the unit name and class name for the object; and the Instantiation section, where you will enter the object name that you will refer to in the program. Once you choose the interface name in the first section, the list of interfaces defined in the IDL file are shown in the drop-down list (the first item in the list being the default interface), where you can choose the specific interface name for which you are writing the object implementation. Once you choose the specific interface name from the list, the wizard automatically fills the unit file name (appending the word Server to the interface name), the object class name (appending the word Impl to the interface name), and the object name (appending the word Object to the interface name). You can change these names if you wish to do so. I am leaving the default names as they are. Click the OK button at the end to make the new unit file part of the project.

If you examine the generated source file for the object implementation, you will notice that the wizard automatically generates the constructor, the operations defined in the interface, and the getter and setter methods for the attributes, all as empty methods. You will also notice that the implementation class is derived from the _sk_randNumber class, which was generated in the skeleton file by the IDL compiler. Finally, the wizard also fills the code to instantiate the object in the main() function in the server application cpp file. At every point during the development cycle, you will notice that the C++Builder 6 wizards generate a lot of VisiBroker-compatible code for you automatically. Now let's fill the empty methods so that our object really does something when requested by the clients. After filling all the methods with appropriate code, the program looks as displayed in Listing 10-5.

Listing 10-5: randNumberServer.cpp

```cpp
//-------------------------------------------------------------------------
#include <vcl.h>
#include <math.hpp>
#pragma hdrstop

#include <corba.h>
#include "randNumberServer.h"
//-------------------------------------------------------------------------
#pragma package(smart_init)
randNumberImpl::randNumberImpl(const char *object_name):
        _sk_randNumber(object_name)
{
    // Initialize the random number generator
    Randomize();
    // set default frandMin and frandMax values
    fRandMin = 0;
    fRandMax = 10;
}


char* randNumberImpl::visitorName()
{
    if (fVisitorName != NULL)
        return fVisitorName.c_str();
    else
        return NULL;
}


CORBA::Long randNumberImpl::getRandNbr()
{
    return RandomRange(fRandMin, fRandMax);
}


CORBA::Long randNumberImpl::randMax()
{
    return fRandMax;
}


CORBA::Long randNumberImpl::randMin()
{
```

```
    return fRandMin;
}

void randNumberImpl::randMax(CORBA::Long _randMax)
{
    fRandMax = _randMax;
}

void randNumberImpl::randMin(CORBA::Long _randMin)
{
    fRandMin = _randMin;
}

void randNumberImpl::visitorName(const char* _visitorName)
{
    AnsiString fTempStr(_visitorName);
    fVisitorName = fTempStr;
//    CORBA::string_free(const_cast<char*>(_visitorName));
}
```

As you will notice in the program listing, I created the application to demonstrate using the VCL non-visual objects in a CORBA application and included the math.hpp header file to make use of the VCL implementation of the random number generation functions. The attributes defined in the IDL file have enabled the IDL compiler and the CORBA Server Wizard to create appropriate access methods, but if we need to save these attribute values as properties of the object, we need to have corresponding variables defined in the object implementation class. I defined three variables under the protected section of the class definition as you will see in Listing 10-6, the header file for the object implementation class. In the constructor, I initialized the random number generator and the lower and upper limit to be used in the random number generation function.

Listing 10-6: randNumberServer.h

```
//------------------------------------------------------------------------

#ifndef randNumberServerH
#define randNumberServerH
#include "RandInterface_s.hh"
//------------------------------------------------------------------------
class randNumberImpl: public _sk_randNumber
{
protected:
        AnsiString fVisitorName;
        long fRandMin;
        long fRandMax;
public:
        randNumberImpl(const char *object_name=NULL);
        char* visitorName();
        CORBA::Long getRandNbr();
        CORBA::Long randMax();
```

```
        CORBA::Long randMin();
        void randMax(CORBA::Long _randMax);
        void randMin(CORBA::Long _randMin);
        void visitorName(const char* _visitorName);
};
#endif
```

The CORBA Client Application

Now let's continue with creating a client application that can make use of this object. Compared to the server object implementation, we have very little to do for the client to use the CORBA objects. The main task is to obtain the object reference through the _bind() method call and then access the methods as we normally do for any standard VCL object. However, you have to keep in mind that the return value types from the method calls are compliant with standard ANSI C++ style data types, not the VCL types. This is because the stub and skeleton files generated by the IDL compiler are compliant with the ANSI C++ language and not just specific to C++Builder or VCL. The same reasoning is valid while writing the object implementation; if we intend to make the object implementation VCL compliant, we need to do the conversion of VCL data types to C++ data types (as used in the stub and skeleton files), so our object can make use of the advanced VCL objects without compromising the ability to implement the CORBA interface.

I implemented the client application by choosing the CORBA Client icon in the Multitier page of the New Items dialog and clicking the OK button. The CORBA Client Wizard is displayed and looks like Figure 10-5. The default project is of Windows Application type. Click OK to accept the default settings.

Part 2

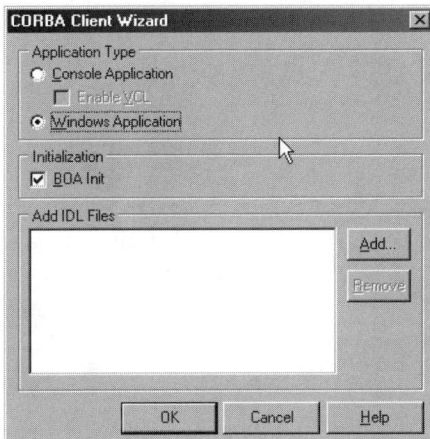

Figure 10-5: The CORBA Client Wizard

For the most part, this is a VCL-based Windows application. I provided a few edit boxes and buttons to set the random number range lower and upper limit values, as well as enter the user name, and set these values through the object's setter methods. I provided a few label components to display the greeting message if the user entered a name and to display the random number obtained from the server object. I also provided a list box to display system messages or messages trapped in the catch blocks and a help button to display some help text in a separate window. The client form looks like Figure 10-6. Listing 10-7 displays the client application program source.

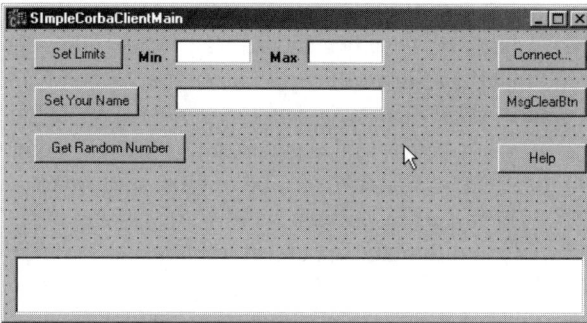

Figure 10-6: The Client application main form

Listing 10-7: SimpleCorbaClientForm.cpp

```cpp
//--------------------------------------------------------------------------------

#include <vcl.h>
#pragma hdrstop

#include "SimpleCorbaClientForm.h"
#include "HelpFormUnit.h"
//--------------------------------------------------------------------------------
#pragma package(smart_init)
#pragma resource "*.dfm"
TSImpleCorbaClientMain *SImpleCorbaClientMain;
//--------------------------------------------------------------------------------
__fastcall TSImpleCorbaClientMain::TSImpleCorbaClientMain(TComponent* Owner)
        : TForm(Owner)
{
}
//--------------------------------------------------------------------------------
void __fastcall TSImpleCorbaClientMain::GetRandNbrBtnClick(TObject *Sender)
{
    AnsiString fYourName(rnVar->visitorName());
    long newRandNbr = rnVar->getRandNbr();
    if (fYourName != "") {
        hellowLabel->Caption = "Hello " + fYourName;
    }
    long randLowerLimit = rnVar->randMin();
    long randUpperLimit = rnVar->randMax();
    AnsiString Limits("( between ");
```

```
    Limits += IntToStr(randLowerLimit);
    Limits += " and ";
    Limits += IntToStr(randUpperLimit);
    Limits += " )";

    AnsiString randLabel("The random number ");
    randLabel += Limits;
    randLabel += " is ";
    randLabel += IntToStr(newRandNbr);
    rnLabel->Caption = randLabel;
}
//---------------------------------------------------------------------------
void __fastcall TSImpleCorbaClientMain::SetLimitBtnClick(TObject *Sender)
{
    try {
        AnsiString fLowerLimit(MinValue->Text);
        AnsiString fUpperLimit(MaxValue->Text);
        if (fLowerLimit == "")
            return;
        if (fUpperLimit == "")
            return;
        long frandLower = StrToInt(fLowerLimit);
        long frandUpper = StrToInt(fUpperLimit);
        if (frandUpper <= frandLower) {
            MsgList->Items->Add("Error - Range upper value must be higher than lower
                                value !");
            return;
        }
        // Calls to the CORBA server object methods
        rnVar->randMin(frandLower);
        rnVar->randMax(frandUpper);
    }
    catch (Exception &e) {
        MsgList->Items->Add(e.Message);
    }
}
//---------------------------------------------------------------------------
void __fastcall TSImpleCorbaClientMain::SetNameBtnClick(TObject *Sender)
{
    try {
        AnsiString yourName(VisitorName->Text);
        if (yourName == "")
            return;
        rnVar->visitorName(yourName.c_str());
    }
    catch (Exception &e) {
        MsgList->Items->Add(e.Message);
    }
}
//---------------------------------------------------------------------------
void __fastcall TSImpleCorbaClientMain::MsgClearBtnClick(TObject *Sender)
{
    MsgList->Items->Clear();
}
//---------------------------------------------------------------------------
void __fastcall TSImpleCorbaClientMain::FormActivate(TObject *Sender)
```

Part 2

```
{
    try {
        rnVar = randNumber::_bind(NULL);
        MsgList->Items->Add("Connected to the server");
    }
    catch (Exception &e) {
        MsgList->Items->Add(e.Message);
    }
}
//-----------------------------------------------------------------------

void __fastcall TSImpleCorbaClientMain::ConnectBtnClick(TObject *Sender)
{
    try {
        rnVar = randNumber::_bind(NULL);
        MsgList->Items->Add("Connected to the server");
    }
    catch (Exception &e) {
        MsgList->Items->Add(e.Message);
    }
}
//-----------------------------------------------------------------------

void __fastcall TSImpleCorbaClientMain::HelpBtnClick(TObject *Sender)
{
    HelpForm->ShowModal();
}
//-----------------------------------------------------------------------
```

This is not a pretty application implementing enterprise-level features, but I believe this application would certainly help someone understand the process of creating simple CORBA applications and kick-start the thought process. If that happens to the reader, I will be satisfied that I am successful in this attempt. From here, let's move on to the Portable Object Adapter and examine how to implement the POA architecture into your VisiBroker applications.

The Portable Object Adapter

The Portable Object Adapter (POA) is a piece of software that forms part of the server-side ORB. It is responsible for activating and deactivating the servants. A servant includes system resources such as CPU and memory allocated for an object. When an object is idle, the resources may be deallocated, and when the object is accessed (by a client), the resources are reallocated. This resource allocation and deallocation are termed *activation* and *deactivation* of the objects. When an object is deactivated, its state is preserved to persistent storage and retrieved again while activating the object. All this is done by the POA and is transparent to the client. A CORBA implementation like VisiBroker provides all this functionality internally and is transparent to the client.

The POA features can be customized by properly setting the POA policies. A POA is characterized by a set of policies. A *policy* is an object that controls the behavior of the associated POA and the objects that the POA manages. The policies are set programmatically when the POA is created, and remain unchanged for the lifetime of the POA. If we do not set any policies explicitly when a POA is created, the default values for all the policies are set automatically. An application can have more than one POA, and each POA may have its own set of policies. The default POA is the rootPOA, and all other POAs form children within the hierarchy originated from rootPOA. In short, POA policies are rules by which the POA functionality can be customized, per our application needs. The POA policies govern features such as the object threading model, object lifespan, object ID assignment, servant retention, implicit activation, and so on. Also, all the objects managed by a specific POA are governed by the policies set for that POA while creating the POA object.

The *object threading policy* may have a value of ORB_CTRL_MODEL, which means that the POA is responsible for assigning requests to the threads in the (default) multi-threading model, or it may have a value of SINGLE_THREAD_MODEL, which means the object requests are handled sequentially.

The *lifespan policy* guides how the object's lifespan is managed by the POA. The permitted values are TRANSIENT or PERSISTENT. The transient object references become invalid when the POA is deactivated or the server goes down. On the other hand, the persistent objects outlive the process in which they were created, since they make use of the complete ORB capabilities to persist across server restarts. The default value for this policy is that the objects are transient.

The *servant retention policy* indicates whether the servant should be deactivated after completing an object invocation, as identified by the NON_RETAIN value. If the RETAIN value is set (the default value), the servant is not deactivated after an object invocation is complete.

The *object ID assignment policy* indicates how the objects' IDs are assigned. The value of USER_ID for this policy indicates that the application assigns the IDs to the object programmatically. If we set this to SYSTEM_ID, the POA assigns the object IDs.

The *object ID uniqueness policy* indicates whether the servant will be shared by multiple objects. The possible values to this policy are UNIQUE_ID, which means that a servant supports only one object, and MULTIPLE_ID, which means that a servant can support multiple objects.

The *bind support policy* is a policy specific to VisiBroker. It controls the registration of POAs and the objects with the osagent. A POA alone may be

Part 2

registered with the osagent, and a client may include the POA name and the object ID in the bind request so that the osagent will easily forward the request. A value of BY_INSTANCE indicates that all the objects are automatically registered with the osagent. This value must be used along with the PERSISTENT and RETAIN policies. When the value is BY_POA, it means that only POAs are registered with the osagent. This is the default value and must be used along with the PERSISTENT policy. A value of NONE indicates that neither the POAs nor the objects are registered with the osagent.

There are more POA policies than discussed here, and I would recommend that you refer to the VisiBroker documentation.

We will now modify our earlier example, which was built to use BOA, so that the client and server communicate through the POA. To successfully convert a BOA-based server to a POA-based server, we need to perform the following steps.

1. Instead of initializing the BOA, we should now obtain a reference to the rootPOA. The resolve_initial_references() method with a string argument value "RootPOA" on the ORB object returns a reference to the CORBA object, which should be narrowed (downcast) to get the rootPOA reference.

   Set the appropriate POA policies to be used while creating the child POA. This is done by creating an array of policies and setting appropriate values to them.

2. Obtain a reference to the POA manager from the rootPOA. This is done by executing the the_POAManager() method on the rootPOA object.

3. Create the child POA with the policies array created above. This is done by executing the create_POA() method on the rootPOA object. This method takes three arguments: a name to the child POA, the reference to the POA manager object, and the policies array for the child POA.

4. Create an instance of the implementation object. This object acts as the servant object for the child POA.

5. Provide an ID to the servant object. This is a two-step process: First obtain an object ID reference by invoking the string_to_objectId() method on the portable server object, which takes a single argument, the object name; then activate the servant object with the object ID on the child POA.

6. Activate the POA manager by executing the activate() method on the POA manager object.

7. Finally, execute the run() method on the ORB object. This will wait for client requests to be processed by the child POA.

The modified server application, with the POA-related code, is displayed in Listing 10-8.

Listing 10-8: CorbaPoaApplication\SimpleCorbaServer.cpp

```
//------------------------------------------------------------------------------

#include <vcl.h>
#pragma hdrstop

//------------------------------------------------------------------------------

#include "randNumberServer.h"

#include <corba.h>
#pragma argsused
main(int argc, char* argv[])
{
    try
    {
        // Initialize the ORB
        CORBA::ORB_var orb = CORBA::ORB_init(argc, argv);
        // Obtain a reference to rootPOA. First we get a reference to the
        // CORBA object. Then we should narrow it to get the rootPOA reference.
        CORBA::Object_var obj = orb->resolve_initial_references("RootPOA");
        PortableServer::POA_var rootPOA = PortableServer::POA::_narrow(obj);

        // Create an array of policies. Each element in the array takes a
        // single policy definition. The array is zero-based.
        CORBA::PolicyList policies;
        policies.length(1);
        policies[(CORBA::ULong)0] = rootPOA->create_lifespan_policy(
                        PortableServer::PERSISTENT);

        // get the POA Manager from the rootPOA.
        PortableServer::POAManager_var poa_manager = rootPOA->the_POAManager();

        // Create randNbrPOA with the right policies. This is the child POA
        // under the rootPOA. To create the child POA, give a name, POA manager,
        // and the policies array.
        PortableServer::POA_var randNbrPOA = rootPOA->create_POA("rand_number_poa",
            poa_manager, policies);

        // The implementation object is the servant object for the child POA.
        randNumberImpl randNumberServant;

        // Provide an ID for the servant object. This is a two-step process.
        // 1. Obtain an ID from the object name string.
        PortableServer::ObjectId_var randNbrObjId =
            PortableServer::string_to_ObjectId("randNumberObject");
        // 2. Activate the servant object with the object ID on the randNbrPOA
        randNbrPOA->activate_object_with_id(randNbrObjId, &randNumberServant);
```

Part 2

```
        // Activate the POA Manager
        poa_manager->activate();

        // Wait for incoming requests
        orb->run();
    }
    catch(const CORBA::Exception& e)
    {
        Cerr << e << endl;
        return(1);
    }
    return 0;
}
//----------------------------------------------------------------
```

When the server application uses POA in place of BOA, we need to modify the client application to use the object through the child POA that receives the client requests. The changes on the client side are very minimal. Just initialize the ORB in the program main function (for a console application) or the WinMain function (for a Windows application); obtain the object ID using the object name and executing the string_to_objectId() method on the portable server object; and execute the _bind() method with two arguments: the child POA name and the object ID obtained in the previous step. These steps may be executed all in the main function or another appropriate method (as we did in the FormActivate event handler), as appropriate to your application, but they must be executed to get the object reference before you try to execute the operations on the object. Listing 10-9 displays the WinMain function where I initialized the ORB, and Listing 10-10 displays the FormActivate event handler where I implemented the remaining steps.

Listing 10-9: CorbaPoaApplication\SimpleCorbaClient.cpp—WinMain function

```
//----------------------------------------------------------------

#include <vcl.h>
#pragma hdrstop
//----------------------------------------------------------------
#include <corba.h>
USEFORM("SimpleCorbaClientForm.cpp", SImpleCorbaClientMain);
USEFORM("HelpFormUnit.cpp", HelpForm);
//----------------------------------------------------------------
WINAPI WinMain(HINSTANCE, HINSTANCE, LPSTR, int)
{
    try
    {

        Application->Initialize();
        // Initialize the ORB
        CORBA::ORB_var orb = CORBA::ORB_init(__argc, __argv);

        Application->CreateForm(__classid(TSImpleCorbaClientMain),
```

```
                                    &SImpleCorbaClientMain);
        Application->CreateForm(__classid(THelpForm), &HelpForm);
        Application->Run();
    }
    catch (Exception &exception)
    {
        Application->ShowException(&exception);
    }
    catch ()
    {
        try
        {
            throw Exception("");
        }
        catch (Exception &exception)
        {
            Application->ShowException(&exception);
        }
    }
    return 0;
}
//-------------------------------------------------------------------------
```

Listing 10-10: CorbaPoaApplication\SimpleCorbaClientForm.cpp—FormActivate event handler

```
//-------------------------------------------------------------------------
void __fastcall TSImpleCorbaClientMain::FormActivate(TObject *Sender)
{
    try {
        // Get the object id (randNumberId)
        PortableServer::ObjectId_var randObjId =
            PortableServer::string_to_ObjectId("randNumberObject");

        // bind the object id with the object name to get the object reference
        rnVar = randNumber::_bind("/rand_number_poa", randObjId);
        MsgList->Items->Add("Connected to the server through POA");
    }
    catch (Exception &e) {
        MsgList->Items->Add(e.Message);
    }
}
//-------------------------------------------------------------------------
```

Part 2

The Interface Repository

An interface repository is like a database of interface definitions and is useful for access by the client applications. If the client has an object reference, it can retrieve the corresponding interface from the interface repository. The information that the client application can obtain from the repository is similar to the interface descriptions stored in the IDL files, but it is stored in the form of object hierarchies so that the client application can access it during run time. An interface repository may contain ModuleDef objects, InterfaceDef objects, and OperationDef objects, which store information about modules, interfaces within modules, and operations on the interfaces, respectively. The information is stored in terms of objects so that by making method calls on these repository objects, we can obtain the information we are interested in.

If you have worked with version control tools, you may be familiar with repositories. Repositories are like databases and can be accessed programmatically to store and retrieve information belonging to the repository. A typical programming environment may provide you with the ability to maintain multiple repositories of source code that you are building in your organization. You might build a repository during the development phase, a different repository during the testing phase that contains different versions of the programs, and yet another repository deployed to the production environment, which contains the production-release binaries, and so on. I am giving this analogy to give you the idea that you may build and maintain any number of repositories (containing any set and version of its members) as your business requirements demand. You may use VisiBroker tools, or you may want to build your own custom tools to maintain these interface repositories. For more information on interface repositories, please refer to the VisiBroker documentation.

The Object Activation Daemon (OAD)

The Object Activation Daemon (OAD) is the implementation repository service provided by VisiBroker. Objects registered with the OAD service may be activated automatically when a client request is received for an object. The OAD provides the run-time repository of information on the classes and the objects supported by a server. Any client that supports the standard IIOP protocol can activate the server objects through the OAD. The oadutil program is used to register or unregister object implementations with the OAD or list already registered object implementations. The OAD itself may be started by running the oad program at the command prompt. For more information on the OAD, please refer to the VisiBroker documentation.

The Naming Service

The naming service associates (or binds) a name to an object within a namespace. The naming service helps the clients access the objects through the names identified in the namespace. The osagent associates a name to the object through the interface definition, and every time you change the interface name, you have to recompile your application to make sure that the osagent takes the new name. Also, the osagent can bind only one name to an object. But by using the naming service, you can define one or more logical names to objects and bind the objects during run time. Object names defined within a naming service are hierarchical data structures rather than simple strings; however, we can convert these logical names to equivalent string values. The NamingContext object is used by the object implementations to bind a logical name to the object. The NamingContextExt interface must be used to use logical names of objects converted to strings. For more information on the VisiBroker naming service, please refer to the VisiBroker documentation.

CORBA development itself deserves exclusive attention and is not the main focus of this book. In this chapter, I introduced you to the process of building CORBA applications using the Borland C++Builder 6 and Visi-Broker tools. VisiBroker offers a lot more than what we discussed in this chapter, and if you are a serious developer interested in CORBA development, I would recommend going through the VisiBroker manuals for further information.

Simple TCP/IP Applications

TCP/IP has established itself as the defacto standard protocol for the majority of client-server applications and has also become the lower-level protocol for several other popular high-level protocols, including HTTP, SOAP, IIOP, DCOM, and so on. These other protocols actually formulate a layer above the TCP/IP protocol, whereas TCP/IP itself focuses on packaging the data and sending it across the network to the receiving end. In this section, we will pay some attention to how to build custom distributed applications, without using any of the standard high-level protocols we have been discussing so far.

For TCP/IP to serve as the base communication protocol, both the server computer and the client computer must be running the TCP/IP software, as provided by many operating systems today such as Windows, UNIX, Linux, and so on. TCP/IP applications use the mechanism of sockets.

Simple TCP/IP Protocol

Developing TCP/IP applications using C++Builder is very easy, since almost every type of protocol or service is supported by the robust VCL architecture and its components. For example, we have VCL components to develop almost any type of TCP/IP-based applications, such as socket-based servers, clients, HTTP applications, FTP, NNTP, POP3 applications, and so on. Typically, a TCP/IP server application provides a specific service, either one of the standard services or you may build your own service. A service is identified by a port number on the operating system. The port number may be considered a numeric identification of a service name. The service names to port numbers mapping is saved in a services file stored in a specific location on the operating system. On Windows-based operating systems, it is usually the \drivers\etc directory under the Windows System32 directory, whereas on UNIX-based operating systems, it is the /etc directory. If we are building a custom service in our application, we must enter an entry into the services file mapping the service name to the port number. We can use our own port numbers. But we should not use the port numbers used by the standard service names, such as ftp, telnet, smtp, and so on.

Building our own custom service means establishing an application-level protocol between the client and server modules. In simple terms, the client should understand and interpret the message sent by the server, and the server should, in turn, interpret correctly what the client is communicating. This may even be considered as specifying the rules by which the client and server communicate with each other to the extent of interpreting each individual byte received from the sender. This is all we have to implement. The rest is taken care of by the VCL-based TCP/IP socket components, which package the message and send it to the recipient on the other end. In this section, we first examine the flow of logic between the client and server and then discuss an example application where we build a custom server and its client module.

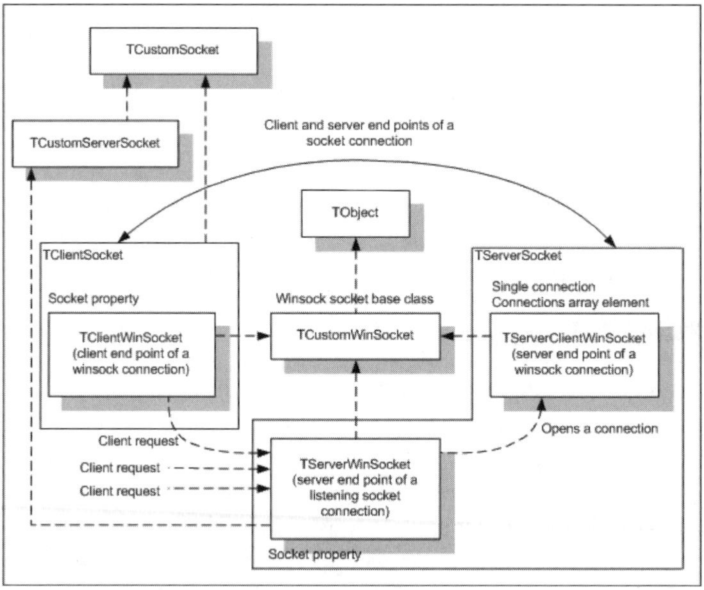

Figure 10-7: VCL socket components and their interactions

On Windows-based operating systems, the Winsock library provides the Microsoft implementation of the TCP/IP sockets. Since C++Builder is a Windows-based development tool, the VCL components are designed to hide the complexity of using the Winsock library and provide us with a very simple event-based socket model. All through our discussion, we have been noticing that the Borland VCL components are really cool tools, and the socket components are no exception to that fact.

Figure 10-7 on the previous page displays the typical VCL components that we use in building socket-based TCP/IP applications and their interactions.

There are two types of VCL objects that implement sockets. One type is a set of non-visual objects derived from TObject directly that implements the Winsock functionality. The base class in this hierarchy is the TCustom-WinSocket. There are three main descendants from this base class that participate in maintaining socket connection end points and perform the actual task of sending and receiving the data packets. These are the TClientWinSocket object, which represents the client end point of a client-server connection, the TServerWinSocket object, which represents the listening end point on the server side, and the TServerClientWinSocket, which represents the server end point of a client-server connection.

The second type is a set of non-visual components derived from TComponent that provides user access through the Component Palette. The TCustomSocket forms the base class for this type of object. The TClientSocket component is directly derived from the TCustomSocket and publishes all the properties, methods, and events relevant to a client connection. A server socket has to implement additional functionality, such as the ability to differentiate a listening connection from an actual server connection and accept and maintain connections from multiple clients. Therefore, these additional features are implemented in the TCustomServerSocket, which is the direct descendant of the TCustomSocket. Now the TServer-Socket component is derived from the TCustomServerSocket and publishes all the necessary properties, methods, and events for a server connection.

The Socket property of the TClientSocket component is an object of the TClientWinSocket class, and the Socket property of the TServerSocket component is an object of TServerWinSocket. The Connections property of the TServerWinSocket (the listening socket) represents an array of TServerClientWinSocket objects (in other words, the set of server-side end points of client connections).

Part 2

Blocking and Non-blocking Connections

The connection that we wish to establish between the client and server may be of one or two types: a blocking connection or a non-blocking connection. A blocking connection, as its name suggests, blocks the application when a read/write operation occurs on the socket port and releases the application only after the read/write is complete or cancelled. This is not usually a preferred or recommended method because the application's normal flow is interrupted every time a socket read/write occurs. However, if you have to use blocking type socket connections, it is recommended to spawn a separate thread to perform the blocked read/write operation, so the normal flow is performed in the main thread of the application. The socket read/write over a blocking connection is also called a synchronous read/write operation.

On the contrary, a non-blocking type connection performs asynchronous read/write, which means that the normal flow of the application is not interrupted or blocked due to a socket operation. The socket awakes every time a read/write occurs and performs the operation without impacting the program's normal flow.

How Do Clients Establish a Connection with the Server?

Let's now examine the sequence of events that take place when a client tries to establish a connection with the server. A server's service is published through the services definition file on the client's operating system. The client application uses the TClientSocket component, and the server application uses the TServerSocket component.

The server's Service, or Port, property is set to the appropriate value in the server module. Also set the ServerType property to stNonBlocking (to indicate a non-blocking connection) or stThreadBlocking (to indicate a blocking type connection). When the server application is started, the Active property of the server socket object must be set to true, which means that we are opening the server connection to listen to the client's requests. Opening a server socket only means that the server's Socket (as identified by the TServerWinSocket object) is ready to listen to the client's requests; however, the TServerWinSocket object does not perform the actual read/write operation.

When a client request is received by the server's Socket object, it opens a new connection (as identified by the TServerClientWinSocket object) if the request is accepted and then passes the connection's properties to the client. The client then updates its own properties, which reflect the server-side end point of the connection and completes the connection. Once the connection is established, the server's Socket object is not concerned about the server-side connection object, except when we explicitly attempt to access the object through the Connections array of the Socket object either to forcibly terminate the server connection or for any other purpose or when the client itself terminates the connection after it is done with its task.

It is the server-side connection object (an instance of the TServerClient-WinSocket class) that performs the actual socket read/write operations on the server-side, while the client's Socket object performs the client-side socket read/write operations.

Both the client's end point and the server's end point of the connection have the same type of event handlers for sending and receiving the data packets, as well as responding to the exceptions. For example, when the connection object at one end point executes a SendBuf() method, which writes data to the socket, the other end points wake up with a read event handler. Similarly, if the connection object at one end point attempts to close the connection, the other end point's OnDisconnect() event handler is triggered.

The SendBuf() method takes two arguments; the first argument is a void pointer to the buffer containing the data to be sent, and the second argument is an integer indicating the number of bytes you want to send in one send request. The method returns an integer value indicating the actual number of bytes sent. It is worth noting a couple of points here. First of all, the buffer may be larger than what we are sending in one method call. Secondly, WinSock may not send all the bytes as we requested in the second argument. Let's consider a scenario where the buffer size may be 10,000 bytes; we may be intending to send 5,000 byes (identified by the second argument) in one method call, but WinSock may only send 3,600 bytes, for example, identified by the return value. The programmer does not control how many bytes the underlying WinSock DLL actually sends. Neither is it recommended to hard-code such a value in the program. Therefore, the best strategy to send the entire buffer contents is to keep executing the SendBuf() method within a loop until all the bytes are sent. Listing 10-11 displays an example of such a loop where I am attempting to send all the contents of the buffer repeatedly. You can use this sample code in an appropriate event handler or method implementation, as triggered by the user's request to send the data.

Part 2

Listing 10-11: SendBuf() method in a loop

```
// fBuff is the buffer containing the actual stream of data
// fVBuff is the void pointer to the buffer.
void* fVBuff = static_cast<void*>(reinterpret_cast<char *>(fBuff));

// f_total_bytes_tobe_sent is the total size of the buffer.
int f_bytes_sent = 0;
bool f_send_complete = false;
int f_total_bytes_sent = 0;
int f_remaining_bytes = f_total_bytes_tobe_sent;

while (!f_send_complete) {
    f_bytes_sent = Socket->SendBuf(fVBuff, f_remaining_bytes);
    f_total_bytes_sent += f_bytes_sent;
    f_remaining_bytes -= f_bytes_sent;
    fBuff += f_bytes_sent;
    fVBuff = static_cast<void*>(reinterpret_cast<char *>(fBuff));
    if (f_total_bytes_sent >= f_total_bytes_tobe_sent)
        f_send_complete = true;
}
```

This example indicates a situation where the number of iterations executed by the loop is determined by the program, depending on the actual size of the buffer and how much is sent in each iteration. For each execution of SendBuf(), the OnRead event handler on the client socket is triggered, which means the complete package is received by the client in multiple iterations of the OnRead event handler. Therefore, it would be our job to assemble all the packets together on the client side. An interesting observation is that the server-side program may know when to terminate sending, as we noticed in the above code block, but the client-side program does not have a way to know when to identify that a packet has been completely received. Therefore, we should employ some mechanism to identify the beginning of the response message from the server. I would prefer to do this by a packet-begin signature. Then the client can examine the packet received in every OnRead event handler execution to find the packet-begin signature in the beginning of the packet. If it finds one, then it is the beginning of the packet, and if not, it is the next sub-packet in sequence of the previous main data packet.

Custom App Server Model

Let's now go through an example where I demonstrate the different event handlers on the client side as well as the server side in a non-blocking type client-server application. When the client sends a greeting message, the server acknowledges the client with a reply-greeting message. Since this is a client-server model, you can test this example by invoking multiple clients either from the same machine or from multiple machines. You can marshal any type of data between the client and the server. Listing 10-12 displays the custom server implementation, while Listing 10-13 presents the custom client implementation using TCP/IP sockets. Both the server and the client are VCL-based Windows applications. The client has four buttons, one message list box, and one TClientSocket component. A label is also used to display the return message from the server. The buttons are used to connect to the server, disconnect from the server, send a greeting message to the server, and clear the messages in the message list as well as the label caption. The server module uses a message list and a TServer-Socket component.

Listing 10-12: Custom TCP/IP socket-based server

```cpp
//----------------------------------------------------------------------

#include <vcl.h>
#pragma hdrstop

#include "TCPIPServerMain.h"
//----------------------------------------------------------------------
#pragma package(smart_init)
#pragma resource "*.dfm"
TTCPIPServerForm *TCPIPServerForm;
//----------------------------------------------------------------------
__fastcall TTCPIPServerForm::TTCPIPServerForm(TComponent* Owner)
    : TForm(Owner)
{
    PKT_BEGIN = 0xF0F0F0F0;
}
//----------------------------------------------------------------------
void __fastcall TTCPIPServerForm::FormResize(TObject *Sender)
{
    if (Height > 300)
        Height = 300;
    if (Width > 400)
        Width = 400;
}
//----------------------------------------------------------------------
void __fastcall TTCPIPServerForm::ServerSocket1ClientConnect(
        TObject *Sender, TCustomWinSocket *Socket)
{
    AnsiString fMsg("Client connected - client Id ");
    fMsg += IntToStr(Socket->SocketHandle);
    MsgList->Items->Add(fMsg);
}
//----------------------------------------------------------------------
void __fastcall TTCPIPServerForm::ServerSocket1ClientDisconnect(
        TObject *Sender, TCustomWinSocket *Socket)
{
    AnsiString fMsg("Client disconnected - client Id ");
    fMsg += IntToStr(Socket->SocketHandle);
    MsgList->Items->Add(fMsg);
}
//----------------------------------------------------------------------
void __fastcall TTCPIPServerForm::ServerSocket1Accept(TObject *Sender,
        TCustomWinSocket *Socket)
```

Part 2

```
{
    AnsiString fMsg("Client connection accepted - client Id ");
    fMsg += IntToStr(Socket->SocketHandle);
    MsgList->Items->Add(fMsg);
}
//---------------------------------------------------------------------------
void __fastcall TTCPIPServerForm::ServerSocket1ClientError(TObject *Sender,
    TCustomWinSocket *Socket, TErrorEvent ErrorEvent, int &ErrorCode)
{
    AnsiString fMsg("Socket error occurred. Error type - ");
    if (ErrorEvent == eeGeneral)
        fMsg += "General Error - Error Code -";
    if (ErrorEvent == eeSend)
        fMsg += "Send Error - Error Code - ";
    if (ErrorEvent == eeReceive)
        fMsg += "Receive Error - Error Code - ";
    if (ErrorEvent == eeConnect)
        fMsg += "Client Connect Error - Error Code - ";
    if (ErrorEvent == eeGeneral)
        fMsg += "Client Disconnect Error - Error Code - ";
    if (ErrorEvent == eeAccept)
        fMsg += "Client connection accept Error - Error Code - ";
    fMsg += IntToStr(ErrorCode);
    MsgList->Items->Add(fMsg);
    ErrorCode = 0;
}
//---------------------------------------------------------------------------
void __fastcall TTCPIPServerForm::ServerSocket1Listen(TObject *Sender,
    TCustomWinSocket *Socket)
{
    const AnsiString fMsg("Server socket is opening to listen for client
                          connections...");
    MsgList->Items->Add(fMsg);
}
//---------------------------------------------------------------------------
void __fastcall TTCPIPServerForm::FormActivate(TObject *Sender)
{
    ServerSocket1->Active = true;
}
//---------------------------------------------------------------------------

void __fastcall TTCPIPServerForm::ServerSocket1ClientRead(TObject *Sender,
    TCustomWinSocket *Socket)
{
    try {
        int fRsize = Socket->ReceiveLength();

        // allocate char buffer to read input from socket, and typecast it to void
        char *fRbuff = new char[fRsize];
        void *fVRbuff = static_cast<void *>(fRbuff);

        // read from socket, into void buffer, and typecast to char buffer again
        int fBytesReceived = Socket->ReceiveBuf(fVRbuff, fRsize);
        fRbuff = static_cast<char *>(fVRbuff);
        char *fRbuffPtr = fRbuff;

        unsigned long fPktSign;
        std::memmove(&fPktSign, fRbuffPtr, sizeof(fPktSign));
        fRbuffPtr += sizeof(fPktSign);
```

```
    if (fPktSign != PKT_BEGIN) {
        MsgList->Items->Add("Error in the incoming data packet ");
        return;
    }


    // determine the completre data packet size
    int fPktSize = 0;
    std::memmove(&fPktSize, fRbuffPtr, sizeof(fPktSize));
    fRbuffPtr += sizeof(fPktSize);
    if (fBytesReceived != fPktSize) {
        MsgList->Items->Add("Error receiving the packet ");
    }
    // determine how many more bytes are to be received in the data packet
    int fRemainingBytes = fPktSize - sizeof(fPktSign) - sizeof(fPktSize);

    char fTempStr[256];

    std::memmove(fTempStr, fRbuffPtr, 4);
    fRbuffPtr += 4;
    fTempStr[4] = '\0';
    const AnsiString fClientType(fTempStr);
    fRemainingBytes -= 4;

    std::memmove(fTempStr, fRbuffPtr, 5);
    fRbuffPtr += 5;
    fTempStr[5] = '\0';
    const AnsiString fReqCode(fTempStr);
    fRemainingBytes -= 5;

    std::memmove(fTempStr, fRbuffPtr, fRemainingBytes);
    fTempStr[fRemainingBytes] = '\0';
    const AnsiString fReqMsg(fTempStr);

    if (fReqCode == "GREET") {
        AnsiString fTempMsg("Greeting message received from ");
        fTempMsg += fClientType;
        fTempMsg += " Client - Connection Id - ";
        fTempMsg += IntToStr(Socket->SocketHandle);
        MsgList->Items->Add(fTempMsg);

        AnsiString fReplyMsg("Hello client - Your Id is ");
        fReplyMsg += IntToStr(Socket->SocketHandle);

        int fSendBufSize = 0;
        fSendBufSize += sizeof(PKT_BEGIN);
        fSendBufSize += sizeof(int);    // for packet size
        fSendBufSize += 5;              // for msg code
        fSendBufSize += fReplyMsg.Length();

        // allocate the buffer for the datapacket
        char* fSbuff = new char[fSendBufSize];
        char* fSbuffPtr = fSbuff;

        // First unsigned long variable (usually 4 bytes on 32 bit machine)
        // would be the packet begin signature
        std::memmove(fSbuffPtr, &PKT_BEGIN, sizeof(PKT_BEGIN));
        fSbuffPtr += sizeof(PKT_BEGIN);

        // Next int variable would be the total packet size
```

Part 2

```
                    // which includes the packet begin signature
                    std::memmove(fSbuffPtr, &fSendBufSize, sizeof(fSendBufSize));
                    fSbuffPtr += sizeof(fSendBufSize);

                    std::memmove(fSbuffPtr, fReqCode.c_str(), fReqCode.Length());
                    fSbuffPtr += fReqCode.Length();

                    std::memmove(fSbuffPtr, fReplyMsg.c_str(), fReplyMsg.Length());
                    fSbuffPtr += fReplyMsg.Length();

                    void* fVSbuff = static_cast<void *>(fSbuff);
                    const int fBytesSent = Socket->SendBuf(fVSbuff, fSendBufSize);
                    if (fBytesSent == fSendBufSize) {
                        AnsiString fMsg("Reply greeting sent to client ");
                        fMsg += IntToStr(Socket->SocketHandle);
                        fMsg += " successfully";
                        MsgList->Items->Add(fMsg);
                    }
                    else {
                        AnsiString fMsg("Sending reply message to client ");
                        fMsg += IntToStr(Socket->SocketHandle);
                        fMsg += " failed";
                        MsgList->Items->Add(fMsg);
                    }
                    delete [] fSbuff;
                }
                delete [] fRbuff;
            }
            catch (Exception &ex) {
                MsgList->Items->Add(ex.Message);
            }

}
//---------------------------------------------------------------------------
```

Listing 10-13: Custom TCP/IP socket-based client

```
//---------------------------------------------------------------------------

#include <vcl.h>
#pragma hdrstop

#include "TCPIPClientMain.h"
//---------------------------------------------------------------------------
#pragma package(smart_init)
#pragma resource "*.dfm"
TForm1 *Form1;
//---------------------------------------------------------------------------
__fastcall TForm1::TForm1(TComponent* Owner)
    : TForm(Owner)
{
    PKT_BEGIN = 0xF0F0F0F0;
}
//---------------------------------------------------------------------------
void __fastcall TForm1::FormResize(TObject *Sender)
{
    if (Height > 300)
        Height = 300;
    if (Width > 500)
        Width = 500;
```

```cpp
}
//----------------------------------------------------------------------------
void __fastcall TForm1::ConnectBtnClick(TObject *Sender)
{
    try {
        ClientSocket1->Active = true;
    }
    catch (Exception &ex) {
        MsgList->Items->Add(ex.Message);
    }
}
//----------------------------------------------------------------------------

void __fastcall TForm1::DisconnectBtnClick(TObject *Sender)
{
    try {
        ClientSocket1->Active = false;
    }
    catch (Exception &ex) {
        MsgList->Items->Add(ex.Message);
    }
}
//----------------------------------------------------------------------------

void __fastcall TForm1::ClientSocket1Connect(TObject *Sender,
    TCustomWinSocket *Socket)
{
    MsgList->Items->Add("Connection established with the server");
}
//----------------------------------------------------------------------------

void __fastcall TForm1::ClientSocket1Disconnect(TObject *Sender,
    TCustomWinSocket *Socket)
{
    MsgList->Items->Add("Disconnected from the server");
}
//----------------------------------------------------------------------------

void __fastcall TForm1::ClientSocket1Error(TObject *Sender,
    TCustomWinSocket *Socket, TErrorEvent ErrorEvent, int &ErrorCode)
{
    AnsiString fMsg("Socket error occurred. Error type - ");
    if (ErrorEvent == eeGeneral)
        fMsg += "General Error - Error Code -";
    if (ErrorEvent == eeSend)
        fMsg += "Send Error - Error Code - ";
    if (ErrorEvent == eeReceive)
        fMsg += "Receive Error - Error Code - ";
    if (ErrorEvent == eeConnect)
        fMsg += "Client Connect Error - Error Code - ";
    if (ErrorEvent == eeGeneral)
        fMsg += "Client Disconnect Error - Error Code - ";
    fMsg += IntToStr(ErrorCode);
    MsgList->Items->Add(fMsg);
    ErrorCode = 0;
}
//----------------------------------------------------------------------------

void __fastcall TForm1::ClearBtnClick(TObject *Sender)
```

Part 2

```
{
    MsgList->Items->Clear();
    MsgLabel->Caption = "";
}
//-------------------------------------------------------------------------

void __fastcall TForm1::GreetBtnClick(TObject *Sender)
{
    try {
        if (!ClientSocket1->Active) {
            MsgList->Items->Add("Client not yet connected ... ");
            return;
        }

        // This is the actual buffer that stores the data packet to be sent
        fSBuf = new char[256];
        // This is a moving pointer to the buffer
        char * fSBufPtr = fSBuf;

        const AnsiString fClientType("BCB6");
        const AnsiString fReqCode("GREET");
        const AnsiString fGreetMsg("Hi Server ! This is your BCB6 Client !!!");

        int fPktSize = sizeof(PKT_BEGIN);
        fPktSize += fClientType.Length();
        fPktSize += fReqCode.Length();
        fPktSize += fGreetMsg.Length();

        char fTempStr[256];

        // First unsigned long variable (usually 4 bytes on 32 bit machine)
        // would be the packet begin signature
        std::memmove(fSBufPtr, &PKT_BEGIN, sizeof(PKT_BEGIN));
        fSBufPtr += sizeof(PKT_BEGIN);

        // Next int variable would be the total packet size
        // which includes the packet begin signature
        std::memmove(fSBufPtr, &fPktSize, sizeof(fPktSize));
        fSBufPtr += sizeof(fPktSize);

        // Next 4 bytes would be the client type - here it is BCB6
        std::strcpy(fTempStr, fClientType.c_str());
        std::memmove(fSBufPtr, fTempStr, fClientType.Length());
        fSBufPtr += fClientType.Length();

        // Next 5 bytes would be the request code - here it is GREET
        std::strcpy(fTempStr, fReqCode.c_str());
        std::memmove(fSBufPtr, fTempStr, fReqCode.Length());
        fSBufPtr += fReqCode.Length();

        // Next set of bytes (till end of the packet)
        // would be the message
        std::strcpy(fTempStr, fGreetMsg.c_str());
        std::memmove(fSBufPtr, fTempStr, fGreetMsg.Length());
        fSBufPtr += fGreetMsg.Length();

        // cast the buffer to a void pointer
        fVSBuf = static_cast<void *>(fSBuf);
        // Since our data packet is really very small (<256 bytes total)
```

```
            // We can assume that WinSock will send them all at once
            const int fBytesSent = ClientSocket1->Socket->SendBuf(fVSBuf, fPktSize);
            if (fBytesSent == fPktSize)
                MsgList->Items->Add("Greeting message sent successfully ");
            else
                MsgList->Items->Add("Error in sending greeting message ");

            delete [] fSBuf;
        }
        catch (Exception &ex) {
            MsgList->Items->Add(ex.Message);
        }
}
//---------------------------------------------------------------------------

void __fastcall TForm1::ClientSocket1Read(TObject *Sender,
        TCustomWinSocket *Socket)
{
    // obtain read buffer size from socket
    int fRSize = Socket->ReceiveLength();

    // allocate char buffer to read input from socket, and typecast it to void
    char *fRBuff = new char[fRSize];
    void *fVRbuff = static_cast<void *>(fRBuff);

    // read from socket, into void buffer, and typecast to char buffer again
    const int fBytesReceived = Socket->ReceiveBuf(fVRbuff, fRSize);
    fRBuff = static_cast<char *>(fVRbuff);
    char *fRbuffPtr = fRBuff;

    unsigned long fPktSign;
    std::memmove(&fPktSign, fRbuffPtr, sizeof(fPktSign));
    fRbuffPtr += sizeof(fPktSign);
    if (fPktSign != PKT_BEGIN) {
        MsgList->Items->Add("Error in the incoming data packet ");
        delete fRBuff;
        return;
    }
    int fPktSize = 0;
    std::memmove(&fPktSize, fRbuffPtr, sizeof(fPktSize));
    fRbuffPtr += sizeof(fPktSize);
    if (fBytesReceived!= fPktSize) {
        MsgList->Items->Add("Incoming packet size does not match the msg size");
        delete fRBuff;
        return;
    }

    char fTempStr[256];
    std::memmove(fTempStr, fRbuffPtr, 5);
    fRbuffPtr += 5;
    fTempStr[5] = '\0';
    const AnsiString fReqCode(fTempStr);

    const int fMsgSize = fPktSize - sizeof(fPktSign) - sizeof(fPktSize) - 5;

    std::memmove(fTempStr, fRbuffPtr, fMsgSize);
    fRbuffPtr += fMsgSize;
    fTempStr[fMsgSize] = '\0';
    const AnsiString fMsg(fTempStr);
```

Part 2

```
        std::memmove(fTempStr, fRbuffPtr, fMsgSize);
        fRbuffPtr += fMsgSize;

        if (fReqCode == "GREET") {
            MsgLabel->Caption = AnsiString(fMsg);
        }

        delete [] fRBuff;
    }
    //-------------------------------------------------------------------------
```

This example shows you how to implement custom marshalling in case you plan to build a client-server model yourself. However, architectures such as CORBA, COM/DCOM, and DataSnap are designed in order to avoid the custom marshalling and relieve you of a lot of the burden. Among all these types of architectures, we notice that DataSnap is a much higher-level architecture, it is built over DCOM, TCP/IP sockets, and HTTP protocol, and it is much easier than using any of these other protocols directly.

A Simple FTP Client

Here I will present a simple FTP client application using the TNMFTP component from the FastNet page of the Component Palette. This is just a client application, which can connect to a remote FTP server. Though it is a simple application, I attempted to provide the minimum necessary features, such as connecting through a proxy server, downloading a file from the server, or uploading a file from your local workstation to the server. You may also set the type of server host, whether it is a UNIX-based or Windows-based server. If you do not choose one, it assumes the server to be a UNIX-based host. Listing 10-14 displays the complete program for this application. It is also provided on the companion CD.

Listing 10-14: Simple FTP client application

```
//---------------------------------------------------------------------------

#include <vcl.h>
#pragma hdrstop

#include "FTPClientMain.h"
//---------------------------------------------------------------------------
#pragma package(smart_init)
#pragma resource "*.dfm"
TFTPClientMainForm *FTPClientMainForm;
//---------------------------------------------------------------------------
__fastcall TFTPClientMainForm::TFTPClientMainForm(TComponent* Owner)
    : TForm(Owner)
{
}
//---------------------------------------------------------------------------
void __fastcall TFTPClientMainForm::FtpConnectBtnClick(TObject *Sender)
```

```
{
    try {
        if (IfProxyServer->Checked)
        {
            NMFTP1->Proxy = ProxyServerTxt->Text;
            NMFTP1->Proxy = StrToInt(ProxyPortTxt->Text);
        }
        if (HostUnix->Checked)
            NMFTP1->Vendor = NMOS_UNIX;
        else if (HostWindows->Checked)
            NMFTP1->Vendor = NMOS_WINDOWS;
        else {
            MsgList->Items->Add("Host not selected - setting to Unix / Linux");
            NMFTP1->Vendor = NMOS_UNIX;
        }

        NMFTP1->Host = HostTxt->Text;
        NMFTP1->Port = StrToInt(PortTxt->Text);
        NMFTP1->UserID = UserIdTxt->Text;
        NMFTP1->Password = PassTxt->Text;
        if (!NMFTP1->Connected) {
            NMFTP1->Connect();
            MsgList->Items->Add("Connected to the host");
        }
        else
            MsgList->Items->Add("Connection is already active");
    }
    catch (Exception &ex) {
        MsgList->Items->Add(ex.Message);
    }
}
//------------------------------------------------------------------------------
void __fastcall TFTPClientMainForm::FtpDisconnectBtnClick(TObject *Sender)
{
    try {
        if (NMFTP1->Connected) {
            NMFTP1->Disconnect();
            MsgList->Items->Add("Disconnected from the host");
        }
        else
            MsgList->Items->Add("Connection not active");
    }
    catch (Exception &ex) {
        MsgList->Items->Add(ex.Message);
    }
}
//------------------------------------------------------------------------------
void __fastcall TFTPClientMainForm::ClearMsgsClick(TObject *Sender)
{
    MsgList->Items->Clear();
}
//------------------------------------------------------------------------------
void __fastcall TFTPClientMainForm::DirChangeBtnClick(TObject *Sender)
{
    NMFTP1->ChangeDir(ChDirTxt->Text);
}
//------------------------------------------------------------------------------
void __fastcall TFTPClientMainForm::FtpFileDirNameListClick(
    TObject *Sender)
```

Part 2

```
{
    try {
        NMFTP1->Nlist();
    }
    catch (Exception &ex) {
        MsgList->Items->Add(ex.Message);
    }
}
//-----------------------------------------------------------------------------
void __fastcall TFTPClientMainForm::FtpFileDirListClick(TObject *Sender)
{
    try {
        NMFTP1->List();
    }
    catch (Exception &ex) {
        MsgList->Items->Add(ex.Message);
    }
}
//-----------------------------------------------------------------------------
void __fastcall TFTPClientMainForm::FtpClearListClick(TObject *Sender)
{
    FileDirList->Items->Clear();
}
//-----------------------------------------------------------------------------
void __fastcall TFTPClientMainForm::FileBrowseBtnClick(TObject *Sender)
{
    try {
        String f_curdir = ExtractFileDir(Application->ExeName);
        SetCurrentDir(f_curdir);
        AnsiString fUploadFile;
        OpenDIalog->FileName = "";
        if (OpenDIalog->Execute()) {
            fUploadFile = OpenDIalog->FileName;
        }

        f_curdir = ExtractFileDir(Application->ExeName);
        SetCurrentDir(f_curdir);
        LocalFileUpTxt->SetTextBuf(fUploadFile.c_str());
    }
    catch (Exception &ex) {
        MsgList->Items->Add(ex.Message);
    }
}
//-----------------------------------------------------------------------------
void __fastcall TFTPClientMainForm::FileUploadBtnClick(TObject *Sender)
{
    if (RemoteFileUpTxt->Text != "")
        NMFTP1->Upload(LocalFileUpTxt->Text, RemoteFileUpTxt->Text);
    else
        MsgList->Items->Add("Remote file name should be filled");
}
//-----------------------------------------------------------------------------
void __fastcall TFTPClientMainForm::FileULAbortBtnClick(TObject *Sender)
{
    NMFTP1->Abort();
}
//-----------------------------------------------------------------------------
void __fastcall TFTPClientMainForm::NMFTP1Failure(bool &Handled,
    TCmdType Trans_Type)
```

```
{
  switch (Trans_Type) {
    case cmdChangeDir: MsgList->Items->Add("ChangeDir failure"); break;
    case cmdList: MsgList->Items->Add("List failure"); break;
    case cmdUpRestore: MsgList->Items->Add("UploadRestore failure"); break;
    case cmdUpload: MsgList->Items->Add("Upload failure"); break;
    case cmdDownload: MsgList->Items->Add("Download failure"); break;
    case cmdAppend: MsgList->Items->Add("UploadAppend failure"); break;
    case cmdReInit: MsgList->Items->Add("ReInit failure"); break;
    case cmdAllocate: MsgList->Items->Add("Allocate failure"); break;
    case cmdNList: MsgList->Items->Add("NList failure"); break;
    case cmdDoCommand: MsgList->Items->Add("DoCommand failure"); break;
                    default: ShowMessage("Unrecognized command failed."); break;
  }
}
//-----------------------------------------------------------------------------
void __fastcall TFTPClientMainForm::NMFTP1Error(TComponent *Sender,
    WORD Errno, AnsiString Errmsg)
{
   AnsiString S("Error ");
   S += IntToStr(Errno)+": "+Errmsg;
   MsgList->Items->Add(S);
}
//-----------------------------------------------------------------------------
void __fastcall TFTPClientMainForm::NMFTP1ConnectionFailed(TObject *Sender)
{
   ShowMessage("Connection Failed");
}
//-----------------------------------------------------------------------------
void __fastcall TFTPClientMainForm::NMFTP1Status(TComponent *Sender,
    AnsiString Status)
{
   try {
       MsgList->Items->Add(NMFTP1->Status);
       MsgList->Items->Add("Last WinSock error: "+IntToStr(NMFTP1->LastErrorNo));
       if (NMFTP1->BeenCanceled)
           MsgList->Items->Add("Input/ouput operation canceled");
       if (NMFTP1->BeenTimedOut)
           MsgList->Items->Add("Operation timed out");
   }
   catch (Exception &ex) {
       MsgList->Items->Add(ex.Message);
   }
}
//-----------------------------------------------------------------------------
void __fastcall TFTPClientMainForm::NMFTP1TransactionStart(TObject *Sender)
{
   MsgList->Items->Add("Starting data transaction");
}
//-----------------------------------------------------------------------------
void __fastcall TFTPClientMainForm::NMFTP1TransactionStop(TObject *Sender)
{
   MsgList->Items->Add("Transaction Complete");
}
//-----------------------------------------------------------------------------
void __fastcall TFTPClientMainForm::NMFTP1InvalidHost(bool &Handled)
{
   // to write code here.
   MsgList->Items->Add("Invalid host; re-enter the host");
```

```
    Handled = true;
}
//----------------------------------------------------------------------------
void __fastcall TFTPClientMainForm::NMFTP1HostResolved(TComponent *Sender)
{
    MsgList->Items->Add("Host Resolved");
}
//----------------------------------------------------------------------------
void __fastcall TFTPClientMainForm::NMFTP1ListItem(AnsiString Listing)
{
    FileDirList->Items->Add(Listing);
}
//----------------------------------------------------------------------------
void __fastcall TFTPClientMainForm::NMFTP1UnSupportedFunction(
     TCmdType Trans_Type)
{
  switch(Trans_Type)
  {
    case cmdChangeDir: ShowMessage("ChangeDir not supported"); break;
    case cmdList: ShowMessage("List not supported"); break;
    case cmdUpRestore: ShowMessage("UploadRestore not supported"); break;
    case cmdUpload: ShowMessage("Upload not supported"); break;
    case cmdDownload: ShowMessage("Download not supported"); break;
    case cmdAppend: ShowMessage("UploadAppend not supported"); break;
    case cmdReInit: ShowMessage("ReInit not supported"); break;
    case cmdAllocate: ShowMessage("Allocate not supported"); break;
    case cmdNList: ShowMessage("NList not supported"); break;
    case cmdDoCommand: ShowMessage("DoCommand not supported"); break;
  }
}
//----------------------------------------------------------------------------
void __fastcall TFTPClientMainForm::NMFTP1Success(TCmdType Trans_Type)
{
    int I;
    switch(Trans_Type)
    {
        case cmdChangeDir: MsgList->Items->Add("Directory changed to '" + ChDirTxt->Text
                                         + "'"); break;
        case cmdList: MsgList->Items->Add("List success"); break;
        case cmdUpRestore: MsgList->Items->Add("UploadRestore success"); break;
        case cmdUpload: MsgList->Items->Add("Upload/Download success"); break;
        case cmdAppend: MsgList->Items->Add("UploadAppend success"); break;
        case cmdReInit: MsgList->Items->Add("ReInit success"); break;
        case cmdAllocate: MsgList->Items->Add("Allocate success"); break;
        case cmdNList: MsgList->Items->Add("NList success"); break;
        case cmdDoCommand: MsgList->Items->Add("DoCommand success"); break;
    }
}
//----------------------------------------------------------------------------
void __fastcall TFTPClientMainForm::NMFTP1PacketSent(TObject *Sender)
{
    AnsiString S(IntToStr(NMFTP1->BytesSent));
    S += " bytes of "+IntToStr(NMFTP1->BytesTotal)+" sent";
    MsgList->Items->Add(S);
}
//----------------------------------------------------------------------------

void __fastcall TFTPClientMainForm::FTPDownloadBtnClick(TObject *Sender)
{
```

```
    if (RemoteDownloadFile->Text != "") {
        if (LocalDownloadFile->Text != "")
            NMFTP1->Download(RemoteDownloadFile->Text, LocalDownloadFile->Text);
        else
            MsgList->Items->Add("Local file name should be filled");
    }
    else
        MsgList->Items->Add("Remote file name should be filled");
}
//-------------------------------------------------------------------------
```

Summary

We started the chapter with an overview of the CORBA object model,
focusing our attention on VisiBroker, the stub and skeleton programs generated by the IDL compiler, and how marshalling takes place in a typical
CORBA application. Then we discussed the Interface Definition Language
and the idl2cpp compiler in more detail, and we examined the contents of
some of the files it generates. We also discussed the idl2cpp mapping to
some extent. Our discussion continued with a sample application based on
the Basic Object Adapter, followed by a discussion of the Portable Object
Adapter, which replaced the BOA in the recent CORBA specification. We
have also seen how to replace the BOA-based code with POA-based code
in assisting programmers to migrate their applications to the newer version
of VisiBroker. We concluded our discussion on CORBA with a little attention to the Interface Repository, Object Activation Daemon, and the
Naming Service.

Our discussion then turned to building simple TCP/IP socket-based
applications using VCL components provided by Borland. We examined a
simple client-server example to see how to implement custom marshalling
between the client and server. Finally, I presented a simple FTP client application using the TNMFTP component.

Part 2

## Chapter 11

Building BizSnap Applications (XML and Web Services)

Introduction

BizSnap is the technical name that Borland uses to identify its web services architecture. As most of you already know, the web services technology is becoming popular very fast, and almost every development tool in the market is making an attempt to provide support in building and using web services in your applications. C++Builder 6 (and Delphi 6) provides this functionality in the standard Borland way (or the VCL way). The beauty of the Borland technology is that it seems to me that Borland not only provides object-oriented technology-based tools but also implements in its own methodology. For example, whatever new technology is invented in the industry (either by themselves or by others), Borland provides a very simple (and componentized) way of using that technology (however complex the technology is) in its tools. I don't have to quote examples; every component in the VCL/CLX architecture is an example.

As you might have already realized by now, I will present the BizSnap architecture in the same style as I did with other distributed architectures; first I will go over the general concepts and principles behind the technology and then jump into the discussion on Borland's style of implementation.

Web services are independent (self-contained and modular) server applications that can be accessed by clients over the Internet, not necessarily by web browsers alone. In fact, the web services are not designed (or intended) for direct human interaction, but a web server application may access information published as web service modules on another host and reinterpret that information to its own browser-based clients in a different way. The three core technologies that underlie the web service development are the

429

HTTP protocol, XML documents, and the Simple Object Access Protocol (SOAP). When a web service module is requested by its client to provide some information, the web service module prepares the information in the form of an XML document, packages the XML document as a SOAP packet, and finally transmits the packet over the Internet as an HTTP response message. This is a very short and crude way of looking at a web service. We will go through the details in the subsequent chapters. In an earlier chapter, we discussed how an HTTP message looks and what its contents are. In this chapter, we will go over the structure of an XML document and the related terminology, followed by a SOAP packet structure and Borland's SOAP components.

XML Overview

The concepts of HTML are extended to another very useful and powerful markup language called Extensible Markup Language, or XML. Please note that XML is not derived from HTML; rather its concepts are inherited from the Standard Generalized Markup Language (SGML), which is the ancestor of all the markup languages. Both HTML and XML are derived from SGML. While HTML has more rigid rules due to the fact that HTML content is designed for presenting data to the user through browsers, XML is open for expansion, as its name suggests, because it is designed to describe the data (rather than the visual presentation of data) in a structured way. You can even design your own customized language using the concepts and principles outlined in XML. Another difference between the two languages is that HTML documents are parsed by the browser applications running on the client systems since they translate the information contained in the documents to make a visual presentation; XML documents are parsed by parser applications, which usually run in the background mode and translate the contents of the documents into a form that is understood by the program that has requested parsing.

While this book does not intend to go into the depths of XML specification, I will bring to your attention some important concepts and terminology so that your job of programming C++Builder applications is easier. For more in-depth information on the subject, I recommend that you read books and materials that cover XML exclusively.

XML Documents

As you can easily guess, files containing information structured in XML are termed "XML documents." There are other file types that we come across while using XML, but an XML document is one that contains the structured information. I will present here some important features about XML documents. The concepts outlined in this section will become clearer in the subsequent sections.

XML documents present data in a text-based style. Fundamentally, XML is a markup language and hence organizes data between begin and end tags, such as <customer> …. </customer>, which indicates that the information contained within these tags belongs to a customer.

XML documents are hierarchical in presentation, containing a number of nodes. This means that each element in an XML document is identified as a node, and a node can be contained by another node as well as contain other child nodes itself.

The process of reading an XML document and interpreting its nodes and their attributes is called *parsing*. It is comparatively easier to develop algorithms that parse XML documents than normal text documents because of the recursive nature of the nodes. Almost all the major software vendors have already come up with their own XML parsers that are designed to work with multiple programming languages.

The World Wide Web Consortium (W3C) is standardizing the XML specification, and many software vendors are contributing to this process. By standardizing the XML document specification, it is possible to direct the different software vendors, developers, and users around the world to follow a standard in designing their business documents. The nice part of XML is that the document structure (known as a *schema*) and its content (the document itself) can be specified as XML documents. This will make business-to-business (B2B) communication across heterogeneous environments very easy. Imagine a scenario where a company that sells its products accepts purchase orders from its customers electronically via XML documents and sends copies of sales orders back to the customers electronically in the form of XML documents. Another company that is interested in purchasing goods from the first company will place its purchase order electronically as an XML document and receive a copy of the sales order as an XML document. Both companies can process the XML documents and save the contents in their systems. The first company might have implemented its system as a Borland DataSnap application written in C++Builder, while the second company might have developed all its systems in a Java-based environment (or for that matter, it could be a legacy

COBOL-based application). As long as you can generate XML documents from a legacy system and parse incoming XML documents, it does not matter what platform on which the internal systems are implemented.

For a company to implement successful B2B applications, a few things are required: utilities that can generate XML documents from their internal database systems and parse the XML documents received from their business partners, and a way to communicate with the external world.

The Document Object Model

The Document Object Model (DOM) treats an XML document as a tree of nodes with a single root node holding the rest of the contents of the document as child nodes. The concept of a parent-child relationship between the nodes is not limited to two levels. A child node to the root node may further contain child nodes, whose child nodes may contain their own child nodes, and so on.

The nodes of an XML document are elements of the document; as mentioned earlier, the elements of an XML document form a hierarchical structure. For example, if the XML document refers to sales order information, <salesorder> becomes the root node and may contain a single <customer> node and one or more <item> nodes. The <customer> node may further contain child nodes, such as <name>, <address>, <city>, <state>, <country>, <phone>, and so on. The <item> node is repeated each time for an item in the sales order. Listing 11-1 displays a sample XML document containing these simple nodes. The first line of the document is a processing instruction called an XML declaration. It specifies to the parser that the document conforms to version 1.0 of the XML specification and it uses utf-8 character encoding style. The standalone attribute (with the value "no") indicates that the document is dependent on an external file by the name of sodtd.dtd for its document-type definition, as specified by the second line. The DTD file may also be retrieved from a URL specified in the second line in place of the filename. The XML declaration is optional, but it is recommended since it supplies useful information.

Listing 11-1: Sample XML document

```
<?xml version="1.0" encoding="utf-8" standalone="no" ?>
<!DOCTYPE salesorder SYSTEM "sodtd.dtd">
<salesorder>
                    <customer>
                    <name>Satya Kolachina</name>
                    <address>450 Some Street</address>
                    <city>Some City</city>
                    <state>IL</state>
```

```
                    <country>United States</country>
                    <phone>(999)-999-9999</phone>
                    </customer>
                    <item>
                            <product>computer desk</product>
                            <price>$123.40</price>
                            <salestax>$10.00</salestax>
                    </item>
                    <item>
                            <product>executive chair</product>
                            <price>$100.00</price>
                            <salestax>$8.10</salestax>
                    </item>
    </salesorder>
```

The nodes that contain the text value for the node are considered the leaf nodes and will not contain further child nodes.

The nodes of an XML document provide a structure to the data presented in the document, as you can see in the above document. A single XML document can easily present data from multiple data objects or tables in a database. In the above example, if a sales order needs to be stored in a relational database, it is typically stored in two different tables, a sales order header table and a sales order item table. For every single entry in the sales order header table, one or more entries will be stored in the sales order item table, since a header contains only the information that occurs once on a sales order and there could be more than one item on the order. Each item on the sales order may represent a product ordered by the customer, and a sales order usually belongs to one customer. By putting the same information in an XML document, we are not only giving a structure to the data but also linking related data objects together. Thus, an XML document looks like a printed form or a hard-copy report containing data from multiple sources, but it has more functionality than a form or report because the business process that is going to receive the document may internally parse the contents and reuse the data electronically within their system; they cannot do the same with a form or a report.

The elements in XML documents may have attributes that describe the characteristics of the element. Attributes are name-value pairs that do not usually become the content of the element; rather they may describe the value contained by the element. We may, however, design nodes where the child nodes may be redefined as attributes of a parent node, instead of being child nodes. If a parser encounters an XML document, as shown in Listing 11-2, the name, address, city, state, country, and phone are treated as attributes of the customer element, and the product, price, and sales tax are treated as attributes of the item element. If an element describes a node, we have to follow the rules for defining a node, and if the element describes an attribute of a node, we have to follow the rules for defining the attribute.

Part 2

Listing 11-2: Sample XML document

```
<?xml version="1.0" encoding="utf-8" ?>
<salesorder>
                    <customer    name="Satya Kolachina"
                                 address="450 Some Street"
                                 city="Some City"
                                 state="IL"
                                 country="United States"
                                 phone="(999)-999-9999">
                    </customer>
                    <item        product="computer desk"
                                 price="$123.40"
                                 salestax="$10.00">
                    </item>
                    <item        product="executive chair"
                                 price="$100.00"
                                 salestax="$8.10">
                    </item>
</salesorder>
```

A programming language like C++, Delphi, or Java can access the contents of an XML document through a parser, which is an interface implemented by a software vendor to convert the nodes of an XML document into content understood by our application program. Commercially, a DOM is implemented by a vendor as a set of interfaces that represent a parsed XML document. Microsoft provides one such powerful implementation of DOM through its COM architecture, which by default is used by C++Builder 6 XML objects. The two ways to define a document structure illustrate that we can define our document structure in a flexible way. However, for the parser to validate an XML document, we need to tell the parser what our XML document looks like. The characteristics of an XML document's elements may be predefined as a document-type definition (DTD). Listing 11-3 displays the DTD for the sample XML document in Listing 11-1.

Listing 11-3: Sample DTD

```
<!DOCTYPE salesorder> [
<!ELEMENT salesorder (customer)>
<!ELEMENT salesorder (item)*>
<!ELEMENT customer (name, address, city, state, country, phone)>
<!ELEMENT item (product, price, salestax)>
<!ELEMENT name (#PCDATA)>
<!ELEMENT address (#PCDATA)>
<!ELEMENT city (#PCDATA)>
<!ELEMENT state (#PCDATA)>
<!ELEMENT country(#PCDATA)>
<!ELEMENT phone (#PCDATA)>
<!ELEMENT product (#PCDATA)>
<!ELEMENT price (#PCDATA)>
<!ELEMENT salestax (#PCDATA)>
]>
```

Typically, a DTD contains declarations for the document type and element types. The <!DOCTYPE salesorder> declaration specifies that the document is of type salesorder, which also forms the root node of the document. The next two lines specify that the document contains a single occurrence of an element of type customer and one or more occurrences of an element of type item. The * following the closing parenthesis of an element declaration specifies that this element may occur multiple times within its parent element; in this case, the parent element is the sales order. This means that the salesorder document type contains one element of customer type and one or more elements of item type. Following this notation, the next two lines describe the child elements of the customer and item elements, respectively. Then, each of the child elements are further specified of type #PCDATA. The elements that are identified of type #PCDATA contain values for the element and hence become the leaf nodes. Leaf nodes do not contain any child nodes.

Specifying the DTD in an external file and linking it to the XML document through the <!DOCTYPE ...> declaration is a nice way to share the single DTD file among many XML documents, but keeping the DTD in a separate file is not required; rather, we can code the DTD contents within the XML document itself after the XML declaration.

Part 2

XML Namespaces

We discussed namespaces in C++ programs in one of the earlier chapters. Namespaces provide a way to uniquely identify objects or entities in the enterprise programming environment where people might use the same names for entities that describe standard business data objects in the real world. For example, to describe entities such as customer, product, and price, most of us would use the entity names customer, product, and price, respectively, because this is the way that industry understands those business entities. Very few of us might use a prefix or suffix to distinguish our entity names from those of other programmers. This problem is more prevalent in objects and documents such as XML documents, which are exchanged across the business groups or organizations over the Internet. Once we publish our documents on the Internet, we do not have control over who is accessing our documents and how they are going to use them in their business applications. At the most, we can secure access to our document by restricting access to only a certain identified number of authorized individuals. The XML namespaces are used to uniquely identify our XML documents and DTD files. The namespaces enable us to make sure that pairs of XML tags representing elements (and any associated attributes) do not conflict with one another.

Uniform Resource Identifiers (URIs) are usually used to declare a namespace, since URIs provide uniqueness in the Internet-enabled world. Listing 11-4 shows a revised XML document from Listing 11-1.

Listing 11-4: Sample XML document using a namespace

```
<?xml version="1.0" encoding="utf-8" standalone="no" ?>
<myorg:salesorder>
                    xmlns:myorg="http://www.myorg.com/sales">
                    <myorg:customer>
                        <myorg:name>Satya Kolachina</myorg:name>
                        <myorg:address>450 Some Street</myorg:address>
                        <myorg:city>Some City</myorg:city>
                        <myorg:state>IL</myorg:state>
                        <myorg:country>United States</myorg:country>
                        <myorg:phone>(999)-999-9999</myorg:phone>
                    </myorg:customer>
                    <myorg:item>
                        <myorg:product>computer desk</myorg:product>
                        <myorg:price>$123.40</myorg:price>
                        <myorg:salestax>$10.00</myorg:salestax>
                    </myorg:item>
                    <myorg:item>
                        <myorg:product>executive chair</myorg:product>
                        <myorg:price>$100.00</myorg:price>
                        <myorg:salestax>$8.10</myorg:salestax>
                    </myorg:item>
</myorg:salesorder>
```

From this listing, we can see that the xmlns keyword associates the myorg namespace with the URI http://www.myorg.com/sales. The URI may be pointing to the DTD, which we explicitly specified earlier. Once we associate the DTD to a namespace, every element in the document is prefixed with the namespace prefix, which is myorg in this case.

XML Schemas

An XML schema provides a way to define the structure of an XML document like a DTD, but an XML schema is much more powerful than a DTD. A schema describes the elements that an XML document may contain and the rules that the elements must follow in order for the document to be valid for that schema. In other words, XML schemas specify the grammar for the XML documents. A schema may also specify the actual data types of each element's value. The W3C standard for XML schemas is continuously evolving.

What is TXMLDocument?

Having learned a little bit about XML documents, let's see which components C++Builder 6 gives us to work with XML documents. The first and foremost VCL component is the TXMLDocument, which can store an

XML document's contents; the contents might be loaded from an XML file or from a string value that is built programmatically, or the component might be used to create a new XML document. You can find this component in the Internet page of the Component Palette. C++Builder 6 comes with a number of interfaces, as defined in the XMLDOM unit file; these interfaces are defined as supported by the W3C documentation. Some of these interfaces appear as properties of the TXMLDocument component. If a DOM vendor were compliant with W3C's definition of the XML interfaces, then you would be able to use that vendor's DOM implementation in C++Builder 6, which supports the Microsoft DOM by default. You would need to register other vendors' DOM on your computer before you could use it. Let's now examine the properties, methods, and events of TXMLDocument.

The DOMVendor property represents an object of a class descendant of the TDOMVendor class, which identifies a registered DOM implementation. As discussed earlier, parsing an XML document requires the set of DOM interfaces, which may be accessed through this object. Once an appropriate DOM vendor object is assigned to this property, the TXMLDocument object automatically obtains the corresponding DOM interface and assigns it to the DOMImplementation property. C++Builder 6 comes with the DOM implementation from Microsoft and IBM and an Open DOM implementation. To use a specific vendor implementation, you must include the corresponding header file supplied with C++Builder 6, such as msxmldom.hpp, ibmxmldom.hpp, or oxmldom.hpp. By default, the MSXML is available, which is Microsoft's XML DOM implementation. You may use another vendor's DOM implementation. For that you should derive a class that is a descendant of TDOMVendor and override the methods Description(), which returns a string identifying the vendor, and DOMImplementation(), which returns the top-level interface, IDOMImplementation. Then you should register this vendor by calling the global function RegisterDOMVendor(). To unregister a DOM vendor, you should call the global UnregisterDOMVendor() function. The function that registers the vendor is usually invoked while initializing the unit (or the custom package that is going to contain the compiled code for the custom DOM vendor class), and the function that unregisters the vendor is usually invoked while exiting the unit (or the package). Both of these methods take a single argument, which is an instance of the class that descends from TDOMVendor. The XMLDOM unit provided with C++Builder 6 maintains a list of DOM vendors available for your application. The header file corresponding to the XMLDOM unit is automatically included when you include the header file containing the definition of the class that descends

Part 2

from TDOMVendor. When the custom DOM vendor is registered using the RegisterDOMVendor() function, your custom DOM vendor is added to the global DOM vendor list maintained by the XMLDOM unit.

The DOMImplementation property represents the IDOMImplementation interface, which is the top-level interface for the DOM implementation. Normally when the DOM vendor is set, the value of this property is automatically set. You may also obtain the interface by invoking the GetDOM() global function, passing the short vendor description (as is returned by the Description() method described earlier), and setting this property directly to indicate which DOM interface you are going to use. If we set this property, we do not have to set the DOMVendor property, but one of these two must be set before we attempt to use the XML document. Having access to the IDOMImplementation interface means we can have access to the other interfaces and will be able to parse the XML document.

The DOMDocument property represents the IDOMDocument interface. When a DOM implementation interface is identified either by directly setting its value or by setting the DOMVendor property, the IDOMDocument interface is automatically available through this property if you desire to have direct access to the interface. But the complete functionality to work with the nodes of the XML document is handled for you by the TXML-Document component. It is therefore recommended that you use the TXMLDocument component, rather than attempting to access the interface directly. However, if you wish to access the underlying interfaces directly, you should have sufficient knowledge of the W3C XML specification of DOM and its interfaces.

The Active property is analogous to opening a dataset. Similar to the way you connect a dataset to the corresponding database connection before attempting to open the dataset, you have to set the source of the XML document (by setting the FileName property or the XML property) and an appropriate DOM implementation to be able to parse the document (by setting the DOMVendor property or DOMImplementation property) before attempting to set the Active property to true. However, if you do not mention the XML source, a new empty XML document is created for you. Similarly, if you do not set either DOMVendor or DOMImplementation, the default DOM vendor, which is MSXML, is considered as set in the XMLDOM unit. I prefer to be specific with respect to component properties, rather than depending on default values, as I believe that default values usually go with some assumptions which may not always suit my needs. When you open an XML document (or activate it, as it is alternatively called), a sequence of events happen; the BeforeOpen event is triggered first, where you can perform any tasks that need to be executed before the document is opened, the parser is loaded and the document is parsed, and finally the AfterOpen event is triggered, where you can execute any tasks required after opening the document.

The FileName property identifies the name of the disk file that is associated with the TXMLDocument object. It may be an input file or an output file. For example, if you set FileName while attempting to read an XML document, it will open the XML document from the file. Similarly, if you created a new XML document or made changes to an already opened XML file, and then executed the SaveToFile() method, the document would be saved with the name set to the FileName property; in the process, it may overwrite an already open document.

The XML property is a TStrings object and contains the string form of an XML document. For example, each item in the XML strings object may represent an individual line of the document. This form of representation of the document is useful for transmitting a string value from one system to another or one application to another, or saving to a stream or file, and so on, but it is not convenient for navigating through the nodes of the document. Therefore, the strings form of the XML document may be used as a source of XML for a TXMLDocument object.

The DocumentElement property (of type _di_IXMLNode) represents the root node of the XML document. You are already aware that the XML documents are hierarchical in nature, and hence accessing the root node gives you access to the complete XML document. Similarly, if you replace the root node, you are actually replacing the whole XML document itself. DocumentElement is accessible only after you activate the document by setting the Active property to true.

The ChildNodes property represents the list of child nodes of the document and is identified by the interface IXMLNodeList. The Node property represents the document node of the XML document and is identified by the IXMLNode interface. The StandAlone property represents the standalone attribute of the XML declaration in the document. Similarly, the Version and Encoding properties describe the corresponding attributes of the XML declaration.

The SaveToFile(), SaveToStream(), and SaveToXML() methods save the document to a file, stream, or string, as the method name suggests. Each of these methods accepts a single parameter—a filename, a stream object, or a string, respectively. The corresponding methods to load an XML document are LoadFromFile(), LoadFromStream(), and LoadFromXML(), respectively. The Refresh() method reloads an XML document from the file. The AddChild() method adds a child node to the current object; if the current object is a TXMLDocument, the method adds a new child node to the document itself. To add a child to a parent node, invoke the AddChild() method of the parent node instead, since the method preserves the parent-child relationship. The method returns an interface pointer (of type IXMLNode) to the node. The method takes either the tag name of the new node itself or the tag name along with the namespace URI. The Create-Node() method may be used to create a node of any type and therefore accepts an additional argument indicating the node type and returns an interface pointer (of type IXMLNode) to the node. The CreateElement() method creates a new element node with the associated tag name and namespace URI and returns an interface pointer (of type IXMLNode) to the node.

The IXMLNode interface represents a node in the XML document and is widely used by many methods in the TXMLDocument component. The properties and methods of the IXMLNode interface let us work with the characteristics of a node, such as adding and modifying child nodes for a node, querying for the child nodes, the parent node, or siblings, and so on.

In Chapter 9, "Developing DataSnap Applications," we discussed the TXMLBroker, TXMLTransform, and TXMLTransformProvider components, which are used to connect to an XML data source and transform an XML document to a data packet or a data packet to an XML document. However, these components directly work with XML files rather than the TXMLDocument object.

Also, please note that this discussion on XML documents will help you understand the concepts behind building the data packets in SOAP objects. As long as you are working with C++Builder 6 (or Delphi 6) and its VCL components, most of the time you do not have to manually create XML documents; either you will be converting data packets to XML documents using the transformation components, or the SOAP components will package your data into an XML/SOAP packet structure and transmit them directly to the recipient.

SOAP Overview

SOAP is the acronym for Simple Object Access Protocol. There is much more to understand about the concepts behind the SOAP protocol. In this section, we focus our attention on this topic to enable us to build working systems around this technology. We know that HTTP is an application-level protocol to exchange messages between the client (the browser) and the server (the web server). Similarly, SOAP is also an application-level protocol designed to interact with server objects located anywhere in the intranet or Internet domain and exchange messages with them. In the context of our discussion, an application or module that initiates a request to exchange a SOAP message may be viewed as the client, and the application or module that accepts such a message exchange and provides a response message may be viewed as the server. A SOAP message is simply a well-formatted XML message containing SOAP elements. This is the reason we took the time to explain the XML documents, elements, schemas, and namespaces at the beginning of this chapter.

Your application might have been developed in Delphi, C++Builder, .NET, Java, or any other language of your choice, and similarly you might have used any database of your choice; as long as you can map your application's data types in terms of XML data types or in terms of a predesigned XML schema data type, your application can effectively provide services to the external world using the SOAP technology. That is the beauty of using XML as the standard for formatting SOAP messages. A SOAP message exchange involves mainly two steps: formatting the message and sending the message to the other end of the communication channel (either the client or the server). We have learned that a SOAP message may be formatted using XML. The next step involved is transmitting this message to the other end, which also needs an established protocol that the message recipient can understand. SOAP messages may be transported using HTTP protocol, which is widely used in many implementations of SOAP. However, SOAP messages may also be transported using message queue middle-ware software, such as MSMQ, or MQ Series, or a low-level protocol, such as TCP/IP.

The important point to remember here is that formatting a message is different from transporting it. An analogy to this scenario would be if you prepared a gift pack that you wished to send to your friend in a different city. You may send it by ground transport, air transport, courier, or mail service, any of which could use its own method of transport, but it is required that the city in which your friend lives have a receiving agent that can receive the package and deliver it to your friend. The transport of data packets follows the same line of thought. The computer (or device in general) that is going to receive the message on behalf of the recipient application must be able to understand the transport protocol that the sending machine is using. Once you have formatted your message (in XML) and handed it over to the transport protocol (such as HTTP or SMTP), your job is over. It is the transport protocol's job to repackage your message (if necessary) and send it; the receiving end of the same transport protocol knows how to unpack the message and deliver it to the receiving application in the form in which you packed it originally. Since HTTP is a widely used and implemented protocol on a variety of platforms and operating systems, in

Part 2

our upcoming discussion and examples we will be using the HTTP protocol as the transport layer for the SOAP messages. Also, C++Builder's web services components support HTTP protocol.

At this time, I would like to bring to your attention that exchanging messages using SOAP technology might impact performance compared to traditional CORBA, DCOM, RMI, or any similar protocols, since the data is transported in text format and since there is twofold data conversion involved (once to convert the original data packets on the sender side and the second time to convert the converted message back to the original format on the recipient side). But the advantage is the ability to communicate with heterogeneous systems and platforms spread across the Internet. It is also worthwhile noting that every distributed computing architecture has its own purpose, advantages, and drawbacks, and we should use the appropriate technology that a situation demands.

Web Services

Web services are applications or modules that are designed to expose one or more services to the external world, which may be viewed as consumers of the services. They are typically self-contained and provide functions that may be used by other user applications located anywhere on the Internet or intranet. It is important to note that web services are loosely coupled functions because they do not dictate how the consumers of the web services must be implemented or on what platform they should be implemented; rather, their interfaces are simply published in the form of a contract in a language known as Web Services Description Language (WSDL). As long as the published WSDL document is not changed, the clients of the service do not realize it even if we change the implementation of the particular service. A WSDL interface document is necessary for a web service to be usable by external applications.

Building and Using Web Services in C++Builder 6

SOAP objects are implemented as invokable interfaces. *Invokable interfaces* are interfaces (classes containing pure virtual methods) that are compiled to contain run-time type information. The run-time type information is used on the server side for the purpose of interpreting the method calls from the clients and marshalling data between the server and the client. The clients of a web service can only use the methods defined in the invokable interfaces. IInvokable interface is the base interface for all the invokable interfaces.

Building SOAP Server Applications

A typical web service application built in C++Builder 6 (or Delphi 6) contains a few core components, each of which performs a specific task. Most of the components are present in every web service application. The main difference between web service applications is the specific interfaces and their implementation classes. We now go through each of these functional elements. The first element is the web module, which interacts with the web server in receiving HTTP/SOAP requests and sending the HTTP/SOAP responses. It also hosts other components such as dispatcher and invoker. The next element is a soap dispatcher component, which auto-dispatches the SOAP messages to an invoker object with a specific pathinfo string value. Every incoming message with the specific pathinfo string is identified as a SOAP message. The invoker object interprets the messages received from the soap dispatcher, and invokes the implementation object of the corresponding invokable interface. There will be an invokable interface and the corresponding implementation object for every web service. Each web service may be treated as an object (a type of distributed object) and may expose any number of methods. The main difference between a SOAP object and other distributed objects we have discussed so far is that the SOAP objects are published through a web server, and the interfaces are accessible to the client through the published WSDL documents via Internet, and hence there is literally nothing to be deployed. Figure 11-1 displays a typical SOAP application and the associated components.

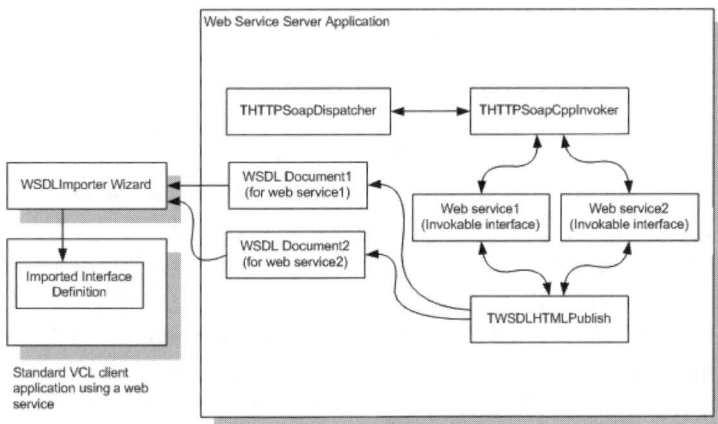

Figure 11-1: SOAP application and components

C++Builder 6 provides VCL-style components to enable developers experienced with the VCL architecture to build web services. Conceptually, a web service server is built on the same concepts of a WebBroker application. The server application uses a web module to host the three necessary components—THTTPSoapDispatcher, THTTPSoapCppInvoker, and TWSDLHTMLPublish. The THTTPSoapDispatcher responds to the incoming SOAP messages by forwarding them to the THTTPSoapCppInvoker component, which interprets the request messages and invokes the appropriate invokable interface implementation. The TWSDLHTMLPublish component publishes a list of Web Services Description Language (WSDL) documents for the web services. Let's examine the characteristics of these components to better understand their contribution in building web service applications.

When you create a web service server application using the SOAP Server Application Wizard, the THTTPSoapDispatcher component is automatically added to the web module, and it registers itself with the web module as an auto-dispatching object. This component does not interpret the incoming SOAP messages; rather, it just dispatches the messages to an invoker object. The Dispatcher property identifies the invoker object, which receives the SOAP messages and interprets them for further processing. The WebDispatch property identifies a TWebDispatch object and is used to describe the HTTP messages, which need to be handled by the auto-dispatching component to which it is assigned. For example, for the THTTPSoapDispatcher component, it identifies the incoming HTTP requests with the pathinfo string beginning with the value "soap." This value may be changed in the Object Inspector if your SOAP object should be accessed through a different URI. Also, please note that the SOAP object is not accessed directly by specifying a URI; rather, it is accessed through the WSDL document published by the WSDL publisher component. We will discuss the process of importing a WSDL document in your client application later in this chapter.

The THTTPSoapCppInvoker is the invoker component that receives the SOAP messages dispatched by the SOAP dispatcher, interprets them to identify which invokable interface should be called, and then finally executes the method (specified by the client) on the invokable interface. There are not any properties that we set explicitly for this object.

When you add an interface to your SOAP server application using the SOAP Server Application Wizard, the wizard automatically adds an invokable interface to your application, which is derived from the IInvokable interface and is given the interface name you provided to the wizard with the letter "I" prepended. You add your own methods (as pure virtual methods) to this interface in the header file that is automatically generated by the wizard with the same name as the interface name you specified to the wizard. The wizard also adds an implementation class to the application with a cpp file name that is the same as the interface name. The implementation class is created with the letter "T" prepended and the string "Impl" appended to the interface name. For example, if you provided the interface name as HelloWorld, the interface name created in the header file is IHelloWorld and the implementation class is named THelloWorldImpl. The implementation class is derived from the TInvokableClass class and the interface you created. The TInvokableClass automatically provides a few features to your invokable interface implementation. The invocation registry knows how to invoke an object of TInvokableClass (or its descendant) since the TInvokableClass has a virtual constructor allowing the registry to supply an invoker in a web service application with an object of the invokable class, which can handle the incoming SOAP request messages. The TInvokableClass has built-in object lifetime management and can free itself when the reference count becomes zero. The SOAP object has to have built-in lifetime management, since the invoker component (such as the THTTPSoapCppInvoker) does not know when to free an interface implementation object. This feature relieves the programmer from handling the object reference count and the associated object destruction when not needed. The wizard also automatically generates a factory method, which generates an instance of the implementation class when demanded by the invoker. The method is given the interface name appended by the string "Factory." For the HelloWorld interface, the factory method name is HelloWorldFactory. You should not remove any part of the code from this method, but you may add any code within this method that needs to be executed during object initiation. You may add any number of interfaces to your application, and for each interface, the wizard adds a cpp file and the corresponding header file containing the interface definition and implementation class.

The TWSDLHTMLPublish component publishes the WSDL documents within the web service server application for each of the interfaces. The URI to access the WSDL document for your interface is <your web service application URI>/wsdl/<interface name>. For example, if you deployed your HelloWorld.exe web service application containing the IHelloWorld interface in the cgi-bin directory of your web server path deployed on your local host, the corresponding WSDL document may be accessed using a URI similar to the following:

```
http://localhost/HelloWorld.exe/wsdl/IHelloWorld
```

Part 2

The TWSDLHTMLPublish component automatically registers itself with the web module as an auto-dispatching object. This enables the web dispatcher to automatically dispatch all the HTTP messages with the specified pathinfo string starting with "wsdl" to this object without a need to implement action items. This is the default setting made to the PathInfo property of the WebDispatch component by the wizard when the SOAP server application is created. It may be changed to another value if needed.

Let's now create a web service server application. The WebServices page in the New Items dialog contains the icons to initiate the SOAP application wizards. Figure 11-2 displays the WebServices page. There are four icons in this page. The SOAP Server Application icon initiates the wizard to create a SOAP server application, which hosts the individual web service objects. The SOAP Server Data Module icon initiates the wizard to add a data module exclusively designed to work in SOAP server applications. The SOAP Server Interface icon initiates the wizard to add a new web service interface to the current SOAP server application. When you first create the SOAP server application, you are asked to confirm whether you would like to add a web service interface at that time. If you click the Yes button, the wizard displays the SOAP Server Interface Wizard. You can also add a new interface to an existing SOAP server application. The fourth icon is the WSDL Importer and is used to import a WSDL document to a client application.

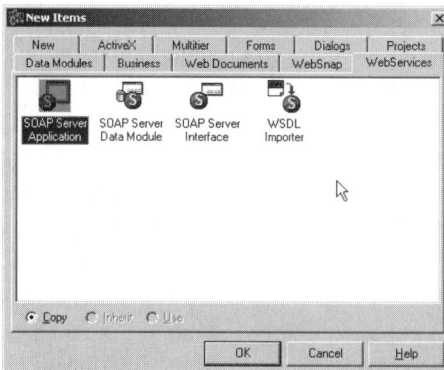

Figure 11-2: WebServices page in the New Items dialog

In the WebServices page of the New Items dialog, double-click the SOAP Server Application icon. The wizard displays a dialog as shown in Figure 11-3, where you choose the type of web service application. The web service application types are similar to the traditional WebBroker and WebSnap application types. Select CGI Stand-alone executable and click the OK button.

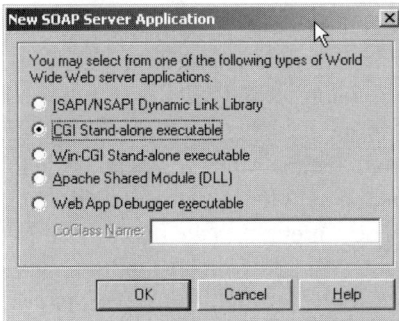

Figure 11-3: New SOAP Server Application type dialog

The wizard creates the SOAP server application and then displays a confirmation box, as shown in Figure 11-4, where you can choose whether you would like to create an interface at this time. I would like to create an interface and therefore click the Yes button. If you say No at this time, you can add the interface from the WebServices page of the New Items dialog. Once you choose to create the interface, another dialog, as shown in Figure 11-5, is displayed where you can enter the interface name. The interface name you enter in this dialog is used to create the invokable interface definition, the implementation class name, and their filenames, as discussed earlier. You may change the filename in this dialog if you wish. Also in this dialog, you will choose the Service Activation Model, either Global or Per Request. If you choose the Global activation model, a single instance of the object is created to handle all the client requests. If you choose the Per Request activation model, a new instance of the web service object is created for every client request.

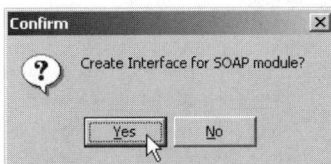

Figure 11-4: Confirmation dialog to create an interface

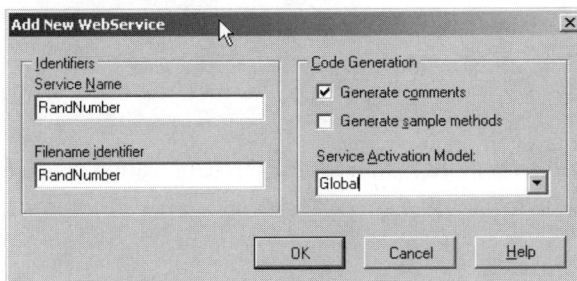

Figure 11-5: Add New WebService dialog

I am now going to implement the web service to generate a random number within a range of lower and upper limits; hence I named the interface RandNumber. The wizard creates the interface definition in the header file, as shown in Listing 11-5. If you examine the header file, you will notice a couple of additions that I made. I included the Math.hpp header file to include the Math unit functions, since I want to execute the random number generation functions. I also added a new method to the public section of the interface definition. This is where you will add your custom methods. However, since this is an interface definition, you should define them as pure virtual methods. I added the method GetNextRandNbr(), which does not take any arguments and returns a random number as a long variable.

Listing 11-5: RandNumber.h

```
// ********************************************************************** //
// Invokable interface declaration header for RandNumber
// ********************************************************************** //
#ifndef    RandNumberH
#define    RandNumberH

// Include this header file for random number generation functions
#include <Math.hpp>

#include <System.hpp>
#include <InvokeRegistry.hpp>
#include <XSBuiltIns.hpp>
#include <Types.hpp>


// ********************************************************************** //
// Invokable interfaces must derive from IInvokable
// The methods of the interface will be exposed via SOAP
// ********************************************************************** //
__interface INTERFACE_UUID("{8A792627-9672-4E59-8D68-07F22CB3CE16}")
    IRandNumber : public IInvokable
{
public:
    // Define your custom method as pure virtual method
    // You will implement the method in the cpp file
    virtual long GetNextRandNbr(void) = 0;

};
typedef DelphiInterface<IRandNumber> _di_IRandNumber;


#endif // RandNumberH
//---------------------------------------------------------------------
```

Listing 11-6 shows the program listing for the implementation class. This is a very simple implementation of a web service.

Listing 11-6: RandNumber.cpp

```cpp
// ************************************************************************ //
// Implementation class for interface IRandNumber
// ************************************************************************ //
#include <vcl.h>
#pragma hdrstop

#if !defined(RandNumberH)
#include "RandNumber.h"
#endif


// ************************************************************************ //
//  TRandNumberImpl implements interface IRandNumber
// ************************************************************************ //
class TRandNumberImpl : public TInvokableClass, public IRandNumber
{
public:

    // define the custom class variables and methods here.

    int randMin;
    int randMax;
    virtual long GetNextRandNbr(void);

  /* IUnknown */
  HRESULT STDMETHODCALLTYPE QueryInterface(const GUID& IID, void **Obj)
                        { return GetInterface(IID, Obj) ? S_OK : E_NOINTERFACE; }
  ULONG STDMETHODCALLTYPE AddRef() { return TInterfacedObject::_AddRef();  }
  ULONG STDMETHODCALLTYPE Release(){ return TInterfacedObject::_Release(); }

  /* Ensures that the class is not abstract */
  void checkValid() { delete new TRandNumberImpl(); }
};

// Implementation of the custom method.
long TRandNumberImpl::GetNextRandNbr()
{
    return RandomRange(randMin, randMax);
};

static void __fastcall RandNumberFactory(System::TObject* &obj)
{
  static _di_IRandNumber iInstance;
  static TRandNumberImpl *instance = 0;
  if (!instance)
  {
    instance = new TRandNumberImpl();

    // You may add custom initialization code here
    // set the default values for the randMin and randMax variables
    instance->randMax = 100;
    instance->randMin = 10;
    Randomize();
    // Custom initialization code ends here
```

```
    instance->GetInterface(iInstance);
  }
  obj = instance;
}

// *********************************************************************** //
// The following routine registers the interface and implementation class.
// *********************************************************************** //
static void RegTypes()
{
  InvRegistry()->RegisterInterface(__interfaceTypeinfo(IRandNumber));
  InvRegistry()->RegisterInvokableClass(__classid(TRandNumberImpl), RandNumberFactory);
}
#pragma startup RegTypes 32
```

Remember to check the project options to make sure that the Use dynamic RTL option in the Linker page and the Build with runtime packages option in the Packages page of the project options settings are unchecked, since this is a web application. Build the project to create the executable file. The created executable is a CGI executable, and therefore you can easily deploy it to any web server, just like you did a WebBroker application. When you try to access the executable over the Internet through a browser, the browser displays the list of web services published by this application, as shown in Figure 11-6. The figure shows two web services, IRandNumber and IWSDLPublish. The second web service is included automatically for every web service server application you build using C++Builder 6.

Figure 11-6: RandNbrService Service Info Page

If you click the WSDL link next to the IRandNumber service, you will see the WSDL document in XML format, as shown in Listing 11-7. You can copy the contents of this document from your browser to an XML file. The WSDL document may also be accessible through the URI. You may build a client application to access this web service in a platform other than C++Builder or Delphi and still be able to access the WSDL document without any difficulty. The platform where you are building your client application should be able to interpret the contents of the WSDL document and provide you with the necessary infrastructure to access the web service. For example, you may try building a client for this web service in Microsoft VB .NET, C# .NET, or a Java client.

Listing 11-7: WSDL document for IRandNumber web service URI
http://localhost:8040/cgi-bin/RandNbrService.exe/wsdl/IRandNumber

```xml
<?xml version="1.0" ?>
<definitions xmlns="http://schemas.xmlsoap.org/wsdl/"
    xmlns:xs="http://www.w3.org/2001/XMLSchema" name="IRandNumberservice"
    targetNamespace="http://tempuri.org/" xmlns:tns="http://tempuri.org/"
    xmlns:soap="http://schemas.xmlsoap.org/wsdl/soap/"
    xmlns:soapenc="http://schemas.xmlsoap.org/soap/encoding/">
    <message name="GetNextRandNbrRequest" />
    <message name="GetNextRandNbrResponse">
        <part name="return" type="xs:int" />
    </message>
    <portType name="IRandNumber">
        <operation name="GetNextRandNbr">
            <input message="tns:GetNextRandNbrRequest" />
            <output message="tns:GetNextRandNbrResponse" />
        </operation>
    </portType>
    <binding name="IRandNumberbinding" type="tns:IRandNumber">
        <soap:binding style="rpc" transport="http://schemas.xmlsoap.org/soap/http" />
        <operation name="GetNextRandNbr">
            <soap:operation soapAction="urn:RandNumber-IRandNumber#GetNextRandNbr"
                style="rpc" />
            <input>
                <soap:body use="encoded"
                    encodingStyle="http://schemas.xmlsoap.org/soap/encoding/"
                    namespace="urn:RandNumber-IRandNumber" />
            </input>
            <output>
                <soap:body use="encoded"
                    encodingStyle="http://schemas.xmlsoap.org/soap/encoding/"
                    namespace="urn:RandNumber-IRandNumber" />
            </output>
        </operation>
    </binding>
    <service name="IRandNumberservice">
        <port name="IRandNumberPort" binding="tns:IRandNumberbinding">
            <soap:address location="http://localhost:8040/cgi-
                bin/RandNbrService.exe/soap/IRandNumber" />
        </port>
    </service>
</definitions>
```

Building SOAP Client Applications

We have noted that building SOAP server applications is comparatively much easier than building many other distributed objects. In this section, we will go through the steps involved in building a SOAP client application. We will use the WSDL document created in the previous section and try to build a standard VCL client application to use the IRandNumber web service.

Part 2

1. Create a standard VCL-based Windows application. Then from the WebServices page of the New Items dialog, double-click the **WSDL Importer** icon to start the wizard that imports a WSDL document. The WSDL Import Wizard is displayed, as shown in Figure 11-7.

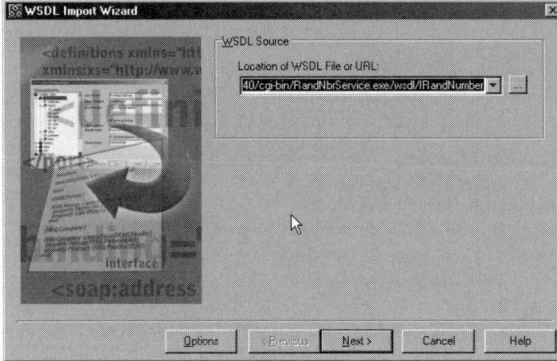

Figure 11-7: WSDL Import Wizard

2. For the location of the WSDL file, enter the URI of the WSDL document and click the **Next** button. If you typed the URI properly (or entered the filename if you have the WSDL document in the form of a file), the wizard imports the web service interface definition published by the WSDL document and shows the screen displayed in Figure 11-8.

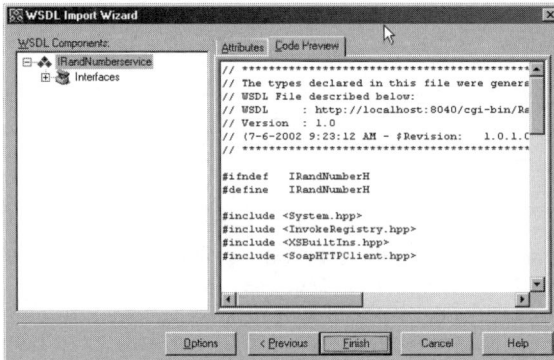

Figure 11-8: Imported interface Code Preview window

When you save the project files, the imported cpp and header files are saved with the default name (taken from the interface name) if you do not change the default name. However, you may change the default name, if you prefer. I saved the files with default names.

3. On the main form, drop a label to show the random number when retrieved from the web service, a list box to display messages, and two

buttons: one to activate the event handler that retrieves the random number and the other to activate the event handler that clears the messages in the list box. Also drop a **THTTPRio** component from the WebServices page in the Component Palette. This is a very simple client application. The THTTPRio component is used to generate statically linked calls to invokable interfaces on the remote web service server application. It uses HTTP messages to call the remote interfaced objects using SOAP. For the THTTPRio component, set the three important properties Port, Service, and WSDLLocation in the Object Inspector. If you were successful in importing the WSDL document, you will see these values in the drop-down list in the Object Inspector.

In the OnClick event handler of the GetRandNbrBtn button, write the code to call a method on the remote web service. First we declare an interface reference and then attempt to initialize this reference by querying on the THTTPRio component. Once we get the valid interface reference, execute the method as if you are executing a method on a local object.

Listing 11-8 displays the client application source.

Listing 11-8: RandNbrClientMainForm.cpp

```cpp
//---------------------------------------------------------------------------

#include <vcl.h>
#pragma hdrstop

#include "RandNbrClientMainForm.h"
#include "IRandNumber.h"
//---------------------------------------------------------------------------
#pragma package(smart_init)
#pragma resource "*.dfm"
TRandNbrClientMain *RandNbrClientMain;
//---------------------------------------------------------------------------
__fastcall TRandNbrClientMain::TRandNbrClientMain(TComponent* Owner)
    : TForm(Owner)
{
}
//---------------------------------------------------------------------------
void __fastcall TRandNbrClientMain::GetRandNbrBtnClick(TObject *Sender)
{
    try {
        // declare an interface variable
        _di_IRandNumber iRandNbr;
        HTTPRIO1->QueryInterface(iRandNbr);
        if (iRandNbr) {
            MsgList->Items->Add("Attempting to connect to the web service");
            AnsiString fMsg("The next random number is ");
            fMsg += IntToStr(iRandNbr->GetNextRandNbr());
            RandNbrLabel->Caption = fMsg;
            MsgList->Items->Add("Obtained random number from the web service");
        }
```

Part 2

```
    }
    catch (Exception &ex) {
        MsgList->Items->Add(ex.Message);
    }
}
//---------------------------------------------------------------------
void __fastcall TRandNbrClientMain::FormResize(TObject *Sender)
{
    if (Height > 300)
        Height = 300;
    if (Width > 400)
        Width = 400;
}
//---------------------------------------------------------------------


void __fastcall TRandNbrClientMain::ClearMsgBtnClick(TObject *Sender)
{
    MsgList->Items->Clear();
    RandNbrLabel->Caption = "";
}
//---------------------------------------------------------------------
```

SOAP-based Multi-tier Distributed Applications

In the previous example we saw how a simple web service can be implemented. Now I will discuss how to implement a SOAP server application that can interact with a database and function similar to a DataSnap server application. The SOAP Server Data Module wizard located in the WebServices page of the New Items dialog is used to build a data module based application, which asks only one input from you, the data module name, as shown in Figure 11-9, and creates a data module class for you.

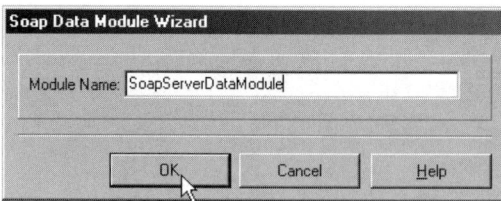

Figure 11-9: SOAP Data Module Wizard

The newly created class is derived from the TSoapDataModule component and the IAppServerSOAP interface. The IAppServerSOAP interface is very similar to the IAppServer interface and provides support through the SOAP protocol. The TSoapDataModule component itself implements two interfaces (IAppServer and IAppServerSOAP) and encapsulates the functionality of an application server using SOAP protocol to develop SOAP-based multi-tiered database applications. Since your data module is derived from TSoapDataModule, it inherits all the functionality necessary for an application server in your application. The corresponding client application uses a TSoapConnection component to generate calls to the application server. When these calls are received by your web service application, the invoker automatically forwards them to the SOAP-based data module. Since this architecture is built upon the DataSnap framework, web services built using the SOAP server data module can be accessed by clients built using the TSoapConnection component, which is again built upon the DataSnap architecture. Therefore, it is almost a requirement to build the clients using the C++Builder 6 (or Delphi 6) platform. In my opinion, this is a very good technology to extend your current DataSnap-based (or earlier MIDAS-based) applications to provide web-based access.

Building the Server Module

Building the server module is simpler than our earlier example.

1. Create a SOAP server application, as described in the previous example, and add a SOAP server data module.

2. On the data module, add one each of the **TADOConnection**, **TADOTable**, and **TADOQuery** components from the ADO page in the Component Palette and two **TDataSetProvider** components from the Data Access page. I named one provider TableProvider and the other QueryProvider.

3. Set the DataSet property of the TableProvider to the TADOTable component and the QueryProvider to the TADOQuery component. After adding these components, the SOAP data module looks like Figure 11-10.

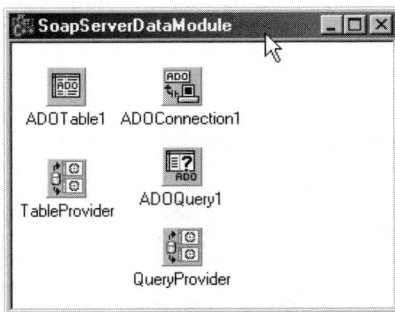

Figure 11-10: SOAP data module with components

4. Save all the project files with names of your choice in a directory of your choice. I am using the Northwind sample database provided with Microsoft SQL Server.

5. Set the ConnectionString property of the TADOConnection component to connect to this database. Set the LoginPrompt property to **false**,

Part 2

since you are already setting the user ID and password in the connection string. For your comfort level, make sure that the connection works by setting the Connected property to **true**. Then set the Connected property to **false** again. I generally prefer to connect to the database while the server module starts up, as a general practice.

6. Write the OnCreate event handler of the data module where you can establish the connection to the database. This is the only piece of code that I am implementing in the web service server, and therefore Listing 11-9 displays this code block only. I am not attempting to display all the source code generated by C++Builder automatically for you when you create the application (and the data module); however, you can access the code on the companion CD for this example.

Listing 11-9: OnCreate event handler of the data module

```
void __fastcall TSoapServerDataModule::SoapDataModuleCreate(
    TObject *Sender)
{
    ADOConnection1->Connected = true;
}
//---------------------------------------------------------------------------
```

Remember to check the project options, as you did for the previous example, and compile the application. Deploy the generated executable file in the cgi-bin sub-directory of your web server home directory.

Now let's discuss creating the client application. The client application is very similar to the DataSnap client application that we created in an earlier chapter. The main difference is that we use a TSoapConnection component to connect to the application server in the current example because the server module implements SOAP protocol. The client main form looks similar to Figure 11-11. Listing 11-10 displays the complete source code for the client application.

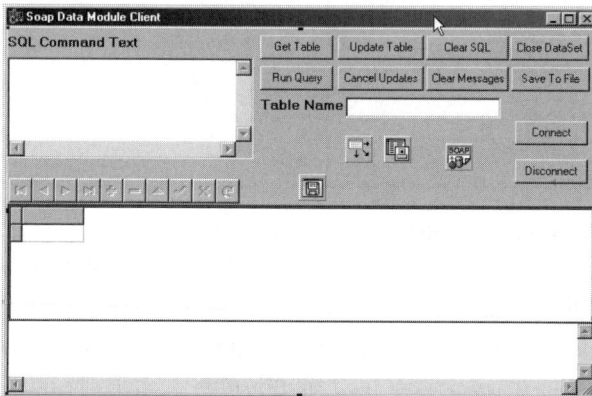

Figure 11-11: Client main form for the SOAP-based server data module

Listing 11-10: SoapDataModuleClientMain.cpp

```cpp
//---------------------------------------------------------------------------

#include <vcl.h>
#pragma hdrstop

#include "SoapDataModuleClientMain.h"
//---------------------------------------------------------------------------
#pragma package(smart_init)
#pragma resource "*.dfm"
TSoapDataModuleClientMainForm *SoapDataModuleClientMainForm;
//---------------------------------------------------------------------------
__fastcall TSoapDataModuleClientMainForm::TSoapDataModuleClientMainForm(TComponent*
    Owner)
    : TForm(Owner)
{
}
//---------------------------------------------------------------------------
void __fastcall TSoapDataModuleClientMainForm::FormResize(TObject *Sender)
{
    if (Height < 410)
        Height = 410;
    if (Width < 620)
        Width = 620;
}
//---------------------------------------------------------------------------
void __fastcall TSoapDataModuleClientMainForm::ConnectBtnClick(TObject *Sender)
{
    try {
        if (!SoapConnection1->Connected) {
            SoapConnection1->Connected = true;
        }
        MsgList->Lines->Clear();
        MsgList->Lines->Add("Connection established with the web service");

        ConnectBtn->Enabled = false;
        DiscBtn->Enabled = true;
        AnsiString currDir = ExtractFileDir(Application->ExeName);
        SetCurrentDir(currDir);
        SaveDialog1->InitialDir = currDir;
        SaveDialog1->Filter = "Data files (*.dat)|*.DAT";
    }
    catch (Exception &ex) {
        MsgList->Lines->Add("Error connecting to the web service");
        MsgList->Lines->Add(ex.Message);
    }
}
//---------------------------------------------------------------------------
void __fastcall TSoapDataModuleClientMainForm::DiscBtnClick(
    TObject *Sender)
{
    try {
        if (SoapConnection1->Connected) {
            SoapConnection1->Connected = false;
        }
        ConnectBtn->Enabled = true;
        DiscBtn->Enabled = false;
        MsgList->Lines->Clear();
```

Part 2

```
                 MsgList->Lines->Add("Disconnected from the web service");
                 CloseDataSetBtnClick(NULL);
        }
        catch (Exception &ex) {
            MsgList->Lines->Add("Error disconnecting from the web service");
            MsgList->Lines->Add(ex.Message);
        }
}
//----------------------------------------------------------------------------
void __fastcall TSoapDataModuleClientMainForm::GetTableBtnClick(
        TObject *Sender)
{
    try {
        const AnsiString tableName(TableNameEdit->Text);
        ClientDS->Close();
        if (tableName == "") {
            MsgList->Lines->Add("Table name empty. Please enter table name");
            return;
        }
        SoapConnection1->Connected = false;
        ClientDS->ProviderName = "TableProvider";
        ClientDS->CommandText = tableName;
        ClientDS->Active = true;
    }
    catch (Exception &ex) {
        MsgList->Lines->Add(ex.Message);
    }
}
//----------------------------------------------------------------------------
void __fastcall TSoapDataModuleClientMainForm::RunQueryBtnClick(
        TObject *Sender)
{
    try {
        const AnsiString sqlCommandText(SQLText->Text);
        ClientDS->Close();
        if (sqlCommandText == "") {
            MsgList->Lines->Add("Please enter SQL command ");
            return;
        }
        SoapConnection1->Connected = false;
        ClientDS->ProviderName = "QueryProvider";
        ClientDS->CommandText = sqlCommandText;
        ClientDS->Active = true;
    }
    catch (Exception &ex) {
        MsgList->Lines->Add(ex.Message);
    }
}
//----------------------------------------------------------------------------
void __fastcall TSoapDataModuleClientMainForm::UpdateTableBtnClick(
        TObject *Sender)
{
    if (ClientDS->Active) {
        if ((ClientDS->ProviderName == "TableProvider") &&
            (ClientDS->CommandText != "")) {
            // If the client dataset is currently connected to the table provider
            // with a table name and is open, then you can initiate updates
                const int errors = ClientDS->ApplyUpdates(0);
                if (errors > 0)
```

```
                        MsgList->Lines->Add("One or more records failed to update");
                    else
                        MsgList->Lines->Add("All changes applied to the database");
            }
            else {
                MsgList->Lines->Add("Dataset not open. Update not possible");
            }
        }
    }
//----------------------------------------------------------------------------
void __fastcall TSoapDataModuleClientMainForm::CancelUpdatesBtnClick(
        TObject *Sender)
{
    // if no records changed, there is no need to call CancelUpdates
    if (ClientDS->ChangeCount > 0)
        ClientDS->CancelUpdates();
}
//----------------------------------------------------------------------------
void __fastcall TSoapDataModuleClientMainForm::ClearSQLBtnClick(
        TObject *Sender)
{
    SQLText->Lines->Clear();
}
//----------------------------------------------------------------------------
void __fastcall TSoapDataModuleClientMainForm::ClearMsgBtnClick(
        TObject *Sender)
{
    MsgList->Lines->Clear();
}
//----------------------------------------------------------------------------
void __fastcall TSoapDataModuleClientMainForm::SaveBtnClick(
        TObject *Sender)
{
    try {
        if (SaveDialog1->Execute()) {
            ClientDS->SaveToFile(SaveDialog1->FileName);
            MsgList->Lines->Add("Client dataset saved to local file " +
            SaveDialog1->FileName);
        }
        else
            MsgList->Lines->Add("Saving client dataset to local file cancelled");
    }
    catch (Exception &ex) {
        MsgList->Lines->Add("Exception occurred while saving client dataset to local
            file");
        MsgList->Lines->Add(ex.Message);
    }
}
//----------------------------------------------------------------------------
void __fastcall TSoapDataModuleClientMainForm::CloseDataSetBtnClick(
        TObject *Sender)
{
    if (ClientDS->Active)
        ClientDS->Active = false;
}
//----------------------------------------------------------------------------
```

Summary

In this chapter I focused my attention on two main topics—basic understanding of XML terminology and building web services using the SOAP protocol. I started the chapter with an introduction to XML and continued with XML documents and the document object model. Then I discussed basic features of DTDs, XML namespaces, and schemas. However, I did not provide an elaborate discussion on any of these concepts, since this book is not intended for that purpose. Then I gave some attention to the TXMLDocument, Borland's way of accessing an XML document and its characteristics.

My discussion continued with a brief overview of SOAP concepts, web services, and how Borland attempted to simplify the whole process for its developer community. I continued with a simple SOAP web service and the corresponding client module, followed by Borland's extension of DataSnap architecture using the SOAP protocol.

Finally, I reiterated the fact that Borland has done a commendable job in providing a very simplified approach and component set for building SOAP-based applications for the general public, as well as building SOAP-based multi-tier DataSnap applications.

Chapter 12

Miscellaneous and Advanced Topics

Introduction

So far we have discussed Windows development, advanced database development, and distributed object development using different technologies. In this chapter we will cover three main areas: the cross-platform component library, custom component development, and object linking and embedding (OLE) to embed/invoke external COM server objects.

The Cross-platform Component Library

Until the previous edition of C++Builder, Borland had been concentrating on strengthening its VCL architecture for both the C++Builder and Delphi platforms. During 2001, Borland released its first version of the Component Library for Cross-platform development (CLX for short, pronounced "clicks") for both the Windows and Linux operating systems. Along with it, the Linux development tool Kylix, which is Delphi for Linux, was released. At the time of publication, the official commercial release of Kylix was Kylix3, which includes support to distributed/Internet technologies such as WebSnap and web services. Kylix3 is a RAD tool incorporating both the Delphi and C++ languages for Linux programmers, enabling rapid development of enterprise-class applications.

The CLX library contains components and classes that are compatible across the Windows and Linux operating systems. CLX is based on the same design concepts Borland implemented for the VCL framework. Since VCL is based on the Win32 API and other Windows programming elements exclusively, it is not possible to port VCL as it is; hence, Borland designed the CLX library, modeling it on those objects of VCL that are conceptually portable to the Linux operating system, and with the

461

underlying library supported by TrollTech's Qt API. Therefore, you will notice a lot of similarity between VCL and CLX, and their properties, methods, and events. However, it is necessary to remember that CLX does not replace VCL on Windows, nor is it a copy of VCL ported to Linux. For the purpose of enabling the current VCL community to smoothly port their applications, Borland made every effort to make the two component architectures similar. This is certainly appreciable by users of Borland tools.

The CLX library is comprised mainly of four parts. The first part is the BaseCLX containing the base library of classes, such as streams, files, object and string lists, and the printer and canvas objects. The classes provided by the BaseCLX are general purpose in nature and are common to both the VCL and CLX frameworks. These are usable directly in our applications and used by the other three parts of the CLX library, as well as the entire VCL framework.

The next part is the VisualCLX, which provides the set of components needed to design the user interfaces. Conceptually, this is where the main difference lies between the Windows and Linux operating systems, due to the differences in the architecture between the Win32 library on Windows and the X-windows library on Linux. The Qt library is designed (by TrollTech) to cover these differences and provide a unique application programming interface (API) to the developer community to enable cross-platform user interface development. The Qt library internally works with these varying GUI architectures, without surfacing the architectural differences in the API. A windowed control in VCL is called as a widget control in CLX, the term "widget" coming from the X-windows architecture. Therefore, the Windows version of CLX also uses the TWidgetControl in place of TWinControl, since the component names have to be unique.

The third part of CLX is the DataCLX, which provides the set of components and classes to develop robust database applications. Again, Borland's efforts are commendable in the design of dbExpress as the cross-platform component library. In fact, Borland provided a version of dbExpress to VCL developers, too. Application developers and architects intending to port their applications from Windows to Linux should strongly consider using the dbExpress library instead of other database connectivity architectures. The InterBase Express component set is also available in the DataCLX component framework if your application is developed to use InterBase databases alone. The very popular BDE and ADO frameworks are not supported in DataCLX because ADO is Microsoft COM-based and is therefore a Windows-specific architecture, and BDE is a bulky and outdated technology. The dbExpress framework replaces ADO very well with respect to supporting multiple databases as well as being a cross-platform technology.

The fourth and final part of CLX is the NetCLX, which contains the components and classes to enable development of cross-platform networking and Internet applications, including WebSnap and Web Services.

Since Qt is a library available on other operating systems, such as Sun Solaris, HP-UX, and Mac OS, it may be possible in the future for Borland to release a version of CLX on these platforms very easily. Therefore, it is now time that we start thinking about cross-platform development.

> **Note:** It is my wish that CLX will be available on many operating systems other than Windows and Linux. Borland has not committed to anything on this matter to my knowledge. My wish may come true if there is enough market support for the architecture.

In this book I am not attempting to discuss the CLX component library at length. For the most part, developing CLX-based applications in C++Builder 6 is very similar to developing VCL-based applications. The New Items dialog provides icons representing the CLX Application, CLX Thread Object, CLX Form, and so on. Once you choose the CLX Application type, the Component Palette is redisplayed with pages containing CLX component sets. Every time you choose the application type as CLX/VCL, the corresponding component library is redisplayed. Therefore, you are not permitted to mix the two architectures. It does not even make sense to attempt mixing two distinct architectures. As a broad general principle, anything exclusive to a Windows operating system, such as COM/DCOM/ MTS/ADO/ActiveX technology (and hence DataSnap), is not available and not supported in the CLX library. The Component Palette pages that are available in the VCL framework but not in the CLX framework are System, DataSnap, BDE, ADO, FastNet, DecisionCube, QReports, Win3.1, Samples, ActiveX, COM+, Servers, and Office2k. Most of the Win32 page components are made available in the Common Controls page in the CLX framework, with a few differences (addition of new components and removal of some VCL components).

If you desire to migrate your VCL-based applications to the Linux platform, you are advised to first convert your VCL applications to CLX architecture on the Windows platform. This ensures that your programs will compile in Linux with fewer surprises or failures. The next step is to convert any Windows-specific API calls to the corresponding CLX API calls if available. If no such corresponding CLX components or API methods are available, you will have to manually convert those API calls to Linux-specific API calls.

What does BaseCLX Contain?

We have learned that constituents of BaseCLX are common to both the VCL and CLX frameworks. Before we examine this in more detail, let me also make it clear that since VCL is Windows-specific and CLX is cross-platform by design, the internal implementation of the classes provided by BaseCLX may be different in these architectures; what is common is the way we use them, though. Now we will examine some of the classes belonging to BaseCLX, and in the process, we will also discuss any specific differences between VCL and CLX.

INI Files and Windows Registry

It is a common practice that many applications store their configuration information in a file. On the Windows operating system, we call this an INI file (INI stands for the first three characters of the word "initiation"). The format of an INI file is very standard and simple. It contains several sections of information, each section having a heading followed by configuration parameters relevant to that section as name-value pairs in the name=value format. Listing 12-1 displays one section of a sample INI file. The file may contain several sections.

Listing 12-1: Sample INI file contents

```
.
.
.
[DBSTART]
DBTYPE=INTERBASE
DATABASE=MYDATABASE.GDB
MAXSESSIONS=10
CONNECTTIMEOUT=5
.
.
.
```

TIniFile and TMemIniFile are the two classes provided by the BaseCLX to work with the INI files. On Linux, both classes are identical in their features, while on Windows they differ in the way they write output to the file. TIniFile works with the disk file directly every time you perform read and write operations, whereas TMemIniFile works with the internal memory buffer and updates the disk file only when you execute the UpdateFile() method. Both classes take the INI filename as an argument to the constructor. If the file does not exist, the constructor creates it for you. If you do not qualify the filename with the appropriate path information, the constructor looks in the Windows home directory, which is the standard location on Windows-based systems. You need to include the inifiles.hpp include file in order to use these classes. Table 12-1 shows the properties and methods supported by these classes.

Table 12-1: Properties and methods supported by TIniFile and TMemIniFile

Property	Description
CaseSensitive	This is a Boolean property and indicates whether the section and key names are case sensitive. This property is not available for TIniFile on Windows.

Method	Description
DeleteKey(const AnsiString section, const AnsiString key)	If the specified key exists in the specified section, the value is erased. If the key does not exist or the section does not exist, it does nothing.
EraseSection(cons AnsiString section)	This method removes the specified section, all the keys, and their values from the INI file. If the section cannot be removed, an exception is raised.
ReadSection(const AnsiString section, Strings* keys)	This method reads all the key names of the specified section into the Strings object.
ReadSections(Strings* sections)	This method reads names of all the sections into the Strings object.
ReadSectionValues(const AnsiString section, Strings* values)	This method reads values for all the keys in the specified section.
ReadString(const AnsiString section, const AnsiString key, const AnsiString default)	This method returns the string value for the specified key in the specified section. The third parameter is the default value to be returned by the method if the section or key or value does not exist. The method returns an AnsiString value. There are similar read methods to read other data types, such as Boolean value, date, datetime, time, float, and integer and binary values.
UpdateFile()	This method flushes the buffered contents of the INI file to the disk file. This method is mainly useful for the TMemIniFile class, which buffers the contents (and updates the buffer) for every write operation.
ValueExists(const AnsString section, const AnsiString key)	This method checks if the specified key exists in the specified section and returns a Boolean value as true or false accordingly.
WriteString(const AnsiString section, const AnsiString key, const AnsiString value)	This method writes (or updates) a string value for the specified key in the specified section. If the section or the key does not exist, the method creates one and writes its value. There are similar write methods to write other data types, such as Boolean value, date, datetime, time, float, and integer and binary values.

Part 2

Listing 12-2 displays a sample code snippet showing the usage of the TIniFile and TMemIniFile classes to create the section displayed in Listing 12-1. The listing displays two different event handlers, both doing the same task, but one is using TIniFile, while the other implements TMemIniFile.

Listing 12-2: Sample code using TIniFile and TMemIniFile

```
void __fastcall TForm1::CreateIniBtnClick(TObject *Sender)
{
    TIniFile* newIniFile = new TIniFile(ChangeFileExt(Application->ExeName, ".INI"));
    try {
        newIniFile->WriteString("DBSTART","DBTYPE","INTERBASE");
        newIniFile->WriteString("DBSTART","DATABASE","MYDATABASE.GDB");
        newIniFile->WriteInteger("DBSTART","MAXSESSIONS",10);
        newIniFile->WriteInteger("DBSTART","CONNECTTIMEOUT",5);
    }
    __finally {
        delete newIniFile;
    }
}
//-------------------------------------------------------------------------

void __fastcall TForm1::CreateMemIniBtnClick(TObject *Sender)
{
    TMemIniFile* newMemIniFile = new TMemIniFile(ChangeFileExt( Application->
        ExeName, ".INI"));
    try {
        newMemIniFile->WriteString("DBSTART","DBTYPE","INTERBASE");
        newMemIniFile->WriteString("DBSTART","DATABASE","MYDATABASE.GDB");
        newMemIniFile->WriteInteger("DBSTART","MAXSESSIONS",10);
        newMemIniFile->WriteInteger("DBSTART","CONNECTTIMEOUT",5);
        newMemIniFile->UpdateFile();
    }
    __finally {
        delete newMemIniFile;
    }
}
//-------------------------------------------------------------------------
```

Similar to creating the INI files, the Windows application extensively uses the Windows registry, which is a database containing key entries in a hierarchical structure. There are two classes, TRegistry and TRegistryIniFile, provided in the VCL architecture to work with the Windows registry. Since the registry is a Windows-specific feature, these classes are not available as part of BaseCLX. They work similarly, but the TRegistryIniFile is derived from TCustomIniFile class, which is also the ancestor class to the TIniFile and TMemIniFile classes. Because of this, the TRegistryIniFile class may be used instead of the TRegistry class, if you have plans to port your Windows-based application to Linux in the future or to write code that is very similar to creating INI files.

You do not need to have much knowledge of Windows registry operations to work with this class, since it provides a very simple interface, hiding the complex registry structure. In simple terms, the TRegistryIniFile class simulates the registry usage to that of the INI files. However, the limitation of the TRegistryIniFile class is that it assumes that the root key is the HKEY_CURRENT_USER key. Since the TRegistryIniFile class is simulated as a TIniFile class to represent the registry, we need to draw a comparison between the elements of the registry and INI files. An object of TRegistryIniFile is instantiated with an AnsiString argument called File-Name. The argument FileName fundamentally represents a subkey under the HKEY_CURRENT_USER key. A section in the INI class represents a key in the system registry, and individual name-value pairs within a section represent data values under a key.

In this section, I will pay some attention to the TRegistry class (although it is not part of BaseCLX) for the benefit of VCL developers. The TRegistry class is declared in the registry.hpp include file, which must be included in your application if you wish to work with this class. The properties and methods of the TRegistry class are displayed in Table 12-2. The class provides a big list of methods, but I will present only a subset of them here.

Table 12-2: Properties and methods supported by TRegistry

Property	Description
Access	This property indicates the access level to be used while opening the keys with the current instance of the TRegistry object. The possible values include KEY_SET_VALUE to indicate permission to set a key's value, KEY_CREATE_SUB_KEY to indicate permission to create subkeys, and KEY_QUERY_VALUE to indicate permission to query the data value of a key, among many other access level indicators. KEY_ALL_ACCESS provides the highest level of access. To activate the access level during the lifetime of the object, we set this property value after instantiating the object.
CurrentKey	This property specifies the currently open registry key (of type HKEY). The current key changes to the value specified in the OpenKey() method. All the operations that operate on a key work on the current key. If the current key is changed by executing the OpenKeyReadOnly() method, then only read/query-related methods operate on the current key. This is a read-only property.
CurrentPath	The CurrentPath indicates the full (AnsiString) registry path of the current key from the root key. Every time the current key is changed, the CurrentPath also changes automatically to represent the current key. This is a read-only property.
LazyWrite	The LazyWrite (Boolean) property indicates how the write operation should be performed on the keys when they are closed. By default, when the registry object is created, this property is set to true, which means the key values are updated when they are closed. However, keep in mind that it may happen, that the process of writing the key value may take longer than for the close operation to complete its execution. If this property is set to false, the change made to the key values are immediately applied, but the process may consume more resources.
RootKey	When the registry object is created, the root key is set to HKEY_CURRENT_USER by default. However, we can change the value by setting this property.

Method	Description
CloseKey()	This method writes the value of the current key and closes it. Usually it is recommended to close the key after the read or write operation is complete.
CreateKey(const AnsiString key)	This method creates a new subkey under the current key with an access level of KEY_ALL_ACCESS by default. To create an absolute key, we should prepend the key name by a backslash (\), which creates the key as a subkey under the root key. The method returns true or false, depending on whether the key creation was successful. To set values to a key, we should use one of the write methods.
DeleteKey(const AnsiString key)	This method deletes the specified key and its associated data values. The method returns true or false, depending on whether the key deletion was successful.

Part 2

Method	Description
GetKeyNames(TStrings* keys)	This method returns the list of all the subkeys under the current key in the argument strings object.
GetValueNames (TStrings* values)	This method returns the list of the names of all the data values associated with the current key.
HasSubKeys()	This method returns a Boolean value true or false, depending on whether the current key has any subkeys.
KeyExists(const AnsiString key)	This method searches the system registry for the specified key and returns true or false, depending on whether the key exists.
ReadString(const AnsiString valueName)	This method returns an AnsiString value of the specified data element under the current key. If there is no such data element, an empty string is returned. If the requested data element value is not a string, an exception is thrown. There are other read methods to read several other data types, such as float, integer, date, time, datetime, currency, bool, and so on.
RegistryConnect (const AnsiString compName)	This method connects the current registry object to the system registry on another computer. Before invoking this method, you should set the root key value for the current registry object to HKEY_USERS or HKEY_LOCAL_MACHINE. If the connection is successful, the method sets the root key value to the root key on the remote computer. The method returns true or false, depending on its execution success or failure.
ValueExists(const AnsiString valueName)	This method returns a Boolean value true or false, depending on whether a value exists for the specified data element name under the current key.
WriteString(const AnsiString valueName, const AnsiString value)	This method writes the string value for the specified data element under the current key. If the specified data element already exists, its value is replaced with the new value; if not, it is created with the specified value. You should use other write methods for other data types such as float, date, time, datetime, interger, bool and so on.

Non-visual Containers

Container is the word that applies to objects that have the ability to contain other objects. Containers may be visual objects or non-visual objects. I am not discussing the visual containers here because they are not part of the BaseCLX framework. Later in this section, we will spend some time discussing some commonly used visual containers (belonging to the VisualCLX framework).

For a C++ programmer who does not use a framework like VCL/CLX, the only containers available are through the use of STL (Standard Template Library). This chapter discusses the container objects provided by the BaseCLX framework. Since the subject of containers is huge with regards to the types of containers provided in the VCL/CLX, attention will be paid to just a few of these classes, but I encourage you to refer to the manuals on the others.

TStrings and TStringList

TStrings is a container class that maintains a collection of strings and corresponding object pointers. This is a base class and contains pure virtual methods. Therefore, the class cannot be directly used to instantiate an object; rather, a descendant class must be used. Examples of its descendants are the TStringList (non-visual) object, which has implemented all the properties and methods of the base class, and the Items property of the TListBox (visual) object.

The Add method lets you add a string item to the list, and the AddObject method lets you add an object with an associated string (e.g., object name). The Strings property is an array of the strings, and the Objects property is an array of object pointers. Both these arrays are accessed by an index, which varies from 0 to one less than the number of items in the list. To add an object to the list, first the object has to be created and then the pointer is passed along as a parameter to the method call.

Signatures of these methods are given in Listing 12-3.

Listing 12-3

```
int __fastcall Add(const AnsiString S);
int __fastcall AddObject(const AnsiString S, System::TObject* AObject);
```

Both the methods return the index of the added string (and object). When the list is destroyed, the strings are destroyed but the associated objects are not, because the string list object does not own them. They have to be destroyed by the developer, separately. In some programming circumstances, it may even be necessary to destroy the objects before the pointers to these objects are destroyed along with the string list (if the list is the only place where the pointers are stored). Otherwise, the object pointers may not be available to access the objects for the purpose of destroying. However, if the objects assigned to the string list are owned by another component, the owner component takes care of destroying the objects and the developer does not have to worry about it; this is particularly the case with objects created at design time using the IDE.

When the objects are accessed using the Objects property, the pointer returns references to an object of type TObject. Hence, it is necessary to typecast the object to the appropriate type before using it, as shown in the Listing 12-4.

Part 2

Listing 12-4

```
// the statements that create a string list and assign an object to it
TStringList *st = new TStringList();      // create a string list
St→AddObject(ListBox1→Name, ListBox1);   // assign a Listbox to the list

. . . . . . . .
. . . . . . . .
. . . . . . . .

TListBox* lb = (TListBox*)st→Objects[I];  // to access the list box object
AnsiString lbName = st→Strings[I];        // to access the corresponding string object
```

Table 12-3 summarizes a list of the most commonly used properties and methods of the string list object.

Table 12-3: Properties and methods of TStringList

Property	Description
CommaText	Returns the string list object contents as comma-separated text
Count	Returns the number of items in the list
Names	Contains an array of names if the string list contains strings of name-value pairs
Objects	Contains an array of TObject*
Strings	Contains an array of AnsiString objects
Text	Returns the contents of the string list object as text, separating individual items with a carriage return and linefeed
Values	Contains an array of values if the string list contains strings of name-value pairs

Method	Description
BeginUpdate() and EndUpdate()	These methods help the TStrings object to track when the list object is being updated and when the update is complete, respectively. Descendants of the TStrings class may use this information to hold and start repainting the portion of the screen where the visual data is being updated to avoid flicker during the update process.
Delete(int index)	Deletes an item located at a specified (zero-based) index position from the string list object. If an object is associated with the item in the list, the reference of the object is also deleted from the list (the object itself is not deleted).
Exchange(int index1, int index2)	Swaps the positions of strings (and any associated objects) located in the positions index1 and index2
IndexOf(AnsiString str)	Returns the index position of the associated string. If the specified string does not exist in the list, −1 is returned.
Insert(int index, AnsiString s)	Inserts a string into the string list object at a specified location
InsertObject(int index, AnsiString s, TObject object)	Inserts a string and the associated object into the string list object at a specified location
LoadFromFile(Ansi String file)	Loads the string list object contents from the specified file. The individual strings must be separated in the file by carriage return and linefeed characters. Only strings are loaded from the file, not the associated objects.
LoadFromStream (TStream *stream)	Loads the string list object contents from the specified stream object. The stream object is a descendant of the TStream class. The stream object should have been created by the SaveToStream method.

Method	Description
Move(int currIndex, int newIndex)	Moves the string (and the associated object, if any) located at the currIndex position to the newIndex position
SaveToFile(Ansi-String file)	Saves the string list object contents to the specified file. The individual strings are separated in the file by carriage return and linefeed characters. Only strings are saved to the file, not the associated objects.
SaveToStream (TStream *stream)	Saves the string list object contents to the specified stream object. The stream object is a descendant of the TStream class. The programmer has to create the stream object that is passed as an argument to this method. After using the stream object, again the programmer has to delete the stream object explicitly.

Another interesting feature of the TStrings object is its ability to store name-value pairs as an individual names list and value list associated with their string. This is very useful for storing property values read from a property file. An example is given here:

```
userid=satya
password=kolachina
```

If strings of this type are stored as items in the list, the string userid=satya is stored as an item in the list. The complete string can be accessed from the Strings property, the value userid can be accessed from the Names property, and the value satya can be accessed from the Values property.

TList and TObjectList

The TList class is a non-visual container that maintains a list of pointers to any type of object. Therefore, the TListBox object (which is a visual component and also a container itself) may be contained within a TList object by storing its pointer as an item in the TList container or TObjectList object. The objects stored in the TList object can be any descendants of TObject. The features provided by TList include the following:

■ Maintains a list of object pointers

■ The number of items in the list is indicated by the Count property.

■ The Delete(int index) method deletes the object pointer at the specified index, and the Remove(void *ptr) method deletes the object pointer ptr.

■ Deleting an item from the list does not destroy the original object; only the object pointer is lost. In fact, if the list is the only location where the pointer is stored, it is advised to destroy the object before deleting the item from the list. Otherwise, the programmer will lose the object pointer and cannot destroy the object later.

■ Similarly, destroying the TList object itself does not destroy the objects whose pointers are contained in the list.

Part 2

■ The list can contain NULL pointers, and to delete all the NULL pointers from the list, the Pack() method must be called.

The TObjectList object descends from the TList object and adds more control to the programmer.

■ Objects whose pointers are contained in the TObjectList object can be owned by the list object that can take the responsibility of destroying them when they are deleted from the list or when the list object is itself destroyed. This is controlled by the Boolean property OwnsObjects, which, when set to true, leaves the responsibility of destroying the owned objects to the list object.

■ The Remove(TObject *ptr) method has been overridden in TObjectList to accept a pointer to the TObject class rather than a void pointer, which is the case with the TList object.

■ Call Extract(void *item) to remove an object from the list without freeing the object itself. After an object is removed, all the objects that follow it are moved up in index position and Count is decremented.

Streams and Streaming

One of the best features of the VCL/CLX component library is the ability to save the object's state to a stream and retrieve it later from the stream. There are many VCL/CLX objects that provide this feature through a pair of functions, SaveToStream(TStream *stream) and LoadFromStream(TStream *stream). TStream is the base class for BaseCLX (VCL/CLX) style streams. Do not confuse these stream objects with the C++ IOStreams. The BaseCLX functionality is always available on top of whatever standard C++ language provides.

TStream defines all the base functionality of a stream that can read from or write to various kinds of storage media, such as disk files, dynamic memory, and so on. Stream objects permit applications to seek an arbitrary position in the stream, either for the purpose of reading or writing. It is the responsibility of the programmer to interpret the data read by mapping to the appropriate object's structure or data layout. In simple terms, any object's contents can be saved to a stream, provided that methods similar to those mentioned above are made available by the respective component writers. The main features of streams are data access from an arbitrary position in the stream and a unified data access technique without regard to the storage media of the stream. The descendant class that derives from TStream takes care of the media access techniques, and hence it is the responsibility of the component writers and not the application programmers.

TStream also introduces methods that work in conjunction with components and filers for loading and saving components in simple and inherited forms. These methods are called automatically by global routines that initiate component streaming. They can also be called directly to initiate the streaming process. These are ReadComponent, ReadComponentRes, WriteComponent, WriteComponentRes, etc.

Two important properties of the TStream object are Position and Size. Position indicates the current location of the stream pointer (similar to the file pointer) from the beginning of the stream. Size indicates current memory (in bytes) of the stream. Methods that load (or add) contents to the stream set the Size property of the stream internally; setting this value explicitly has no effect. When the TStream (descendant) object is created, Size is 0 and Position is 0. As data is added, the size grows, and the current pointer location moves away from the beginning of the stream. After the data is added and before it is read, the stream pointer has to be set to the beginning (or any appropriate location in the stream) explicitly by the programmer; otherwise, access violations occur. When data is read from the stream from a location by a specific number of bytes, it only means that the data is copied from the stream to another memory location by a specified number of bytes, the stream pointer is moved forward by the same number of bytes, and data is not removed from the stream. To read the same set of bytes, move the stream pointer back by the same number of bytes and do another read. To clear the contents of the stream object, the descendant class must implement a corresponding method.

The descendants of TStream, as defined in the VCL/CLX, are explained below. The purpose of these stream objects may be different based on their design, but they all share the same streaming features explained above. VCL inherited more stream objects than the CLX framework from the base TStream class, as indicated here:

- **TFileStream**—This stream object makes it easy to read from and write to a disk file. Component writers can implement methods to save the components' status to disk file and rebuild the component status back from the disk file. There is a Seek(int offset, Word origin) method that must be used to position the stream pointer at an appropriate location before a read or write operation begins. In fact, some of the VCL/CLX components currently support this feature (and even some third-party vendor components support this feature). This stream object is available in both the VCL and CLX frameworks.

Part 2

- **TMemoryStream**—This stream object makes it easy to read from and write to a memory stream. By saving the components' status to the memory stream, application developers can develop uniform and unique logic to save the component status and transmit across the network to other computers, where the receiving applications can restore the components if they know the object structure that the stream contains. This can be used as a simple alternate method to transfer objects across the network without bothering to learn complex architectures like DCOM and CORBA. Moreover, technologies like COM/DCOM/ActiveX are platform-specific. However, component writers have to implement methods to save the object status to the memory stream. Some of the VCL/CLX components currently support this feature (and even some third-party vendor components also support this feature). This stream object is available in both the VCL and CLX frameworks.

- **TStringStream**—This stream object provides file-like access to create string objects, as opposed to a more structured AnsiString object. It is useful as an intermediary object that can hold text as well as read it from or write it to another storage medium. This stream object is available in both the VCL and CLX frameworks.

- **TWinSocketStream**—This stream object is only available in the VCL framework. It provides services that allow applications to read from or write to socket connections using the WinSock library API. Socket connections are of two types: blocking and non-blocking. In non-blocking socket connections, the read or write across the socket is performed asynchronously, and hence the events are fired only when the socket is ready for read or write and data is awaiting at the port. But in case of blocking connections, the read and write occur synchronously, and the client application cannot do anything else as long as the read or write operation is in progress or waiting. Since the reading process cannot wait indefinitely until the socket is ready for reading with data at the port, the TWinSocketStream object provides a waiting feature with a timeout mechanism. It is required to read over the blocking socket. More on sockets was discussed in Chapter 10 along with distributed application development using TCP/IP sockets.

- **TBlobStream**—This stream object is currently only available in the VCL framework and is designed to enable reading and writing BLOB field data in a database table. The BLOB field in a table is designed to hold Binary Large OBjects, including pictures or large memos. Every time the BLOB field data is read from or written to a table, it is necessary to create a TBlobStream object to enable this read or write operation. There are two ways to create this stream object. Using the new operator and passing two arguments (the BLOBField object and the stream access mode) to the constructor creates an instance of the TBlobStream object to operate on the specific BLOBField of the table. The second way is to call the CreateBlobField method on the TTable object and provide the same two parameters. In either case, the stream object is instantiated, and it is the programmer's responsibility to delete the object after use. It is also important to keep in mind that there is no terminating character that identifies the end of a BLOB stream data, and hence the parameter count (which is an integer value) must be supplied with the exact number of bytes to be transferred.

■ **TOleStream**—This stream object is also available only in the VCL framework because OLE is a Windows-specific technology. This object reads and writes information over a streaming interface that is provided by an OLE object.

Graphics at a Glance

Let's first look at the process of working with the low-level graphics API in Windows and imagine the situation if we don't use the VCL/CLX framework. Using the Windows GDI (Graphical Device Interface) directly to include graphics in their applications requires the programmers themselves to manage graphic resources directly. There are such wide varieties of display devices and driver software provided by different vendors that the Windows operating system should support the graphic output display. The Windows graphics device context is designed to handle the intricacies of different devices and provide a unique interface for the Win32 programmer. Win32 help defines a device context as a structure that defines a set of graphic objects and their associated attributes and the graphic modes that affect output. The graphic objects include a pen for line drawing, a brush for painting and filling, a bitmap for copying or scrolling parts of the screen, a palette for defining the set of available colors, a region for clipping and other operations, and a path for painting and drawing operations. In its simplest definition, the device context is a block of memory containing the data structure as defined earlier and managed by the GDI. Before we do any operation on drawing graphics, it is necessary to obtain a handle to the device context from Windows. The direct Win32 functions to retrieve a handle to a device context are given in Listing 12-5.

Part 2

Listing 12-5: Win32 functions to retrieve a device context handle

```
// creates a device context for a device with a specified name
HDC hdc = CreateDC (DriverName, DeviceName, Output, lpInitData);
// returns device context for the window's client area
HDC hdc = GetDC(some_handle);
// returns handle of a display device context for the specified window
HDC hdc = GetDCEx(some_handle, …);
// returns device context for the entire window
HDC hdc = GetWindowDC(some_handle);
```

After obtaining the device context, the programmer then uses its associated functions to perform the necessary drawing tasks. After the device context is no longer needed, it should be released back to Windows either via the ReleaseDC() function (if you used GetDC(), GetDCEx(), or GetWindow-DC()) or via the DeleteDC() function (if you used CreateDC()).

The VCL/CLX framework made this task very simple by providing a set of objects to manage these resources. By using these objects, the programmer does not have to bother with managing the resources. The interface that VCL provides is through the Canvas property of the specific component, which handles the drawing tasks. The Canvas property is an instance of the TCanvas class, which is a direct descendant of the TPersistent class.

TCanvas

TCanvas provides an abstract drawing space for objects that must render their own images. It is derived directly from the TPersistent class. It encapsulates the graphics device context in VCL (for Windows) and the paint device (Qt Painter) in CLX (cross-platform) framework. The properties and methods of this object are exposed to the programmers through the Canvas property of the specific component with which the programmer is working. It is the responsibility of the component writers to expose the Canvas property. The TCustomControl and TGraphicControl classes include the Canvas property in their ancestor class so that component writers can provide the drawing canvas to their users. Controls derived from TCustomControl, such as TDBGrid, provide the Canvas property to the windowed/widget controls (i.e., controls able to receive input focus). Controls derived from TGraphicControl, such as TImage, provide the Canvas property to non-windowed/ non-widget controls (i.e., controls that do not receive input focus). Standard windowed/widget controls, like button, check box, and edit control, etc., know how to draw themselves and do not need to descend from TCustomControl; hence they are derived directly from TWinControl (which is also the ancestor of TCustomControl).

The important properties of the TCanvas object are Pen, Brush, and Font, which are instances of TPen, TBrush, and TFont, respectively, which are the graphic objects that provide different styles, colors, etc. that affect the appearance of the drawing. Accessing the Canvas property of a VCL control opens a channel of drawing capabilities to the programmer.

Visual Container Components (in VisualCLX)

Until now we have been discussing the BaseCLX classes. Now let's throw some light on a couple of visual containers supported both in the VCL and CLX frameworks. To conserve space, I am only going to discuss a few visual components in this section. In fact, many VCL features and components discussed in earlier chapters are supported in the CLX framework with the limitations discussed earlier.

TListBox

Container objects have the ability to contain other objects. An example of a visual container is a TListBox object that contains a list of strings displayed in a visual list box. Here the TListBox object acts like a container, and each of the AnsiString objects are contained within the container. The contents of a list box formulate an object of TStrings class. We are familiar with this class, and we know that it is a non-visual container.

A container object may also be contained in another container object. TList is a non-visual container that maintains a list of pointers to any type of object. Therefore, the TListBox object (which is a container itself) may be contained within a TList object by storing its pointer as an item in the TList container or TObjectList object.

This chapter discusses the container objects provided by the VCL framework. Since the subject of containers is huge with regard to the types of containers provided in the VCL, attention will be paid to just a few of these classes, and the reader is encouraged to refer to the manuals on the others.

TListView

Another visual component, TListView, is an example that contains containers within another container. The list view object is used to display rows and columns of data, preferably in display mode, as the name suggests (to display editable rows and columns, TStringGrid and TDBGrid objects may be used). The individual items of a list view object are instances of the TListItem object, and the list of these objects is contained in the TListItems object and identified by the Items property of the list view. The TListItems object has methods to add, delete, insert items, clear the list, etc. The list also has the methods BeginUpdate() and EndUpdate(), which, unlike the TStrings class, disable and enable screen painting of the list view object to avoid screen flicker during the update process. Each of the items in the list is a TListItem, which in turn has a property called SubItems, an instance of TStrings, to contain strings that appear as sub-items to the main list item. It is also important to note that the individual instances of the TListItem object are owned by the TListItems object, which is owned by the TListView instance. Because of this hierarchy of ownership, when the topmost object is deleted, it takes the responsibility of deleting the components it owns, and this responsibility is carried forward by the hierarchy of components in the object. This is one of the features that make VCL a strong architecture, relieving the programmer from the task of destroying the objects.

Custom Component Development

In this section we will discuss how to build custom components. We will mainly concentrate on building VCL components, but the same concepts can be used for CLX component development. Recall the VCL architecture that we discussed in the beginning chapters of the book. We learned that the classes that are derived from the TComponent class provide certain behavior to the objects, such as the ability to be hosted in the Component Palette, be manipulated in the form designer, contain other components, and so on. The component framework offered by C++Builder enables us to create our own components to perform a specific task without just being satisfied with what is shipped with the product. A well-designed custom component behaves in all respects like the components shipped with C++Builder, and the functionality offered by the custom components is only limited by your imagination. This opens a business avenue for software vendors to design special-purpose components or general-purpose components. In fact, many vendors already provide custom components, which naturally mix with the VCL framework. Your custom component may perform tasks of any complexity. For example, you may create a custom component that manages appointments and scheduled tasks, and one custom component each for an appointment and a scheduled task, respectively. These three components together may implement part of a calendar application, such as Microsoft Outlook.

Since VCL architecture originated with the Delphi product, it has been a business practice by many vendors to first develop components for the Delphi platform using the Object Pascal language and then port them to the C++Builder platform and provide appropriate header files. Though this is acceptable in the Delphi-based developer community, for many programmers who are dedicated exclusively to the C++ language, such as those coming from other C++ platforms like Microsoft Visual C++, this practice may seem odd. Additionally, many programmers may not be willing to develop components that way. In fact, this practice may even convey the wrong message that this is the only way to build VCL (or CLX) components. I would like to take the opportunity to clarify that it is not required to build VCL components in Delphi in order to use them in C++Builder. In fact, C++Builder is itself competent enough to build custom components. In this section, we will discuss the steps involved in creating VCL components in C++Builder.

It is necessary to understand the main difference between creating custom components and using existing components. The difference is that while creating components, you are playing the role of a component writer (and designer) and not an application programmer; therefore, you would be accessing those parts of the component classes that are normally not accessible to those who use the components and you would also be adding new parts to the classes and setting access levels for these parts. In summary, a component writer has complete access to the component classes.

TComponent forms the base class for all the components. However, depending on the type of component, you may need to choose a different base class. To build a windowed control, you need to have TWinControl in VCL or TWidgetControl in CLX as the base class; to build a graphic control you should choose TGraphicControl; and non-visual components should be sub-classed from TComponent. You may also subclass from any of the windowed controls in order to inherit the behavior of the specific windowed control as a base component behavior. There are occasions where you would need to derive subclasses from the ancestors of a TComponent, such as TObject and TPersistent, in which case the derived class cannot be deployed to the Component Palette since it does not represent a component. But it still can be used in other components or applications.

One of the important features of components in C++Builder is that the behavior of objects is controlled through properties, methods, and events. Properties represent a component's characteristics identified by the class variables. Properties provide either read-only or read-write access to the users as required by the specific property. In the application program, an object's property is typically read when it is specified in the right-hand side of the expression and is set to a new value when it is specified in the left-hand side of the expression. Inherently, we implement the getter method to read a property value and the setter method to write a property value. Properties may take any of the simple data types, enumeratated types, arrays, sets, and objects. It is the component writer's responsibility to initialize the appropriate values or instantiate the objects when needed and destroy them when the component itself goes out of scope if the property represents an object. A component's methods are designed to perform a variety of tasks, such as hiding the complexity of an operation, setting several properties at once, and so on. Since components are designed to create objects during run time, their methods provide a very handy way of altering their state at any time.

The event-driven programming model (also called the delegation model) has been very successful, and it tightly integrates a business scenario within an object if the events are better designed and implemented. In fact, it is the event-driven nature of the VCL that makes C++Builder a distinct C++ implementation, compared to some other commercial C++ implementations available on the market. Now the CLX component framework extends this event-based programming model even to Linux applications. The C++ language is not event-based by nature. But the component framework built by Borland has imparted that characteristic to C++Builder. I am so impressed with this feature that I recommend that those C++ developers who are not C++Builder users take a look at this feature.

Implementing Component Properties and Methods

Implementing properties involves a few tasks on our part as component writers. We have to provide the property declaration, declare class data members to store property values, and then finally implement the property access methods. The property declaration should be made either in the public or __published section of the class.

Components have a design-time interface and a run-time interface. The design-time interface contains published properties, which are changeable in the Object Inspector. These are declared in the __published section of the class. The run-time interface contains unpublished properties, which are only accessible during run time. Usually, properties that have read-only access or those that can be set after run-time initialization of the component are provided through the run-time interface only by declaring them in the public section.

A typical property declaration is displayed in Listings 12-6 and 12-7 and identified by the __property keyword. In the examples, the property is defined as a Boolean value by the name IsPermitted. The corresponding class data member that stores the property value is defined by prefixing "F" to the property name, as in FIsPermitted. The property declaration looks like an expression, where the left-hand side of the expression is the name of the property, and the right-hand side constitutes the access definition for the property enclosed within curly braces. The read access to the property is identified by the keyword read and is equated to the corresponding field name or method name. If the field name is provided, the property is read from the field directly, as in Listing 12-6; if the method name is provided, that method is identified by a declaration and the corresponding implementation, as in Listing 12-7. Similarly, the write access is identified by the keyword write and is equated to the field name or the method name, as appropriate. If the property setters and getters have more complex logic to be performed, the access methods are the best choice. If we are using the access methods to access properties, then it is recommended to declare them as private, since it is not a good practice to let the access methods be public. In addition, the property declaration may also contain a default value assigned to the default keyword.

Listing 12-6: Sample published property—direct access

```
//-------------------------------------------------------------------------

#ifndef NewComponentH
#define NewComponentH
//-------------------------------------------------------------------------
#include <SysUtils.hpp>
#include <Classes.hpp>
//-------------------------------------------------------------------------
class PACKAGE TNewComponent : public TComponent
{
private:
    bool FIsPermitted;        // data member that holds property value
    :
    :
__published:
    __property bool IsPermitted = {read=FIsPermitted, write=FIsPermitted};
    :
    :
};
```

Listing 12-7: Sample published property—using access methods

```
//-------------------------------------------------------------------------

#ifndef NewComponentH
#define NewComponentH
//-------------------------------------------------------------------------
#include <SysUtils.hpp>
#include <Classes.hpp>
//-------------------------------------------------------------------------
class PACKAGE TNewComponent: public TComponent
{
private:
    bool FIsPermitted;                    // data member that holds property value
    bool __fastcall GetIsPermitted();                  // getter method
    void __fastcall SetIsPermitted(bool isPermitted);  // setter method
    :
    :
__published:
    __property bool IsPermitted = {read= GetIsPermitted, write= SetIsPermitted };
    :
```

Part 2

```
    :
    };
    :

    // The access method implementation in cpp file
    //
    bool __fastcall TNewComponent::GetIsPermitted()
    {
        return FIsPermitted;
    }

    void __fastcall TNewComponent::SetIsPermitted(bool isPermitted)
    {
        FIsPermitted = isPermitted;
    }
```

The properties declared as protected are only accessed by the class members where the property is declared or by the descendant classes, not by any applications that instantiate the component objects. The protected properties of an ancestor component may be published or made public by a descendant component, in which case the property declaration just contains the __property keyword followed by the property name (as in __property AdditionalCaption) because the actual declaration for the property was provided in the ancestor class. In this case, these properties are accessible in the descendant classes, either during run time (if declared as public) or design time time (if declared as published). Please remember that published properties are also public but not vice versa. In other words, the published access level is the highest level, followed by the next level, public, then protected, and finally private.

We implement component methods as either public or protected. However, the property access methods are implemented as private. Methods are not declared as published because the Object Inspector does not provide design-time access to methods. By defining certain methods as virtual, we enable the descendant classes to implement their own implementation of the method, overriding or augmenting the base class method. We discussed in Chapter 2, "C++ Advanced Concepts," the virtual methods and how the object class type information is used while performing late binding.

Implementing Component Events

Events provide a link between an occurrence in the system and a program block (also known as an event handler) that responds to that occurrence. The occurrences of the events are captured and published by the component writers, and the event handlers are implemented by the application developers. Examples of events include user interaction events such as clicking a button or typing letters from the keyboard, mouse interaction events, and state-change events such as the event representing when a dataset is opened or closed or a record pointer is moved across records in the dataset. The state-change type events provide more control in your hands as a component writer, rather than the user-interaction events, which are controlled by some occurrence external to your component or the application that uses the component. There is no end to the list of examples. In fact, by designing events, you are providing hooks to the application developers, where they can write their own program blocks to respond to the event.

Designing events for your component involves determining the type of the event. The standard type TNotifyEvent is defined in the Classes unit (Classes.pas and Classes.hpp files) as a type-definition (typedef) to a pointer to a method with the __closure keyword. It takes a single parameter, which is a pointer to the TObject type, as shown in Listing 12-8. Because an event is a pointer to an event handler, the type of the event property must be of a closure type. In addition, the __closure keyword enables the Object Inspector to identify the method definition as an event and displays the event name in the Events tab page.

Listing 12-8: TNotifyEvent typedef

```
typedef void __fastcall (__closure *TNotifyEvent)(System::TObject* Sender);
```

Notice that the above declaration indicates that an event defined of standard event type passes only one parameter to the event handler, a pointer to the object that has received the event. Also, this type of event is only one-way, which means that it cannot send a return value to the default event handler. For example, if the user clicks a button, the OnClick event is triggered on the button component, and the event handler receives the pointer to the button component as the single parameter. If the event handler has to convey something back to your default event handler, this type of event should not be used. You need to design an event type that sends more parameters to the event handler for which you would have to define the event type similar to the TNotifyEvent and add more parameters as required. An example event type is shown in Listing 12-9. This new event type generates an event handler that sends a reference to a Boolean parameter Permitted. The application developer sets a value for this parameter, and the default event handler you provided for the event captures the value and acts accordingly.

Listing 12-9: TNewEventType typedef

```
typedef void __fastcall (__closure *TNewEventType)(System::TObject* Sender, bool
    &Permitted);
```

When the application developer double-clicks on an event name in the Object Inspector, the IDE automatically adds an empty event handler with the parameters specified in the event type, whether it is the standard

TNotifyEvent type or your custom event type. The IDE names the event handler by prefixing the name of the component to the event name (excluding the prefix On). For example, if you named a TButton object OkButton in your application, the OnClick event handler generated by the IDE for this button is named OkButtonClick.

Listing 12-10 displays a typical declaration of an event and the associated class member data variable. Remember that an event declaration is merely a method pointer declaration with a specific signature.

Listing 12-10: Sample code defining an event

```
//----------------------------------------------------------------------

#ifndef NewComponentH
#define NewComponentH
//----------------------------------------------------------------------

#include <SysUtils.hpp>
#include <Classes.hpp>

typedef void __fastcall (__closure *TNewEventType)(System::TObject* Sender, bool
    &Permitted);
//----------------------------------------------------------------------
class PACKAGE TNewComponent: public TComponent
{
private:
    TNewEventType FOnPermission;    // data member that defines event method pointer
    :
    :
__published:
    __property TNewEventType OnPermission = {read=FOnPermission, write=FOnPermission};
    :
    :
};
```

Overriding Default Event Behavior

For an event to be fired, the component writer should provide the code in some method. As an example for standard events supported by VCL components shipped with C++Builder, Borland implemented methods that trigger the events at appropriate times, such as an OnClick event fired when you click a button component. This is implemented by VCL designers through the Click() method, which is protected and virtual. In fact, the methods that support event triggering are protected (so that they are only accessible to the descendant classes, and application programs do not directly execute them) and virtual (so that you can override them in your components derived from VCL components).

If an event needs to exhibit default behavior, you may implement it through your own method by overriding the protected method implemented in the base component from which you derived your component (if the event was originally implemented by the base component), by calling the inherited method, or doing both. If you override the base component method, you can modify the internal event handling, and if you call the inherited method, you can maintain the standard handling, including the event handler implemented by the application developer. Even if you override the base component method, make it a point to call the inherited method first so that you allow the application developer's implementation of the event handler to execute before your custom event handling. However, you may call the inherited method after your custom handling code if that is the way your component should work. If you added a new event in the component, then you should declare the method that triggers the event as virtual and in the protected section.

It is always recommended that while designing component events, the default execution of the component should not depend on implementation of the event handler by the application developer. If the application developer does not provide such an implementation, the component should behave normally with the default behavior. However, the component may not behave as expected by the application developer without some specific event handler implementation. For example, while implementing drag and drop, the OnDragOver event handler may be implemented for a target control to indicate if it can accept the dragged item when dropped by the user. If the user does not implement the event handler for this event for a particular control, then that control behaves normally without expecting (and without accepting) the dragged object to be received. After all, the events are meant to be implemented as part of the customization of the component's behavior.

Listing 12-11 displays sample code to show how you could override the protected method from the base class in order to provide the default event handling. In the example, the Click() method of the standard TButton component is augmented (assuming that the component is derived from the TButton class). I am still calling the base component's Click() method in order to preserve the standard way of triggering the event.

Listing 12-11: Sample code overriding the base component's method

```
void __fastcall TMyNewButton::Click()
{
  TButton::Click();    // preserves the standard behavior of the event
  // you may write your custom handling code here …
}
```

Registering the Components

When we develop components, we typically make them available in the Component Palette whether they are visual or non-visual in nature. To make a component available in the Component Palette, at a minimum you have to provide the necessary code to register your component with the IDE. In a single programming unit, you may be providing more than one component, and you may register them all at once. When you create a component through the IDE using the dialog opened with the File | New Items | New | Component options, the IDE automatically creates the Register() function to register the component. Listing 12-12 displays the registration code generated by the IDE for my sample component. Notice that the RegisterComponents() global function is called with the name of the Component Palette page on which the component should be placed and the classes array containing the component classes.

Listing 12-12: Code to register the sample component

```
namespace Mynewbutton
{
    void __fastcall PACKAGE Register()
    {
        TComponentClass classes[1] = {__classid(TMyNewButton)};
        RegisterComponents("Satya's Components", classes, 0);
    }
}
```

You may register several components at once using code similar to Listing 12-13. You first create an array of TComponentClass items and assign the metaclass of each of your new components to the array. Then call the RegisterComponents() method with three parameters. The first parameter is the name of the Component Palette page where the component should be placed. If the specified page exists, the components are placed on that page; otherwise, a new page with the given name is created, and the components are placed. The second parameter to the method is the component classes array, and the third parameter is the highest index size of the component classes array. In a zero-based array indexing, the value is n–1, where n is the size of the array.

Listing 12-13: Code to register the sample component

```
namespace MynewComponents
{
    void __fastcall PACKAGE Register()
    {
        // Declare a component array to hold the new components
        TComponentClass classes[3];
        Classes[0] = __classid(TMyNewButton);
        Classes[1] = __classid(TMyNewLabel);
```

```
        Classes[2] = __classid(TMyNewComboBox);
        RegisterComponents("Satya's Components", classes, 2);
    }
}
```

In this chapter I described the custom component building process in general. However, component building is itself a huge set of tasks. There are many topics, such as message handling, creating graphics for your components, creating property editors, and so on. Believe it or not, one could write a book exclusively on component writing.

Miscellaneous Programming Features

So far, we have discussed the CLX component framework and custom component development in this chapter. At this time, I would like to direct your attention to some of the miscellaneous and advanced features that are very useful in application development.

Variant and OleVariant

The Variant class is the C++ implementation of the Object Pascal intrinsic Variant data type. It is designed to hold variables whose data types are not known during compile time. It is able to automatically recognize the actual data type of the variable (or object) being stored at run time. Most of the basic data types, including TDateTime and AnsiString, are converted automatically. Variant is widely used in applications where the data type is unknown at compile time, such as while implementing generic dataset-based applications. OleVariant is derived from Variant and is used especially to represent COM automation objects or data passed over a COM interface. When an OleVariant object is used to represent a COM automation object, it can be used to get and set properties or to execute method calls on the automation object. The methods that we use most of the time to work with automation objects are given here. There are two special OleVariant values: Unassigned, which represents that the OleVariant object has not been assigned to any COM automation object, and NULL, which indicates that the OleVariant object is unknown. Both Variant and OleVariant types can contain arrays of varying size and dimension with elements of any of the data types they support.

The CreateObject(const String& ProgID) method should be used to instantiate a COM automation object identified by the ProgID program identifier. The pointer to the COM automation object is returned as of type Variant. Before we try to access the properties and methods of any automation object, we must first create it using this method. If the ProgID

Part 2

argument does not represent a valid COM automation object, the EOleSysError exception is thrown.

The GetActiveObject(const String& ProgID) method is used to obtain a pointer to the IDispatch interface of the currently active object of the class identified by the ProgID argument. ProgID is the program identifier for the class of the active object from the OLE registration database. If the method fails to return the requested interface pointer, the EOleSysError exception is thrown. If the automation object is not running or not registered, the CreateObject method must be used to run it.

The OleFunction(const String& name, ...) method is called to execute a method call on the object (which returns a value to the caller object) represented by the current OleVariant. The method takes the name of the method on the COM automation object that should be executed as the first argument. After the first argument, I put an ellipsis because we have a number of overloaded versions of this method. In one variation of the method, the second argument is a reference to an object of the TAutoArgsBase class, which is used to wrap an array of TVariantT values to be used as arguments to the dispatch interface method. The TVariantT is a templatized class that is associated with and derives indirectly from a Windows VARIANT or VARIANT-derived data type. Other variations of the OleFunction method include a number of overloaded templatized functions, which may take from 1 to 32 arguments. The arguments to these methods can be of any C++ data type or class type. To put it simply, we are free to pass up to 32 arguments to the COM interface method through the OleFunction method call. If the target interface method does not take any arguments, we do not have to pass any. The value returned by the COM interface method is in turn returned by the OleFunction method as a Variant data type.

The OleProcedure(const String& name, ...) method is called to execute a method call on the object (which does not return a value to the caller object) represented by the current OleVarient. The method is overloaded and takes arguments in a way similar to the OleFunction method. If the target interface method does not take any arguments, we do not have to pass any.

The OlePropertyGet(const String& name, ...) method is called to retrieve a property value of the object represented by the current OleVariant. The first argument is the name of the property whose value should be retrieved. Arguments may be passed to the property get method on the interface object in a way similar to the OleFunction method, with an exception that the OlePropertyGet method is overloaded with templatized versions permitting up to ten arguments at the maximum. If the target interface property get method does not take any arguments, we do not have to pass any. The requested property value is returned as a Variant data type.

The OlePropertySet(const String& name, ...) method is called to set a property value of the object represented by the current OleVariant. The first argument is the name of the property whose value should be set. Arguments may be passed to the property set method on the interface object in a way similar to the OleProcedure method, with an exception that the OlePropertySet method is overloaded with templatized versions permitting up to ten arguments at the maximum. If the target interface property set method does not take any arguments, we do not have to pass any. The OlePropertySet method does not return any value.

The GetElement() method is used to return the value of the specified element from a Variant (or OleVariant) array. The value returned by the method is of Variant data type. Similarly, the PutElement() method must be used to set the value of the specified element in a Variant (or OleVariant) array. Both the methods take one to five arguments, each indicating the element index in the specific dimension, and support up to five dimensions.

Now I will take you through the steps to create a sample application in order to demonstrate using the OleAutomation features. We will build this example in three stages. In the first stage, we will implement code that uses simple OleVariant methods to launch the OLE automation server objects such as Microsoft Word, populate the Word document by creating a table in the document, and populate the cells of the table from the values retrieved from a dataset. In the second stage, we will see how easy it is to access the COM automation applications through the COM server components provided in the Office2k page of the Component Palette. In the third stage, we will examine how to use the OleContainer component to embed OLE automation objects into your own application.

1. Create a standard VCL-based Windows application.

2. Drop one each of the **TADOConnection**, **TADOTable**, and **TDataSource** components. Using ADO is my choice, but you may use any of the database connectivity frameworks in your program; it does not impact the concept I am demonstrating in the example.

3. Drop a page control component on the form and create two tab pages. On the first tab page, drop a **TDBGrid** component to show the data retrieved from the underlying database table. It is not otherwise required in the example. Also, add three **button** components to the first tab page of the page control; we implement the OnClick event handlers of these buttons to launch the Office application, close the Office application, and finally populate a Word document with dataset contents.

4. Add a list box to the main form where you can display the messages. Add another button on the main form to implement logic to clear the message list box. Set the ConnectionString property of the ADO connection component to connect to a database of your choice. Make the necessary property settings for the ADO table, data source, and grid components. In the form constructor, activate the database connection and open the table. Now implement the logic for the three buttons, as shown in Listing 12-14. I used some global AnsiString variables in the program, which are defined in the form header file, as shown in Listing 12-17.

Listing 12-14: OleAutomationClientMain.cpp

```cpp
//---------------------------------------------------------------------------

#include <vcl.h>
#pragma hdrstop

#include "OleAutomationClientMain.h"
//---------------------------------------------------------------------------
#pragma package(smart_init)
#pragma link "Word_2K_SRVR"
#pragma resource "*.dfm"
TOleAutomationClientForm *OleAutomationClientForm;
//---------------------------------------------------------------------------
__fastcall TOleAutomationClientForm::TOleAutomationClientForm(TComponent* Owner)
    : TForm(Owner)
{
    ADOConnection1->Connected = true;
    ADOTable1->Active = true;
}
//---------------------------------------------------------------------------
void __fastcall TOleAutomationClientForm::NewOfficeApplBtnClick(
        TObject *Sender)
{
    if (WordAppl->Checked) {
        officeApplType = "Word.Application";
        officeApplTypeCaption = "Microsoft Word";
    }
    else if (ExcelAppl->Checked) {
        officeApplType = "Excel.Application";
        officeApplTypeCaption = "Microsoft Excel";
    }
    else if (AccessAppl->Checked) {
        officeApplType = "Access.Application";
        officeApplTypeCaption = "Microsoft Access";
    }
    else if (PowerPointAppl->Checked) {
        officeApplType = "PowerPoint.Application";
        officeApplTypeCaption = "Microsoft PowerPoint";
    }
    else if (OutlookAppl->Checked) {
        officeApplType = "Outlook.Application";
        officeApplTypeCaption = "Microsoft Outlook";
    }
```

```
    else {
        officeApplType = "none";
        officeApplTypeCaption = "none";
    }

    try {
        if (officeApplType == "none") {
            MsgList->Items->Add("Proper Office application type must be selected");
            return;
        }
        OfficeApplication  = Variant::CreateObject(officeApplType);
        OfficeApplication.OlePropertySet("Visible", true);
        AnsiString docOpenMessage(officeApplTypeCaption);
        docOpenMessage += " has been launched. You may start using it.";
        MsgList->Items->Add(docOpenMessage);
    }
    catch (Exception &ex) {
        MsgList->Items->Add("Error in launching Microsoft Office application");
    }
}
//---------------------------------------------------------------------------
void __fastcall TOleAutomationClientForm::CloseOfficeDocClick(
    TObject *Sender)
{
    if ((!OfficeApplication.IsEmpty()) && (!OfficeApplication.IsNull())) {
        OfficeApplication.OleFunction("Quit");
        OfficeApplication = Unassigned;
        AnsiString docOpenMessage(officeApplTypeCaption);
        docOpenMessage += " has been closed.";
        MsgList->Items->Add(docOpenMessage);
    }
    else {
        AnsiString errMsg(officeApplTypeCaption);
        errMsg += " is already closed";
        MsgList->Items->Add(errMsg);
    }
}
//---------------------------------------------------------------------------
void __fastcall TOleAutomationClientForm::AddContentsBtnClick(
    TObject *Sender)
{
    OleVariant Template = EmptyParam;
    OleVariant NewTemplate = False;

    if (officeApplTypeCaption == "Microsoft Word") {
        Variant wordDocuments = OfficeApplication.OlePropertyGet("Documents");
        Variant wordDoc = wordDocuments.OleFunction("Add", Template, NewTemplate);

        if ((!ADOTable1->Active) || (ADOTable1->RecordCount <= 0))
            return;

        int fRows = ADOTable1->RecordCount + 1;
        int fCols = ADOTable1->FieldCount;

        Variant docRange = wordDoc.OleFunction("Range", Template, Template);
        Variant docTables = wordDoc.OlePropertyGet("Tables");
        Variant docTable = docTables.OleFunction("Add", docRange, fRows, fCols);

        // Fill the first row of the table to contain
```

Part 2

```
            // database table field names
            for (int k=0; k < ADOTable1->FieldCount; k++) {
                AnsiString fieldHeading = ADOTable1->Fields->Fields[k]->FieldName;
                Variant cell = docTable.OleFunction("Cell", 1, k+1);
                cell.OlePropertyGet("Range").OleFunction("InsertAfter",
                fieldHeading.c_str());
            }

            // Fill the subsequent rows of the table to contain
            // data from the table
            ADOTable1->First();
            for (int i=0; i < ADOTable1->RecordCount; i++) {
                for (int j=0; j < ADOTable1->FieldCount; j++) {
                    AnsiString fieldValue = ADOTable1->Fields->Fields[j]->AsString;
                    Variant valueCell = docTable.OleFunction("Cell", i+2, j+1);
                    valueCell.OlePropertyGet("Range").OleFunction("InsertAfter",
                    fieldValue.c_str());
                }
                ADOTable1->Next();
            }
            ADOTable1->First();
            AnsiString curdir = ExtractFileDir(Application->ExeName);
            curdir += "\\OleWordTestDocument1.doc";
            wordDoc.OleProcedure("SaveAs", curdir.c_str());
            CloseOfficeDocClick(this);
        }

}
//---------------------------------------------------------------------------
void __fastcall TOleAutomationClientForm::ClearMsgBtnClick(TObject *Sender)
{
    MsgList->Items->Clear();
}
//---------------------------------------------------------------------------
```

Using Office 2000 Automation Objects

The Office2k page in the Component Palette provides a number of VCL components encapsulating the Microsoft Office automation servers and objects. The task of launching an Office application and populating the data is made quite simple by the use of these components. However, you need to have knowledge of the Office automation object models and their properties and methods to programmatically access the Office documents. You may refer to Microsoft documentation such as MSDN for more details on this subject.

To implement stage 2 of the example, you need to add another button to the first tab page of the page control. We implement our logic in the OnClick event handler of this button, as shown in Listing 12-15.

Listing 12-15: OleAutomationClientMain.cpp—stage 2 addition

```
//---------------------------------------------------------------------------
void __fastcall TOleAutomationClientForm::NewWordDocumentMethod2Click(
    TObject *Sender)
```

```
{
    OleVariant Template = EmptyParam;
    OleVariant NewTemplate = False;
    OleVariant FileName;
    OleVariant FileFormat;
    OleVariant docIndex = 1;
    OleVariant tableIndex = 1;

    if ((!ADOTable1->Active) || (ADOTable1->RecordCount <= 0))
        return;

    int fRows = ADOTable1->RecordCount + 1;
    int fCols = ADOTable1->FieldCount;

    // connect to the word automation server
    try {
        NewWordAppl->Connect();
    }
    catch (Exception &exception) {
        MsgList->Items->Add("Erron connecting to Microsoft word automation server");
        Abort();
    }
    NewWordAppl->GetDefaultInterface()->Visible = True;

    // add a new document to word application object
    // and assign it to the word document object
    NewWordAppl->Documents->Add(Template, NewTemplate);
    NewWordDoc->ConnectTo(NewWordAppl->Documents->Item(docIndex));
    NewWordDoc->get_Tables()->Add(NewWordDoc->Range(Template, Template), fRows, fCols);

    // Fill the first row of the table to contain
    // database table field names
    for (int k=0; k < ADOTable1->FieldCount; k++) {
        AnsiString fieldHeading = ADOTable1->Fields->Fields[k]->FieldName;
        NewWordDoc->Tables->Item(tableIndex)->Cell(1, k+1)->
            get_Range()->InsertAfter(StringToOleStr(fieldHeading));
    }

    // Fill the subsequent rows of the table to contain
    // data from the table
    ADOTable1->First();
    for (int i=0; i < ADOTable1->RecordCount; i++) {
        for (int j=0; j < ADOTable1->FieldCount; j++) {
            AnsiString fieldValue = ADOTable1->Fields->Fields[j]->AsString;
            NewWordDoc->Tables->Item(tableIndex)->Cell(i+2, j+1)->
                get_Range()->InsertAfter(StringToOleStr(fieldValue));
        }
        ADOTable1->Next();
    }
    ADOTable1->First();
    AnsiString curdir = ExtractFileDir(Application->ExeName);
    curdir += "\\OleWordTestDocument2.doc";
    FileName = curdir;
    NewWordDoc->SaveAs(FileName, EmptyParam, EmptyParam, EmptyParam, EmptyParam,
        EmptyParam, EmptyParam, EmptyParam, EmptyParam, EmptyParam);
    NewWordAppl->Disconnect();
}
//--------------------------------------------------------------------------
```

Part 2

The TOleContainer Component

In the previous two sections, we discussed how to launch the COM/OLE server objects externally, which means these servers are launched external to your application although you are able to access them from your VCL-based application. In this section we will examine the TOleContainer component, which will enable you to embed an OLE object into your own application.

The System page in the Component Palette has a component called the TOleContainer, which is very useful in embedding external objects using Microsoft's Object Linking and Embedding (OLE) technology. The TOleContainer component encapsulates the OLE technology and lets you embed OLE objects in your application to make those objects appear to be part of your application. When you run an application containing this component, you will be able to access all the OLE objects registered on your computer.

When you drop a TOleContainer component onto a form, it looks similar to a palette. However, you have to load the OLE object of your choice, either during design time or run time. Let's examine a few methods of this component to understand the features it exposes.

The CreateObject(AnsiString ProgId, bool Iconic) method adds the required OLE object to the container, as specified by the ProgId programmatic identifier (such as word.document, excel.sheet, and so on). The second argument to the method indicates whether the specified object should be shown in normal style (when false) or as an icon (when true).

The CreateObjectFromFile(AnsiString FileName, bool Iconic) method loads the required OLE object from the specified file.

The LoadFromFile(AnsiString ProgId) method loads the required OLE object from the specified file. The file should have been created by the SaveToFile() method for the TOleContainer component. If there was an OLE object in the container before, it would have been destroyed, discarding the changes made by the user before loading the new object. The LoadFromStream and SaveToStream methods work the same way with a stream instead of a file.

The DestroyObject() method destroys (or unloads) the loaded OLE object from the container. The InsertObjectDialog() method displays the Insert Object dialog (which is used to load the object during design time) so that the user can select during run time the OLE object type to be loaded from the displayed list. This method returns a Boolean value of true if the dialog box was successfully displayed and the user pressed the OK button after selecting an item in the list; otherwise, it returns false.

The CreateLinkToFile(AnsiString FileName, bool Iconic) method adds a linked OLE object to the specified file. The UpdateObject() method updates the contents of an outdated linked OLE object.

Now we will complete stage 3 of our example. To implement this, we need to make changes to our form.

1. Add a **TMainMenu** component from the Standard page of the Component Palette, two radio buttons representing Word and Excel, a **TOleContainer** component from the System page, and three buttons to the second tab page of the page control. Use one button to launch the Office document into the OLE container, as indicated by the radio button, the second button to unload the launched OLE object from the container, and the third button to invoke the Insert Object dialog to enable the users to choose an OLE object from the list.

2. Implement the event handlers, as displayed in Listing 12-16.

Listing 12-16: OleAutomationClientMain.cpp—stage 3 addition

```cpp
//---------------------------------------------------------------------------
void __fastcall TOleAutomationClientForm::LaunchOfficeApplBtnClick(
    TObject *Sender)
{
    if (WordAppl2->Checked) {
        officeApplType = "Word.Document";
        officeApplTypeCaption = "Microsoft Word";
    }
    else if (ExcelAppl2->Checked) {
        officeApplType = "Excel.Sheet";
        officeApplTypeCaption = "Microsoft Excel";
    }
    else {
        officeApplType = "none";
        officeApplTypeCaption = "none";
    }

    try {
        if (officeApplType == "none") {
            MsgList->Items->Add("Proper Office application type must be selected");
            return;
        }
        OleContainer1->CreateObject(officeApplType, false);
        OleContainer1->DoVerb(ovShow);
        AnsiString docOpenMessage(officeApplTypeCaption);
        docOpenMessage += " has been launched in the ole container. You may start using
                          it.";
        MsgList->Items->Add(docOpenMessage);
    }
    catch (Exception &ex) {
        MsgList->Items->Add("Error in launching office application in ole container");
    }
}
//---------------------------------------------------------------------------
void __fastcall TOleAutomationClientForm::UnloadOfficeApplBtnClick(
```

Part 2

```
      TObject *Sender)
{
    try {
        // destroy the current object contained in the OleContainer
        OleContainer1->DestroyObject();
        MsgList->Items->Add("Ole Container is cleared");
    }
    catch (Exception &ex) {
        MsgList->Items->Add("Error in unloading object from ole container");
    }
}
//-----------------------------------------------------------------------
void __fastcall TOleAutomationClientForm::InsertOleObjectBtnClick(
      TObject *Sender)
{
    try {
        // Invoke the Objet Insert dialog
        OleContainer1->InsertObjectDialog();
    }
    catch (Exception &ex) {
        MsgList->Items->Add("Error in launching the insert object dialog");
    }
}
//-----------------------------------------------------------------------
```

Now the example is complete. The program header file is displayed in Listing 12-17.

Listing 12-17: OleAutomationClientMain.h

```
//-----------------------------------------------------------------------

#ifndef OleAutomationClientMainH
#define OleAutomationClientMainH
//-----------------------------------------------------------------------
#include <Classes.hpp>
#include <Controls.hpp>
#include <StdCtrls.hpp>
#include <Forms.hpp>
#include <ComCtrls.hpp>
#include "Word_2K_SRVR.h"
#include <OleServer.hpp>
#include <OleCtnrs.hpp>
#include <DBGrids.hpp>
#include <Grids.hpp>
#include <DB.hpp>
#include <ADODB.hpp>
#include <Menus.hpp>
//-----------------------------------------------------------------------
class TOleAutomationClientForm : public TForm
{
__published:        // IDE-managed components
    TPageControl *PageControl1;
    TListBox *MsgList;
    TTabSheet *TabSheet1;
    TButton *ClearMsgBtn;
    TButton *NewOfficeApplBtn;
    TButton *CloseOfficeDoc;
    TRadioButton *WordAppl;
```

```
        TRadioButton *ExcelAppl;
        TRadioButton *AccessAppl;
        TRadioButton *PowerPointAppl;
        TRadioButton *OutlookAppl;
        TDBGrid *DBGrid1;
        TDataSource *DataSource1;
        TADOConnection *ADOConnection1;
        TADOTable *ADOTable1;
        TButton *AddContentsBtn;
        TButton *NewWordDocumentMethod2;
        TWordApplication *NewWordAppl;
        TWordDocument *NewWordDoc;
        TTabSheet *TabSheet2;
        TOleContainer *OleContainer1;
        TRadioButton *WordAppl2;
        TRadioButton *ExcelAppl2;
        TButton *LaunchOfficeApplBtn;
        TButton *UnloadOfficeApplBtn;
        TButton *InsertOleObjectBtn;
        TMainMenu *MainMenu1;
        void __fastcall NewOfficeApplBtnClick(TObject *Sender);
        void __fastcall CloseOfficeDocClick(TObject *Sender);
        void __fastcall ClearMsgBtnClick(TObject *Sender);
        void __fastcall AddContentsBtnClick(TObject *Sender);
        void __fastcall NewWordDocumentMethod2Click(TObject *Sender);
        void __fastcall LaunchOfficeApplBtnClick(TObject *Sender);
        void __fastcall UnloadOfficeApplBtnClick(TObject *Sender);
        void __fastcall InsertOleObjectBtnClick(TObject *Sender);
private:                    // User declarations
        AnsiString officeApplType;
        AnsiString officeApplTypeCaption;
        Variant OfficeApplication;
        Variant WordApplication;
        Variant ExcelApplication;
        Variant AccessApplication;
        Variant PowerPtApplication;
        Variant OutlookApplication;

public:                     // User declarations
        __fastcall TOleAutomationClientForm(TComponent* Owner);
};
//---------------------------------------------------------------------------
extern PACKAGE TOleAutomationClientForm *OleAutomationClientForm;
//---------------------------------------------------------------------------
#endif
```

Summary

This chapter is dedicated to discussing some advanced and miscellaneous topics. I started the chapter with an introduction to the CLX component framework and how it resembles the VCL framework. I continued my discussion on CLX by identifying its four main parts, and spent some time explaining the BaseCLX classes and how they share common features with VCL. The topics that I addressed included working with INI files and the

Windows registry, non-visual containers, stream objects, and the graphic canvas class, along with a few commonly used visual containers.

My discussion then shifted to custom component development, where I discussed the need for custom components, principles of component development, how to add properties and events to components, overriding the default behavior of events, and registering components with the IDE. Though I mentioned VCL throughout my discussion on component development, most of the principles remain the same for developing the CLX components.

My final topic was a discussion on Variants, OleVariants, OLE containers, and Office2k objects provided in the VCL framework. The OLE technology, which is the predecessor to COM, is exclusively a Windows-based technology like COM. Therefore, features discussed in this third section are not applicable to the CLX environment. In this section I first discussed the Variant and OleVariant classes and provided an example to show how we can invoke COM servers like Microsoft Windows and Microsoft Excel by executing method calls on the OleVariant objects. The second part of the discussion focused on the Office2k objects provided in the C++Builder 6 Component Palette and gave an example for a different way of invoking the Office 2000 server objects. I also added a third dimension to the same example by embedding an OLE object in an OLE container component provided in VCL.

Index

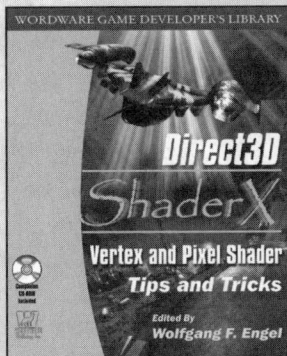

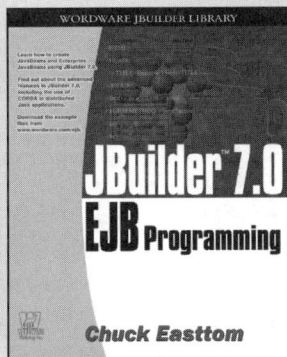

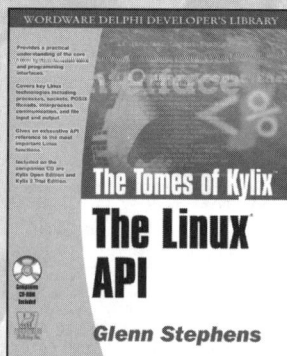

About the CD

The CD includes sample projects and the C++Builder 6 Enterprise 60-Day Trial.

The sample projects are organized by chapter number in the Code folder. The files can be installed in any folder on your hard drive. The projects were all created, compiled, and tested using C++Builder 6 Enterprise Edition. Thus, if you have a different edition, you may not be able to compile some of the projects unless you make some changes.

The project files contain the packages described in the Project Options dialog. When you attempt to open a project, C++Builder 6 notifies you if it does not have one or more packages installed that are specified in the project files. You may ignore these messages and continue opening the project. After you open the project successfully, make sure you remove those package names that do not exist in your edition of C++Builder 6 from the project definition if you attempt to compile a project with an edition of C++Builder 6 other than Enterprise. However, if the particular package is required by the project (because one of its constituent components is used in the project) and you don't have it in your edition of C++Builder 6, the project will not compile.

As a simple check to find out whether a particular project will compile in your edition of C++Builder 6, follow this guideline: As you go through a particular chapter, identify the components discussed in that chapter and check the C++Builder 6 Component Palette to see if you have the corresponding components. If you don't have those components, the projects created for that chapter will not compile; if you do have those components, the corresponding projects will compile.

To install the trial version of C++Builder 6, you will need a serial number and authorization key. In the C++Builder 6 Enterprise 60-Day Trial folder on the CD, double-click **Install.exe**. In the screen that appears, click **Step 1: Get Your Install Key** and then click **Register Here**. This procedure takes you to the Borland web site where you register to receive the serial number and authorization key that you will need for the installation step. For more information about the trial version, see the readme.txt file in the C++Builder 6 Enterprise 60-Day Trial folder.

✖ **Warning:**   Opening the CD package makes this book nonreturnable.

CD/Source Code Usage License Agreement

Please read the following CD/Source Code usage license agreement before opening the CD and using the contents therein:

1. By opening the accompanying software package, you are indicating that you have read and agree to be bound by all terms and conditions of this CD/Source Code usage license agreement.

2. The compilation of code and utilities contained on the CD and in the book are copyrighted and protected by both U.S. copyright law and international copyright treaties, and is owned by Wordware Publishing, Inc. Individual source code, example programs, help files, freeware, shareware, utilities, and evaluation packages, including their copyrights, are owned by the respective authors.

3. No part of the enclosed CD or this book, including all source code, help files, shareware, freeware, utilities, example programs, or evaluation programs, may be made available on a public forum (such as a World Wide Web page, FTP site, bulletin board, or Internet news group) without the express written permission of Wordware Publishing, Inc. or the author of the respective source code, help files, shareware, freeware, utilities, example programs, or evaluation programs.

4. You may not decompile, reverse engineer, disassemble, create a derivative work, or otherwise use the enclosed programs, help files, freeware, shareware, utilities, or evaluation programs except as stated in this agreement.

5. The software, contained on the CD and/or as source code in this book, is sold without warranty of any kind. Wordware Publishing, Inc. and the authors specifically disclaim all other warranties, express or implied, including but not limited to implied warranties of merchantability and fitness for a particular purpose with respect to defects in the disk, the program, source code, sample files, help files, freeware, shareware, utilities, and evaluation programs contained therein, and/or the techniques described in the book and implemented in the example programs. In no event shall Wordware Publishing, Inc., its dealers, its distributors, or the authors be liable or held responsible for any loss of profit or any other alleged or actual private or commercial damage, including but not limited to special, incidental, consequential, or other damages.

6. One (1) copy of the CD or any source code therein may be created for backup purposes. The CD and all accompanying source code, sample files, help files, freeware, shareware, utilities, and evaluation programs may be copied to your hard drive. With the exception of freeware and shareware programs, at no time can any part of the contents of this CD reside on more than one computer at one time. The contents of the CD can be copied to another computer, as long as the contents of the CD contained on the original computer are deleted.

7. You may not include any part of the CD contents, including all source code, example programs, shareware, freeware, help files, utilities, or evaluation programs in any compilation of source code, utilities, help files, example programs, freeware, shareware, or evaluation programs on any media, including but not limited to CD, disk, or Internet distribution, without the express written permission of Wordware Publishing, Inc. or the owner of the individual source code, utilities, help files, example programs, freeware, shareware, or evaluation programs.

8. You may use the source code, techniques, and example programs in your own commercial or private applications unless otherwise noted by additional usage agreements as found on the CD.

✖ **Warning:** By opening the CD package, you accept the terms and conditions of the CD/Source Code Usage License Agreement. Additionally, opening the CD package makes this book nonreturnable.